A Theory of Economic Systems

STUDIES IN SOCIAL DISCONTINUITY

Under the Consulting Editorship of:

CHARLES TILLY
University of Michigan

EDWARD SHORTER
University of Toronto

The list of titles in this series continues at the end of this volume.

A Theory of Economic Systems

MANUEL GOTTLIEB
Emeritus Professor of Economics
University of Wisconsin
Milwaukee, Wisconsin

1984

ACADEMIC PRESS, INC.
(Harcourt Brace Jovanovich, Publishers)

Orlando   San Diego   New York   London
Toronto   Montreal   Sydney   Tokyo

ACADEMIC PRESS, INC.
Orlando, Florida 32887

United Kingdom Edition published by
ACADEMIC PRESS, INC. (LONDON) LTD.
24/28 Oval Road, London NW1 7DX

Library of Congress Cataloging in Publication Data

Gottlieb, Manuel.
    A theory of economic systems.

    (Studies in social discontinuity)
    Bibliography: p.
    Includes index.
    1. Comparative economics. I. Title. II. Series.
HB90.G67 1983   330   83-9995
ISBN 0-12-293780-5

Contents

8. Institution of Property

9. The Economic System as a Whole

Preface

In this preface I wish to state what this book is about, how I came to write it, what relationship it has to past and contemporary theorizing in its field, why the book is needed, and to whom it may appeal. This book is a systematic inquiry in the form of an essay on the nature of historical economic systems. It deals with their relationships to each other and to their peripheral areas and the ways in which they and their components have evolved over time. *Historical* systems are here defined to be those associated with developed societies marked by widespread literacy at least among the elite of the society, written records and law, food growing by settled agriculture, the use of iron in utensils and implements, and the formal emergence of precious metals as money. By the *nature* of systems is meant the principal ingredients and processes that together make up the systems' defining conditions. The systematic inquiry embodies an attempt at theory that seeks to probe at a generalized level but that does not attempt systematic codification of available empirical knowledge or a critical evaluation of the theoretical literature available in the field. I draw from that literature chiefly for illustrative purposes and only occasionally to combat adversary views.

The book is arranged in four distinct parts. The first part (Chapter 1) is introductory and is concerned with laying out the frame of reference, basic definitions of the terms involved in economic systems, methodological issues, and the bounds of the inquiry. As drawn, these bounds exclude analysis of economic systems of primitive and archaic societies and thus center our field of interest on historical economic systems.

The second part (Chapters 2–5) is devoted to elucidation and cataloging of the first major component of economic systems: modes of production or forms of productive organization. My usage of the term *modes of production* is derived from Marx but is more narrowly construed than in most Marxian writings. I have accordingly uncovered 10 distinct modes of production, more than Marx pointed to or than Marxists generally recognize. Hence one of my major findings, argued in the conclusion of Chapter 4, is that economic systems in a stable equilibrium are commonly multimodal, with different modes sometimes dominant in different fields of economic activity (agriculture, industry, wholesale trade, urban services, etc.). Special analysis is provided (Chapter 5) of the major ways in which use of economic resources is coordinated both within and between modes. One of these ways is of course the markets so familiar to students of Western economic theory. But equally valid and in widespread use are two other ways: rationing and central planning. It thus becomes clear that economic systems differ according to the way they pattern the use of these three methods of resource coordination.

Chapters 6–8 comprise the third part, designed to cover the role of the state and the public economy in economic systems. I deal first with the economic functions commonly exercised by states in historic life and variously implemented by them. My list of functions is narrower than those commonly attributed to government because my concern is only with economic functions having primary impact on economic behavior. It is of course very much a matter of judgment whether the three major functions I have identified—regulation, public works, and income redistribution—are adequate, or whether additional functions could be drawn into the analysis (e.g., defense and education). The economic work of the state is by no means exhausted in the narrow exercise of these (and even broader) functions because the state contributes substantially to the process of institutionalization; this topic is surveyed in Chapters 7 and 8, which deal with money and property, respectively. These chapters are prefaced by a short section in which the concept of institution is developed in the light of available sociological literature.

The fourth part (Chapter 9) is a summary in which the whole theory of an economic system, as elucidated in previous chapters, is put together and explored in the light of three basic concerns: (1) treatment of change in culture, institutions, and technology; (2) ways in which separate economic systems may be drawn into meaningful multinational gestalts or orders; and (3) problems of system classification. In conclusion, the last section lists eight broad family types of systems into which most, if not all, historically experienced systems may fit.

Because the essay form does not call for critical evaluation of the literature in the field (or disclosure of preconceptions), the reader may be assisted by a brief summary of my own doctrinal orientation and my relationship to major figures in the field, past and present. My doctrinal relationship to theorizing in the field of economic systems was laid out partly in the mid-1950s in an enlarged version of my 1952 theory paper dealing with Marx, Veblen, Weber, Roepke, and Sombart. Beyond that, the footnotes and the balance of the bibliography exhibits my enormous dependence upon Marx, who is recognized as the primary founder of the discipline of comparative economic systems and as the special creator of one of its key conceptual components, that of modes of production.

I have also drawn extensively from Adam Smith, whose *Wealth of Nations* is still a gold mine of information relating to my subject and concerns. Of more recent writers there may be mentioned Max Weber, Alfred Marshall, and J. M. Keynes, who were always consulted about any relevant topic. Of the Marxian successors, my favorite is V. I. Lenin, the founder of the contemporary communist movement. Milton Friedman figures in this book chiefly as a negative influence, to be steadily opposed when he crosses my path on issues of substance and methodology, but otherwise to be avoided. I have drawn much from economic historians, who have sought to portray economic systems and the way in which they have evolved, but economic historians do not *think* much about what systems are, or where and how their boundaries are to be drawn, which is the major concern of this book.

Of more contemporary craftsmen in the field—Polanyi, Sweezy, Amin, Wallerstein, Lange, and others—my book will speak for itself, for here and there I have had the need to refer to them and to indicate the relationships among us. Some readers may find a connection between my work and that of Althusser and Balibar, for like them I have attempted a critical reworking of the concept of mode of production. Unlike them, however, I have shaped the concept so that it points in new directions, whereas they are content, despite the subtlety and sophistication of their analysis, to stay in the traditional Marxian ruts. There is no need to speak of the whole tribe of Western (chiefly American) textbook writers in the field, for apart from occasional items of information garnered from them, I have found them to be of little use.

The book will be useful to readers who, like the author, are dissatisfied with our habitual tendency to presuppose that economic systems exist without ever carefully probing the grounds for their existence. In the absence of that probing we have oscillated in the past between two equally repellent ideological types of system concepts. One of these, the Marxian, reduces all economic systems to five or six basic types and all modern (Western) nineteenth- and twentieth-century systems into two classic molds: capitalism and imperialism. At the other pole, modern Western economic theory effects a more radical shrinkage in system variety, for it presupposes that there is only one coherent rational kind of system, revolving around private enterprise, rational choice, and markets, and that all others are a tissue of fraud, force, and error. Both schools thus deprive different societies, so far as their economic arrangements go, of any distinctive identity. It is my aim in this book to provide this sense of identity without submerging the shared inheritance and mechanisms that link all societies and constrain the choices they may make.

This book should also appeal to all social scientists who in their varied fields of specialization—geography, sociology, economic history, political science, and economics—feel the need to develop an adequate, logically defensible scheme of analysis relating to economic systems, their defining characteristics, and their broad classes. I expect it will appeal most to thoughtful persons in all countries who are trying to work out an independent line of development with a distinctive national character. I expect it will appeal least to dogmatic Marxists and to dogmatic Western market theorists, for whom all such writings as this are anathema.

In its original plan this book would have been lengthened to include three chapters of case studies of economic systems, thus illustrating how the theory of the book could be put to use. During composition of the case studies, the writing was drawn out and six long chapters resulted. They were too much to include in this work, partly because of sheer bulk and partly because the focus of writing inevitably shifted from exposition of theory to historical narration. The case studies thus became suitable for an audience to whom this more generalized work would not have appealed; they will (one hopes) be published separately in due course.

The preparation for this book involved scanning the professional literature for relevant contributions. Regrettably but unavoidably, that search was often incomplete. Some important writings that should have influenced the treatment of some of the major themes in this book were omitted and have come to my attention since the manuscript was brought to completion in the summer and fall of 1982. The writings that I most regret missing include important works by Frederick L. Pryor and Nicholas Georgescu-Roegen. Pryor's treatment in 1973 of the institution of property and industrial organization makes an important contribution to the subject. His later work, which also appeared in this Social Discontinuity Series, is more ambitious and its attempt at quantification and empirical verification is almost breathtaking. His failure, however, to distinguish between villages found in advanced civilizations and in near-primitive societies makes his empirical results inconclusive for any study of historical economic systems.[1] Georgescu-Roegen gave a probing and philosophically illuminating critique of Western economic theory for ignoring entropy and the role of exhaustible resources, and for its warped account of the process of production—themes that are central to this book.[2]

---

[1]Frederick L. Pryor, *Property and Industrial Organization in Communist and Capitalist Nations.* Bloomington Ind.: University of Indiana Press, 1973;—*The Origins of the Economy. Comparative Study of Distribution in Primitive and Peasant Economies.* New York: Academic Press, 1977. My attention to Pryor's work was drawn by his suggestive paper, "The Classification and Analysis of Precapitalist Economic Systems by Marx and Engels" *History of Political Economy*, XIV, winter, 1982, pp. 521-542.

[2]Nicholas Georgescue-Roegen, *The Entropy Law and the Ecoomic Process.* Cambridge: Harvard University Press, 1971.

It is also regrettable that I missed the significant study of Jeffrey M. Paige, published in 1975. He worked out a suggestive theory of rural economic organization and class conflict in the export agriculture of developing countries in the post-1946 world. His schema partly coincides with that set forth in this work and partly cuts across it.[3]

In quite another field of scholarly writing—dealing with the latest phase of the developing institution of money—two significant works, both published in 1980, were missed. If utilized, they would have entered into our treatment of the IMF and gold demonetization, central themes in Chapter 7.[4]

Finally, an important book by Douglas C. North, *Structure and Change in Economic History*, published in 1981, came to our attention too late to be worked into the theoretical development incorporated in this work. His book is an attempt to explain the shifting panorama of economic systems from the unduly narrow base of modern Western economic theory of rational market choice with the addition of two additional constructs: ideology and the state. In any revised version of this book his work would be taken into account.[5]

---

[3]Jeffrey M. Paige, *Agrarian Revolution. Social Movements and Export Agriculture in the Underdeveloped World.* New York: Macmillan, 1975.

[4]Milton Gilbert, *Quest for World Monetary Order. The Gold-Dollar System and its Aftermath.* New York: 20th Century Fund, 1980: Richard N. Gardner, *Sterling-Dollar Diplomacy in Current Perspective. The Origins and the Prospects of our International Economic Order,* 3rd ed. New York: Columbia University Press, 1980.

[5]Douglas C. North, *Structure and Change in Economic History.* New York: Norton, 1981.

A Note on Background

My interest in attempting a generalized theory of economic systems was first aroused in 1950–1951 at a seminar by Talcott Parsons at Harvard University, where I was belatedly seeking a doctorate after 7 years of employment in government during the war and its aftermath. Parsons was then in the final stages of preparation of *The Social System*, which was circulating in his seminar in multilith together with a host of supporting materials, alternative drafts, and the major contents of an allied publication. I was enormously impressed with Parson's ambitious theorizing and I perceived that it allowed full scope for the development of subsystems in special fields of behavior, such as economics, that would fit into the social system. In consequence I composed a paper for a session of the American Economics Association meeting at Christmas 1952 under the ambitious title, "Theory of an Economic System." Though the paper made a certain stir, aroused favorable comment from no less than Frank Knight and Joan Robinson, and was later singled out in a methodological review by Henry Briefs as an outstanding example of "holistic method," as an effort in theoretical construction it was pretty much still-born, though echoes and certain elaborations of that paper, published a few years later, entered into this book.

This early writing prepared me for a second formative experience, namely an invitation to spend 2 years (1971–1973) in Tanzania as Research Professor at the University of Dar es Salaam, the state university of a newly formed East African state then attempting an ambitious program of socialist reconstruction under the leadership of that remarkable nationalist leader, Julius Nyerere. The country was in a process of political transformation, and the university was a focus of political debate and controversy sparked chiefly by the valiant efforts of a group of Marxist and neo-Marxist intellectuals assembled from East and West and places in between to turn President Nyerere's program leftward. The chief forums for policy discourse in the country were seminars held at the university in which papers, frequently circulated in advance, were read and subjected to keen critiques from an audience drawn from the university's advanced students and faculty, visiting scholars, and a circle of interested persons from government service. I stirred one of these seminars with a paper composed in September–October 1971 and bearing the title "Pluralist or Unitary Economic Systems: A Contribution to the Dialogue between Western Social Science and Marxism." It was later presented at the initiative of the redoubtable Ali Mazrui, who presided over a session of the East African Social Science Conference then meeting in Kampala (Christmas 1971) and was also published. In that paper I gave an early statement of the concept of mode of production that is developed in this work, and elaborated on three of the modes then not widely recognized: the direct commodity producer, the corporative mode, and the public mode. I emphasized that economic systems combined different modes of production and thus distinguished between the unitary and pluralist approach to economic systems. I also attempted there a version of the concept of *socialist economy* given full exposition in this book, combining the two central notions of socialization of industry and centralized economic growth planning to guide new investment. My stint of university teaching at Dar es Salaam centered on a course on comparative economic systems, and students at the university who were channelled into that course had exposure to an unusual body of instruction. The Marxists in the department sought in a departmental meeting to make me refashion the course outline, which, as the Tanzanian departmental chairman, a Harvard graduate, noted, was generously detailed. (His own were usually curt.) At one time I was reproached by my East German colleague for labeling the current prevailing Western economy "the mixed economy." "We usually entitle that 'imperialism,'" he objected. I stated that I was aware of that nomenclature, but did not think it suitable because, in the nationalist revolution of our times, most of the subjects of imperialism had become self-governing states. The attempt at suppression failed and I taught the course as outlined. After returning to the United States my curriculum of instruction at the University of Wisconsin–Milwaukee for the next 5 years always included a course on comparative economic systems in which the lines of thinking set forth in this book were worked out in classroom lectures, discussion, and examinations.

My conviction is that no form of economic system is inherently superior to others—that private enterprise as a form of property and business organization is not sanctified as an infallible recipe for bringing prosperity and economic growth to peoples near and far, and that socialism is not the inevitable wave of the future, nor is it even especially desirable. Although societies have been revolutionized, chiefly after disaster in prolonged war, more commonly revolutionary changes in economic systems have developed slowly as societies have changed in class alignment, in attitudes, in methods of production, and in political capacity, and as the various elements of an economic system have evolved and taken new forms. As the reader will see, in modern times—roughly over the past two centuries—change in economic systems has been cumulative, sweeping, and has had outcomes differing radically from initial positions. This process of historic change is too interesting and challenging to permit taking sides, especially from the comfortable position of the more or less detached onlooker. This is not to say that institutionally shaped economic systems may not at times become radically unsuited to the needs and temperament of the people whose activities are embraced by it. Something like that happened to the forms of nineteenth-century capitalism as it extended into the twentieth century. The tendency to instability deeply rooted in that system was aggravated particularly by a disturbed, war-shaken environment and by the development of a higher standard of living and a wider industrialized network, which made the consequences of that instability more intolerable. There was a need to implant new regulative processes and institutions that would assume responsibility for masterminding economic development, maintain a more stable course of economic growth, and, especially, prevent the downward spirals to which unrestrained capitalism was particularly prone. The society at many points had become restless with its inherited institutions and creeds and so was ripe for change. Accordingly, a phase of societal change occurred—extended and drawn out in some societies of the Western world, more concentrated in others, and revolutionary in some in which new institutions of government and a radical growth in the public mode of production and in schemes of public finance helped to transform the economic system. But even here the institutional regrowth was largely initiated in the older society, and vast changes in modes of production and in class alignment that supported the new system had gradually come into existence in the older society. The lines of continuity and of cumulative process were by no means breached in all areas.

But though the thinking embodied in this book is premised on no general preference for any one kind of economic system, that thinking does allow a certain positive role for collectivism in institutions and nonmarket controls in response to needs induced by dislocation, impoverishment, and development. I may cite here the apologia on this point set forth in my doctoral dissertation, later published in revised form in 1960:

> By dislocation is meant serious injuries to the productive organism at home or, with reference to sources of supply or markets, abroad. By impoverishment is meant shrinkage of national income per capita and reduced levels of consumption relative to those expected norms around which incentives are organized and income budgets are balanced. By development is meant economic flow on an expanding scale as contrasted with the mere reproduction of the social economy on an unchanged basis. This study was written on the assumption that relative to the ability of any given society to handle large-scale overhead political organization and directive mechanisms, successful societal response to impoverishment, dislocation and developmental needs will generate collectivism and controls. Con-

versely stated, collectivism and controls are the dimension of positive response to marked needs growing out of impoverishment, dislocation or development. Just as the maintenance of life in a besieged city requires increased solidarity and sharing, as a herd under attack may band together for mutual protection, so social patterns under strain will tend to become more cohesive and solidaristic.

A Note on References

All works are cited by author, shortened title, and year of publication. Where this year of publication is significantly different from year of *first* publication, the year of first publication is cited in the footnote text. Where first publication was delayed significantly, the year or period of original writing if known is specified. This information will help to identify a given work as occurring in the "early," "mature," or "late" writings of an author, or sometimes the historical epoch imprinted on the writing. In the reference list the year of first publication or writing immediately follows the title of the work except where that year is designated in the title. This information is then followed by bibliographical data on the edition I used in preparing this volume. Classical writings of Antiquity and the Early Middle Ages, published all over the world in countless editions and appearing in numerous collections—such as the works of Aristotle, Plutarch, Plato, Herodotus, Livy, the Bible, and the Koran—are cited with sufficient particularity (volume, book, chapter, paragraph, or line number) to identify the passage in all or nearly all forms of publication. Because the date of original publication or writing is rarely known, the dates usually cited for classical writings are dates of editions of English translations used for cited passages. The major works referenced of Marx and Engels are separately identified with their year of initial publication or writing. Minor works or shorter pieces with few exceptions are cited as they have been republished in the authoritative English edition of the *Collected Works*, utilized in this work up to the seventeenth volume, including writings up to December 1860. The volume number cited will indicate the time-period of origin. I have found it convenient to confine my utilization of encyclopedias to the well-known (to the older generation of social scientists) *Encyclopedia of the Social Sciences*, appearing between 1930 and 1934 in 15 volumes.

The reference list at the end of the book is an alphabetized list of works directly cited in the footnotes. Thus this list does not make up a bibliography in the true sense of the word of either all writings consulted or utilized at one stage or another in the preparation of this work or of writings in various languages significantly related to the subject matter. Since this work is an outcome of studies carried on over three decades of teaching and writing, the list of all writings that entered into these studies is too voluminous to publish here. The preparation of a bibliography of writings entering into the history of debate on the subject is itself a monographic task best attempted in the context of a history of thought on the subject.

Acknowledgments

Thanks are owed and are here expressed to the following people, who in ways large and small helped in the writing of this book: William F. Halloran, Dean, College of Letters and Science, University of Wisconsin–Milwaukee, for special arrangements to provide typing and secretarial assistance; Frank P. Zeidler, Phyllis Hopkinson, Douglas E. Booth, Elizabeth Kohlenberg, and an anonymous reviewer for helpful suggestions on revision of an earlier manuscript version; Dee Alexander and Arlene Handrich for their careful typing of a difficult manuscript; Charles Tilly, coeditor of the Studies in Social Discontinuity Series, for support and helpful suggestions; and, above all, Margaret R. Gottlieb, my wife, for her endless patience in reading and editing preliminary draft versions, proofing all galleys and page proof, and prodding me to awareness of deficiencies, which she managed to detect no matter how they were smoothed over.

A Theory of Economic Systems

1

Introduction

METHODOLOGY

The objective of this book is to work out the defining conditions of an economic system, the relationship of economic systems to each other and to their peripheral areas, the broad classes of systems thus defined that have historically appeared, and to note the way in which economic systems evolve or change over time. First, then, we must consider what is meant by the term *system* and what range of conduct is subsumed within the scope of the word *economic*.

For sociocultural purposes, the concept of *system* denotes a set of elements with a sufficient degree of interdependency such that a change in any element or in the whole set will be conducted through some of the elements, consequently altering all or nearly all of them. Systems will thus vary along a continuum from the "congeries" state, in which there is a total lack of *conductivity* or integration, to varying degrees of integration.[1] We shall presuppose at the outset that economic life has a sufficient degree of conductivity among its defining elements so that the true earmarks of a system emerge.

This book does not regard economic systems as concrete entities, existing in a material form. Like beauty, they dwell in the eye of the beholder in the light of the defining conditions that set forth the specific features ascribed to

---

[1]Talcott Parsons did not explore the implications of the term *system* in his important work *The Social System*, but "interaction" of actors in structured situations or "consistency in shared cultural patterns relative to actor-motivations" appear central to his use of the system concept. See *Social System*, 1951, pages 1 ff., 11 ff., 17 ff. Pitirim Sorokin specifies more clearly the varying degrees of integration in sociocultural systems and both general and differential conductivity within these systems on both the cultural level and the social-action level. See *Social and Cultural Dynamics*, 1941, pages 3 ff., 11 ff., 31 ff. For Sombart a body of knowledge becomes a science only insofar as its elements are organized into a "system," perhaps by the archetonic skill of the author. See *Die Drei Nationalökonomien*, 1929, pages 178 ff. Admittedly, the element of the archetonic, which Sombart drew from Kant, is there.

them. Economic systems are heuristic constructs contrived by an observer to facilitate comparison of the essential features of different sets of economic arrangements and conditions found in different societies or in the same society at different time periods. These constructs possess an objective reality only in terms of a particular set of defining criteria—and to the extent that the criteria have revealed the most conductive, essential, and fundamental of the conditions and relations appearing in economic life.

But how can we establish degrees of conductivity and essentiality in the different sets of economic relations and conditions found in different societies and historical epochs? Obviously no simple, objective method can make this determination. Nor can we, by experimentation, modify in some given society a particular economic condition or relation and then—holding everything else constant—record the effects of the modification. The development of peoples and societies is never-ceasing. Even when social relations or cultural beliefs or social institutions appear to be unchanged, their prolonged existence over time will change their nature as live traditions harden into dogma or as continuous repetition solidifies what originally was fluid. Because words change their meanings, beliefs and traditions expressed in language will eventually shift their meanings.

The physical environment, moreover, rarely remains constant. The inevitable drift of migration redistributes populations in novel patterns as well as opens up new areas for settlement. Over and beyond these influences, human history has responded to the staccato rhythms of technical inventions and innovations in tool making, food growing, the domestication of animals, the control of water, the production of metals and ceramics, and transportation. Thus for periods long enough to be relevant, social change is too continuous and pervasive to permit direct observation of the effects of single changes in economic life in a particular country or region. Yet even if we were certain about particular effects, we could not be certain that they would appear in other societies and regions that are subject to a similar stimulus of change. The effects themselves vary in accordance with the plasticity of social organization, the prevailing level of wealth and income, and the degree of social cohesion or differentiation.

If we cannot use the method of actual or virtual experimentation, neither can we use the related positivist method that in recent decades has become canonical in Western economics. By this method, the primary test of the validity of a hypothesis or *theory* lies in its ability to predict rather than the validity of its assumptions.[2] Predicting the outcome of the application of a hypothesis, derived from one set of facts and applied to a distinctly different set, makes a valuable test of its merits. Although our inquiry could use this

[2]Friedman, *Essays in Positive Economics*, 1953, pages 8 ff., 23 ff.

approach, it would nevertheless be ill-advised to limit the methods of proof to formal predictions. The theory itself is too provisional to apply to facts that lack quantification and relate to a wide range of societies with differing institutions for control of behavior.[3]

The means of determining degrees of conductivity and essentiality will be a mixture of methods long in use in the fields of comparative sociology and comparative economic systems. Our method here partially relies upon the analysis of processes that must run their course in all societies regardless of the forms of social organization. It is frankly eclectic and synthesizing, utilizing selections from historical or monographic literature of factual findings relevant to issues being considered. Also, our method involves the unfolding of a succession of Weberian *ideal types*. Like Weber, we find that "the more inclusive the relationships to be presented, and the more many-sided their cultural significance has been, the more their comprehensive systematic exposition in a conceptual system approximates the character of an ideal type, and the less it is possible to operate with one such concept both in the 'logical sense' but also in the 'practical sense'." We thus, following Weber, operate with a wide range of "ideal types—ideal-typical generic concepts—ideas in the sense of thought-patterns which actually exist in the minds of human beings—ideal types of such ideas—ideals which govern human beings—ideal types of such ideals—ideals with which the historian approaches historical facts—theoretical constructs using empirical data illustratively—historical investigations which utilize theoretical concepts as ideal limiting cases," all belonging to the sphere of the cultural sciences for application to the field of historical socioeconomics to which Weber specifically addressed himself.[4]

Both the research methodology employed and the diffuse nature of the subject matter preclude any rigor or conclusiveness in the results reached. We can rest assured, however, that economic life in different societies has always appeared to observers to be significantly structured. A vast literature has evolved from contributors in all the social sciences—historians, economists, sociologists, anthropologists, and geographers. Their studies, dealing with specific features of economic life in different societies and historical periods, provide the raw material for our own study. That material, which is selectively reviewed, constitutes the basis of this volume.

---

[3]Though the Friedman methodology is now applied to a broad range of social behavior, including marriage, family size, crime, and the law, in its initial formulation it related to "the kind of economic system that characterizes Western nations." See Milton Friedman, *Essays in Positive Economics*, 1953, pages 41 ff.

[4]Weber, *Methodology of Social Sciences*, 1904–1917, pages 63 ff., 96 ff. Weber specifically noted that "the scientific investigation of the general cultural significance of the socioeconomic structure of the human community and its historical forms of organization is the central aim of this journal" (page 67).

Because rigor is eschewed at the outset, we can only speak provisionally of our subject matter, *economic systems* or the complex of more or less persistent arrangements governing economic behavior. We commence provisionally, like Hegel, so that the subject matter itself at length gains finality through its own development: "The very point of view, which originally is taken on its own evidence only, must in the course of science be converted to a result."[5] We shall see in the end how firm and credible that result will be.

THE SCOPE OF THE *Economic*

At the outset we need to reach clarity on the character and scope of the behavior to be included under the rubric of the *economic*. Two divergent streams of thought present different views about economic behavior. Established usage in Western economic thought, which more or less crystalized in the past half-century, holds that economic behavior involves the administration of scarce and inadequate resources to minister to multiple ends. The resources include our natural environment, our own efforts and talents, and all that we have accumulated in facilities and goods. Resources have been called inadequate because of the endless expansibility of the human wants that underlie the uses for these resources. In its most recondite and rigorous form, this reduces economic behavior to a form of behavior found in all areas of life, where choice must be affected by the terms on which alternatives are offered in the family, in military strategy, in philanthropy, in the jockeying for position and compromise in palaces and legislative chambers.[6] This concept of economic behavior almost precludes the notion of an economic system except one which institutionalizes this philosophy of choice itself by rational individuals each with isolated want-patterns and coming into juxtaposition in markets for exchange of goods or services or ideas. For that reason, modern Western economics tends to recognize only two kinds of economic systems: the rational kind using logical relationships to achieve economic ends, and the abnormal kinds, which are not very feasible except by the use of

---

[5]Hegel, *Science of Logic*, 1817, page 27.

[6]This philosophy of the "economic" was set forth classically by Lionel Robbins in his famous essay *An Essay on the Nature and Significance of Economic Science*, 1932. It draws upon the economic theory of Pareto (*Manuel D'Economie Politique*) for whom economic behavior was strictly logical conduct to overcome "obstacles" to satisfy "wants." Robbins drew most fully upon the classical work of Wicksteed *The Common-Sense of Political Economy*, 1910, especially the introductory chapter, "Administration of Resources and Choice between Alternatives. Price and the Relative Scale." On the tendency of this concept of economics to turn itself into a universal social science, see such works as Becker and Landes, *Essays in the Economics of Crime and Punishments*, 1974.

force or fraud.[7] Rejection of this concept of the *economic* does not mean that the analysis of choice that has been developed by Western economists should not be utilized where it is appropriate.[8]

The concept of the *economic* underlying this work is quite different from the modern Western concept: it is concrete, historically bounded and by its very nature social. At its core, the concept refers to the totality of the behavior by which the members of a society seek to provide for their needs in an unruly and frustrating environment through material production whose products, after suitable exchange and distribution, are either accumulated as a stock of wealth for later use or to facilitate further production of goods or services, or are utilized by members of the society for current use. The central object dealt with by economics is thus the social process of production and the related social processes of exchange and distribution. The things that are produced make up the social product of society and are either used for current consumption or are accumulated into a standing stock of wealth. This classical view of economic behavior developed by the Physiocrats and Adam Smith, prevailed in the works of John Stuart Mill and Karl Marx. Formally, this view was still held by economist Alfred Marshall, working at the end of the nineteenth century.[9] Its central terms were *production, distribution,* and *wealth.*

The advantage of the classical view for purposes of comparative system analysis is that it focuses upon core processes of economic behavior regardless of the social form in which this behavior is carried on or the ideas which the

[7]A comment of Marx in an early work about "the singular manner" of economists is still relevant. "There are for them only two kinds of institutions, those of art and those of nature. Feudal institutions are artificial institutions, those of the bourgeoisie are natural institutions. In this they resemble the theologians, who also establish two kinds of religion. Every religion but their own is an invention of men, while their own religion is an emanation from God. In saying that existing economic conditions—the conditions of bourgeois production—are natural, the economists give it to be understood that these are the relations in which wealth is created and the productive forces developed conformably to the laws of nature. . . . They are eternal laws which must always govern society. Thus there has been history, but there is no longer any." See Marx, *Poverty of Philosophy,* 1847, page 174.

[8]That was the position of the distinguished Polish Marxist economist Oscar Lange, who in his unfinished treatise, *Political Economy,* included an analysis of this discipline that he called *praxeology,* which was defined as a science auxiliary to political economy. See Lange, *Political Economy,* 1959, page 200.

[9]What is surprising is that this concept of *production* as the core of socioeconomic phenomena was also held by Max Weber when he was still engaged in working out a system of socioeconomics. "[What] we call, in the widest sense, 'social-economic,' is constituted by the fact that our physical existence and the satisfaction of our most ideal needs are everywhere confronted with the quantitative limits and the qualitative inadequacy of the necessary external means, so that *their satisfaction requires planful provision and work, struggle with nature and the association of human beings*" [italics added]. See Weber, *Methodology of Social Sciences,* 1904–1917, page 64.

actors hold about their behavior. Thus, we are no longer confined to behavior governed by rational choice and the maximizing calculus. We deal instead with the entire field of behavior involved in the relationship of human society to its material environment, and the wresting from that environment of those materials needed for sustaining and carrying on life.

The most essential material products are, of course, foodstuffs including fibers or skins as a source of clothing, organic energy and body-building materials. Activities of agriculture, food gathering, hunting, animal husbandry, and fishing are still fundamental in modern societies, not just in primitive ones, although most people do not directly participate in them. Later chapters frequently refer to the agricultural sector.[10]

By the first century A.D., mastery of metals, especially iron, began to rival foodstuffs as an essential material of life. Metals in turn have been rivaled in essentiality by the burgeoning world of energy to drive both the world's work, travel, play, and home operation. Many materials of small import in themselves may play a critical role as catalysts or trace elements needed for a chemical process. The measure of essentiality in the modern productive process has thus become elusive and complex, depending upon the scale of production as well as the technology used. The activity of production thus includes not only the processes of fabrication of end products, either used for consumption or accumulated, but all requisite subordinate and ancillary processes, including experimentation and research, transportation and communication, financing, and management operations.

The activity of production runs beyond processes of current production and extends to processes of expanded reproduction—often more extended, complex, and roundabout—by which part of the material social product is accumulated for further productive or consumptive use. Accumulation may take the form of new facilities of production laid out sometimes in wholly new communities or of revamped, renovated, or enlarged older facilities. Accumulation on some scale is carried out by nearly all economic decision makers using their own resources to improve or expand their immediate facilities for living and working. Often, however, decision makers, especially for larger projects, will call upon producers with specialized skills, implements, and facilities who collectively make up a separate branch of industry that has existed in some form in all historical economic systems. This division of labor between specialized investment producers and investment decision makers is paralleled by a corresponding division of labor between the activity of saving, by which a fraction of income or social product is set aside for purposes of

[10]In an earlier paper I once characterized man's primary want as "food, his basic occupation, agriculture and his basic resource, fertile land." See Gottlieb, "Ayres and Economic Theory," 1960, page 47.

accumulation and the activity of investment by which accumulation is carried out. Not all savers wish to have care and oversight of the investment facilities that have been associated with their saving; and, conversely, many economic decision makers who are able to use new investment opportunities effectively can provide only a fraction (sometimes a very small fraction) of the savings required. The hiatus between saving and investment makes arrangements possible that provide both incentives and security for savers who place their resources in the hands of investors for effective use. Because that hiatus often takes a pecuniary form, it offers an opening wedge to financial institutions at a certain stage of their development (amplified in Chapter 7 on money) to gather up monetary savings and, with created bank credit, to finance and monitor large-scale investments.

The channelling of accumulation into consumptive, public, and industrial forms—corresponding, for example, to investment in improved housing, public parks, and industrial plants—will considerably influence the growth of material production and the ability to satisfy human needs and wants. The process of accumulation was thus one of the central concerns of classical economists, from Adam Smith to Karl Marx. Because that process may take on different institutional forms, it should be pivotal in any comparative study of economic systems.

SERVICES

In its earlier phases, classical economics was satisfied that material production for both consumption and investment purposes could serve as the yardstick and measure the performance of different economic systems.[11] Many economists of Marxian persuasion, especially those in the Soviet Union, still include only material goods in the social product.[12] In the Western world, we have learned that it is unwise to put that much stress on the materiality of products. We cannot ignore the huge productive effort ministering to needs and wants that are every bit as important and essential as those that are served by material goods. We cannot consider the erection of an opera house as productive if not considering as productive the opera performance. We can-

---

[11]As Marx showed in his extended commentary on the theories of *unproductive labor*, Smith's treatment, which Marx to a large extent followed, was extensively criticized by most economists writing in the first half of the nineteenth century. See Marx, *Theories of Surplus Value* I, 1862–1863, pages 152–304, especially the criticisms of Garnier (pages 183 ff.), Ganilh (pages 203 ff.), Say (pages 266 ff.), and Senior (pages 287 ff.).

[12]"The aggregate social product, and therefore also the national income, are created by workers employed in the various branches of *material* production." See Institute of Economics, 1954, page 240.

not count the drugs dispensed by the pharmacist as valuable and not deem the services of the pharmacist, the nurse, or the healing art of the physician equally valuable. We cannot count as a product the toys and games made to entertain children and not count as a product those who entertain children with games and play.[13] We cannot count as a social product the books published by the printer yet ignore the work of the teacher who expounds them or the critic who reviews them. We are in this work at one with modern Western economics that the materiality of the product is not the sole criterion of productive effort and that the performance of service as well as the fabrication of a product should enter into the concept of social production that is used as a basis for comparative analysis of economic systems.

But should *all* services performed in the society be construed as part of the process of social production? Readily includable are those services that enter into or assist directly or indirectly the process of material production itself. Joining them are the essential services that transport goods, convey information, supply fuel or energy, make needed repairs on buildings or equipment, and provide research or experimentation to aid in product development or assist buyers in making purchase decisions. Includable too are those services of home cleaning, cooking, entertaining, instruction, and health care that minister with skill to the needs of people who pay for these services. By thus invoking the *marketability test*, which was theoretically developed in early national income theory, we include in the productive process the work of the first vocational specialists in early civilizations, such as the priest or diviner, the healer, the teacher, the musician, the bard, and the servant.[14] The marketability test recognizes (1) that the labor force, whether dedicated to the performance of services or the production of goods, is a homogeneous entity; and (2) that there is a tendency toward the equalization of earnings in various occupations. In Marx's example, the exchange process causes both tailoring, which makes the coat, and weaving, which makes the linen, to become reduced to the "common character of human labor." The exchange process also reduces the work of healing, teaching, home cleaning, and the like to that same common denominator. Logically, then, we cannot follow Marx in declaring that "human labour-power in motion" becomes of value "only in its congealed state, when embodied in the form of some object" and not when embodied in the form of some service deemed valuable by its

[13]Marx conceded that "it may seem strange that the doctor who prescribes pills is not a productive labourer, but the apothecary who makes them up is. Similarly the instrument maker who makes the fiddle, but not the musician who plays it." Marx, *Theories of Surplus Value* I, 1862–1863, page 185.

[14]See especially the pioneer work of Simon Kuznets, *National Income*, 1941, pages 6 ff., 31 ff.

observer or recipient.[15] The Marxian insistence on the materiality of social product is equally untenable for analysis of pre-industrial societies where so much exploitation took the form of enforced personal service or contemporary industrial societies where service performers outnumber product producers.[16]

The marketability test also encompasses the various mercantile services provided by traders and merchants who assemble supplies and products from producers and then either arrange for further transportation and marketing outside the area or else undertake to provide storage so that these products and supplies will be available to local consumers. This work removes from individual producers two functions that they will typically be unsuited to

[15]This analysis wherein the "congealed state" of the product of labor plays a central role is found in the most difficult part of *Capital*—the early chapters on simple forms of value in relation to commodities and exchange. See Marx, *Capital* I, 1867. Marx warned his French reading public (in the foreword to the first French translation of *Capital*) that they would find this "rather arduous." The high level of abstraction in which the spirited analysis is carried on permits some of its conclusions or postulates to escape critical attention. See especially, Marx, *Capital* I, 1867, "Preface to the French Edition," page 21; page 2; pages 41–46. Marx's postulate of the materiality of the "commodity," "The Relative Form of Value," (see Marx, *Capital* I, 1867, pages 49 ff.) is the more questionable because it violates the principle he established early in his analysis that the "varied bodily form" of different commodities did not invalidate their common "value-form" (page 47); that "productive activity" generically "is nothing but the expenditure of human labour-power" regardless of its varied objects; and "that in the world of commodities the character possessed by all labour of being human labour constitutes its specific social character" (page 67). Marx warned even more strongly in his conclusion that "the equality of all sorts of human labour is expressed objectively by their products all being equally values," so that "the mutual relations of the producers, within which the social character of their labour affirms itself, takes the form of a social relation between the products" (page 72). This analysis itself would almost call for recognition of services as well as physical products as "commodities" exchanged among "producers" because in the early communities in which "simple commodity production" was prevalent, many important producers performed services that were handled, valued, and dealt with as commodities in the markets of that time.

[16]It is thus no objection to the inclusion of marketed services in the social product for present purposes that an enormous amount of exploitive services as servant work is thereby included. Marx notes that the British 1861 census reported that over a million household servants were employed in the U.K., whereas persons employed in factories numbered only 775,534 persons. "What a convenient arrangement it is that makes a factory girl to sweat twelve hours in a factory, so that the factory proprietor, with a part of her unpaid labour can take into his personal service her sister as maid, her brother as groom and her cousin as soldier or policeman!" See Marx, *Theories of Surplus Value* I, 1862–1863, page 201. In his *Capital* I, he cites that same census servant count as 1,208,648, and also enumerates a total of 1.6 millions employed in textile factories, metal industries, and mines altogether. He notes a tendency to increase "on a constantly extending scale of the ancient domestic slaves under the name of a servant class." See Marx, *Capital* I, 1867, page 446. That is a significant finding about the English economic system of the day.

perform themselves: (1) transporting goods in quantity to more distant markets, requiring movement of large masses of goods in one cargo shipment or convoy; (2) selling the products directly to consumers. In the retailing function, one storekeeper can display the products of many producers. By concentrating them with sufficient variety under one roof, the dealer facilitates their exhibition to would-be buyers whose field of choices is widened and whose task of procurement is eased. The merchant accomplishes these functions by a double process of exchange and price setting. He must buy with some skill and art because he must buy before he sells, and he must correctly anticipate the price at which he is likely to sell. He must then set a second set of selling prices or, as was often the case in older societies and in such modern fields as real estate, new and used automobiles and electric appliances, *negotiate* selling prices with individual customers in bargained transactions, with an eye to changing economic conditions and the danger of either running out of stock or holding too many of his goods unsold. It is a tribute to the analytic genius of Plato that although he held the merchant in low repute and would not (with Aristotle) admit him to citizenship in his ideal state, still he showed full awareness of the important economic service provided.[17]

On the Marxian side there is again dissent. Marx was prepared to recognize the productive functions in storage, warehousing, and transportation to be regarded as "production processes continuing within the process of circulation." But he excluded the activity of "buying in order to sell" or "buying

---

[17]The genius of Plato discerned these significant functions performed by dealers despite his distaste for their work and though he would not allow them citizenship in his ideal state. "To find a place where nothing need be imported is well-nigh impossible. . . . Then there must be another class of citizens who will bring the required supply from another city. But if the trader goes empty-handed, having nothing which they require who would supply his need, he will come back empty-handed. . . . And therefore what they produce at home must be not only enough for themselves, but such both in quantity and quality as to accommodate those from whom their wants are supplied. . . . Then more husbandmen and more artisans will be required. . . . Not to mention the importers and exporters who are called merchants? . . . Then we shall want merchants? . . . And if merchandise is to be carried over the sea, skillful sailors will also be needed, and in considerable numbers? . . . Then again, within the city how will they exchange their production? . . . Clearly they will buy and sell. Then they will need a market-place and a money-token for purposes of exchange. . . . Suppose now that a husbandman or an artisan brings some production to market, and he comes at a time when there is no one to exchange with him—is he to leave his calling and sit idle in the market-place? Not at all; he will find people there who seeing the want undertake the office of salesmen . . . commonly those who are the weakest in bodily strength [whose] duty is to be in the market and to give money in exchange for goods to those who desire to sell and to take money from those who desire to buy." See Plato, *Republic*, bk. 2, pages 370–371; Aristotle, *Politics*, bk. 8, ch. 9. In Plato's *Laws*, he evinces little appreciation for the function of commodity exchange, commerce is reduced to the smallest scope, and only aliens can be retail traders.

and selling with the entailed costs of accounting, bookkeeping, correspondence, etc."[18] Marx ignored the large amount of knowledge required of the merchant regarding the different varieties of products handled, their liability to spoilage, their suitability for different uses, and the comparative risks in carrying inventories under changeable conditions. For modes of production that depend upon market exchange to achieve the requisite distribution, it is inconsistent with Marx's own theory of the historically determined mode of production to deny the mode the method of exchange appropriate to it. For these reasons we rank mercantile services among those contributing to social product.

We encounter more of a problem in handling services rendered within the home or family. Much of the business of life is conducted at home. Here is where children are raised and nurtured, where the sick are often cared for, where food is prepared for eating, where the home is furnished or decorated and where much of the entertainment or play experienced by most people is actually provided. The home is where clothing is often made or at least repaired, cleaned or laundered. It is also where most sexual satisfaction is obtained—a prime need—expensive to satisfy in the marketplace. The real value of household production was especially evident under earlier conditions, when readymade articles of food and clothing were unavailable. Never-ceasing woman labor, unassisted by processed foods from the market, or piped and heated water and electric appliances was the rule.[19]

Our problem, however, is not in recognizing the reality of household production, which has been shamefully neglected both in Marxian and modern economics.[20] Our problem lies in the limited degree of conductivity or interaction of household production with the other components of economic systems that will be central in this work. Until recent times, household production was carried on mostly by hand, using only traditional methods and simple equipment. There was no close association between the mode of

[18]Marx, *Capital* III, 1864–1865, pages 266 ff., 282, 289.

[19]Possibly overblown is the picture of the "good wife" in the Bible, Prov. 31: 13–22, "She seeks wool and flax, and works with willing hands, she is like the ships of the merchant, she brings food from afar. She rises while it is yet night and provides food for her household and tasks for her maidens. She considers a field and buys it; with the fruit of her hand she plants a vineyard. She girds her loins with strength and makes her arms strong. She perceives that her merchandise is profitable. Her lamp does not go out at night. She puts her hand to the distaff, and her hands hold the spindle. . . . She is not afraid of snow for her household, for all her household are clothed in scarlet. She makes herself coverings; her clothing is fine linen and purple."

[20]Three exceptions in American economic literature are the following: the charming and still illuminating essay of Wesley C. Mitchell, "The Backward Art of Spending Money," see Mitchell, pages 3–19; the brilliant work of T. Scitovsky. *Joyless Economy*, 1976; and Veblen, *Theory of the Leisure Class*, 1899.

household production and the other modes of production. Then, too, household production was governed by the form of family and marriage institutionalized in a given society. Once shaped, domestic institutions often tend to be unaffected by changes developing elsewhere in the economic system. Perhaps channels of interaction between household production and other facets of economic systems are more obscure and difficult to trace. Certainly, quantitative information about household production in earlier societies is virtually unknown. So for these reasons we must leave untreated in this work the role of household production, hoping that at a later time this deficiency may be corrected.

Government services are another troublesome category for which the market test is not applicable. If a state produces goods sold to the public or performs a service purchased voluntarily, we are dealing with a special form of production handled by the state. But what about the broad range of services performed on authority of the state and financed through a compulsory levy on the incomes and property of taxpayers that is enforced by its legislators, judges, magistrates, tax collectors, policemen, soldiers, and priests? Here Marx was happy to follow Adam Smith in ruling that "the labour of some of the most respectable orders in the society is, like that of menial servants, unproductive of any value . . . the sovereign . . . with all the officers both of justice and war who serve under him, the whole army and navy are unproductive labourers."[21] That was of course congenial to Marx's philosophy in which the state is usually pilloried as an immense apparatus that orders the resources of society at the behest and for the use of the ruling class. The Marxist texts along that line, drawn from various writings of Marx and Engels, were assiduously collected by V. I. Lenin, the founder of Russian communism, to drive home the theme of the class-state or the state as an instrument of class-rule.[22]

But side by side with this notion of state power, Marx and Engels gave some expression to the common finding that states, however twisted by class-rule, have positive social functions to perform. These functions were given comprehensive statement in Engel's well-known condemnation of any theory

---

[21]See the citation from Smith with commentary by Marx, *Surplus Value* I, 1862–1863, page 160.

[22]Lenin, *State and Revolution*, available now in many editions and English translation. Marx's description of French state power built up already at the time of the absolute monarchies is typical: "This executive power with its huge bureaucratic and military organization, with its extensive and artificial state machinery, a horde of half a million officials in addition to an army of another half a million, this frightful body of parasites wound like a caul about the body of French society and clogging its every pore." See Lenin, *State and Revolution*, 1917, pages 24 ff.

of the state resting solely upon force and domination. He noted "common interests the safeguarding of which had to be handed over to individuals, even though under the control of the community as a whole: . . . the adjudication of disputes; repression of encroachments by individuals on the rights of others; control of water supplies, especially in hot countries; and finally, when conditions were still absolutely primitive, religious functions." He observed that such offices are "naturally endowed with a certain measure of authority and are the beginnings of state power." With increasing density of population, these communities are grouped in "larger units" with "organs to safeguard common interests and to guard against conflicting interests" in the context of "the increasing number of conflicts with . . . other groups." This independence of social functions in relation to society increased "until it developed into domination over society." What was originally the servant then became the lord, but always "the exercise of social function was everywhere the basis of political supremacy; and further that political supremacy has existed for any length of time only when it fulfilled its social functions."[23] Engels possibly downplayed the role of defense among these "common interests," for among primitive and developing peoples alike—especially those settled in agricultural communities—the constant struggle to defend the homeland against encroachments by competing peoples, particularly nomadic pastoral-warrior peoples, virtually dictates the need for state formation to defend the home territory, or growing out of this, to extend through conquests to gain more arable land, slaves, and booty.

The development of civil process to eliminate standing blood feuds derived from ancient quarrels and antagonisms is also a requisite for peaceful relationships among peoples drawn from many ethnic and tribal groups. Adjudication of disputes may be the starting point of law, but this soon evolves into formulation of standing rules to minimize disputes or to provide a guide for their settlement. The conduct of religious services by officers of government is a natural function for peoples who believe that every major decision of personal or group life should only be taken after determining the will of the gods or at least by seeking their favor.

Control of water supplies by means of public works projects is only one example of the power that government assumed from the earliest times in settled societies. Other necessary projects have been building of harbors and dock facilities, the construction of roads, and where possible the deepening of rivers or the digging of canals for interior transportation. Other public

---

[23]I have encapsulated here a more extended—and at times confused—text whose point of departure is an effort to explain how "domination and subjection" have arisen. See Engels, *Herr-Dühring's Revolution*, 1877–1878, pages 203–205.

works projects are the building of dams and reservoirs to permit irrigation and to hold down floodwaters, and the construction of dikes along lower basins or river settlements to minimize flood damage.[24]

Finally, as means of exchange evolve and ultimately precious metals in bars, rings, or plates are pressed into circulation, government assumes the function of facilitating the ready acceptance of money by minting precious metals in standard units of weight and fineness for public use, and by stamping and sealing each minted piece with identifying signs.

Despite these positive functions of government, the state may well concurrently serve class interests or may be used to enrich and gratify the possessors of state power. In the folk legends of every ethnic group are tales of the occasional great kings who ruled benevolently. But it is far more common to expect the worst—and repeatedly receive it. The vast resources utilized by government may trickle down into only miniscule amounts of social welfare. But although the functions of government are often carried out unfairly or wastefully, the functions themselves should not be eliminated as basic features of economic organization. The exercise of these functions, whether proper or improper, must be included within our concept of an economic system, because the services rendered by governments entail the use or abuse of economic resources and, to varying degrees, augment the mass of social product.

Transactions

The human interaction that sustains production in all of its forms and sectors has been usefully classified by one of our great institutional theorists, John R. Commons, under the heading of *transactions*.[25] A major and familiar category is that of *bargaining transactions* in which two or more parties negotiate or reach agreement involving terms of exchange for some appropriate thing or service or right. These transactions raise issues of fraud, enforceability, and fairness that may be subject to review by some kind of judicial process. The content of the bargaining transaction at its fullest specifies price, quality, quantity, and other aspects such as time, warranty, and tie-ins. Full bargaining in the modern Western world is rarely experienced by consumers except in real-estate markets and in places where used goods are traded. The scope of bargaining is reduced if the terms of the contract are stereotyped or one-sidedly laid down so that it only remains to specify the quantity to be purchased and the time of delivery. The leading example of full bargaining in the modern

---

[24]See ch. 6, pages 250 ff., this volume.
[25]Commons, *Institutional Economics*, 1934, pages 59 ff., 754 ff.; Commons, *Economics of Collective Action*, 1950, pages 43 ff., 352 ff.

Western world occurs with a service, not a product. It is the so-called collective bargaining of trade unions with employers. Though quantity of employment or jobs is not specified or subject to negotiation, the terms of employment, the conditions of work, arrangements for termination, and work-load features or the equivalent in piece-rate specifications are all subject to negotiation.

A second major category of transactions involves rationing decisions by authoritative bodies enforcing over time and within an organization or community a plan of distribution of benefits or of resource use. Distribution of supplies within a tribe or village involves a *rationing transaction* in a simple form. The levy of taxes and the apportionment of grants and subsidies by governments are a notable type case of *rationing transactions*. The immense structures of private government in large trade unions or corporate complexes, cooperative associations, trade associations, and international syndicates also operate by means of rationing transactions.

The third class of transactions shows up whenever interaction between parties of higher and lower statuses relates to performing a service under direction. These *managerial transactions* are the characteristic modes by which surplus products are appropriated by ruling classes. Managerial transactions may differ in the range of authority involved, in the scope for consultation, and in the sanctions available for imposing authority on recalcitrant or disobedient performers. At one extreme is the master-slave relationship in which lines of authority are drawn sharply, an attitude of submission is expected, consultation is negligible, and resistance to authority is met by physical punishment. At the other extreme, participation in decision making is widely diffused, authority is weak, and enforcement sanctions are limited and come slowly into play. Transactions of different types can become linked within an organization where at different levels rationing, bargaining and managerial transactions are concurrently carried on.[26]

The actors involved in these transactions will also run a broad gamut. The most common decision-making unit is the individual household, traditionally a solidary body of kinfolk who share consumption and earnings. At the opposite pole from the detached household is the sovereign state itself. Between the small household communities and the state are a wide variety of organizations that may be grouped under a few broad categories according to the function performed. The most important category is a group brought together for productive purposes: to assemble automobiles, build a dam, or operate a department store, postal station, or school. Almost as important and of more recent vintage is the investing association, which serves as a

---

[26]I have drawn upon a somewhat fuller summary of the Commons schemata in my paper "Toward a Sociological Economics," 1957, pages 349 ff.

vehicle for persons who pool funds, supplies, or patronage. It can result in an insurance association, a bank, a cooperative, or an investment trust.

Another kind of decision-making unit is a regulative association that usually arises to promote the general welfare of a group united by some common bond of interest or faith and—in early societies—kinship. Sustained membership entails diffuse loyalties to the organization and attitudes of fraternity and sharing. However, the association is tangential because it arises in a society as an outgrowth of a basic social interest at the point where this can be promoted by means of a special organization. Through the association rules and procedures are established to regulate a given field of activity. An association may be predominantly recreational, social, or religious. It is primarily economic when it functions as an agency for administering husbandry in village agriculture or for fixing standards of service, terms of procurement, or disposition. The pure type of the economic association is the village community, the guild, the trade union, the trade association, the farmer's grange, and the medical association.[27]

ROLE OF THE NONECONOMIC AND UNDERSTANDING

Although all phases of economic activity and transactions are drawn into our concept of an economic system, not all of this behavior need be overtly economic in its outer bearings or appear as economic behavior either to the actors concerned or to contemporary observers. Every society tends to de-economize purely economic relationships, infusing into them or giving increasing scope to affective and expressive aspects of behavior, and then organizing them into going concerns that can take on some deeper meaning for the individuals concerned. Thus the bare repetition of instrumental economic behavior over time will change the nature of the behavior. As such, it will induce the formation of habits and customs that ultimately provide their own forms of motivation and proximate goals. Any standard of living, once achieved, tends to become prescriptive and internalized into aspiration levels and the moral psyche. After it has become habitual, work too provides its self-reward as a mode of attaining legitimate status in a society.

Any particular economic relationship incapable of mobilizing the support of effective noneconomic motivations probably tends to be inherently dysfunctional. As such, it becomes the source of personality maladjustment and social strain.[28] Thus, we agree with Karl Polanyi's far-reaching generalization

[27]These two paragraphs encapsulate the gist of an extended discussion in Gottlieb, "Toward a Sociological Economics," 1957, pages 351–358.

[28]I summarize here a line of argument first developed in my paper "The Theory of an Economic System," see Gottlieb, "Theory of an Economic System," 1953, page 355; later

that "man's economy, as a rule, is submerged in his social relationships" so that the "economic system" will appear to be run "on non-economic motives." We also agree with his further conclusion that the human economy is "embedded and enmeshed in institutions, economic and non-economic."[29]

The enmeshment is of course reciprocal, for if the noneconomic institution is a crucial agency in carrying out economic functions, it in turn will be molded partly to meet economic requirements. Because the survival of the society involves a minimum level of economic performance and adaptability, even hardened custom bends under sufficiently strong economic pressures. Collective wants, as Alfred Marshall pointed out, are molded by new activities. But this adaptability is not swift and automatic; it involves reshuffling of priorities and takes effect through a process of cultural growth. Thus the economic and noneconomic ways and means of economic life mutually condition each other as aspects of a shifting cultural process.[30]

That shifting cultural process and the institutions in which it takes form cannot be analyzed except in terms of the logical category of *understanding*. This category, however, finds no place at all in the current positivist methodology of Western economics. Its methodological presuppositions, worked out initially in German idealist thought, were applied to the social sciences by a distinguished group of German thinkers in the late nineteenth century, among whom Max Weber and Werner Sombart were outstanding.[31] There was a twofold focus in the concept as applied to the social sciences: (1) shaping theoretical categories couched in the subjective point of view and addressed

---

enlarged upon in "Perspectives for Analysis of Economic Behavior," see Gottlieb, "Analysis of Economic Behavior," 1967, pages 129 ff.

[29]Polanyi, *Primitive, Archaic, and Modern Economies*, 1944–1966, pages 139–174, especially page 148: "The instituting of the economic process vests that process with unity and stability; it produces a structure with a definite function in society; it shifts the place of the process in society, thus adding significance to its history; it centers interest on values, motives, and policy. Unit and stability, structure and function, history and policy spell out operationally the content of our assertion that the human economy is an instituted process." Where the present author differs from Polanyi is in the special institutional categories he has developed that are drawn chiefly from the study of primitive and archaic societies.

[30]This paragraph is plucked with very little alteration from Gottlieb, "Theory of an Economic System," 1953, n. 28, page 356.

[31]Weber, *Methodology of Social Sciences*, 1904–1917; Weber, *Economy and Society*, 1921, pages 3 ff.; Sombart, *Die Drei Nationalökonomien*, 1929, pages 193–233. The German category "Verstehen" was developed formally by Dilthey for whom *Erlebnis* (experience) was central to the cultural sciences. "We understand ourselves and others only by inserting our own experienced life into every form of expression of our own and others' lives." See Habermas, *Knowledge and Human Interests*, 1968, 145 ff. The great Indian sociologist–economist, Radhakamal Mukerjee, evinced an interesting appreciation of the category of "Verstehen" in *Institutional Theory of Economics*, 1941, pages 18 ff.

to motivations and values which condition behavior; and (2) an effort to trace the connection between these individual motivations and the generally prevailing creeds and norms bearing social approval and thus implicit in the "spirit" of a society or institution.[32]

Norms, values, and motives can only be evaluated in terms of meaning both for individual actors and for the society as a whole by seeking to understand them in both these senses. There should be no need for perfect consistency between institutionalized social creeds or beliefs and internalized moral values and motivations, contrary to John Kenneth Galbraith's assertion.[33] The psyche is notoriously capable of compartmentalization, so that incompatible beliefs can be held simultaneously without invalidating each other. This scope for divergence increases with nonempirical beliefs both at the cognitive and cathectic levels. Talcott Parsons has shown why it is not possible in a complex social system "for a single pattern-consistent system of value-orientation to be completely and evenly institutionalized in all of the roles within the social system."[34] The relationship between a prevailing social ethic and lines of motivation consistent with it were handled with special skill by Thorstein Veblen, who laid crucial emphasis on the extent to which members of a social order tend to seek the approval and esteem of others in order to be fully satisfied with their conduct.[35]

Perhaps the effort to understand relevant features of economic systems will, for present purposes, be satisfied by the identification of *themes*—a term derived from literary usage, in which the same motif (say, conflict between father and son) may appear in different episodes of a novel.[36] If we find a given value favored in behavior and lauded as a virtue in practical life, and

[32]Talcott Parsons in his essay "Weber's Methodology of Social Science," (see Parsons, "Introduction," 1947) in Weber's *The Theory of Social and Economic Organization*, which contained the introductory chapters of the later translated *Economy and Society*, emphasized the first of the two foci noted in the text but neglected the second, which in Weber's work was illustrated by his effort to trace out the attitude "which seeks profit rationally and systematically" in the manner of Benjamin Franklin. See Weber, *Protestant Ethic*, 1904–1905, page 64.

[33]"It is now necessary to summarize and to reaffirm a rule. The relationship between society at large and an organization must be consistent with the relation of the organization to the individual. There must be consistency in the goals of the society, the organization and the individual. And there must be consistency in the motives which induce organizations and individuals to pursue these goals." See Galbraith, *New Industrial State*, 1967, page 159. There is considerable merit to the chapter and to the related discussion of goals and motives.

[34]Parsons, *Social System*, 1951, page 356.

[35]This shows up in all of Veblen's works but especially in *Theory of the Leisure Class*, 1899, in which the ability of a prevailing creed or ethic to drive behavior was related to the widespread desire to win social approval by significant peers.

[36]Linton, "An Anthropological View of Economics," 1953, page 308.

correspondingly it is enshrined in art and creed as an eternal verity or a necessity of nature, the same theme will run through personal motives and ideologies. Max Weber conducted this research for thematic consistency in his inquiry into the connection between the Lutheran and Calvinist creeds and the capitalist ethic. The extended controversy aroused by Weber's inquiry suggest that caution is needed in such inquiries. The evidence available is not compelling, so that qualified investigators can reach highly divergent conclusions. An even more clear-cut case of congruent thematic values may be found in eighteenth-century England: the institution of private property, the paramount ideal of natural rights as a basis for political organization, and the parliamentary state to achieve ordered liberty.

PRIMITIVE AND ARCHAIC SYSTEMS EXCLUDED

The close connection between economic systems and social organization—cast together or shaped jointly—makes it necessary to simplify our task and to exclude from our analytical quest those early economic systems most fully identified with their social context in so-called primitive and archaic societies.[37] Of course, these societies have structured economic arrangements that provide incentives for performance of requisite economic functions. But very clearly, before animal and plant breeding, regular agriculture, settled habitation, and the development of bronze and iron for tools, weapons, and utensils—that is, before the emergence of societies going well beyond the range of the tribal network of clan communities—class differentiation was and still is rudimentary. In such developing societies the bond of kinship ties is extremely close. Any economic organization is submerged in the social organizations, and money and markets have hardly emerged or are experienced only in rudimentary form. Rights to personal possessions related almost entirely to personal effects, weapons, and utensils that might be buried or passed on to the surviving kindred in the proper line of descent. The scale of economic organization in these societies is almost minute. A differentiated economic language has not yet come into existence. Under these circumstances, it would hardly contribute to the analysis of economic systems of the more advanced societies if we included these early systems in our survey.

We thus part company with Polanyi and Veblen, who turned to primitive societies for their most important concepts and frames of reference. Such retreat to a distant past may, as with Veblen, yield insights suggesting a line

---

[37]"The study of comparative economic systems may fruitfully include the less-developed countries, but not primitive economies." See Bornstein, *Comparative Economic Systems*, 1971, page 15.

of filiation of values and motives that ordinarily lie submerged and that can only be brought to light by a kind of psychoanalytic pre-history. But it is unnecessary to retrace his steps, and in any case these findings are far too conjectural for use in a work of this kind devoted to historical societies that long ago cut their umbilical cords with their remote beginnings. Although Polanyi's main categories for defining an economic system—redistribution, reciprocity, ports of trade, symmetry and centricity—may be useful in describing and comparing primitive and archaic societies, they do not seem especially illuminating or useful for purposes of description or analysis of what can be called *historical* societies and their economic systems.[38]

Whereas the line we mean to draw between primitive and historical societies is almost self-evident, the concept of an *archaic* society perhaps needs elucidation, since we mean to exclude early societies with incomplete evolution from the primitive level.

Drawing from and adding to material in a recent work of Talcott Parsons, we can specify significant criteria for distinguishing the major features that differentiate advanced from archaic societies:[39]

1. a cosmological religion that has broken through to philosophical levels of generalization and systematization;
2. mastery of an alphabet and a system of writing with a corresponding level of education that has extended literacy through the upper class and made written records and written law a common practice;
3. evolution of a coined money to facilitate commodity production and marketing or an equivalent token of wide acceptance and stable value;
4. transcending the ties based on kinship and forging new loyalties to a territorial state with a formal political structure and crystallized body of law;
5. mastery of iron and its utilization in weapons, tools, and utensils;
6. mastery of the arts of navigation and ship building to permit ready movement on navigable rivers and coastal waters;
7. development of a productive agriculture and forms of animal and crop husbandry that can yield, under favorable conditions, a considerable surplus of food, skins, and fibers.

The archaic societies do not satisfy these criteria. Among them are the Dahomey society on which Polanyi has written a full monograph; Hellenic society down to the sixth century A.D.; early phases of ancient Egypt, Mesopotamia, China, and the Indus Valley; as well as the advanced Native Amer-

---

[38]Polanyi, *Primitive, Archaic and Modern Economies*, 1944–1946, pages xxi ff., 148 ff.
[39]Parsons, *Societies*, 1966, ch. 4. I have added 3, 5, 6, 7 to the Parsonian list.

ican societies in the New World—the Aztecs, Mayas, and Incas. Having iron ore plentiful and within easy access was generally an important prerequisite in the mastery of metallurgy. After learning how to get the heat needed for smelting, the use of iron became widespread and helped to account for the military prowess that built large territorial states. Broadly speaking, use of iron began between the seventh and tenth centuries B.C.[40] Equally important, however, was the development of a written language, the formation of a cultural tradition fixed in a body of writing that was shared by large numbers of people, and mastery of navigational skills and boat building. The emergence of formal markets and a well-defined money was essential in facilitating the impersonal dealing necessarily involved in the movement of goods over wide areas that was needed to bring together and into common use a range of products such as basic metals, including iron, gold, silver, and copper; livestock and domesticated animals for meat, fiber, skin, and draft labor; and bread-grain surpluses.

The advanced societies of the ancient world were usually located in fertile river valleys. However, advanced culture and great states soon widened their domain to encompass outlying, less-developed peoples, some of them nomadic, and others living in rugged mountain country or on islands. Thus the distinction between *center* and *periphery* is by no means unique to modern society, but is nearly a constant feature of social and economic systems. Advanced culture is essentially mobile, transmitted from the center to the periphery. It gradually widens its field of action and the peoples included within it. This widening process and the societies that grew out of it will of course be treated in this volume, partly because class differentiation was steadily generated by this interplay between settled and peripheral domains. Although this interplay sometimes yielded a plentiful supply of captives held in slavery, sometimes through conquest warlike peripheral peoples actually developed new forms of class dominion. Because the advanced societies were commonly bounded by developing societies in an earlier stage of cultural growth, economic systems as well as societies had fluid and elastic borders.

Our primary reason for excluding from the analysis of this book economic systems of primitive and archaic societies—namely, that these systems were deeply submerged in their social organization—has certain reverse implications for those economic systems that are central to our analysis. These sys-

---

[40]For timing in different areas on development of iron-working cultures that roughly followed bronze culture by about a thousand years, see Kroeber, *Anthropology*, 1923, 727 ff. Kroeber believes that by the seventh century B.C. iron was "in common use for hoes, plows, hatchets, needles and domestic purposes" in China and somewhat later among other Old World peoples.

tems, we should not forget, are mere fragments of the total social organization into which *they* are fitted. The involvement is, in every sense of the word, thorough. This entails recognition, as previously urged, that the economic system cannot be regarded as an empirical self-contained or closed set of interconnections but only as a phase or cluster of a larger whole.

At the outset we must recognize that some of the functional requirements of the economic system will be discharged through agencies arising elsewhere in the social order. Conversely, certain strains that originate in economic activities will find their ultimate issue elsewhere.[41] We are not able, within the compass of this work, to explain the whole economic process or to tie up all the loose ends. We must also invoke other phases of social organization—such as the state, the church, or the family—without deriving them from their elementary grounds or reducing them to their simplest forms.

The section immediately following presents an analysis of the *functions* of an economic system, the priorities or the emphases given the various functions, and the functional prerequisites for continuous and stable economic performance. Not all the functions related to the economy are examined. One very important function, that of preparing young workers ready and schooled for economic action in its social contexts, cannot be explored in its earliest stages; the nurturing and socialization of the immature child are the functions of the family and related agencies (including church and school) that must be excluded from our scrutiny. Likewise, although government looms in our work as an important economic actor, the mechanism of government itself and the way it relates to dominant and elite classes of the society and the process of institutionalizing the form of government itself cannot be adequately treated here. In *this* sense, our primary field of analysis is the economic system itself, though we recognize it is deeply involved in the noneconomic.

FUNCTIONS OF AN ECONOMIC SYSTEM

Preliminary to the task of developing the defining characteristics of an economic system is the specification of the functions that a system would carry out. The notion of *function*, as related to system, was first developed in the sciences of biology and physiology and it described the purposes fulfilled by given organs and tissues of the body during their normal behavior. These purposes were, of course, imputed to the organ or tissue by the analyst and

---

[41]Gottlieb, "Economic System," 1953, page 352.

were not supposed to have an independent psychic existence of their own. They were objective functions, not subjective purposes. In the social sciences, the concept of function became prominently developed as objective functions in the work of anthropologists who commonly found that the subjective explanations offered by observed peoples to account for aspects of their behavior were usually mythical or allegorical. Close observation of behavior indicated that the actual function performed by a given usage would bear little relationship to its formal or express purpose.[42] This concept was borrowed, with suitable adaptations, by sociologists who continued the now well-established tradition of imputing to the functions an objective character not found in the avowed purposes of the social actors. Sociologists were thus concerned with the *latent*, not the *manifest*, functions, to use the language of R. K. Merton, a functional theorist well-known some 30 years ago.[43] This was consistent with the Marxist principle of the "veil of ideology" that often evolves to obscure and mystify the real connections in historical action.[44]

When the concept of function was carried into economics its character was somewhat altered. Economics increasingly became a policy science oriented to advising governments about proper economic courses of action.[45] The statement of functions increasingly took on the character of deliberated goals that could then be utilized as a standard of judging economic policy or evaluating economic systems. As the search for "goals" grew fashionable in the early decades after World War II, functional analysis became well accepted in Western economics—at least in this form.[46] Wherever such goals have been closely adapted to the needs of a particular economic system or to the adverse comparison, as is frequently the case, of rival present day socialist and Western systems, they are unsuitable for our purposes: to determine the character of the governing conditions of *all* economic systems

[42]See especially Malinowski, *Theory of Culture*, 1944, pages 67–74; Linton, *Study of Man*, 1936; Kroeber, *Anthropology*, 1923, pages 304 ff.

[43]Merton, *Social Theory*, 1949, pages 46–79; Parsons, *Social System*, 1951, pages 20 ff., 167 ff., 476 ff.

[44]"Whilst in ordinary life every shopkeeper is very well able to distinguish between what somebody professes to be and what he really is, our historians have not yet won even this trivial insight." Marx and Engels, *German Ideology*, 1932–1933, page 64. On the "fetishizing" of social relations and the false consciousness thereby produced in Marx's view, see the interesting work of Jürgen Habermas, *Knowledge and Human Understanding*, 1968, pages 59 ff.

[45]For an extended comment on this, see Gottlieb, "Mukerjee," 1971, pages 45 ff.

[46]Two of the more interesting volumes developing "goal" analysis are A. D. Ward, *Goals of Economic Life*, 1953; and K. E. Boulding, *Principles of Economic Policy*, 1958. Logically enough, Boulding couples with his statement in 5 chapters of objectives of economic policy, 11 chapters devoted to the "application" of "policy." See also Grimes and Clark, *Goals of Economic Policy*, 1955; D. L. Dewey *et al.*, "Standards for Performance," 1960, pages 1–26.

except primitive and archaic.[47] For these purposes we may draw upon a statement of functions prepared by me some 15 years ago.[48]

The most important and widely recognized of the functions, which follows directly from the primary nature of economic behavior, is the successful consummation of productive effort by effective organization and utilization of productive resources.[49] Success can be scaled in two different dimensions. One is concerned with high levels of *efficient performance* per unit of input resources utilized, yielding for an appropriate set of input resources the largest available quantum of output of desired goods or services. Our measures of efficient performance may be ambiguous and there may also be a range of uncertainty about application of this standard to different economic systems; yet unquestionably, significant differences in efficiency can be detected. Certainly the desire for efficient performance will vary in different societies in accord with a greater or lesser acceptance of traditional technologies and standards of living that are internalized into aspiration levels. For that reason, we cannot accept the dogmatic principle, embedded in classical political economy, that "every man desires to obtain additional wealth with as little sacrifice as possible."[50] Anthropological research demonstrates, however, that improved technologies and devices as well as new materials, recipes, agricultural products, and ways to work metals, once initiated in a given culture area, become readily distributed to adjoining peoples. This rapid process of cultural diffusion of technology would not be possible if there were not con-

[47]Thus, J. M. Montias in. his interesting book *The Structure of Economic Systems*, 1976, developed a set of "desiderata that appear to be present in the prevailing norms of most systems in the modern world," and he enumerated 14 desiderata including national strength (y6), provision of social services and public goods (y4), widely dispersed economic decisions (y9), a tolerant attitude toward uninformative competitive advertising (y10), and removal of workers' alienation (y12). Obviously, this goes far beyond the needs of a more general theory of economic systems. The report of a Presidential Commission of notables on "National Goals" is not very helpful for our purposes. See President's Commission on National Goals, *Goals for Americans*, 1960.

[48]Gottlieb, "Analysis of Economic Behavior," 1967.

[49]In the Parsonian scheme, the sole function attributed to the economy as a subsystem in the society is to *produce* so as to yield income or consumer satisfaction. See Parsons and Smelser, *Economy and Society*, 1957, pages 22 ff., 55 ff; Parsons, *Sociological Theory and Modern Society*, 1967, pages 228, 232 ff., 359 ff. It is very strange that Boulding's comprehensive treatise on "policy," for which standards are so important, omitted the standard of output itself or productivity. His four policy objectives, each with their own chapters, were the following: economic progress, economic stabilization, economic justice, and economic freedom. See Boulding, *Principles of Economic Policy*, 1958.

[50]Senior, *Political Economy*, 1836, pates 66 ff. This was one of the four "postulates" of economic science.

siderable receptivity and curiosity about new and improved devices, artifacts, skills, and materials making for more efficient or serviceable production.[51]

Beside the norm of efficiency, the consummation of productive achievement implies the goal or standard of *full utilization of productive resources*. The economic goal is not furthered if some producers must be involuntarily idled when the desire for output or goods is still unsatisfied and when means of production are at hand. Idleness was common in all earlier economic systems, but usually it was due to physical disasters that destroyed the means of production or hindered or disrupted transportation that provided the necessary materials. The issue of stable employment could arise only with the development of the capitalist economy in the eighteenth and nineteenth centuries and its concentrated production for wider markets. This was perhaps Keynes's central message—that the quest for efficiency in a decentralized market economy did not of itself produce high and stable levels of employment. He argued that attempting to achieve efficiency in resource allocation by decentralizing decision making, so that business managers could freely move in and out of commodity and credit markets, tended to destabilize aggregative activity. In the 1940s and 1950s this was widely conceded in Western economics and was reflected in the established field of "business cycles." Hence, earlier standards for evaluating economic systems all emphasized the role of stable employment. The record of the Great Depression demonstrates that this standard could at times become crucial.[52]

A second major function to be performed by an economic system arises from the need to provide some form of *distribution* of the results of productive efforts among suitable claimants. This need, of course, is to a very large degree determined by the organization of production itself. The relations of production will always be the point of departure for distributive patterns because these relations will govern which parties in the first instance have access to

---

[51]In his great work still in progress, Needham exhaustively traces the origin, transmission, and flow of cultural inventions and technical devices between the high cultures of Asia, northern Africa, and Europe. See Needham, *Science and Civilization China*, 1954–1978. More generally on diffusion, see any standard anthropological treatise (e.g., Kroeber, *Anthropology*, 1923, chs. 11–14).

[52]Thus, the literature noted previously (Ward, *Goals of Economic Life*, 1953; Boulding, *Principles of Economic Policy*, 1958; Grimes and Clark, *Goals of Economic Policy*, 1955; A. L. Dewey *et al.*, "Standards of Performance," 1960) emphasizes the standard of stable employment. It finds a curious reflection in Frank Knight's scheme as a need "to adjust consumption to production within very short periods." See Knight, *Economic Organization*, 1933, pages 14 ff. In recent decades "Friedmanism" has tended to expunge this issue from the record by shaping a vision of the macroeconomics of a decentralized business economy as strongly tending to equilibrium and high levels of stability except for disturbances by government or by monetary disorders.

the facilities of production and therefore exercise control over the product.[53] That control must allow, however, for the need to sustain with adequate incentives and rewards the productive effort mobilized in the process of production itself. However, though production relations may provide the starting point for distribution, they do not govern it all the way or in all economic systems. That was the position taken and argued by John Stuart Mill and Leon Walras, and their classical discussion on the subject is still pertinent. Unlike production, which depends, Mill argued, upon a condition that "partakes of the character of physical truths," distribution is a "matter of human institution only" and as such "depends upon the laws and customs of society." Although this overstates the case, it does emphasize that distribution is affected, to some degree, by social organization and by varying standards of equity held in different societies. The methodological implications of this observation were spelled out by Walras, who set up the domain of *pure economics* for the study of social riches characterized essentially by the relation of men to things and motivated by considerations of interest and by the canon of efficiency. Parallel to pure economics was the domain of *social economics* that was concerned with the relations of men to each other in the distribution of things. These relations were fundamentally moral and social in character, and they were decided by men with primary reference to their sense of justice.[54]

Both Mill and Walras believed that distribution was mainly given a social character by action of government exerting its authority over the institution of property and appropriating through taxation a share of the social product. But apart from the action of government, the standards of "fair shares" or "just rewards" that the economic actors themselves seek to uphold does influence the shares and rewards actually received. By affecting the rewards needed to motivate high levels of productive performance, those standards may well affect market outcomes. And such standards may be sustained by various kinds of producer regulative associations—such as guilds, trade unions, village communities, and cooperatives—that play important roles in economic life.

---

[53]"The structure of distribution . . . is completely determined by the structure of production, not only in its object, in that only the results of production can be distributed, but also in its form, in that the specific kind of participation in production determines the specific forms of distribution, i.e., the pattern of participation in distribution." See Marx, *Grundrisse*, 1857–1858, page 95.

[54]Mill, *Principles of Political Economy*, 1848, pages 199 ff.; Walras, *Elements of Pure Economics*, 1877, pages 76 ff. See also Walras's *Études d'économie sociale*. 1896 (component essays were written and in part published in three prior decades). For precisely these reasons Walras argued that the institution of property and taxation were subjects of *social economics*. See especially "Théorie générale de la société," Walras, *Études d'économie sociale*, 1896, pages 147–172.

Though historical distribution of the social product is thus influenced by some prevailing sense of social justice or equitable dealing, this has no universal form nor can it be reduced to a single standard. Much will depend upon (1) the sense of equality of right or condition in which members of a society evaluate their own roles and those of others; (2) degree in which differential social standing is inherited; (3) the extent to which individuals are free to express their grievances; (4) the availability of education that enlarges the mind and stimulates mental activity; and, (5) the proportion of "this worldly" or "other worldly" orientations.

Just as there is no simple or single historical form of justice institutionalized in all economic systems, so there is no accepted philosophic explanation as to what justice really is. The latest effort to work out a philosophical analysis of justice that draws heavily upon accepted Western economic theory is that of John Rawls. He boldly postulated an imaginary dialogue among a conclave of creatures devoid of present interest or memory and without even a defined time sense—in effect, disembodied intelligences with an appetite for rational debate about abstract principles. They allegedly committed all later societies to the social state we have achieved in the Western World and excluded all other alternatives.[55]

For our purposes, from the welter of philosophic debates on justice we may extract the core notion: that some form of *equality* of condition or of opportunities, treatment, and status underlies the claim for justice. We can thereby, if only in a rough way, quantify the degree of fulfillment of the distribution function in various economic systems by their inclination toward equalitarianism.[56]

Closely akin to justice in distribution as an economic function is that of *freedom of choice*. Thus there are choices of where to live, of occupation or vocation, and of the use of income or possessions. The notion of freedom and even of choice is complex, with many levels: (1) the inner psyche; (2) the absence of obstacles to the realization of desires; and (3) the availability

[55]Substantially that, bathed in rhetoric, is presented in John Rawls's *A Theory of Justice*. We are bound by a contract reached by disembodied intelligences, with a veil of ignorance shrouding every conception of present interest or status, debating abstract principles of justice and deciding unanimously on the two principles that very evidently would be suitable for that curious "original position" (pages 118 ff.) and for that reason irrelevant to the actual world.

[56]In his still-useful survey of the attributes of actions that entitle them to be regarded as unjust or just, John Stuart Mill emphasized the notion of equality, along with its conjunct idea *impartiality*, which "often enters as a component part both into the conception of justice and into the practice of it, and, in the eyes of many persons constitutes its essence." See Mill, *Utilitarianism*, 1859–1861, page 42. See Hawtrey, *Economic Problem*, 1926, pages 227 f.; Tawney, *Equality*, 1929; Boulding, *Principles of Economic Policy*, 1958, pages 83–109; Hayek, *Constitution of Liberty*, 1960, pages 85–102.

of the capacity to execute choice. Freedom can be both conditioned and transcendent, and the laws through which freedom is organized also limit it. Freedom seems to be essentially plural and oftentimes conflicting. A particular category of freedoms—to use and dispose of property—may curtail the political freedoms of disadvantaged groups. Political freedoms may flourish only in an atmosphere of economic freedoms. The hierarchy in which freedoms—and the obstacles to freedoms—are ranked will influence judgments about the importance of particular freedoms.[57]

We can leave it to the ethical philosopher to unravel these tangles. For present purposes, we need only assert that aside from efficiency, full employment, and equity, there is in economic life a fundamental value in free choice of livelihood, home, and use of one's resources. Free choice is valued in Keynes's eloquent words as "the best safeguard of the variety of life which emerges precisely from this extended field of personal choice."[58]

Of the various limitations on freedom of choice that enter into economic systems, the most important is surely that which determines social status and occupation by the accident of birth, binding descendants to the same work, the same status, and sometimes the same place. These confinements are not always felt as onerous, for there is security in the accustomed and the known, and in the natural transmission from parent to child. But curiosity and search for novel experience are ingrained tendencies of human nature.[59] The restriction of upward and horizontal mobility hardens lines of class distinction and tends to underuse reservoirs of talent and ability, gradually to weaken the ability of ruling classes themselves to fulfill a leadership role. It is noteworthy that although economic systems that encourage upward or horizontal mobility may be more socially and politically unstable, they will exhibit more dynamism, better development, and possibly higher productive levels.[60]

The other main impact of freedom on economic systems is in sumptuary and other codes that tend to stereotype dress and style of habitation, or to prohibit transactions or usages deemed offensive or improper (such as gambling, sale of sexual favors, and loans at interest).

Freedom or liberty was the central value of the culture of nineteenth-century capitalism, and it has become virtually the obsession of the neoliberalism

---

[57]Bronfenbrenner, *Ethics*, 1955, pages 157–170; Knight, *Freedom and Reform*, 1947, a collection of essays dominated by the concept of freedom.

[58]Keynes, *Theory of Employment*, 1936, pages 380 f.

[59]In the sociology of W. I. Thomas and F. Znaniecki, one of the four perennial "wishes" of human nature was the wish for novel or new experience. See Thomas and Znaniecki, *Polish Peasant*, 1919, pages 21 f., 72 f.

[60]See the classic work of Pitirim Sorokin, *Social Mobility*, 1927. An entire school of Italian sociologists placed great weight on this process of circulation of elites as developed by Pareto and Mosca.

of our day.[61] It is properly included in our listing of the economic functions to be variously served by economic systems.

Of a more tangible—and hence less ambiguous—nature is the fourth major economic function, that of *promoting economic progress.* Few would deny progress the rank of a cardinal function. It is readily quantified as output per manhour.[62] Though simple in measurement and end result, many forces can contribute to its achievement: the advance of knowledge, specific inventions, accidental discoveries, rewards especially established to cultivate it, interaction with distant peoples, the development of new sciences, the accumulation of wealth invested in industrial pursuits, and the spread of trade that enlarges markets and creates incentives for improved methods of production.

It is now a truism to say that economic progress is not automatic or thrown off as a by-product of the quest for other economic objectives. When the resistance to innovation is considerable, new wealth may accumulate in unproductive forms that minister to high living standards of the opulent few. In part, such resistance seems inevitable: progress often generates societal disturbance. Those injured by progress usually try to halt its course. Those benefited by progress are commonly widely scattered, and they passively adapt to its diffuse benefits. The faster the pace of progress, the more pervasive is the uncertainty and the greater is the concern for protective arrangements, as Joseph Schumpeter emphasized in his epochal *Theory of Economic Development.* This work, published originally in 1912, only spelled out the logic that Adam Smith 136 years before had made the central theme of his *Wealth of Nations*—"the progressive state" with increasing division of labor and capital accumulation. Yet little attention was given after Adam Smith, save by Karl Marx, to this central fact of economic progress, which is now the cardinal theme of all economics.

We now turn to the last of the basic functions—that of *conservation of our natural environment* as the continuing home of human society. The depletion of the environment is inherent in the use of fossil fuels, which are used up, whereas depletion is only partial with metals because a fraction at least of fabricated metals can be recovered in scrap form after use. Farming may rob soil of its fertility, and forests can be cut down by "clear cutting" rather than by selective timber removal, which retains continuous forest cover. The at-

---

[61]Milton Friedman, *Capitalism and Freedom,* 1962 and Hayek, *Constitution of Liberty,* 1960 (especially the latter) are the peak performances of this school.

[62]The "great multiplication of the productions of all the different arts" that creates that "universal opulence which extends itself to the lowest ranks of the people" is a result of the increase in the "productive powers of labour" that is the mark of the "progressive state." Adam Smith, *Wealth of Nations* 1776, pages 3, 11, 81. I have put together passages from these different texts, but they express a single theme that runs through the entire work. Boulding, *Principles of Economic Policy,* 1958, page 26.

mosphere is readily polluted by chemical waste gases of combustion, just as the surface waters and streams are made into depositories of industrial and urban sewage. In the modern industrial economy, pollution is thus equally at home in all sectors: agriculture, mining, energy utilization, urban waste disposal, and especially the metallurgical industries. In less-industrialized societies, the principal focus of resource conservation involves maintaining soil fertility and preserving forest cover on uplands to reduce both soil erosion and the silting of river channels. As the function of resource conservation has become more important in an industrialized economic life, a considerable economic and technical literature on the subject has emerged.[63]

By their nature, the economic functions cannot be completely carried out when available resources are limited. What is more, carrying out some functions frustrates the achievement of others. Promoting economic progress, which usually calls for investment of additional resources to be used as means of production, often increases inequalities, making society less egalitarian and thereby adding to social tensions. Excessive stress on resources conservation can hamper the process of material production and result in lower levels of productivity as more and more effort is deployed to reduce pollution instead of increasing output.

If freedom is given full rein in economic life, it widens inequalities because of innate disparities in resource endowment and wealth, as well as the potent role of windfalls that tend to cumulate rapidly. The basic economic functions do not always conflict, and over long stretches of time they may tend to reinforce each other synergistically. But in the short run, at least, there is the need in all societies to develop and apply some scheme of functional priorities. Preference must be given to some functions over others in shaping institutions, in the use of tax resources, and in regulating economic life. Such priorities seem a major component of economic systems. As I indicated in a preliminary survey of this subject nearly three decades ago, functional priorities will "be a crucial feature of the larger social order and will be closely integrated with it." As such, they serve as links between the social order and the economic system.[64]

---

[63]For the United States, see the current reports of the Council on Environmental Quality, *Environmental Quality* issued annually since the early 1970s. The outstanding treatise on the subject is by Mills, *Economics of Environmental Quality*, 1978.

[64]"As soon as it is realized that there is not a single order or family of functional objectives which economic systems must subserve but a variety of them operating on different levels and becoming effective in different ways, the way is opened to the realization that in any concrete economic system these functional objectives must be arranged in priorities which lay out their relative value or claim on a limited stock of economic and social resources. . . . The pattern of functional priorities will be a crucial feature of the larger social order and will be closely integrated with it" (Gottlieb, "Economic System," 1956, page 324).

2

The Mode of Production: Early Forms

The process of production is central to economic behavior. Time spent in production dominates the lives of individual producers. The outcome of production determines the scale of both private and public consumption within a society and its standard of living. Therefore, the way in which production is organized or carried on should provide significant grounds for differentiating economic systems.

Production can be regarded from many different perspectives. The *environment* in which work is carried on—whether underground in mines, on water in fishing boats or in overseas vessels, farming the soil, or tending flocks in pastures—provides possible points of differentiation. Then again we can consider factors associated with the *size* of the productive unit: that is, whether the productive unit is a single producer assisted by family members, a small group of fellow craftsmen, or a vast army of laborers mostly unknown to each other scattered in many producing facilities and tied together by impersonal relations and a hierarchy of supervision. The *motivation* of work—that is, whether performed under compulsion or whether induced by hope of reward or by shared purpose and an associated sense of identification—also furnishes bases for differentiation. The method of *recruitment* to the place of work, whether by assignment at birth or by purchase or free choice might also be relevant. The possibilities in work for expressing creativity, design, or scientific research are additionally important. The social status involved in work relations and the place of subordination and authority can occupy telling positions. The forms of *ownership* over means of production and products, the ways in which the means of production are themselves accumulated and adapted for the purpose cannot be neglected. Finally, we should also include consideration of the requirements of the process of continuing or expanded reproduction, which include schooling of new generations of producers, assembly of savings or capital for use in business enterprises, negotiation of

31

terms of partnership, and continuous evaluation of the stock-investment merits of different business enterprises. Because all this can be viewed as part of the totality of social relations involved in the process of reproduction of a modern business economy, the range of concrete behavior relevant for classification in the analysis of productive behavior is broad indeed.

If we turn from this kaleidoscopic array of potential production features relevant to the task of analysis of economic systems to the simple formulas in which Marx (and Marxists) have sought to encapsulate these features, we cannot help feeling puzzled and a bit cheated. The Marxian formula of *mode of production* or its looser German expression (*Produktionsweise*) harbors two related concepts, especially in Marx's earlier writings.[1] One was the *productive forces* (*Produktivkräfte*), embodying apparently whatever contributes to the capacity to produce (including skills, technical knowledge, and the means of production themselves).[2] A second was the *relations of production* (*Produktionsverhältnisse*), often specified as *social relations* of production. Variously emphasized about these social relations of production are four features: (1) they will always involve the way in which labor is joined or connected with the means of production; (2) they involve the totality of relations by which the product is produced and, by implication, exchanged and distributed; (3) in class-exploitative systems, the specific way surplus product is siphoned away from the direct producer is especially strategic; (4) these relations are "social relations" that, in their legal guise, make up corresponding forms of property.[3] Official Soviet Marxism, which in these matters fixes the form of accepted Marxism for the entire Eastern world, has constituted the mode of

[1] Thus the first sentence of Marx's *Das Kapital* refers to the capitalist "mode of production" as "Produktionsweise" and that term invariably appears in Marx's German texts whenever their English version talks about "modes of production." To my knowledge, Marx did not employ the term "mode of production" any more than he employed the term "surplus value," itself a translation with slightly altered meaning from the German *Mehrwert*. See Gottlieb, "Marx's Mehrwert," 1951, pages 164–178.

[2] This concept was probably first elucidated by Marx in an early study coauthored with Engels, written in 1845–1846, which was not published until 1932–1933, *German Ideology*. See Marx and Engels, *German Ideology*, 1932–1933, pages 41 f., 82 f.

[3] Once fixed in the early 1840s, these features of Marx's concept of "production relations" were variously developed in his early writings and appear to be steadily maintained throughout the whole corpus of writings, notably embodied in *Capital* and *Theories of Surplus Value*. I do not believe that the date or frequency of repetition of the various features indicates a greater or lesser importance for Marx. See Marx and Engels, *German Ideology*, 1932–1935, pages 31 ff., 77 ff.; Marx, *Poverty of Philosophy*, 1847, pages 165 f.; Marx *Capital* I, 1867, pages 177–184; Marx, *Capital* II, 1865–1878, pages 34 f.; Marx, *Capital* III, 1864–1865, pages 818f. Lenin in his early investigations into Russian economic development boiled down the mode of production to "the social relations of men in production," which turned into what he described as "the analysis of the social-economic system and consequently of the class structure in Russia," Lenin, *Capitalism in Russia*, 1899, pages 8, 41.

production as a synthesis of the productive forces with the production relations that govern the way labor is combined with the means of production.[4]

We can at the outset cut away one-half of this dialectic unity. What is
denoted as *productive forces* hardly enters into an economic system, as distinct
from making up a presupposition of such a system. In a sense, all economic
systems associated with rudimentary technologies that depend upon human
and animal muscle power, sometimes supplemented by winds or falling waters,
for their primary source of energy fall into a class apart from modern systems
that have mastered the productive forces of fossil fuels and modern machinery. Of course, we have already omitted from consideration the economic
systems of primitive and archaic societies precisely because their development
of productive forces provided an inadequate basis for the differentiation of
economic institutions and processes that are of central interest to us. Perhaps
a specification of *technology* needs to be formally incorporated into a structured concept of an economic system,[5] but that hardly affords a basis for
drawing the whole of the *productive forces* into that concept.

Marx's second concept—of social relations in production—requires further
specification if it is to be helpful and not all embracing. Bukharin informs us:
"In a complicated system of society there are innumerable such relations,
such as, between merchants, bankers, clerks, brokers, tradesmen of all kinds,
workers, consumers, salesmen . . . which all constitute production relations
. . . interwoven in the most varied combinations, the most peculiar patterns,
the most unusual confusions." [6]

Institutional economic theory is challenged to unravel critical focal centers
or clusters of these social relations of production that are sufficiently distinctive in character and coherent in form to make up defining conditions of an
economic system. We propose to do precisely that in this work, with the
many spheres of economic life affected or influenced by the power of the

[4]More or less in this form, see Institute of Economics, *Political Economy*, 1954, pages xiv
ff.; Makhov and Frish, eds., *Society and Economic Relations*, 1966, pages 20–61, especially 30
ff.; Spirkin and Yakhot, *Dialectical and Historical Materialism*, 1971, pages 117–133. Bukharin,
in his talented *Historical Materialism: A System of Sociology* puts these same elements together
but less dogmatically. See Bukharin, *Historical Materialism*, 1923, pages 148 f., 164 ff., 233
ff., and 244 ff.

[5]Werner Sombart was careful to include specification on the level of technique as one of
the three major rubrics within an economic system; the other two were *Geist* (Wirtschafts-
gesinnung) and Form (Regelung und Organisation). See Sombart, *Die Ordnung des Wirtschaft*,
1925, page 20. More illuminating perhaps is the threefold classification of post-Stone-Age
technologies worked out by Patrick Geddes and amplified by Lewis Mumford, *Technics and
Civilization*, 1934.

[6]Bukharin, *Historical Materialism*, 1925, page 147. For a similar emphasis on the "multi-
farious" production relations involved, see Rumyantsev, *Categories and Laws*, 1964, pages 20
ff.

state that Marx equated to the "concentrated and organized force of society," itself "an economic power."[7] Thus, in Chapter 8, we address the forms of ownership that in Marx's view are the legal guise of the production relations as they take shape in the institution of property. We do the same in a parallel chapter (7) on the institution of money, which evolves both as a social and economic force and as a composite result of the power of the state and the elementary needs of the processes of commodity exchange and circulation. Yet again, in Chapter 5, we gather under the three headings of *marketing, rationing,* and *planning* the totality of the relationships involved in the process of coordination of economic resource use within and between the various modes of production. In still another chapter (6), we deal with the ways in which the power of the state regulates, guides, restricts, and otherwise affects economic life.

What is left, then, of the totality of social relations of production is the *mode of production* in the narrow sense of that term: (1) the forms of organization of the productive process or the way capital or land is assembled and combined with labor; (2) the forms of authority or the hierarchy of control embodied in that process or its class structure; the ways in which labor and capital are assembled or allocated to workplaces; and (3) what may be indispensable—the characteristic attitudes of fulfillment growing out of work and the kind of motivation associated with production. These make up a cluster of attributes that can then be defined in certain ideal-type formations that appear and reappear in our more descriptive monographic accounts of economic life and that we term *modes of production* in the narrower sense. The number of these narrower modes is greater than in the Marxist set mostly because our criteria are broadened and because we are no longer seeking to distinguish broad historical epochs of social history via such modes. The same mode may in fact appear in more than one epoch, and each epoch in turn may be characterized by numerous modes.

An arbitrary line can, of course, be drawn between what may be regarded as a mode of production in a narrower sense and what Marx commonly would describe as a special form of that mode that can readily be treated as an independent mode in its own right, depending upon the purposes at hand.[8]

---

[7]Marx, *Capital* I, 1867, page 751.

[8]Thus in the classical work of *Capital* I three *forms* of the capitalist mode of production were traced out, all sharing the common pattern of simultaneous employment of a number of wage laborers by one employing capital: (1) that of "simple cooperation" in which craftsmen, often owning their own tools, share common workrooms and use common storehouses and utensils, or assist each other in lifting heavy weights or erecting some structure, thereby shortening construction time (pages 322 ff.); (2) "manufacturing," in which definite forms of subdivision of labor are crystalized with some adaptation of tools to specialized performance by individual workers who thereby lose their generalized craft skills (pages 336–370); and (3) "machinery and modern industry," distinguished by use of fossil fuels to operate prime movers

We categorically reject as an exclusive basis for defining a mode the mere *legal form* (private, public, feudal, or communal) of property involved. I also categorically exclude the corresponding *economic form of wage labor* (e.g., a labor force made up of individuals deciding individually to accept employment in certain enterprises and receiving for their labor compensation in the form of wages) as the decisive feature for imprinting the character of a mode on its performance. The most diverse forms of economic organization hire and employ wage labor controlled by a hierarchy of management: the socialist state, the cooperative, the Roman army under the Empire, the civil service of a bureaucratic state, the capitalist enterprise, or the modern public corporation. The wage form, however important in its own right, cannot thus be the distinguishing feature of modes of production. Neither can the mere fact of *marketing* its product combine in a single mode of production the wide range of economic organizations whose products and services are marketed or distributed by a process of purchase on a voluntary basis: the independent craft producer, the slave plantation of either the Graeco-Roman world or of the New World in the sixteenth to nineteenth centuries, the feudal manor, the socialist industrial trust, the capitalist enterprise, the public corporation, the marketing cooperative, and the municipally owned waterworks.

The fact of *profit* is a critical feature of all enterprises that earn income by producing commodities or services sold in markets. For them profit is the net residual after making payments to factors of production whose cooperation is obtained by a predetermined compensation set before results of production are available for distribution. The most diverse forms of economic organization experience profits as a form of income under the constraint of uncertainty as a constant condition of economic life.[9] Of course, the recipi-

---

linked to systems of machines only supervised or monitored by workers (pages 371–503). Of "simple cooperation" Marx said that it is "a specific form of the capitalist process of production" and constitutes "the first change experienced by the actual labour-process when subjected to capital" (page 335). Even manufacturing to him was an incomplete form of the capitalist mode of production, because "handicraft skill is the foundation of manufacture" whose process is basically under the control of the workmen (page 367). Only with the emergence of modern industry did the capitalist mode of production, having acquired new energy sources and new tools for working metal and manufacturing precise component parts, develop complete control over the process of production, including the speed of work itself and the instruments by which it is carried on, and finally adopts the machine, "its characteristic instrument of production," and acquires for itself a "fitting technical foundation" by learning how to make "machines with machines" (pages 384 ff.). Whether we deal with Marx's trinity of "forms" of the capitalist mode of production or treat these as independent modes does not raise an issue of principle, only of convenience in exposition.

[9]This insight we owe to the classical work of Frank Knight, *Risk, Uncertainty and Profit*, 1921. Profit emerges as the income share distinguished by its *residual* character after available incomes are utilized for meeting obligations to those factors of productions whose compen-

ents of profits will vary, as will the extent to which profits and losses serve
as motivating forces for the disposition and deployment of the means of production or for enlarging the process of accumulation that adds to the stock
of means of production.

From all this it is clear that there is no definitive list of the modes of
production that cannot readily be split up or augmented by fission, whenever
an investigator finds it useful to do so. For a work of this type, dealing with
comparative economic systems, modes should be defined wherever possible
with sufficient generality as to permit cross-cultural and historical comparison
and specification. Modes, however, should be defined with sufficient particularity to correspond to a distinct form or complex of production relations
and not to an entire amalgam of institutions, culture patterns, and forms of
government, such as the so called Asiatic mode of production, which a recent
critic, after exhaustive analysis, suggests be given the "decent burial it deserves."[10] In the remaining sections of this chapter we examine the simpler
and earlier appearing modes, many of which are found even in advanced
economic systems. In the chapters that follow, later and more complex modes
are presented.

---

sation has been expressly determined beforehand. Marx recognized that the New World slave
plantations were, in this respect, profit-seeking enterprises because the bulk of their product
was sold after the harvest was processed and sold at prevailing prices; the resulting proceeds,
after paying all the expenses of production, were of course considered as a form of profits.
The pyrotechnics of Soviet economists seeking to assimilate the use of "profits" as a category
of income in their socialist economy to a mere "accounting" device (recognized as such by
Stalin), has been fascinating to behold. See, e.g., Institute of Economics, *Political Economy*,
1954, pages 615 ff.

[10]Anderson, *Lineages of the Absolutist State*, 1974, page 548. The suggestion for burial follows from a near-exhaustive account of the evolution of the concept in the writings of Marx
and Engels in the light of an earlier literature traced and critically evaluated by Anderson
(pages 462–549). For a new exhaustive account that closely follows the Marx–Engels writings,
see Krader, *Asiatic Modes of Production*, 1975. To his credit, Marx let slumber—chiefly in his
notebooks, correspondence, occasional newspaper articles, and some early "rough drafts"—
his efforts in the late 1850s to formalize a concept of an "Asiatic mode" as an alternative line
of development from primitive communal society for Oriental or Asiatic peoples. The concept
was an ingenious but unacceptable amalgam based upon stereotypes inherited from Montes-
quieu and Hegel; it presupposed some "unchanging" or uniform Asiatic or Oriental culture
and historic pattern of civilization and presented unclear notions about the role of irrigated
agriculture and hydraulic control systems, the alleged absence of private property in land, and
the ubiquitous presence of an autarchic village community. Though usually Y. Varga is insightful in his criticism of Soviet orthodoxy, his recent attempt to resuscitate the "Asiatic
mode" as a viable concept fails on all counts, though his criticism of the more or less
mechanical application of European historical patterns to Asia is quite correct. See Varga,
Politico-Economic Problems, 1963, pages 330–351.

VILLAGE COMMUNITY MODE

Probably the oldest of the historically formed modes of production that have played roles in the economic systems under review is that of the village community that took shape among many cultures in an early phase of their agricultural life and that in various forms persisted among many peoples to the present century. Marx took only peripheral notice of the community as a fact of economic history, not only because basic research on the community came after his own schematic account in the 1840s of industrial evolution but also because he associated the surviving forms of the community in Russia and in India with "Asiatic" backwardness. Later, the debate among Russian revolutionists regarding the possible role of the still-extant Russian village community in preparing for socialism brought the community to Marx's attention.[11] By that time, investigators had established the widespread antiquity of the village community as a form of agricultural production, with common ownership of land often allocated by village elders to eligible village families based upon need. Though land was privately worked, with abundant mutual aid, the organization of husbandry was collective. Thus fields were all plowed, seeded, and cultivated to the same set of rotating crops, but after harvesting, the fields would be turned into a common pasture for village livestock. Individual plots within the farm fields used by the cultivating families were not fenced off or enclosed. Dwelling areas and small garden plots were purely private. The use of woodlands and pastures and frequently the care of flocks tended by a village herdsman were purely collective. For mutual protection and sociability, the dwelling areas, together with temples, shrines, wells, or

[11]In *Contribution to the Critique of Political Economy* (Marx, 1859) and as well in *Capital* I (Marx, 1867) itself, Marx took note of the "spontaneously developed form" of "associated labour" which "we find on the threshhold of the history of all civilized peoples." In its primitive form "we can prove it to have existed amongst Romans, Teutons, Celts and even to this day we find numerous examples . . . in India" (Marx, *Capital* I, 1867, page 77 n. 1). In the same volume, see the extracted description of the division of labor in the Indian village community (page 357). The debate with Russian revolutionaries was incited by the despised Bakunin–Tkachov center then established in Switzerland (1873–1874) and also by later queries from Russian socialist thinkers with Marxist sympathies. At about the same time Marx had occasion to return to his earlier studies of communal Indian land tenure in the course of commenting upon a treatise on the subject based primarily upon reports by English administrative officers and translations of Indian documents. Relevant documents include two articles by Engels, short letters by Marx, a long unpublished essay by Marx on the Russian commune, and finally Marx's detailed commentary on Maxim Kowalewsky's 1879 work on communal land tenure. See Marx and Engels, *Russian Menace*, 1848–1894, pages 203–241. Substantially the same documents may be found in Marx and Engels, *Selected Works*, 1845–1895, vol. 1, pages 387–412; vol. 3, pages 152–161. See also Krader, *Asiatic Modes of Production*, 1975, pages 343–412.

other common village facilities, were grouped at the center of the village area. These were surrounded by an area for garden plots, which in turn were surrounded by fields, pastures, and woodlands.[12] The Indian village community was somewhat distinctive because it endowed itself with village servants who, as carpenters, teachers, healers, or other special craftsmen, served the village and were rewarded with a share in the harvest. Nearly everywhere elected village officers discharged supervisory and watchman duties.[13]

Land holdings of village families tended to be vested in the family as soon as good farmland became scarce or when the land's value was increased by draining, clearing, or other improvements. The practice of reallocating arable plots under communal land tenure was relinquished nearly everywhere, with notable exceptions in the East African community, in the more advanced Amerindian communities in Latin America, and in the Russian village community through the twentieth century.[14] Marx noted that "the dualism inherent" in the village community endowed it with a special vitality "since on the one hand communal property and all the social relations which accrue from it give it a solid base, whereas the private house, the parcelled cultivation of arable land and the private appropriation of the fruits of labour allow development of the individual which was incompatible with the conditions obtaining in more primitive communities."[15]

This very dualism, as Marx pointed out, easily became a source of disintegration, often due to increased density of settlement and either dying out of long-tenured families or multiplication of heirs with no place in the village. This readily made for differentiation in the village of a class of eligible "holders" and an understratum of landless servants, a common occurrence in village communities of the East and West and in the New World. Village overlords

[12]For surveys of this literature, commenced by G. Ludwig v. Maurer (1851–1853) and Baron v. Haxtaufen (1847–1852) with evidence on ancient German and contemporary Russian village communities, see Luxemberg, *Einleitung in die Nationalökonomie*, 1925, pages 79–88, 146–150, 151–160, 170–186; Kropotkin, *Mutual Aid*, 1890, pages 105–128; Weber, *General Economic History*, 1923, pages 3–25. For an older useful survey, see Seligman *et al.*, *Encyclopedia of Social Sciences*, 1930–1934, vol. 15, pages 253–259.

[13]Marx, *Capital* I, 1867, page 357; R. Mukerjee, *Institutional Theory of Economics*, 1941, pages 214 ff.; Maine, *Village Communities*, 1871. On the generally elected village officers, see Homans, *English Villagers*, 1941, pages 290–308.

[14]The tradition of common land tenure was so strong among Russian peasants that in the Revolution of 1905 and in the period following their political representatives advocated nationalization of land, eventually carried out in the 1917 Revolution. See the extended analysis in Lenin, *Selected Works*, 1907, vol. 3, pages 218 ff., "The Agrarian Programme of Social-Democracy in the First Russian Revolution of 1905–7." For a vivid account of the role of communal land tenure in a Mexican village with a substantial carryover from the pre-Spanish period, see Lewis, *Life in a Mexican Village*, 1951, 113 ff.

[15]Marx and Engels, *Selected Works*, 1845–1895, vol. 3, page 155.

and headmen or *caciques* could also readily appropriate wasteland, forests, and pastures, which really make up the economic reserves of the village community and without which it is hardly sustainable. Even in the solidary Russian village, the growth of commercial agriculture and the heavy pressure of taxation heightened differentiation within the community, converted weaker members into wage laborers, and enriched stronger members by loan usury and by larger farming operations using lands acquired by lease from weaker members.[16] The Indian village community was disfigured by cast segregation.

These tendencies to disintegration were strong enough to have wiped out the form of the village community from many of the early economic systems treated in this work, probably in the Graeco-Roman world, and possibly also

[16]On these tendencies to disintegration, see Marx and Engels and Weber as well as the well-known works of Russian Marxists making their case for the "disintegration" of the village community: Plekhanov, *Selected Philosophical Works*, 1883–1913, vol. 1, pages 271–310; Lenin, *Capitalism in Russia*, 1899, pages 172 f., 346 ff. European Marxists attracted to the young Tanzanian republic, established in 1960 with socialist aspirations, made the mistake of expecting the same process of "differentiation" experienced in Russia in the nineteenth century to spring up in East Africa, where tendencies to commercial agriculture were much weaker and where clan and village traditions were much stronger. Hence my survey of tendencies to differentiation in Tanzanian agriculture and rural society aroused among local Marxists a good deal of anger and frustration. See Gottlieb, "Tanzanian Agricultural and Rural Society," 1973, pages 241–261. However, the results of my research were apparently given due regard by senior Marxist onlookers in the Soviet Union, who have concluded that "studies of the late medieval and early capitalist stages of development of Europe are not always justified in the context of Tropical Africa, with its unique features that influence the establishment of capitalism here." See Ivanov, *Agrarian Reforms*, 1979, pages 116 ff. Taking issue with the results of the household income and expenditure survey, which showed that when mean household income of the three broad classes of income recipients were expressed on a per capita basis, Ivanov argued that the small spread of mean per capita income disclosed is "not applicable to extended African families" however suitable it may be for the American family because of central control of income and expenditure within the "extended family" (page 116). But my article showed full awareness of the "extended family" with its pooling of income within the household (hence the importance of expressing household income on a per capita or member basis) and of the extended loan support given households by "relatives" who do not participate in direct household pooling. Secondly, Ivanov emphasizes tendencies to exploitation *within* household groups and the larger family. "Thus in the case of African villages exploitative relations and economic inequality already emerge within the framework of family cooperation" (page 117). But that was precisely the argument of my paper, especially in households with plural marriage. "Probably the most significant line of inequality runs not *between* households but within households with preference in consumption, a lesser share of the drudgery of field work, high status and esteem and finally disproportionate amounts of sexual gratification awarded to older males. At the opposite pole are wives upon whom are concentrated the burdens of psychological subjection, continuous personal service and a never-ceasing round of domestic and field labour." See Gottlieb, "Tanzanian Agricultural and Rural Society," 1973, page 259. Ivanov also errs badly in contraposing my estimate of 16,000 peasant-employers with another well-founded earlier estimate of some 500,000 employers by the

in the Chinese.[17] But nearly everywhere except in the New World it left as its inheritance the farming village whose unenclosed farm properties, made up of fragments of "strips" in different fields cut down or augmented by inheritance or purchase, provided a mute testimonial to the power of the village community in older times.[18] Even till modern times, in many countries community land was retained in pasture and woodlots and in rights to graze village livestock in once-harvested fields. These inherited fossil fragments of the once-live village community made the process of enclosure a revolutionary act with a decisive effect on economic life.[19] Where this revolution did not occur, there was left behind a residue of tradition of peasant cooperation

---

knowledgeable Hans Ruthenberg. My statistic was of employers hiring *year-around* helpers with a clear-cut employee status. Searching for evidence of part-time hiring, I found that very extensive, chiefly around the harvest period, affecting some 10% of farm households and involving some 10% of marketed farm output. See Gottlieb, "Tanzanian Agricultural and Rural Society," 1973, page 248. Thus there is no contradiction between my results and Ruthenberg's except that my results were derived from the first major countrywide census of agriculture carried out in Tanzania and hence, with all the limits of census data, had stronger footing than the mere "estimates" or "guesses" of Ruthenberg. What is more, I carefully sought to analyze the character of this part-time employment, the extent to which it was reciprocal among different housholds or concealed growing class differentiation. See Gottlieb, "Tanzanian Agricultural and Rural Society," 1973, pages 248 ff. Although the Ivanov work is a serious study, its methods of debate with Western analysts could stand some improvement.

[17]Weber believed the "clan economy" still existing at his time in the Chinese village "where the clan has its little ancestral temple and its school and carries on tillage and economic life in common" was a residual legatee of an earlier form of Chinese village as "clan community." Weber, *General Economic History* 1923, page 22; *Religion of China*, 1916, pages 86 ff.

[18]"The agricultural land lies on all sides of the hamlets and there are in India no farms in the sense of stable and compact agricultural properties. There are only fragments of land and each farmer cultivates as his 'holding' a number of these fragments which lie scattered in the fields surrounding the villages, intermixed with strips cultivated by other farmers," P. K. Mukerjee, *Economic Surveys*, 1959, page 20; G. Myrdal, *Asian Drama*, 1968, vol. 2, pages 1371 ff.; R. Mukerjee, *Planning the Countryside*, 1945, page 129. A department of the Soviet government functioned in the 1920s to promote consolidation of scattered "strip holdings," up to 10 or 20 strips in a holding. Lewin, *Russian Peasants and Soviet Power*, 1968, page 29; Carr and Davies, *Foundations of a Planned Economy*, 1974, pages 243 ff. The consolidation of scattered small parcel holdings of Kikuyu farmers, carried out on a massive scale by the then colonial-settler government in the late 1950s and early 1960s, was the basis for establishing the present African-dominating, white-tolerating republic of Kenya. See T. W. Hutchinson, *Africa and the Law*, 1968, page 52. Among the Ukara in the Lake Victoria region fragmentation of holdings has resulted in the average separate land-piece of 1/20 of an acre (page 53). For a valuable worldwide survey of "fragmentation" of peasant land holdings, see Woytinsky and Woytinsky, *World Population and Production*, 1953, pages 491 ff., covering Belgium, Switzerland, France, Bulgaria, Romania, China, and Indochina.

[19]On enclosures, see the insightful treatment of Moore, *Dictatorship and Democracy*, 1966, pages 426, 513 ff., 9 ff., 20 ff., 360 f., 64.

and mutual help that played a large role in reinforcing the move toward large-scale cooperative forms of husbandry and marketing.[20]

SIMPLE COMMODITY PRODUCER MODE

The disintegration of the village community leaves clusters of commercial farmers or peasant proprietors whose produce is exchanged for essential or desired goods and services that cannot be produced in the farming village. "The great commerce of every civilized society," reported Adam Smith, "is that carried on between the inhabitants of the town and those of the country [consisting] in the exchange of rude for manufactured produce."[21] Where peasant proprietors dispose of their whole product, they will draw the immediate benefits from the exchange. More generally, however, the larger part of the marketable produce of villagers is extracted from them by landlords, masters, or tax collectors to whom the benefits of agricultural production largely accrue.

This great exchange between countryside and town in part boils down to an exchange between agriculture and industry, which involves an exchange of agricultural produce for metal goods of all kinds. Metals are generally found in the uplands or in the more rugged country where outcroppings of ore veins are more likely to have become exposed, especially by the cutting of rivers into rock formations. The skills of mining are joined to the even more difficult crafts of crushing and smelting ores, and then separating by use of alloys and solvents the different metals often found in undesired compounds. The arts of the miner and smelter call for distinctive means of production that must be located generally near the mining sites and accessible fuels. Ordinarily they will be concentrated in a few places. Fabricators with various craft skills who work with refined metal will be more plentifully distributed but specialized each to their kind—skills with bronze or copper, gold or silver, or iron. A specialized fabricator with his tools, alloys, forge, and

---

[20]Polish Marxist sociologist B. Galewski correctly pointed out that the "collective farm, having arisen on the grounds of the former village community, generally constitutes its continuation." See Galewski, "Social Organization," 1968, page 125. In quite another tradition, the village community was the basis for much of the economic program of Mahatma Gandhi. See the collection of his writings on village economics, Gandhi, *Village Swaraj*, 1921–1947.

[21]Adam Smith, *Wealth of Nations*, 1776, pages 356, 358. Varying his formulation a bit, Marx declared: "The foundation of every division of labor that is well developed and brought about by the exchange of commodities is the separation between town and country" for which he cites as authority J. Steuart who he says "handled this subject best." See Marx, *Capital* I, 1867, page 352 n. 1.

bellows, and with skill in his work, will generally be located in a central place where he can supply various metal requirements: the government's for armament and minting, villagers' for plows, axes, utensils, and weapons, and other artisans' and producers' for metal goods or tools in their work. Even country smiths, specialized in repairing and fabricating iron tools and articles used in farming, sometimes locate in country towns to service the needs of a number of farming villages.[22]

The extent of specialization in metal work by the first century B.C. in China is indicated by the various classes of craft workmen with specialized skills in metal work enumerated in a contemporary work on artisan crafts: lower alloy founders, higher alloy founders, bell founders, plough makers, sword-smiths, minters.[23] In early China, specialized tools and equipment for work with metals and ores included special pliers and tongs; heavy hammers or trip-hammers operated either by human, animal, or water power; rope-suspended pile drivers; files sometimes equipped with guide rods; wire-drawing setups for drawing ductile metal into wire; double-acting piston bellows to produce a high blast in the blast furnace; and a treadle-operated tilt-hammer (an extremely simple device that enables the pounding work to be done with the feet and the weight of the whole body instead of with the hands or arms).[24] The development of productive forces in metallurgy in the economic systems with which we are now dealing—in the late Iron Age—would not be possible without separation of metal work from agriculture and full-time specialization of miners, smelters, and metal fabricators into distinct industries with evolved craft skills, representing the beginning of professional metallurgy.

Historically, the commerce between town and country rested on more than this important exchange between metal producers and agricultural producers. The peasant villager of old acquired simple skills of working wood with simple tools: a knife, and perhaps an ax, a hammer, or a mallet of some kind. But to make complex craft products out of wood—such as wheels and carriages, chairs, seaworthy boats, or cabinets—required the skilled facility with woodworking tools for cutting, drilling, joining, planing, or sawyering that could only be acquired by a professional woodworker with his toothed

---

[22]Rogers, *Six Centuries*, 1883, page 46; Homans, *English Villagers*, 1941, pages 225, 286 f., 361. In his interesting paper on this mode of production, K. D. Kelly points out that "the first craftspeople detached from agricultural work are smiths," though there is some doubt whether timing can be specified that exactly. See Kelly, "Independent Mode of Production," 1979, page 41. Outlying European peoples counted the smith among the oldest crafts producing for sale, identified as such in the oldest Germanic sagas. See Kulischer, *Allgemeine Wirtschaftsgeschichte*, 1925, vol. 1, page 71.

[23]Needham, *Science and Civilization in China*, 1954–1978, vol. 4, pt. 2, pages 11 ff.

[24]Needham, *Science and Civilization in China*, 1954–1978, vol. 4, pt. 2, 51 f., 54 f., 59 ff., 135 ff., 184 ff.

saws, hammers, plane, lathe, dowels, measures, plumb lines, and squares.[25] The peasant villager would ordinarily be unable to afford the services of a professional carpenter. But those who had control of the surplus product of the villager—the government official, the tax collector, the landlord, the local priest or ruler—would all have the means and the motives to employ the carpenter's services. The professional woodworker also constructed for other craftsmen the wooden utensils, tables, or structures they needed, and he probably put together the machines made of wood for milling, weaving, and spinning, as well as wagons, boats, and carriages.

There are similar details in the other crafts dealing with hides and leather, glass, cloth, clay and stones, fur, feathers, and salt. To different degrees they all eventually separated themselves out of domestic rural industry carried on in village households. By developing professional skills and specialized tools and equipment they learned to do their work efficiently and to reach standards of quality much higher than were possible in the peasant household. As specialized facilities for weaving, fulling, and dyeing developed, which the peasant villager could not duplicate, he utilized also the services of these expert artificers with their specialized equipment even in the one field of industry—fibers and textiles—that for long remained within the scope of peasant households as a major field of rural domestic industry.[26]

The division of labor between agriculture and industry is by no means a local one. For some industrial materials, especially salt and scarce minerals like gold, silver, tin, and mercury, it is necessary to go far away. As Marx emphasized, the starting point of this division of labor will frequently be that "different communities find different means of production, and different means of subsistence in their natural environment [so] their modes of production and of living and their products are different [calling] forth the mutual exchange of products and the consequent gradual conversion of those products into commodities."[27] But wherever they are located, most of these industrial producers—miners, craftsmen, and service performers—are small-scale producers carrying on their crafts in small shops or enterprises. For the most part, the products exchanged take the form of commodities tendered by

---

[25]Needham, *Science and Civilization in China*, 1954–1978, vol. 4, pt. 2, pages 50 ff., 53 ff., 62 f.

[26]Marx, *Capital* I, 1867, pages 748 f.

[27]Marx, *Capital* I, 1867, pages 351 f. The currents of trade, traced by recent investigators of precolonial central and eastern Africa—centered in distribution of high-quality salt, the demand for which was found to be "persistent and wide-spread," as well bar iron and copper—gives an inkling of the widespread trade that must have sparked the early economic development of European peoples. See Gray and Birmingham, *Pre-Colonial African Trade*, 1970, pages 1 ff., 25 ff., 28 ff.

simple-commodity producers or offered for sale by dealers and peddlers who facilitate the exchange process.

There are four main classes within the simple-commodity producer mode (SCPM). The largest in importance and the backbone of this producing stratum are the peasant proprietors and their near-counterparts, fishermen and the pastoralists who in earlier times migrated with their herds. Almost as numerous are town artisans and craftsmen whose callings run a wide range: ironsmiths, coppersmiths, silversmiths, tailors, dyers, tanners, weavers, fullers, and building tradesmen of all kinds, including masons, carpenters, and stone-workers. The third class of the SCPM is much smaller in number and embraces fewer callings because it carries on the exchange process itself. The retail dealers, and the whole tribe of peddlers and market caterers of all kinds, generally fall within this category. Their second cousins, however, the wholesale dealers operating between countries and using large means of transportation by caravan or ship, mostly fall outside the SCPM category. In earlier societies, wholesalers and retailers probably had little specialization beyond that of dealing in foodstuffs, metal goods, money exchange, money loans, and the like.

The fourth category of the SCPM was not recognized at all by Smith or by Marx, the performer of skilled services. The service performer was well established in many callings when whole branches of commodity production were as yet undeveloped.[28] The healer or doctor is the best known of these professionals and was probably among the first to become specialized in the primitive community. These traditional healers acquired elementary techniques of surgery, extraction of diseased teeth, and bonesetting for fractures. They searched their environment for materials, chiefly from plants and animals, that could provide healing or analgesic services. Going hand in hand with disease treatment was ministry to assuage anguish and grief and vent anger or frustration by practices of divination, exorcism, or hypnotism. Though the two branches of traditional medicine were frequently practiced together, they tended to separate in the higher cultures. By the time modern economic systems took shape, the medical healer or traditional doctor was a well established professional with specialized utensils, a vast store of knowledge, and an enormous pharmacopoeia. One talented East African people, for instance, had detailed knowledge of "thousands of plants, each of which had several uses, including some 400 specifically medicinal plants with their own medical names."[29]

[28]In a relatively neglected section of *The Principles of Sociology*, Herbert Spencer provided an interesting survey of the early professions. See Spencer, *Principles of Sociology*, 1896, vol. 3, pages 37 ff., 179 ff., 185 ff., 201 ff., 217 ff., 235 ff., 261 ff., 274 ff., 286 ff., 294 ff., 304 ff.

[29]For a survey of "traditional healers" in Tanzania, estimated to number some 38,000 full-time practitioners supported out of fees paid by the African public, see Gottlieb, *Health Care*

Nearly as well established as the healer was the tutor or teacher (of whom the philosopher Plato was the prototype); the minstrel or poet or dramatist; the architect who served primarily upper classes or state agencies; the surveyor whose skill with geometry and measuring devices aided in determining boundaries; the notary or local writer who could inscribe legal documents of record; and the attorney or advocate (who under Roman law was not supposed to work for hire yet managed all the same to receive his honoraria). These professionals make up the fourth branch of the SCPM. They give this mode strength, dignity, and sometimes professional representation because their way of life puts them in sympathy with the mode as a whole in its humbler callings.

The characteristics of the SCPM have not been worked out except for one of its principal categories, that of the peasant proprietor, whose economics was brilliantly elucidated by the martyred Russian agricultural economist, A. V. Chayanov.[30] The characteristics of the simple-commodity producer (SCP) as craftsman have been comprehensively drawn up by Werner Sombart in laying the groundwork for the emergence of what he termed *modern capitalism.*[31] Generally speaking, the SCPM involves ownership of the means of production (land, tools, buildings, libraries, records, utensils, inventories) by the craftsman, dealer, farmer, or professional. The producer incorporates into his work a skill or art only gradually learned by a more or less formal apprenticeship or course of study. The SCP does most of the work of the enterprise assisted at best by family members or one or a few helpers who are generally apprentices but may be wage laborers. The essential character of the SCPM is undermined if the SCP becomes dependent on hired labor for much essential work; at this point, the SCP metamorphoses into a capitalist producer.

The SCP is the sole manager and planner of the enterprise and commonly handles personally all critical negotiations regarding terms or conditions of service or disposal or purchase of necessary materials. The SCP sells or markets a variable fraction of his product or service. A smaller fraction is typical for the peasant household, which commonly feeds itself from its own crops and animal husbandry, resides in shelter built on the spot out of local materials, and provides for itself many of its other needs. A much larger fraction of marketed output is characteristic of the miner or urban SCP—the crafts-

---

Financing, 1975, pages 16–25, especially 25 n. 1 and the literature cited there. Polynesian and higher culture New World Indians developed valuable medical skills according to Heyerdahl, *American Indians in the Pacific,* 1952, pages 655 ff.

[30]Chayanov, *Theory of Peasant Economy,* 1925. He was, interestingly enough, a victim of the Stalinist purges connected with the collectivization drive of the early 1930s.

[31]For an exemplary treatment of the subject, see Sombart, *Der Moderne Kapitalismus,* 1902, vol. 1, pages 75–194.

man, professional, or dealer. In either case the marketed product or service is sold for prices or fees that are either set at some customary norm or are negotiated in organized local markets under conditions arranged to provide for fair dealing. Thus the SCP knows the categories of *price, market, money,* and *profit.* Like the capitalist producer, the SCP figures net income, after deducting expenses, and thinks of income as a kind of profit, though in reality "profits" are largely the earnings of the SCP's own labor. As a profit maker, the SCP is instantly sympathetic to the capitalist producer for whom, of course, profits are much more the return on capital invested, monopolistic position, or special business ability.[32]

Though the SCPM is characterized by a strong tendency to equalization of earnings and a uniform state of social equality, this by no means results in a condition of equal incomes within given craft communities or peasant villages. Statistical information collected by Werner Sombart from a variety of European centers of craft production from the thirteenth to the nineteenth centuries show an artisan income stratification whereby the bottom 60% of the craft producers will earn less than a quarter of the income of the top 20%, disregarding a handful of peak-income craft performers whose incomes will be 20–50 times that of the bottom level. The weaver trades were characteristically poorer and the baker and the butcher trades were characteristically well off. These earning differentials owe partly to variations in physical strength, health, and number of family helpers, to capital invested in inventories, and to possession of skills specially desired. Among peasant villagers, too, there is a similar differentiation of earnings, though possibly with a narrower range.[33]

The SCP appears to have, as Marx noted, a leaning to the patriarchal form of family, a restricted orbit of exchange, a developed sense of both ownership and personal independence, and—in Marx's judgment—a tendency toward an alienated form of consciousness. This Marx attributes to the SCP's "own social action in a division of labor" that takes the form of the objects [money and price] that "rule the producers instead of being ruled by them."[34] This tendency to fetishism of the SCPM seems very questionable. The very re-

---

[32]In nearly the whole of this paragraph and in the following treatment of the SCP, I have drawn on text originally published in Gottlieb, "Pluralist or Unitary Economic Systems," 1972, pages 80 ff.

[33]Sombart, *Der Moderne Kapitalismus,* 1902, vol. 1, pages 80 ff.

[34]Marx, *Capital* I, 1864–1865, pages 77 ff.; Marx, *Capital* III, 1864–1865, pages 325 ff., 332 f., 804 ff.; Engels, *Herr Dühring's Revolution,* 1877–1878, pages 371f. The circumstance that SCP functions on a *family* basis, with use of all family members whose work must be coordinated by the family head, supports the Marxian suggestion that this mode is inherently patriarchal. But only a careful survey of family patterns in the SCPM could prove the hypothesis.

stricted orbit of exchange means that SCPs will know very well with whom they deal and the division of labor by which they make their living by serving their neighbors. Peasant producers, whose products move into remote markets and who depend upon some impersonal market price, may be more confused about their role in a social division of labor.

In their periods of greatest strength, the major types within the SCPM—trader, peasant, craftsman, professional—appear together and give each other mutual support. That appeared to be the case in the early phase of the Graeco-Roman republics. However much disfigured by slavery, the prime actors in these republics were sturdy producers in field, craft, shop, and merchant store. They had a fierce loyalty to their society, a ready willingness to take up arms to defend it, and a pride in its institutions and its principles of equal treatment under law. The society in which the peasants functioned pushed them up against their commodity compeers, linked within a network of mutually beneficial commodity exchange. Though intellectuals disparaged the trader or merchant, it is doubtful that practical people shared this view, for their town life was centered on their market place (*agora, forum*) with its facilities for meeting and exchange. Athens in its heyday was a commercial center of some importance and Roman law, venerated by all alike, put emphasis on fair dealing in trade and commerce.[35]

In the medieval period, the independent peasant proprietor dropped nearly out of the exchanging circle. Most of the peasant's marketable product was appropriated by the manorial lords, the ruling church, or the power of the state. But in the towns the SCPM achieved a wide leeway for independent action with chartered liberties extorted from kings and liege lords. Town guilds were entrusted powers of local government and oftentimes with their armed forces, as in the great Italian and German mercantile republics, wielded independent state authority over broad territories. Thus an urban SCPM could become strong even though its rural peasant base was in subjection. Guild organization not only wielded power but preserved its egalitarian character by the institution of apprenticeship and by limiting division of labor within the workshop. "If circumstances called for a further division of labor, the existing guilds split themselves up into varieties or founded new guilds by the side of the old ones."[36] Through the guild scheme of apprenticeship

---

[35]"Peasant agriculture on a small scale, and the carrying on of independent handicrafts . . . form the economic foundation of the classical communities at their best, after the primitive form of ownership of land in common had disappeared, and before slavery had seized on production in earnest," Marx, *Capital* I, 1867, page 334 n. l. In another context, Marx stated the "form of free self-managing peasant proprietorship of land parcels . . . constitutes . . . the economic foundation of society during the best periods of classical antiquity . . . ," See Marx, *Capital* III, 1864–1865, page 806.

[36]Marx, *Capital* I, 1867, page 359.

and schooling every matured craftsman could normally expect to head an independent craft enterprise in the practice of his calling.

Later on, the balance between the different types or forms of SCPM turned variously in different countries and at different times. In the English economic system of Marx's day, the urban SCPM functioned well, though much of its industrial base was displaced by capitalist enterprise. But, as in the medieval world, the rural SCPM had been displaced, not by feudal production but by the capitalist farm. In that era in America, the SCPM was supreme in northern agriculture as the free family farm; in the South the plantation with its army of enslaved laborers was the prevailing mode.[37] Perhaps only in France did the SCPM hold its widest sway in the nineteenth century when it was dominant in agriculture, town crafts, the professions, and small industry.[38]

In the capitalist world of the later nineteenth century and throughout the twentieth century, SCPs have lost out in a variety of fields in which they were formerly preeminent, such as shopkeeping, tailoring, and dressmaking, and the SCP has nearly disappeared from the world of manufacturing proper, mining, wholesale trade, banking, and heavy construction. Despite these defeats, the SCPM has failed to disappear as Marx continually predicted that it would.[39] Though the large-scale department store, mail-order house, or chain network has taken over most of retail distribution, many small stores remain. Floral shops, gas stations, restaurants, garages, movie theaters, bowling halls, taverns, hardware stores, shoe stores, and drug stores anchored in the professional trade of the pharmacist are only some of the stores and shops dominated by the SCPM in the eighth decade of the twentieth century in the United States of America.

[37]Marx always distinguished between the form of "peasant proprietor" grown out of the European world of dissolving feudal or communal forms of rural society and the "new world farmer" who has much easier access to land and who farms on quite a different scale and rarely rents his land. That hardly bars including the New World farmer and the Old World peasant proprietor or their counterparts in other continents in a single social form for purposes of analyzing comparative economic systems.

[38]Marx once sarcastically noted that "the largest French manufacturers are petty bourgeois compared with their English rivals." See Marx and Engels, *Collected Works*, 1841–1860, vol. 10, page 116. Alfred Marshall believed "the equal division of property made for industrial quietism; and in spite of the exceptional brilliancy of her engineers, France owes relatively little to the aid of mechanical power in manufacture." See Marshall, *Industry and Trade*, 1919, pages 113 ff.

[39]The many-sided, frequently repeated, persistently held doctrine of the disappearing nature of the direct commodity producer in a fully developed capitalist society dates at least from the *Communist Manifesto*, persists through the latest writings of Marx and Engels, and was critically reviewed in the great revisionist debate of the early 1900s. See Lichtheim, *Marxism* 1961, pages 289 ff.; P. Gay, *Dilemma of Democratic Socialism*, 1962, pages 166–220. "The lower strata of the middle class—the small tradespeople, shopkeepers, rentiers, the handicraftsmen and peasants—all these sink gradually into the proletariat, partly because their di-

In agriculture, the victory of the direct producer in most of the world has for its foundation the unsuitability of large-scale production with its personnel specialized in a narrow set of detailed operations. The diversified husbandry of the family farm with its scattered theater of operations does not permit either the standardized operations or the close supervision required for employees. The capitalist farm has a hard time holding labor attracted to urban centers with diversified job opportunities and higher wage levels. In the field of building, the general contractor is often primarily a skilled building tradesman who in rural areas and small towns contracts for building work to carry out with one or more assistants or to subcontract to specialized craftsmen. The work of personal service—including nearly all the practicing professions and the new world of repair activity on both traditional products and the new consumer appliances and vehicles—all bear the stamp of the SCPM.

The SCPM, we need remark, has in many fields maintained its place only by relinquishing much of its freedom of action. In the field of petroleum product distribution, the gasoline service station operator is in most areas of the United States only nominally independent because he is bound to a particular product source with whose brand he is stamped and whose main line and sidelines he must carry to retain his franchise. The privilege of cancellation of contract on very short notice puts this nominally independent dealer in a condition of near bondage that has often led to overt dealer revolts and hostility to the master, the integrated petroleum company.[40] Although the same is true for "branded" retail outlets generally, even when they are independently owned and operated, it is not true for those forms of branded distribution for which the brand is created by an association of retail dealers

---

minutive capital does not suffice for the scale on which modern industry is carried on and is swamped in competition with the big capitalist, partly because their specialized skill is rendered worthless by new methods of production." See Marx and Engels, *Communist Manifesto*, 1848, pages 491 f., 494, 498. Other texts were cited in full in Gottlieb, "Pluralist or Unitary Economic Systems," 1972, page 81 f., n. 16.

[40]From the earliest days of the Standard Oil monopoly, the efforts by that company to regiment under corporate control distribution of their product in bulk stations aroused strong opposition from independent wholesalers who did not like to be converted into branded distributors. After the automobile came into widespread use, the oil companies after some experimentation with company-operated stations with employed labor shifted over to leasing stations to independent operators subject to onerous lease provisions. These usually required certain hours of operation to be maintained around the clock, and certain quantities of product to be distributed, combined with the main brand company-supported lines of accessories. Service operators were denied the ordinary rights of employees, including collective bargaining and retirement and health benefits. Leases could be cancelled on very short notice, as low as 10 days and commonly 30 days. See Engler, *Politics of Oil*, 1961, pages 43 ff.; U.S. Senate Committee on Interior and Insular Affairs Hearings, *Market Performance and Competition*, 1973, pt. 1, pages 10–60; 1973, pt. 2, pages 572 ff., 584 ff., 530 ff., 577 ff.

arranging for a common supply, national advertising, planning, and other functions.

The SCPM has also held its own by increasing the relative amount of work performed by employees, and oftentimes the owner participates only slightly in the main work carried out by the enterprise, which then is more properly classified under the capitalist mode of production. Because the borderline between the two modes is hard to draw by a mechanical formula, at different stages of their life cycle, and sometimes at different seasons of the year, an enterprise may appear predominantly under the one or the other heading. The world of SCPM is continually breeding and producing capitalist producers, though the converse, a regression to SCPM status, rarely occurs.[41]

SLAVE MODE

The slave mode (SM) of production belongs to a broader class of unfree labor modes characterized by an objectively stratified society and an antagonistic relationship between a master class able to exert direct coercive control over a subordinated class of laborers and the means of production utilized. The relationship is objectively exploitative in that its purpose is to take from one class for the benefit of the other. In the apprehension of most members of each class, however, their relationship may be held as mutually beneficial and based upon reciprocal service or merit in either this or another (imaginary) world.

The scope of coercive control in the SM may be very narrow or may extend to all features of life: arrangement of the home; place, method, hours of work; clothing and foodstuffs as provided; forms of play; marriage; and worship or religious observances. The forms of control and the degree to which they are internal or external will vary widely depending upon the isolation of the society and its density of settlement, ethnic makeup, cultural tradition, and opportunities for gain. External controls include the chain or shackles, whipping, branding or mutilation to permit ready identification where needed, fencing or ditching, patrolling, and the like. Internal controls include beliefs that are fully internalized as moral obligations by both classes to induce appropriate behavior with a minimum of coercion.

Whichever the form of unfree labor, the SM cannot function very long and survive as a self-reproducing mode of production unless it is a widely

---

[41]One of the few valid generalizations about SCPM appearing in the chapter of Institute of Economics, *Political Economy*, 1954, devoted to this mode (ch. 4) is the tendency of the mode to "serve as the point of departure for the rise and development of capitalist relations" because of competition among commodity producers leading to enrichment of some and ruin of others (page 69).

prevailing form over a bounded area where it is recognized in law and is given supportive treatment. This follows from the fact that the core of the SM is a coercive relationship. No matter how internalized the subordination may be, in time the relationship will become questioned and resisted by the subordinated class, or at least its boldest and strongest members. Over time in cultural habits and in speech the subordinated class will have become assimilated with the masters. Hence it is not possible to maintain the relationship unless it appears to its members to be a *universal* form that is inescapable. In highly broken country, on archipelagos, or in scattered settlements surrounded by wastelands (deserts, swamps, and the like), or wherever travel is difficult and strangers are inhospitably treated, the bounds of the area can be quite small. In the open plains, where natural boundaries are scarcer, the area must be very considerable if the coercive system is to be maintained. Where the coercive area is not completely closed, as was the case in the antebellum southern United States, and is neighbored by societies in which the ethic and law of bondage are in question, then it is more important that the coercive relationship be sheltered by special protective arrangements of the type embodied in the fugitive slave provision of the American constitution.[42]

With a limitation that will be specified shortly, the mode of production most complete and beneficial to an upper class is unquestionably the classical state of slavery. In its ideal form, this SM involves complete subordination to control in all dimensions of life: obedience to all orders, liability to corporal punishment administered by the master or his agents, appropriation of the products of toil, the requirement to perform all desired services, accommodation when required for sexual access, reproduction of status by offspring, and virtual absence of civil rights. The orders may relate to work, play, mating, housing, diet and time of meals, articles of dress, and sexual access. The latter is usually only sought by males of the master class from desirable sexual objects, usually young slave females. Punishment may be inflicted by whipping, beating, incarceration, chaining, deprival of food or water for a limited period, and other harsh treatment. Civil rights to prevent undue injury to the slave are only nominal because the slave will have little or no access to courts to utilize his legal rights. In any contest between master and slave, the word of the slave must be disregarded to uphold the discipline of the institution.[43] The successful operation of the slave institution inherently involves

[42]For the story of the adoption of this provision (Article IV, Section 2, No. 3, American Constitution), which made escape from slavery much more difficult, see Robinson, *Slavery in American Politics*, 1971, pages 228 ff.

[43]Romans were proud of the slave-protective provisions of their slave code, as were other peoples who took the trouble to work out these provisions; but they are mostly without effect except if members of the master class intercede on behalf of oppressed slaves to redress wrongs. See Davis, *Slavery in Western Culture*, 1970, pages 73 ff.; Winks, *Slavery*, 1973, pages 141 f.

sale or transfer of chattels to adjust settlement patterns to changes in climate or resource use, to allow for sex disparities in particular communities, to allow for altered needs for labor power in different regions and industries, to allow for the partitioning of estates by inheritance, and to redistribute resources among productive enterprises.

The advantages of slavery to a master class are many. In the SM the range of exploitation is widened from both ends. The conditions of life of the slave can be arranged so that in housing, dress, food, and other personal needs, the slave's consumption of goods and services can be held to the minimum. Few sumptuary codes are as stringent as the code of slavery. Only coarse garments needed for protection to preserve health can be provided. Feeding can be confined to rations of nutritious staple cereals and the cheapest kind of animal or vegetable fats and proteins. Housing is a simple frame building with the fewest possible amenities. Both the intensity and hours of work can be stretched to the fullest. Indeed, it is often stretched too far without sufficient rest periods.

There is a tradition among economists that the labor of the slave "is given reluctantly."[44] No doubt it is. But this reluctance to work can be overcome by use of the stick and the carrot. The stick is punishment, which in artful doses and given full visibility provides strong negative incentive for constant exertion. This can of course be supplemented by small rewards, which if they are infrequent and few in number are the more highly valued. It is this combination of negative sanctions and positive rewards that yields results in work camps under the worst working conditions.[45]

The completeness of control that can be utilized by a master maximizes the potential of enslavement as a means of exploitation. The slave has abundant reasons to cherish the goodwill of the master, to seek continually to become ingratiated, and to aim constantly to please because the master has so much ability to hurt or injure as well as to bestow favors, including the ultimate boon of emancipation.

Nor did Romans flinch from carrying out one of the more brutal provisions of their slave code requiring the execution, according to what Tacitus called "ancient custom," of every slave residing in a household where a master or one of his family was presumably murdered by a slave belonging to the household. In the instance noted by Tacitus, *Annals of Imperial Rome*, bk. 14, A.D. 61, the number of slaves about to be executed was very large, some 400, and "a crowd gathered eager to save so many innocent lives." The humanitarian residues, as Pareto would describe them, were not dead to Romans of that period. After debate, the Senate voted for execution to make sure that every slave had ample incentive out of fear for their own lives to (*watch for* and) intercede to protect the life of the master or his family members.

[44]Cairnes, *Slave Power*, 1862, page 28.

[45]That was the central disclosure of the concentration camp regime of the Soviet archipelago as depicted in the work of Solzhenitsyn, *Gulag Archipelago*, 1960s.

The other two standard economist complaints about the SM are that slave labor is "unskillful" and is "wanting in versatility."[46] These complaints make no allowance for the widespread use of slaves in household service where considerable skill is involved in a wide variety of duties like cleaning, food handling, nursing and child care, personal grooming. In most systems of slavery slaves are widely trained in artisan crafts and even in professional pursuits such as those of the teacher, clerk, healer, or musician. This was notably true of the Graeco-Roman world, where the slave artisan, clerk, civil servant, shopkeeper, building trade worker, and carpenter frequently functioned on the jobs alongside their free counterparts or their masters.[47] Russian landlords of the nineteenth century, who treated their serfs in many essential respects like slaves, commonly singled out suitable younger serfs for apprenticeship in desired crafts and for formal schooling.[48]

Because practice of a skill would ordinarily make a slave more valuable to the owner, it could readily bring with it somewhat easier treatment and better working conditions. Thus slaves could aspire to master skilled crafts for the same reason as free workers: to improve their conditions of life. Indeed, the harsher life condition of the ordinary slave could very well make the learning and the later exercise of a craft skill a momentous occasion. Urban slaves practicing a craft or skilled labor, who were leased out for independent hire or even under self-management for payment of a fixed rental, were often able to work for their own emancipation by installment-purchase arrangements, a common practice in the Graeco-Roman world and well protected in law.[49] In the American South, however, a strong tradition developed to discourage skill formation among slaves—attributable to the abnormal environment of this particular slave society with its increasingly strong attachment to personal freedom and universal civil rights. Slave insurrections and escapes were often engineered by slaves or free blacks with advanced skills. Moreover, slave-

[46]Cairnes, *Slave Power*, 1862, page 28.

[47]The role played in Roman law by the slave agent who was allowed to represent the master in a variety of business transactions indicates the penetration by the slave of business management or proprietorial roles. Jolowicz and Nichols, *Roman Law*, 1932, pages 83 f., 256 f. See also Jones, *Later Roman Empire*, 1966, vol. 2, for use of slaves as estate managers, in public service, and of course as personal servants (696 f., 851 f., 836 f., 833 f.). For skilled crafts among slaves, see Finley, *Ancient Economy*, 1973, pages 74, 76 ff., 44, 58, 64.

[48]In the three Kropotkin country estates that Peter Kropotkin knew well as a young lad, skilled training was frequently noted for fine embroidery, piano-tuning, doctoring, and agronomy. See Kropotkin, *Memoirs of a Revolutionist*, 1899, pages 50 f., 56 ff. Gogol in his classic account of the swindler buying "dead souls" (still retained on tax lists) has his readers in stitches as serf owners seek higher prices for those dead serfs with artisan skills. See Gogol, *Dead Souls*, 1842, pages 11 ff., 61 f.

[49]Finley, *Ancient Economy*, 1973, pages 64 ff., 76 ff.

holders had access to a free wage-earner class capable of supplying artisan skills.[50]

Slavery not only maximizes exploitation of slave labor; it also provides to the master class a valuable supplement in the form of social esteem and sexual gratification virtually at will and under favorable conditions. This gratification satisfied what Malthus called the single most intense human want other than for food.[51] This is most readily provided where plural marriage is accepted in the culture; but where it is not, females of the master class manage to adjust to the double standard that in any case shadows monogamic marriage. Nearly everywhere it gives a special premium to the sexually attractive female slave, and this master-slave relationship invariably leaves its trail in the form of a mestizo population.[52] To that extent sexual gratification with slaves tends to undermine the institution of slavery itself because masters are often reluctant to have their own offspring live as slaves; favored female slaves will tend to be emancipated or treated as if emancipated; and the homogenization of the slave and master population will tend to erase the readily recognized ethnic stamp of the slave and thus facilitate his or her assimilation.

We may thus dismiss the claim that the slave mode as a general rule is

---

[50]Gutman in his magnificent critique, *Time on the Cross, Slavery and the Numbers Game*, shows the fallacy in the analysis by which Fogel and Engerman in their *Time on the Cross* conclude that 11.9% of rural slaves were artisans, that slaves virtually dominated "the top non-ownership management" of large plantations, and that a high fraction of urban artisans were slaves whose services were hired out. See Gutman, *Time on the Cross*, 1975; Fogel and Engerman, *Time on the Cross*, 1974, pages 48–82.

[51]Malthus postulated his entire work on population on two human wants: "First, that food is necessary to the existence of man. Secondly, that the passion between the sexes is necessary and will remain nearly in its present state." See Malthus, 1799, page 8. In later editions, the two postulata were consolidated: "After the desire of food, the most powerful and general of our desires is the passion between the sexes, taken in an enlarged sense" (page 481).

[52]After the abolition of serfdom in Russia, Kropotkin's father once confided to the son that though his punishment of serfs was at times severe, he never took advantage of his maids as did a neighboring serf owner upon whom the peasant women had planned to inflict a "terrible punishment." See Kroptkin, *Memoirs of a Revolutionist*, 1899, page 61 f. "The sexual exploitation of female slaves by white men was the most disgraceful . . . aspect of Jamaican slave society. It was common practice for a white man visiting a plantation to be offered a slave girl for the night." Winks, *Slavery*, 1973, page 149. Portuguese Brazil was the highpoint of miscegenation in Latin America. Gilberto Freyre declares that the Portuguese planter "without leaving his own lands could have as many women as he wished in addition to the legitimate one he had brought from Portugal"; the result has been "stabilization of mixed-bloods in a new ethnic type." See Freyre, *New World in the Tropics*, 1963, pages 69, 119. American slaveowners or overseers lagged somewhat in utilizing their sexual access, as the statistics of our mulatto population inherited from slavery indicate, with a range of 13–20% for slave population and a much higher percentage of the free Negro population. Note "fancy-girl" slave markets with their much higher prices. On "miscegenation," see Genovese, *Roll Jordan Roll*, 1976, pages 413–431. The topic is unending, and Genovese's references will suffice.

unprofitable, that is, does not yield to the master class enough advantages to justify its continuation, provided of course that it can be upheld and administered without excessive reliance upon direct coercion. If the enslaved are determined to revolt and therefore must be kept chained or maintained under virtually military guard, as in a concentration camp, and if the institution of slavery is itself under question, then of course slavery can not be profitable. Before the nineteenth century, in nearly all of human society it was possible to maintain without excessive direct coercion the institution of slavery among most ethnically unrelated peoples, and even frequently among an ethnically homogeneous or kindred people (as among the Chinese, Russians, Africans, Semites, and Latins). Throughout most of history it was not the state of slavery that was questioned; it was the presupposition of freedom that was strange. Freedom was conceived of as inherent only in one's homeland where one had inherited or maintained rights and obligations bound in community. Wrenched from that community or invaded by a technologically and militarily superior people, one had no rights except such as would be granted by the mercy of one's hosts. If captured in war, one's life was forfeit and either death or some form of slavery was a near-universal expectation. Slavery was justified as an institution by the ancients in these very terms, and against this background of thinking slaves could frequently be armed and induced to fight for the master class, sometimes without even the promise of emancipation as a reward.[53]

Because a matured bourgeois society only emerges in very special conditions as an upshot of a series of historical developments, the SM encountered few impediments historically. It is found in many societies at or near the primitive level and through the Bronze and Iron ages. In North America it was a developed institution among Pacific Coast Indians. It has been a general feature of the Malay Archipelago, among Polynesians, and among Africans north of the Zambesi. It prevailed widely among all Indo-European peoples, Semitic peoples, and the ancient Egyptians. It was found as an important institution in the Graeco-Roman world from its earliest years, in China, in the Moslem world, in the early medieval world, and in the New World

---

[53]Enlistment of slaves in the Roman legions was ordinarily prohibited, but in several national emergencies it was successfully carried through, as after the catastrophe of Canae in 216 B.C. at the critical point of the Second Punic War. Some 8000 slaves "healthy and in the prime of life," according to Livy's account, were "bought from owners at the public expense having first been asked individually if they were willing to serve"; apparently they successfully served. See Livy, *History of Rome* 29 B.C.–A.D. 17, bk. 21, para. no. 57. Interestingly enough, after two years of military service emancipation was promised as a reward in the coming battle for any man "who brings from the field an enemy's head"; but the transportation of "heads" was so disorganizing during battle that the order was given to drop the heads and keep on fighting (bk. 24, para. no. 14 f.).

throughout Latin America, the Caribbean, and the southern portion of the United States.[54] Slavery readily takes the form of subjugating one people commonly regarded as "barbarian" or "inferior" by another, but it also arises within ethnically homogeneous peoples when socioeconomic stratification gives rise to upper classes or castes that consider themselves superior and worthy of masterhood. Additionally, it can arise as a form of collecting tax tribute from village communities, from inability to repay debt, or from the sale of children by families seeking refuge from famine.

Because the SM was so readily established or evolved and appears so advantageous to masters, there is something problematic about the mode's continual tendency either to disappear or to turn into less rigorous forms of unfree labor. We can account partly for this by sex disparities associated with beginning forms of slavery. Under the earliest conditions, these disparities took the form of enslavement only of female captives retained as war booty for household service or concubinage, as among the Trojan women who appear in classical Greek tragedies.[55] Where the hostile soldiers are captured and not slaughtered, large numbers become available at one time. They are readily accommodated in three forms of gang labor: in mines, on galleys, or on large plantations. The Roman latifundium evolved to meet the needs of large acreages of fertile land expropriated from enemy peoples and staffed with a labor force of purchased or leased war captives handled as slaves.

In household service, with its call for ceaseless and undivided attention, the slave finds it virtually impossible to reproduce, except among the females as concubines. Sometimes the domestic slave achieves a degree of intimacy that often results in emancipation after a lifetime of personal service. In any case, offspring tend to be emancipated. By contrast, in the brutal labor of mine or galley and of the plantation with its tradition of gang labor, the slave is deprived of home life and is converted into a work animal under conditions that do not usually permit reproduction.[56] Even where sex disparities are

[54]For surveys of prevalence see the articles under the heading of "slavery" by B. J. Stern for "primitive," W. L. Westermann for "ancient," and M. M. Knight for "modern" in Seligman *et al.*, *Encyclopedia of Social Sciences*, 1930–1934, pages 73–84 and in the extended bibliography, 88 ff., items by Nieboer, Hobhouse, Westermarck, Sumner, Henshaw, Meyer, Mendelsohn, Frank; see also, D. W. Davis, *Slavery*, 1970, pages 44–77.

[55]From Euripides, *Andromache*; *The Trojan Women*; Aeschylus, *Agamemnon*; from Sophocles, *Electra*. Nor did the dramatists have to recall the anguish from a remote past. Three times between 427 B.C. and 416 B.C., Thucydides records, after storming a city the victors destroyed the male survivors and enslaved women and children. See Thucydides, *History of the Peloponnesian War*, fifth century B.C., ch. 10, page 69, ch. 13, pages 47 f., ch. 17, page 116.

[56]"The workers have no families and do not reproduce themselves. The permanence of such plantations is therefore dependent upon slave hunts, either through war or through periodical raids on a large slave hunting territory such as Africa. . . . The slaves are without

avoided and mating among slaves is permitted with arrangements for family domiciles, harsh treatment by brutal overseers accustomed to the ready use of the lash breaks the spirit, affecting the ability to reproduce or else inducing a definite resistance to childbearing.[57] Hence the common theme of the SM is that it does not adequately reproduce, that is, does not permit enslaved peoples enough domestic facilities and freedom in their domestic arrangements to induce them to raise families and thus to reproduce not only biologically but socially, thereby providing a new generation of young slaves who will serve a new generation of masters. Nonreproduction was the nemesis of the SM in the Graeco-Roman world and in Islamic and Chinese societies where slave employment was chiefly in household service. Nonreproduction was the uniform characteristic of slave societies in Latin America and in the Caribbean, as has been frequently noted.[58] Without a fresh supply of new slaves obtained at the frontier by pillaging, conquest, or slave trading, the slave mode of production would tend to dry up. The outstanding exceptions to this were in the two great continental areas where forms of slave estate farming evolved—in Russia and in the southern United States—with a high degree of exploitation combined with successful reproduction.[59] By a striking historical coincidence, slavery was abolished in both countries in the same decade of the nineteenth century.

---

families and without property and are herded together in barracks, combining dormitory, pesthouse, and cell for confinement against escape. Work goes forward under strict military routine, beginning with an answer to reveille in the morning, with march in closed ranks to and from work and issue of clothing by a warehouse to which it must be returned." See Weber, *General Economic History*, 1923, page 80. (Weber had an expert knowledge from his doctoral dissertation of Roman agrarian institutions). See also Malthus, *Principle of Population*, 1799, pages 232 ff.

[57]Resistance of slave women to child-bearing is frequently indicated. Weber, *General Economic History*, 1923, page 81; Knight, *Slave Society in Cuba*, 1970, page 78; Curtin, "Epidemiology and the Slave Trade," 1968, page 213 ff. "Of all forms of breeding that of human cattle is one of the hardest." Clapham and Power, *Cambridge Economic History of Europe*, vol. 1, page 235.

[58]Furtado, *Economic Growth of Brazil*, 1961, pages 127 ff.; Curtin, *Atlantic Slave Trade*, 1969, pages 28 ff. The sheer statistics were overwhelming. Brazil imported altogether some 3.6 million slaves mostly before 1850; yet the slave population enumerated in 1872 counted only 1.5 million slaves. Cuban slave importation was heavy and between 1835–1864 brought in nearly 390,000 slaves; yet the slave population in 1871 was less than 300,000. Knight, *Slave Society in Cuba*, 1970, pages 53, 63, 79. Genovese put it simply: "The less than 400,000 Africans imported into the North American British colonies had become a black population ten times greater by 1860, whereas despite much larger importations by Jamaica, Saint-Dominique, Brazil and Cuba these and other slave countries struggled to balance imports against mortality in order to hold their own in population." See Genovese, *Roll Jordan Roll*, 1976, page 57.

[59]With all its flaws, the Fogel and Engerman *Time on the Cross*, and the parallel work of Genovese, *Roll Jordan Roll*, both emphasize the achievement of North American slave masters

Feudal Mode

The weaknesses of the slave mode and the difficulty of successfully utilizing its potential for exploitation without hampering reproduction, biological and social, necessarily led to forms of exploitation of unfree labor that may be called *serf* or *feudal mode of production.* This mode embodies a set of relations that permit effective exploitation by methods of coercive control that widen the laborer's scope in a delimited quantum of free time for independent decision-making and responsibility, give the laborer greater control over his family and domestic arrangements. The former condition creates an economic basis for improved incentives and enterprise; the latter fosters greater social esteem and standing, which assures reproduction.

The serf form for accomplishing this end result involves the following elements:

1. The power of the state is in the hands of the master or his agent.
2. The whole land is owned or controlled by the master, though the laborer is vested with possessory rights over his homestead, allotted fields, farm equipment, livestock, and household goods.
3. Social subordination of the laborer who has, however, rights to his family and to marriage, and who is free from corporal punishment at will.
4. Obligation by the laborer to give either labor service, money, or products to the master, more or less exhausting the surplus of the laborer over subsistence.[60]
5. Restricted ability of the laborer to move.

---

over some two centuries in handling their African slaves and acculturating them—by harsh dealing, by paternalistic arrangements, by permitting enough domestic life, and by the attraction of a higher cultural state. The sullen and withdrawn African became a cooperative, Christianized, English-speaking Afro-American adapted to subordination. The critical work of Gutman, David and Temin, and other *Time on the Cross* critics has adequately shown that this productive and reproductive achievement of southern slave masters was achieved by steady doses of coercive handling (chiefly whipping), that family breakup was a common experience, and that exploitation greatly exceeded the mere 10% of social product calculated by Fogel and Engerman. A similar achievement is to be accorded Russian masters who imposed a slave state on the village communities of their own people, drawing partly on subordination inherited from the early Kievian state and partly on the reaction to prolonged Mongol rule. See Fogel and Engerman, *Time on the Cross*, 1974; Genovese, *Roll Jordan Roll*, 1976; Gutman, *Time on the Cross*, 1975.

[60]The habit of appropriating the surplus of the cultivator over his subsistence had become so ingrained in the culture of earlier centuries that the young science of economics simply presupposed that *that* surplus was the natural *rent* of land. In the memorable words of Petty, whom Marx called "the founder of modern political economy" (from Engels, *Herr Dühring's Revolution*, 1877–1878, page 262): "Suppose a man could with his own hands plant a certain

In its European form, the serf mode was typically implanted in village communities by having dominant demesne holdings, under seignorial control, interspersed with serf holdings. The demesne holding enabled the masters to participate in the production process by recruiting and directing the labor that produced the surplus product. The demesne, however, was not essential, especially for a nonresident master with interest elsewhere or without a permanent vested place in the village. Hence feudal appropriation could be successfully organized without a demesne holding, as in Japan, by collecting a surplus product (or its equivalent in money) as rent transferred as a reward to the owner or controller of the land. Because, as we shall see in Chapter 8 on property, the institution of ownership requires the support of government, the same transfer can be viewed as either a tax or a rent, depending on the nature of that support, the extent to which rights of tax collection are vested in the collector, and the character of the collector's local involvement.[61]

Social subordination may be inscribed in law codes, or else it may take the form of a general obligation to give deference and support as needed. In India, this subordination kept degraded castes, whose touch or even shadow was deemed polluting, confined to the most menial and low-paid labor. In its European form, subordination involved vassalage: the promise to obey and serve.

The power of the state reduces to an effective monopoly of local coercion according to established norms and authority, both to judge controversies in formal trials or hearings and to punish offenders and make settlements.[62] In

scope of Land with Corn, i.e., could Digg, or Plough; Harrow, Weed, Reap, Cary home, Thresh and Winnow, so much as the Husbandry of this land requires; and had withal Seed wherewith to sow the same. I say, that when this man had subducted his seed out of the proceed of his harvest, and also what himself hath both eaten and given to others in exchange for Clothes, and other Natural necessities; that the Remainder of Corn, is the natural and true Rent of the Land for that year; and the medium of seven years, or rather so many years as make up the Cycle, within which Dearths and Plenties make their revolution, doth give the ordinary Rent of the Land in Corn." Cited Marshall, *Principles of Economics*, 1890, page 635 n. l.

[61]See Footnote 10 for discussion of the so-called Asiatic mode of production in which the issue of state ownership of land or state property in land and the character of the surplus product as tax or rent come into question. The demesne was relatively weak in most of Germany for reasons well-stated by Weber, *General Economic History*, 1923, pages 72 f. Japanese serfs lived in well-organized village communities from which armed retainers (samurai) had been withdrawn and settled in castle towns of the some 250 fiefs in which the country was divided. See T. C. Smith, *Agrarian Origins of Modern Japan*, 1971, pages 54 ff., 182 f., 203 f., 181.

[62]This power of judicial administration is the underpinning of the mode as Weber and Homans make very clear. Homans, *English Villagers*, 1941, ch. 20, Weber, *General Economic History*, 1923, pages 65 ff.

medieval Europe the serf might at times bear arms and have some training in soldiering, but his arms were inferior and all heavy armament (including armor and horse) were used only by the master and his entourage.[63] Yet in its West European form, this status of subordination and deference yielded ultimately to some sense of independence nourished by the privacy of the home, the strength of the village community, calls for military service, and sometimes the possibility of appeal to a higher kingly authority.[64]

Claim to ownership of village land or its proper "holding" was central to the authority of the master. In European forms of serfdom, it was constantly reasserted with every new incumbency. The rights of the old holder (and some of his property) expired with his death or retirement, but the new holder could only take possession on receiving an express grant from the master or his agent after swearing the oath of fealty.[65] This sense of ownership and control in the land was continuously exhibited in prohibitions on use and access to pasturage, woodlands, and running waters and on hunting wild game. In India and the Near East, although ownership might belong nominally to some higher national authority, such as king or emperor, in practice the local representative collected primarily in his behalf, turning over a portion of taxes to the central ruler.

Basic ownership of land is consistent with possessory rights of serf-tenants over allotted fields, homestead, and chattels because these rights are subject to judicial administration controlled by the master or his agent. Restricted ability to move involved a formal bonding to the estate or manor. In practice this assured the manor a stable labor supply except in time of disaster and a means to control (and tax) exodus from the estate of surplus younger laborers or girls for whom there was no productive place. In England, hardly an instance has come to light in which a request to move away or leave the manor was not granted with payment of the requisite tax (or fine).[66] The dispersion

[63]The manorial lord in his heyday was a "warrior" on horseback, "body and soul." Serfs were called into service as foot soldiers or orderlies and had no right in ordinary times to bear arms. See Thierry, *Norman Conquest*, 1825, vol. 1, page 91; Bloch, *Feudal Society*, 1939–1940, vol. 1, pages 250, 257, 289; Homans, *English Villagers*, 1941, pages 248, 329.

[64]The plays of the great Spanish dramatist de Vega, writing in the early decades of the seventeenth century, the dusk of Spanish serfdom, illustrate the audacious spirit of peasant villagers in their struggle against feudal oppression. See especially *Peribanez* and *Fuenteovejuna*.

[65]The manuals for holding hallmotes in the fourteenth and later centuries described the service of fealty thus: "Hear this my Lord! I Roger will be faithful and loyal to thee, and faith to thee will bear of the tenement that I hold of thee in villeinage, and will be justiciable by thee in body and chattels. So help me God and his saints." Homans, *English Villagers*, 1941, page 255; on vassalage generally, see Bloch, *Feudal Society*, 1939–1940, vol. 1, pages 145–163.

[66]Postan, *Medieval Economy and Society*, 1972, page 162.

throughout agricultural country of walled free market towns—"nonfeudal islands in the feudal seas," as Postan called them[67]—steadily attracted recruits seeking their fortune from the adjacent countryside. Although it was not easy to find a place in town, growth of industry and trade accommodated more people. Also, the failure of towns, especially the larger ones, to reproduce themselves, chiefly because of unsanitary conditions in their close quarters, opened room for rural immigration even under stationary economic conditions.[68]

The obligation to give service in money or products did not usually take the form of a single billing for so many total hours of labor service and/or so much by way of money value in goods, like the annual net balance due of a modern income tax. It was usually a composite total made up of a wide variety of takings, sharings and pluckings under many different headings, taking advantage of the ownership rights of masters and special needs of serf households. The core of the billing reduced to a share in the basic grain crop—in wheat, barley, oats, corn, or rice, according to the cultivated staple—or labor service in plowing, cultivating, and harvesting the crop on the master's land. Labor service for these purposes was usually very detailed, East

[67]Younger sons with no place in the village, or younger daughters for whom marriage could not be arranged, left the village to try their fortune elsewhere. See Homans, *English Villagers*, 1941, pages 133, 139. Postan describes the towns as follows: "Medieval towns were precisely that . . . non-feudal islands in the feudal seas; places in which merchants could not only live in each other's vicinity and defend themselves collectively but also places which enjoyed or were capable of developing systems of local government . . . exempting them from the sway of the feudal regime." Postan, *Medieval Economy and Society*, 1972, page 239. Add to merchants, craftsmen, and the fraternity—or, as Weber put it, "brotherhood in arms for mutual aid and protection"—and the rule that "town air makes free" if the countryman has become resident and thus a citizen. See Weber, *General Economic History*, 1923, ch. 28, especially pages 317 ff., 329 f.; Mundy and Riesenberg, *Medieval Town*, 1958, pages 43 f. and readings indicated there; Mumford, *City in History*, 1961, chs. 9–11.

[68]The longstanding failure of urban communities until modern times to biologically reproduce themselves is well-established in demographic literature. Drawing upon an extensive analysis of differential mortality and fertility for urban and rural parishes in England and on the Continent in the eighteenth and early decades of the nineteenth century, Malthus concluded that "There certainly seems to be something in great towns and even in moderate towns peculiarly unfavourable to the very early stages of life," so that "to fill up the void occasioned by this mortality in towns . . . a constant supply of recruits from the country is necessary." See Malthus, *Principle of Population*, 1799, pages 283 f. "Rural communities have been the centers of production of a surplus of human beings, and the urban communities the centers of their consumption." See Sorokin and Zimmerman, *Rural–Urban Sociology*, 1929, page 44, 215 f., and for certain limitations of this generalization for the later nineteenth century and twentieth century, pages 422 ff. Reaching the same conclusions, see Russell, "Population in Europe," 1972–1976, vol. 1, pages 48, 64; Haines, "Fertility and Marriage," 1980, pages 151–158.

and West, for the various farm operations.[69] Where crop deliveries were involved, sometimes the harvested crop was transported to special places for threshing operations under the observation of the landlord or tax collector.[70] The obligation for service then specified carting or carrying landlord produce either to the nearest market town or to the main residence of the master.[71] When the hunting season came around, the serf was obligated to feed the pack. "On certain days, the tenant brings the lord's steward perhaps a few small silver coins or, more often, sheaves of corn harvested on his fields, chickens from his farmyard, cakes of wax from his beehives on the arable or the meadows of the demesne."[72]

Nearly universal was the arrogation by the landlord of the monopoly (banalités) of local facilities frequently used by villagers: service of the bull or boar for stud purposes; use of the grinding mill, the baking oven, or the winepress; or the brewing of beer.[73] Very widespread was the arrogation of tithing revenues nominally paid to the local church for religious services.[74] There was also a basic head tax (tallage).[75] All the fines paid in the village community for violating the bylaws or order of the community were harvested by the master, who presided over the village community court.[76] Then there were the dues payable at critical stages of the family life cycle, such as when a younger son left the village or entered the church, or upon the marriage of a daughter, or on the succession of the landlord's heir to the hold-

[69]Marx had great fun in excoriating for all time the Danubian Boyars whose greed for "labour-service" was set forth in a state document analyzed in *Capital* I, 1867, pages 235–242. The labor services are described in contemporary documents "in elaborate detail," often specifying allowances of food, drink, or money paid in "reprisal." See Homans, *English Villagers*, 1941, pages 257 f., 261 ff. For the Asiatic provinces of Ottoman Turkey, see Gibb and Bowen, *Islamic Society*, 1950, pages 240 f.

[70]Gibb and Bowen, *Islamic Society*, 1950.

[71]Homans, *English Villagers*, 1941, pages 257 f.

[72]Bloch, *Feudal Society*, 1939–1940, vol. 1, page 250.

[73]Bloch, *Feudal Society*, 1939–1940, vol. 1, pages 251 f. Use of *banalités* was widest in French feudalism but present also in Germany and England. Weber, *General Economic History*, 1923, page 72.

[74]Bloch, *Feudal Society*, 1939–1940, vol. 1, page 252; Homans elaborates on the tithing revenues, the *avowson* of a parish rector as a source of landowner profit, and the substitute priest or "vicar." See Homans, *English Villagers*, 1941, ch. 24. Rogers estimated the total income yielded by the parish church at 40% of the manorial revenue but he does not allow for diversion for manorial use. See Rogers, *Six Centuries*, 1883, pages 161 f.

[75]Commonly masquerading as a "gift," it was an aid or tallage (*taille*) or *demande, queste,* or *bede* but sometimes frankly called *toulte* from the verb *tolir,* "to take." See Bloch, *Feudal Society*, 1939–1940, vol. 1, pages 252 f.; Homans, *English Villagers*, 1941, pages 227, 237, 275 ff.

[76]Hallmote records show this made up a copious collection. See Homans, *English Villagers*, 1941, page 227, ch. 20; Postan, *Medieval Economy and Society*, 1972, page 139.

ing.[77] Not counting the tithing to the church or special taxes levied by kingly authority or many special labor services provided, a recent historian of the English feudal mode has estimated that the total of the due payable by an average villein household reached 50% of the household output, a level that came to be regarded as the "landlord's normal 'rake-off'."[78] That is consistent with the considered judgment of a widely respected European economic historian writing a half-century ago that the total take of the European feudal mode came to 67% of the peasant output, with the *Grundherr* sharing the take evenly with crown and church.[79] A detailed survey of the burden on European villagers from the wide variety of dues and services still owed to their seigniors in the eighteenth and nineteenth centuries indicated that these fractions of village output of the feudal mode in its full vigor had not diminished much over the intervening centuries.[80] By contrast, it appeared that the feudal take by overlords from the Japanese village had diminished considerably as a fraction of output during the $2\frac{1}{2}$ centuries of the Tokugawa regime. Though the Japanese overlord still maintained a very stern regime in the village and punished instantly and severely any show of recalcitrance or insubordination, the village take had been reduced to some 30% of village output. The reasons for reduction were (1) new assessment levied on the village as a whole in a single billing, (2) allowance for a higher standard of living for the wealthier landowning peasant families that controlled the village and managed most of the farming, and (3) choosing not to tax unduly the rising levels of productivity due to improved husbandry or skill.[81]

[77]Homans, *English Villagers*, 1941, pages 252 ff., 144 ff., 133 ff.

[78]Postan, *Medieval Economy and Society* 1972, page 140.

[79]Kulischer, *Allgemeine Wirtschaftsgeschichte*, 1925, vol. 1, page 160 ff.

[80]Blum sums up his survey with the assertion that "when the attempt is made to add up the charges that rested upon the peasants of the servile lands, the totals reach seemingly incredible proportions." As he added up charges, they were sometimes 20% or less in certain parts of Saxony and on East Prussian royal manors; they appeared only a bit heavier in various districts of Switzerland. But in the Danubian provinces, in the Baltic provinces of Russia and Poland, in most of France, in Austrian Silesia, and in German and Slav crownlands, the feudal take of seigniors ran from a fourth to a third with supplementary takes for allied institutions of church and state. See Blum, *End of the Old Order*, 1978, pages 73–79.

[81]There seems to be much evidence to sustain Barrington Moore's judgment that feudal extraction from the villages in the Tokugawa period left "an increasing surplus among those peasants who were energetic enough to add to their output," despite respect for the maxim, 'Peasants are like sesame seeds; the more you press, the more comes out.'" See Moore, *Dictatorship and Democracy*, 1966, pages 241, 254. Smith's investigations suggested that though the feudal take by overlords was rarely less than 30% at the end of the Tokugawa regime and was sometimes more, yet the villagers retained for themselves the larger part of the growth in product and improved husbandry associated with the development of craft trades, wider markets, extension of irrigation, and the spread of improved techniques. See T. C. Smith, *Agrarian Origins*, 1959, pages 160, 181.

It is standard to explain the master–serf relationship in feudal society by saying that service was reciprocal: that the master and his armed knights gave protection while the enserfed villagers worked the land and gave personal service. The neat explanation, however, fails to note that the protection most needed was against the protectors themselves.[82] This high pitch of exploitation is sometimes traced to "custom" without allowing for how custom evolves or became established.[83] Very obviously that amount of nonreciprocal exchange cannot become institutionalized at the level of production at the time except by extreme pressure on life and limb and by a continual local show of force. Experience with slavery had shown that total subjugation— enchainment and use of the lash—was inadvisable and ineffectual, and eventually that opinion became incorporated into the common belief. Hence, while pressing hard, it was necessary to provide enough leeway for the subjugated class to breathe, react, and function as a social body. The loyalty of the peasant was needed in severe military contests. A semblance of rights and some civic personality for the vassal had to be recognized; those rights evolved with occasional appeals to the highest kingly level and with continual consultation in manorial courts and asssemblies.

In time it became clear that there was value in accepting the level of "custom" as a benchmark in resolving controversies. It was easier for the master to delegate the function of local estate management to an agent, the *reeve* or *bailiff*. Thus the absentee lord evolved.[84] To the villagers, custom functioned

---

[82]Oddly enough, feudal society performed very poorly in protecting its villagers from continued pillaging between the eighth and tenth centuries by bands of Saracens, Hungarians, and Northmen. Bloch puts it as follows: "That a handful of robbers perched on a hill in Provence should have been able for nearly a century to spread insecurity all along an immense mountain chain and partially close some of the vital routes of Christendom; that for even longer little detachments of horsemen from the steppes should have been left free to ravage the West in all directions; that year after year . . . the ships of the North should with impunity have hurled themselves against the shores of Germany, Gaul and Britain pirate bands eager for pillage; that in order to appease these brigands it should have been necessary to pay heavy ransoms and ultimately yield extensive territories to the most redoubtable of them—all these are surprising facts." Bloch, *Feudal Society*, 1939–1940, vol. 1, page 52.

[83]Statements of these customary rents and services were drawn up in formal documents by sworn juries of villeins recorded in hallmote records, and reference was commonly made in the language of the day to the "custom of the manor." "There are few words," says Homans, "which occur more commonly in English documents of the Middle Ages than custom, *consuetudo*," The term customer (*custumarius, consuetudinarius*) "was a common synonym for villein." See Homans, *English Villagers*, 1941, pages 9 f., 271 f., 140 f. Controversies were commonly resolved by having knowledgeable neighbors swear as to the custom involved. But as Marshall wisely pointed out: "[I]n fact the payment and dues, which custom is supposed to stereotype, nearly always contain elements which are incapable of precise definition . . . ." See Marshall, *Principles of Economics*, 1890, page 638.

[84]The key fact, of the evolution of the *absentee lord* who drew revenues from the manor and paid only an occasional visit to it, was closely associated with *multiple ownership* of manors.

as an imperfect protection against the total oppression inherent in the overlord to whom they had to pledge obedience and service. The overlord, armed to the teeth, had the apparatus of the law on his side. Yet, to safeguard its vital interests, the village community had to resist encroachments and struggle to enlarge its freedoms. Legal contests, involving appeals to the authority of the king or church, would sometimes smolder for generations.[85] Under pressure, the level of custom could drift.[86] In the century after the eleventh-century survey of Domesday Book, manorial profits in England are estimated to have risen by some 60% and again by as much in a half-century. Some of this came from growth in manorial population, but it also reflected improved productivity and enhanced exploitation. With changing social conditions and new socioreligious stirrings of Protestantism, the latent tension triggered mass peasant insurrection that broke out in England after visitations of famine and the Great Plague.[87]

The decline or disintegration of the feudal mode was nearly everywhere an extended process. The disappearance of the manorial regime, with its centrally worked demesne estate, scaled down the local demand for labor services for which a compensatory payment either in products or money was commonly exacted. Yet the proclamation or grant of formal freedom and the spread of freehold farming did not change the past, and sometimes a surviving

---

Imperial crown domains numbered hundreds of individual manors. As Homans notes: "The relations between lord and man . . . were . . . seldom a matter of face-to-face contact. If the lord held many manors, he probably would not reside at any for more than a week or two during the year." See Homans, *English Villagers*, 1941, page 229. William the Conqueror held some 1500 manors and many higher Norman lieutenants held manors up to three digits. Thierry, *Norman Conquest of England*, 1825, vol. 1, page 307. The great "honorial complexes" contained "hundreds of manors in all parts of the country" and like manors possessed by monasterial orders (with widespread properties) these "acquired most of the features of institutionalized landownership." Postan, *Medieval Economy and Society*, 1972, pages 103 f. Postan notes that "a large number of manorial estates were too far removed from the lord's physical presence and had to be left in charge of local agents occasionally controlled by intermittent audits or visitation." Marriage of wealthy family heirs or heiresses consolidated princely holdings. In consequence, Postan concludes that apart from home-farms of Benedictine abbeys "few demesnes still functioned under the direct management of their lords" (page 116).

[85]See an interesting case detailed by Homans, *English Villagers*, 1941, vol. 1, pages 276 ff. of the Halesowen Manor with a "century and a half of bad feeling between a lord and his tenants" (page 284).

[86]Postan, *Medieval Economy and Society*, 1972, page 187.

[87]The characteristics of the famine of 1315–1317, "one of the most spectacular in the 14th and 15th centuries," are explored together with the Great Plague of 1348 in Miskimin, *Early Renaissance Europe*, 1975, pages 26 ff. The drop in population in Europe was around 40%. "Whereas land had been scarce before the series of plagues, labor had now become the key factor in agricultural production" (page 29). Rogers gives a colorful account in "The Famine and the Great Plague," *Six Centuries*, 1883, ch. 8.

core of economic privileges and payments persisted even in Western Europe to the nineteenth century.[88] The privilege of judicial administration and the collection of fines remained in the hands of aristocratic landowners long after serfdom proper had disappeared. In Russia the so-called abolition of serfdom in 1861 only extended to peasant communities new rights in exchange for a complex arrangement of payments and performances binding them for generations ahead.[89] The feudal mode was a widely prevalent form in the whole of the Turkish empire through to the nineteenth century.[90]

The feudal mode in Western Europe was almost inherently rural, involving a subject peasantry bound to the soil in vassalage. But the feudalism in Russia during the eighteenth century and up to 1861 had an extensive experience

[88]Marx declared that "serfdom had practically disappeared in the last part of the 14th century." See *Capital* I, 1867, page 717. Dobb properly qualifies this judgment by noting that many bondsmen continued to serve under the Tudors and that the House of Lords rejected a bill for the manumission of villeins. He noted that obligation to grind at the lord's mill, payment of heriot, custom works, and even "harvest journeys" survived to the end of the sixteenth century. See Dobb, *Studies*, 1947, pages 51, 65 f. In France and Western and central Europe Blum sought to enumerate the percent of peasants who enjoyed full or partial freedom from seigniorial authority, and he found that Poland and the Danubian provinces had the largest fraction of free peasants, running up to 30%, even where personal thralldom had totally disappeared. Blum, *End of the Old Order*, 1978, pages 29 ff., especially 33.

[89]A comprehensive analysis of the serf-emancipation program put into execution by Russian czarism in 1861 and the years following was published by A. Gerschenkron in "Agrarian Policies," 1965. Under the terms of this emancipation, the peasants were given collective ownership via the *mir* for minimal land allotments for which they had to make annual payments, and thus bondage of individual *mir* members to the *mir* continued after 1861. Since the allotments were insufficient for livelihood, peasants leased land or pastures from landlords and provided in exchange labor services, often with plow and horses, just as under serfdom. This whole system of traditional technique, collective peasant responsibility, labor service on landlord lands, and dependence from a base of small allotments with substantial money taxes due—all this made up the Russian mode of production of *otrabotki*, of which Lenin gave a striking analysis in *Capitalism in Russia*, 1899, pages 190–213. It was not a stable form, for peasants tried to move away from it and capitalist agriculture tended to supplant it; yet some 22 years after serf emancipation, *otrabotki* was predominant in nearly 40% of European Russia (pages 196 f.). Stripped of its coercive elements, *otrabotki* is merely a specifically Russian form of the landlord-tenant mode.

[90]Gibb and Bowen, *Islamic Society*, 1950, pages 237 ff.; the spirit of the regime is indicated by the etymological origin of their word for peasant, *ra'iya*, which originally meant "cattle at pasture." There was a profusion of special taxes and dues including special taxes on vineyards, fruit orchards and vegetable gardens (pages 241 f.). Delivery obligations were strict and ra'iya were bound to the soil except with landlord permission (page 242). In the Arab provinces, the peasants were termed *fellahin*, they too were bound to the soil (pages 260 f.) and were subject to maximum drainage by hereditary tax collectors who had become landowners *de facto*, especially in Egypt. Here, in the main, the Ottoman Turks merely took over an exploitation pattern that had become established under the Pharaohs, amplified and routinized under the Graeco-Roman rule, continued under the Umayyad and Abbasid caliphates, and was transmitted to later regimes.

with use of serf labor in mines and industrial establishments.[91] Therefore in principle the feudal mode extended to urban workshops or mines worked by serf labor, especially if workshops were established on the estates. Because such workshops could not be self-supporting by raising their own foodstuffs and supplying their own subsistence from fields and husbandry, such undertakings would require more entrepreneurial skill to organize the work, provide the equipment, and market the product to provide subsistence support. Most feudal lords were content to confine their entrepreneurial activity to supervision of their agricultural estates. They also proved willing to work out exchange relationships with commercial towns chartered or established in their midst.

PEON MODE

The slave and feudal modes are undisguised forms of class rule and appropriation. However, that outright form of appropriation can become inconsistent with a culture's new assumptions of personal dignity and worth enshrined in its evolving principles of law and faith. Under those conditions coercion must be more subtly applied by depriving the village community of adequate amounts of fertile land or by direct imposition of tax and labor responsibilities resulting in a cumulative buildup of individual debt. The laborer is thus bonded to his work in an estate or to a tenant holding until the debt is redeemed. Such debt is also caused by advances of working capital to commence farming operations until the harvest is reaped from field or stock. A standing burden of debt will accumulate (1) if a poor rate of compensation for estate or for other work is paid, (2) if the tenant's share of his crop on crop-sharing arrangements is too low, (3) if merchandise and farm supplies are advanced on a credit basis at high interest, or (4) if the accounts are fraudulently manipulated. Usually tenant debts involved some combination of these tactics. Peonage results when debtors are not permitted to leave the estate without discharge of debt and if masters, either directly or intermediately through police and administrative authorities under their control,

---

[91]Tugan-Baranovsky, *Russian Factory*, 1898, ch. 3. Spurred on by decrees from Peter the Great, by 1725 some 233 factories or mills were staffed with serf labor; by 1762 that number was raised to 982, involving some 45,000 serf workers, and by 1825 some 90,000 outright "serf" and so-called "possessional" workers. A major center for serf-staffed industrial enterprise was in the Ural iron-producing area where even after serf "liberation" a residue of owner control lingered. See also, Bendix, *Work and Authority*, 1956, pages 128 ff., a remarkable and rare study of management ideologies and strategies in the early phase of industrialization. Serfdom, said Lenin, "to this day" [1899] "leaves its impress on quite important aspects of life in this mining area." See Lenin, *Capitalism in Russia*, 1899, pages 530 ff.

enforce the master's right to compel labor service. Because the kingpin of the coercion arises out of credit advances, commodity purchases, and resulting debt, the commercial exchange between master and peon becomes critical. For their own advantage, merchants sometimes join estate-owners in drawing the major profit from peonage.

The peon mode presupposes a high degree of social subordination of the peonized population. Peonage became the matured Hispanic form of organizing agricultural, shop, and mining work for the acculturated Amerindian peoples of Latin America.[92] When the slave mode in the New World had to be dissolved, it was replaced in the Black Belt of the American South, in Cuba, and elsewhere with some condition of peonage. Forms of peonage are also reported for the Philippines, the Danubian provinces, and twentieth-century China.[93] Because the liberated slaves in the American South and Cuba had neither ownership of land nor working capital of livestock and equipment, they were naturally dependent upon the former slave master or whoever would grant them credit to operate tenant farms when they declined staying on at the old plantation.

In the more advanced Amerindian settlements in Mexico, the Andean plateau, and Central America, Spanish colonists and *conquistadores* stole and expropriated, or arranged the purchase at low prices, of choice communal farmlands.[94] Unused desirable lands for which indigenous title could not be established were routinely assigned to haciendas. Remaining communal lands—confined mainly to steep mountains or inaccessible areas—were insufficient to provide for the natives' needs, especially when the demographic losses associated with Spanish takeover were made up. The conquest was effected through (1) the superior weaponry of the Spaniard and his use of

[92]In its mature state, before the social revolution commenced in 1910, over half of the farmland in Mexico was included in a few thousand large haciendas. Lewis, *Life in a Mexican Village*, 1951, pages xxvi f. Around 1960, large multifamily estates operated 81% of farmland in Chile, 75% in Peru, 53% in Brazil, 45% in Columbia and Ecuador, 41% in Nicaragua; and estate owners own most or much of the land operated as small minifundia averaging a few hectares each and leased from the haciendas. See Feder, *Rape of the Peasantry*, 1971, pages 48, 57, 104 f. If allowance were made for quality of land, the share owned by estate owners would even be greater (pages 54 f.). The UN estimated that in 1951 estates over 15,000 acres accounted for half of all agricultural land in Latin America. See Tannenbaum, *Ten Keys to Latin America*, 1960, pages 77 f.

[93]In 1910 an estimated 1/3 of the Mexican population were in a state of peonage; in the Philippines the estimate ran to 20% in 1928. See Seligman *et al.*, *Encyclopedia of Social Sciences*, 1930–1934, vol. 12, pages 69 ff. Marx's fleeting notice of peonage relations, which he described as a form of "hidden slavery" with advances repayable in labor "handed down from generation to generation," called attention in a footnote to their prevalence in Mexico and in the Danubian provinces. See Marx, *Capital* I, 1867, page 168.

[94]See Frank, *Mexican Agriculture*, 1979, page 69.

horses, mules, and protective armor; (2) the rather gentle inefficiency of Indian villagers when confronted with predatory force and fraud; (3) mass use of terror to punish any attempt at rebellion or resistance; and (4) systematic destruction of the ruling native elites (or their eventual assimilation by marriage into colonialist society). Peasant villagers, at first forced by state or local decrees to work on the haciendas, were later readily recruited for such work because their cramped communal lands were inadequate or could not yield the surpluses needed for taxes. In some parts of Latin America, the haciendas were laid out on such a large scale that pureblood or mestizo communities were actually nested on assigned plots under the direct control and tutelage of the hacienda.[95] Supplementary features of the hacienda system of labor were occasional use of corporal punishment, oppressive charges for use of hacienda consumption facilities, like the grinding mill, and of course the complete social subordination of the peon to his master or *patron*.[96]

The hacienda with its peonage mode of production took form in the sixteenth and seventeenth centuries in response to the stimulus by the European market for tropical crop staples, gold and silver to be converted into money, and other valuable raw materials. Theorists of "underdevelopment" have presupposed that the stimulus governed the response, as if class stratification and exploitative relationships could only evolve to meet market needs from the outside.[97] It is therefore important to note that stratification and tribute patterns in the most advanced part of the Amerindian world in Mexico and Peru were not imposed by Spanish *conquistadores* upon an idyllic communal society. For the most part, the agricultural population was already accustomed to acceptance of class rule and payment of tribute both in personal services and products. At the outset, the Spanish conqueror in effect replaced and in part was assimilated into the local ruling class.[98] Some form of stratified society would necessarily have evolved to enable this new ruling class to extract the largest possible amount of service and goods for which they could

[95]An interesting account for Mexico and Central America, with unquestioned parallels in South America, is found in Wolf, *Sons of the Shaking Earth*, 1959, pages 195 ff. See also the two reports about the Peruvian hacienda of Vicos which with American financing was given land reform, Holmberg, "Vicos," 1971, 531 ff.; Vazquez, "Vicos," 1971, 558 ff.; see also, Feder, *Rape of the Peasantry*, 1971, pages 140 f., 149 f., 152 f., 116 f., 130 ff; Tennenbaum, *Ten Keys to Latin America*, 1960, page 78.

[96]On use of private violence or whippings now increasingly delegated to the local police or gendarmerie, see Feder, *Rape of the Peasantry*, 1971, pages 154 f., 128; "The whipping post" was possessed "by every hacienda," Wolf, *Sons of the Shaking Earth*, 1959. Tepoztlan villagers so informed Lewis. *Life in a Mexican Village*, 1951, pages 111 f.

[97]See the various writings of A. G. Frank collected in two of his earlier volumes: *Capitalism and Under-Development*, 1969; *Latin America*, 1970.

[98]Lewis, *Life in a Mexican Village*, 1951, 81 ff.

find use. Peonage was the mode of production that developed in the light of both the market opportunities found in the advanced societies of the Old World and the production capabilities that could be shaped up in the New World.

To a surprising degree peonage is still the prevailing contemporary mode of production in Latin America. Yet the Mexican Revolution of 1910, the Cuban Revolution of 1959–1960, and the wave of so-called land reform inspired by Castro have here and there broken up latifundia, led to reform legislation, or permitted peasant unions to come into existence—thus leading to significant weakening of the peon mode of production.[99] This mode has also been significantly weakened in the United States by the development of well-capitalized "agribusiness" plantations using high-grade agronomic skills and employing wage labor, by the social emancipation of black people following the civil rights revolution led by Martin Luther King in the 1950s and 1960s, and by the subsequent political emancipation resulting therefrom.

LANDLORD MODE

One way of dissolving the unfree labor mode (slave, feudal, or peon) is by the development of capitalist agriculture in relatively large farms that use wage labor under capitalist management. This was the classical outcome in England and East Prussia, and the mode of production it formed is presented in Chapter 3. Another way to end subjugated labor is for holdings in the village community to become vested in the peasants and not in the feudal overlord. Landlord property is then vestigial or falls away. That fortunate outcome, aided by revolution and favorable legislation, occurred in France, much of southern and western Germany, and Japan.

But a third mode of production, involving landlord–tenant relations, overshadows the other two in territories where feudal, serf, or slave agricultural production was well established. It emerged in Russia as one of the forms of agricultural enterprise in the tangled skein of agrarian development in the 50 years following the formal abolition of serf-slavery in 1861. It was the predominant form of agricultural production in England's first colony, Ireland, where the English landed-proprietor lorded it over tenant smallholders. It played a significant role in the late Roman Empire, in Italy throughout the medieval period, and in most of Southeast Asia under colonial domination. Alongside peasant proprietorship, it became the established mode in most of China. Because landlord–tenant farming is sometimes considered an aberrant

[99]Feder, *Rape of the Peasantry*, 1971, pt. 3; Horowitz, "Alliance for Progress," 1970, pages 45–62.

form of capitalist farming—distinguished by its stagnant technology and the absence of significant entrepreneurial function by the landowner—it has not usually been considered a distinct mode of production. Just as frequently it is deemed a diluted form of the feudal mode of production rooted in serfdom or peonage. Here, as with other modes of production, the pure mode, delineated here as an ideal type, may in some cases be adulterated in practice or share certain features of one or more related modes, especially in a process of transition.

The main features of this landlord mode (LM) may be schematically outlined as follows:

1. Small-scale production units managed and organized by a tenant farmer and his family, using only occasional hired labor.

2. Clear-cut and permanent class stratification with a relatively small class of landowners who rent out their land in small allotments to tenant farmers, either on a sharecrop basis, a cash-rental basis, or a combination of the two for relatively short terms.

3. Basic capital in clearing, fencing, draining, or hedging the land—improvements that in Marshall's words "are slowly made and slowly worn out"—is provided by the landowner or has been appropriated from earlier tenants; capital in equipment, livestock, seed, and working supplies is provided by the tenant or jointly by the landlord and tenant.[100]

4. Terms of sharecropping are negotiated with each tenancy but tend to become stereotyped over broad areas and are relatively slow to change; market forces commonly affect cash-rental terms, which are dependent upon expected commodity prices and farm productivity.

5. Many landlords are absentee or are represented by agents.

6. With noteworthy exceptions, neither landlords nor tenants are able, as a general rule, to carry out the entrepreneurial function by adjusting farm technology or husbandry; in other words, farm technology tends to be stationary and traditional.

7. Social subordination of tenants to landlords is not primarily feudal but bourgeois; that is, it involves the respect of an employee for his employer or the poor man for the wealthy man with a formal equality of rights and mutual respect for persons.

8. Upward mobility is possible: some tenants become owners in their own right and, by good fortune, in time become landlords, whereas, conversely, some landlords who dissipate their capital drop out of the landlord class.

9. The landlord class, with its property stake, higher incomes, and capacity

[100]Marshall, *Principles of Economics*, 1890, page 635.

for investing in higher education, tends to become a political and social power in rural society and, as such, a *gentry class.*

The LM is not found wherever there are landlords who *rent* farms to tenants. As Marx contended: "Where the landlords have to deal with a class of large capitalists who may, as they please, invest their stock in commerce, in manufactures or in farming, there can be no doubt that these capitalist farmers, whether they take long leases or no time leases at all, know how to secure the 'proper' return of their outlays." The result is the capitalist, not the landlord, mode of production. With regard to Irish tenants, Marx went on to detail the circumstances that made Irish tenancy a classic example of the landlord mode. His analysis has immediate reference to tenant-financed farm improvements and proposed legislation that made such improvements or their undepreciated residue compensable upon expiration of a tenant lease. The discussion touches upon the basic character of the landlord mode and on nearly all the propositions outlined above.

> On the one side you have there a small class of land monopolists, on the other a very large class of tenants with very petty fortunes, which they have no chance to invest in different ways, no other field of production opening to them, except the soil. They are therefore forced to become tenants-at-will. Being once tenants-at-will, they naturally run the risk of losing their revenue, provided they do not invest their small capital. Investing it, in order to secure their revenue, they run the risk of losing their capital too.
>
> A tenant having incorporated his capital, in one form or another, in the land and having thus effected an improvement of the soil, either directly by irrigation, drainage, manure or indirectly by the construction of buildings for agricultural purposes, in steps the landlord with demand for increased rent. If the tenant concedes, he has to pay the interest for his own money to the landlord. If he resists he will be very unceremoniously ejected, and supplanted by a new tenant, the latter being enabled to pay a higher rent by the very expenses incurred by his predecessors, until he also, in his turn, has become an improver of the land and is replaced in the same way, or put on worse terms. In this easy way a class of absentee landlords has been enabled to pocket, not merely the labour, but also the capital, of whole generations, each generation of Irish peasants sinking a grade lower in the social scale, exactly in proportion to the exertions and sacrifices made for the raising of their condition and that of their families. If the tenant was industrious and enterprising, he became taxed in consequence of his very industry and enterprise. If on the contrary he grew inert and negligent, he was reproached with the "aboriginal faults of the Celtic race."[101]

An editorial in the *Times London* had advanced the argument that the relation between Irish landlord and tenant was like that between "two traders"

---

[101]Marx, "Irish Tenant Rights," 1853, pages 58 f. The article was followed by repeated references to the same issue later in the year. See Marx and Engels, *Ireland and the Irish Question,* 1845–1891, pages 67 ff., 70 f., 77 ff.

and that if a landlord deliberately injured a tenant, he would find it "harder to get another." Against this, Marx rejoined that "the more a landlord injures one tenant, the easier he will find it to oppress another. The tenant who comes in, is the means of injuring the ejected one, and the ejected one is the means of keeping down the new occupant."[102]

There may be some exaggeration in Marx's account of wholesale landlord expropriation of both the capital and the surplus product of Irish tenant farmers of the midnineteenth century. But there can be little doubt that market relations work very ineffectively in such an environment. In England, as a contrast, farming tenants had more standing and capital, were now enjoying the suffrage in parliamentary elections that gave them a certain measure of influence, worked often with written leases that they negotiated with landlords or agents, and had the resources to defend their interests in English courts and before local juries.[103] Yet many small capitalist farmers were not properly repaid for their improvements, and certainly smaller tenants had few alternative fields of investment open to them and their capital except farming, as Marx recognized in his later writings about English tenant farming.[104]

[102]Marx, "Irish Tenant Rights," 1853, pages 58 f.

[103]In Adam Smith's time only a lease for life of 40 shillings or more yearly entitled the lessee to vote in parliamentary elections. But the yeomanry voted so that "the whole order becomes respectable to their landlords." See Smith, *Wealth of Nations*, 1776, page 368. Writing some 60 years later, the younger Mill could salute as voters, farmers with long leases frequent in northern England and universal in Scotland. But as Mill stated in his 1839 essay "Reorganization of the Reform Party," the capitalist tenants-at-will in south England had, he felt, "slavish deference for their landlord, the notion that their vote goes with their rent" and some time must elapse before they awake from their "habitual servitude" to landlords. See Mill, *Essays on Politics and Culture*, 1831–1870, page 275. Another knowledgeable contemporary thought that "even the freehold for life would permit subservience." See Rogers, *Six Centuries*, 1883, page 478. Writing some years later, Alfred Marshall emphasized that "custom has always given the English tenant some partial security for compensation for improvements made by him; and legislation has recently caught up custom, and even passed it. The tenant is now practically secure against the raising of his rent on account of increased yield of the soil due to improvements of a reasonable nature made by himself; and on leaving he can claim compensation for the unexhausted value of them, to be fixed by arbitration." See Marshall, *Principles of Economics*, 1890, page 658—the extended footnote on the legislation.

[104]In working out in 1864–1865 the treatment of rent and landed property in his third volume of *Capital*, Marx reenunciated the doctrines of his 1853 *Tribune* articles: with emergence of the "capitalist tenant" "all relations which arose out of the old rural mode of production are torn asunder" (England), while in Ireland the tenant pays a rent which not only absorbs a part of his profit and wage but "expropriates his small capital" invested in improvements in the land. See Marx, *Capital* III, 1864–1865, page 625 f. But Marx recognized that the typical English farming tenant, especially smaller ones, "are destined and compelled by education, training, tradition, competition, and other circumstances to invest their capital as tenants in agriculture. They are forced to be satisfied with less than the average profit and to turn over part of it to the landlords as rent" (page 626). And earlier, he cited extensively from

Hence, though it may appear to be only a difference in degree, we hold with Marx that the difference between Irish and English farm tenancy is one of kind. In Ireland, class stratification between landlord and tenant was so complete, relative bargaining power between landlord and tenant so unequal, and legal capability of protecting tenant property interests so nearly lacking that we must acknowledge a unique landlord–tenant mode of production.[105]

The case of American northern tenant-farming relationships raises somewhat different issues than the comparable English case noted above. Class stratification in the North American circumstance is incomplete and partial. Much tenancy continues the incumbency of a farm family who remain in possession but in quasi-retirement status. Other tenancy is pursuant to liquidation of a farm estate settlement where no family heir wants to farm immediately but where sale is not feasible. A significant number of North American farmers commence farming as tenants but at a later stage of their farming career take on ownership status. Terms of rental are not stereotyped. Just as Marx placed the English tenant capitalist farmer in the category of *English capitalist mode of production*, so we can put the American tenant farmer in the category of the *direct commodity producer*, family-farm subtype.[106]

---

a publication that alleged that "all the efforts of the numerous agricultural associations throughout the country must fail to produce any extensive or really appreciable results in the real advancement of agricultural improvement, so long as such improvements mean in a far higher degree increased value to the estate and rent-roll of the landlord, than bettering the condition of the tenant farmer or the labourer" (see pages 620 f.). Marx cites later a lecture given by a knowledgeable authority on rural real estate who declared that smaller parcels generally rent at excessive rates "because the competition is usually greater for the latter . . . as few small farmers are able to turn their attention to any other business than that of farming" (page 629). From all this, we infer that the dependence of the Irish tenant on his landlord was not unique to the social circumstances of Irish farming but tended to apply to all landlord-tenant relations; that tenant-capital invested in the land by its proper husbandry would always tend to favor the landlord and work against the "rational development of agriculture for the tenant farmer avoids all improvements and outlays for which he cannot expect complete returns during the term of his lease" (page 620) but that this tendency worked more completely or intensively when tenants were predominantly small and poorly financed than when they were more mobile and could better attend to their interests.

[105]This also follows J. S. Mill, who believed that landed property in Ireland was on another footing than in England and Wales. See Mill, *Principles of Political Economy*, 1848, bk. 2, ch. 11, par. 6.

[106]A good standard account of the stepladder theory of farm tenancy in the northern states of the United States is found in an early agricultural economics text: H. C. Taylor, *Agricultural Economics*, 1919. In two chapters (20 and 21) dealing with farm tenancy before and after 1890, at which time periodic comprehensive census surveys became available, he pointed out that when farm operators are classified by age bracket that the tenant fraction of younger operators under 25 years of age is very high (72.2%), but that for each successive age bracket the fraction falls to only 18.6% for operators aged 55 years and older (261 ff.). Combine this

Some comments are in order about the defining features of the LM. The stratification between landlord and tenant classes is functional and not biological. Individual tenants may prosper, accumulate, and pass into the landlord class, usually only after the lapse of one or more generations. The stratification makes of the two classes noncompeting groups that are, however, very unequally affected by opportunities arising in other modes of production in society, especially the capitalist mode. Landlords commonly have a wider range of action and social mobility. With their landed property as a base, landlords may readily invest and participate in mining, industrial, transportation, or mercantile ventures, usually at home, sometimes abroad. Thus the landlord class, while retaining their farm properties, may diversify their fields of investment and interests. Tenants are more confined in their income, interests and travels. Rent levels and conditions of tenant farming will be affected only by major changes in the relative demand and supply of farm tenancies because of substantial diversion of tenant labor from farm fields to new jobs in industry or trade.

A standard charge of classical economists from Adam Smith to John Stuart Mill is that the LM leads to the neglect of the entrepreneurial function, thus tending to keep agriculture on a traditional level of husbandry and technology. Under the sharecrop or *metayer* system, "it could never be to the interest of cultivators to lay out, in the further improvement of the land, any part of the little stock which they might save from their own share of the produce, because the lord, who laid out nothing, was to get one-half of whatever it produced." The tithe, Smith noted, though but a tenth of the produce, is "found to be a very great hindrance to improvement. A tax therefore which amounted to one-half, must have been an effectual bar to it."[107] If the cul-

---

fact with others: that a large number of tenants are linked by first-degree kinship relations (up to 40% in the state of Wisconsin, Seligman *et al.*, *Encyclopedia of Social Sciences*, 1930–1934, vol. 6, page 126), that 80% of landlords rented only one farm, and that lease terms do not appear stereotyped (Taylor, *Agricultural Economics*, 1919, pages 285 ff.)—and the case for the stepladder theory is made, though a fraction of tenants did not make it through to ownership. From the mid-1920s onward, that fraction rose, in the northern and western regions rising from 26.6% (1920) to 30.5% (1935), which aroused widespread concern that the stepladder was failing. See Rochester, *Why Farmers Are Poor*, 1940, pages 45 f., 47 ff., 288 ff.; U.S. Department of Agriculture, *Yearbook*, 1940, pages 887 ff. Remedial programs were devised easing terms of credit for qualifying tenants. It turned out that the stepladder is less serviceable in periods of declining farm incomes and of depressed farm prices. The revolutionary change in farm conditions after 1940 restored the stepladder, and in 1975 the tenancy fraction of American farm operators had fallen to its lowest level since nationwide statistics were collected in 1890—11.3% of all farms. See U.S. Bureau of the Census, *Statistical Abstract*, 1979, page 686.

[107]Adam Smith, *Wealth of Nations*, 1776, page 368.

tivator pays a cash rent, the situation is not much better. Any improvement of husbandry or equipment that increases the relative productivity of the farm thus increases the rent that can be paid. "When the lease comes to be renewed, the landlord commonly demands more rent."[108]

Both landlord and tenant working together clearly have a joint interest in improving the land, but they have no easy way to effectuate that interest in LM. Any basic improvement, such as better drainage, improved methods of cultivation, or new equipment, almost always involves some change in husbandry or the way the tenant applies his effort. It is not possible to draw a categorical separation between improvements in the land—by better drainage, improved fertilizer, or use of new plant varieties or insecticides—and improved methods of working the land—by more intensive cultivation, use of better equipment, deeper plowing—and rule that one category of improvements is the function of the landlord and the other of the tenant. The improvements that result in higher yields often require both a changed method of working the land and different equipment. The landlord cannot make it his function to improve only the land, leaving to the tenant responsibility for its cultivation.

It is not easy to estimate in advance the benefits that a given improvement will generate so as to rule fairly on any change in rent that may be appropriate. Moreover, it is not easy for the two parties involved in partnership to negotiate with each other. "It seldom happens," generalized Smith—who on the whole was fond of landed proprietors and country gentlemen—"that a great proprietor is a great improver." His very "conceit of his own superior knowledge . . . in most cases ill founded," is likely to be costly to the tenant and, Smith believed, "ought always to be considered as an additional rent."[109] From this vantage point, the proprietor deals with an illiterate peasant, accustomed to following tradition and skeptical of changes that will make his work more burdensome, with questionable benefits. But supposing that the peasant reached a suitable agreement with the proprietor willing to provide the necessary additional capital to finance improvements that would, over time, build the earning power and the value of the farm; what assurance could there be for him that premature death might not throw the property under the control of a new landlord with other ideas?[110] Under these circumstances, the best form of husbandry for the LM is traditional and customary husban-

---

[108]Adam Smith, *Wealth of Nations*, 1776, page 368.

[109]Adam Smith, *Wealth of Nations*, 1776, pages 363, 783.

[110]This hazard of succession, even when extended as in France of Smith's day to 27 years from the commencement of a lease, is a period "still too short to encourage the tenant to make the most important improvements." See Adam Smith, *Wealth of Nations*, 1776, pages 369 f.

dry, or precisely the level of technology that Lenin ascribed to the landlord-rental or cropsharing system, *otrabotki,* prevailing in Russia after the termination of slavery in 1861—"by its very nature based on routine technique or the preservation of antiquated methods of production."[111] This tendency to routine technique and use of antiquated methods may perhaps be abated if landlordship is carried out on a small scale and in a plebeian atmosphere experienced in the unusual circumstances of Japanese village development during the late Tokugawa regime and the Meiji Restoration.[112]

The LM will not necessarily dominate the areas where it flourishes. Often it will be only one of the prevailing modes in a dispersed agrarian field where independent peasant proprietors and feudal–peon relations bound by debt serfdom are interspersed, holding their own side by side with capitalist wage-labor farm holdings.

Lenin's analysis of social and economic development following the abolition of Russian slavery emphasized this interspersion of various modes of production, usually in the same region but oftentimes within a single estate.[113] The American South, where the post-Bellum plantation evolved into a share-cropping system of peonage, had a more homogeneous character, at least in the fairly well-defined region of the Cotton Belt.[114]

[111]*Otrabotki* system, as Lenin pointed out, was a transitional system "combining the features of both the corvée [pre-1861 serfdom] and the capitalist system" (using wage-labor and capitalist investment in equipment) with most of landlord land leased to peasants farming with their own implements on a sharecrop basis or for money (194f). Lenin, *Capitalism in Russia,* 1899, pages 194 f., 219 ff., 235 ff.

[112]This LM is a classical instance of what can be called *plebeian landlordism.* It evolved out of the serf village community by processes of internal differentiation resulting from inequalities between original settler and migrant families by (1) the buildup of rich peasant properties with servants and hirelings originally accommodated to family status; (2) the development of improved technology and commercial farming (breweries, tanneries and related processing enterprises); (3) the decline of the "cooperative family group" and the rise of formal wage-labor or tenancy running the gamut of sharecropping; (4) a modified form of sharecropping with the sharing ratio fixed annually after an estimate of the coming harvest was made, a stipulated payment in kind for a 5-year term, a rent in kind fixed for some years but payable in money, a real money rent fixed and paid in money. See T. C. Smith, *Agrarian Origins,* 1959. As Barrington Moore put it, "a landlord class emerged out of the peasantry . . . as a result of the advent of commercial farming." By the late 1930s, 47% of the land was farmed by tenants, about 40% of whom owned land of their own. Moore, *Dictatorship and Democracy,* 1966, pages 282 ff. About half the crop went to the landlord (page 285). The plebeian and small-scale character of the Japanese landlord-tenant mode enabled it to develop a progressive technology and some of the highest crop yields in the world.

[113]Lenin, *Capitalism in Russia,* 1899, pages 194 f., 199 ff.

[114]Ransom and Sutch, *One Kind of Freedom,* 1977, portrayed a familiar picture well delineated in monographic literature on the aftermath of slavery but with the aid of newer research methods. A somewhat softened picture may be found in Wright, *Political Economy of the Cotton South,* 1978, especially ch. 6.

In one lifetime, farm tenants in the LM may shift into the wage-labor class or find themselves bound by peonage. The pre-Communist Chinese agrarian situation had such a heterogeneous character: contemporary residents of a single peasant village can recollect all these modes of production experienced in their family during their lifetime.[115] The LM in China often degenerated into a kind of feudal peonage often accompanied in the late Manchu period by corrupt local officials, clerks, and policemen who, with the assistance or in collaboration with cliques of educated notables and landlords, carried out a merciless exploitation of villagers (whether owners or tenants) and small traders and craftsmen.[116] These associated features of the LM have generated the suggestion, now converted into Communist Party dogma, that the LM in China embodied a special form of feudalism.[117] But these feudal features of the LM are quite separable from it. The early peasant movement in the 1920s, culminating in the great Chinese Revolution of this era, was quite clearly aimed not at the LM itself but at these feudal features. "The main targets of attack by the peasants," wrote Mao Zedong in his famous 1927 report on the Hunan peasant revolt, "are the local tyrants, the evil gentry and the lawless landlords." Landlords were weakened economically by peasant actions to freeze rent levels, check tenancy accounts, reduce interest rates on loans, and prohibit the cancellation of tenancies by landlords. Drastic action was taken against local tyrants, or "evil gentry" and their underlings in local government who acted as "virtual monarchs of the countryside." The movement also targeted gambling and opium smoking.[118]

As used in the Chinese context, the term *gentry* only denotes academic degree-holders eligible for high state positions and who thus were local notables in their own right. The term *evil gentry* would then refer to greedy or

---

[115]See especially Jan Myrdal, *Report from a Chinese Village*, 1963, accounts of Pai Yu-teh (pages 78 f.), Mau-Ke-yeh (pages 95 f., 107 ff.), Li Hai-yuan (pages 143 ff.), Ching Chung-ying (pages 156 ff.), Fu Hai-tsao (pages 167 ff.), Ma Chen-hai (pages 178 ff.), and Li Yiu-hua (pages 356 ff.). This stands out in the villager accounts collected by Myrdal. Villagers frequently described their debt bondage; with debt the tenant couldn't move (pages 95, 108 f., 144 f.).

[116]An authoritative study of local government in the Manchu period gives a valuable detailed account of the structure of local government, of the role played by local gentry (landowner, retired and officials-on-leave, or other) and of the immense corrupt levying on the peasant community. T'ung-Tsu Ch'u, *Local Government in China*, 1962. Evil gentry were a category already established in the mideighteenth century when an imperial edict was issued stating: "Previously the official-gentry in the various places relied upon their influence and were arbitrary and tyrannical in their native places, bullied their neighbors, and constituted a great source of harm to the local area" (pages 189 f.).

[117]Mao Tse-Tung, *Selected Works*, 1926–1957, vol. 1, pages 97 f., 99; vol. 2, pages 309, 341 f.; vol. 3, pages 247 f.; Institute of Economics, *Political Economy*, 1954, page 35.

[118]Mao Tse-Tung, *Selected Works*, 1926–1957, vol. 1, pages 25 ff., 35 ff., 39 ff.

unscrupulous officials who misused their powers of office or the privileges of the degree-holding class and who collaborated with the bureaucracy in oppressing the common people. Mao himself, in building up his victorious revolutionary coalition movement, which won supreme power in China in 1949, drew a very clear line between the *evil gentry* and the *enlightened gentry*. The latter "cooperated with us in the past, continue to cooperate with us at present, who approve of a struggle against the United States and Chiang Kai Shek and who approve of land reform."[119] That the gentry class ran a broad spectrum in social attitudes, source of income, and political behavior is well established in sociological works on this class.[120]

[119]Mao Tse-Tung, *Selected Works*, 1926–1957, vol. 4, page 209.
[120]Chung-li Chang, *Income of the Chinese Gentry*, 1962; Fei Hsiao-Tung, *China's Gentry*, 1947–1948.

3

Modes of Production: Capitalist and Corporate

CAPITALIST MODE

Continuing the catalogue of the modes begun in the last chapter, we turn to the capitalist mode, the best-known of all, since upon it both modern and Marxian economic theory has focused its attention. At the center of this mode is the *capitalist enterprise* in which we can distinguish the following dramatis personae: (1) capitalist–entrepreneurs who, seeking profits, have invested equity capital in the enterprise; (2) capitalists who have invested loan capital and landowners who have permitted the use of real estate sites for a set return; (3) suppliers who for negotiated prices make available raw materials, parts, equipment or services; (4) laborers recruited and assembled for work in the enterprise in return for wages; (5) customers who buy the product or service at prices or markups established by, or negotiated with, the enterprise.

The essential difference between the capitalist enterprise and the craft enterprise of the SCPM is that enough workers are involved and the enterprise has sufficient complexity that the sole function of the equity capitalist is to perform the entrepreneurial tasks. This work entails (1) establishing the enterprise in the first instance and from time to time reestablishing it in either new activities or locations; (2) recruiting workers and devising suitable conditions of work; (3) setting individual tasks before the assembled workers and coordinating their respective movements; (4) providing and designing the facilities of work; (5) arranging on terms that are satisfactory for procurement from suppliers and for disposition of the product to customers. Now and then small capitalists will take a direct hand in productive work, but in the main, capitalists arrange for the work itself to be done by hired wage earners. In the larger enterprises even supervision and direct management will be hired out, though the task of coordinating the supervisors and guiding their work remains an essential entrepreneurial task.

This analysis of the capitalist enterprise differs in two important respects from the Marxian analysis. First, following Alfred Marshall, it relates profits earned to the composite of the investment of equity capital and the entrepreneurial work of the capitalist.[1] Profits cannot be accurately described solely as a return on equity capital invested without allowing for entrepreneurial performance. Loan capital cannot usually be attracted to an enterprise unless sufficient equity capital is there to give assurance that whoever discharges the entrepreneurial function will have a stake in prudent management and will take a prior risk of loss before other creditors are adversely affected. Thus the entrepreneurial function itself under normal circumstances cannot be exercised without investment of equity capital. That investment in turn calls for the exercise of the entrepreneurial functions. They go together, with profits the reward for the collaborative effort.

Second, profits are a residual, delayed, and *uncertain* income. They are residual because they are what remains of the proceeds of sale or the net value of additions to inventory for a normal economic period, after payments have been made to all other parties—laborers, capitalists, landowners, government, suppliers—whose cooperation with or contribution to the enterprise has been obtained by the promise of specific payments over relatively short time periods. After making these payments, some of the proceeds must then be set aside to allow for (1) contingent and noninsurable risks arising at some future time out of operations in the past period; and (2) the need ultimately to replace or carry out major rebuilding of facilities and equipment, which wear out by usage and by mere exposure to the elements.

If demand for the product by customers diminishes or falls away before the investment in the enterprise has been completely recouped—which will happen if the customers' real purchasing power or their ability to sustain their outlays has declined, or if superior products have been developed by other producers—then the productive life of the enterprise may be jeopardized, with the value of the equity investment destroyed. The creditors of the enterprise will have the first claim on what viable assets may be extracted from it for conversion to other uses or as salvage. Thus the total profit earned by any enterprise will be definitely established only with its *winding up and its liquidation.* Prior to that event all distributions of profits are, strictly speaking, *advances* on profits. Hence the well-known conservatism of capitalists in both estimating and drawing on their profits, however lucrative they may appear to be.

While the profit maker must always bear in mind the possibility of loss that may wipe out his equity capital, he also harbors hopes for good fortune

[1] Marshall, *Principles of Economics,* 1890, chs. 7 and 8.

or windfall that will lead to successful operations, to increase the profits and boost the value of both his business and his equity capital. Thus the profit maker is an inveterate optimist. He builds a business based on speculation that future conditions will favor the undertaking and produce riches. This uncertain, speculative, acquisitive, and future-oriented aspect of profit seeking—this sense of gambling for large stakes—distinguishes it above all from investment returns on loan capital as interest or earnings of the landlord paid as rent for the leased use of land.[2]

In its simplest form the capitalist enterprise involves the *equity investment* of a single capitalist or, more realistically expressed, his family, because its members are usually drawn into the enterprise as junior partners, though control and ownership is concentrated in the senior family head. Frequently, however, the capital for the undertaking or the business entrepreneurial skills required are too much for the resources of the family of a single capitalist, which at times "puts too many eggs in one basket." Hence, the capitalist enterprise has developed the *partnership*, a kind of brotherhood of capitalist families embodied in a formal agreement that lays out respective mutual contributions by way of capital and entrepreneurial responsibility, as well as principles of sharing in the fruits thereof. The consent of the partners is needed at every stage and for every operation. If they can no longer function with complete agreement, they will then try to negotiate the terms for the breakup of the partnership. If this cannot be negotiated, then judicial processes that developed in most societies where the capitalist enterprise has functioned, preside over this breakup.

The partnership enlarges the scope of the capitalist enterprise, endows it with more continuity, multiplies the entrepreneurial and investment resources that can go to work, and frequently provides a fraternal element in what otherwise is a very cold and impersonal set of relationships. But the very solidarity of the partnership and the unanimity of its every action make it difficult for very many persons to become drawn to it unless they are in a junior status or can accept the leadership of a dominant partner or are in certain professional fields. These deficiencies of the partnership arrangement are remedied by the corporation. But as we shall see in the following section, the corporation usually evolves into a form of organization so distinctive, and with resources so commanding, that it opens the way to a new mode of production.

---

[2]There are, of course, second-rate entrepreneurial decisions to be made even in loan investments and land rentals. The credentials of would-be borrowers and tenants must be scrutinized, suitable contracts drawn up, and the necessary guarantees or security provided to reduce risks.

ORDERING PRINCIPLE: COMPETITION

Although the capitalist enterprise is the heart of the capitalist mode of production, it does not exhaust the mode. A single enterprise or a handful of enterprises could not make up a capitalist mode of production because an essential principle of that mode would be lacking—namely, rivalry of producers competing for supplies and materials, for the hiring of labor, and for customers. In its earliest phases where the capitalist mode of production is insecurely established and occupies only a small part of the field of production, competitive rivalry will be less against other capitalist enterprises than against other commodity-producing modes: the enserfed village, the slave plantation or shop, the village community, craft guilds, or public enterprise. There may be a deeper kind of rivalry, too, against the natural economy itself and a simple scheme of life with an undeveloped level of productive forces. Here the effort will be threefold: (1) to awaken new wants which can only be satisfied by the exchange process; (2) to seek to mobilize or attract labor not otherwise fully occupied in the natural economy; and (3) to provide outlets for raw materials or village products that can be traded or exchanged for the goods available from capitalist enterprise.

But as capitalist enterprise grows, inevitably its essential *ordering principle, competition,* will have wider play. Even among capitalist producers of different goods—satisfying different wants and moving in different markets—there will be competition in the hiring of labor, searching out the most satisfactory kind of labor that can be recruited, and providing terms of compensation and working conditions that are attractive in the light of alternative opportunities. Once workers are apprenticed or trained, their range of opportunities may be narrowed. But decisions to search out apprenticeships or learning opportunities in the different fields will be influenced by the attractiveness of employment in those fields. Opportunities will inevitably be greater in the larger urbanized areas than in smaller population centers. In these larger areas competitive forces will have a wider field of action in shaping labor markets and in equalizing terms of compensation. This process of equalization, which of course is very crude under early conditions, must allow for differential advantages or drawbacks associated with different employments catalogued by Adam Smith under five broad headings: (1) agreeableness or disagreeableness of the employments; (2) the easiness and cheapness or the difficulty and expense of learning them; (3) constancy or inconstancy of employment; (4) the small or great trust that must be reposed in the employee; (5) probability or improbability of success in them.[3]

[3]Adam Smith, *Wealth of Nations,* 1776, pages 100 ff.

Earning differentials will only take shape where fields of employment are "well known and long established," when these trades are in their normal state and suitable for primary breadwinners, not for subordinate members of households.[4] The base for the wage level established by capitalist enterprise will in its earlier phases be little better than earning levels among independent craft producers, or within village communities and available to members of SCMP households who do not inherit the main farm holding or succeed to the craft shop of the father. The habits of work formed in the struggle for existence in villages and craft shops will fix the standards of the intensity and extent of labor offered in labor markets. And the standards of living—basic cereals making up the main food, adequate clothing for the body in inclement weather, stimulants, artifacts, and household furnishings—will at the outset be borrowed from the simpler and earlier conditions prevailing in the economy when capitalist enterprise is launched. Those standards of working and living thus make up the subsistence base of the *real wage level* of the capitalist sector that the classical economists, from Adam Smith to Marx, recognized as culturally shaped to accommodate the habits and social needs of the population.[5] This variable base of standards gave to some workmen a real wage level founded upon wheaten bread and leather shoes, and to other workmen, oatmeal as a main cereal and wooden clogs for footwear.[6] Once shaped, that money wage level or, strictly speaking, the wages structure, would tend to fluctuate with market forces, regularly rising and falling in business cycles, and following the changing course of price levels as they run their long-run secular movements.

Real wages are more problematical. For a long time they were influenced chiefly by four factors. (1) Good or bad harvests, which make food, the dominant item in the workman's budget, cheap or expensive.[7] (2) Manufactured goods, the main product of the capitalist mode of production, tended to become cheaper in real terms and thus gradually became accessible to wage-earner budgets, eventually to be incorporated into the social habits and requirements making up the "standard of living" of at least higher-strata work-

---

[4]Adam Smith, *Wealth of Nations*, 1776, pages 114 ff.

[5]"The power of the labourer to support himself, and the family which may be necessary to keep up the number of labourers, . . . depend . . . on the quantity of food, necessaries and conveniences become essential to him from habit. . . .It varies at different times in the same country, and very materially differs in different countries. It essentially depends upon the habits and customs of the people." See Ricardo, *Principles of Political Economy*, 1817, 52 ff.

[6]Adam Smith, *Wealth of Nations*, 1776, pages 76 f.

[7]Adam Smith noted that wage rates did not fluctuate with short-term market fluctuations in the price of food, so that periods of "plenty" (or low food prices) were not followed by wage reductions and "place" differentials in wages did not correspond to the same differentials for food prices. See Adam Smith, *Wealth of Nations*, 1776, pages 74 ff.

men.[8] (3) Such goods, passing by osmosis into the standard of living and wages of the common body of wage earners, can only stay there if the workmen have sufficiently high aspiration levels and moral stamina to uphold and maintain wage standards, resisting all the while the encroachments of employers to reduce them. (4) That moral stamina would be reinforced or undermined by the balance of demand and supply for wage earners that is governed chiefly by (a) the rate of inflow of new wage earners migrating from overpopulated village communities or from the declining handicraft trades and rural industries adversely affected by capitalist production; (b) the demand for additional wage labor arising out of new capital accumulation and the spread of capitalist production to new wants and newer production

[8]The tendency of manufactured goods to "diminish gradually" in real price was found by Adam Smith in his celebrated survey of price trends for the different classes of products to apply to "manufacturing workmanship . . . without exception" in consequence of better machinery, greater dexterity, a more proper division and distribution of the work—"all of which are the natural effects of improvement." This tendency he found greatest in metal goods or hardware, was present in "joiner's work and the coarser sort of cabinet work" (though not offsetting the rise in the real price of barren timber), in fine weaving, and in textile products like hose. Adam Smith, *Wealth of Nations*, 1776, pages 242–247. The gradual incorporation of these manufactured products into the standard of living of "the most common artificer or day-labourer in a civilised and thriving country" (England, of course) was detailed in Smith's remarkable peroration to the capitalist mode of production early in his work, which I cannot forbear citing:

> Observe the accommodation of the most common artificer or day-labourer in a civilized and thriving country, and you will perceive that the number of people of whose industry a part, though but a small part, has been employed in procuring him this accommodation, exceeds all computation. The woollen coat, for example, which covers the day-labourer, as coarse and rough as it may appear, is the produce of the joint labour of a great multitude of workmen. The shepherd, the sorter of the wool, the wool-comber or carder, the dyer, the scribbler, the spinner, the weaver, the fuller, the dresser, with many others, must all join their different arts in order to complete even this homely production. How many merchants and carriers, besides, must have been employed in transporting the materials from some of those workmen to others who often live in a very distant part of the country! How much commerce and navigation in particular, how many ship-builders,, sailors, sail-makers, rope-makers, must have been employed in order to bring together the different drugs made use of by the dyer, which often come from the remotest corners of the world! What a variety of labour too is necessary in order to produce the tools of the meanest of those workmen! To say nothing of such complicated machines as the ship of the sailor, the mill of the fuller, or even the loom of the weaver, let us consider only what a variety of labour is requisite in order to form that very simple machine, the shears with which the shepherd clips the wool. The miner, the builder of the furnace for smelting the ore, the feller of the timber, the burner of the charcoal to be made use of in the smelting-house, the brick-maker, the brick-layer, the workmen who attend the furnace, the mill-wright, the forger, the smith, must all of them join

fields; and (c) mechanization of work processes within the capitalist sector permitting fewer workmen to produce the same output.[9]

The net balance of outcomes varied widely in different eras and countries wherever the capitalist mode of production became established without a uniform trend of behavior. Hence the same development of the capitalist mode of production that can build up a rising level of working-class prosperity (as at times in North America with interspersed periods of advance and retrogression elsewhere) can elsewhere leave real wage levels stagnating at a very low level, and sometimes drag them below subsistence.

There is little basis for Marx's negative prognosis that the real wage level of wage earners will decline, with increasing unemployment and growing pauperism. He felt so certain about this prognosis that he denominated it an

---

their different arts in order to produce them. Were we to examine, in the same manner, all the different parts of his dress and household furniture, the coarse linen shirt which he wears next [sic] his skin, the shoes which cover his feet, the bed which he lies on, and all the different parts which compose it, the kitchen-grate at which he prepares his victuals, the coals which he makes use of for that purpose, dug from the bowels of the earth, and brought to him perhaps by a long sea and a long land carriage, all the other utensils of his kitchen, all the furniture of his table, the knives and forks, the earthen or pewter plates upon which he serves up and divides his victuals, the different hands employed in preparing his bread and his beer, the glass window which lets in the heat and the light, and keeps out the wind and the rain, with all the knowledge and art requisite for preparing that beautiful and happy invention, without which these northern parts of the world could scarce have afforded a very comfortable habitation, together with the tools of all the different workmen employed in producing those different conveniences; if we examine, I say, all these things, and consider what a variety of labour is employed about each of them, we shall be sensible that without the assistance and co-operation of many thousands, the very meanest person in a civilized country could not be provided, even according to, what we very falsely imagine, the easy and simple manner in which he is commonly accommodated. Compared, indeed, with the more extravagant luxury of the great, his accommodation must no doubt appear extremely simple and easy; and yet it may be true, perhaps, that *the accommodation of an European prince does not always so much exceed that of an industrious and frugal peasant, as the accommodations of the latter exceeds that of many an African king, the absolute master of the lives and liberties of ten thousand naked savages.*" See Adam Smith, *Wealth of Nations*, 1776, pages 11 f. (emphasis added).

[9]A celebrated example of (a) was the vast influx into the English labor market in the first half of the nineteenth century of Irish villagers because of stagnant economic conditions in Ireland and a wave of higher fertility which doubled Irish population in a half-century. Marx believed that mechanization under (c) was triggered in the developed capitalist mode of production by higher real wages, so that "the absolute increase in capital is accompanied by no corresponding rise in the general demand for labor." See Marx, *Capital* I, 1867, pages 638 ff.

"absolute general law of accumulation" for the capitalist mode of production.[10] Since the capitalist mode inherits a subsistence level from earlier societies, there would hardly be room for the continued erosion of that real wage level. The Marxian prognosis also does not allow for the fact that the capitalist mode in industry is a relatively late arrival among modes. For most of its history it recruits its growing labor force by attracting migrants from other production modes—chiefly village communities and simple commodity producers, often coming from a considerable distance. The capitalist volume of employment can only increase on a considerable scale if it recruits labor by offering attractive employment and wages. At a later stage in its career, of course, the capitalist mode of production might well have produced conditions of health and sanitation sufficiently high and conditions of life sufficiently good that its industrial population could reproduce itself or even produce occasionally a slight net growth from its own demographic resources.[11]

If the market forces via competition broadly shape both the structure and level of wages associated with the capitalist mode of production, these forces

---

[10]Marx, *Capital* I, 1867, page 644. Having written that and probably realizing that his generalization outstripped the evidence that could sustain it, Marx went on to limit his own generalization with this qualification: "like all other laws, it is modified in its working by many circumstances." A feeble law to be thus circumscribed in its operation. In his commentary directly following, Marx spells out the factors in the capitalist mode of production which he believed determined that "in proportion as capital accumulates, the lot of the labourer, be his payment high or low, must grow worse." The law of mechanization which "always equilibrates the relative surplus-population . . . to the extent and energy of accumulation, this law rivets the labourer to capital more firmly than the wedges of Vulcan did Prometheus to the rock" (page 645). And in the extended sections of the chapter following (pages 648–712), Marx sought not to *prove* the validity of the law over an extended period of time but to "illustrate it" by examining wage and labor conditions for the weakest sections of the working class (migratory agricultural laborers, the agricultural village workers, low-paid industrial and cottage domestic workers) and better-paid workers at moments of "crisis," as when affected by cyclical unemployment. The illustrations show stark human need and deprivation but hardly sustain the generalization that Marx sought to illustrate. Orthodox Marxists have been loath to give up the doctrines of the master, and the Soviet Institute of Economics textbook, *Political Economy*, 1954, page 150 f., still gives obeisance. The dean of Marxist economists, Varga, presents almost a repudiation in *Politico-Economic Problems of Capitalism*, 1963, pages 111 ff. In his elucidation of "laws of the Capitalist Mode," Amin deals only peripherally with Marx's "law of immiserisation," noting in one context that only union struggles can raise real wages but then again assuming a constant wage-share of national product. See Amin, *Unequal Development*, 1973, pages 76, 221, 273.

[11]See this volume, ch. 2, n. 68 on the tendency of earlier urban populations not to be demographically self-sustaining. Extraordinarily striking is the tendency in the nineteenth century of fertility rates to fall and population growth to slow up in the advanced European countries where the capitalist mode of production was making most headway: Great Britain, France, Belgium, and, to a lesser extent, Germany.

do not function as effectively in fixing working conditions and hours of work, which must be directly established and administered by the capitalist–entrepreneur. The development of modern industry provided the capitalist with strong inducements to intensify the process of production by speedup and longer hours of work to obtain full utilization of his expensive equipment; at the same time his control over the speed and rhythm of work became governed by his prime movers and gearing ratios built into his equipment. The gaslight and other artificial illumination made it possible to work not only by day but also by night, so that the ancient diurnal rhythm of work was finally overturned. Work previously limited from dawn to dusk could now go on round the clock. Especially where the labor force was recruited mostly from its weaker members, with little bargaining power or resistance to the encroachments of capital, as in the newer textile factories employing mostly women and juveniles, the capitalist mode of production produced a havoc that could only be checkmated by the power of the state to establish reasonable hours of work, decent working conditions, adequate ventilation, and safety devices to minimize bodily damage of workers by such hazards as industrial accidents, dust, and poisonous gases.[12]

Market forces had, of course, a freer hand in shaping by competition the prices at which capitalist enterprise bought its materials or supplies and sold its products to its customers. These forces could be effective even when the number of competing firms was very few—provided access to entrance in the field to new capital was unblocked either to existing or to newly established firms. In the short run, a capitalist enterprise could take advantage of a favorable market conjuncture and make extra profits by raising selling prices above those governed by normal costs. But because knowledgeable customers might then favor new competing firms, many if not most capitalist firms developed policies of establishing selling prices at or near competitive norms and rationing supplies among customers when short so as to retain customer loyalties. Changed methods of production leading to reduced costs were generally followed by reduced prices or the equivalent in quality improvements. As previously noted, the tendency of prices for manufactured goods in the capitalist mode of production to fall with improved methods was discovered by Adam Smith in 1776 and was formulated by him as a near universal law of the capitalist mode of production.[13]

The same competitive process that equalized prices to normal costs for given commodities also equalized profit margins earned by equity capital within a broad zone of variation for the different branches of capitalist en-

---

[12]See Marx, *Capital* I, chs. 10; 15, sec. 39. This was possibly the central contention of my earlier study. See Gottlieb, "Marx's Mehrwert," 1951, pages 164–178; see also Meek, 1952.
[13]See A. Smith, *Wealth of Nations*, 1776, pages 11 f. (cited in ch. 3, footnote 8, this volume).

terprise. As for excess profits owed to particular advantages of landed sites, it transferred them to landlords in the form of rent. Thus through competition the capitalist mode of production established a two-tier self-regulating process in which prices for the use of production factors—*land, labor* and *loan capital*—were adjusted on one level. At another level those factor prices and the prevailing technique and scale of production resulted in cost prices for the products which in turn governed product prices. Any change in the condition of demand or supply at either the product or the factor level, or the presence anywhere of dissatisfied demanders or suppliers, would tend to force some production factor prices to change, and these changed prices would in turn destabilize other prices, thus inducing altered scales of production and affecting product quantities for the different branches of production. It is doubtful that the capitalist mode of production ever achieved a perfect equilibrium in all of its prices for products and factors. Economic history indicates that a tendency to equilibrium has been at work so that most prices and quantities remain in a near-equilibrium zone; if out of that zone, they tend to move toward it. Modern Western economic theory is concerned almost solely with working out the ideal form of the mechanics of this tendency to equilibrium.

MERCANTILE CAPITALISM

The capitalist mode has achieved its greatest success in industry, in which it came to dominate the advanced Western countries by the end of the nineteenth century. But it by no means commenced with industry. Its earliest phases are probably found in the field of *wholesale trade.* Already in antiquity there was the merchant—with his expensive means of production invested in caravans, supply depots, navigable ships, and warehouses, inventories which moved at a relatively slow rate. The merchant was the first capitalist. By the nature of his calling, he was a profit maker, functioning in a world of uncertainty and speculation. He invested his capital in inventories that he then made more valuable, chiefly by moving them to places where they were considered more desirable than at their production center. His principal capital was, of course, his mercantile skills and knowledge.[14] To help operate his

---

[14]The skill and knowledge acquired only by extended experience and close attention to a wide range of details involved partly mastery of the characteristics and ways of evaluating varieties of products handled (see a list of 288 spices alone), skill in avoiding sharp practice in necessary dealings with suppliers and customers or "sharing" contracts, knowledge of credit devices and credit reputation, understanding of factors affecting future values in commodity markets, knowledge of trustworthy merchants and dealers in foreign centers, and knowledge of various national coinages and monies. See the compendium of materials on these subjects published in Lopez and Raymond, *Medieval Trade,* 1967.

means of production he often hired workers, purchased slaves, or took on apprentices or helpers drawn from within the extended family.[15]

The rich merchant was the backbone of the upper stratum of many of the urban communities of the Graeco-Roman world, above all in Athens, where it was the boast that "the magnitude of our city draws the produce of the world into our harbour."[16] With his train of employees, agents, helpers, and partners, the rich merchant likewise dominates the patriciate of the great Italian and German mercantile-states of the medieval period.[17] The case has been well-made that many, perhaps most, of the wholesale traders of the world of antiquity and the medieval period were small operators, belonging to the SCPM.[18] The craft trader's world would continuously sprout capitalist merchantry, whereas the latter, whenever meeting upsets, managing poorly, or losing its entrepreneurial skills, would decline and fall away. The institution of the periodic fairs—which reached their highest European development in the thirteenth and fourteenth centuries—were the homing ground of many small but also of some large merchants.[19] The rich Islamic, Jewish, Japanese, Chinese, Italian, Portuguese, Germanic, Russian, Indian, and English merchant—and thus the merchant capitalist enterprise—is a well-established figure in folklore, fiction, and history.[20] Doubtless, then, authentic capitalist enter-

[15]A Constantinople raw-silk dealer was prohibited from engaging a helper except on a month-to-month basis, but employment of a helper who had not completed a monthly term of employment was fined. Lopez and Raymond, *Medieval Trade*, 1967, pages 20 f. The role of the extended family in the solidarity of the trading enterprise was extensively explored by Max Weber in his study of trading enterprises in the Medieval period. See Weber, "Zur Geschichte der Handelsgesellschäfte," 1889, ch. 3. The legal ramifications of the extended family are especially well treated in this work. The extended family includes not only blood-kin but household servants living in the household (pages 349 f.).

[16]Cited from the funeral oration of Pericles. See Thucydides, *History of the Peloponnesian War*, fifth century B.C., bk. 1, ch. 6, sects. 38 f.

[17]Most illuminating are the full histories of some of the great medieval capitalist merchant undertakings, De Roover, *Medici Bank*, 1963; Lane, *Andrea Barbarigo*, 1944. On this merchantry in general, see Pirenne, *Medieval Europe*, 1933, pages 16 ff., 26 ff., 45 ff.; Boxer, *Fidalgos*, 1948; Carus-Wilson, *Merchant Adventurers*, 1962; Rörig, *Medieval Town*, 1955, pages 45 ff., 85 ff., 123 ff.

[18]Sombart, *Der Moderne Kapitalismus*, 1902, vol. 1, ch. 7, pages 162–189; later literature cited by Pirenne, *Medieval Europe*, 1933, page 162 n. l.

[19]Weber, *General Economic History*, 1923, pages 220 ff.; Pirenne, *Medieval Europe*, 1933, pages 97 ff.; Lopez and Raymond, *Medieval Trade*, 1964, pages 79 ff.

[20]To cite only the case of Japan, it seems well-established that the great merchant princes of Osaka and Kyoto at the end of the Tokagawa period financed the Meiji overturn that opened up a new socioeconomic and political regime in Japan. And these merchant princes made their fortunes chiefly with operations in Japanese long-distance internal commerce. See Eihiro Honjo, *History of Japan*, 1935, pages 324 ff. As for Jewish traders, Pirenne, *Medieval Europe*, 1933, page 11, states that Jews were so active in regular commerce that the words Judaeus and Mercator would appear synonymous in the Carolingian period.

prise, played an important role in advanced early economic systems in the form of the wholesale merchant firm wherever long-distance trade was conducted on land or sea.

It has been suggested that this trade was noncapitalistic because it was organized and carried out as a monopoly.[21] The evidence for this is scant indeed. Early merchant activities, especially long-distance trade, were organized for mutual protection both en route and at trading stations that were usually maintained by special grants from local authorities or by treaties of friendship between established governments. In places where merchants were organized in strong guilds, these grants would secure more profitable terms of trade.[22] But except for a long period in the Dark Ages when only Byzantine merchants had access to the mercantile basin drained by the Black Sea, trade was generally open to most organized merchant groups from many trading centers. Among these centers, both during and after the Graeco-Roman period, intensive commercial rivalries invariably developed. Moreover, within each major trading center the interests of large numbers of small or plebeian traders—whose ventures aided by commenda finance, played vital roles in reviving medieval commerce in the Middle Ages—could never have been properly accommodated by organized cartels, pooling earned profits by some established formula. Such agreements would have been handicapped by limited record-keeping and payment in coin. Also, the traditions of early merchant capital favored individual enterprise, open dealing, and private appropriation. Even in the late medieval period, the more concerted forms of international trade that were developed did not involve pooling of trading profits or general agreements on volume and price, but only provided for certain common overhead facilities at ports and trading stations and mutual assistance.[23]

---

[21]"The precapitalist merchant drew *his* profit from his possession of a monopoly." See Amin, *Unequal Development*, 1973, page 32. This monopoly was allegedly more complete "in proportion to the distance over which the trade was carried on and to the rarity of the goods involved." "When the merchants were not grouped in independent cities or in castes, or differentiated ethnically or by religion, they organized themselves into closed groups like the 'merchant-adventurers' in Europe or the corporations that existed in China" (pages 32 f.). Dobb comes close to same position. See *Development of Capitalism*, 1947, pages 88 ff.

[22]Some examples of limited cartels formed by traders of one center in particular kinds of markets are found in Lopez and Raymond, *Medieval Trade*, 1967, pages 126 ff.

[23]The Company of the Merchant Adventurers and of the Staple, which formed in the closing phases of the Middle Ages in the rising national states of Europe to supersede local urban trading guilds, were designed to "regulate the trade of individual merchants, not to engage in trade themselves in their collective capacity." See Postan, *Medieval Economy and Society*, 1972, pages 245 ff.; Dobb, *Development of Capitalism*, pages 111 ff. Whenever trade with a given center is first initiated, profits will often be greater as with Portuguese trade in the sixteenth century with Japan and China. But this monopoly of trade was soon broken up

But were these early merchant princes of the ancient, medieval, Muslim, and Asiatic societies capitalist undertakings in the Weberian sense? That approach concedes that earlier merchants had the acquisitive urge and the business temper as well as the "will and wit" to search out "every chance of profit."[24] Weber further agrees that profits, the net return of a business enterprise after paying business expenses, is a true characteristic of capitalist enterprise. But Weber denies that these early merchants earned their profits in the "spirit of modern capitalism" because:[25]

1. They did not practice double-entry bookkeeping or rational capital accounting.
2. They maintained no clear separation between household and business assets.
3. Their trading activity was episodic and lacked continuity.
4. Their enterprises were conducted in a "traditionalistic spirit."
5. Their labor force was not hired in a free labor market.

While the bookkeeping records of early merchants were not in ideal form, they did permit at any time a full statement of a given proprietor's assets and net worth, and for each trading venture they yielded an exact summation of income and expenses. The former was needed both for statements of credit and to serve as the basis for testamentary disposition. The latter was needed because many trading ventures were carried out by partnerships frequently involving shares by many investors (in so-called commenda agreements) with the net gain to be recorded and shared in an agreed fashion.[26]

But aside from direct profit accounting, are we certain that profit estimation by early merchants was so much below the standards of nineteenth century capitalist enterprise? Merchants at both periods had many opportu-

---

by competition from Dutch and English and later French merchant capital. As Marx pointed out, generally "monopoly of the carrying trade disintegrates, proportionately to the economic development of the peoples, whom it exploits at both ends of its course." See Marx, *Capital* III, 1864–1865, page 329.

[24]Weber, *Economy and Society*, 1921, page 1614.

[25]From his earliest presentation on this theme, from the 1904–1905 essays on the "Protestant Ethic and the Spirit of Capitalism" through his last performance in his lectures on the *General Economic History*, Weber made the case for the uniqueness of "modern capitalism," following in this respect the earlier work of Sombart. See Weber, *Protestant Ethic*, 1904–1905, pages 65 ff.; *Economy and Society*, 1921, pages 90 ff.; *General Economic History*, 1923, page 276. On Sombart's related position, see Lane, *Enterprise and Secular Change*, 1953, pages 25 ff.

[26]Weber confirms that the commenda is "found in Babylonian and Arabian as well as Italian law and in a modified form in the Hanseatic." See Weber, *General Economic History*, 1923, page 206. Weber's early dissertation on trading companies in the Middle Ages focused on the commenda relationships and their legal forms developed in selected Mediterranean cities.

nities for trading ventures embodying differing risks, promising different rates of return, and tying up capital over time. A merchant needed to choose among proffered ventures without being able to reduce them to actuarially equivalent risk-free levels. Such choices were made at both times on the basis of rough surmises founded on information (woefully inadequate), prior experience (not precisely analogous), and with guidance from talk in the market place. Neither then or now could these choices be made on the basis of yield estimates ground out with actuarial precision. As Keynes advised us about modern investment planning, "the outstanding fact is the extreme precariousness of the basis of knowledge on which our estimates of prospective yield have to be made."[27]

The mixture of household and business assets prevailed through near modern times; under the surface, it still exists. Creditors always extended credit to a capitalist enterprise assured that all household assets, beyond those needed for a bare living, could be drawn upon under the law of bankruptcy if needed to pay debts. Many a small business establishment raised capital at a critical juncture by mortgaging the home or pledging gold or silver plate as security for a loan. A small corporation often had poorer credit standing than a capitalist enterprise precisely because creditors could not reach into the corporate leaders' household assets or other investments to satisfy indebtedness.

Early trading activity did take the form of apparently discontinuous trading ventures. But these ventures were launched by merchants working full time in their business and schooled in its principles and methods. The merchant was continuously active; only his ventures were discontinuous.

Among merchants early and late, the balance between "traditionalistic" and innovating entrepreneurship was mixed, though doubtless bold innovation took on different forms in earlier centuries. Few merchants could *become* wealthy by merely running a "traditionalistic" business with the "traditional amount of work, the traditional manner of regulating relationships with labour and the essentially traditional circle of customers."[28] This axiom is borne out by occasional biographical information about earlier merchants or businessmen who achieved wealth by either innovating and doing novel things or else doing the same thing in novel ways and places.[29] The implication in

---

[27]Keynes, *General Theory*, 1936, page 149.

[28]Weber, *Protestant Ethic*, 1904–1905, page 67.

[29]Thus a Chinese historian writing some 2000 years ago turned his attention in his biographical sketches to a few of the great "moneymakers" of the period who are generally characterized as acquiring mercantile wealth by "buying cheap and selling dear." Szuma Chien, *Records of the Historian*, 120 B.C., pages 152, 414. But he shows awareness now and then that more was involved, doing "what others spurned," locating in strategic places, (page 413) or performing odd services like selling preserved tripe, sharpening knives, or hawking drinks (page 428). A contemporary economic Chinese historian, Ku Pan, discussing other cases of wealthy

Weber's analysis that older merchants were often "traditionalistic" is the nub of Joseph Schumpeter's contention in a series of works commencing in 1912, which argued that most capitalist businessmen, both old and new, were "followers," functioned effectively only in the domain of "tried experience and the familiar motive," and that nontraditionalistic innovating behavior could only be expected of "rare" birds.[30]

Weber's final charge—that the merchant labor force of older times was not a free labor force—has, of course, much truth. In Graeco-Roman times slaves were widely used on ships as means of propulsion.[31] Slaves were widely used as confidential agents and secretaries by Jewish merchant traders of Cairo in the tenth to twelfth centuries A D. and were almost adopted into families.[32] Older Chinese merchant accounts frequently mention recruiting a sales force by purchase of suitable slaves.[33] The merchant labor force in these early times

---

businessmen in early Han China listed one who grew wealthy preparing "delicately flavored sheep stomach and other dried meats," another on "bean relishes." See Ku Pan, *Han Shu*, 1950, page 410. Crassus was celebrated for his extraordinary wealth and his talent as a Roman politician and general. But he commenced his career from ordinary circumstances and made a fortune out of public calamities by buying up properties of persons in need of quick sale, families just put on the proscribed list or with houses caught in or near a fire. He assembled a crew of builders and architects who could presumably restore the damaged buildings and, according to Plutarch's possibly exaggerated account, ended up owning "most of Rome." See Plutarch, *Lives*, "Crassus," page 650 f. He was an entrepreneur all the way, never appearing in the law courts without carefully prepared speeches "and undertaking the whole management of the case" (page 653). A Jewish medieval scrap dealer is recorded as having purchased the famous bronze Colossus from the Muslim authorities and shipping it away as 900 camel loads of bronze. See Goitein, *Jews and Arabs*, 1955, pages 101, 105.

[30]Schumpeter, *Business Cycles*, 1939, pages 98 f. For the fullest statement of this theory of entrepreneurship, see Schumpeter, *Theory of Economic Development*, 1912. There are good grounds for believing that Schumpeter exaggerated the scarcity of the innovating temperament, as I argued in an earlier essay. See Gottlieb, "Schumpeter's Thought," 1959, pages 1–42. The point is that the charge of "traditionalistic" behavior can be leveled at many capitalists at all times, and that there is little evidence to suggest that the balance of innovating and traditionalistic behavior among merchants was very different in earlier or later periods.

[31]Weber, *General Economic History*, 1923, page 203.

[32]Goitein, *Mediterranean Society*, 1967–1971, vol. 1, pages 132 ff. Male slaves, writes Goitein, "were mainly employed in positions of trust. . . . The acquisition of a male slave (or "ghulam") was a great affair on which a man was congratulated almost as if a son had been born to him . . . for a slave performed tasks similar to those of a son."

[33]One successful moneymaker took slaves and captives who were distressing to others and "commissioned them to make profits by selling fish and salt as traveling traders or resident merchants or by cart with mounted retinue." See Ku Pan, *Han Shu*, 1950, page 455. Szuma Chien commented on this case that the master "let his slaves become rich and powerful while utilizing their abilities to the full." See Szuma Chien, *Records of the Historian*, 1979, page 426. In the later Tang and Sung periods accounts of wealthy merchants mention less staffing a merchant service with slaves but rather hiring "pedlars and lesser merchants among whom he shares the task." See Shiba Yoshinobu, *Commerce and Society in Sung China*, 1968, pages 194 ff.

was not hired in a free labor market. But it had to be recruited, trained, and induced to loyal performance by suitable inducements, including adequate compensation. Merchants hired assistants and associates drawn especially from the extended family or else appointed agents who worked on commission. Navigational officers and craftsmen on Graeco-Roman ships were free seamen.[34] The sea law of Rhodes, codified in late Roman times, states that seamen were paid in wages by the year, by a fixed sum per voyage, and finally even by a portion of freight receipts.[35] The seamen who worked on medieval merchant ships as free men were paid wages; generally they also enjoyed certain rights to engage in a little shipping trade on their own account. The Venetian medieval economy revolved around maritime trade, thus depending on a large proletariat trained to undertake both seamen and sea-fighter missions.[36]

The earlier West European medieval merchant, especially the Italian merchant from the tenth century onward has been celebrated for his skill, audacity, and enterprise—not so much, as Lopez and Raymond point out, by his business records but by the medieval town that was his masterpiece, "with its art, its religion, its literature, its atmosphere of free opportunity."[37] Within the realms of Islam and rabbinic Judaism, where the merchant was cherished for his way of life and where his values were enshrined in central religious teachings, is it so strange that mercantile enterprise itself should be any less celebrated?[38] And although most biographical evidence of merchant activity

---

[34]Weber, *General Economic History*, 1923, page 203.

[35]Lane, *Enterprise and Secular Change*, 1953, page 16.

[36]Lane, *Venice*, 1973, pages 126, 116 ff. "In Venice's biggest industry, shipping, there was no guild organization. Seamen were too numerous and too varied in status. When not 'signed on' for a voyage, they were caulkers or fishermen or coopers or engaged in some other occupation. At sea they were traders as well as sailors or oarsmen."

[37]Lopez and Raymond, *Medieval Trade*, 1967, page 409.

[38]Islam has not been without its detractors of commerce, including Ibn Khaldun, who declared that "honest traders are few." See Ibn Khaldun, *Muqaddimah*, 1377, page 312. Under many Muslim rulers, especially after the Turkic invasions, properties of rich traders could be arbitrarily sequestered. But the Prophet Muhammed had himself engaged in trade, gave trading profits a clear blessing in the Koran, and left a tradition which clearly honored merchant enterprises. See Rodinson, *Islam and Capitalism*, 1966, pages 12 ff.; Goitein, *Jews and Arabs*, 1955, pages 38 ff., 103 ff. As Weber emphasized in his "Sociology of Religion," after the first eschatological period when the religion turned into a warrior faith, the basic ethic of Islam favored a this-worldly orientation without an inherent asceticism or mysticism and with rejection of magic. See Weber, *Economy and Society*, 1921, pages 623 ff. In the heyday of the Moslem Empire under the Abbasids, an extensive trade with both the Far East and Europe and Byzantium brought what a recent authority terms a flourishing period for many towns and a definite emergence of a "new and rich Moslem bourgeoisie." Ashtor, *The Near East*, 1976, page 112. The features of Islam which favored mercantile activity were reinforced among Jews, who as a pariah people were deprived of settling on land and were required to make their living in urban pursuits, either petty crafts, moneylending and above all trade. As

has failed to survive from the remote past, it seems reasonable to project into the facts of wholesale commerce and the existence of merchant wealth the enterprise and activity that alone made that wealth possible.[39]

AGRARIAN CAPITALISM

As the first major field for the development of capitalist enterprise, wholesale or long-distance trade—with its conjunct fields of insurance and loan finance—created a kind of "mercantile capitalism." The second major field for this mode has been *agriculture* itself; its starting point was feudal production in overlordship of a village community. As this mode dissolves, it can convert into the landlord mode, degenerate into peonage, or combine the two modes. But it can also turn easily into capitalist enterprise if the landed proprietor (1) asserts his overriding property interest in the land itself, (2) clears away the village communities and their open fields and commons for the combined uses of tenants and lord, and (3) establishes or "encloses" large farm properties out of arable fields already available. Farm workers are readily recruited as wage laborers from the expropriated villagers cleared from the estate.

If the landed proprietors decide to work the available property themselves and manage it as a large-scale farming enterprise, they have at hand all the elements of capitalist production: (1) free laborers looking for work, (2) en-

---

Werner Sombart in his classical work, *The Jews and Modern Capitalism*, 1911, pages 202 f., pointed out, Talmudic Judaism almost constituted a schooling in mercantile enterprise with its emphasis on account-keeping, rational calculation of gain, riches as a reward for good behavior, and pragmatic adaptability.

[39]This "mercantile capitalism" has validity not only as a theoretical construct but as a social-class phenomenon. It was the express contention of Alexander Hamilton—a very perceptive observer of class alignments in the American bourgeois society in which he participated as a revolutionist, political leader, and businessman (in New York City, one of America's largest mercantile-industrial centers)—that the merchant was the "natural representative" of urban direct commodity producers as artisans and manufacturers. His argument is worth citing in detail. "Mechanics and manufacturers will always be inclined, with few exceptions, to give their votes to merchants in preference to persons of their own professions or trades. Those discerning citizens are well aware that the mechanic and manufacturing arts furnish the materials of mercantile enterprise and industry . . . are immediately connected with the operations of commerce. They know that the merchant is their natural patron and friend and . . . that . . . their interests can be more effectually promoted by the merchant than by themselves. They are sensible that their habits in life have not been such as to give them those acquired endowments, without which in a deliberative assembly, the greatest natural abilities are for the most part useless. . . . [Hence] artisans and manufacturers will commonly be disposed to bestow their votes upon merchants." See Hamilton, Madison, and Jay, *Federalist*, 1787–1788, page 167. He amplified the argument in the next article (page 170).

trepreneurs with an adequate supply of capital invested in suitable means of production for saleable commodities, and (3) an adequate market for the most saleable of all commodities—food staples. As Marx observed: "The ancient proprietor of land, if he is rich, needs no capitalist in order to become the modern proprietor of land. He needs only to transform his workers into wage-workers and to produce for profit instead of for revenue. Then the modern farmer and the modern landowner are presupposed in his person."[40] That scenario presupposes only that the proprietor is willing to become entrepreneurial—to withdraw from his dignified patrician status and invest himself as well as his resources in farming.

Many English landowners took seriously to farming ventures and retained a "home farm" whose cultivation was under their management. The East Prussian Junker was a landowner (*Grundherr*) with aristocratic pretensions; this rural patriarch in the eighteenth and nineteenth centuries converted his tenants, with their cottage rights, into wage-laborers on a rationalized farming estate, hiring Polish migratory field hands to help with the harvests.[41] Capitalist farming enterprises have been built up in many other countries: China, Japan, India, Latin America, and the American South, American cattle ranching and intensive fruit growing, in which picking is the main labor operation.

After the abolition of serfdom in Russia in 1861, the development of capitalist farms by entrepreneurial landed proprietors was a notable phase of agricultural development analyzed by Lenin.[42] But capitalist farming would have been crippled at birth had it depended upon landed proprietors to invest not only their resources but themselves in the business of farming. Though frequently found, it was nevertheless exceptional. The established life-style of the landed proprietor was inappropriate to farm entrepreneurship. One way out was for the landed proprietor to rent his lands to a capitalist farmer with the necessary entrepreneurial skills. This arrangement took place widely in England, and fortunately the story of that development was told by Marx in one of his memorable historical sketches.

It is a "slow process," notes Marx, "evolving through many centuries." The first form of the farmer was the bailiff, himself a serf with a position

[40]Marx, *Grundrisse*, 1857–1858, page 277. Marx's prefatory comment to the cited remarks is also interesting. "There can therefore be no doubt that *wage* labour in its classic form, as something permeating the entire expanse of society, which has replaced the very earth as the ground on which society stands, is initially created only by modern landed property, i.e., by landed property as a value created by capital itself."

[41]Weber, *Essays in Sociology*, 1906–1921, "Capitalism and Rural Society in Germany," pages 380 ff.; *General Economic History*, 1923, pages 109 ff.

[42]See especially the interesting story of the development of a capitalist farm out of a proprietorial estate, "The Story of Engelhardt's Farm," in Lenin, *Development of Capitalism in Russia*, 1899, pages 219–224.

like the old Roman *villicus*. He was replaced in the second half of the four-teenth century by a farmer whom the landlord provided with seed, cattle, and implements, and who still operated like a peasant but on a larger scale, even hiring wage laborers. In time he became a "half-farmer" by advancing a share of the agricultural stock, the landowner furnishing the remainder. This intermediate form quickly disappeared in England, converted into the farmer proper "who makes his own capital breed by employing wage-labourers, and pays a part of the surplus product, in money or in kind, to the landlord as rent." His position improved with the "theft" by enclosure of the common lands of the village, which allowed him to augment his stock of capital without cost while supplying more manure for soil enrichment. The practice of long leases, then widely indulged, yielded the capitalist farmer its "golden fruit" because the steady inflation of gold prices in the sixteenth century lowered the real value of wages and rents paid, thus enabling him to "grow rich" at the expense of both his landlords and laborers.[43]

"It is therefore precisely in the development of landed property, that the gradual victory and formation of capital can be studied, which is why Ricardo, the economist of the modern age, with great historical insight, examined the relations of capital, wage-labour and ground rent within the sphere of landed property, so as to establish their specific form."[44] When landed property evolves in this way, it can legitimately be entitled "agrarian capitalism."

Industrial Capitalism: Six Behavioral Laws

The development of the capitalist mode of production was slower in industry than in agriculture largely because of the resistance of the craftsman with his guild traditions and the tenacious hold of guild organizations. Additionally, men having sufficient capital to invest rarely possessed the entrepreneurial skills and experience with production needed for the success of large-scale industrial enterprise. Certain critical improvements in *technology* were needed: metalurgical furnaces with stronger blasts, advances in casting and working metal, the ability to pump water out of deep mines, better navigational aids, and developing the arts of making glass and paper. An important role was

---

[43]Marx, *Capital* I, 1867, ch. 29. The long gold-price inflation of the sixteenth and seventeenth centuries made the issue of desirable long-term rental arrangements a much-debated issue in England on which Adam Smith had some interesting comments. See A. Smith, *Wealth of Nations*, 1776, pages 34 ff.

[44]Marx, *Grundrisse*, 1857–1858, page 252.

played by the great monarchs in Western Europe who used their royal power to finance improved technology that furthered their military power.

The industrial capitalists had a more varied origin than the capitalist farmers. Some of them were merchants who organized rural domestic industry by providing materials and arranging for sale in distant markets, thus undermining the independence of the domestic craft workers.[45] Others were master craftsmen who accumulated starting capital or teamed up with capitalists to undertake both production and marketing. Still others were highly placed adventurers who obtained royal backing and patents to carry out, with monopoly privileges, new and difficult manufacturing processes. Since credit is often given to the man without fortune "but possessing energy, solidity, ability and business acumen," he then is enabled to "become a capitalist."[46]

Once workmen with craft skills were brought together under capitalist control in manufacturing, whether to carry out an improved technology or to utilize an old one, the circumstance of their working in close juxtaposition on a limited round of operations promoted new specializations among them. Gradually, their operations grew disconnected from the customary sequence, to become the specialized work of particular operatives who then developed skill and dexterity by narrowing their fields of action. The needlemaker of the Nuremberg Guild was the cornerstone on which English needle manufacture was raised. In Nuremberg, however, a single artificer had performed a series of perhaps 20 operations one after another, whereas in England there were soon 20 needlemakers side by side, each performing only one of those

---

[45]The "putting out" system whereby cottage industry was subordinated to merchant capital was first studied by Marx as a detailed stage in the development of the capitalist mode of production but has since been given close scrutiny by many outstanding students of industrial organization. See Marx, *Capital* I, 1867, ch. 15, sec. 8, pages 459–480. For later studies, see those referenced by Fay, "Putting Out System," 1930–1934, vol. 12, pages 7 ff.; Coleman, *Economy of England*, 1977, pages 76 ff.; Lenin, *Capitalism in Russia*, 1899, pages 386 f., 476 ff.; Cippolla, *Economic History*, 1972–1976, vol. 1, pages 247 ff.; Dobb, *Development of Capitalism*, 1947, pages 138 f., 143 ff., 230 f., 265 f.

[46]A partial text of Marx's statement on the subject is worthy of citation: "Even when a man without fortune receives credit in his capacity of industrialist or merchant, it occurs with the expectation that he will function as capitalist. . . . He receives credit in his capacity of potential capitalist. The circumstance that a man without fortune but possessing energy, solidity, ability and business acumen may become a capitalist in this manner—and the commercial value of each individual is pretty accurately estimated under the capitalist mode of production—is greatly admired by apologists of the capitalist system. Although this circumstance continually brings an unwelcome number of new soldiers of fortune into the field and into competition with the already existing capitalists, it also reinforces the supremacy of capital itself, expands its base and enables it to recruit ever new forces for itself out of the substratum of society." See Marx, *Capital* III, 1864–1865, page 600.

20 operations, with the resulting miracle of productivity that Adam Smith made so well-known in his celebrated chapter on Division of Labor.[47]

This *subdivision of labor* was the basis for the *mechanization of production*, in which machines were developed that replaced the skill of craftsmen. New sources of power were devised to drive machinery, achieved at first in channeled falling waters, then in the steam engine, in turn replaced or supplemented later by the internal-combustion engine, the electric dynamo, and the motor. Coal, the fossil fuel first used, was later supplemented or partially replaced with energy derived from oil and natural gas, and finally uranium. Though the industrial revolution drew strength from improved technologies developed in many European countries and in China, it was perfected in its early phase in England. There a special interest was taken in the application of the natural sciences to technology; there, too, the power of guild monopolies had been broken and entrepreneurial skills were widely cultivated. We need not detail here the oft-told, highly dramatic stories of the inventions in metallurgy, textiles, and power-driven machinery that led to such wonders of the nineteenth century as the great textile mills, the railway locomotive, the deep mine, the oceangoing steamer. The new technology inevitably spread from one product to another, leading to new industries that superseded the old craft methods.

Six laws of behavior for that completed form of the capitalist mode of production—which Marx called "machinery and modern industry"—can be laid down:

1. Capitalist industrial production is usually associated with high rates of reinvestment of earned profits plowed back to serve the needs of expanded reproduction. Marx remarked: "At the historical dawn of capitalist production—and every capitalist upstart has personally to go through this historical stage—avarice, and the desire to get rich, are the ruling passions." That passion calls for stinting of luxury consumption and the utmost parsimony. At a later stage, "enjoyment" is given freer rein and a "conventional degree of prodigality, which is also an exhibition of wealth and consequently a source of credit, becomes a business necessity." But this prodigality in the capitalist

---

[47]Marx, *Capital* I, 1867, ch. 14, especially sec. 1. The Smith account of pin manufacture—which in my active teaching career, students invariably read if they take a course on the history of economic thought—is found in *Wealth of Nations*, bk. 1, ch. 1. For a more extended modern account, see Dobb, *Development of Capitalism*, 1947, pages 123 ff. Smith boasted that by division of labor, 10 workmen could produce upwards of 48,000 pins a day. Marx described how in one day one workman can superintend four machines, each making 145,000 needles per day. See Marx, *Capital* I, 1867, page 460. And for an account which lays more stress on the promotional role of government and of royal finance in patented or sponsored undertakings, see Nef, *Industry and Government*, 1957, pages 58 ff.

mode merely keeps up with accumulation that is still the supreme law, or "Moses and the Prophets."[48]

2. As the capitalist mode of production develops in the various branches of industry, its technology is improved and extended, so that its level of productivity continuously increases in a way unknown to any previous mode of production. The principle pursued—of "resolving each process into its constituent movements" without any regard to their possible execution by the hand of man—"created the new modern science of technology." That science is ever being perfected and pressed into the service of production. "Modern industry never looks upon and treats the existing form of a process as final. The technical basis of that industry is therefore revolutionary, while all earlier modes of production were essentially conservative."[49]

3. The combination of an increased investment in new plant construction with an increase in production to serve constantly widening markets necessarily made the pace of industrial activity, and the whole economy that now depended upon industry, very unstable. "The enormous power, inherent in the factory system, of expanding by jumps, and the dependence of that system on the markets of the world, necessarily beget feverish production, followed by overfilling of the markets, whereupon contraction of the markets brings on crippling of production. The life of modern industry becomes a series of periods of moderate activity, prosperity, over-production, crisis and stagnation."[50] Economic growth occurs in periodic waves of very short duration— from 4 to 5 years for forms of movement dominated by investment in inventory, the first form of cycles noted by Marx and Engels. Interspersed with these and somewhat more variable are longer movements—from 7 to 15 years in duration—dominated by fluctuations in investment in plant and equipment, railway construction, and shipbuilding. This international rhythm Marx took close account of in his *Capital* and related writings.[51] Much less obtru-

---

[48]Marx, *Capital* I, 1867, pages 593 ff.

[49]Marx, *Capital* I, 1867, page 486.

[50]Marx, *Capital* I, 1867, page 453.

[51]The existence of both the "short cycles" and so-called "major cycles" for the United Kingdom in the first half of the nineteenth century has been exhaustively demonstrated by the detailed research, now unfortunately much neglected, of Gayer, Rostow, and Schwartz. The statistical methodology was unfortunately drawn from the National Bureau of Economic Research and the influence of "short" cycles, conclusively demonstrated by activity of prices and of exports and imports, was not removed from the statistical data on the longer waves so that identification of these is a bit muddied. Short cycles had an average duration of 51.7 months between 1790 and 1850. Major cycle movements cannot be ascertained precisely, but the duration is a good deal longer. See Gayer, Rostow, and Schwartz, *Growth and Fluctuation*, 1953, vol. 2, pages 594 ff., 551 ff. The Marx and Engel writings in the entire pre-*Capital* period have generally presupposed the short cycle though the close analysis that Marx gave after establishing residence in London in the 1850s was between 5 to 7 years for the cycle

sive, and unnoticed by Marx, was a still longer pattern of instability in urban building, with a duration from 12 to 30 years. It ran its course in England through the eighteenth and nineteenth centuries; for the United States, Germany, and elsewhere, all through the nineteenth century.[52] This notable instability of the capitalist mode of production derives from its most basic characteristics: its drive to accumulate, its penchant for progress, its search for wider markets, its investment always geared to shifting expectations of future prospects. Production will always release as much income entitled to purchase as it produces goods seeking customers. But the use of income in expenditure, especially on durable goods and construction, can either be deferred or accelerated (aided by newly created bank credit), thus causing contractions or expansions in spending.

Production fluctuates readily.[53] The "superficiality of political economy," Marx wrote (as true today as 117 years ago), "shows itself in the fact that it looks upon the expansion and contraction of credit, which is a mere symptom of the periodic changes of the industrial cycle, as their cause."[54] Of

---

movements after 1842. See Marx and Engels, *Collected Works*, 1841–1860, vol. 9, page 228; vol. 10, pages 490–510; vol. 11, pages 175, 359. The minor cycle in England and international economic life subsided in the 1850s and the major cycle became more conspicuous so that in his writings on the cycle for *Capital*, Marx generally refers to the cycle as "decennial." See Marx, *Capital* I, 1867, pages 5 f., 632 f., 667 f.; *Capital* III, 1864–1865, pages 489 ff.

[52]See Gottlieb, *Long Swings in Urban Development*, 1976, and references to works by Abramovitz, Cairncross, Thomas, and Weber cited there. For English long swings, see especially pages 192 ff. and Charts 7.2 and 7.3, pages 215 f.

[53]"So soon as the factory system has gained a certain breadth of footing and a definite degree of maturity, and especially so soon as its technical basis, machinery, is itself produced by machinery; so soon as coal mining and iron mining, the metal industries and the means of transport have been revolutionized; so soon, in short as the general conditions requisite for production by the modern industrial system have been established, this mode of production acquires an elasticity, a capacity for sudden extension by leaps and bounds that finds no hindrance except in the supply of raw materials and in the disposal of the produce" (Marx, *Capital* I, 1867, page 450). In winding up his discussion, Marx generalizes thus: "The enormous power, inherent in the factory system, of expanding by jumps, and the dependence of that system on the markets of the world, necessarily beget feverish production, followed by overfilling of the markets, whereupon contraction of the markets brings on crippling of production. The life of modern industry becomes a series of periods of moderate activity, prosperity, overproduction, crisis and stagnation" (page 453).

[54]Marx, *Capital* I, 1867, page 633. That superficial view had been undermined by the theoretical work on business cycles and macroeconomics heading up in work of J. M. Keynes and the familiar multiplier-accelerator model of fluctuation taking off from Keynes. But the new monetarist philosophy spearheaded by the popular Milton Friedman, the new prophet of "free trade" or as he calls it "free choice," is eliminating "business cycles" from the curriculum of graduate study and research in the United States since depressions and recessions are attributed almost exclusively to disturbances in credit management by central banks as shown by one major index, the index of the quantity of money stocks. The longer depressions

course, as we shall see later, the credit system evolved by the capitalist mode of production can be an auxiliary force, sometimes to offset and moderate, sometimes to intensify cyclical instability.

Marx was wrong, however, in expecting instability and average unemployment constantly to expand.[55] But certainly instability increases as the respective proportions of durable goods and private construction augment in total social product. And the coalescense of different cyclical rhythms in a period of common depression can lead to unusually severe or protracted depression, especially where there have been underlying changes in economic relations induced by major wars after which imperfect readjustments have been made.

4. The capitalist mode of production tends to be destructive of the health and life of the miner, factory worker, and industrial operative. It produces harsh, hurried, and dangerous conditions of work in factories, mills, and mines because management sets the speed and conditions of work.

5. Capitalist production, especially in its later industrial phase, has proved destructive to the ecological environment. Collecting population in great centers, it pollutes the surrounding waters and streams with its human and industrial wastes. Stripping the nonarable soil of its forest cover, it increases water runoff and soil erosion, causing the level of silt to rise and producing dangerous floods. It pollutes the ambient air with poisonous fumes from its furnaces, mills, refineries, earth churnings, and diggings.

6. The capitalist mode of production gives its greatest service to its most knowledgeable and best-informed buyers, who know how to exert market pressure and reward performance. Most consumers, on the other hand, are imperfectly informed about modern technology, nor do they have time or

---

associated with major declines in urban building and construction are attributed by Friedman to monetary disturbances. See Friedman and Schwartz, *Monetary History*, 1963. The evidence for long building swings is simply not recognized in his text though a footnote briefly notes the evidence assembled by Moses Abramovitz (page 43). The long depression of 1882–1885 with its well-known financial crisis phase is sort of attributed to exchange or financial adjustments (page 100); the severe panic of 1884 was confined largely to New York (this without evidence). The protracted depressions of the mid-1890s are attributed to lack of confidence in the gold standard which had been firmly reestablished in 1879 and was on a solid footing but allegedly was endangered by the "agitation over silver" (page 104). In a more refined statistical analysis focusing on major economic fluctuations, explanation is in terms of "changes in the stock of money as related to changes in income and prices," all three treated as annual aggregates. Annual data serves very poorly for cyclical analysis and especially when the aggregates do not focus on investment goods or building or employment and the concrete factors that led to a change in those critical magnitudes. See Friedman and Schwartz, "Money and Business Cycles," 1963, pages 32–78, especially 50 ff.

[55]Marx, *Capital* I, 1867, page 644 (by implication) and expressly in his earlier writing, Marx and Engels, *Collected Works*, 1841–1860, vol. 9, page 228.

means to conduct proper market research. Furthermore, they are often susceptible to marketing advice even from parties whose profit-seeking interests are demonstrably adverse to their own well-being.

The guilds deliberately sought to develop high standards of workmanship. But guild restrictions and government controls characteristic of the mercantilist period were abandoned or repealed in the nineteenth century, in some fields earlier. Hence newer branches of industry, such as coal mining, unaffected by guild or government quality controls, exhibited tendencies to adulteration even in the seventeenth century.[56] In the capitalist mode's heyday in the nineteenth century, when most consumer goods were touched at one stage or another by capitalist enterprise, the scope for adulteration was considerably widened. A French chemist in a mid-nineteenth century treatise on "sophistication" enumerated multiple methods of adulteration. He named 6 for sugar, 9 for olive oil, 10 for butter, 12 for salt, 19 for milk, 20 for bread, 23 for brandy, 24 for meat, 28 for chocolate, 30 for wine, 32 for coffee—all to achieve greater profitability by deceiving the customer.[57] Some of this adulteration was worked by retail dealers, but much was traceable to processors, wholesalers, and manufacturers. Textile manufacturers were fully responsible for adulterating cloth by adding inferior fibers. For example, low-grade animal hair customarily supplied one-third the weight of products of the American woolen industry in the 1880s.[58] The adulteration of foodstuffs horrified the British public in the 1860s through the revelations of a parliamentary investigating commission that found substances in bakery products.[59]

Consumers may respond to evidence of adulteration by turning toward

[56]Good and bad coals were indiscriminately mixed with slate or stone, all graded at the higher price. See Nef, *British Coal Industry*, 1932, vol. 2, pages 240 ff.

[57]Cited in Marx, *Capital* I, 1867, pages 248 f. A similar comprehensive listing was published in 1820 and 1855 in England. In 1860 competent professional authorities found after testing only 3 pure samples of coffee in 34 examined; all 49 samples of examined bread contained alum; only 8 pure samples of cocoa of 56 tested, and so on. See Chase and Schlink, *Your Money's Worth*, 1928, page 95; Seligman *et al.*, *Encyclopedia of Social Sciences*, 1930–1934, vol. 6, page 298. Engels in his 1845 study of English working-class life reported extensive adulteration in the form of "tainted meat," sugar mixed with pounded rice, chicory with coffee, cocoa mixed with brown earth, flour mixed with gypsum or chalk, and so on. See Marx and Engels, *On Britain*, 1845–1895, pages 104 ff.

[58]Wells, *Recent Economic Changes*, 1889, pages 187 f. He reported a similar adulteration of silk fiber with cheaper-grade fibers, up to 60%.

[59]Marx, *Capital* I, 1867, pages 248 ff. Concern for bad working conditions for bakery workers and their long hours was quite subordinated to revelations about unsanitary food practices in London bakeries. Precisely the same kind of subordination occurred after Upton Sinclair published his revelations about conditions in Chicago meat-packing plants and the public responded to the need for pure-food law controls more quickly than to the need for legislation on hours of work, working conditions, and wages. See Downs, "Afterword," 1960, 345 ff.

higher-priced merchandise of the same class. But producers who quickly learned that many customers were dissatisfied with the cheaper products adulterated the higher-priced goods in their turn. Sometimes new materials devised by chemistry—to maintain a product's freshness, for instance, or add to a good taste or appearance—could be dangerous to life because they were carcinogenic, toxic, or potentially dangerous in other ways. But not all producers adulterated, and to the extent that an independent merchantry survived, the merchant would often obtrude his own informed judgment on the producer by declining to sell shoddy or adulterated merchandise. However, in its later course the capitalist mode of production tended to develop its own specialized distributive facilities through branded retailers or wholesalers. Furthermore, quality knowledge is rare among merchants who must handle a wide variety of products and have no access to scientific testing devices or laboratories. Commonly, though, a merchant was so interested in promoting quick sales that he was taken in by manufacturer's salesmanship. "Let the buyer beware"—*Caveat emptor*—was the basic premise of the capitalist mode of production. Therefore, the buyer, when neither protected by law nor by well-informed social organizations, had to beware of plenty.

THE QUASI-PUBLIC CORPORATION MODE: STRUCTURE

The *quasi-public corporate mode* involves business organizations that resemble the capitalist mode in many critical respects:

1. Its primary purpose is to carry on gainful business for private advantage.
2. It invests capital in commodity production for profit, buying its raw materials and supplies and disposing of its products in commodity markets.
3. It arranges for its own marketing and must regulate the rate of its production to the demand of customers.
4. In the absence of government controls, it tends to pollute the environment with its waste products and irresponsibly exploit natural resources.
5. Employing wage labor, it often abuses and overstrains its work force.
6. In its efforts to cajole patronage from final consumers, it may use deception and trickery.

The quasi-public corporate mode does not consist of *all* business corporations; many are small businesses that now appear in the outward guise of corporations. Such a guise may readily be obtained for payment of a small registration fee by merely filing certain *general* information with authorized state agencies—even when few persons are associating themselves or their resources to form a corporation.[60]

The quasi-public business corporation, by contrast, is defined essentially by sufficiently large size so that "a large measure of separation of ownership and control has taken place through the multiplication of owners" whose securities or claims to ownership are regularly traded in public markets.[61] Not all large-size corporations are quasi-public. The Ford Motor Co., until it went "public" in 1956, was controlled and substantially owned by members of the Ford family, who with their limited number of associated stockholders operated a private company.[62] The Aluminum Corporation for many years of its existence was a closely held company dominated by the Mellon family, though its stock was regularly listed in one of the minor security exchanges and a small fraction of its stock was traded there.[63] Nor is security trading or listing on a "minor security exchange" the differentiating fact. The common stock of the largest banks and insurance companies is generally traded on the minor exchanges although many of them are clearly "quasi-public."

In each country the quasi-public corporations must be identified individually. In the United States, nearly all of the corporations whose common stock is listed on the major security exchange, the New York Stock Exchange (NYSE), would be quasi-public, because the rules of the exchange permit listing only when security ownership has been broadly diversified and when there is effective public reporting of corporate operations and finances. Though an adjunct to quasi-public corporations, with a function of providing a market for their securities—along with, it should be noted, the securities of governments—the stock exchange began as an autonomous body. A collection of professional brokers and security dealers set about in the early 1800s to organize a securities market. Such a market could only develop and

---

[60]These statistics of the total number of active corporations are regularly reported by the U.S. Internal Revenue Service in their published annual reports, Statistics of Income, Corporation Income Tax Returns. Some 2 million business corporations were reported active in the mid-1970s. See U.S. Bureau of Census, *Statistical Abstract*, 1978, page 570.

[61]We drew here on the magisterial work of Berle and Means, *Modern Corporation*, 1932, pages 4 ff. Though in their initial formulation, the quasi-public corporation is defined only by reference to the "large measure of separation of ownership and control [which] has taken place through the multiplication of owners" (page 4), as their discussion continues two additional characteristics are derived, "almost as typical of the quasi-public corporation as the separation itself—mere size and the public market for its securities" (page 5). Without relatively large size, the quasi-public corporation would be unstable; and without the public securities market, it could not come into existence.

[62]Details of going "public" are recounted in the work of the Soviet economist S. Menshikov, *Millionaires and Managers*, 1960, pages 285f.

[63]Berle and Means, *Modern Corporation*, 1932, page 6.

win the confidence of investors and other interested parties by taking steps to assure that a sufficient number of independent stockholders were involved to make up a "fair market" and that adequate disclosures would be made of market transactions and of corporate information. Starting off with minimal requirements for "listing," since 1916 the NYSE—in its own interests as well as in those of the investors it serves—has required quarterly reports of earnings and balance sheets, immediate reporting (now by electronic devices) of dividends and stock splits, and other information to facilitate market appraisal of value.[64] This information is supplemented and extended by a network of publications media—some publishing daily and others intermittently—providing both commentary and organized research, all with a bearing on the corporate world and its securities.[65] Since the Roosevelt New Deal of the 1930s this informational flow has been considerably augmented by full disclosure to accompany any public offering of new corporate securities, detailed quarterly financial statements of all corporations with marketable securities, and records of dealings by corporate insiders in the corporate securities concerned.

The *security market* has been perfected as a marketing instrument with the increase in the number of participatory corporations with marketable securities. In 1874, the NYSE listed only 152 stocks by nearly as many corporations. The number of listed stocks by 1955 had risen to 1532 (for 1084 corporations).[66] Beside the New York Stock Exchange, the American Stock Exchange (organized in 1910) listed some 1200 common stocks that could not meet the more stringent listing requirements of the older market; they are generally of much smaller size and hence have a turnover volume of a fifth of the senior exchange.[67] A large number of the smaller corporations, including insurance companies and banks, have securities traded exclusively in regional exchanges or in dealer-made markets operating "over the counter" and usually paying higher commissions than brokerages on the main exchange, without public reporting of either price or number of shares traded.

[64]Writing in 1932, Berle and Means—who certainly qualify as independent and knowledgeable observers of the corporate scene—wrote of the requirements for listing that their scope and detail is "constantly extending . . . towards an increasingly full and increasingly prompt disclosure of information leading the open market to appraise the stock with full knowledge of the facts. . . ." See Berle and Means, *Modern Corporation*, 1932, page 297.

[65]Berle and Means, *Modern Corporation*, 1932, pages 294 f.

[66]New York Stock Exchange, *1955 Year Book*, 1955, page 31; U.S. Senate Subcommittee on Securities, Committee on Banking, Housing, and Urban Affairs, *Securities Industry Study*, 1973, pages 89 f.

[67]U.S. Senate Subcommittee on Securities Committee on Banking, Housing, and Urban Affairs, *Securities Industry Study*, 1973, pages 89 f.

Some of these corporations would fall under the "quasi-public" category.[68] Hence, there is no definitive exact inventory of quasi-public business corporations available for citation.

In 1932, in a classic study of the quasi-public corporation, Berle & Means illustrated this inexact inventory by classifying the status of control of the largest 200—12 of which were found to be privately owned and controlled by entrepreneurial capitalist families.[69] They made, however, no claim to have inventoried all the corporations that in their judgment would have been effectively "quasi-public." Neither has John Kenneth Galbraith, who in 1967 devoted an entire work to the quasi-public corporation catalogued the list or sought to estimate its approximate number.[70] From the facts already cited it appears that in the United States there are probably some 4000 well-established quasi-public corporations. It is noteworthy that they predominate in the published statistics of dollar revenues, value of total assets, and employment, all of which are classified under the broad heading of the corporate sector as a whole or at best the nonfinancial corporate sector, which includes the immense number of small proprietorial businesses that wear the corporate guise.

CHARACTER OF THE CORPORATE MODE

What then distinguishes the quasi-public corporation as a distinct mode of production? Five features can be singled out for special attention:

1. The quasi-public corporation shows the hankering after or search for monopoly power and for the giant size and ready capacity for growth that enable monopoly power to be achieved.
2. A professional class of managers emerges. Hierarchically organized, in the main it is salaried but is also reimbursed by profit sharing. It is entrusted with control over the enterprise and the carrying out of entrepreneurial functions. The obverse of this also holds: owners of com-

[68]For many years the SEC estimated the year-end market value for large over-the-counter (OTC) companies with more than 300 shareholders of record. The number of companies so qualifying rose from 3500 in 1952 to 4100 in 1963. The market value in 1968 of large OTC companies was estimated at $220.7 billion or about one-third the NYSE companies. By contrast, companies listed on other exchanges in 1968 had a market value of only $5.1 billion and the American Exchange market companies had a market value of only $49.6 billion. See Goldsmith, *Institutional Investors*, 1973, pages 429 ff.

[69]Berle and Means, *Modern Corporation*, 1932, page 95.

[70]Galbraith, *New Industrial State*, 1967. Galbraith variously talks about the largest 200 or 500 nonfinancial corporations; he distinguishes between the Entrepreneurial and the Mature Corporation (pages 91 f.) but fails to give their number.

mon stock have mainly divested themselves of effective participation in controlling the corporation by deliberately opting for diversified portfolios.

3. The mechanism of the securities market enables fixed capital to be readily attracted by issuance of new corporate securities that appeal to investors.

4. An overlordship of corporate management is held by overlapping circles of corporate notables wielding titular authority as boards of directors nominally elected by stockholders.

5. The hold of corporate overlordship was significantly weakened in recent decades by the tumorous formation of widely assorted corporate "conglomerates" without long-run staying power and harboring the possibility of future corporate abuse, crisis, and breakdown.

These distinguishing features need to be elucidated at some length. First of all, the hankering for *monopoly* was central to the quasi-public corporation from its first emergence in the joint stock companies of the seventeenth and eighteenth centuries, in which the corporate form—clearly recognizable and carrying with it the issuance of marketable securities—was found. These companies were established with legal privileges and monopoly authority to conduct business in certain areas or in certain commodities.[71] This hankering was also clearly visible in the corporations chartered in the eighteenth and nineteenth centuries to operate or build, with the assistance of the power of eminent domain, public utilities and usually given an exclusive service grant in a given terrain or service field. These corporations built the London city waterworks, public docks for ocean shipping, railways, canals, gaslight plants, and gas distributive facilities. Marx commented in 1867 that the world would still be without railways if it had had to wait until "accumulation had got a few individual capitals far enough to be adequate for the construction of a

---

[71]During the seventeenth century much of the foreign trade of England was in the hands of these foreign trading joint stock companies—the East India Co., the Africa Co., the Russian Co., the Levant Co. The power of note issue and public banking was conferred as a monopoly on the Bank of England, organized as a joint stock corporation. Common stock was not widely distributed; e.g., the great East India Co., late in the eighteenth century was owned by about 80 men, "many of whom were in close touch with its administration." See Marshall, *Industry and Trade*, 1919, page 312. The boards of these companies were self-perpetuating and Walter Bagehot in his classical study points out how carefully young merchants were recruited at an early age for service on a board, on which eventually by order of seniority they would take a turn at the governorship. See Bagehot, *Lombard Street*, 1873, pages 198 ff. Of these old corporations, the Hudson Bay Co. still operated in the 1970s under its 1670 charter. See Dewing, *Financial Policy of Corporations*, 1919, vol. 1, pages 25 ff. Adam Smith gives a detailed account of the major joint stock companies active in his time. See *Wealth of Nations*, 1776, pages 699–716.

railway"—accomplished "in the twinkling of an eye by means of joint-stock companies."[72]

Stock investment in these early corporations was very widespread. The British stock market, which had been dominated by government issues, naval bills, and the like, now had manias of enthusiasm for these new securities and the new world of industrialization carried with them.[73] The potential power of monopoly was considerable and the corporate franchises readily granted by Parliament laid few restraints on profit-making.[74] For railways the realization of monopoly power would await the merger into giant regional trunk networks. The process of merger and intracorporate acquisition that went on in England in the 1840s soon had parallels in the American and French scenes, where corporate promoters and the first generation of railway tycoons built up the trunk systems that yielded the first of the major industrial quasi-public corporations with widely distributed security holdings.

Though some business concerns without monopoly power or any special claim to legal privileges—such as insurance companies, banking companies, trading and mining companies, or ordinary manufacturing firms—reached out for corporate form along with canals, railways, and chartered utilities, the effective move toward quasi-public status in industry commenced only with the movement toward business combination, which made headway in the last three decades of the nineteenth century. The earliest chosen instrument for combination was a *deed of trust*, by which the resources of the combining firms were placed under the control of a self-perpetuating group of trustees. Beneficial interest in the trust estate was allocated by trust shares, kin to shares of common stock, that were distributed among members of the combination in proportion to the rated value of their contribution. In the United States, some 40 companies operating in or around the petroleum business came to-

---

[72]Marx, *Capital* I, 1867, page 628.

[73]English business cycles and economic growth in the first half of the nineteenth century was carefully studied by a team of American researchers whose results were published in two volumes in 1953. See Gayer, Rostow, and Schwartz, *Growth and Fluctuation*, 1953. The corporate sector was sufficiently important that the team found it necessary to construct an index or set of indexes of security prices, to which 100 pages of their work is devoted, and included in the same is a valuable chapter, "The Institutional Background of the Share Indexes," I 406–454, with a detailed account of the investment boom, especially in railways in the 1830s and 1840s (pages 434–439).

[74]Clapham, *Economic History of Modern Britain*, 1926–1938, vol. 1. He traced the history of the rise of trunk systems "by agreements and common directorships" (page 391) and the extended effort of a parliamentary committee headed by Gladstone to develop regulatory authority over rate levels and operations affecting the public. "Amongst many other things the committee learned . . . how systematically the companies felt for the maximum revenue by constant experimental shifting of rates and fares" (page 418). Rail opposition to regulation blocked passage of effective regulation (pages 418–424).

gether in the original Standard Oil Trust of 1882.[75] The Rockefeller lead was soon followed in other industries.

The deed of trust was a flexible business form that served the early purposes of business combination. But the ideal form for such combination was unquestionably the *holding company*, a corporation chartered by friendly state governments. Endowed with broad operating powers, it was permitted to own stock in other corporations.[76] By the time the holding company of the Standard Oil combination, Standard Oil, (N.J.), was dissolved in 1911 by order of the Supreme Court, the companies whose resources were pooled in the combination had been augmented by acquisition of competing firms and in part by fresh investment. The effect of dissolution was to spin off 33 disaffiliated corporations—each endowed with the same set of stockholders and patterns of stockholdings, and launched in turn on the same course of reproduction on an expanding scale by acquisition of competing firms, by fresh investment, and sometimes by formal fusion with each other or with competing firms.[77]

The process of business combination to form monopolist enterprises by

[75]Hidy and Hidy, *Pioneering in Big Business*, 1955, Table 2.

[76]The essential place of the holding company or "parent company" in the American corporate system, since initially established in the 1890s, has proved remarkably stable except in one field—electric utilities. Ultimate dissolution was enacted in 1935 of holding companies found to be in control of operating utilities scattered over widely extended areas and hence presumably lacking in management economies or any regional grid system. See the extended discussion of the 1935 Public Utility Holding Co. Act in Dewing, *Financial Policy of Corporations*, 1919, vol. 2, pages 999 ff. But Dewing also makes clear that there is no clearcut dichotomy between "holding companies" and "operating companies" or "subsidiaries," since most corporations own some stock in other corporations and the percentage of stock which is deemed to be "controlling" will differ widely from case to case. See Dewing, *Financial Policy of Corporations*, 1919, ch. 32, 966 ff. Using broad criteria, Berle and Means found that in 1928, 70% of the corporations listed on the NYSE were holding companies. See *Modern Corporation*, 1932. Using more precise criteria, Bonbright and Means, in their 1932 monograph *The Holding Co.* (cited here as summarized in Dewing, *Financial Policy of Corporations*, 1919, vol. 2, page 982 n. x.) found that of 97 large industrial corporations in 1929, 21 were solely holding companies, 5 were "parent companies primarily holding," 8 were "parent companies equally holding and operating," 59 were "parent companies primarily operating," and 4 were "operating companies." The role of holding companies was noticed by Lenin as a "cornerstone" of the corporate system enabling a "comparatively small capital to dominate immense spheres of production." See Lenin, *Imperialism*, 1917. He argued that effective control over a subsidiary corporation could be achieved with only 40% of the shares. He would have been surprised at the American development, two decades after he wrote, by which a 10% stockholding could be determinative of "control." See Dewing, *Financial Policy of Corporations*, 1919, vol. 2, pages 969 ff.

[77]Cook, *Petroleum Industry*, 1941, pages 5 ff. For a detailed account of the growth activities of Standard Oil Co., New Jersey, see Hidy and Hidy, *Pioneering in Big Business*, 1955, vol. 2.

merger, under a holding company or the large umbrella of an operating corporation, accelerated around the turn of the century, at which time it became almost an epidemic. Some 87 corporate promotions involving the merger of competing firms in the same or in similar product markets were carried out in 1899. In the following three years there were 151 such promotions on record, predominantly for the business motive of achieving monopoly positions.[78] A considerable proportion of these promotions turned out unsuccessfully in the sense that the monopoly position attained by merger could not be upheld or that the enterprises' earnings after merger did not attain the standard achieved before merger.[79] In this period, however, the quasi-public corporation outside of the public utilities became an established institution. The oligopolistic character of American industry was also set—this character reinforced later by the merger movement of the 1920s, whose booming stock prices facilitated corporate mergers that steadily increased to a peak in 1929 of 1245 business disappearances, as they are called, at "a pace matching the earlier watershed year of 1899."[80]

Conservative judgment maintains that this era of consolidation "substantially tightened the oligopolies and increased concentration in such major fields as steel, oil, machinery and copper."[81] The merger movement expanded again in the rising stock market, to reach a crest in 1966–1968. In each of the latter two years the fraction of all manufacturing and mining assets absorbed by merger exceeded the fraction of 1929. As in earlier movements, larger firms were "relatively more active acquirers throughout" with a "rapid increase in the number of relatively large firms being acquired" resulting in increased "overall concentration."[82]

A similar process of concentration occurred in Europe and Japan, where the process of corporate merger in quasi-public corporations lacked any impedance in law. The great Japanese holding companies—in which dynastic merchant–industrial families controlling major banking institutions developed

---

[78]Markham, "Evidence and Findings." 1955, pages 149 ff.; Lintner, "Expectations, Mergers and Equilibrium," 1971, pages 101 ff. Dewing did a special monograph in 1914 on corporate promotions and combinations and his chapter on the subject, "Industrial Combinations," is illuminating. The early wave of consolidations, following the depression of the middle 1880s involved the "typical trust form . . . in which a Board of Trustees assumed ownership of the corporate shares of numerous small, previously competing concerns," with competition effectively stifled. From 1895 onward, the New Jersey-style holding company became the predominant form. See Dewing, *Financial Policy of Corporations*, 1919, vol. 2, pages 876 ff.

[79]Dewing, *Financial Policy of Corporations*, 1919, pages 879 ff.; Lintner, "Expectations, Mergers and Equilibrium," 1970, pages 102 ff.; Markham, "Evidence and Findings," 1955, pages 163 ff.

[80]Lintner, "Expectations, Mergers and Equilibrium," 1970, pages 103 f.

[81]Lintner, "Expectations, Mergers and Equilibrium," 1970, pages 103 f.

[82]Lintner, "Expectations, Mergers and Equilibrium," 1970, pages 104 ff.

dominant positions in major fields of industry, finance, trade and commerce— exceeded even the American pattern of concentration.[83]

At the outset, the quasi-public corporation tended to be a primarily national institution nesting under the protection of a friendly nation–state whose territory it was seeking to dominate in a given product field. But in countries such as England, Germany, and France, whose economies were oriented toward a substantial amount of foreign trade, these corporations soon crossed the national frontiers or moved into colonial territories controlled by the home power. In all fields in which a monopoly position required control of access to strategic raw materials—like iron, aluminum, and petroleum—or in fields where new technology gave predominance, the quasi-public corporation became international, seeking raw materials or establishing branches or subsidiaries abroad. Lenin highlighted this international scope of the movement for concentration of control among corporate combines by associating this movement with a tendency toward export of capital: "Typical of the old capitalism, when free competition had undivided sway, was the export of *goods.* Typical of the latest stage of capitalism, when monopolies rule, is the export of capital."[84]

Export of capital was truly on an extraordinary scale around the turn of the century.[85] But a large part of the capital exported by Western Europe in the century before 1914 was virtually portfolio investment—the purchase of investment securities issued as much by governments as by private corporations, as in the case of French loans to Russia or West European investment in American railways.[86] As Lenin points out, portfolio investment often was associated with special agreements that resulted in industrial advantages for bankers or furthered export interests of the lending country.

But for the most part, portfolio investment did not extend the power of the quasi-public corporation abroad.[87] For that, direct investment was needed—typically experienced in mining investment, oil drilling and refining or extractive industries generally, and such specialty products as the Singer sewing machine or soft drinks. The heyday of direct investment for the mul-

---

[83]Norman, *Modern Japanese State,* 1975, pages 219 f., 238 f., 315 f.; U.S. Tariff Commission, *Implications of Multinational Firms,* 1973, pages 849 ff.; Allen, *Japan's Economic Policy,* 1980, pages 47–62.

[84]Lenin, *Imperialism,* 1917, page 72.

[85]At its peak in 1913, foreign investment took one-half of British savings, and it is estimated that one-tenth of British national incomes was the return on foreign investment. See Cairncross, *Home and Foreign Investment,* 1953, pages 2 f.

[86]In 1870, government bonds made up some two-thirds of British foreign investment; the great bulk of French foreign investment in 1913 was in loans to government, primarily to Russia but also to Greece, the Balkans, Turkey, Austria-Hungary—nearly all repudiated during World War I. See Cairncross, *Home and Foreign Investment,* 1953, pages 183, 224.

[87]Lenin, *Imperialism,* 1917, pages 76 ff.

tinational corporation came after World War II with the American capital movement abroad, largely to Canada, Western Europe, and selected Latin American states, or to a circle of industrializing, cheap-labor states under American influence, such as Taiwan, South Korea, and Singapore. In 1966, a U.S. census of manufacturing firms with foreign affiliates enumerated some 3400 firms with 23,000 foreign affiliates. The book value of direct U.S. foreign investment went up from $11.8 billion in 1950 to $78.1 billion in 1970.[88] An equally large foreign investment has occurred in the service sector in such fields as chain-store retailing, hotels, airlines, insurance, and banking.

The urge to monopoly is rarely given complete fulfillment except in the public utilities, which are awarded legal privileges. Some independent enterprises will resist combination. In any case, national monopolists will tend to compete against one another in a world market, leading to a persistent pattern of oligopoly, in which a few large firms coexist with each other. Lenin stressed that such a pattern of oligopoly "leads right up to monopoly for a score or more of giant enterprises can easily arrive at an agreement, while on the other hand the hindrance to competition, the tendency toward monopoly, arises from the very dimensions of the enterprises."[89] The scope for this monopoly and the possibility of its actualization are actually reduced as the number of oligopolists increases, as new technologies develop alternative processes for satisfaction of the same want or need, and as international rivalry increases between different monopolist centers.

Quite exceptional in the monopolist pattern was the position of refined petroleum products—which proved far superior to any other material for obtaining illumination, lubrication, or operation of an internal-combustion engine. Here the margin for monopoly profits was very wide. In most monopolized products the margins were far narrower, and control of access to production by new enterprises was more limited. Accordingly, the efforts of monopoly power consisted largely, as Galbraith has emphasized, in trying to stabilize price levels for the monopolized products at levels sustainable over time and yielding "satisfactory" but not excessive rates of profit within a framework of "acceptable" relationships among the oligopolist firms.[90] Where

---

[88]See U.S. Tariff Commission, *Implications of Multinational Firms*, 1973, pages 86 ff.

[89]Lenin, *Imperialism*, 1917, page 14.

[90]Though Galbraith makes a major point in his works of denying that quasi-public corporations are guided by profit maximization, it turns out that this denial of maximization is short-term only; Galbraith holds there is "more emphasis on security of earnings and growth," or "some combination of security, growth and profit." See Galbraith, *Economics and Public Purpose*, 1973, page 86. By "growth" Galbraith means growth in sales, but he agrees that corporate management would be very dissatisfied with growth in sales and constant net revenues or falling profit margins. Clearly Galbraith's thesis—that corporate management aims only at a "minimum" profit return—is inconsistent with the recognized high levels of earnings

monopoly positions were more assured, as with railroads and public utilities generally, in the more advanced countries the scope for monopoly profit making was checked by state regulation of rates and prices or by the development of outright state operation and management.

Along with monopoly or oligopolistic control, a major differentiating feature of the quasi-public corporation is the emergence of a class of professional salaried managers, entrusted with control over the enterprise and carrying out entrepreneurial functions. Concurrently, of course, the ordinary stockholder has gradually abdicated any real authority over the corporation, so that the focus of "ownership" is no longer the corporation itself but only the security held. Dynastic figures from prominent capitalist families with great inherited wealth have occasionally played a management role in a few quasi-public corporations—most notably in recent years Henry Ford II (for Ford Motor Co.), Howard Hughes, and David Rockefeller (for Chase Manhattan Bank).[91] But clearly such involvement is the exception for older corporations founded by capitalist entrepreneurs long since passed away. Even where dynastic families inheriting from the entrepreneurial founders have business interests and capacities, they rarely choose to invest themselves so fully in the work of a particular corporation that they seek a controlling position in it. Influence and guidance can be achieved with lesser visibility. Because a managerial profession has evolved that can readily be drawn upon to take on the burden of control and management, the dynastic families—nestled around personal holding corporations, trust funds, and benevolent foundations—can readily relinquish playing a personal role in the quasi-public corporations that they collectively control.

---

of successful major corporations. See Galbraith, *New Industrial State*, 1967, pages xviii, 168, 171. In a later work, Galbraith conceded that there is "often a choice between profits in the short run and profits based on larger volume in the more distant future," so that "the conflict between profits and growth thus diminishes, the longer the period of calculation." See Galbraith, *Economics and Public Purpose*, 1973, page 111 n. 3. We thus agree with Paul Baran and Paul Sweezy that profit maximization with quasi-corporate, as distinct from capitalist, enterprise is marked by a "longer time horizon" and a more rational calculation. See Baron and Sweezy, *Monopoly Capital*, 1966, pages 47 ff. Mandel, *Late Capitalism*, 1972, contends further in accordance with our argument that strong competitive pressure on oligopolistic corporations has substantially eroded away their monopoly power so that, in his language, "monopolies cannot emancipate themselves from the law of value" (page 548). See also, entire analysis, pages 538 ff.

[91] Besides these scions of well-known wealthy families, there are, of course, the "new wealth-holders," 35 of whom were enumerated by *Fortune* magazine in 1957 as having personal wealth in excess of $75 million, associated in almost every case with high position in a major business corporation. The list included J. Paul Getty, H. L. Hunt, A. Davis, J. P. Kennedy, Sid Richardson. For a convenient summary, see Lundberg, *Rich and Super-Rich*, 1968, pages 37–87. Drawing on other listings Lundberg adds to the number.

The managerial profession has branched off and developed from the "chief clerks" whom Adam Smith in 1776 believed to be capable of carrying out the function of "inspection and direction" of the "great works" committed to their care.[92] Since then, the clerks have both multiplied in number and developed a wide range of specializations. At its widest scope, this managerial profession has now been estimated, on the basis of sample surveys, to include one in seven employees. The number of employees functioning as "managers and administrators" in 1978 was counted by the U.S. Bureau of Labor Statistics at some 10 million; or—omitting school administrators, restaurant, cafeteria, and bar managers, officials and officers in public administration and health administration—some 8.5 million.[93]

This army of managers and administrators has a twofold division. They are on the one hand divided by specialization for different functions such as finance, engineering, marketing, buying, office managers, sales, accounting, and production. They emerge as specialists from schools of business administration or professional schools, where increasingly most of them are trained. They are also divided by the scope of their authority into (1) low-level management charged with responsibility for a shop, a store, or an operating division of a company; (2) medium-level management in places where low-level managers need to be supervised and guided; and (3) high-level management, made up of line and staff agencies that are responsible for overall firm guidance and control. And at the highest level of all are some 5000 upper corporate executives who possess many of the characteristics of the businessman entrepreneur.[94] Highly motivated and dedicated to their work of successful management, they are exceedingly well-paid, not only in terms of salary and generous arrangements for retirement pay but also by participation in profit-sharing bonuses, stock-purchase options, elaborate fringe benefits, and high social status.

Galbraith makes much of the seeming contradiction that though managers' ownership stakes in the quasi-public corporation are so limited, their drive to successful profit performance is so high. From the lowest rung to the highest, the management calling is measured by performance for the company in terms of both profits and sales. Managers can only rise to high position

[92] Adam Smith, *Wealth of Nations*, 1776, page 49. Noteworthily, in his analysis of the quasi-public corporations of his day, he complained of the corporate staff that "like the stewards of a rich man, they are apt to consider attentions to small matters as not for their master's honour." Negligence and profusion "must always prevail, more or less, in the management of the affairs of such a company" (page 700).

[93] Koontz and O'Donnell, *Principles of Management*, 1955, pages 3 f.; U.S. Bureau of Census, *Statistical Abstract*, 1978, pages 418, 420.

[94] For the estimate of 5000 upper executives in quasi-public corporations, see Lundberg, *Rich and Super-Rich*, 1968, pages 532 ff.

in the hierarchy by excelling in the performance of the managerial function and by the ability to build and maintain good *esprit de corps* in their staffs. Though the profession of managers is partly self-recruited—male children raised in high-level managerial families will have greater access to schooling and opportunities—to a substantial degree the process of personnel selection and promotion from the ranks is uninfluenced by pedigree, ethnic background, or personal wealth. Therefore, able men and women with low social background but with demonstrated business ability and skill in their specialties may readily rise in managerial ranks.[95] The typical business leaders of the early 1950s entered a business career at the age of 22 years and "freely shifted jobs and companies until about 29 years old when they joined their permanent firms" and reached a high executive position when 47 years old.[96]

Even in 1865 Marx observed that corporations showed "an increasing tendency to separate the work of management from the ownership of capital," eliminating the pretext "for the confusion of profit-of-enterprise and wages of management."[97] By the 1980s there can be little doubt that in the large quasi-public corporation the separation between management and ownership of capital is relatively complete. Nor does this separation mean the divestment of the top wealth owners. They are thereby released to pursue their personal interests, look after their investment portfolios, or seek a never-ceasing round of pleasure and travel untroubled by pressing business concerns. Enough of their class is still engaged in corporate overlordship—seated in corporate directoral boards or private investment or commercial banking centers—to give oversight to managerial selection and from time to time to make the managerial shifts that are so newsworthy. The permanence of the corporate system is thereby given assurance as a steady supply of fresh talent moves up the managerial hierarchy and renews top corporate leadership.[98]

A good overall measure of managerial performance in the quasi-public corporation is provided by the stock market, where investors, continually engaged in the portfolio shiftings, expose to clear view the corporate winners and losers. This activity serves as a barometer for corporate overlordship—to be reviewed shortly—by indicating that something is amiss in current managerial functions. Even more importantly, the stock market serves as a ready

[95]Drawing upon a 1955 study by W. Lloyd Warner, 43% of top business executives "started as clerks and salesmen, 24% as professionals, 14 % as skilled or unskilled labourers." See Lundberg, *Rich and Super-Rich*, 1968, page 562. Increasingly, a university degree is a prerequisite for success.

[96]Lundberg, *Rich and Super-Rich*, 1968, pages 561 f. W. Lloyd Warner later summarized his own research, see *Corporation*, 1962, pages 16 f., 51 f.

[97]Marx, *Capital* III, 1864–1865, page 389.

[98]There is no doubt that this social mobility of talent from the lower ranks of the society considerably strengthens the corporate mode of production.

means for channeling fresh equity capital to winning corporations enabled by their high stock-market values and security acceptability among investors (including mutual and pension funds) either to issue new stock on advantageous terms for purchase on the market or for acquisition of existing firms by the merger route. Corporate expansion by merger is demonstrably dependent upon relatively high stock-market values that permit the firms which are swallowed up to accept newly issued corporate stock as good purchase money.[99] The corporate winners too are able to borrow huge sums by issuance of bonds or short-term notes sold to investors, including financial institutions and pension funds. Thus the very publicity of corporate life and the system of full disclosure of corporate earnings and stock-market values encourages investors to invest fresh capital in deserving corporations.

The system of capitalist enterprise was enabled by commercial banks to transfer short-term or current capital among capitalist firms and industries.[100] But capitalist enterprise found it difficult to finance capital expansion except out of retained earnings—which Galbraith erroneously makes the hallmark of the quasi-public corporation. Of course, the corporation depends heavily upon retained earnings favored by affluent stockholders to minimize payment of personal income taxes and to transform income into capital gains. But new security issuance has played an important role in financing capital expansion. For the nonfinancial corporate sector as a whole, including the world of smaller proprietorial corporations, the share of "external financing"—involving issuance to investors of bonds or stocks—made up some 27% of total gross capital outlay in the 1946–1958 period, as compared with 35% and 38% in the previous expansion periods, 1901–1912 and 1923–1929. That fraction rose to 35% in the 1952–1968 period.[101] In the 1946–1958 period, new stock issuance to investors was on a comparatively small scale—only

---

[99]Lintner, "Expectations, Mergers and Equilibrium," 1970, pages 105 ff.; Markham, "Evidence and Findings," 1955, pages 153 f., 172 f.

[100]This function of commercial banks was given special notice by Ricardo, *Political Economy*, 1817, pages 48 f.: "In all rich countries there is a number of men forming what is called the moneyed class . . . [who] live on the interest of their money which is employed in discounting bills or in loans to the more industrious part of the community. . . . The capital so employed forms a circulating capital of a large amount and is employed in larger or smaller proportions by all the different trades of a country. . . . When the demand for silks increases, and that for cloth diminishes, the clothier does not remove with his capital to the silk trade, but he dismisses some of his workmen, he discontinues his demand for the loan from bankers and moneyed men; while the case of the silk manufacturer is the reverse: he wishes to employ more workmen, and thus his motive for borrowing is increased; he borrows more, and thus capital is transferred from one employment to another. . . . " By lending chiefly on bills of exchange, bankers and moneyed men provided capitalist production only with a small fraction of their needed current capital and little of their fixed capital.

[101]Goldsmith, *Capital Funds*, 1965, page 117; *Institutional Investors*, 1973, page 173.

some $26.5 billion with annual issues fluctuating between $1 and $3 billion.[102] But beginning with 1969 and 1970, the corporate sector commenced more intensive utilization of the securities market and the net volume of newly issued securities rose to levels fluctuating between $30 and $40 billion yearly.[103] New common stock issues peaked in 1972 with a total of $10.3 billion, with approximately $8 billion each in 1976 and 1977. Bond and note issuance in each of those years reached the $50 billion mark.

Issuance of new corporate securities is the main way in which the quasi-public corporation utilizes the securities market to obtain fresh capital. Another mode of security issuance involves the process by which smaller concerns, mostly proprietorial, are drawn into the corporate system by acquisition or merger. Typically, such acquisition is paid for by issuance of new stock or by an exchange of stock that incorporates fresh assets into the corporate system. For large concerns alone, corporate assets acquired by merger peaked at $11 billion in 1969 and have run about $5 billion in the first 8 years of the 1970s.[104] Owners of the acquired firms who have received the new common stock will then seek through piecemeal sale or by so-called "secondary" security distribution to diversify their portfolios. Such distributions play an important role in stock-market trading.[105]

In recent years, in addition to these avenues of distribution of new securities to strengthen the quasi-public corporation, corporations have successfully appealed to investors to take all or a significant fraction of their dividend entitlements in the form of new stock securities. This method enables small sums to be regularly invested without inconvenience or payment of brokerage fees.

The *stock market or public market* for securities of quasi-public corporations thus permits successful corporations that have won and retain investor favor, as reflected in favorable levels and trends of security prices, both to raise fresh capital by cash issuance of new securities or to acquire existing enterprises by exchange of securities or tender of securities via the merger route. This mechanism for the mobilization of fixed capital for corporate use requires the action of two adjuncts of the corporate system: (1) the stock market itself with its ready facility for sale or purchase of securities, and (2) the network of security dealers and investment bankers who serve as an intermediary be-

---

[102]Goldsmith, *Institutional Investors*, 1973, page 165.

[103]As his volume was in final preparation, Goldsmith noted that in 1969 and 1970 stock issue financing had increased appreciably. See Goldsmith, *Institutional Investors*, 1973, pages 133 f.; U.S. Bureau of Census, *Statistical Abstract*, 1978, page 552.

[104]U.S. Bureau of Census, *Statistical Abstract*, 1978, page 580.

[105]Goldsmith reported that block distributions through the NYSE amounted to about one-eighth of all new issues of marketable common stock. See Goldsmith, *Capital Funds*, 1965, page 238.

tween investors and corporations. The latter adjunct stands ready to introduce new blocks of securities by negotiated purchase of an entire issue by a group of security dealers, each of whom takes a "share" of the issue, which is then peddled to knowledgeable investors on terms considered attractive relative to the going price level for securities of comparable quality.

The investment banker is a large-scale security dealer with sufficient investor following, corporate connections, public standing, and capital to originate security flotations by direct dealing with the issuing corporation. The group of dealers taking a "share" of the issue form a temporary "syndicate" bound together by a formal agreement. Syndication permits dealers all over the country and in major financial centers abroad to reach local investors, thereby achieving a broader and diversified security distribution. Forming and reforming in syndicates puts all investment bankers in close association with each other. Out of this activity a hierarchy of leadership and influence have evolved with certain old and well-established investment bankers, such as the former Morgan-Stanley Co., high in the pecking order.[106] A major corporate promotion such as is involved in arranging for a combination of many firms into a single corporation will repay the investment bankers involved with a generous profit by way of commission on security sale and a bonus share of stock.[107] But the ordinary security issuance by an established quasi-public corporation will involve moderate commissions that run between 1 and 3% on high-grade bonds and considerably more on common stock garnished with attractive banker's options for a few years at a price somewhat above the public offering price. Gilding it a bit, the well-informed A. S. Dewing said, "Considering the risk involved, the responsibility, the intelligence, and by no means of inconsiderable importance, the time required to achieve a standing in the business world, no business involving the same amount of risk is con-

---

[106]The historic leadership role in the New York financial and corporate community of the J. P. Morgan & Co. is well-demonstrated and clearly shows up in the biographies of J. P. Morgan and in such accounts of contemporary financiers as Bernard Baruch, whose memoirs give many revealing accounts of the power and influence of the Morgan Co. See Baruch, *My Own Story*, 1957, pages 125 f., 149 f., 211 f., 203 f. As late as 1939, this influence persisted and shows up clearly in the TNEC Hearings on investment banking, in which revelatory letters by Charles E. Mitchell, chairman of Blyth & Co. (NY) were made official record. See TNEC, *Concentration of Economic Power*, 1940, pages 11,549–11,604. One letter noted the advantage for Blyth & Co. of maintaining a large deposit with the Morgan Banking Co. to get "inside the tent;" another noted the "historical relationship" between houses of "good reputation" (pages 11,569 f.); another related the experience of the participation by Blyth in a telephone call from a Morgan partner asking for confidential information about business dealings and profit record and inventory to complete a survey of "street conditions" (pages 11,583 ff.).

[107]The profit taking by J. P. Morgan & Co. on the formation of the merger of iron and steel concerns into the U.S. Steel Corporation in 1901 was spectacular.

ducted on so narrow a margin of profit."[108] Many public utility issues and all corporate offerings in many states have their flotation commissions determined by competitive bidding.[109]

The stock market and investment-banker machinery not only serve the fixed capital needs of the quasi-public corporations. They also equilibrate the demand and supply of investable funds among other claimants for the use of long-term capital: state and local governments, the national government, mortgage-lending corporations holding local mortgages (thus providing capital to farmers and homeowners), and foreign corporations and governments with access to the American capital market. All these forms of capital compete against each other in the securities market. Thus we cannot agree with Lenin that the change from "the old type of capitalism, in which free competition predominated, to the new capitalism, in which monopoly reigns, is expressed among other things by a decline in the importance of the Stock Exchange." The stock exchange, he believed, was the "indispensable regulator" of the "old capitalism."[110] No view could be more mistaken or drawn from partial facts that cannot stand generalization. The quasi-public corporation is closely linked and tied to the stock market and to its adjuncts—the investment bankers and security dealers and brokers. The security market in turn grew in importance with the rise of the corporation and the investment banker, who achieves his influence over the quasi-public corporation, as we shall soon see in considering corporate overlordship, because of his role in the securities market. Meanwhile, the common stockholder has relinquished to professional management and overlordship most of the incidents of control over the quasi-public corporation because inexpensive and efficiently organized security markets have made it possible for investors to withdraw capital from particular corporations with the greatest of ease. The stock market, the stock investor, professional corporate management, the investment banker, and the securities industry all make up an institutional complex that has evolved with the quasi-public corporation.

We turn to the subject of *corporate overlordship* formally embodied in *boards of directors*. These boards are elected by common stockholders and hold nominal authority over the quasi-public corporations. The number of directors per corporation averages around 13 but may fall as low as 3 or exceed 30.[111] Their principal nominal powers are (1) appointment or replacement of the

---

[108]Dewing, *Financial Policy of Corporations*, 1919, pages 1100 ff., Dewing showed that "syndicate" profits were high when stocks were readily selling in booming times and were poor in dull markets.

[109]Dewing, *Financial Policy Corporations*, 1919, pages 1045 ff.

[110]Lenin, *Imperialism*, 1917, pages 41 ff.

[111]Koontz and O'Donnell, *Principles of Management*, 1955, pages 292 f.; Koontz, *Board of Directors*, 1967, page 118.

chief executive officer of the corporation, (2) deciding on dividends or the periodic allocation of earnings between dividends and "retentions," and (3) approval of new security issuance, of mergers, or of corporate acquisitions that, together with corporate retentions, will govern the pace of corporate growth.[112] Beyond these powers, there is a diffuse function of discussion and counsel on basic corporate policy sometimes consisting merely in raising "discerning" questions.[113]

One-third to one-half of the directors of quasi-public corporations are chief executives drawn from upper management levels—a larger fraction in smaller, a smaller fraction in larger, corporations (although there are a few giant corporations with directorates entirely made up of senior full-time executives). A significant number of directors, indicated on one survey to be one-fifth of their total number, represent substantial holdings of stock. Commonly, large stockholders do not make personal appearances on corporate boards; the aggregate stockholdings of directors for the 200 largest nonfinancial corporations were found to be just 6% of the available common stock.[114]

One-seventh of the directors are drawn from banks, brokerage firms, or investment banks. Legal counsel contributed 11.6%. A fraction of directors is drawn from the military—in 1946 only 4.6%—but it may be presumed that the fraction is higher now with the much greater role of defense spending.[115] An unimportant fraction was drawn from community or academic notables.

These directors by no means are divided into autonomous boards, each with authority over a separate corporation. There is an enormous number of interlocks with two or more corporations sharing the same director or—an even more common pattern—a nest of corporations with mutually interlocking directorships centering usually in major investment or commercial banks. These interlocks were clearly identified in a congressionally sponsored investigation of the late 1930s of the largest 200 nonfinancial and the largest 50 financial corporations. Only 25 of these corporations had no director in common with at least one other corporation in the list. Between them, 400

---

[112]Koontz and O'Donnell, *Principles of Management*, 1955, page 254; Dewing, *Financial Policy of Corporations*, 1919, vol. 1, pages 91–96, 95 f., 142.

[113]On this diffuse function and the role of "discerning" questions, see two Harvard Business School faculty studies: Copeland and Towl, *Board of Directors*, 1947; Mace, *Directors*, 1971, pages 23 ff.

[114]These statistics are drawn from two separate surveys: one published in 1945, covering 155 giant corporations; the other published a year later and covering 521 companies. See Koontz and O'Donnell, *Principles of Management*, 1955, page 263.

[115]Koontz and O'Donnell, *Principles of Management*, 1955, pages 263 f.; writing in 1956, C. W. Mills in his well-known book *The Power Elite*, 1956, was able to list only 14 prominent military figures who had moved after military service into executive positions in giant corporations (page 214). The number now is presumably much greater.

men held nearly one-third of the 3544 directorshps. And 151 corporations, holding three-quarters of the combined assets of the entire group, had inter-locking directorships with at least three others in the group.[116] The corporate board of such an institution as Morgan Guaranty Trust Co. or Chase Man-hattan Bank will read like a roster of major corporate executives of the largest American corporations. And the partners or senior officers of each of the major investment banks will be seated on the corporate boards of dozens of corporations. Investment banks represented on corporate boards naturally have an "inside track" at the handling of corporate security issues or flota-tions. The intricate pattern of these corporate interlocks suggests a filiation of intercorporate influence and demonstrates the emergence of a common climate of opinion, though on what scale and to what effect, little as yet is concretely known.[117]

Lack of knowledge about the influence of special groups on corporate boards of directors may partly derive from the fact that directorate boards themselves play little role in corporate affairs. Directors are commonly se-lected and nominated by corporate management, which controls the proxy machinery of stockholder election.[118] It is frequently indicated that directors who become abrasive or divisive at board meetings are commonly terminated from board membership at the next election.[119] The search for qualified new directors willing to serve is usually carried out by management, not by stock-holders or directors.[120] Board meetings are generally of short duration, from

[116]National Resources Committee, *American Economy*, 1939, pages 158 f.

[117]In the late 1930s, Paul Sweezy, doing the research for the National Resources Committee volume noted above (n. 116), allocated 106 of the 250 giant corporations surveyed into eight broad "interest groups" headed by major corporate-financial or dynastic interests. This allo-cation gave full consideration to corporate directoral interlocks, stock ownership patterns, common affiliations with investment or commercial banks, and intangible personal relation-ships. Writing in 1966, Paul Sweezy (and his associated author, Paul Baran) argued that "a whole series of developments have loosened or broken the ties that formerly bound the great interest groups together." See Baran and Sweezy, *Monopoly Capital*, 1966, pages 17 ff.

[118]Writing in 1932, Berle and Means attributed control of proxy machinery to manage-ment, to the Board of Directors or alternatively to "control." See *Modern Corporation*, 1932, pages 87, 244 f., 139. A comprehensive treatise on proxy contests for corporate control made it very clear that management solicits proxies and is the active party in control of the proxy machinery. See Aranow and Einhorn, *Proxy Contests for Corporate Control*, 1957, pages 20 ff., 23 ff., 217 ff., 249.

[119]Mace, *Directors*, 1971, pages 16, 33 ff., 94 ff.; Copeland and Towl, *Board of Directors*, 1947, pages 164 f.

[120]Mace, who served on and worked with corporate boards for the past 25 years and conducted extended interviews in preparing his volume, has many illuminating experiences that back up the statement made in the text. See Mace, *Directors*, 1971, pages 94 ff. See also Jurau and Louden, *Corporate Director*, 1966, pages 207 ff., 218 f. Turnover on corporate boards is marked, partly because of high average age of board members and changes in their personal circumstances. On board turnover, averaging about 7% per year, see Copeland and Towl, *Board of Directors*, 1947, pages 26 ff., 172.

1 to 2½ hours, and are held either monthly or quarterly.[121] Director compensation is nominal, and because most board members have full-time responsibilities in other organizations, they cannot give much of their time and attention to corporate affairs that they pass on in director's meetings, let alone actually challenge management.[122] Even the function of selecting a new chief executive, regarded as "the most important single decision" of the board of directors, is commonly assumed by the incumbent chief executive who will select and groom a successor for the position.[123]

Only if a corporation is doing poorly for a series of reporting periods will a board begin to question management strategy. If the situation goes from bad to worse and if strong directors perhaps representing important stockholding interests take the lead, then the board may seek to play an independent role and replace the incumbent chief executive with a nominee of their choice, in relation to whom the board will again play a subordinate role. An alternative scenario is for stockholder dissatisfaction with declining earnings and suspended or curtailed dividends to result in a grotesquely low level of stock-market values relative to the value of corporate assets, thus inviting a "takeover" bid from a stronger company with aggressive management.[124] That may lead to a proxy fight or to a negotiated takeover with a new management in control.

We turn now to the final major feature of the quasi-public corporation selected for comment—the tumorous recent growth of *corporate conglomerates*. The drive toward monopoly of the earlier quasi-public corporations was built around two facets: (1) horizontal combination of firms competing in the same product market, and (2) vertical combination of firms controlling the critical inputs of a manufacturing process: key raw materials or patents, essential transportation facilities, and occasionally wholesale and retail marketing.

Though many of the corporate combinations were not capable of holding

[121]"The upper limit to the length of the board meeting is commonly a half day for any one meeting." See Copeland and Towl, *Board of Directors*, 1947, page 276. In one board that was clock-timed, board meetings averaged 133 minutes when "outsiders" were on the board and 303 minutes with a wholly "insider" board. See Copeland and Towl, *Board of Directors*, 1947, pages 277 f. Mace reported meeting-time length as "anywhere from 1 to 2½ hours." See *Directors*, 1971, page 11. One-half of the corporations surveyed in 1961 and again in 1965 had 10–12 board meetings yearly; the other half met quarterly. Koontz, *Boards of Directors*, 1967, pages 156 f.

[122]That conclusion saturated the Mace report. See *Directors*, 1971, pages 179 f.; see also Koontz, *Board of Directors*, 1967, page 227.

[123]Jurau and Louden, *Corporate Director*, 1966, page 97; Mace, *Directors*, 1971, pages 65 ff., 188 ff.

[124]This situation is often indicated in the growing literature on corporate takeovers, mergers, and proxy fights. See Vice, *Strategy of Takeovers*, 1971; G. S. Hutchinson, *Acquisitions and Mergers*, 1968.

their own and lost their monopoly position in the fields taken over, yet the combinations had a rationale in a claim to economies of scale, market control, and a basis for comprehensive product planning.

Where product lines were highly diverse, as in electronic equipment—which includes a wide range of consumer products and of heavy industrial products—quasi-public corporations such as Westinghouse and General Electric Co. brought together a very large number of product lines. Where critical raw materials had worldwide distribution, the corporation followed them. Mining concerns frequently branched into related minerals that were joined together in mineral ore sites or veins. The General Motors Corporation branched off into diesel locomotives, household appliances, aviation engines, earth-moving equipment, and a variety of other durable goods.[125]

The fastest growing segment in the last two decades of the corporate world has not been the integrated combination, either vertical or horizontal, but conglomerates. Though the term defies precise definition, it points to the assembly under a single corporate umbrella of highly unrelated types of business, from life and property insurance, car rentals, and motel and hotel chains, to airlines, chemical concerns, food companies, and shoe manufacturing.[126] The latest merger movement during 1960–1977 involved the acquisition of some 20,000 firms with a total value of over $25 billion (counting only the value of larger firms with assets of $10 million or more). And these mergers have been classified by the Federal Trade Commission primarily for three-quarters of the assets acquired, as "conglomerate" in character.[127] In consequence, a series of giant corporations such as ITT, Litton Industries, Textron, and Gulf & Western have emerged with hundreds of operating units, continually engaged in shuffling their portfolio of managed concerns, steadily acquiring new ones, and occasionally dropping unsuccessful ones. Conglomeration has spread from regular conglomerates to the established single-line giant corporations. Thus Mobil Oil acquired Montgomery Ward. The daily newspaper brings such news as one of the giant steel companies' obtaining an acceptance to a takeover bid of a Milwaukee-based $100 million concern involved in insurance, business forms, and building materials.[128]

[125]See the fascinating business memoirs of Alfred P. Sloan, *My Years with General Motors,* 1963, ch. 19.

[126]On the difficulty of drawing a precise line between "conglomerate" and other corporations, see Edwards, *Business Concentration and Price Policy,* 1955, "Conglomerate Business as a Source of Power," page 331 n. 1.

[127]See U.S. Bureau of Census, *Statistical Abstract,* 1978, page 580. The best appraisal of this merger wave is the thoughtful study of conglomerate mergers by Steiner, *Mergers, Motives, Effects, Policies,* 1975, ch. 1.

[128]*New York Times,* August 1980. Steiner's figures are arresting. The 25 most active acquirers between 1961 and 1968 acquired 695 companies with a value of some $20 billion. See Steiner, *Mergers, Motives, Effects, Policies,* 1975, pages 11 ff.

In his apologetics for the giant corporation, Galbraith has noted that the conglomerate—"one of the more notable developments of recent times"—combines "great size with highly diversified lines of manufacture."[129] In the long run it also displaces local management and ownership, overspends in the process of acquiring control, multiplies corporate bureaucracy, facilitates the manipulation of accounts "among the various corporate entities [engaged in] . . . one gigantic game of financial ledgerdemain."[130] Financial drainage occurs from the so-called "fat cats," where corporate expansion policy has been conservative, resulting in the accumulation of large liquid assets. Unrelated as product lines may be, they still support an obvious tendency to "tie-in" sales in which patronage is encouraged among members of the corporate chain, thus distorting normal market affiliations. Above all, they harbor the tendency to waste and inefficiency arising from the overcentralized administration that burdened many of the earlier industrial combinations bringing together firms with the same or similar product lines and technologies. This tendency may be temporarily held at bay by an especially brilliant management team or by the inertial tendency of the acquired firms.[131]

The conglomerates rely heavily upon continual increases in reported earnings and advancing stock market prices. Understandably, the tendency to corporate conglomeration was viewed very skeptically even by the Nixon Administration when antitrust measures were first taken to check conglomeration in its most extreme form.[132] Some of the ills in the American economy showing up in the late 1970s and early 1980s may have been related to the conglomerate movement permitted to reshape the American corporate structure in the last two decades.[133]

[129]Galbraith, *New Industrial State*, 1967, page 26. Steiner discusses the value of diversified holdings under the "synergistic," effect which he views a bit optimistically. See Steiner, *Mergers, Motives, Effects, Policies*, 1975, pages 38 ff.

[130]I cite here from Dewing's critique of the utility holding companies broken up by federal statute because they involved "conglomerate" corporate systems. See Dewing, *Financial Policy of Corporations*, 1919, page 1012*uuu*.

[131]Steiner is properly unconvinced by conglomerate enthusiasts like N. Jacoby that a "new management science" via computers is the driving force behind conglomeration. See Steiner, *Mergers, Motives, Effects, Policies*, 1975, pages 62 ff.

[132]An English journalist, Anthony Sampson, in his best-selling paperback, *The Sovereign State of ITT*, 1973, has given a flashy but fascinating account of the successful resistance of the ITT Corporation under Harold Geneen to the trust-busting efforts of the Nixon Administration to hold back acquisition by ITT of the Hartford Insurance Co. The ITT case entered into the scandal that ended the Nixon presidency.

[133]One observer believes that the decline in productivity since 1965 is "associated with the increase in conglomerate mergers." Another notes that conglomerate mergers have not improved the quality of corporate management. A common concern "of a growing number of experts" is that top conglomerate managers are "becoming more like bankers than managers of industries." A partner in a leading investment banking firm believes that a single executive

In view of the many common features of both, the distinctions I have made between the capitalist and the corporate modes may appear to many readers of this work as overdrawn. I might have called the new mode "corporate capitalism," to accentuate its links with and its outgrowth from the capitalist mode proper, had it not been convenient earlier in our analysis to attach the label of capitalism to distinctive forms of capitalist enterprise, the wholesale merchant and the capitalist farmer. But apart from this essentially secondary semantic issue, there is surely enough newness in the corporate system and enough distinctive in its mode of economic performance and social relationships to warrant its consideration as a separate mode of production.

Looking at the corporation only in its early stages, Marx did not hesitate to declare that since it takes the form of "social capital," it amounts to no less than "the abolition of capital as private property within the framework of capitalist production itself."[134] Looking at the corporation a half-century later, with its gigantic proportions and massive concentration—involving for some products worldwide planning and resource allocation—Lenin exclaimed that this led "right up to the most comprehensive socialization of production," dragging, so to speak, the "capitalists against their will and consciousness into some sort of a new social order," transitional "from complete free competition to complete socialization."[135]

That judgment is reinforced if we then have regard for the features of a corporate system not pushed to the forefront when Marx or Lenin wrote, and take note of the professionalization of management and of the entrepreneurial function itself inherent in the matured form of the quasi-public corporation, the transformation in the style and substance of property from concrete business establishments to marketable securities, the whole development of the securities market and its agencies, and the rise of new control groups and cliques associated with corporate overlordship. And if we then

---

cannot effectively master four to five different businesses. A survey of corporate management found no "excellently managed" companies in unrelated conglomerates, partly due to executive time and energy being absorbed by merger and acquisition activity. Big conglomerates were found to have more layers of management than nonconglomerates. A Justice Dept. study in 1979 concluded that "available evidence indicates that conglomerate mergers did not promote productivity of managed units." See Crittenden, "After Wave of Mergers," 1982. Steiner concluded his evaluation of the larger economic effects of conglomerate mergers with the suggestion that "how seriously one views these considerations is a matter of taste" and not an "overriding social concern." See Steiner, *Mergers, Motives, Effects, Policies,* 1975, page 312. Would Steiner change his mind 7 years later on that favorable view?

[134]Marx,*Capital* III, 1864–1865, page 436.
[135]Lenin, *Imperialism,* 1917, page 25 (and for the same idea, pages 51, 153 f.).

reflect on how the corporate world has achieved for itself a new economic mechanism, a *capital market*, by which long-term capital can by market processes be allocated to successful corporations, do we not have every right to contrapose the "new" against the "old" as distinct though related modes of production?

4

The Mode of Production: Conclusion

THE COOPERATIVE MODE

Like the quasi-public corporation, the *cooperative mode of production* grew out of the world of capitalist enterprise. The earliest local cooperative societies with distinctive cooperative characteristics appeared in the sixteenth century and were well known by the tail end of the seventeenth century. But these early societies had a purely local existence and were unrecognized in law. Most of these societies were "mutual aid—friendly societies" providing pensions for widows and orphans or providing for some kind of sickness benefit.[1] A persistent strain of diffuse and largely undocumented mutual aid and cooperation lingered among European villagers as an outgrowth of the village community's participation in organized summer livestock tending in the highlands, milling of grain, construction of dwellings and barns, sinking of deep wells, and a variety of other local purposes.[2]

Cooperative trading societies founded in the late 1700s and early 1800s pursued a desultory and scattered career. They disappeared almost as fast as they were founded—until 1844, when the famous Rochdale Pioneers established its trading cooperative venture on a set of principles that were quickly emulated. It became the center of an amazing worldwide cooperative growth in the latter half of the nineteenth century.[3]

[1]On this early record of "friendly societies," see the summary account in the treatise of Lord Beveridge, *Voluntary Action*, 1948, pages 21 ff. Beveridge takes note of a chapter in Daniel Defoe's *Essay on Projects*, 1696, to "friendly societies." The oldest recorded such society was incorporated in 1555. The table of early societies founded in Britain before 1800 shows 191 societies still functioning in 1905. The "recognized membership" of friendly societies in the early 1800s neared a million, and Clapham believes their activities served as a screen for union or guild objectives. See Clapham, *Economic History of Modern Britain*, 1926–1938, vol. 1, pages 210 f., 295 ff.
[2]Kropotkin, *Mutual Aid*, 1902, pages 190 ff.
[3]See the interesting accounts collected in Kress, *Introduction to the Cooperative Movement*, 1941, ch. 1, pages 3–21.

Cooperative production societies or workshops were chiefly outgrowths of the socialist enthusiasm of the early nineteenth century. They probably reached their climax in the cooperative workshops launched by the French revolutionary republic of 1848—which, as Marx caustically noted, "was forced to proclaim itself a republic surrounded by social institutions" with a department of labor authorized to establish cooperative people's workshops, national *ateliers*.[4] Cooperative production societies were supported throughout the Western world by communities of dedicated workmen searching for a new form of productive organization that would not be subordinated to business enterprisers. The experiments generally proved short-lived, either because marketing of the product was found difficult in a technologically changing world or because working capital could not readily be obtained by borrowing from banks or by purchase on credit. Especially in the United States and the United Kingdom, many successful producer cooperative societies eventually turned into workmen's corporations by hiring more and more of the needed labor force from workmen who did not make the necessary capital subscriptions, while many shareholders—perhaps after retirement or moving away—ceased to work in the enterprise.[5] Hence we will consider producer cooperatives only in the form of the collective or cooperative farm, which managed to survive in a competitive world and has played a major role in the socialist economies of our time.[6]

Like the quasi-public corporation, the cooperative enterprise raises its capital by public subscription from shareholders who in annual meetings elect a

[4]As Beatrice Webb (AKA Beatrice Potter) portrayed the early movement of cooperation in the first three decades of the nineteenth century, it largely consisted of cooperative workshops, predominantly cornmills and baking societies; and the number of these "union Shops reached up to 300 or 400 by 1832." See B. Potter, *Cooperative Movement*, 1891, pages 49 ff. For a somewhat later detailed account of these British producer cooperatives, which by 1892 had nearly died out, see B. Jones, *Cooperative Production*, 1894, pages 774 f. Cooperative workshops were abundant in France also and reached a climax in the first phase of the 1848 revolution which put a socialist, Louis Blanc, in the new government. See Marx and Engels, *Collected Works*, 1841–1860, vol. 10, pages 55, 63 f.

[5]Thus in 1930 the 356 French producer cooperative societies, with 17,108 stockholding members, employed 5694 "auxiliary employees" who presumably were not shareholders. In 1929 the 20-some cooperative producer enterprises in the U.S. had 1405 shareholders, of which only 421 were employed currently in the enterprises. See Seligman *et al.*, *Encyclopedia of Social Sciences*, 1930–1934, vol. 12, page 460 ff., The British cooperative cotton factories were particularly subject to this tendency. See B. Jones, *Cooperative Production*, 1894, pages 752 ff.

[6]By way of requiem to this form of producer urban cooperation, it deserves note that a 1929 survey of them showed that, outside of Italy and the USSR, some 720 societies were functioning in 29 countries with a membership of 134,000 persons. See Seligman *et al.*, *Encyclopedia of Social Sciences*, 1930–1934, vol. 12, page 462. In a later survey most of these societies were still going. See Digby, *World Cooperative Movement*, 1947, pages 57–62.

board of directors or a set of management committees. But the role of share-holding is quite different in the cooperative. Share contributions are small in amount and may be acquired on the installment plan with a small cash do-nation and by dedication of dividends earned. Shares can only be rewarded with a fixed and minimal interest payment. Shareholding is open to any pa-tron of the cooperative and all shareholders are fully ranking members of the cooperative entitled to its patronage dividends and to participation in annual meetings and voting. Despite possibly unequal shareholdings, all cooperative members have an equal vote. There is no market for shares, and shareholders are nearly always neighbors or fellow-urbanites who may conveniently pa-tronize cooperative facilities and readily participate in membership activities of a managerial or educational sort. Shareholders in a cooperative are thus associated together in a much more vital and pervasive relationship than shareholders in a quasi-public corporation brought together mainly by access to an international securities market and the accident of a particular diver-sification strategy.

The social strata that launched the corporative and cooperative movements were quite different. Corporations were launched by prosperous bourgeois or successful capitalists, and the great corporations were promoted by major investment bankers with the support of the investing middle class. The co-operative movement, by contrast, was initially drawn from the middle and upper ranks of the peasant proprietors, artisans, and wage earners, whose small cash savings were pooled to found a humble shop to handle goods at retail, to market local produce, or to provide local services.[7] From the outset the movement—which still shows signs of its origins—was charged with eth-ical purposes. It strove to improve the living and working conditions of hum-ble people, to develop their business capacities, to make for a more democratic form of business organization with egalitarian distribution of benefits.[8] In line

---

[7]It was a movement, said the perceptive Alfred Marshall who was one of few major econ-omists to take serious note of the cooperative movement, "by the weak to help the weak." See Marshall, *Industry and Trade*, 1919, page 290. Though a working-class and farmer move-ment, in the main, the cooperative movement did not draw from or obtain the support of the poorest stratum of wage earners or of tenant farmers without an ownership stake in the land. This stands out clearly in Cole, *A Century of Cooperation*, 1944. As Jacob Baker pointed out, "the very wealthy and the very poor sometimes belong to consumer cooperatives, but the great bulk of their members are workers with reasonably steady jobs and fair pay." In farming, he pointed out, "membership of agricultural cooperatives consists almost entirely of small and middlegrade farmers." See Baker, *Cooperative Enterprise*, 1937, page 81. See also Kress, *Introduction to the Cooperative Movement*, 1941, pages 160 f.

[8]Boulding, *Organizational Revolution*, 1953, stated that cooperative organization differs from other business organization "in that it is usually charged with ethical tone and is the object of much ethically motivated behavior" (page 150). This tone was obviously strong in the pioneer phase of the movement, and however diluted in the practical endeavors of operating

with this deeper purpose, the ethic of the cooperative movement has always been associative, not competitive. Cooperative leaders are distressed if the boundaries of particular societies overlap so that there is competition for membership. Cooperative societies are inherently prone to federation—to carry out on a regional or even national level those tasks which run beyond the scope of a local society, such as to produce commodities or arrange for importation of supplies that will be regionally or nationally used, or to set up banks and insurance companies servicing local cooperatives or their members. The principle of democratic control by active members with finance the servant and not the master applies to the federal institutions as to local societies.[9] Cooperatives compete not with each other but primarily against the noncooperative world of business.

ESSENTIAL PRINCIPLES OF COOPERATION

The essential principles of cooperative business organization are already indicated:

1. To achieve control by patrons as shareholding members of a local society that provides a facility to give retail service in goods distribution; to arrange for loans, insurance, or medical care; or to assemble, process, and market local produce;

2. To resist the tendency to quality deterioration or adulteration and marketing ensnarements and sales promotion by both capitalist and corporate enterprise in their dealings with weak buyers;

---

a complex business organization, ethical purpose is still there. Cole has emphasized there "is no necessary connection between the cooperative movement and any sort of social idealism" and that though the movement has never shed its "idealistic aspects" "it has never limited its appeal to those for whom its ideals count." See Cole, *British Cooperative Movement*, 1951, page 20. This means that most patrons and members of the cooperative societies are drawn to it by its practical benefits. But the activist core of the movement who predominate at membership meetings and contribute to committees and auxiliaries are attached to its ideas and ideals. And though the farmers' cooperative movement in its later phases had few aspirations for overall economic reform, yet that movement was saturated with a class philosophy of farmer antagonism to middlemen and a strongminded kind of agrarian idealism.

[9]"As soon as cooperative movement in any country has reached a certain stage of development the cooperative societies begin to form federations . . . to develop the spirit of solidarity among the societies [and to carry out] bulk purchases and if possible organize production. . . ." See Gide, *Consumers' Cooperative Societies*, 1917, page 153. The character of the federal system built up by the English and Scotch cooperative movements was reviewed in detail by Sydney Webb and Beatrice Webb, *Consumer's Cooperative Movement*, 1921, ch. 2.

3. To combat product or service monopolies by developing alternative sources of supply;
4. To provide simple, nonornamental facilities of optimum size that can be fully utilized in service, thus making for efficient operation and reduced overhead costs while avoiding the idle capacity endemic to competitive marketing establishments;
5. After paying for all operating expenses—including interest expense on share capital and setting aside proper reserves for expansion for education and other social service—to distribute profits of operation as patronage dividends, prorated according to volume of patronage.

Other principles of cooperative organization have been variously followed, including cash trading, sale at prevailing market prices, regular and frequent membership meetings for the discussion of the society's business, both sexes to have equality in membership rights.[10] But the above five principles are nearly universal in the true cooperative movement. The achievement of quality control and the avoidance of quality deterioration were major objectives in the minds of the Rochdale cooperators. Certainly there has always been adequate motivation to make concern for quality a basic standard of cooperative purchasing and manufacturing.[11] Farmers in both Europe and America soon learned that their efforts to market their products cooperatively would be greatly enhanced by taking measures to improve the conditions of production and quality of the resultant product by selective breeding, careful grading, and packing.[12] In nearly all Western countries governmental stan-

---

[10]These were spelled out in the original rules of the Rochdale Pioneers. See Kress, *Introduction to the Cooperative Movement*, 1941, pages 24 ff.

[11]Concern for quality stands out clearly in the 1857 publication by a prominent Rochdale Pioneer, G. J. Holyoake, *Self-Help for the People: The History of the Rochdale Pioneers*. "These crowds of humble workingmen, who never knew before when they put good food in their mouths, whose every dinner was adulterated, whose shoes let in the water a month too soon, whose waistcoats shone with devil's dust, and whose wives wore calico that would not wash, now buy in markets like millionaires and as far as the pureness of goods goes, live like lords" (page 28). Writing as an "enquiring outsider" who had taken a good look at the cooperative movement (as a member of President's Inquiry on Cooperative Enterprise), Jacob Baker commented frequently on the concern for quality which he noted in cooperative marketing activity. See Baker, *Cooperative Enterprise*, 1937, pages 88, 108, 122.

[12]In his 1913 treatise on agricultural cooperation, G. Harold Powell abundantly demonstrated how most efforts by farmers to market their products cooperatively were accompanied by efforts to improve quality, to enforce rigorous standards of product, and to develop efficient and honest systems of packing and grade-labeling. See Powell, *Cooperation in Agriculture*, 1913. Thus Danish cooperative farmers pioneered in cow breeding and cow testing to eliminate unproductive cows (pages 89 ff.); California fruit growers learned to fumigate cooperatively on a district-wide basis, thus improving pest control; American and Danish farmers developed careful systems of egg handling by control of production at the source and by careful grade-

dards provide some check on adulteration and merchandise fraud by misleading advertising or packaging. Furthermore, the general consumer's
movement with its research activities and publications has educated many
ultimate consumers to higher standards of purchasing, to which merchants
and manufacturers in turn have reacted. The work of the cooperative movement has tended in the same direction.[13]

Because patronage was to be promoted by efficient merchandising, avoidance of sales-promotion and advertising gimmicks has been another appealing
objective of the cooperative movement. Regular provision for "education"
has always been a major feature of cooperative organizations—though under
this heading some cooperatives have undertaken "intensive advertising" and
permitted sales promotion by paid canvassers.[14]

The tendency to idle capacity in competitive retail and service establishments is nearly endemic—mostly because of the ease of entry with limited
capital requirements, the attraction of self-employment in a business career,
the hope for ultimate high profits, and the high rate of turnover in retail
trade and service. Retail markups have tended to be relatively low on things
bought habitually and of which the customer is a good judge. But on other
items, in Alfred Marshall's view, the markups can be overly generous.[15] Under earlier or rural conditions in which customers have had limited mobility,
the nearest store or dealer with a relative monopoly can command a hand-
some price.[16] The typical remedy for this local monopoly is the establishment

---

labeling (pages 161 ff.); and California citrus-fruit growers learned to control fruit rots by
careful standardized picking and grading of fruit at or near the source (pages 210 ff.).

[13]A prudent merchant who seeks to build up a loyal patronage will also seek to avoid
adulterated products or fraudulent merchandise, for a frustrated customer turns upon the merchant who misled him, not upon the supplier. The question is who is the better merchant
and buys more carefully?

[14]See, for example, Fite, *Farm to Factory*, 1965, pages 27 ff., 38. The expenditure on
"education" includes the building of schools, organization of lectures, and provision of lending
libraries. In his informed commentary on the British cooperative movement, Alfred Marshall
merely noted the stores spend nearly £100,000 annually on education. See *Industry and Trade*,
1919, page 291 n. 1. See also the informed account of Jacob Baker, *Cooperative Enterprise*,
1937, pages 173 ff.

[15]Marshall, *Industry and Trade*, 1919, page 810. In his 1889 address before the British
Cooperative Congress Marshall stated: "Retailers as a body kept more shops than was necessary, spent far too much trouble and money on attracting a few customers and then in
taking care that those few customers paid them in the long run . . . for those goods which
they had bought on credit." See Pigou, *Memorials of Alfred Marshall*, 1956, page 231.

[16]As Chamberlin pointed out in his classical *Theory of Monopolistic Competition* "People not
only buy where prices are cheapest; they also trade at the shop which is most conveniently
located." See Chamberlin, *Monopolistic Competition*, 1933, page 236. The relative monopoly
of the small-town dealer was most nearly absolute of all, as the recent work of Ransom and

of another nearby competitive enterprise that shares the business, causing lower earnings for both. This multiplication of enterprise will continue until trading costs have been driven up and net earnings are at the barely sustainable level.

Though cooperatives thus possess a relatively wide potential for saving through more efficient operation, it is an open question how much of this potential has actually been realized. There are indications that retail cooperatives, in England especially, have developed a larger volume of trade per employee and presumably more efficient levels of store operation.[17] And the regular payment of substantial cooperative purchase dividends strongly suggests that cooperative marketing has yielded extra profits beyond reward for capital invested or return to management.[18] A tendency has been observed for retail markups to drop in areas where a cooperative enterprise is brought into operation.[19] But cooperative marketing has not proven more efficient than the food supermarkets that in mid-century America pioneered low markups in American food retailing and efficient methods of operation. Nor is there indication that cooperative general retailing has been more efficiently conducted than the mail order and chain retailing begun in the late nineteenth century by Sears, Roebuck, & Co. and Montgomery Ward, and later by J. C. Penney. It deserves notice, however, that in England chain-merchandising and department store operations were pioneered by the cooperative movement.[20]

The record of achievement is stronger on the successful combat of monopolies by cooperative movements developed in strength at the wholesale level. The field of combat was pursued through a wide range of consumer

---

Sutch has persuasively argued. In the great farming regions, wrote Veblen who knew them well, "any given town has a virtual monopoly of the trade within the territory tributary to it." Town merchants, he felt, adjusted their markups to what the traffic would bear. See Veblen, "The Country Town," 1923, pages 411 f. See also Ransom and Sutch, *One Kind of Freedom*, 1977, ch. 7.

[17]Florence, "Cooperatives," 1968, vol. 3, pages 393 f; Cole, *British Cooperative Movement*, 1951, page 64; Baker, *Cooperative Enterprise*, 1937, page 79.

[18]The national average in Great Britain of retail cooperative society surplus (after deduction of interest), stated as percentage of sales, ran to 13.4% in 1912; in Scotland, 16.1%. But as Cole pointed out, this was not evidence of more efficient operations since "before 1914 Cooperative prices were well above the prices of competitive private traders." He believed, however, that in the 1920s and 1930s co-op pricing was reduced to the private trader level, so that the average co-op dividend, which in 1948 and 1949 ran to one-fifth per pound of purchase, reflects co-op differential earnings over private trade. See Cole, *British Cooperative Movement*, 1951, pages 49 ff.

[19]Baker, *Cooperative Enterprise*, 1937, pages 100, 148 f.

[20]See Digby, *World Cooperative Movement*, 1947, page 28; Marshall, *Industry and Trade*, 1919, pages 289 f.

goods—from galoshes to electric light bulbs, margarine, flour, fertilizer, sugar, and refined petroleum products.[21] The extended campaign by the first generation of farm cooperatives in the 1870–1880 period to challenge the patent monopoly of farm implement makers on reapers, cultivators, and harvesters was unsuccessful but the effort was a valiant one.[22] The co-op refineries and marketing systems in the United States, along with other independent refineries and marketing chains, made a real contribution in the battle against monopoly pricing in that field.[23] But at best the cooperative movement can only move against monopoly formation in fabricated consumer goods or farm supplies and the simpler types of farm equipment. The cooperative movement cannot reach back to attack monopoly at the producer goods level or in fields of heavy industry.

RETAIL MARKETING CO-OPS

The field especially suited for the cooperative mode of production is preeminently retail trade in urban communities for staple consumer goods and services—with backup support at the wholesale level and a limited number of consumer goods factories that can be taken on at the cooperative wholesale level. Starting from that simple Rochdale beginning, in a century of operation the British cooperative movement built up 127 department store facilities, 11,567 grocery stores, and significant numbers of dairy shops, boot and shoe stores, furniture and hardware stores, and scattered facilities in such areas as paints and wallpaper, hairdressing, and tailoring. These stores accounted by 1950 for some 10% of total British retail turnover. Cooperative trade then was carried out in about a thousand local societies (which for large cities such as London will have hundreds of thousands of members and numerous stores) with some 10 million members—embracing, with their families, about a third of the British population.[24] Though the cooperative movement in Great Britain grew steadily for over a century, since World War II there are signs that growth has slowed to a halt. In the last two decades the cooperative movement has barely held its own.[25] Retail cooperative development has attained

[21]Baker, *Cooperative Enterprise*, 1937, pages 150 ff.

[22]Kile, *Farm Bureau Movement*, 1921, pages 21 ff.

[23]Partly due to Howard A. Cowden, the leader of the CCA, which led the way in co-op refining and oil production, farm co-ops in the U.S. in 1971–1972 provided 32% of petroleum products used by farmers. See Abrahamsen, *Cooperative Business Enterprise*, 1976, page 113; Fite, *Farm to Factory*, 1965, pages 35 ff., 126, 147, 161 ff.

[24]Cole, *British Cooperative Movement*, 1951, pages 37 ff; Digby, *World Cooperative Movement*, 1947, pages 27 ff.

[25]Florence, "Cooperatives," 1968, page 393, seeks to explain what in 1968 he called the "relative cooperative stagnation."

a somewhat higher level in Scandinavian countries but slightly lower levels in German- and Slavic-speaking areas and among Mediterranean peoples.[26] The cooperative movement itself fostered the growth of efficient, massive retailing networks that provide effective competition at low markups. Small, private enterprise trade has everywhere survived by catering to the very poor, and the migratory, or to the very rich and those affluent customers with special tastes for high-priced, stylish goods.

In countries with a developed cooperative movement, cooperative retailing is supplied up to two-thirds by cooperative wholesaling.[27] Over the years cooperative wholesalers have moved back to the manufacturing or growing level to produce or process a fraction of the retail goods handled: foodstuffs, leather goods, textiles and clothing, metal goods and jewelry, home appliances and brushes, soap, tobacco products, pharmaceuticals, pottery, paints and varnishes, and furniture. In the British Isles, the two large wholesale unions have alone 230 factories and over 58,000 employees.[28] Manufacturing has probably been better developed in the Scandinavian countries, but in other countries cooperative-controlled manufacturing is more limited. The reasons for the limited share of retail turnover that can be handled cooperatively at the manufacturing level are many: goods too risky to undertake because of uncertain future demand, highly capitalized services of supply that can best be undertaken on an international scale, products that must be imported, and high technology products. In socialist countries cooperatives have been excluded from participating in or organizing manufacturing, though their scope in retail distribution has been widened by official discrimination against private dealers. Though the principles of the cooperative movement have been ostensibly sponsored by socialist regimes, local cooperative societies in fact have often—especially where Soviet influence and example have been dominant—lost much of their organizational autonomy and control over their regional and wholesale activities of supply. During the Stalinist period in the Soviet Union, autonomous social organizations could not survive unless rigidly controlled by the party-state machinery. The once-thriving cooperative societies that had grown up in precommunist Russia were cut down at the roots.[29]

---

[26]See the surveys of cooperative movement in different countries in Digby, *World Cooperative Movement*, 1947, ch. 4; Abrahamsen, *Cooperative Business Enterprise*, 1976, ch. 7.

[27]Digby, *World Cooperative Movement*, 1947, page 36.

[28]Digby, *World Cooperative Movement*, 1947, page 39.

[29]Digby, *World Cooperative Movement*, 1947, pages 54 f; Kress, *Cooperative Movement*, 1941, pages 42 ff. In its later emasculated form cooperative trade accounted in the mid-1950s for 27% of all Soviet retail trade, mostly serving the rural population. Institute of Economics, *Political Economy*, 1954, page 676. After careful portrayal of the developed form of consumer cooperation in the Soviet Union—with its 73 million members in 45,000 local or primary

An adjunct field for urban cooperation is provided by mutual credit societies, which provide safe outlets for membership thrift and a source of small loans. In Europe these societies, fostered chiefly by artisans and small traders, achieved security in lending by obtaining endorsements either of the whole society or of a few members, borrowers being required to purchase shares which provide equity capital to the society.[30] In the United States these financial institutions, called "credit unions," were generally tied to the employer, with employees being shareholders and with security for the loan provided by withholding from payroll. The European societies function very much like the American mutual savings banks or mutual savings and loan associations, which—though substantially free from private profit making—are not subject to democratic control by members and hence are more readily vulnerable to utilization by officials or by special interests.[31]

---

societies and complex hierarchy of regional and national administrative bodies and total employment of a million persons in 1935—the Webbs went on in the 1937 "Postscript" to the second edition of their work to recite how cooperative retailing in cities was simply eliminated by "drastic transfer from the voluntary cooperative societies to various governmental organs of the magnificent central stores and mechanized bakeries in all but the smallest cities of the USSR." See Webb and Webb, *Soviet Communism*, 1935, pages 235 ff., 948 ff.

[30]Digby, *World Cooperative Movements*, 1947, pages 75 ff.; Baker, *Cooperative Enterprise*, 1937, pages 94 ff.

[31]The most common kind of insider manipulation found on boards of directors of the mutual savings and loan associations, which now predominate as custodians of savings deposits, is probably found in the operation of an insurance agency in coordination with mortgage lending, a combination which a federal regulatory official stated "occurred with remarkable frequency." A congressman at the hearing noted it was a "common practice" to tie in a construction loan with the use of a "particular real estate agent." Builders, developers and other individuals in "some business activity related to home construction, buying and financing" have "organized and formed" savings and loan associations and divestment of such interests has never been required by state or federal supervisory bodies. See U.S. Committee on Government Operations, Hearings, *Federal Home Loan Bank Board*, 1962, pages 17, 550 560. A scholarly paper has shown that the "mechanism by which management converts its power position into personal gain" results in a lesser degree of efficiency than prevails in the non-mutual saving and loan (i.e., stock) association. See Nichols, "Stock versus Mutual Savings and Loan Associations," 1967, pages 337–346. The most overt and broadly publicized proceeding which exposed conflict of interest and insider manipulation in the savings and loan movement was related to the strong position achieved by Mortgage Guaranty Insurance Corporation (MGIC), a Wisconsin-chartered corporation formed in 1956 to insure home mortgage loans primarily held by savings and loan associations, whose mortgage holdings were generally not insured by FHA at an interest charge of 0.5%. The FHA insurance charge involved deliberate initial overpricing for the range of loans in which more than 10% was paid down or in which loan duration was under 25 years. Federal Housing Authority borrowers were, however, entitled to a refund on the liquidation of their loan by a payment from loan reserves, which at the time MGIC was established amounted to $131 per transaction. See Fisher and Rapkin, *Mutual Mortgage Insurance Fund*, 1956. MGIC was required

FARM CO-OPS

Rural communities have shown themselves to be even more prone than urban communities to cooperative organization. The independent peasant-
proprietor or family farmer has even greater need than the industrial urban
worker for cooperative action. He is more dependent on nearby dealers or
financial institutions for supplies, marketing access, local processing and stor-

---

by the Wisconsin Insurance Commissioner to set up a reserve for unusual losses which in
1959, shortly before the Insurance Commissioner resigned to join the MGIC board of directors, was made available for distribution to stockholders after 15 years. At that time the
national leaders of the savings and loan movement, including four past presidents of the Savings
and Loan League, one a former chairman of the Federal Home Loan Bank Board (which
regulates all federally chartered S&Ls), acquired stock in MGIC and joined its board of directors. A special stock issue was prepared in September 1959 for exclusive sale to "certain
selected executives of mortgage lending institutions" and other selected insiders according to
the exact text of the prospectus filed with the Securities and Exchange Commission. These
officials were later described as located "particularly in states where MGIC was then licensed
to do business." Some 74,000 shares were sold to 146 officials and employees of 81 S&L
associations and 7038 additional shares were sold to 10 persons otherwise associated with the
mortgage lending business. At about the same time a favorable ruling was obtained from IRS
making nontaxable the 50% of MGIC premiums put into the rapidly mounting contingency
reserve which could be used for stockholders on a delayed basis. To achieve all this, options
for purchase of the special stock issue were distributed widely to key officials and congressmen
including—and this made a nationwide scandal—Bobby Baker, then secretary of the Democratic Majority group, closely associated with Lyndon Johnson, the former leader of the Senate
Majority and incumbent Vice President. For that and similar indiscretions Bobby Baker was
sent to prison. The Home Loan Bank Board disclosed that nearly a quarter of all MGIC
insurance written in 1962–1963 originated from S&Ls whose officers or directors owned stock
in MGIC. "The most critical potential conflict of interest between the interests of the officers
and the association arises when the former goes through the process of deciding whether to
require insurance or to make a loan at a higher rate of interest or charge without insurance."
Federal Home Loan Bank Board, *Statement*, 1964, page 23. These citations and the related
analysis are drawn from an unpublished paper by the author growing out of inquiries launched
into MGIC scandals at the time of the 1966 gubernatorial election campaign in Wisconsin.See
Gottlieb, "Mortgage Credit Insurance," 1969. At the time a full search was conducted into
the MGIC reports, Wisconsin insurance commissioner reports, newspaper articles in the Wisconsin Press (especially the Madison *Capital Times*), congressional hearings into the Bobby
Baker affair and into the Home Loan Bank Board and financial institutions generally. See
especially, U.S. Senate Committee on Rules and Administration, *Financial or Business Interests*,
1964, pages 32–37. In December 1967, Congress passed corrective legislation by which nontaxable income put in contingency reserves had to be invested in a special issue of noninterest
bearing, nontransferable U.S. bonds. See *Congressional Record*, 1967, H. 16638. Oddly enough,
there was no commotion at S&L membership meetings over corruption of their officers by
favored participation in MGIC. In a real cooperative movement the benefits of "integration
backward" to cooperative suppliers would be arranged so that the benefits of integration would
go to the underlying cooperatives rather than to their officers.

age, and credit. He also functions in a more traditional community with deeper fellowship ties. He has greater need for credit support to finance a new cycle of crop production by purchasing seeds, fertilizer, and new equipment or to overcome the economic disaster of a ruined crop or drouth. More experienced in commodity marketing and business management than his urban cooperative compatriots, he is even more prone than they to jealousy of the middleman's profits—where the fruits of his field labors have often gone to rest. Hence it is not surprising that the gospel of cooperative organization both in the New and in the Old World and in undeveloped as well as developing countries sprouted abundantly in the later nineteenth and throughout the twentieth centuries.

Three generations of American farmer organizations have preached the gospel of farmer cooperation and have given practical assistance to farm co-ops. These organizations include (1) the 1867 National Grange, which organized many cooperative stores and marketing associations; (2) the valiant Farmers Alliance movement of the 1880–1890s, (3) the Farmers Union, launched in Texas in 1902, with locals active in purchasing and marketing services especially in western and midwestern states, with emphasis in the fields of livestock, grain marketing, and petroleum-product distribution; and (4) the American Farm Bureau Federation, formed as a national body in 1919 and unique with its connection with the agricultural extension agent movement.[32]

[32]Scroggs, "Historical Highlights," 1957, pages 3–56; Fite, *Farm to Factory*, 1965, pages 1–16. On the Farmers Alliance which came to a climax in the Populist Movement, see the interesting portrait by Goodwyn, *Democratic Promise*, 1976, especially ch. 5. The integrity of the Farm Bureau, the most recent and conservatively oriented of American nationwide farm organizations, has been challenged by Mancur Olson, in his recent searching inquisition into that movement in *Collective Action*, 1965, pages 149 ff. This organization, he states, was "created by the government" because of governmental support for county agents functioning under the general authority of the extension departments of state agricultural universities. It has been more cogently contended that the Farm Bureau movement was sparked and guided in its formation by Big Business distressed by the radicalism of earlier agrarian revolt. See along these lines McConnell, *Decline of Agrarian Democracy*, 1953, pages 160 ff. The first "farm bureau" was started by a local chamber of commerce in Binghamton, NY, as one of its "bureaus" to improve farming. See Kile, *Farm Bureau Movement*, 1921, ch. 7. Both views are one-sided. Abler and more conservative (because more prosperous) farmers were unquestionably drawn to extension activity by which they could keep abreast of improved farming methods. Conversely, county agents needed the assistance of local farming circles to serve as conduits for their work. Thus the stimulus of government funds (for county agents) and business support of a more conservative farm organization merely served as points of crystalization of a new farmer's movement. As McConnell emphasizes, "nothing is more illusory . . . than the impression that the Farm Bureau is not an organization of actual farmers" busily at work in their county organizations, their affiliated business organizations, their ladies' and youth auxiliaries. See McConnell, *Decline of Agrarian Democracy*, 1953, page 175. Mancur Olson's

Vital functions are performed for farmers by purchasing cooperatives, which make farm supplies and materials available, such as insecticides, livestock feed, fertilizer, petroleum products, and seed; and by marketing cooperatives. The latter provides facilities for local crop or product storage, canning, processing, and shipment to distant markets—here the local grain elevator, dairy creamery, or cheese-making plant, and there the packing plant where fruits or vegetables are sorted, washed, and graded—then often canned, frozen, or dried and packed for shipment. In the United States farmer membership in cooperatives, though decreasing because of decline in the number of farms and farm population, in 1976 numbered some 7.6 million farmers (or over three times the number of farms in operation) and involved a total volume of business of over $40 billion.[33] For a recent representative period the cooperative share of gross farm output marketed was 25% for cotton and cotton products, 73% for dairy products, 24% for fruits and vegetables, 35% for grain and soy bean meal and oil—27% for all farm products. The cooperative share was somewhat smaller for farm supplies purchased: 16% for feed and seed, 30% for fertilizer and lime, 32% for petroleum products, and 17% for all farm supplies and equipment.[34]

Cooperative marketing of citrus fruits, carried through in recent years to canning of the fresh and frozen product, played a pioneering role in the development of marketing standards and grades.[35]

European farmers, except possibly the British, have been as prone to cooperative marketing and purchasing as the American with high fractions of

---

argument that large Farm Bureau membership was due in good measure to the Farm Bureau tie with extension agents is undermined by the continued success through the 1960s and 1970s of the Farm Bureau, though early in the 1950s by administrative action of the Department of Agriculture and concurrent action by state legislatures, the work of local extension agents was divorced from local Farm Bureaus. The detailed story of this disaffiliation, ultimately supported by extension leadership at the state agricultural universities and by the national leadership of the Farm Bureau itself, was laid out by William J. Block, in *The Separation of the Farm Bureau and the Extension Service*, 1960, chs. 8–14. Olson argues that the mere limitation in 1921 of explicit or blatant participation in organizational work of local farm bureaus by county agents "accounted for the decline in membership [of farm bureaus] at the very time the organization was expanding its programs." See Olson, *Collective Action*, 1965, page 151. If Olson's inferences are to be accepted, the more serious curtailment of county agent association with local farm bureaus in the early 1950s should have pretty much wiped out the Farm Bureau movement. Yet the Farm Bureau movement thrives today.

[33]U.S. Bureau of Census, *Statistical Abstract*, 1978, pages 686, 689.

[34]Abrahamsen, *Cooperative Business Enterprise*, 1976, 109 f.

[35]Digby, *World Cooperative Movement*, 1947, pages 117 f.: Abrahamsen and Scroggs, *Agricultural Cooperation*, 1957, pages 382 ff. Control of processing in the major product categories is concentrated, according to the well-informed National Commission on Food Marketing, *Food from Farmer to Consumer*, 1966, pages 51 f.

raw milk to cooperative dairies or creameries, and of cereals and fruit.[36] Co-operative marketing of grain output in British Commonwealth countries such as Australia and Canada is much farther developed than in the United States.[37] Cooperative organizations in Scandinavian countries such as Denmark and Sweden have achieved extraordinary high output percentages of cooperative marketing.[38] Japanese farm cooperatives have established control over marketing of rice, cocoons, dairy products, and fruits.[39] In France—indeed, in most wine-growing countries—a large part of wine output is in the hands of cooperative associations who frequently own and operate the wine presses and attend to blending, storage, and bottling.[40]

In the United States cooperative development of rural electricity production and distribution and rural telephone networks, encouraged by government assistance and long-term low-interest loans, predominates in the field.[41]

Still more striking is a development of credit cooperatives that channel farmers' savings and serve as a means of mobilizing low-interest loans, both short- and long-term. These were pioneered in Germany by Raiffeisen societies made up of local farmers willing to stand surety for short-to-medium-term productive loans made to a member with two local sureties. A fraction of the borrowings would be subscribed as member shareholding on which interest would be paid. Local thrift was thus encouraged while outside capital could be mobilized with little investor risk. Association of these societies in a federal union added to their prestige, provided needed auditing and research services, and permitted the circulation of farmer thrift among societies. The farmer credit society spread—often with government aid and stimulus—throughout Europe; it also made impressive progress in pre-1917 Russia and took root in major areas of southeast Asia under colonial control.[42]

In the United States, the rural cooperative movement became strong enough to obtain comprehensive legislation over a 50-year period that laid

[36]Abrahamsen, *Cooperative Business Enterprise*, 1976, pages 133 ff.

[37]Digby, *World Cooperative Movement*, 1947, pages 110 f.

[38]Digby, *World Cooperative Movement*, 1947, pages 94 f., 97 ff.; Abrahamsen, *Cooperative Business Enterprise*, 1976, pages 138 ff.

[39]Abrahamsen, *Cooperative Business Enterprise*, 1976, page 147. Though attempts at farmer cooperation had emerged in earlier centuries, the present Japanese system of farm cooperatives was established from above by government which financed it by low-interest loans and tax remittances after the Meiji restoration. See Seligman *et al.*, *Encyclopedia of Social Sciences*, 1930–1934, vol. 6, pages 395–398.

[40]Digby, *World Cooperative Movement*, 1947, pages 116 f.

[41]Abrahamsen, *Cooperative Business Enterprise*, 1976, pages 238, 296 ff., 399; Abrahamsen and Scroggs, *Agricultural Cooperation*, 1957, pages 63, 287; Kress, *Cooperative Movement*, 1941, page 100.

[42]Digby, *World Cooperative Movement*, 1947, pages 63–74; Powell, *Cooperation in Agriculture*, 1913, ch. 11.

out, with initial federal funding, a network of farmer-controlled financial institutions. These were at first given the right to issue tax-exempt bonds in making loans to local cooperatives or to local farm credit societies made up of shareholding borrowers. The financial institutions specialize in dealing with farm mortgages, short-term credit, and loans to cooperative societies, as well as to farm mutual insurance and electric societies. In each instance the controlling boards of local societies are elected by shareholding farmer-members, and the board members of the regional credit institutions are elected by the local cooperative societies. While originally the top executives in the system were governmentally appointed and were controlled by a Federal Credit Agency established in 1933, federal control has increasingly been cut down as the original governmental contributions to capital have been repaid and replaced with equity drawn from shareholdings and from the accumulation of reserves. In mid 1977, farmer-controlled credit institutions had outstanding mortgage and medium-term loans of $35.6 billion reaching about a million farm establishments.[43] Impressive lending support has also been provided rural electricity and telephone and general marketing co-ops.

Perhaps more than urban cooperatives, farm cooperatives tend to draw support from the more prosperous—in this case, farmers with large farm properties and a higher degree of commercialization in their activities and interests. In an early polemic on this question, Lenin, who had a sharp eye for tracing class differentiation, uncovered a rare statistical tabulation of dairy cooperative German farmers in 1895 classified by size of farm, embracing altogether 148,000 farms and slightly over a million dairy cows. It turned out that less than 1% of small farms under five acres belonged to dairy cooperatives, whereas a third of the larger farms with 25–50 acres or more belonged. Though making up only some 6% of the cooperative dairy farmers, this group owned a good third of the milk cows supplying the dairies. The next larger size-class of farm with a holding of from 50 to 125 acres and a mean dairy herd of 9.6 cows contributed some 39% of the cooperative dairy herd. Lenin had no trouble ridiculing the claim that farm cooperation was of primary benefit to small and medium-size farmers.[44]

Though few statistics are available, the charge is often advanced that Indian rural credit cooperatives are dominated by and serve the interests of the larger farm operators and landlords.[45] Thirteen American states permit voting in farm cooperatives based upon participation so that participants with a larger

[43]U.S. Bureau of Census, *Statistical Abstract*, 1978, page 541; Abrahamsen, *Cooperative Business Enterprise*, 1976, pages 321–343; Gee, *Social Economics of Agriculture*, 1932, pages 245 ff.

[44]Lenin, "Agrarian Question," 1902, vol. 4, pages 283 ff.

[45]Bettelheim, *India Independent*, 1968, pages 196 ff.; Gunnar Myrdal, *Asian Drama*, 1968, vol. 2, pages 1039 ff., 1334 ff.

volume of turnover will have multiple votes. Most states, however, and the controlling federal statutes, specify that members may have only a single vote, which is the prevailing practice.[46] In any case, no evidence has been adduced that on any appreciable scale bona-fide smaller farmers, when meeting all proper eligibility requirements, are denied access to use facilities of co-operative marketing or credit institutions. Nor does the practice of exclusive dealing with association members impair or undermine the democratic or bona-fide character of the cooperative, as Mancur Olson argues, so long as association membership is open on nondiscriminatory terms to all local farmers operating within the marketing territory concerned.[47]

Though rural or farmers' cooperation has stronger roots and probably a greater scope for development in most countries than urban working-class cooperation, like the latter it is equally adjunct in character as a mode of production. By that I mean that both forms of cooperation are auxiliary to

[46]Abrahamsen and Scroggs, *Agricultural Cooperation*, 1957, pages 240; Abrahamsen, *Cooperative Business Enterprise*, 1976, page 195; Kress, *Cooperative Movement*, 1941, page 256.

[47]In his very one-sided analysis of the Farm Bureau cooperative movement, Mancur Olson (see *Collective Action*, 1965, pages 154 ff.) argues that "proof that the interest of the political arm of the Farm Bureau is important even in the management of the business side of the movement is found in the fact that *some of the business enterprises are not allowed to sell their product to anyone who is not, and will not become a member of the political organization.*" (Italicized in the original; page 154). The restriction in question is misconstrued. Where a farm cooperative is predominant in a given territory and does not need to encourage patronage from nonmembers, it is in a position to force membership as a price of obtaining the commercial benefits of the cooperative. Whether such forced membership is advisable or not is another question, because it certainly does not strengthen the "political arm of the movement," though it does augment the revenues of the organization and the circulation of its periodicals. Olson also argues that in some Farm Bureau state organizations, notably Illinois, cooperatives are "controlled by a lobbying or legislative organization" on a statewide basis and thus inferentially not by its members. See Olson, *Collective Action*, 1965, pages 155 ff. Reference here is to the practice in Illinois of adopting the *centralized* type of cooperative association formed on a statewide basis, "started on the Pacific coast and spread widely over the country particularly between the years 1921–5." According to Gee, at the end of 1925, there were some 74 such centralized associations with 879,170 members. "In its actual functioning the centralized association is not greatly different from the federated." See Gee, *Social Economics of Agriculture*, 1932, pages 356 ff. In Illinois and adjoining states centralized associations were sponsored and controlled by the State Farm Bureau organization whose members made up the local associations. Olson calls the state organization a "lobbying or legislative organization." See Olson, *Collective Action*, 1965, page 155. That it is by its activity, but in form the state Farm Bureau is controlled by a delegate convention assembled from local bureau chapters, and elected statewide officers supervise the statewide cooperative business organizations, thus functioning in the role of a federated wholesale organization. This mode of organization is perhaps especially appropriate for mutual insurance companies that cannot by their nature be organized and carried on at a local level, except, as in the case of fire insurance, where there is special value in local underwriting and control of insurance organization. See Powell, *Cooperation in Agriculture*, 1913, ch. 13.

another mode. Urban cooperation is essentially auxiliary to the capitalist–corporate mode and competitive to the direct commodity producer mode. It is auxiliary to the first two modes in retail and wholesale distributive activity and a small fraction of manufacturing. By its competitive efforts it can displace the direct commodity producers with small retail shops. Marx was thus correct in his early judgment that urban cooperation could not displace or by itself revolutionize the economic system then prevailing, which was predominantly based upon capitalist and corporate enterprise.[48]

Farm or rural cooperation is auxiliary to the direct commodity mode and thereby even to the small capitalist farmer. The latter's market position is buttressed by his ability through cooperative membership to control his marketing, to carry out the necessary processing, packaging, bottling, or canning activities, to arrange for long-term credit at low interest rates, and through group purchasing and even manufacturing to combat monopoly control on prices for farm supplies. Thus the ability of the family farmer or grower to survive in the nineteenth and twentieth centuries has been assisted by the great role of farm cooperation in obtaining for the farmer better markets and extending his field of investment from his own farm enterprise to the collection, marketing, and financial facilities upon which he is dependent. It is noteworthy that Marx, when indicting the family farm or peasant proprietor as a declining institution, took no cognizance of the possibilities for farmer cooperation—then of course only in its infancy.[49]

Even though an auxiliary mode, the cooperative has effects far beyond its own limited numbers. It establishes at the core of economy an egalitarian sector dedicated to the principle of producer democracy. It schools broad masses in the art of mutual cooperation in business pursuits, and it has provided to millions of persons practical schooling in the problems of economic management. For a socialist economy, it provides a basis for superseding or checking the potent role of the private trader without seeking to involve the state in retail trade management. It also provides socialism with a way of transcending the hold of the individual farmer, with his inherent acquisitiveness, by substituting various forms of cooperative farming that have the advantage of permitting large-scale mechanization.

[48]"We acknowledge," Marx wrote in the official report of the Provisional Council of the First International to the 1866 Geneva Congress of the International, "the cooperative movement as one of the transforming forces of the present society based upon class antagonism . . . . Restricted however to the dwarfish forms into which individual wage slaves can elaborate it by their private efforts, the cooperative system will never transform capitalistic society"—for which purpose control of the state power is needed. Moreover, he noted, "cooperative stores" touch "but the surface of the present economic system" whereas "cooperative production attacks the groundwork." See Marx, *First International*, 1864–1872, pages 27–28.

[49]Marx, *Capital* III, 1864–1865, pages 807 ff.

No wonder Lenin, in the closing months of his life, looked to the cooperative movement as a means of developing collective enterprise along lines that would strengthen the worker–peasant alliance that had made the Russian Revolution and brought the Soviets to power. The New Economic Policy established market relations as a way of coordinating resource use; it legalized the peasant as trader and the principle of private trade carried on even by state enterprises with the aid of a noninflationary money. What more did they need for socialism, Lenin argued, now that they had established a socialist state power that retained ownership and control of all heavy industry, transport, land dealing, banking, and foreign trade? Only educational work among the peasantry and the urban population, he said—to found cooperative societies out of the millions of small peasants and to develop cultured traders out of the populace so that they "induce absolutely everyone to take not a passive but an active part in cooperative operations" to ensure that "really large masses of the population actually take part." Yet even with the state providing inducements by way of initial funding or tax advantages, it would take a long time—"at best . . . one or two decades"—to organize this work which "is adjustable to the most ordinary peasant and does not demand anything higher of him" but which does require achievement of literacy, the habit of "book-reading." "All we actually need under NEP is to organize the population of Russia in cooperative societies on a sufficiently large scale, for we have now found that degree of combination of private interest, of private commercial interest, with state supervision and control of this interest, that degree of its subordination to the common interests which was formerly the stumbling-block for very many socialists . . . is this not all that is necessary to build a complete socialist society out of cooperatives, out of cooperatives alone, which we formerly ridiculed as huckstering and which from a certain aspect we have the right to treat as such now, under NEP?" If the whole of the peasantry, Lenin pleaded, had been "organized in cooperatives, we would by now have been standing with both feet on the soil of socialism."[50] Lenin died before he could implant these principles deeply in the minds and hearts of his party comrades. Within half a decade, they were tearing up the New Economic Policy (NEP) itself and the revival of voluntary cooperation associated with this policy.

Lenin probably hoped that under the fostering auspices of a socialist worker's state, farmer cooperation in marketing, processing, and credit activities would spread to communal use of land and joint forms of farming. There is, of course, a tendency for farmer cooperation to move into adjunct fields of production, such as joint purchase and use of individual machines too bulky and expensive for a single farm to operate effectively, joint investment, shar-

[50]Lenin, "On Cooperation," 1923. See Lenin, *Selected Works*, 1971, vol. 3, pages 760–766.

ing a stud bull or boar, pooled livestock herds shepherded to higher pastures, and cooperative development and maintenance of irrigation facilities.[51] Cooperative farming has been successfully operated in communities that share commitment to a communal life, as among the Hutterites and the Israeli kibbutzim.[52] Such communities are established at the outset with communal financing and recruitment only among devoted followers. Elsewhere, many group farms have been established by governments seeking to settle landless laborers or tenant farmers on newly opened reclamation projects, on estates seized from European colonists, or from haciendas established in the New World centuries ago.[53] Farming families living and working on adjoining fields rarely feel enough solidarity of purpose and mutual good faith to turn over their farm, stock, and equipment to some newly born collective enterprise made up of themselves and their neighbors. If only a few join together, insufficient economies of scale would be realized to reap the advantages of large-scale farming, and they would also experience the hassles of partnerships. Such small-scale farming partnerships have been favored in France based on lease agreements running only for 9 years and with a limit of 10 members.[54]

[51]On these extensive tendencies to partial group farming, see two works on group farming: Schiller, *Cooperative Integration in Agricultural Production*, 1966; Dormer, *Cooperative and Group Farming*, 1977. Schiller describes machinery pools in England and Norway (page 168), Netherlands labor-hiring associations and West German spray irrigation on field crops (pages 169 f.), cooperation in South Baden in hybrid corn cultivation, rearing of young cattle, pasture associations, pig fattening (pages 170 f.), common Scandinavian cowsheds (page 173), cooperation in machinery use in Germany (pages 11 ff.). In the Dormer work we learn about 12,000 machinery co-ops that sprouted up in French agriculture after World War II (page 333).

[52]There are some 24,000 Hutterites living in 232 colonies with communal agriculture and 238 kibbutzim (and moshavim) with a total population of 100,000. See Dormer, *Cooperative and Group Farming*, 1977, pages 45 ff. Emigrating from the Austrian Tyrol in the sixteenth century, the Hutterites reached the U.S. in the 1870s with their communal traditions and sharing patterns intact (pages 66 ff.). The kibbutzim are the product of the zealot faith of young Israeli and Zionists with funds raised from fellow believers to build a national homeland (pages 54 ff.)

[53]Group farming projects have been variously maintained in Asia, Africa, and Latin America on lands newly opened for settlement by governmental reclamation activity or on estates taken over from colonists or in a few cases expropriated from local landlords or on lands purchased by government for the purpose. See surveys of such group farming in Sri Lanka, India, Mexico, Tunisia, and elsewhere in Schiller, *Cooperative Integration in Agricultural Production*, 1966, pages 104 ff., 114 f., 134 ff., 159 f., 130 f.; Dormer, *Cooperative and Group Farming*, 1977, pages 199 ff., 231 ff., 289 ff.

[54]Of 2753 limited-partnership farming French projects by the end of 1972, blood relatives were involved in 68% of the instances and 55% of the partnerships were two-member cases. The 1972 full ha. size of partnership lands was 91 ha. with individual farms at 20 ha. See Dormer, *Cooperative and Group Farming*, 1977, pages 335 ff. A similar move toward group farming was apparently commenced in Japan after World War II with 6275 group farms mostly in rice culture and embracing 21–50 households each. See Dormer, *Cooperative and Group Farming*, 1977, pages 315 ff. Schiller reported that 261 joint cultivation societies were

But if many seek to join together, the need to coordinate their work and facilities would make it necessary to establish a management structure and involve cumbersome requirements as to record keeping and report filing. It would be hard to overcome rivalries and festering grudges inherited from the past.

Significantly enough, the communes launched in the enthusiasm of the Russian Revolution did not prove attractive to their neighbors, despite credit assistance from government and favorable taxation. Soviet villagers with their deep communal traditions resisted the constant urging of their government to establish joint farming ventures. When collective farming was implanted on Soviet villages in 1929–1931, even minimal peasant cooperation could not be obtained without grant to each peasant family of a small plot where some livestock could be tended and where a small farm could be operated. Even after collective farms in Poland and in Yugoslavia had been functioning for several years, once government pressure to maintain them was relaxed and peasants were allowed to withdraw with their farm holdings, most of the collectives disintegrated.[55] Wherever the memory and style of life of private farming is still alive—with its self-reliance, independence, and the scope given for the possessory instincts—it is dubious that any generation of farmers would ever voluntarily turn over on any scale their individual farms to large-scale group farming, however communal their mode of land tenure, however accustomed to mutual-help activities and formal cooperation, and however great the benefits ultimately to be gained from group farming with the aid of modern machinery.

PUBLIC MODE

The *public mode of production* is especially difficult to work out conceptually as productive activity. Classical economic theory envisaged economic resources as being utilized only by households for purposes of consumption or

---

formed in Spain, and by 1965 they involved some 15,000 families. See Schiller, *Cooperative Integration in Agricultural Production*, 1966, page 125.

[55]Over the decade 1965–1975, farm output in the five East European states with collectivized agriculture experienced a somewhat slower rise in average annual farm output than in the two Eastern socialist countries where private farming predominated. U.S. Congress Joint Economic Committee, *East European Economies*, 1977, page 294. Where the peasantry had been more roughly manhandled, as in the Soviet Union, and was assigned much smaller private plots than in Eastern socialist countries with collectivized agriculture, farm productivity has been rising even more slowly. On the 1956 crisis that brought Gomulka to power and forced dissolution of Polish collective farming, see Brzezinski, *Soviet Bloc Unity*, 1960, ch. 11, especially pages 154 ff., 342 ff.

by business establishments for purposes of profit making. Government existed only as a kind of epiphenomenon which constituted a "burden" on producers because of its taxes on their income. Yet collective needs and wants are universal in all societies, and though they can be exaggerated in their scope, and their fulfillment may generate waste and exploitation, they are nonetheless genuine. Government services may be intangible. Providing for order and defense, for example, may take the form of preventing ills and hurts rather than eliciting goods and boons. But services are needed as well as tangible things—man lives not by bread alone—and services of prevention are just as real as services of commission. All this has been argued in our introductory chapter.

Thus, we define the public mode of production very simply as that part of the labor force, together with its invested resources utilized in administration, defense, and other duties, engaged full time in the work of government. It will include servants and retainers of a prince or emperor and his royal establishment; soldiers and officers serving in the armed forces of the state; legislators and officials charged with the responsibility of both making and enforcing laws; employees of the postal service, armories, naval yards, and waterworks in public operation; ministers in a state church, if there is one; workers at public mints that coin money; rangers at forest preserves; teachers at public schools and institutions of higher learning. In the socialist economies the public mode encompasses all workers in industrial establishments owned and operated by the government service, as well as personnel of planning agencies, research establishments, and the like.

The core of the public mode, where its characteristics are most deeply impressed and unambiguously established, is in the general services of administration. There ready channels of communication and transportation for persons and goods are provided, public security and order are maintained, frontiers are administered and relationships with other societies are monitored, institutions of justice are established to resolve controversies and to enforce the common law, public records and granaries and armories are maintained for emergency use, and facilities are provided for national celebration and sharing. This core area is characterized by three major characteristics: (1) relative incommensurability of costs and benefits, handicapping rational decision making; (2) diffuseness and intangibility of most benefits that cannot be readily appropriated by individual persons; and (3) need for financing by compulsory levy or taxation.

The short-run costs of public service, at least those out of pocket, may be readily established and often estimated in advance. The worth of the benefits provided over the large number and variety of persons and communities affected, many with distinctive circumstances, will be impossible to measure exactly; even very knowledgeable persons can gauge them only broadly and with great difficulty. Hence, there is a strong tendency to continue on with any scheme of public service that has survived the past and proved not too intolerable, and perhaps to arrange from time to time for incremental changes, waiting each time to observe the full effects. Many of these effects work their way slowly and are subject to marked disproportionalities of response with unseen threshhold limits and areas of rising crescendos. Hence under the best of circumstances rational decision making in organizing and modifying the public mode of production is exceedingly difficult—even in well-ordered states where smooth channels of communication permit a ready exchange of opinions between rulers and ruled, and where adequate records and up-to-date information exist about the society and its public services and resources.

Most benefits of the core area of public service will be diffuse in character, not targeted on individual beneficiaries who may choose to receive or utilize them and thus to appropriate their benefits.

Because of these characteristics, the core area of public service cannot be self-financing by any scheme of fee or charge-for-service pricing. Citizens or state-subjects cannot choose how much of the state services they will recognize and pay for. Because the core services must be supported by a compulsory levy on the community to bring in the needed revenues, the work of tax collecting and tax administration is a strategic part of the core public service inherent in the state itself.

Customarily, employees of the public mode, especially in the core area of public service, are sworn to a special fealty to the state service they have undertaken. Many members of this service wear special insignia or clothing so that they and their mission can be readily identified. Their offices are in public buildings. Members too are often commissioned to bear arms or to command armed detachments so that their orders to any and all may be instantly obeyed. Officers of such detachments who wield special discretion are usually carefully identified and labeled by law, which spells out their prerogatives and duties. In earlier and simpler state systems the number of offices and officeholders for the public service were limited and enactments governing the same were relatively few. But in the more advanced societies—with their greater concentrations of population and a more highly developed set of production modes yielding ample taxable surpluses to the state—systems of state service have been accordingly elaborated, with more careful provision made for supervision and control by a hierarchical organization of public service.

Hierarchy allows for greater specialization of function and takes cognizance of the need for supervision to prevent abuse of power or authority by local members of the service. Hence the spelling out of duties and responsibilities by enactment is multiplied in law codes. Agencies are instituted whose sole function is to check upon or audit the performance of other agencies. Primary courts are established to hear and resolve controversies; higher courts are also instituted to which appeal can be taken against judgments deemed improper or unsupportable. And because the public service nearly always harbors authority for using coercion to enforce commands or requests, authority to act is often spelled out in wearisome detail with frequent requirements for maintenance of written records ("files") and the submission of detailed reports to higher authorities. All this spells out the basic syndrome of the public mode of production: use of authority, enmeshment in red tape, hierarchy in administration, rootedness in tradition, diffuse loyalties claimed and often given.[56]

STAFFING OF THE PUBLIC MODE

The quality of public service has been greatly improved by recruiting for public service through open written examinations in which applicants for positions are tested for performance. The pioneer society for the development of a merit selection of officials based upon examinations is unquestionably classical China, where by the seventh and eighth centuries A.D. the highest stratum of officials was recruited by means of examinations. The integrity of the examinations—especially at the highest level, where they were conducted by the Emperor himself—was zealously preserved even through the imported Manchu regime. Though a formalistic emphasis on style and penmanship became increasingly important, the philosophic classics of early China are no mean training grounds for the intellect, so that persons awarded the highest offices tended to uphold high standards. However, at the lower level the conduct and grading of examinations was frequently corrupt and fraudulent.[57]

---

[56]Our text only highlights the main features of Max Weber's classical presentation on "Bureaucracy." See Weber, *Economy and Society*, 1921, pages 956–1005.

[57]The great Manchu emperor, K'ang-Hsi, observed that "Even among the examiners there are those who are corrupt, those who do not understand basic works, those who ask detailed questions about practical matters of which they know nothing, those who insist entirely on memorization of the Classics and refuse to set essays, those who put candidates from their own geographical area at the top of the list." The emperor at times conducted examinations himself as he did with the 183 re-examined . . . candidates in 1700, "grading their papers by four ranks in different categories" and as he usually did with the highest level exams in the Hanlin Academy, where he would "scrutinize them in batches of ten before the exam, write out the questions myself in the . . . Palace under the eyes of the senior officials." See Spence, *Emperor of China*, 1957, pages 50 f. The celebrated seventeenth century novel by Wu Ching-Tzu, *The Scholars*, is about scholars or students engaged in the quest for academic distinction, favorable test ratings in the examinations, and ultimate appointment to the civil service. The novel brings to light the eerie juxtaposition in the civil service of deep corruption mingled with the highest loyalty, as one local regime marked by "the reciting of poetry, the moving of chesspieces and the singing of operas" is followed by another regime highlighting "the clang

Not until the seventeenth century in Europe was a beginning made with civil service. In the rising state of Prussia a succession of able Electors established a formally organized bureaucracy; already by the early 1700s it was recruited in large part by written examinations, which presupposed a university training in law and cameralistic science.[58] A similar development in England and France had to await the mid nineteenth century—though Marx found reason to praise the English civil servants whose vigilant administration of the Factory Acts elicited his high commendation.[59] Oddly enough, English merit examinations commenced with the schooling and selection of civil servants trained for work in India. From that branch of service, the merit system was applied to the domestic civil service in mid 1850s and at about the same time in France. A corresponding development in America came only in the later decades of the nineteenth century, to spread incompletely throughout the federal government and more slowly still among states and local governments.[60] By the latter half of the twentieth century, the civil service principle was well established throughout the advanced countries of the Western world. This involves not only recruitment of the public service primarily by means of competitive examination, but also a far-reaching kind of political neutrality and protection of the civil rights of public employees against deprival of office except for cause.

Compensation for officeholders in the public service is usually twofold: (1) a set salary or compensation by the state, and (2) perquisites of office by way of gifts or gratuities offered or extorted from those who seek the service or favor of government. The first form of compensation is shared with other modes of production—such as capitalist, corporate, or cooperative enterprise—that depend upon hired labor. The level of compensation tends, of course, to be higher for work that is more honorific. In recent times it is

---

of a balance, the rattle of an abacus and the thud of bamboo rods" (page 89). An exhaustive study finds that "corruption was rife in the examination system despite the strong regulations to prevent it and the severe punishments imposed on some offenders." See Chung-Li Chang, *Chinese Gentry*, 1955, page 197.

[58]A fascinating account is provided by Finer, *Modern Government*, 1934, ch. 28, pages 724 ff.

[59]Finer, *Modern Government*, 1934, chs. 29–32. According to Finer, until 1855 British civil service was in the hands of the ruling political party and "used to bribe and reward their followers" and according to the permanent Secretary of the Treasury in 1848 was "overstaffed, inactive and incompetent . . . the last chance of a livelihood for young men who were too stupid to be successful in the open competition of the professions outside" (pages 760 f.). Yet Marx, who knew well the work of the civil service who staffed the investigatory commissions and factory inspectorate, had only the highest praise for this branch of public service as "competent, as free from partisanship and respect of persons." See Marx, *Capital* I, 1867, page 9.

[60]Finer, *Modern Government*, 1934, ch. 33.

triply compounded by (1) bearing the promise of regular increases by way of promotion to higher-ranking posts or in the same post because of seniority; (2) usually involving a lifetime career where dismissal or demotion except for grave cause and only after a quasi-judicial hearing is extremely rare; and (3) finally terminating at an advanced age by the grant of a lifelong pension (given in public service long before it became customary for other employees).

The second form of emolument was widely prevailing in public service of imperial China and Rome where auditing and supervision of lower levels of administration, especially dealing with granting of licenses, judicial determinations or collection of taxes was difficult to arrange. Morale of public service had long been undermined or destroyed in these regimes by repeated pillaging of the state coffers by civil war, by repeated usurpation of office, and by the erosion of any generally accepted moral creed restraining the acquisitive impulse. Corruption of public service has been widely experienced in American municipal and state government, especially in earlier decades. And the prevalence of corruption and its widespread acceptance has been regarded as a major problem of public administration in many of the newer African countries and most of southeast Asia.[61]

Corruption is scarcely unique to public service. It has been reported as plaguing the first generation of corporations trading abroad in the eighteenth century.[62] It is still reported as a particular problem in the purchasing service

[61]For S.E. Asia Gunnar Myrdal, in *Asian Drama*, 1968, vol. 2., devotes an entire chapter to corruption, "Corruption: Its Causes and Effects" (ch. 20). Ann Seidman, who had extensive experience in the newer countries of both East and West Africa, recognized the problem of corruption but found it was traceable chiefly to "foreign firms." See Seidman, *Development in Sub-Saharan Africa*, 1974, pages 204, 244 f. Without playing down the role of foreign firms, S. P. Huntington, *Political Order in Changing Societies*, 1968, finds many reasons why "modernization" tends to breed corruption—especially where political parties are weak, or where family, clan or clique predominate or in bureaucratic centralized societies (pages 59–71). Perhaps corruption will be specially prominent in countries such as Ghana, where the forms of traditional society were eroded centuries before an effective state system evolved and where the tasks of the public sector were extended over modes of production in which the small trader, individual farmer, or merchant was still predominant.

[62]"Nothing can be more completely foolish than to expect the clerks of a great counting-house at thousand miles distance . . . should upon a simple order from their masters, give up at once doing any sort of business upon their own account . . . and content themselves with the moderate salaries which those masters allow them. . . ." See Adam Smith, *Wealth of Nations*, 1776, page 603. There was so much corruption at the head of the East India Company administration of India, charged Edmund Burke in one of his memorable prosecution addresses on that subject before the House of Lords—then sitting as a high court to hear charges of Articles of Indictment—that they could not have been taking it with their own hands, "for then they must have as many hands as one of the idols of an Indian temple." See Burke, *Burke's Works*, 1910–1917, vol. 1, page 135. The Articles of Indictment specify only a few of the takings and "presents" for which evidence was apparently on hand. See Burke, *Burke's Works*, 1910–1917, vol. 4, pages 220–533; vol. 5, pages 2–62.

of modern corporations. Corruption has been endemic for over a century in the music publishing and broadcasting industry.[63] It has even been cited as a major problem of the cooperative store where accounting for inventory and trading losses is difficult to tie down.[64] But the scale of corruption is far greater in the public mode of production, especially where that mode seeks in its regulatory and taxing activities to restrain, draw upon, or check the interests of private wealth in the capitalist, the corporate, and even on occasion the cooperative modes.[65] Wherever there is a hiatus between the power of wealth given organized form and the power of government, especially when this latter power is exerted through a system of checks and balances involving many layers of authority, corruption becomes the agency by which wealth seeks to assert its power.[66] Corruption, however, is not a universal or inherent feature of public service. Under modern conditions of income distribution and auditing, it can be held down to a workable minimum especially in societies with a well-organized state, a comprehensive and vigilant police service, dedication to public service as a high-ranking social ideal, a well-paid public service, and a law code consistent with the predominant norms of the society and not its outdated moral creeds.[67]

[63]Coase, "Payola," 1979, pages 269–328. This exhaustive study traces bribery of musical performers or broadcasting "disc-jockeys" as merely the latest version of early bribery to musical performers or band leaders to advertise or show favour to music being published.

[64]Webb, and Webb, *Soviet Communism*, 1935, page 236.

[65]See U.S. Senate Select Committee on Presidential Campaign Activities, *Senate Watergate Report*, 1974, vol. 2, ch. 6, showing the connection between the Dairy Cooperatives, a cash contribution of $100,000 to Kalmbach in 1969, the 1971 price-support decision by the President and the DA decision-making process, and the Milk Producers' contribution activity in 1971 and 1972.

[66]Edmund Burke, who knew well the power of money in politics, warned the House of Lords in his opening address (1788) on the prosecution of Warren Hastings that "enormous wealth has poured in this country from India through a thousand channels." He later that year warned the Lords that "Today the Commons of Great Britain prosecute the delinquents of India—Tomorrow the delinquents of India may be the Commons of Great Britain. We know I say and feel the force of money." See Burke, *Burke's Works*, 1910–1917, vol. 1, pages 17, 449.

[67]An NBER Conference volume dealing with the "Economic Analysis of Political Behavior" devoted one of its sessions to "Corruption as a Feature of Governmental Organization," with the main paper by A. C. Banfield and "Comments" by M. W. Reder and S. Rottenberg. See Landes, *Economic Analysis of Political Behavior*, 1975, pages 518–616. There was very little analysis of corrupters, though much of the corrupted and how difficult corruption is to eradicate or suppress completely, thus leading to the concept of an "optimal" amount of corruption (pages 590 f.). That is similar to the concept in the text of a "workable minimum" of corruption which is hardly "optimization."

TECHNOLOGY OF THE PUBLIC MODE

The core area of the public mode of production, like all modes, has a specific technology that has influenced the mode's scope and performing power. That technology has two broad divisions: civilian service and military service. Each has numerous special subdivisions. There are five principal means of production for the civilian branches: (1) assembly halls and chambers for consultation, adjudication, and debate; (2) offices as places to store records, coordinate information, prepare reports, and make decisions; (3) mints or currency printing establishments where money is coined or currency is printed, stored, and issued; (4) treasuries where funds or their accounts and surrogates are kept and paid out; and (5) jails, prisons, and police stations where the domestic military arm of the state is deployed for the enforcement of law. The improvements of technologies in building, communication, and transportation have widened the scope of effective operation of this division of the public mode to increase the optimal size of state that can be effectively supervised from a single center. Even more, the development of the new science and technology of rapid computation has made possible detailed record keeping for an entire nation with less time and effort than would have been required for a small community a century ago.

The development of technology in the military branch of the public mode has been more complex and transformative. One decisive change for historical economic systems came early when ownership and control of means of production in military service was shifted from the popular militia—made up of citizen soldiers providing their own equipment under local leaders and oftentimes supplying their own provisions—to a centrally controlled standing army recruited, armed, and provisioned by the state.[68] The citizen army, which in the early Roman Republic was assembled annually, was the true basis for the democratic phase of the early Roman and Greek city republics.[69] The au-

---

[68]This decisive change was both described and recognized as constitutive in the writings of Max Weber and the interesting treatise of Adam Smith on the military segment of the public economy. See Weber, *Essays in Sociology*, 1906–1921, pages 228 f; *Economy and Society*, 1921, vol. 2, pages 980 ff., 1359 f.; *General Economic History*, 1923, pages 324 f., 329 f.; A. Smith, *Wealth of Nations*, 1776, pages 654 ff.

[69]"The basis of democratization is everywhere purely military in character; it lies in the rise of disciplined infantry, the *hoplites* of antiquity, the guild army in the middle ages." See Weber, *General Economic History*, 1923, page 325. Memorable is the account of Polybius, the Greek historian who observed at close quarters the Roman Republic in its finest days, when both its top military commanders (consuls) and 14 military tribunes were elected annually by the people in assembly, and met annually with all younger Romans called up for military service. The conscripts were then divided and enrolled into companies and legions falling into

tocracy of the empires that followed corresponded to the larger standing armies on which they depended. A remnant of this earlier mode of public production was reflected in the constitutional protection in the United States for the right of citizens to bear arms as a base for the popular militia and as a counterweight to the power of the central state with its standing army.[70] The most formidable of those popular militia armies in early times was that of Asian pastoral peoples whose large herds of horses were used both for travel and food. With their great skills in horsemanship, weapons manufacture, and iron making, such fast-moving predators as the Huns and Mongols were dangerous to adjacent societies whenever, as Adam Smith noted, their forces could be united under a single leader.[71]

A decisive change in military technology that had important repercussions in the form of governmental organization and social structure was the conjunct development around the ninth and tenth centuries of the nailed horseshoe, the winged spear and the hanging iron stirrup—which enabled a squad of armoured soldiers on horses to mount a terrifying assault charge on ground troops. The nailed shoe protected the beast's vulnerable hooves, while the stirrup gave the rider enough support to permit a violent strike with the spear readily withdrawable because the wings made for limited penetration into a body. There is much evidence to support Lynn White's contention that the armored mounted soldier became the dominant military force around the ninth to tenth centuries A.D., and that thereafter popular militia levies played a smaller role or fell by the wayside. A new class of warrior aristocrats emerged who could draw upon the large resources required to support horseman, a groom and the horse with adequate provisions, opportunity for training, and practice and armor, and this new class or modified form of an older class developed the characteristic features of much that is denominated "feudalism."[72]

---

classes depending upon age and the equipment they were required to bring by their assessed wealth capacity. They elected their immediate commanding officers (centurions), swore their oaths, and were then ready for mobilization. See Polybius, *Histories*, 155–125 B.C., bk. 6, paras. 19–25.

[70]"A well-regulated militia, being necessary to the security of a free state, the right of the people to keep and bear arms, shall not be infringed." U.S. Constitution, Amend. 2. That provision should be interpreted in the light of the calculation made at the time of the adoption of the Constitution that the population and resources of the United States would not permit a standing army, wholly controlled by the central government, greater than 25,000–30,000 men while opposed to them would be a militia of "half a million citizens with arms in their hands, officered by men chosen from among themselves. . . ." See Hamilton, Madison, and Jay, *Federalist*, 1787–1788, page 243.

[71]Adam Smith, *Wealth of Nations*, 1776, pages 654 f.

[72]For the laying out of the remarkable historical and archaeological research on the horseshoe, winged spear, and iron stirrup and the evaluation of its consequences, see the brilliant

A still more momentous change in the military arts was associated with the development in the late medieval era of gunpowder and firearms of different sizes and capacity. Some hurled huge missiles that in Machiavelli's view could batter down "even the strongest walls"; others shot only a pellet capable of penetrating a knight's armor.[73] These new weapons ultimately revolutionized not only war but also, in Engels' words, "the political relations of domination and subjection."[74] Although handguns could be effectively owned and operated by militiamen, that was not true of the heavier cannon, the armed naval vessel, or the fortifications emplaced to defend strategic areas. The development and improvement of firearms, artillery, and naval power went hand in hand in the fifteenth and sixteenth centuries with the emergence of the central core of national states; their large standing armies and navies from then on were the central feature of the public mode of production in the Western world. The development and refinement of technology in the capitalist and corporate modes of production in the nineteenth and twentieth centuries were marked by a corresponding development of the public mode of production in its military branches.

Of course weapons manufacture narrowly construed has never been wholly or even predominantly a branch of public service. All modes draw raw materials, equipment, and auxiliary supplies from other modes specializing in such items. The public mode is no exception. Weapons in early days were chiefly the product of the craft skill of direct commodity producers as armorers, smithies, and shipbuilders. In the earliest phase of firearms manufacture, craftsmen as bell-founders, accustomed to work on bronze, alternately turned to cannon or church bells.[75] Nearly all bronze, iron, and steel, or other metals required for weapons manufacture has always been produced by the mode of production, in recent centuries chiefly capitalist or corporate, that specialized in those products. But government armories, naval yards, and arsenals have played a distinguished role. The Venetian Arsenal—in the me-

---

work of L. White, Jr., *Medieval Technology and Social Change*, ch. 1, pages 1–38. As Cipolla notes, good authority has it that the horseshoe was known to the Celts before the Roman conquests. But the horseshoe was not used on any scale on the Continent, as White points out, until the ninth to tenth centuries A.D. See C. M. Cippolla, *Before the Industrial Revolution*, 1976, page 169.

[73]Machiavelli, *The Prince*, 1513–1521, ch. 17.

[74]Engels, *Herr Dühring's Revolution*, 1877–1878, page 190. I cite one of many signal theses elucidated in Engels's summary disquisition on sociopolitical aspects of war and the military as connected to economic systems (pages 190–198). Smith also emphasized the importance of firearms and gunpowder. See A. Smith, *Wealth of Nations*, 1776, pages 60 f. (As this manuscript is sent off to press, the reader's attention is called to the set of brilliant articles on military technology by Engels published in Marx and Engels, *Collected Works*, 1841–1860, vol. 18.)

[75]Cippolla, *Guns, Sails and Empires*, 1965, pages 21 ff., 33 f.

dieval epoch, the largest producing enterprise yet known and immortalized in Dante's Inferno—produced the naval supplies and the great galleys that usually led out their merchant fleets.[76] Work in state factories in the Late Roman Empire, manned by a conscripted labor force, was largely devoted to government supplies of weapons and military supplies. The public economy of the mercantilist epoch in Western Europe was dominated by the effort of the Great Powers to foster arms manufacture, to organize the collection of saltpetre, to improve casting processes in the making of cannon.[77] In the nineteenth and twentieth centuries the balance turned, and such capitalist and corporate enterprises as Krupps, Skoda, Vickers-Maxim, and Putiloff were the great arms producers, especially of heavy armament. Because the new technology of missile and atomic power is far too dangerous to entrust to private enterprise functioning on a market basis, that technology—shaped almost totally in government laboratories, research institutions, and industrial facilities—is now wholly in the public mode. In the United States it has become, as we shall see, a hybrid mode with a mingled public–corporate character.

PUBLIC MODE: UTILITIES

Outside the core area of civil and military public administration there is a wide field of public service often distinguished by the capacity to finance itself in whole or in large part from sale of services or products produced and marketed on an open-access basis at prices or fees fixed in public schedules. Outstanding in this field are agencies such as TVA (Tennessee Valley Authority), Bonneville Power Administration, the postal service, communication and railway transportation when operated by government (as they are over most of the world), armories and naval establishments to produce weapons or warships, canals, and toll roads. Also to be included under this heading are public-serving activities such as the cleaning, repair and maintenance of streets, waterworks and sanitation departments that distribute clean water and collect and dispose of solid and liquid wastes. Here also are the bulk of commercial, industrial, or financial enterprises governmentally owned and operated in socialist economies. In this field of public service there is a lesser use, or the complete absence, of authority to force a behavior along wanted lines

---

[76]Established in 1104 and enlarged in 1473, it contained a shipyard, a provisioning center for vessels, and a munitions works, employing up to 16,000 workmen. See Mumford, *City in History*, 1961, pages 323 f.; Lane, *Venice: A Maritime Republic*, 1973, pages 14 f., 163 f., 333 f., 362 ff.; Dante, *Divine Comedy*, 1307–1321, canto 21, lines 5–16; Storti, *Venice: A Practical Guide*, 1981, page 97.

[77]Nef, *Industry and Government*, 1957, pages 59 ff., 88 ff.

or to prevent proscribed behavior from occurring. Much of the work accomplished in this field has an industrial or commercial character. Relations at work generally resemble those in other fields of wage labor, and the protection and tenure commonly given to civil servants by civil service laws is here often scaled down. Government, whether large or small, is the employer, and the upper officialdom is commonly included in the comprehensive civil service. Top direction is provided by politically appointed or elected officers of government and policies are governed by enactments of legislatures.

Beyond this fringe field of public service, there is a penumbra of quasi-public service enterprises or agencies that have a hybrid character, part public and part private. This hybrid field is especially wide in the United States, where a deliberate effort has been made to allow private enterprise under special regulation and public control to carry out what in effect are public services. This penumbral field is almost entirely organized as quasi-public corporations endowed with special public authority, usually that of eminent domain, so that they can acquire land or real estate needed for their operations. These corporations are usually given monopoly authority to operate in a given area and hence are required by law to give service to all who seek it in the area, subject to charges that are usually regulated by law or by special regulatory agencies. Here the communist theoretical concept of "state-monopoly-capital" is most appropriate, as these enterprises bear a hybrid character in which special state regulation is supposed to offset or neutralize the monopoly power exercised.[78] Among them are railroad corporations, utilities producing and distributing electric power, the telecommunications network using the radio broadcast spectrum, natural gas distributing utilities, natural gas and oil pipelines, local bus companies and transit services, and telephone and other communication systems. Where interstate operations are involved, the regulatory authority is a national agency. Wherever the primary form of service is local distribution, state regulatory control is imposed. But most fields of service entail joint control in which the national government regulates interstate operations while yielding to local control where local distribution is involved. The relative importance of the regulated utilities has risen considerably in the twentieth century. In 1965, for example, some 7.8% of Gross National Product (GNP) was attributed to utilities, with a net capital investment in them of $131 billion. From one-third to one-half of the quasi-

[78]The concept is expounded in many Soviet texts and an adequate résumé of official doctrine may be found in Institute of Economics, *Political Economy*, 1954, pages 324 f. There it is baldly stated that it signifies: "subjection of the State machine to the capitalist monopolies and their using it to interfere in the country's economy" (pages 324 f.). The crudities of this version were clearly pointed out by the talented Soviet Marxist, Varga, *Politico-Economic Problems of Capitalism*, 1963, pages 51–74.

public corporation sector is made up of regulated utilities, which took the lead in developing the corporation as an institution for modern industry.[79]

The power of monopoly can, of course, be limited by the range and attractiveness of alternative sources of supply. In the United States, the monopoly power of the railroads was especially great when they controlled the chief means of intercity transportation of bulk supplies by use of machine power. Competition of railroads with each other was at best transitional.[80] But the opening up of coast-to-coast navigation via the Panama Canal, the construction of large and deep internal waterways within the continent, culminating in the Saint Lawrence Seaway, the development of a vast public highway system on which private vehicles, trucks, and buses could easily move, to provide both speedy personal transportation and pickup and delivery service, the building of a network of airports that enabled speedy long-distance aircraft transport—all took away from railroad business, forcing the virtual abandonment of much passenger service by rail and now making it necessary to free railroad corporations of many regulatory restrictions imposed upon them.

The monopoly-granted municipal bus systems that operate a franchised local transit service on public streets often compete poorly with the private vehicles available to most urban households. Electricity and gas serve different purposes but they can be substituted for each other in the operation of water heaters, kitchen ranges, ovens, and furnaces. Gas, coal, and electric furnaces compete against oil burners, and all three are rivaled now by new heat-conserving wood-burning fireplaces and stoves that are especially feasible in rural wooded areas. The wired telephone and telegraph systems and international cable services are subject to potent competition from the newer technology of wireless telecommunication using the short-wave spectrum.[81]

Though the force of competition against franchised monopolies is consid-

---

[79]There are different estimates of the volume of income or output originating in the utility sector as a fraction of gross national output or national income. In his investigation of regulated utilities Melville J. Ullmer stated their output as a fraction of GNP in 1929 dollars over a 9-year moving average; he found the utility share or fraction of that GNP rising from 5.9% in 1886 to 17.5% in 1950. See Ullmer, *Transportation, Communications, and Public Utilities*, 1960 Table 22, page 82. A standard text in the field drawing upon statistics showing percentage of national income originating therein finds that regulated utilities in 1965 contributed 7.8% to national income. See Phillips, *Economics of Regulation*, 1965, page 8. The Ullmer measure is of "gross output" inclusive of materials purchased, the Phillips estimate is of "value added."

[80]Kahn, *Economics of Regulation*, 1971, vol. 2, has effectively rebutted the claim that ICC regulation was devised in the 1880s chiefly to restrain price cutting by railroads competing with each other.

[81]The cited work of Kahn especially, as well as the newer literature which he seeks to evaluate arguing for substantial reduction or complete elimination of utility regulation, deals extensively with the role and development of competition among franchised services.

erable, it by no means provides full protection to all or even to most users of a franchised service. Heavy bulk commodities—such as grains, coal and building materials—that do not move readily on highways in areas or directions for which waterways are not available, will continue to be dependent upon rail transportation. Entire communities dependent upon transportation facilities either for crucial industries or shipping points could lose their economic base if transportation charges were radically raised or access was altered. To turn monopoly power loose on captive shippers with a sizeable potential for exploitation and economic disruption is very difficult to carry through a legislative assembly such as the U.S. Congress.[82] So whether monopoly is absolute or limited by potential competition, the need for service regulation is compulsory and tends for protective reasons to spread to regulate the terms on which competition too will be permitted to function.

Nor can effective regulation be confined only to terms on which service is rendered. A uniform accounting system must be designed and imposed to show investment in service property and a level of net income that is adequate. The characteristics of service, and not only end prices, should be spelled out in terms of frequency of carriage, shutdowns or other service lapses, warranties, connection charges, and areas of service to be provided. This now involves licensing for all major construction projects and approvals needed for termination of service facilities. Regulated and regulators thus come to know each other well, and frequently the personnel shift from one side to the other. Executives in regulated companies obtain representation on regulatory commissions, while public commissioners or staff members may be drawn by attractive salary offers to utility service. But though they have intimate dealings with each other, the proceedings are always of an adversary character, open to the public and to interested groups in extended fact-finding quasi-judicial hearings. The initiative in action is commonly taken by the regulated utility that proposes, with the commission either concurring, rejecting, or disposing on modified terms. Because the regulatory body has few final enforcement powers, any change in regulatory policy or statutory basis will have uncertain application until controversies wend their way through the court system, sometimes taking years before issues are settled. Where regulation bears lightly—as in many states on local municipal utilities—the regulatory admixture to the hybrid mode is weak indeed, so that the quasi-public corporations function on their own with some public limitation on

---

[82]This reluctance to turn large numbers of shippers and entire industries and communities over to the mercies of profit-seeking monopolists, which railroads could easily be if unrestrained by law, clearly shows up in the House of Representatives debates on the Rail Act of 1980. See *Congressional Record*, July 24, 1980, H 6405 ff.; *Congressional Record*, September 5, 1980, H 8339 ff.; *Congressional Record*, September 9, 1980, H 8547 ff.

their right to exact price increases. But more commonly and especially where national regulatory agencies are involved, regulatory control is more formidable because it is backed up not only by greater public exposure but by the organized national interest groups drawn from commercial utility users as well as private customers. Thus the regulated utility complex of quasi-public corporations makes up a distinct hybrid mode of production drawing together elements both of the corporate mode proper and of the public mode.

MILITARY–INDUSTRIAL–SCIENCE COMPLEX

The regulated utilities are only one hybrid mode attached to the public and corporate sectors. Another of comparable importance involves the cluster of quasi-public corporations primarily specializing in the design, manufacture, and marketing of military, space, and nuclear technology for which the principal customer is the federal government and its various agencies, chiefly DOD (Department of Defense), NASA (National Aeronautics and Space Administration), AEC (Atomic Energy Commission and its successor agencies). Government has always been vulnerable to the beguiling merchandising methods of producers of goods or services it desires or needs. For that reason many charters of state and local governments in the United States require competitive bidding for printing contracts and public works construction contracts that have dominated their purchasing activities. Requiring competitive bidding has been standard operating procedure in most federal government departments that also maintain major in-house production capabilities for printing and minting operations and for production of weapons or warships in armories and naval yards.

American armed forces were maintained on a very small peacetime scale until World War II. Before then, because military technology did not call for elaborate or formidable pieces of equipment, except for great warships and submarines, the industrial establishments that predominantly catered to governmental buyers played a relatively minor role in the economy. The standard articles of Quartermaster supply—uniforms, blankets, tents, footwear, foodstuffs canned and fresh, medical supplies, bedding, ammunition, small arms, and hand guns—were readily produced by manufacturers of civilian goods. And the construction contractor who sought out public works contracts handled these along with his other construction work for commercial and industrial enterprises. This minor role for the government supplier reached mainly by competitive bidding was revolutionized by the militarization of the American economy in World War II—caused by the nation's rise to world leadership and imperialistic control and the subsequent emergence of a new military, space, and nuclear technology.

The wartime explosion of demand for armaments, weapons, and military supplies ruled out any hope of recourse to traditional methods of competitive bidding and arms-length dealing by government purchasing officers. The production of ordinary consumer goods using scarce materials was drastically curtailed or completely prohibited so that producers everywhere were reaching out for war orders. Meanwhile, procurement officers were handing these out usually with arrangements for provision of capital needed to construct special production facilities or for government construction and outfitting of plants leased out for operation to industrial firms reimbursed on a cost-plus basis. After some experience with this system, government contracts were made renegotiable whereever it seemed that extravagant profits were possible—which in any case were drastically cut down by high rates of wartime income and profits taxation.

These new government–contractor relationships carried over after military hostilities slowed down or disappeared. The struggle for world supremacy, which came to a climax during the war, continued after the war only by other means—chiefly by a furious, intensive, insatiable quest to develop a more powerful technology for producing and channeling an ever-widening potential for destruction that would bend adversaries to our will by the threat of annihilation. There was no question any more of organizing national defense in any meaningful sense of that word, involving training and equipping a nation's manpower to resist an invasion and thus defend its population against the attack of hostile armed forces. After the secret development and successful use of the terror weapon in 1945 that destroyed two Japanese cities and brought Japanese armed forces to accept unconditional surrender, there was a desire to produce more atomic weapons but improved in destructive power, to assure ever-better instruments of delivery by air, land, and sea, and to prepare highly mechanized armed forces to cope with minor challenges or what were called "brush-fire wars." The lead in this new government–contractor partnership was taken by three major branches of government service in the forefront of this quest for destructive power: the administrative nursery for atomic weaponry shaped into the Atomic Energy Commission (AEC); the Air Force, which pioneered the new missile technology and the bold use of what was called strategic air power; and the National Aeronautics and Space Administration (NASA). These government agencies were the prime spawning ground for what was later called by President Dwight Eisenhower the "military-industrial complex"—born, he said, of the "conjunction of an immense Military Establishment and a large arms industry."[83]

The development of atomic power and a nuclear technology in the United

---

[83]The Eisenhower farewell address is republished in Seymour Melman, *Pentagon Capitalism*, 1970, app. B.

States was managed by starting, under the strict holding-company control of the armed forces, two major kinds of autonomous contractor-controlled establishments. One group of these were federally funded research institutions leaning upon and drawing support and staff from major university centers. Prior to the dissolution of the AEC in 1974, there were seven multiprogram research laboratories, controlled chiefly by the Universities of Chicago and California, with the peak institutions being the Argonne National Laboratory and the Los Alamos Scientific Laboratory. Flanking these was a larger group of specialized research laboratories scattered over various university campuses that concentrated on biomedical or various phases of advanced nuclear physics. For engineering development and actual production and fabrication facilities, some 26 establishments were under the control and administration of 20 major corporations, the best-known of whom are Westinghouse, Union Carbide, Allied Chemical Corporation, Aerojet Nuclear Co., General Electric, Monsanto Research Corp.[84] These establishments, many of which included large industrial or testing facilities, were well-scattered over the nation, although some concentration is apparent in Richland, Washington, and Oak Ridge, Tennessee. Only a small, chiefly administrative staff in formal civil service presided over this massive complex of research and production facilities handled entirely by "contractor" relationships and substantially free of the controls and limitations that go with civil service. In its latest transmutation involving planning for the further spread of nuclear power, AEC brought into existence—with the cooperation of the nation's electric utilities—a jointly financed and shared control of two "not-for-profit" corporations, the Breeder Reactor Corporation and the Project Management Corporation to "provide broad-gauged utility participation" in the famous Clinch River Breeder Reactor Plant, lingering in a sort of half-life with the Congress generally favoring its continuation and the Executive branch of government at times strongly opposed. Though predominantly funded by government and deeply involved in the production of plutonium, the key component of our strategic weapon system, this facility is to be separated by layers of "contracts" from direct government operation and control.[85]

The Air Force led the armed forces in utilization of contractor setups partly because this branch of service was relatively new and lacked the substantial in-house engineering and research capability developed over the years by the other two branches of service. "The Air Force sought to leapfrog this hand-

[84]These institutions are listed in the Atomic Energy Commission, *Annual Report to Congress, 1973*, 1974, pages 11 f. under the heading, "Major AEC Owned, Contractor-Operated Facilities."

[85]Atomic Energy Commission, *Annual Report to Congress, 1973*, 1974, pages 26 ff. Some essential government documents were put together in U.S. Congress Joint Economic Committee Hearings, *Fast Breeder Reactor Program*, 1976.

icap in competing for jurisdiction over new weapons systems, turning to private contractors to correct the defect." Hence it brought into existence a "growing band of private companies which took over a substantial part of regular military operations, including maintaining aircraft, firing rockets, building and maintaining launching sites, organizing and directing other contractors. . . ." This had the advantage of "building an enormous industrial and congressional constituency with a stake in maintaining large-scale funding of new weapons systems."[86] This contractor constituency was pyramidally organized heading up in a research-consultant corporation headed by two initially obscure aerospace scientists who soon were joined by concerns with hardware capability that had special access to Air Force contracts. By 1965 the scientists had become multimillionaires by heading up an industrial complex with an annual volume of operations of $500 million and a high place among the top 50 prime governmental contracting corporations.[87]

Being late-born and with more esoteric interests, the space agency NASA was even more fully committed to the contractor principle than the Air Force or AEC. It has been estimated that 95% of the NASA budget was expended by contract. In its formative years, the agency contractually assigned to two giant corporations, AT&T and G.E., large management responsibilities to coordinate and integrate contract work at the various research and field centers. It was NASA policy generally to waive all rights to patents growing out of applied research that government procurement was buying. The resident capabilities that NASA inherited, chiefly that of the Jet Propulsion Lab, was cut down or starved of funds or itself converted into a contracting agency.[88]

Although government staffing, in-house capability, and contract administration has been notably weak in NASA and probably also in the field of atomic energy, it has not been neglected in the Defense Department generally. Hence there has been built up in DOD a counterpart bureaucracy to that of the contracting organizations pursuing and defending what are believed to be government interests in contract negotiations and administration. One part of that bureaucracy has been organized since 1963 as Defense Contract Administrative Services (DCAS), which is responsible for the administration and monitoring of a contract once the separate military services, under the authority of law, have been empowered to obligate government funds by the execution of the contract. Functioning in one national center and 11 regional offices with a staff of over 24,000 persons, DCAS personnel are given a

[86]I cite here from the invaluable work of my former colleague at the University of Wisconsin–Milwaukee, H. L. Nieburg, *In the Name of Science*, 1966, pages 188 ff.

[87]The detail of this depressing tale is set forth in full in Nieburg, *In the Name of Science*, 1966, ch. 11.

[88]Nieburg, *In the Name of Science*, 1966, pages 42, 220, 229, 237, 292 f.

comprehensive mandate to monitor closely all the work of contract implementation including a review of the contractor's compensation structure, his
insurance coverage, and requests for "progress payments" that compensate
for work in progress and thus help to finance working capital. Their responsibilities include determining the acceptability of certain costs; negotiating
prices and supplemental agreements for spare parts; assuring timely notifi-
cation by contractor of anticipated cost overruns of the estimated costs under
cost-type contracts; reviewing and approving or disapproving of the contractor's procurement system; performing necessary screening, redistribution, and
disposal of contractor inventory; monitoring industrial relations matters; ap-
prising the procuring contracting officer of actual or potential labor disputes;
and evaluating and overseeing contractor engineering efforts and engineering
data control systems. In fiscal year 1967, the agency was monitoring 272,000
contracts with a value of $49 billion. To give top Pentagon management an
independent check on the operations both of its contracting and contract
administration officers, a DOD "audit agency" has been established to ensure
detailed compliance with DOD regulations.[89]

The work of contractors is interwoven at every stage with a counterpart
organization at the government level, which includes responsibility for providing financial aid, basic capital funding of facilities, or pieces of equipment
that the contractor does not prefer to procure and manage. In one five-year
period, 13 major prime contractors used $1.5 billion of government property
against $1.4 billion of their own.[90] It includes current "progress" financing
to provide working capital, limited by DOD regulations to not more than
70% of total contract costs, which in one year alone ran to nearly $5 bil-
lion.[91] Reporting is continuous and for many prime contractors may involve
hundreds of reports in a given year. The sharing of responsibility and management is carried through all the way to the level of international sales. The
American armament industry is of course a prime export high-technology
area. Most marketing is channeled through a DOD marketing organization,
with government often taking the lead in pushing sales especially where there
is a foreign policy interest involved.[92] Contractors appear to take marketing

[89]Melman, *Pentagon Capitalism*, 1970, pages 57, 249 f. Melman gives a detailed résumé of
this supervisory work of DCAS drawing upon the 4-volume set of Armed Services Procurement Regulations (pages 37 ff., 43).

[90]Melman, *Pentagon Capitalism*, 1970, page 47.

[91]Melman, *Pentagon Capitalism*, 1970, pages 49 f.

[92]Annual military sales agreements by DOD operating under the Arms Export Control Act
in recent years (1974–1977) have been running between $11 to $12 billion while annual
deliveries have run from one-half to one-third of that. Commercial exports of military ware,
against orders placed by foreign government with private firms, amounts to less than one-fifth
of the government sales program. See U.S. Bureau of Census, *Statistical Abstract*, 1978, page
373. For background on military sales, see Melman, *Pentagon Capitalism*, 1970, pages 92 ff.

responsibility whereever corruption or bribery is employed.[93] And contract completion does not close the relationship, for yet another agency in DOD has the right to seek to renegotiate contracts that are believed to have resulted in improper levels of measurable profit or where the resulting level of price is unconscionable. The personnel on the two sides of the bargaining table tends to become interwoven as prime contractors draw into their staff senior procurement officers who will have know-how in the DOD and may still wield considerable influence.[94]

On the overall efficiency of this hybrid mode of production—variously labeled "Contract State" or "Pentagon Capitalism"—much evidence suggests extensive waste and extravagance. The frantic quest for gold-plated technology and the general use of cost-plus contracting leads to a reckless unconcern for levels of cost. Nieburg asserts that a "voluminous documentation of systematic waste and profiteering is buried in GAO and congressional reports." He fills 11 pages of his work with condensed descriptions of what he calls a "Sample Catalog of Atrocities."[95] Duplicated interweaving of management both by prime contractors and government will, of course, considerably tend to boost supervisory services. Detection of excess profit is not easy because the available profit statistics for quasi-public corporations generally cover total activity on an international basis. The breakdown of net earnings on a particular product or activity is usually inaccessible to outside observers. Cele-

[93]At least that was the case with Textron–Bell and the helicopters that were sold in 10 countries with the aid of bribes amounting to over $5 million, according to an authoritative report of the Securities and Exchange Commission. The Commission report was pursuant to inquiries into Wm. G. Miller, who had been appointed to the Federal Reserve Board (and was later to be Secretary of Treasury) and who was questioned vigorously by Senator William Proxmire at hearings before the Senate Banking Committee. See Proxmire's speech opposing confirmation of the appointment to the Treasury, *Congressional Record*, August 2, 1980, S. 11341 ff. An earlier scandal had implicated the Lockheed Corporation in bribery of foreign government personnel to promote the sale of aircraft; according to Senator Proxmire, some 500 American corporations came forward and disclosed bribery payments abroad to the SEC (S. 11355).

[94]Nieburg, *In the Name of Science*, 1966, pages 272 f. The opposite is, of course, true: top Pentagon policy positions in the services are usually held by top executives from the big corporations. Senator Proxmire reported that the 100 largest military contractors employed almost 2100 retired or former military officers of the rank of colonel or navy captain and above. "Lockheed Aircraft and General Dynamics . . . had respectively 210 and 113 retired high-ranking officers on their payroll." At the end of 1971, an additional 993 retired or former officers had been signed on by contractors and 108 high-ranking Pentagon civilian employees had shifted to the contractor side. "Further, 232 former civilian employees or consultants to defense contractors were hired by the Pentagon." See Proxmire, *Uncle Sam*, 1972, pages 69 f.

[95]Nieburg, *In the Name of Science*, 1966, pages 275–287. This is paralleled by Proxmire's hard-hitting and well-informed critique of wasteful and gold-plated military procurement. See Proxmire, *Uncle Sam*, 1972, pages 39–89.

brated cases are on record of superlatively high levels of profit for particular defense contractors. But cases are also on record where they have lost heavily though not necessarily on their defense business. One available study of net profits on contractor business found these profits moderate as a percent of sales but somewhat higher than the industry average when related to invested capital.[96]

Significantly enough, these two hybrid forms of the public mode of production on a large scale are mainly an American product. The prevalent tendency elsewhere is for public utilities to be owned and operated by the appropriate branch of government—local in some cases, provincial or regional in others; yet in other cases, as with the postal, communication, and rail networks, it may be national. As for the high-technology nuclear and missile industry, it is found abroad in the Western world on a much smaller scale or not at all.

HYBRID MODES

In our extended discussion over this and the preceding two chapters devoted to modes of production, it has been made clear that in many given instances modes of production materialize historically not in pure but in hybrid form. Two leading instances of such hybrid development in the twentieth century American economy—crosses between the public mode and the corporate mode—were elucidated in the preceding section of this chapter. Yet the forces making for hybridization were hardly exhausted on the American scene or with those two examples. Various historical circumstances and the force of changes in technology and social institutions tend to modify the form in which modes of production appear and produce hybridization. This can be readily established if we seek to make a listing of the more prominent examples of hybridization already developed in the literature of political economy.

To continue with hybrid crosses between the public and corporate modes, one has only to recall the early form of the quasi-public corporation in the seventeenth and eighteenth centuries where capitalist development and machine industry was still in an incipient stage. The corporations were primarily trading companies that linked together dynamic European states with overseas peoples having inferior military technology and therefore readily colonized. The agencies for trade, colonization, and empire were quasi-public corporations usually given monopoly authority over a specified territory or trading network and equipped with the power of the state. Imperial authority

[96]Melman, *Pentagon Capitalism*, 1970, pages 63 f.

was at once mercantile, capitalist, and military. The colossal power of empire in India was built up by a chartered profit-seeking corporation, the East India Company, which Marx alleged "conquered India to make money out of it" and "began to enlarge their factories into an Empire when their competition with the Dutch and French private merchants assumed the character of national rivalry."[97] Issuing of a national currency and management of the public debt was assigned in England to a chartered corporate monopoly, the Bank of England, controlled by capitalists as stockholders and managed by their representatives both to make profits and to stabilize the national economy. The English settlements in North America were largely the outgrowth of chartered profit-seeking companies given patents or grants of land and imperial authority. The early stages of imperial development in Africa were pioneered by chartered companies given exclusive grants of territory in return for fulfilling certain obligations. These corporations were variously Dutch, English, and French. These corporations were most active in the seventeenth century but they lingered on well into the nineteenth century. They provided the toehold of imperial authority where European settlement and control of ports and harbors were the startingpoints for colonial division of Africa which exploded late in the nineteenth century.[98]

Nor was it only for purposes of overseas trade and colonial expansion that the hybrid public–private corporation was used. The development of English interior transportation on highways and canals was turned over to profit-seeking private corporations obligated generally to allow passage to eligible vehicles, vessels, or foot-passengers for uniform charges. The English "turnpike trust" was a well-known institution in the eighteenth century and as it was being phased out of highways, it provided the precedent for the establishment of railroads by private corporations.[99] The great canal of Languedoc in France—built at the end of the seventeenth century by the French government—was turned over for upkeep and maintenance to the engineer who

[97]Marx and Engels, *Collected Works*, 1841–1860, vol. 12, page 179. Beginning in 1784 the authority of the Company over its Indian affairs was subject to the superintendence of a government Board of Control, which in 1833 was accorded formal power while the Company was dissolved in its commercial existence—though it still retained influence in the Indian administration.

[98]Hopkins, *Economic History of West Africa*, 1973, pages 87 ff.

[99]Though in general Adam Smith approved of the British system of putting the construction of intercity highways in the hands of turnpike trusts authorized to collect tolls for their use, he did feel the management of those tolls and their magnitude had been "justly complained of" and he believed the excess revenue involved perhaps amounted to half a million pounds. See A. Smith, *Wealth of Nations*, 1776, pages 684 ff. The rise and later fall of the turnpike trust is well portrayed in the classic account of Sidney and Beatrice Webb, *History of Local Government in England*, 1922, vol. 4, pages 152–235.

planned and constructed the work and was given a "present" of the tolls. Adam Smith believed these tolls, which "constitute a very large estate to the different branches of the family of that gentleman" at least provided adequate incentive to keep the canal in "constant repair."[100]

Turning to the junction of the capitalist and public modes of production, the outstanding instance of hybrid development is probably the assignment in the late Roman Republic of public duties involving revenue collection or construction to private contractors or mercantile companies. This struck the attention of Polybius, the Greek historian who lived most of his adult life as hostage in Rome during the second century B.C.: "All over Italy an immense number of contracts . . . are awarded for the construction and repair of public buildings . . . the collection of revenues from navigable rivers, harbours, gardens, mines, lands—in a word every transaction which comes under the control of the Roman government—is farmed out to contractors." There was scarcely a soul who did not have some interest in these contracts and the profits which were derived from them—by purchasing contracts from the awarding authorities ("censors") or acting as partners or providing security.[101] As the empire expanded and the collection of tribute payments became a major state revenue, this collection was assigned to contractors given the authority of tax administration in the conquered territories. The power of these tax-farmers or *publicani* was great enough nearly on one celebrated occasion to block by massed force the administration of justice.[102] Cicero called them— the "respected and well-to-do personages who have contracted to collect your taxes"—a "mainstay" of the "community"; instantly upon trouble in the Roman provinces of Asia Minor with the disruption of tax collecting there would be "collapse of credit at Rome due to the widespread non-payment of debts."[103] The tax-farmers were often organized into "companies" with

[100]A. Smith, *Wealth of Nations*, 1776, page 684.

[101]Polybius, *Histories*, 155–125 A.D., bk. 16, para. 17.

[102]Livy, *History of Rome*, 29 B.C.–A.D. 17, bk. 25, para. 3 f. Two greedy *publicani* who had been reporting imaginary shipwrecks, for which they sought to collect in Rome for alleged losses, were assessed a fine by action of the tribunes who acted in default of delay by the Senate. At the session of the popular assembly where an appeal was taken, the assembled tax-farmers, "shoulder to shoulder, like troops breaking through enemy's line, . . . thrust their way into the space left by the crowd when it was ordered to stand back, hurling insults as they went at tribunes and people alike." It nearly came to blows when the consul Fulvius called out to the tribunes to dismiss the session. Later the Senate, afraid of the precedent, took sterner action.

[103]The cited remarks are from Cicero's oration "On the Command of Cnaeus Pompey," See Cicero, *Selected Political Speeches*, pages 43 f. Cicero was aware of the abuse of authority by the *publicani* and he advised his brother who was serving as proconsul in Asia that coming to term with tax-farmers—a "class to which we owe a great deal and which we have brought into alliance with the public interest"—would be his main problem. If deferred to too much along the line, it will lead to "the utter undoing of the people for whose interests as well as survival, it is our duty to care." Cicero, *Letters to His Friends*, 1978, vol. 2, pages 262 f.

large numbers of subscribers entitled to share in the net revenues available and with some form of delegation of authority and agency control, making them a kind of hybrid of the capitalist and corporate forms. The Roman tax-farming *publicani* faded out as the imperial regime crystallized. But as a hybrid cross between the public and the capitalist modes it enjoyed wide currency throughout the world of Islam and the absolutist state systems that emerged in Europe in the later medieval and mercantilist period—indeed, surviving in France up through the Great Revolution.[104]

The capitalist enterprise itself is readily subject to hybridization as it evolves from or deals extensively with formally independent craft producers. The line between the craft and capitalist enterprise is itself a fluid one, depending upon the degree of reliance for productive labor on the hired workmen rather than the proprietor and his family. There is thus a class of enterprise which is neither fully capitalist nor fully craft–proprietor. Guild rules and traditions sought for a long time to protect against encroachments of this class.

A better-recognized case of the hybrid of craft and capitalist enterprise is found in the "putting out" system. Developed chiefly in the textile trades for operations like weaving, leather work, embroidering, lace making, and straw plaiting, under this system the craftsman and his family, working at home with his own equipment, becomes dependent for his market and some-times for essential work materials upon an outside merchant to whom he may also be indebted for advances. Merchant marketing is almost always required if the product is to be sold in export markets or at international fairs. Dependence is greater if the merchant provides both work materials and disposal of the finished product and if the workman has become separated from his rural setting and a small peasant holding or at least a large garden and some place for animal husbandry.[105] In the later Middle Ages in Western

---

[104]Tax-farming among the Romans was possibly an institution borrowed from the Greek cities where, according to an informed authority, it was "regularly found." See H. Mitchell, *Economics Ancient Greece*, 1940, page 356. Even beyond tax revenues, Gotein found that "farm-ing out" was "rampant in the Byzantine and Persian empires," pervaded the entire public administration in Fatimid Egypt (eleventh to thirteenth centuries A.D.) and included "even a post like that of the head of the police" with power to impose fines to indemnify himself for his purchase of office. See Gotein, *Mediterranean Society*, 1967-1971, vol. 2, pages 354 ff. Selling off the revenues by farming was rampant in many Spanish dominions and in the Turkish empire in the later sixteenth century. See Braudel, *The Mediterranean*, 1949, vol. 2, pages 685-693, 723 f. Tax-farming in France was driven to a high art in the seventeenth and eighteenth centuries and produced a wealthy class of *publicani* that drained the public revenues and helped to make the French tax system so unproductive compared to the British one, as Adam Smith virtually concludes in his informed account of tax administration in both coun-tries. See A. Smith, *Wealth of Nations*, 1776, pages 853 f., 856 f., 871 f.

[105]The "putting out" system is a phase of economic development which has been given close attention by economic and social historians. See the still illuminating survey by E. F. Gay in *The Encyclopedia of Social Sciences*, 1930-1934, vol. 13, pages 7-11; Kulischer, *Allge-*

Europe the entire cloth-making industry of especially fine woolens was organized by merchant entrepreneurs who assembled the necessary raw materials often imported from other countries, organized the markets, and provided
the work to successive series of guild shops and artisans—in a few cases putting the latter to work in workshops controlled by the merchants, particularly
in processes of dyeing and fulling.[106]

The Russian town artisan of the serfdom period was uniquely dependent
upon merchant entrepreneurs.[107] The postserfdom stage of the Russian rural
economy, investigated by Lenin in 1899, was saturated with the development
of small-scale craft-product production in which merchant capital had insin-
uated itself because of its provision of markets and of working capital. Sometimes the merchant function would be taken on by a peasant commissioned
by his village compeers to arrange for the marketing task by traveling to the
big city—and who in time because of his connections and higher earnings
became established as merchant.[108] Side by side with the simpler forms of
manufacture, into which machine industry had not yet penetrated, Marx
found extensive place in England in the mid nineteenth century for domestic
or home workshops wholly dominated not only by merchant intermediaries
but by factories or capitalist workshops whose operations were supplemented
or completed by a large amount of work given out to workers functioning
in their own homes.[109]

The tendency to hybridization was also at work at the other end of the
capitalist spectrum when it was evolving into the quasi-public corporation.
At a certain stage in this evolution, when the corporation is still dominated
by major capitalist founders and has a large number of stockholders, the busi-

---

meine Wirtschaftsgeschichte, 1925, vol. 1, pages 215 ff.; Braudel, *The Mediterranean*, 1949, vol.
1, pages 430 ff.; Earle, ed., *Essays in European Economic History*, 1974, pages 47 ff., 53 ff.,
68 ff., 226 ff., 262 ff.

[106]The development of the "putting out" system in the woolen industry has been exhaustively and perceptively portrayed on the basis of careful research by E. Carus–Wilson in
many of her writings. See especially Carus–Wilson, *Medieval Merchant Venturers*, 1967. (For
emphasis on fulling mills, an early stage of mechanization with water power, see 183 ff., 211
ff.). See also Carus–Wilson, "The Woolen Industry," 1952, vol. 2, pages 355–429.

[107]"Except in the big cities, the Russian artisans accept no work on order. They produce
everything for sale—shoes, slippers, boots, coats, out garments, fur coats.... The artisans
deliver all these items at set prices to merchants who sell them in their shops." From a 1799
account cited in Tugan–Baranovsky, *Russian Factory*, 1898, pages 7 f.

[108]Lenin, *Capitalism in Russia*, 1899, pages 354–413. In the one district with carefully
compiled statistics, Lenin found that 80.6% of the handicraftsmen still engage in agriculture
(page 356), that processes of differentiation quickly sprang up among the Kustar producers
(pages 369 ff.), and that merchant capital sometimes reinforced by making of loans quickly
develops partly among the Kustar producers themselves (pages 386 ff.).

[109]Marx, *Capital* I, 1867, pages 470 ff.

ness is in transition from capitalist enterprise to the matured quasi-public corporation dominated by professional management. These "entrepreneurial corporations"—to use the term given them by Galbraith—were the predominant form of the institution when it was observed and investigated by Lenin during World War I. The form of entrepreneurial corporation is reproduced every time a new major business establishment is born with its multimillionaire founders. The breed is still with us and is not merely a phase of the past.

Fluidity of form and tendency to hybridization are not only characteristic of the later or latest modes of production but also of the earliest. Historians have frequently noted that, especially for earlier periods, it is very difficult to place unfree workers into either "slave," "serf," or "feudal" categories. The label "slave" is often placed in our sources on workers who hold relatively high status in the Roman public service or who conduct their own business establishments, paying regular fees to their "owner," earning the funds needed to purchase their manumission. The characteristics of unfree labor themselves change, sometimes relaxing and at other times stiffening as when, in the late Roman Empire, the nominally free tenant became bound to the estate. The status of the Russian unfree peasant community deteriorated in the seventeenth and eighteenth centuries, and at some stage it turned into a state similar to slavery. Yet for centuries the condition was obviously a fluid one resulting in various "hybrid" states.

Hybridization is frequently found on the fringes of the cooperative movement, resulting from a junction of the cooperative with the capitalist or the corporate mode. Sometimes this junction is only transitional, as when capitalist enterprise seeks to utilize the cooperative movement as a convenient vehicle. Thus cooperative creameries were formed not as a result of the felt needs of dairymen but through the promotional activity of manufacturers of creamery machinery seeking to market their product.[110] Similarly, California mutual irrigation companies originated as subsidiaries of capitalist "land and water companies" that would buy up a large tract of land from Spanish grantholders, develop a waterworks distributive system with canals, pipelines, and reservoirs, then sell to settlers small farm tracts with water rights and shares in the corporation controlling water development. Presumably after settler development was completed the settlers would own a majority of the outstanding common stock, thus controlling the corporation and able to turn it into a mutual service agency.[111] In their early phases some Farm Bureau cooperatives seeking to appease hostile local dealers would pool their orders with certain of the dealers for a reduced markup or service fee.[112] We have

[110]Powell, *Cooperation in Agriculture*, 1913, pages 144 f.
[111]Kile, *Farm Bureau Movement*, 1921, pages 201 ff.
[112]Kile, *Farm Bureau Movement*, 1921, pages 106 f.

already noted that the mutual insurance company and thrift institution often embodies a similar form of compromise between capitalist enterprise and true cooperation.[113]

Does hybridization mean that the modes of production presented in this work have no objective existence and are in historical reality always embodied in mixed hybrid forms? That would go too far, because our historical literature attests to the frequent existence of all of the analyzed modes in various societies with relatively constant features. But no doubt hybridization is very common, especially during transition phases when one mode is growing into another. But even if hybridization were universal and if all historically viable modes exhibited features that to a greater or lesser degree were traceable to other modes, that would not mean that the modal types did not exist—only that their analysis is more complicated because characteristics of behavior in the real world would be drawn from two or more sets of modal types. It is thus fortunate that hybridization is confined to adjacent or closely related modes like capitalist and corporate enterprise, direct commodity production and capitalist enterprise, or to public utilities in twentieth century America, where opposition to public enterprise is too strong for utilities to be in government ownership and operation yet opposition to private monopoly will not permit them to function unregulated by law.

ECONOMIC SYSTEMS AS MULTIMODAL

In the development of our analysis of the various modes of production and of their hybrid forms, it has already become clear that economic systems, which are the subject of this work, will commonly contain at least two modes of production and frequently many more. This is of course true for the cooperative mode earlier described in this chapter as an adjunct mode necessarily playing an auxiliary role in economic systems. The cooperative mode is essentially adjunct to the capitalist and corporative modes in urban trade and production and to the direct commodity producer or small-capitalist production in agriculture. The existing socialist economies allow space alongside the predominant public mode of production for the cooperative mode of production, especially in agriculture but also in retail trade and urban services. And however mutilated and state-dominated this socialist cooperative mode may be, its cooperative features have not yet been totally expunged in the

---

[113]Some state Farm Bureau organizations, instead of establishing their own mutual insurance companies commissioned certain mutual insurance concerns, especially in the field of auto casualty insurance, to sell on special terms to their members car insurance. See Kile, *Farm Bureau through Three Decades*, 1948.

socialist economies.[114] The lines of evolution of both Eastern and Western economies do not appear to allow any place for development of an economic system that would be exclusively cooperative in its mode of production—the stateless "cooperative commonwealth" of sets of associated producers. This does not, of course, rule out the possibility that under altered circumstances, which cannot now be previsioned, at some future time and place a drift to such a commonwealth may occur, perhaps in a world seeking recovery from nuclear ruin.

We cannot, however, rule out in the same way the possibility of an exclusive predominance in the socialist economies—a category we have not yet defined but shall now presuppose—of the public mode of production or the conversion into the public mode of existing marketing and production cooperatives functioning chiefly in the field of agriculture and retail trade. That is the historic objective of Marxist theory and it is made possible by the all-encompassing power developed by the communist state. Stalin in his speculation on this subject in his last theoretical work took care to emphasize that Soviet collective farms did not own the land on which they lived and worked (for land had been theoretically nationalized early in Soviet power) nor did they own the basic machinery utilized (which then was state property hired out for farm use for payment in kind). That left as collective farm property chiefly the product of their labor—a "considerable part" of which goes into the market "and is thus included in the system of commodity circulation." It would be necessary, Stalin reflected, to convert this process of "commodity circulation" into a state-monitored system of "products-exchange" for which he believed only a greater abundance of industrial products available for exchange would be needed, thereby raising collective farm property to the level of "public property" and including farm products wholly within the scope of national economic planning.[115] In his interesting commentary on Stalin's reflections, the Chinese counterpart of Stalin, Mao Tsetung, concurred as to the centrality of the objective of converting cooperative property into socialized public property. He set limits to the increase in national production which would make this possible (a rise in farm income levels

[114]This dual makeup of the socialist economies was clearly set forth in the theoretical swan song of Joseph Stalin written shortly before his death: "Today there are two basic forms of socialist production in our country: state or publicly-owned production and collective-farm production, which cannot be said to be publicly owned. In the state enterprises, the means of production and the product are national property. In the collective farm, although the means of production . . . do belong to the state, the product of production is the property of the different collective farms, since the labor, as well as the seed, is their own, while the land, which has been turned over to the collective farms in perpetual tenure, is used by them virtually as their own property." See Stalin, *Economic Problems of Socialism*, 1952, page 16.

[115]Stalin, *Economic Problems of Socialism*, 1952, pages 69 ff.

from 85 to 150 yuan) and he drily noted that by use of "cadres" and the power of the state with a higher income level the shift could easily be made in the broad state-dominated framework of rural "commune" into which the Chinese collective farms villages had been submerged.[116] We have yet to see whether this transformation can be thus easily accomplished.

Turning to the other modes of production, we find that when looked at closely they all have usually appeared in multiple sets in the economic systems treated in this work. That is especially true of the most basic and long-enduring Simple Commodity Producer Mode (SCPM). In one field of production or another—agriculture, industry, trade, professions, wholesale trade, and construction—SCPM has been present in virtually all economic systems from the classical Chinese Empire and the Graeco-Roman regimes of antiquity up to the contemporary socialist economies. This was conceded by the author of a Marxist classic, Oscar Lange, who characterized the SCPM as a mode which though "never dominant in any period, continually reappears as a subsidiary mode."[117] It was hardly a subsidiary mode in the earlier phases of the Roman Republic—in which Marx hailed the peasant proprietor and his compeers, the small trader and craftsman, as the "economic foundation of society during the best period of classical antiquity."[118] Usually however, the SCPM is not present in full force, as was pointed out (see ch. II, pages 47 f.). Here the small trader has lost his ground, elsewhere the peasant proprietor; in recent history, the urban craftsman, sometimes even the independent professional. But he has been powerful as well as ubiquitous. Over strategic areas of the European medieval world the urban SCPM, organized as town guilds, wielded authority over their walled urban world and even built up extensive maritime empire in the Baltic and Adriatic seas. And nearly everywhere except possibly in England the SCPM as family farmer has carried into the mid-twentieth century. The urban world is still littered with small shops, stores, and offices where the SCPM reigns supreme, even though under conditions of advanced economic development nearly all mining and industry is in the capitalist, corporate, or public sector. The peasant proprietor has dominated the agriculture of all the peoples who have followed the Russian and Chinese lead in building a socialist economy.

If the SCPM has usually been joined together with other modes in making up an economic system, the same can be said of the capitalist mode of pro-

[116]See Mao Tse-Tung, *A Critique of Soviet Economics*, 1958–1959, pages 101, 130 ff., 140. Though Mao chiefly addressed himself to the proposed Soviet textbook on political economy, he thus indirectly confronts Stalin's views on the same subject, and in the final section of the booklet he directly deals with Stalin's pamphlet.

[117]Lange, *Political Economy*, 1959, page 19.

[118]See this volume, ch. 2, Footnote 34.

duction, which has had a similar universal course. In earlier economic systems before the development of machine technology, the capitalist mode was limited chiefly to the field of wholesale trade, which it tended to dominate. It is striking, however, that just in the period when the capitalist mode of production began to take over in industry—in the eighteenth and nineteenth centuries—that the quasi-public corporation appeared first in the field of wholesale (overseas) trade and later in the field of banking, railroads, and canals. By the time that the capitalist mode of production had developed a solid industrial base in metallurgy and textiles and was spreading throughout the commodity world, all the institutions of the corporate mode had become well-established. By the early decades of the twentieth century in the countries in which the capitalist mode of production was most advanced, the corporate mode had become predominant in mining, manufacturing, and in public utilities wherever the public sector did not operate these as a public mode.

The fact that modes of production usually come in pairs, triplets, or quadruplets in economic systems was accorded some recognition by the Marxian hypothesis that a predominant or central mode would coexist with early stages of modes just sprouted or taking root and with decaying stages of modes being superseded.[119] But this hardly answers to the need. Modes deemed to be in a declining state may be disappearing only in certain fields where they are inappropriate to the available technology. That is true of SCPM, which overall has held its own even though in various fields it has been superseded by capitalist, corporate, or cooperative enterprise. Similarly, with all the strength of the corporate mode, it has still left a large space for the capitalist mode in such fields as retail trade, finance, agriculture, and certain kinds of manufacturing. And both the capitalist and corporate modes have had to acknowledge the supremacy of the Simple Commodity Producer in most fields of professional practice and the more specialized kinds of building maintenance and repair, retail trade, or repair services. To be sure, some modes of production have died out in the modern world—notably, the village com-

---

[119]This traditional Marxian *caveat* was repeated by Oscar Lange. "These [five] modes of production . . . roughly correspond to certain periods in the historical development of mankind. Between these periods there are, however, transitional stages when two or more different modes of production exist side by side. Moreover, even in an epoch characterized by a particular mode of production, remnants of some other mode may persist for a long time and may even survive the epoch itself. [How stubborn those "remnants" are.] Under capitalism, e.g., elements of feudalism in many countries survived and still have not been finally extinguished. . . . The elements of other modes of production which are found along with the dominant one are not only those which have survived from the past but also those incipient forms which will develop fully later in the historical process." See Lange, *Political Economy*, 1959, page 19.

munity, slavery, and the serf mode. But it is remarkable how long these modes persisted side by side with other modes in the most incongruous social formations. Thus the slave mode which was well-established in the classical Graeco-Roman world of antiquity and then appeared to dwindle away in its European setting became rejuvenated again in the seventeenth and eighteenth centuries, to reach its climax within the United States republic in the *sixth* decade of the nineteenth century—when the capitalist, SCPM, and corporate modes were also well-developed. We accordingly conclude that the facts of history are better served by the presupposition that modes come in multiple sets with strength in various fields of economic life rather than as predominant wholes. That presupposition has in recent years been given some recognition in Marxist debate though sometimes in curiously limited form.[120]

We can reach the same result of stable multiple modal sets in economic systems even if we accept the argument that one mode is predominant and the others are in a transition state, either coming or going. The pace of coming or going is the controlling fact, not the movement itself. If the movement is very slow relative to processes of life so that any particular generation will orient itself and its life situation to the multiple modes that it inherited and then confronts, then to all practical purposes multiple modes are permanent and stable, not transient and passing. Conversely, if one takes the historical perspective that reduces a whole sequence of generations or centuries into a

[120]Rodinson, *Islam and Capitalism*, 1967. He found in Muslim society various modes of production operative in different sectors of the economy (page 10ff.), with "petty commodity production predominant" in many fields (pages 50 ff.) but a distinctive form of capitalist enterprise in trade and finance. Rodinson found many modes in Islamic agriculture, ranging from village communities to state-ownership and tribute-collecting, with some peasant proprietorship and definite feudal patterns (pages 66 ff.). Another specialist in Islam, Samir Amin *Unequal Development*, 1973, is willing to accept a variant set of Marxian basic modes of production (primitive-communal, tribute-paying village communities, slavery, simple commodity production, capitalist mode) and for all precapitalist modes he believes that economic systems (labeled "socio-economic formations") contain various sets of these modes linked by long-distance merchant trade (pages 17 ff.). "Since a formation is a group of modes of production, every society actually presents the picture of a complex group of more than two classes: feudal lords, serf–peasants, free peasants, commodity producing craftsmen, and merchants in feudal Europe; imperial court and 'gentry' officials, communal peasants, free petty craftsmen, wage-earning craftsmen employed by entrepreneurs . . . and merchants in imperial China" (pages 13 ff., 17 ff., 23 ff.). The capitalist mode was born of the industrial revolution and became worldwide. This mode takes the form of advanced formations with a single "capitalist" mode dominating "peripheral formations" with somewhat distinctive precapitalist modal complexes, (pages 293 ff.). Amin's work has a brilliant side, especially for the analysis of economic systems appearing in earlier societies, but there is a blindness about his blithe assumption of a monopolist "capitalist" system that "tends to become identical with the mode of production that dominates it, whereas all previous formations were stable combinations of different modes" (page 77).

single vista, then instability and transition become very clear not only for the subordinate but also for the predominant modes, because they too are subject to the same process of evolutionary change. The dominant mode itself is not a fixed crystal but a complex of evolving institutions. Marx made that very clear with the capitalist mode of production, which in a few centuries had metamorphosed itself through a sequence of forms: simple cooperation, manufacturing, and modern industry. At a certain stage and under certain circumstances the capitalist mode of production began to metamorphose itself again into the corporate mode, which likewise went through an evolutionary process. Thus whether we take the long or the short view we will deal with multiple modes—in the short run of relatively fixed types, in the long run with evolving and changing forms.

We may gain assurance in the methodological and substantive soundness of the conclusion we have just reached if we make a summary sketch of the main modes of production included in the leading economic systems of the Western world in the decade of the early 1860s and for the same countries a half-century later, just before World War I. In the United Kingdom we find in agriculture two dominant modes—the capitalist farm and the landlord–tenant, one holding sway in England, Wales, and Scotland, the other in conquered Ireland—with dwindling fragments of yeomanry still surviving though rapidly declining in England proper. In industry, trade, and finance we find three well-developed modes: the quasi-public corporation holding forth in banking, insurance, railways, and public utilities; the capitalist enterprise predominant in urban realty, manufacturing, mining, wholesale trade; and the direct commodity producer predominant in retail trade, petty construction, urban artisan services, and the professions. In retail trade there are only the beginnings of the cooperative mode, and the "putting out" system with capitalist control rivals the artisan proprietor in craft shops.

Turning to France in the same period of mid nineteenth century, we find a different modal complex. In finance and in public utilities there is a well developed quasi-corporate sector as in England, though tending to take on hybrid forms with a deep-rooted public mode. In agriculture a strong carry-over from the village community and peasant proprietorship is the dominant mode along with landlord-tenant farming. In industry and trade the capitalist mode—and at that predominantly small-scale—still competes with artisan production carried out by craft producers often under "putting out" control.[121]

Then turning to Germany—or what is shortly to become a united German state—we find in agriculture two predominant modal types with quite different characteristics. In the East is a capitalist–Junker estate with hired mi-

---

[121]I draw this vignette sketch chiefly from Tom Kemp, *Economic Forces in French History*, 1971, ch. 8; Clapham, *Economic Development of France and Germany*, 1921, chs. 1, 3, 6, 7.

gratory and submissive tenant labor, substantively a hybrid form of capitalist and feudal agriculture. In the rest of Germany the independent peasant proprietor dominates—here and there with characteristics of capitalist farming based on hired labor, elsewhere landlord–tenant agriculture. In industry, trade, and commerce we find the field shared between capitalist enterprise and craft and shop enterprise, with only the beginnings of corporate sector and the first sproutings of cooperation and a considerable holdover of medieval guild organization. The labor employed in small handicraft and trader shops with one or two assistants greatly outnumbered labor employed in capitalist enterprise proper. In Prussia by 1846 less than 4% of the cotton-weaving looms of Prussia were power-operated. Linen and woolen textiles were still branches of cottage domestic industry. Of modern industry only the construction of railways had begun in earnest by the mid-century mark. The whole Silesian development of heavy industry was not yet commenced.[122]

Turn now to the United States where modern capitalist industry was advancing with giant strides. American agriculture was sharply segmented in two major modes: (1) family farming usually based upon owned not rented land and (2) slave plantations found in the South and in the border states. A sizable quasi-public corporate sector taking off from railroad and banking corporations had gotten started. Wholesale trade was chiefly in the hands of capitalist enterprise, whereas retail trade and artisan and professional services were in the hands of small proprietors.

Compare the modal complexes in the three countries a half-century later, just before the First World War. In Great Britain agriculture was still segmented. The capitalist farm employing wage labor with rented land had come to prevail even more completely in England proper, but in Ireland a far-reaching program of land reform had bought out, in part driven out, the absentee landlord so that the Irish tenant farmer had become a proprietor.[123] In industry and finance the quasi-public corporation more and more displaced the capitalist enterprise, while the cooperative movement had made sizable

---

[122]Clapham, *Economic Development of France and Germany*, 1921, chs. 2, 4, 5, 7. In the first edition of *Der Moderne Kapitalismus*, Sombart gave a detailed portrayal of the business life of Germany in the middle of the nineteenth century. See *Der Moderne Kapitalismus*, 1902, vol. 1, chs. 18–20. The small-scale, guild-like handwork character of the economy stands out clearly from this account.

[123]The process by which Irish tenants were transformed into landed proprietors involved an extended round of virtual guerrilla agrarian land war (which for a few years put the country under martial law); legislation gave tenants the benefit of improvements on termination of lease, scaled down the power of landlords to evict tenants, disestablished the Episcopal Church, enabled local courts to fix fair rents, and finally provided finance by which tenants could buy out landlord properties at long-term low interest rates. See Clark, *Irish Land War*, 1979; Beckett, *Making of Modern Ireland*, 1966, pages 370 ff., 391 ff., 406 ff.

inroads on the world of the small shopkeeper and the wholesale trading merchant.

In France and in Germany the modal complexes in agriculture remained unchanged, but the capitalist enterprise had greatly undercut the craft producers while in turn the quasi-public corporations had taken over ground from the capitalist enterprise. Though on a lesser scale than in England, the cooperative movement had taken over significant territory from the private trader and the processor of farm goods.

The American modal complex was considerably modified. The quasi-public corporate sector had become predominant in industry, while in public utilities the hybrid modal sector of regulated industries took distinct shape. An agricultural cooperative movement transformed the setting of rural trade. The slave plantation had disappeared—replaced by a landlord–mode with peonage characteristics.

The conclusion to be drawn from this recitation is obvious. It is impossible to analyze *at any one time* the economic system prevailing in the advanced countries of the Western world or to trace the course of economic development in those systems *over time* except in terms of multimodal complex.

Recognition of the plurality of modes commonly found in economic systems points to certain implications with important consequences for economic systems. One of these implications relates to the tendency of modes to compete with each other for limited economic resources and thus to shift the balance of predominance in the mutual relations of these modes. This tendency to competition of modes was especially strong in the sphere of agriculture, in which the slave mode tends to disintegrate and to turn into serf and landlord–tenant modes frequently found side by side. That is especially true for the whole period of classical Graeco-Roman antiquity, for most of the medieval period of European history, for Islam, and for much of Latin America. In modern conditions the landlord and peon mode tend readily, as we have previously noted, to live side by side. The peon mode will tend to be supported by landlords because it binds labor more closely to the estate and makes possible a higher degree of exploitation. But the peon mode may conflict with general ideas and social conditions existing in the society and may not prove feasible over wide areas, while conversely the operation of the peon mode may tend to generate dysfunctional under-class hostility and disaffection. The changing consciousness of the society may also cause a crisis of conscience for peon-exploiters and weaken the will to power which is fundamental to all antagonistic social formations. Here the competition between the modes is affected to a considerable degree by prevailing levels of culture and movements of social consciousness.

The competition of modes can take on various forms. The competition may be very direct and crass—as between the quasi-public corporations that operate vast nationwide systems of chain stores, capitalist chain-store networks, and small-scale store operators. Here modes tend to displace each other by offering a wider field of service, lower markups, or more innovative merchandising techniques. The capitalist and corporate modes are in continuous competition with each other over a broad front of industry, trade, and finance, but here the struggle is both for a common patronage and as well direct acquisition. In the early period of trust formation, the competition was brutal; the resources of Big Business were deployed on various fronts to deprive the competitive capitalist enterprises of their markets, their access to finance and transportation, or to raw materials. More recently, the use of such brutal methods has been abridged, with the competition confined more to struggle for patronage—determined ultimately by ability to carry on production and marketing at lower costs or achieve the capital liquidity needed to handle property succession through inheritance.

In the process of arriving at a mature state the cooperative mode had to live through a period of nearly deadly combat waged by practitioners of the competing modes—corporate, capitalist, and small-scale dealers and traders. Attempts would be made to block access to loan credit, to handicap access to wholesale supplies at the appropriate discount, and to seek by political influence to impose legal disabilities on cooperative enterprise.[124] Between capitalist enterprise and simple commodity producers there was competition for customers between the newer and older technologies, which in most fields gradually forced the simple commodity producers to the wall, in the process writing memorable chapters of economic history.[125]

In European medieval society the struggle between the prevailing modes—enserfed peasant village enmeshed in the manorial economy, and the self-governing town craft and merchant guilds—took partly the form of direct

---

[124]The movement by grain farmers to establish cooperative grain elevators "encountered the most vigorous sort of opposition" from "strongly intrenched line elevators, usually owned by big milling and financial interests [which] . . . enlisted the aid of the railroads in refusing siding privileges, 'forgetting' to furnish cars and 'losing' shipments. The banks refused credit at critical times." See Kile, *Farm Bureau Movement*, 1921, page 57. The first farmers' elevator cooperative organized in 1889 in Iowa encountered the "most vicious competition" by the grain dealers of the state. See Powell, *Cooperation in Agriculture*, 1913, page 127. Efforts to form cooperatives in the southern states by the early Alliance movement "and the opposition it stimulated from furnishing merchants, wholesale houses, cotton buyers and bankers . . . brought home to hundreds of thousands of American farmers new insights into their relationship with the commercial elements of American society." See Goodwyn, *Democratic Promise*, 1976, pages 110 ff. The battle to impose corporate income taxes on cooperatives has still not subsided.

[125]"History discloses no tragedy more horrible than the gradual extinction of the English handloom weavers, an extinction . . . spread over several decades and finally sealed in 1838." See Marx, *Capital* I, 1867, page 431.

competition for underlying village labor. Once an economic foothold was won, the town offered personal freedom and opportunities for social and economic advance. Flight to the town therefore was always one way to escape from feudal bondage. A similar possibility of escape lay in mountainous terrain, where feudal subjection less frequently prevailed. Following the season of famines and plague and demographic collapse that marked the early decades of the fourteenth century, tenant mobility helped to force the estate managers throughout Western Europe to end the harsher forms of feudal subjection.

The second major implication of the diversity of competing modes commonly found in economic systems relates to social friction. Classes corresponding to a given production mode tend to develop a way of life and an outlook or consciousness hostile to other modes of production and classes harbored by them. Thus the feudal lords and their retainers and clerics despised the money-grubbing trader or peasant plowman for their unheroic style of life. The bourgeois in turn held in contempt the wasteful splendor of the feudal lord unable to attend even to his simplest wants. In the New World the hostility generated between the classes associated with the three modes of production—the slave plantation, the capitalist enterprise, and the simple commodity producer—could not in the course of American social development be accommodated within a single state and exploded in the American Civil War. Both the capitalist class and the host of direct commodity producers fanatically opposed trade unions and looked askance on extensions of public enterprise that did not directly benefit them. The functionaries of the communist state are extremely hostile to any form of social thought or practical action carried out by direct commodity producers. Pluralist societies with more than one mode of production are thus antagonistic by their nature because they harbor mutually hostile classes, outlooks, and consciousness. This antagonism makes for an unstable, tension-ridden polity that may break down in civil war unless reconciling political institutions are developed. Foremost among these are the national monarchy, or the constitutionally limited rule of law, the institution of the mandarinate, or elite-symbiosis by which the elite of a class accustomed to rule adapts its makeup and ideas to suit the needs of a rival class. The foremost examplar of such an elite was the English landowning bourgeois aristocracy, which presided over an imperial power that in its heyday sheltered a wide diversity of modes of production both within the British Isles and even more overseas.[126] This development required

[126]Marx, "The Election in England—Tories and Whigs," *New York Herald Tribune*, August 21, 1852; "The Crisis in England and the British Constitution," *New York Herald Tribune*, March 24, 1855 (reprinted in Marx and Engels *Collected Works*, 1841–1860, vol. 11, pages 327 ff.; vol. 14, pages 59 ff.).

a sense of tolerance and relativism in the ruling elite that facilitated empire abroad and the emergence of pluralism at home.[127]

---

[127]This paragraph is extracted with slight revision from Gottlieb, "Pluralist or Unitary Economic Systems," 1972, presented in October 1971 to a seminar at the University of Dar Es Salaam. In the lively oral discussion, attention was called to my comment about "sense of tolerance" and "relativism" in the British "ruling elite" who presided over a vast empire containing many modes of production and hostile classes. I noted in the paper that this elite was thus enabled to manage "empire abroad" and cultivate "pluralism at home" (page 84). John R. Saul (then on campus) who was (and is) a major exponent and leader of Marxism in East Africa called out a vigorous dissent at the mention of "tolerance."

5

Coordination of Resource Use within and between Modes

INTRODUCTION

Because the scope of production extends to activities of exchange, distribution, and accumulation, there must be processes of exchange and distribution whenever ultimate consumption or accumulation does not occur within the producing unit. Some production will, of course, be utilized within producing units to satisfy needs directly experienced or anticipated. Where the producing unit is a collectivity, distribution will follow norms set by authority or culturally evolved within the collectivity, to vary with the strength and status of the persons involved. But where goods or services are not utilized or accumulation carried out directly within the producing establishment, there is need for some process of resource coordination.

This process of coordination will also serve the function of interrelating the various modes of production existing within a given economic system. Each mode in a society does not service distinct sets of needs and consumers, as it were, in vertical compartments. The products or services rendered by the modes make up a mass of social product which is then utilized for purposes of consumption or investment via exchange and distribution. As suggested in the last chapter, there may even be a kind of competition between modes for customer patronage. Rising modes whose products are favored and well-rewarded will tend to displace declining modes that cannot hold their productive resources or prevent the erosion of their economic base. Moreover, the modes widely utilize products of other modes. From all this it follows that the mode of production or any given set of production modes cannot by itself define or constitute an economic system. Processes of exchange, distribution, and resource administration will run between and beyond the modes; therefore these processes have properties that must be separately reviewed. We shall review these processes under three broad headings: markets, rationing, and planning. These processes are found in some form in nearly all economic systems but in proportions that vary widely.

Markets

The market itself in its concrete form is territorially bounded, depending upon the efficiency of transportation and the facilities for transportation. Heavy and bulk goods like ores, timber, food grains, and building materials can move only short distances except with the aid of special long-distance transport facilities. In earlier economic systems high value of metals was due to the relatively high cost of transporting them from scattered sites, often in remote or rather inaccessible places. Water transportation was, of course, available upon navigable stretches of rivers, inland lakes, and interior seas. All the early economic systems were thus based on water transport. The primitive wheeled vehicles, poor roads, and the crude types of harness available—which in the Roman and early medieval world tended to choke draft animals—made long-distance vehicular transportation virtually impossible except for goods exceptionally light for their value like precious metals, silks, spices, and medicinal herbs. Gradual improvement in navigational skills and boat construction led to worldwide shipping in the fifteenth century, thus opening up for the most valuable goods a *world market* in which more and more commodities have been included as transportation has become more efficient. The world market does not imply, as Immanuel Wallerstein supposes, a world economic system. The market is only an agency of resource coordination within and between modes of production carried on in different places both within and between economic systems.

Within a given market, a cross-modal principle generally applies for the same class of product or service. Thus the cotton-marketing organization that serves the slave plantations will also service the landlord–tenant farms or simple commodity-producing family farms with a marketable cash crop. Similarly, the lord of the manor will patronize the same town markets that satisfy the needs of the town bourgeois, of village serfs, or nearby simple commodity producers. Just as different modes of production will throw their respective products into the same market for disposal, so buyers receiving incomes originating from different modes within a given marketing area will draw upon the same textile market for their cloth, the same smithies—or, in modern times, the same garage networks—for vehicle repairs. This cosmopolitan multiclass tendency of markets was conceived by Marx to be a specific by-product of merchant capital. "Since its function consists exclusively of promoting the exchange of commodities, it requires no other conditions for its existence . . . outside those necessary for the simple circulation of commodities and money . . . . No matter what the basis on which products are produced, which are thrown into circulation as commodities—whether the basis of the primitive community, of slave production, of small peasant and petty bourgeois, or the capitalist basis, the character of products as commodities is not altered. . . . Under slavery, feudalism and vassalage . . . it is the slave-owner, the feudal lord, the tribute-collecting state, who are the owners, hence sellers of the products. The merchant buys and sells for many."[1]

Thus the cosmopolitan character of merchant capital brings together many modes of production and forges trading links between communities independent of each other. Quite obviously, if different modes of production are functioning in close juxtaposition to each other and within the same society, then the same market serves different modes and provides the specific means for resource coordination between these modes. The major metropolitan areas of the ancient and medieval world can only be understood as centers of urban production carried on by craft producers, slave shops, or state enterprises and service renderers of all kinds, but also as great mercantile centers where merchant dealers in the different commodity areas serviced the needs of the motley collection of customers drawn from the various modes of production serviced by the city.

Our knowledge of market organization for the early Western world is fullest for the medieval period. Anglo-Saxon records in the eleventh century illuminated this market organization because of the detailed survey of the economy that it produced in the Domesday enumeration of towns; many had mints and each had a market catering to the needs of the adjacent villages, manors, mines, and fisheries.[2] Craft skills in metal working, leather and hides, dyes, and carpentry had already developed to the point where specialization of production with special implements and tools would be feasible only if the needs of a number of farming villages or manors were serviced. These skilled workmen with their ancillary train of merchants and government and church

---

[1]Marx, *Capital* III, 1864–1865, pages 325 f. These extracts from Marx's chapter "Historical Facts about Merchant Capital" more or less presuppose that merchant capital, creating linkages between different modes of production carried out in different countries "rests as a pure carrying trade upon the barbarism of the producing nations, between whom they acted as middlemen" (page 330). But this passes over the function of merchant capital in linking together in a trading complex different modes of production carried on within the same society or region, especially in the imperial nations such as the Assyrian, Persian, or Roman empires—the last of which Marx made specific reference to by saying that in its "later Republic days" merchant capital "developed to a higher degree than ever before in the ancient world" (page 332).

[2]The numismatic records of Anglo-Saxon England of the eleventh century disclose 86 identified mints, and the Domesday survey enumerates some 50 towns exclusive of the large urban communities such as London. See Mund, *Open Markets*, 1948, pages 53 f.; Benton, *Town Origins*, 1968, pages 56 f.

organizations, linked by roadway or waterway to other marketing centers, made up the core of the town. The manorial village itself harbored the commonly used smith, the baker, the miller, and the parish priest—but little else by way of a fully employed craftsman with specialized means apart from agricultural husbandry.[3]

Towns were, in Homan's words, "clearly set apart in the minds of men."[4] The Norman conquerors prohibited sale of cattle except in a market town. Neither market nor fair could be established except by authority of the king or of a great baron. The common law of the time required that a new market could not be established nearer than 6.67 miles from older markets. Intense market development in the early centuries of Norman rule is indicated by the fact that between 1200 and 1483, some 2099 charters for markets and 2315 charters for fairs were granted, mostly before 1300.[5] Hence we can accept the assurance of a recent authority on the period that by 1250 a "network of urban centers" developed, "most of them serving relatively small regions and occupied in commercial and industrial activities."[6]

The network of towns in early China in the Han period must have been denser in the closely settled parts of China partly because of the high grain yields per acre owing to generous use of irrigation and of rice culture in the Yangtze valley. The rich development of urban crafts in metal work, woodwork, textiles, and the building of a relatively dense network of roads and canals facilitated urban–rural trade. The high level of urban crafts in Han China is attested to not only by archaeological diggings but by the magisterial survey of science and technology in China by the great Sinologist, Joseph Needham.[7] Like medieval and most ancient towns, early Chinese towns were walled and moated for security; but unlike Western towns, they were dominated or ruled by officers of central government. As in Western towns, merchants and craftsmen, usually organized in guildlike associations, lived and worked in common quarters of the town.[8] Town markets were supplemented by temporary markets or periodic "fairs" in the rural countryside and on the pastoral frontiers.

[3]Homans, *English Villagers*, 1941, pages 285 ff.
[4]Homans, *English Villagers*, 1941, page 337.
[5]Mund, *Open Markets,* 1948, pages 53 ff.
[6]Postan, *Medieval Economy and Society*, 1942, page 240.
[7]Needham, *Science and Civilization in China*, 1954–1978, 5 vols. The work is still in process. The fields so far covered include civil engineering, nautics, construction including road and bridge building, hydraulic engineering, shipbuilding and propulsion, iron and steel metallurgy, gold and silver metallurgy, and chemistry. For recent archaeological findings, see Hsia Nai, *New Archaeological Finds in China*, 1972.
[8]Balazs, *Chinese Civilization and Bureaucracy*, 1932–1961, pages 67–78. (The chapter cited here, "Chinese Towns," was originally published in 1954.)

Market exchange by its nature tends to be inherently peaceful and voluntary.[9] Application of force tends to deter parties from participating in it. Merchant caravans or ships were usually armed for self-defense, and in new or strange territories, trading and piracy often alternated.[10] But extended, repeated trade requires a footing of peace and mutual goodwill. By coercive measures, trade can be taxed and sometimes requisitioned but only at the cost of dampening incentives to market participation or driving market exchange underground to escape official controls. These dampening effects are minimized if the purpose or effect of the coercive measures is clearly to regulate market conduct, prescribe suitable forms of market exchange, lay down requirements for market publicity, or limit access to the market to licensed traders or marketeers. The degree of dampening varies in each case with the particular set of coercive measures and the degree to which they obtain consensual support of market participants. Thus some forms of price control with prescribed prices may be quite acceptable if the controlled prices satisfy prevailing cost norms, are well within the range of prices previously experienced, and are at least moderately market-clearing—i.e., do not leave dealers or producers with excessive inventories of unsold goods or lead to inventory rundowns with many customers turned away unsatisfied. Other forms of price control may work out disastrously and dry up legal trade completely. Direct violence applied to markets by seizing available market supplies or requisitioning them for unreliable promises to pay at some future time dries up the market process or drives it underground, where its activities are concealed and furtive and its processes are correspondingly inefficient and expensive.

The form of market organization can vary widely in the way it brings together marketing activities. Concentrating market activity in a set spot or facility at given times and standardizing for weights and measures of traded items makes for efficient marketing, provided the facility is not too distant and that sufficient time is provided to clear markets. In Greek cities of the fourth and fifth centuries B.C., commerce was carried on in specially designated marketplaces (*agora*) where different classes of sellers were assigned space. In Rome, a similar special place for marketing (*forum*) was provided in the city center; the concourse of people engaged in marketing (*mercatus*)

---

[9]Thus we disagree with Max Weber, who defines as economic action "any peaceful exercise of an actor's control over resources which is in its main impulses oriented toward economic ends." See Weber, *Economy and Society*, 1921, vol. 1, page 63. Periodic whipping to speed up slave production is a nonpeaceful form of economic action. The quality of "peacefulness" applies far more to *market* behavior where, strangely enough, it is missing from Weber's general analysis of the market concept (pages 82–85).

[10]The Venetian trading caravan was nearly always guided or headed by armed merchant ships. Weber writes: "Commerce by sea is everywhere originally conjoined with piracy." See *General Economic History*, 1923, page 202.

formed the term from which our word "market" was itself derived. The right of instituting a market was a prerogative of the Senate, later of the Emperor, and the rule was that only one market could be organized in a contiguous market area.[11]

Nearly universal in medieval markets was the requirement that wares or services of the same general class should conform to common specifications and be stalled in close juxtaposition with like dealers to permit ready comparison and to facilitate shopping. All transactions needed to be witnessed. To assure adequate market traffic, it was common to regulate the time limits and days of open market. A would-be buyer was severely prohibited from seeking out suppliers so as to negotiate the purchase of goods or materials outside the market. The largest markets were, of course, the great fairs periodically held on regional, national, and international bases at set periods. For these there was the strictest emphasis on principles of fair market dealing: publicity of transactions, standardization of weights and measures, and witnessed dealings.

The one great category of commodities that could not conform to these exacting requirements was the marketing of labor service, which occupies the heart of the capitalist mode of production. Laboring service could not readily be bought and sold in markets organized to assure fair dealing and uniform pricing. Propertyless proletarians of low social status, pressed by current needs to assure livelihood, could not merchandise their services in organized markets.

Nearly everywhere the nature of the work to be performed is specified by employers, not by would-be employees, and employees cannot well appraise the quality of the job they have undertaken to fill until they have become settled in it. Employers rarely have brought to one marketplace in open array the detailed descriptions of the positions they seek to fill, providing adequate specifications of the conditions of work and the rates of pay. Certain professional associations in modern times seek to set up such a "job placement service" but on a restricted scale. Search and screen agencies have sprung up to scout and recruit executive talent. Only a relatively few individuals are willing or able to make an effective market survey especially on a national job-market basis for their skill or talent and acquire or invest in the information needed to protect or further their interests in market exchange.

When the capitalist mode of production was very undeveloped and confined chiefly to agriculture, only under conditions of special scarcity growing out of the depopulation and famine of the fourteenth century could market forces penetrate into the rural scene and give a perceptible lift to levels of earnings and to conditions of work. And precisely under those conditions,

[11]Mund, *Open Markets*, 1948, pages 5 ff.

of course, the state intervened as a class agency to restrain wage increases and to restrict labor mobility.[12] In the later phase of the capitalist mode of production, when industrial work had become predominant, the wage earner had increased mobility to search out job openings within his local residential area or at the farthest extent his urban community, but he suffered here from the "take-it-or-leave-it" philosophy of the capitalist system of hiring labor. Scanty reserves compelled many or most wage earners who had lost a job to accept almost any vacant job in their area of work to avoid missing too many payroll periods. Unforgettable, if slightly exaggerated, is Marx's pen-picture of the demeanor of the parties in this purchase and sale of labor power by free voluntary agreement, "a very Eden of the innate rights of man":

> He who before was the money-owner, now strides in front as capitalist; the possessor of labour power follows as his labourer. The one with an air of importance, smirking, intent on business; the other, timid and holding back, like one who is bringing his own hide to market and has nothing to expect but a tanning.[13]

The core of this relationship is illuminated by the legal language of dependence in which it was expressed up to modern times: that of "masters" and "servants."

This traditional dependent relationship of the wage earner in the capitalist mode of production has been revolutionized in our time by the rise of mass trade unionism, the development of public labor exchange agencies, and legislation that has standardized working conditions and hours of work and set minimum wages. Many Western economists blithely wave away the need for this protective legislation and organization and assume that without it wage laborers can efficiently exploit labor market opportunities.

Just as the conditions for marketing wage labor in the capitalist mode of production gave every advantage of resource, position, and knowledge to employers, so all the protections that earlier societies worked into the commodity market were destroyed by the capitalist entrepreneurs. The traditional medieval organized market was retained for most agricultural raw produce such as foodstuffs, fibers, animal hides, vegetable oils, and dairy products. But fabricated products even when produced from these raw materials were generally marketed outside the restrictions imposed by guild-market controls. In

---

[12]See the excoriating comments of Marx, *Capital* I, 1867, pages 272 f., 738 f. There is some question how effective this legislation was, and competent historians have declared that "In the end economic forces asserted themselves and the lords and employers found that the most effective way of retaining labour was to pay higher wages, just as the most effective way of retaining tenants was to lower rents and release servile obligation." See Postan, *Medieval Economy and Society*, 1972, page 170; Rogers, *Six Centuries of Work and Wages*, 1883, pages 251 f.

[13]Marx, *Capital* I, 1867, page 176.

the capitalist mode of production each producer developed his own marketing procedures and methods. Capitalist merchants went to the countryside to seek out the sources of raw materials and to purchase them outside the frame of a competitive market process. In the same way, the capitalist producer sought to sell his products with his own sales agents either to regional wholesale houses or through his own regional warehouses directly to retail dealers. Products and services could be marketed with the aid of deceptive advertising, labeling, or packaging. Some buyer protection was built into the marketing of products purchased by independent business firms either for resale or for their own utilization. Here product specifications would be shown to buyers and often producers arranged to show their wares at gigantic exhibitions where it would be easy for buyers to make product comparisons in the light of requested terms of sale.

In a few lines of production, such as the contract construction trades, it became customary for producers to submit "bids" for a defined construction project or to submit on request "proposals" with terms of dealing spelled out, thus facilitating competitive marketing. But most consumer goods and services in the capitalist mode of production were marketed under conditions which facilitated deception, discouraged competitive product comparisons, and hindered intelligent marketing action by consumers. In its latest phase, producer domination of consumer markets has been intensified by producer-purchased access to the printed page of newspaper and magazine—even more potently to the television tube, where buyers' favor can be enticed by sexual lures, entertainment, or dramatic exhibitions.

The worst abuses against the consuming public are screened out by government controls such as the Consumer Product Safety Commission in the United States, but these only work *ex post facto* by bringing legal action which at best imposes modest monetary fines. Direct access to the consumer home via the printed page and picture tube is often buttressed by elimination of the independent merchant, whose premises are taken over by producers and converted into a mere sales agency for the distribution of "branded products" advertised in a "national market." Some consumer protection over the years has been eked out by regulatory actions of the state to require disclosure of contents, a statement of true weight, and cautions where consumer health or safety may be involved.

This awful producer power in consumer markets is illustrated by the recent history of the automobile, which could only be certified to consumers for fuel efficiency after an energy crisis of unprecedented dimensions made it a matter of national security that consumers be able to choose their vehicles with knowledge of actual fuel-efficiency information. An economic theory of this producer domination of consumer markets by means of "sale outlays" or product manipulation was worked out by one of the seminal minds of

Western economics, Edward H. Chamberlin, whose *Theory of Monopolistic Competition* (1933) is one of the few original achievements of academic economics of the twentieth century in the United States. It is characteristic of the deterioration of the discipline of formal economics in the Western world that this work, as well as the literature and commentary which it inspired, has been virtually cut away from the intellectual inheritance of the younger generation of economists schooled in the apologetics of Milton Friedman and the Chicago School as a whole.[14]

The principles of market organization have been misapplied not only in the contemporary Western world but also in the Eastern world. Malformation in the East took two principal forms in the Soviet economy. Especially in the Stalinist period of mobilized industrialization, the incentives for industrial production were intensified by a scheme of price control that at prevailing prices left market inventories dangerously short of critical consumer goods—available only sporadically and then only by dint of frequent queuing, thereby increasing the marketing burdens of consumers.[15] An even more wasteful malformation of market principles is found in the so-called peasant market for products grown in the meager land allotments ranging in size from one-half to one acre allowed collective farmers for private cultivation. Peasant cultivators have been allowed to market their privately grown products without price control—but subject to the amazing restriction that individual producers or their collective farm organization must attend to their own marketing if they choose not to sell to state agencies. This prevents the emergence among peasant villagers of specialization in trading on a full-time basis. The consequence is an "erratic and unequal" distribution of privately produced food supplies and wasteful, inefficient carting of sacks and bags to market, even sometimes over long distances by air travel.[16]

---

[14]Chamberlin, "The Chicago School," 1957, pages 296–306.

[15]This was roundly condemned as erroneous doctrine by Khrushchev; namely, the notion that "under socialism the purchasing power of the population should always keep ahead of production as one of the motor forces of our development." That thesis, he said, justified the "shortage of articles of primary necessity and the perpetuation of the ration-card system and its necessity." See Khrushchev, *Report of the C.C. C.P.S.U.*, 1961, pages 138 f.

[16]A case was reported of "peasants with two sackloads of citrus fruits [who] find even an air journey from Transcaucasia to Moscow worthwhile . . . in the absence of a professional trader class and of adequate incentives for official trading initiatives." See Nove, *The Soviet Economy*, 1961, page 212. Soviet statistical reports indicate that around 1960 some 700,000 collective farmers sold their produce at 8000 collective-farm markets in cities, taking up 250 million man-days annually—an admittedly costly method of marketing. See Makhov and Frisch, *Society and Economic Relations*, 1966, page 135. State constriction of the peasant market fluctuates chiefly with the harvest, with a bad harvest inducing officials to relax restrictions on private marketing. The Soviet state is still committed to the objective—theoretically justified by Stalin in his last published writing—that the movement from socialism to communism and

PRICE FORMATION

Through all forms of market organization—whether monopolistic or competitive, well-organized or malformed—will run the category of *price*, which spells out the terms of market exchange. Modern Western economics conceives of price as the indispensable market regulator which, by shifting upwards or downwards, enables markets to be "cleared." But for most services and for many commodities in nearly all economic systems, price may be stereotyped, for the immediate purposes of market clearing—fixed either by tradition or usage at some "normal" acceptable level or set by the state. Under these circumstances, market demand and supply will be adjusted by altering the scope of accommodation of patronage, which is widened or narrowed to more or less desired classes by adjustment of inventories held by dealers or by postponement of demand to some future period by taking an "order" for future sale. Though this is anathema to Western economics—which rests on the principle that only changing price can clear markets—the stereotyping of price was the way in which even a very large commercial institution such as the Bank of England operated its credit discount activities. For three-quarters of a century, in its early decades, they were conducted at a fixed uniform rate—with only intermittent market-induced changes in discount rates in its later history.[17]

In the very well-organized markets—such as markets for public securities, for agricultural staples, and for local produce—prices will, of course, change nearly continuously, influenced by the changing currents of current demand and supply and to an even greater degree by changing expectations of future market conditions and of potential capital gains or losses. At a more sophis-

---

the corresponding conversion of collective-farm property to the level of public property would call for the curtailment and ultimate extinction of the private plot and farm market by "widening the sphere of operation of products-exchange." See this volume, ch. 4 page 175. The Chinese program of collectivization initiated on a nationwide scale in 1955 went on to abolish the private plot and private markets in the wild frenzy of the Big Leap Forward (August 1958–Spring 1959), but in 1961–1962 it was restored with the resumption of private markets, especially in pig supply. For the full story of the Chinese development, see Walker, *Planning in Chinese Agriculture*, 1965. That phase of "wild frenzy" is presented by Franz Schurman under the heading of "the militarization of the peasantry." See Schurman, *Ideology and Organizations*, 1966, pages 479–494. Some echoes of this are found in Mao's published addresses of the period, as yet available only in unofficial English collections. See St. Schram, *Chairman Mao Talks to the People*, 1974, especially "Speech at the Lushan Conference, 23 July 1959," pages 131–146.

[17]"For seventy-six years—from 1st May 1746 to 20 June 1822, the Bank discount rate stood unchanged at 5%. From 1822 to 1839 there were small fluctuations between 4 and 5%." See Keynes, *Treatise on Money*, 1930, vol. 1, pages 186 f. J. Schumpeter declared: "Rationing was not an emergency measure but part of the ordinary routine of banker's banks." See Schumpeter, *Business Cycles*, 1939, vol. 2, page 651.

ticated level, current price will be affected by what Keynes called "second-degree" expectations, namely forecasts of expectations of market price anticipated to be held by other market participants.[18] Such markets are probably inherently *speculative;* price movements in any direction will tend to be augmented by speculative anticipation and psychological contagion that feeds upon itself. This speculative tendency will, of course, be reinforced if the propensity to gamble, discouraged by conventional morality in other fields of economic life, can find here a major outlet.

In between markets with stereotyped price and markets with continually fluctuating market price are the vast bulk of markets dominated by price schedules usually laid down by producers or sellers—but in a few cases where powerful buyers deal with many sellers, by buyers—to regulate terms of exchange.[19] Here the principal task of the dealing parties is to negotiate ancillary terms of sale such as dates of delivery, quantities to be purchased, and trade-in allowances where they are customary. These administered prices will, of course, be changed from time to time chiefly to adjust to changing levels of costs of production or of the desired rate of profit that it is prudent to seek to impose. The profit rate will be higher in enterprises that have a monopoly position based either on legal privilege or on control of some essential supply. Profit markups will be lower in declining industries with excess capacity or in those fields where market demand is relatively weak because alternative means are readily available—including "do-it-yourself"—for satisfying the underlying want to which market demand is related.

It is a common policy of sellers to seek to administer price changes in an orderly way, to avoid frequent alterations of price, which are always upsetting to customers if they are upward and oftentimes if they are downward (why weren't prices reduced before?).[20] Thus alike in various modes of produc-

---

[18]Most of the expert market professionals, wrote Keynes, "are . . . largely concerned not with making superior long-term forecasts of the probable yield of an investment over its whole life, but with foreseeing changes in the conventional basis of valuation a short time ahead of the general public. . . . This battle of wits to anticipate the basis of conventional valuation a few months hence . . . does not even require gulls amongst the public to feed the maws of the professionals;—it can be played by professionals among themselves." This is the second-degree level of expectation. Keynes indicated that we "have reached the third degree when we devote our intelligences to anticipating what average opinion expects average opinion to be." See Keynes, *General Theory of Employment,* 1936, pages 154 ff.

[19]A leading historical example of the supersession of a competitive auction market by a monopsonistic buyer was the break with the petroleum market in the 1880s by the Standard Oil combination, which began the practice followed ever since of "posting" the purchase prices that the pipelines and refineries of the combination would pay. Such "posted" prices apply to many agricultural materials purchased by monopsonistic processors such as sugar refineries, dairies, and canneries.

[20]This analysis of industrial pricing was developed by this author in terms of the theory of monopolistic competition in an earlier paper. See Gottlieb, "Value and Price," 1959, pages 22–38.

tion—in the Soviet economy, among cooperatives, direct commodity producers, public utilities, and government producers, in the capitalist and the corporate modes—price schedules will be set to cover expected costs of production along with a customary profit markup that experience has indicated to be sustainable.

Such slow-changing and semi-rigid price levels may be market-clearing—i.e., at the prevailing price there are no unsatisfied would-be buyers or sellers—but this condition obtains only by sheer happenstance. Usually sellers would like to produce and sell more at the prevailing market price, and often buyers must wait their turn for delayed satisfaction. Under stable conditions changes in market inventories can accommodate small shifts in demand so that markets clear by changing the level of inventories held. For extended periods, sellers may typically be very unhappy with the quantities they are producing and selling at the prevailing price but they do not seek to "clear the market" by reducing their price schedule. This would disrupt orderly marketing procedures, and it would startle competitiors who, of course, would tend to follow suit to the common disadvantage of sellers. Of course, at a certain point of excess capacity sufficiently prolonged, market discipline will break down just as in periods of supply shortage some sellers will be tempted to raise profit markups and take advantage of market bonanza. In the capitalist mode of production, these price breakdowns are more likely to occur than in the matured corporate mode of production, where price schedules almost take on the status of a government tariff or tax schedule.

This whole process of administered pricing for industrial products has developed since the economic reforms of the mid 1960s along very similar lines in the Soviet economy. Here the agencies responsible for marketing industrial output characteristically set prices by norms which are close to their Western counterparts. Prices are designed to cover anticipated costs of production at anticipated rates of capacity usage, the desired allowable net income for the enterprise (net profit markup) and net income of the state in the form of the so-called turnover tax.[21] In practical procedure, an industrial price is set at a level that will allow the enterprise to recoup its expected (planned) costs of unit production and of procurement of needed supplies and materials, sales taxes, what amounts to a corporate income tax, and a rate of profit believed appropriate in the light of the need to stimulate the production of the par-

---

[21]"Costs, the net income of the enterprise, and part of the centralized net income of the State in the form of the so-called turnover tax, all form part of the price of industrial output." Institute of Economics, *Political Economy*, 1954, page 631. As formulated by Alex Nove after the 1965–1967 reforms, industrial prices were set to cover "the average cost of production of all enterprises producing the commodity in question plus a profit margin," formerly expressed as a markup over cost but now computed as a charge on capital assets used. See Nove, *Soviet Economy*, page 146.

ticular product or to regulate the demand.[22] Market-clearing achieved by price variation is implemented through variation in the retail sales turnover tax.[23] Though in earlier years, Soviet prices were centrally set and could not be altered except at high levels of the All-Union government, increased authority is now given (since the reforms of 1965–1966) for ministries and enterprises to set prices conforming to price-control standards. In earlier decades, there were many anomalies in Soviet pricing.[24] Whole categories of industrial products, such as iron ore, were priced at a level covering only 75% of costs of production. Failure to take capital charges into account tended to underprice all capital-intensive methods of production so that hydro-projects were greatly favored to produce electricity over thermal stations using mined coal.[25]

Whether distorted or not, prices in a given economy will tend to influence each other and incentives to produce or purchase. Evaluation of the linkages between prices makes up the principal work of modern economics—which is applicable to all economies where market relations to any degree are found.

RATIONING

Rationing is a stereotyped method of commodity distribution that is pinned primarily to allotment by coupons or other entitlement which qualifies a recipient—a person, a household, or collectivity—to a given quantity of the rationed item. The allotment may be compulsory, as with public schooling available to children required to attend a certified school for certain periods of time. More usually, the allotment is voluntary and must be applied for. Historically, rationing on a community or nationwide basis is usually reserved for emergencies caused by natural or manmade disaster resulting in unusual shortage and the need to sustain community morale by establishing public control over holding and use of certain essential commodities. But other forms of rationing on a more restricted scale are the normal method for the allocation of some resources and products within mass organizations—such as centralized churches, armies, universities, prisons, and welfare institutions.

Rationing is also a common method of commodity distribution among branches of enterprises in the Western world and among industrial enterprises

[22]Even before the 1965–1967 reforms, pricing norms included the need to stimulate production of particular goods "and to regulate the demand for them." Institute of Economics, *Political Economy*, 1954, page 591.

[23]Nove, *Soviet Economy*, 1961, pages 150 ff.

[24]Perhaps the highpoint of these anomalies was the proposal for setting prices for cotton, baked bread, and grain at an identical per-ton price. See Stalin, *Economic Problems of Socialism*, 1952, 19 ff.

[25]Nove, *Soviet Economy*, 1961, pages 150 ff.

of the Soviet economy for many goods and services. Within a solidary or collegial institution, a rationed allotment is received without any passage of money or of formal entitlement. Elsewhere, a rationed allotment usually requires for its completion payment in the current money. During World Wars I and II, goods in critical shortage in the combatant countries that were rationed included basic foodstuffs, fuel, and even use of housing in areas where there was extensive destruction. Despite widespread experience with rationing as a mode of commodity distribution, it now touches chords of extreme ideological sensitivity in the American scene, where any suggestion of rationing arouses categorical and unqualified antagonism.

The earliest peacetime governmental rationing scheme historically recorded is probably food distribution established in the late years of the Roman Republic and for the later imperial years at Constantinople and in limited periods at a few other major urban areas. At Rome, a monthly dole of corn to citizens, established in 58 B.C., continued through some of the sixth century A.D. The dole was designed to win the favor of the Roman street mob, which still retained a semblance of political authority. The dole was limited by Augustus to 220,000 plebeian recipients whose ration tickets by the third century A.D. had become "hereditable and saleable," with the names of authorized recipients engraved on a bronze tablet. The corn ration was then turned into a bread ration by adding baking services. This was later supplemented by a monthly dole of oil and pork during five months of the year. It was once suggested to add a wine ration but this was deterred with the ironic remark, "It only remains to give them fowls and geese." The whole system involved collection of grain in kind from the taxed grain-surplus provinces, provision for shipment by sea and barging to Rome itself, milling of the grain and distribution to 274 bakeries.[26] This initial experience with rationing illustrates the tendency of rationing to become extended and intrenched, like rent control in New York City, where it still lingers from its initial installation in World War II.

Omitting rationing of foodstuffs and water by besieged city populations during the medieval years early and late, and a short episode of requisitioning and rationing during the French Revolution, the next major use of rationing in later centuries beyond a strictly local scene is found in wartime industrial provisionment during the two World Wars of the twentieth century. European countries were forced by critical shortages to schemes of allocation of industrial materials to restricted users in accordance with classified priorities and to widespread rationing among consumers of fuel, foodstuffs, and other essential civilian supplies. For America, comprehensive rationing and alloca-

---

[26]These details are extracted from the recital of the history of public feeding in the Roman Empire by A. H. M. Jones, *Later Roman Empire*, 1966, vol. 1, pages 695–705.

tion had to await the development of the war economy during World War II. At the industrial level, official controls concentrated on curtailing civilian production by limitation or prohibition orders, giving priority to new facility construction related to the war effort, and controlled material allocation to industrial users of three critical materials: copper, aluminum, and steel. "All industrial consumers of basic metals . . . whose consumption of such metals exceeded $5,000 during any quarter, had to apply . . . for all preference ratings covering their requirements for those metals."[27] The need for controlled allocation was sparked by the tremendous expansion in military orders for tanks, aircraft, warships, and transport vessels—for war material of all kinds for a massive military force on air, on land, and on water. These orders called for both conversion of existing civilian facilities and construction on a vast scale of new facilities. The market could not resolve the problems of priorities, time-jams, and the understandable scramble to hoard scarce materials needed for the future. Hence the development of an intricate industrial–military planning and programming effort to maximize war production.[28]

On the consumer side, there was a similar development of rationing for essential consumer products in short supply to hold down mushrooming prices and profiteering and to make sure that affluent people, who could afford higher prices, would not squeeze wage earners and low-income people out of the market for scarce essential consumer goods. The Congress had given the President blanket authority to allocate or ration whenever a "shortage" in the supply of some essential product would threaten the public interest or the national defense effort.[29] Tires were the first civilian product to go into

---

[27]James W. Fesler, War Production Board Historian, who headed up a large staff who collaborated in the report, Fesler *et al. Industrial Mobilization for War. History of the War Production Board and Predecessor Agencies, 1940–1945*, vol. 1, of a set of three volumes dealing with "program and administration," 1947, page 463. The controlled material plan referred to in the text was modified and partially extended to other materials, but in various forms it remained the core program of wartime industrial allocation.

[28]The need for an industrial war-mobilization program was indicated when President Roosevelt on May 16, 1940, following the British defeat in Norway, declared in a message to Congress that he would like to see this country able to turn out 50,000 warplanes annually; he was told by aircraft manufacturers that it would take 5 years to achieve that capability. See Fesler *et al., Industrial Mobilization for War*, 1947, page 40. Once America formally entered the war with the Pearl Harbor attack, which electrified the nation, the President formulated a $50 billion production target for 1942 (for planes, ships, tanks, and guns) which "made men gasp" and "even to experts (seems) . . . unattainable." (page 201). With intense efforts war production in 1942 approached the Roosevelt target, $46.6 billion (page 205). The "must" program of the President for 1943 included 82,000 combat aircraft and 25,000 training aircraft. In 1939 only 1.5% of GNP was for military purposes. The figure rose to 2.8% in 1940, 9% in 1941, 31% in 1942, and in the last quarter of that year it was 40% (page 533).

[29]Redford, *Field Administration of Wartime Rationing*, 1947, page 1.

rationing in January 1942, automobiles were added the next month, gasoline in the Eastern seaboard states in May 1942, and by the end of the year the list included fuel oil and kerosene, stoves, sugar, coffee, typewriters, and heavy rubber footwear. In the next year were added solid fuels (Pacific Northwest only), processed foods, meats, fats, canned fish, cheese, canned milk, and shoes.[30]

The rationing agencies were generally 5600 local boards of unpaid community notables with diverse backgrounds giving voluntary service to what was commonly felt to be the war effort. For some products, they were assigned "quotas" and under standing rules defining eligibility and need, the boards issued purchase permits. For foods and gasoline, a uniform ration card was generally issued to households and vehicle operators either through the public school or local government network. Commercial banks were generally utilized to bank ration currency. Local boards handled special cases, issued supplementary allotments to specified classes of users and took care of emergency needs.[31] An elaborate system of verification of the circulation of "rationing" currency was instituted to cope with the menace of stolen or counterfeit coupons. Even with good will and the utmost loyalty, there was bound to be a substantial amount of noncompliance either through coupon "overissue" at the local board level or through the efforts of organized crime or abuse by business firms granted substantial discretion in the administration of rationing. It is indicated, however, that noncompliance and abuse were held within moderate bounds and that the consumption of rationed items was generally by authorized persons.[32]

Though rationing and allocation superseded the market as an agency for wartime product exchange and distribution, it was allowed to do so only because of the general consensus of national emergency and because the widespread conscription of manpower for field service in the war effort made it almost indecent for civilians at home to shirk the minor bit of cooperation asked of them. Because conventional economic theory with its dedication to market process was comatose, economic leadership in government passed into the hands of nonconformist economists who a generation later would find scant public hearing for their views.[33]

With the end of active hostilities in 1945, allocations, rationing, and price

[30]Redford, *Field Administration of Wartime Rationing*, 1947, page 2.

[31]Redford, *Field Administration of Wartime Rationing*, 1947, page 23 ff., 85 ff., 97 ff.

[32]Thus in the sensitive field of gasoline rationing there was a significant enforcement effort to revoke rations where there was evidence of illicit use of a supposed business vehicle for pleasure or trips to resort areas. In 1944 there were 34,400 local board revocations and 3258 district revocations. See Redford, *Field Administration of Wartime Rationing*, 1947, page 116.

[33]Thus, J. K. Galbraith was chief executive of OPA (price control and rationing) during most of the war; his predecessor was Leon Henderson. In Galbraith's memoirs, two chapters tell the story of wartime price control, rationing, and associated programs. See Galbraith, *A Life in Our Times*, 1981, chs. 8 and 9.

control were soon relinquished. Rationing remained through 1947 only for sugar, and price control affected only housing rentals through to the 1950s. Though a war economy of sorts was reestablished during the Korean War period, it was on a less ambitious scale; and both allocations and rationing were forsworn in the Vietnam effort. For minor or "brush-fire" wars, a mobilized war economy was not needed. Major conflicts would not last long enough for a mobilized economy to be instituted. Hence in the Western world and especially in the United States, the use of rationing and allocation methods of economic control is no longer on the agenda of economic policymakers. Economists consider these methods unsound and destructive, and public opinion—dominated by the affluent—condemns measures that deprive money of its power to purchase when this power is most needed, in periods of shortage.

The latter-day American attitude toward rationing (and all forms of price control except wage controls) is illustrated by the curious form of a rationing plan presented to the U.S. Congress in March 1979. Though this plan was not approved by the Congress, the President was authorized to submit a plan somewhat revised, subject to certain restrictions, and this plan obtained congressional approval.[34]

Consider first the severe degree of shortage required for the rationing plan to come into effect. This was described in general terms as a "severe gasoline shortfall [that] would justify the implementation of rationing," illustrated in the President's plan as a 15% shortfall in petroleum availabilities associated with a 20% shortfall in gasoline availabilities because of a shift of refining toward more essential distillates—such as jet and diesel fuels.[35] A 20% shortfall was finally set by the President as a requirement for Presidential imposition of rationing—subject, however, to a veto by either house of Congress.[36]

---

[34]*Standby Rationing Plan*, 1979. The plan was approved by the Senate, 58–39, on May 9, 1979 (*Congressional Record*, S. 5579) but was defeated by the House (*Congressional Record*, H. 3018), 246–159 after extended debate (*Congressional Record*, H. 2971–3018) on May 10, 1979. A revised plan was accepted by the Senate but barely won out by a vote of 207–205 in the House of Representatives.

[35]*Standby Rationing Plan*, 1979, pages 18 ff., 214 ff.

[36]In the Emergency Energy Conservation Act of 1979, which set forth the will of Congress regarding the preparation of a new rationing plan, the House voted for a straight 20% shortfall as the trigger for rationing, but the Senate believed that a lesser shortfall could trigger an emergency. The compromise embodied in the legislation directed that with a shortfall of 20% or more, the President would have authority to impose rationing, but that with a lesser shortfall, the imposition would require support by a joint resolution. See *Congressional Record*, S. 14710. As Senator Domenici noted, that keeps the Congress "in the chain of decision-making." (See *Congressional Record*, S. 14713.) The presidential standby plan submitted to Congress on June 20, 1980—with a veto right by either House—became, absent a congressional veto, law by July 30, 1980; it stipulated a 20% shortfall as the precondition for rationing. See *Oil & Gas Journal*, June 23, 1980.

Since the degree of gasoline shortfall experienced in the 1973–1974 Arab embargo episode is now estimated at 14%, it is indicated that in American emergency planning, a shortfall of that degree of severity should not result in rationing.[37]

But even a shortage of catastrophic dimensions was thought to warrant only a pseudo-rationing plan which harbored within it a significant degree of rationing by price rather than by need. As modified by congressional intervention after initial presentation to Congress, the plan called for withholding of 5% of the available supply for need rationing administered by states through local ration boards, a 2% national reserve to be administered nationally, and special allotments for priority services including mass transit, farms, businesses, and government agencies using significant amounts of off-highway gasoline. The remaining supplies of gasoline were to be allocated equally to vehicle owners depending upon weight and vehicle class, with allotments graded to average statewide vehicle fuel consumption.[38] Commercial trucks and business vehicles would be treated the same as passenger vehicles in rural and urban areas alike except that scooters and motorcycles would receive only 10 and 20% of a passenger car allotment while trucks between 10,000 and 20,000 pounds would receive an allotment of 2.2 times a passenger vehicle and a truck over 33,000 pounds, 7.0 times a passenger vehicle.[39] It was recognized that millions of vehicle owners would receive ration allotments in excess of their normal driving needs, while millions of other vehicle owners—including most business and trucking firms—would be caught severely short by the allotments.

To equilibrate the market, it was proposed to legalize and facilitate the sale of ration coupons through a specially organized "white market." Low-income households, especially where mass transit was available in the larger cities, would be tempted by high white-market prices to sell their ration coupons. Business firms and high-income households for whom the expense was a negligible factor would appear on the "white market" as buyers. Allotments would be received in the form of a ration check that could be cashed for actual coupons in a "ration bank" which would either be a local financial

---

[37]*Standby Rationing Plan*, 1979, pages 473, 1–8 ff.

[38]The Administration plan originally provided for a ration allotment set at a uniform national level per passenger vehicle. After congressional objections were voiced from states with higher-than-average fuel consumption records per vehicle, the plan was modified to vary the allotment by states according to recorded differentials in average vehicle fuel consumption. This principle was embodied in the formal requirements for a ration plan set forth on October 17, 1979.

[39]The allotment indices worked out in the *Standby Rationing Plan*, (page 35) were illustrative only and were to be prepared from the most up-to-date statistics of average gasoline consumption by type and weight of vehicle.

institution, supermarket, or other appropriate market center. It was projected that the "white-market price" for gasoline would rise over twice the February 1979 prevailing price (75¢ per gal.) to $1.97 per gallon. At the February 1979 price level, the estimated net flow of income from sale of coupon rights was projected at $12.4 billion.[40] The price level would rise because business firms would set their profit markups on a higher base unit cost now inflated by "white-market" gasoline purchases. About one-fifth of American households which do not own vehicles, about a third of all tenant households, would of course bear the burdens of this rationing scheme as the general price level would rise, minimally estimated at .9%.[41] This scheme of "rationing" has many of the characteristics of an "excise tax" on gasoline with a consumer rebate of the proceeds, with an open black market for the affluent to satisfy their fuel needs.[42] This was in 1979–1980 the formal American rationing plan for gasoline to deal with a catastrophic shortage.[43]

Rationing and allocation are, of course, fully at home in the socialist economies following the lead of the Soviet Union. There the method of rationing and allocation became institutionalized in the mobilized planning of the 1930s, when industrial prices were not market-clearing and when plan design was crude. Hence, distribution of industrial products needed to be controlled as in the Western war economies. The massive growth of urban population and the concurrent decline in the output of most consumer goods made it essential to ration and allocate nearly all essential civilian goods: housing, foodstuffs, and other products. In the late 1950s and 1960s, when more refined schemes of pricing, cost accounting, and planning were developed in the Eastern world, it became possible to widen the discretion of enterprise managers to buy material and equipment without allotment in conformance to plan norms by contractual arrangements with customer enterprises. Fewer product targets were spelled out in the annual and five-year plans and more room was left for enterprises and trusts to work out customer relations and product modifications to meet the needs of their contracting partners. Since these enterprise networks must be monitored and are subject to audit and review procedures, much scope for centralized commodity allocation remains— though a wider sphere for enterprise initiative has been achieved.[44]

[40]*Standby Rationing Plan*, 1979, pages 252, 428.

[41]*U.S. Statistical Abstract*, 1978, page 656; *Standby Rationing Plan*, 1979, pages 236, 246.

[42]"There are striking similarities between the effects of an excise tax on gasoline and gasoline rationing with a white market." See *Standby Rationing Plan*, 1979, pages 223.

[43]Congress has not yet acted by appropriating funds for implementation of the plan. See *Congressional Record*, 1980, S. 9549. Of course any rationing fallback plan was anathema to the Reagan administration and the program was dropped.

[44]See Novosti Press Agency Publishers, *Soviet Economic Reform*, 1966; Liberman, *Economic Methods*, 1970; Schroeder, "Recent Developments," 1973, pages 2–11; Nove, *Soviet Economy*, 1961, chs. 9 and 10.

ECONOMIC PLANNING

Planning is the third major method of the coordination of resources and activities both within decision-making economic units and between the modes. This method works out a pattern of coordination of resource use or allocation *over time,* for a future period more or less extended. This method calls for a clear delineation of objectives or goals, a listing of resources to be administered over the future period, and a program of activities in orderly sequence designed to carry out the ascertained objectives. Conceived of in this way, planning is a basic characteristic of human labor geared to serving future needs without direct regard to present drives and immediate impulses. A spider, Marx wrote, "conducts all operations that resemble those of a weaver and a bee puts to shame many an architect in the construction of her cells. But what distinguishes the worst architect from the best of bees is this, that the architect raises his structure in imagination before he erects it in reality."[45] Economic planning is thus an essential feature of orderly use of economic resources that cannot or should not be consumed or utilized as soon as they are made available. Some goods must be laid aside for future use or retained in a contingency reserve; some must be utilized by investment in structure or equipment or facility to enable future production or to provide means of production for an increasing labor force. The more durable and massive the structure or facility, the greater will be the emphasis on designing not merely for *present* needs but for anticipated future requirements—which, of course, may be affected, to some degree, by the very project under design. In the case of many public works, it is costly to add extensions or supplements. Research into future requirements—itself a formidable undertaking— seeks to strike a balance between overbuilding, which results in wasted capacity, or underbuilding, which calls for frequent tearing up and patchwork repairs.

The need for forward planning is greater wherever inputs or incomes are not steadily flowing at a constant rate but appear intermittently or at extended intervals (as on most farms), or are subject to unpredictable variations due to changes in weather or to natural or man-made disasters. Governments especially must plan for coherent financial administration of their expenditures over a forthcoming period in the light of expected needs and anticipated revenues, if the projects or fund uses that capture attention earliest are not to get disproportionate access to resources or make borrowing necessary.

[45] Marx, *Capital* I, 1867, page 178. It is not just the imagination, for as C. R. Noyes pointed out, the central mechanisms for generating behavior in relation to *present* and *future* wants are quite different both in neural and behavioral terms. See Noyes, *Economic Man,* 1948, vol. 1, chs. 2–6.

Adam Smith argued cogently that with the rise in taste for "luxury" and "pageantry" and erecting "splendid public buildings" and "public ornaments"—as well as the still greater pressure for expenditure on standing armies, navies, and fortifications—expenditures usually "become equal" to "ordinary revenues" and will "frequently exceed it" as much in the "sober senate house of a little republic as in the dissipated court of the greatest king" or as we would now say, Superpower.[46] Hence in the more advanced countries the principle of a *budget*—which is merely a plan for orderly expenditure of the revenues from existing or projected taxes expected to be available for a forthcoming period—must have been institutionalized in some form in the long centuries of public finance administration.

Alexander Hamilton, in composing the *Federalist*, could presuppose as common knowledge that "nations in general . . . usually commit the administration of their finances to single men or to boards . . . who digest and prepare . . . the plans of taxation which are afterwards passed into laws. . . ."[47] That was in fact the explicit British arrangement formalized in 1612 by which a board headed by the first Lord of the Treasury—who later became the formal Prime Minister of the cabinet—exercised financial authority over all ordinary departments of government and conducted financial planning. A single fund was later set up for receiving and recording all revenues and expenditures. A complete statement of finances was published at the beginning of the year since 1802 and since 1822 was submitted formally to Parliament.[48] Until after the French Revolution, parliamentary assemblies in Europe were not regularly convened nor expected to enact or approve government budgets, but annual statements of revenue and expenditure were prepared by chancellories and evaluated in some fashion by the highest levels of government.[49] The American arrangements were at the outset looser but from 1802 onwards the Secretary of Treasury submitted to the Congress an annual report on finances and a table of "estimates," thus serving as an incipient budgetmaker at the executive level.[50] At the Congressional level budget responsibilities were shared between the Ways and Means and Appropria-

[46]Adam Smith, *Wealth of Nations*, 1776, page 861.

[47]Hamilton, Madison, and Jay, *The Federalist*, 1787–1788, page 171.

[48]J. Burkhead, *Government Budgeting*, 1966, pages 2 ff; *Encyclopedia of Social Sciences*, vol. 3, pages 38 ff, vol. 6, pages 235 ff. Our very term for "budget" derived from an old English word *bougette*—the sack or pouch from which the chancellor of the exchequer extracted his papers in presenting to Parliament the government's financial program for an ensuing year.

[49]Thus in Austria annual statements of revenue were formally prepared within the executive establishment since 1766 and during most of the eighteenth century in Prussia and the larger German states. A French budget bill was only submitted for parliamentary consideration after 1815. Burkhead, *Government Budgeting*, 1966, pages 7 f, 9 ff.; *Encyclopedia of Social Sciences*, 1930–1934, vol. 6, pages 239 f.

[50]Ford, "Budget Making," 1915, pages 4 f.

tions Committees of the House of Representatives.[51] The increasing scale of federal expenditure which mushroomed during World War I called for formal institution of a budget process. In 1921, the Bureau of the Budget was established under the President to prepare and submit to the Congress an annual budget well in advance of the fiscal year.[52] Municipal and local budgets were generally prepared by a formal process somewhat earlier because of the primary dependence for revenue upon the property tax, which is set for collection at a definite sum once yearly soon after a fresh assessment of property has been made available. That sum became fixed by a process of estimating expenditure requirements for the fiscal year ahead. Constitutions generally limited borrowing to meet special capital needs or, as in Wisconsin, prohibited public debt at the state level in excess of $100,000, and specifically required the legislature to provide an annual tax "sufficient to defray the estimated expenses of the state for each year."[53] Hence for over a century planning for a forward period comprehending all current activities and services of government including public works has been a standard article of governmental finance at the state and local level.[54]

So likewise has planning been an accepted staff feature of business administration grown in importance as business firms have grown larger and operate in a wide range of settings. One principal focus of this business-planning function is short-term planning for procurement, production, and funding to maintain inventory targets and to meet customer needs, either forecast or booked. It was around this function that Keynes devoted one of his most suggestive chapters in the *General Theory,* dealing with what he termed "short-term expectation."[55] These expectations would cover "cost of output on various possible scales" and the "sales-proceeds of this output."[56] To this should be added the optimal range of inventory holdings that would be augmented by current output or depleted by continued utilization of raw materials. Keynes emphasized that the "actually realized results of production and sales of output will only be relevant to employment insofar as they cause a modification of subsequent expectations." He correctly pointed out that a change

[51]Burkhead, *Government Budgeting,* 1966, pages 11 ff.

[52]Burkhead, *Government Budgeting,* 1966, pages 25 ff.

[53]*Wisconsin Constitution,* art 8, Finance, secs. 5, 6.

[54]The so-called "budgetary reform movement"—which called for reorganization of the budgeting process in state and local governments during the early years of this century—did not seek to institute the process of budgeting but only to centralize responsibility for preparing the budget for all executive branches of government in the chief executive and giving to this executive proper staff services assigned to this function. See Burkhead, *Government Budgeting,* 1966, pages 21 ff., and various writings of W. F. Willoughby (cited in Burkhead's bibliography, page 30).

[55]Keynes, *General Theory of Employment,* 1936, ch. 5.

[56]Keynes, *General Theory of Employment,* 1936, page 47.

in expectations or in the character of short-term business planning would only produce its "full effect" on employment "over a considerable period" so that *processes* of change in the business situation may have considerable complexity.[57] This was the starting premise for Metzler's schema of inventory-output fluctuation initially constructed using an accelerator-multiplier model; presented in a pair of brilliant articles published in the 1940s, it was elaborated later into a formal theory of short-term or inventory cycles.[58] Apart from cyclical aspects, an extensive business literature covers the field of business short-term planning.[59]

A second focus of business planning involves long-term projection—which, though it touches all aspects of business operations, comes to a focus in the capital budget. As a formal document the capital budget is a relatively new concept in business administration. But it was a basic feature of any well-managed accumulating capitalist industrial undertaking of the late nineteenth century or early twentieth century. Industrial expansion at a time when industrial technology is being revolutionized is hardly the simple, routine, or transparent business that Kenneth Galbraith portrays.[60] The Galbraith portrayal is least applicable to the construction of a new industrial undertaking that calls for initial approval by entrepreneurial investors of the plan for the capital project, the drawing up of specifications for letting out bids and purchase contracts, and the long period of gestation while the plant is being erected and its equipment assembled. Firms that have integrated the process of production and assume responsibility for production and transportation of essential materials, fabrication of component parts, maintenance of wholesale depots, and retail distribution will thus, at any time, have a variety of in-

[57]Keynes, *General Theory of Employment*, 1936, pages 48 ff.

[58]Metzler, "Nature and Stability," 1941, pages 113–129; "Length of Inventory Cycles," 1947, pages 1–15. Metzler's work was enriched by a series of studies collected together and published by the U.S. Congress Joint Economic Committee, *Inventory Fluctuations and Economic Stabilization*, 1961–1962. See also the more empirically oriented contributions by staff members of the National Bureau of Economic Research: Abramovitz, *Inventories and Business Cycles*, 1950; Mack, *Information, Expectations and Inventory Fluctuation*, 1967; Zarnoviz, *Orders, Production and Investment*, 1973.

[59]Koontz and O'Donnell, *Principles of Management*, 1955, pages 506–541.

[60]Galbraith, *New Industrial State*, 1967, ch. 2; "The Imperatives of Technology" draws the distinction between processes of manufacture of the first Ford car in 1903 and the development of the Mustang in 1964. "In the early days of Ford, the future was very near at hand. Only days elapsed between the commitment of machinery and materials to production and their appearance as a car. . . . If the car did not meet the approval of the customers, it could quickly be changed" (16). But in its first full year of operation, 1904, the Ford Motor Co. produced and sold about 1000 vehicles; only 22,830 vehicles were manufactured by the entire industry. The Ford plant in that year was a pilot plant. See Federal Trade Commission, *Report on Motor Vehicle Industry*, 1940, pages 7 f., 625 f. Within a few years a highly specialized machine technology was developed in the Ford Motor plant.

vestment projects in process with different time rhythms. This itself suggests the need for a plan for an extended forward period providing both for uses of funds and for sources of funds for capital outlay purposes including existing reserves, forthcoming depreciation charges, and outside finance drawn either from new bank borrowing or from issuance of new securities in the capital market. A common period for capital budgeting is now 5 years but plans for a longer term have been developed for public utilities which have vested service rights for given territories.

Investment analysis carried on within the firm had rarely been surveyed by professional economists prior to the research carried out by Ruth P. Mack in the 1930s. At that time, she conducted a survey of investment behavior during 1934–1938 of some 32 companies, out of a total sample of 54 concerns whose financial returns were public documents.[61] She found that "for the most part the very large companies" and a "considerable number of those not so large" used "annual capital expenditure budgets" assuring "periodic and comprehensive review." She found however a considerable range of variation for individual projects when finally authorized and for their initial budgeting.[62] Methods of profitability calculation were still of the relatively primitive "years payout" variety that greatly biases choice for quick-earning forms of investment and discourages acquisition of assets with extended trial or learning periods.[63]

By 1951, when Joel Dean published his monograph *Capital Budgeting*, the level of sophistication found in profitability calculations had been raised.[64] He found long-range development plans that include capital expenditure "not uncommon" but that 5-year plans were very tentative beyond the first 2 years, which Dean found embodied the working limit for serious capital budgeting.[65] Payout periods were still the "criterion commonly used . . . in appraising investment opportunities," though more advanced firms used more refined methods of profit calculation. By the late 1970s, payout calculations were largely superseded by formal profitability measures that allow for earning over the full life of the project and discount for delay. Budgetary constraints within the firm have grown more stringent, while national economic models that on various assumptions project gross national or industrial output permit firms to pin their profitability calculations to these projected aggregates. These projections, of course, do not pinpoint the place of the firm within the industry or the relative role of different classes of output in broad industrial aggregates. Nor can these projections allow for satisfaction of do-

---

[61]Mack, *Flow of Business Funds*, 1941, pages 26 ff.
[62]Mack, *Flow of Business Funds*, 1941, pages 241 ff.
[63]Mack, *Flow of Business Funds*, 1941, pages 255 ff.
[64]Dean, *Capital Budgeting*, 1951.
[65]Dean, *Capital Budgeting*, 1951, pages 556 ff., 565 f, 569 f.

mestic demand by increased foreign imports. The character and scope of these investment projections carried out by different industrial firms is usually kept highly secret except in industries like petroleum, transportation, and refining, where cartelization procedures and "joint ventures" in field development and pipelines permit widespread pooling among elite firms of investment plans.

SOCIALIST ECONOMIC PLANNING

Socialist economic planning carries forward and combines the process of both short-term and long-term business planning by firms and of annual budget making by governmental bodies. As developed in the Soviet economy, socialist economic planning was based upon nationalization of industry, banking, and foreign trade as well as upon the express goal of accelerating the industrialization of the Soviet Union to overtake and surpass the level of production achieved in the non-Soviet world. Nationalization was not merely nominal but was made effective in a twofold sense. Secrecy of both short- and long-term planning within the enterprise was abolished, and a vast forward surge of information flow from enterprises and regional and local bodies to the national center was instituted to permit the review and coordination of local planning. Secondly, there was a nationalization of investable funds wherever they arose within the economic system: as surpluses from state budgets, as depreciation charges retained for use within the producing organization, as credit creation by banks and savings collected by financial institutions from individuals, and finally as profits of enterprise. These funds were nationalized in the sense that utilization of them was projected in an economic plan produced by the highest political authority, pinpointing the use of these investable funds: for new industrial construction and equipment, research and geological prospecting, town construction, and agricultural or other investment purposes. A minor fraction of these funds was authorized for use within the organization, where they were made available for purposes of small-scale investment, repair, or renovation; but the bulk of the funds were reserved for centralized use to finance accumulation within the economy according to a comprehensive plan.[66]

[66]"Non-centralized investments are those made by state enterprises and organizations out of their production development, social and cultural and housing funds, or by means of bank loans and certain special-purpose loans." Berri, *Planning a Socialist Economy*, 1973, vol. 1, page 231. Some of the non-centralized investment is made up of minor repairs (which are not controlled by the central plan); and the line may be drawn by magnitude since investment projects with an estimated cost over 2.5 million rubles must be approved by Ministries or regional agencies. See Berri, *Planning a Socialist Economy*, 1973, pages 242 f. The basic statute of the Socialist Industrial Enterprise in 1965 required that a part of the profits earned by an

Investible funds are only a pecuniary magnitude. If they are to result in accumulation, they must have a real economic basis by way of (a) specialized facilities for planning and designing new investment, (b) a construction and building materials industry and trained labor force able to carry out construction projects, and (c) a machinery-producing industry capable of building the machinery and equipment needed for investment. These domestic resources can be substituted by drawing on the world market, which is open for such purposes by exporting noninvestment goods in order to purchase the needed investment goods, as was accomplished at critical moments in the early stages of Soviet five-year planning. The non-Soviet world was then in the throes of the Great Depression that was especially severe for machinery, equipment, and investment goods industries—which were therefore receptive to Soviet bids for additional business. Even when the Soviets had established a broad-based machinery industry of their own after World War II, they were still anxious to negotiate arrangements for large complex industrial plants with specialized equipment that would probably have been difficult to produce domestically. The specialized means of production in making investment goods are in turn specialized in different kinds of labor skills (carpenter, brick-layer, electrician), of vehicles (trucks, tanks versus passenger cars), and of machinery (printing machines or presses, typing machines, electronic equipment, communication equipment, machine tools, etc). This relative specialization constrains the form that accumulation can take in the forth-coming period unless resources are to be invested in changing the specification. Even the places where investment can be carried on are subject to the constraints of available transportation and power and must have at least minimal urban amenities. This tendency of existing specialization to constrain the form of new accumulation increases because plans for new investment projects often originate with existing enterprises that have been conditioned to work with and adapt to existing specializations.

A new investment plan must look more than a year ahead because of the long gestation period between the approval of an industrial project for new investment and its actual materialization for use. Investments in heavy industry, transportation, and electric power production are especially time-consuming. According to one report, the "total elapsed time between project

enterprise by exceeding plan requirements "shall be left at the disposal of the enterprise as a fund for bettering the cultural and living conditions of its workers and improving techniques," including the "introduction of new production techniques, modernization of equipment"; and the enterprise is also given some leeway in expending its depreciation allowances which in general amount to some 20% of total Soviet investable funds. See collection of documents and papers, Novosti Press Agency Publishers, *The Soviet Economic Reform*, 1965, page 155; Koval and Miroshnichenko, *Fundamentals of Soviet Economic Planning*, 1972, page 180.

initiation and full scale production" averaged "seven to eight years."[67] Elapsed time tends to stretch out when new industrial projects must be accompanied by supportive facilities in town construction, road building, port development, and other ancillary investments. One of the endemic weaknesses of the Soviet planned economy has been a tendency to launch more construction projects than can be digested and properly equipped to function within the planned period. At any time there are an unusual number of construction facilities awaiting the arrival of machinery or equipment needed for functioning and warehouses of equipment and machinery awaiting completion of construction.[68]

It would, of course, be helpful for planning purposes if each batch of new investment would have the same gestation period and commence production at the same time. The planning period could then readily be fitted to the gestation period. But such simplicity is not to be found. Each planning period commences with an outfitting of undigested investment projects carried over from the past planning period, so that they will come to fruition at different points of time, some immediately, some within a few months, some within a year, and others variously in the forthcoming 5-year plan. Then of the new projects launched, those that are made up of additions and extensions to existing facilities—especially where new ancillary supportive investment is not called for—will take effect in much shorter time than those for which a whole parcel of new investment in a fresh environment is projected. Hence any plan for new investment must have both a long-term and short-term character. It must be prepared as a flowchart of the national economy, in which new production facilities will become available in each forthcoming time period. Allowance must be made in the plan for the inputs needed to activate these new facilities, and place must be found for their outputs. This then calls for not merely a plan for new investments but a periodic flowchart of inputs and outputs for the whole economy and for each of its regions, facilities for transportation and housing, major branches of production, and urban centers. There must be assurance not only of *terminal* balance of inputs and outputs

---

[67]Cohn, "Soviet Investment Policies," 1976, pages 457 f. An earlier survey by a Soviet research institution shows that it takes 5–7 years "for new plant to reach full-capacity efficient operation." Novosti Press Agency Publishers, *Soviet Economic Reform*, 1965, page 35.

[68]See sources cited in footnote 74. In his October 1961 report *Program of the Communist Party of the Soviet Union*, N.S. Khrushchev noted in response to critics that "we suffer great losses" from "lack of coordination" between the erection of new industrial buildings and provision of equipment for them. On January 1, 1961, he declared, there were "industrial buildings with a total floor area of millions of square meters that had not been completely equipped and stocks of equipment to the value of hundreds of millions of rubles for which the necessary buildings were not ready." See Khrushchev, *Program of the Communist Party*, 1961, page 152.

at the end of the plan period but of a substantial degree of balance throughout the whole development.

Where the pace of new investment and its facilities is comparatively small compared to the existing stock of production facilities, the plan for new investment may be modeled primarily on the needs and requirements perceived at the outset of the planning period as inherited from the immediate past. But where the pace of new investment is rapid, so that a high fraction of social product takes the form of new accumulations of productive assets, then it is no longer possible to model the pattern of investment to the pre-existing conditions that are the immediate environment of the plan takeoff.[69] The investment plan must allow for the projected needs and requirements of the transformed industrial environment that will materialize at the end of the plan period. The investment plan is not first determined and then a flowchart of inputs and outputs derived; this flowchart and investment plan will mutually influence each other and be synchronized both spatially and temporally. The accumulation of wealth and the improvement in technology, resulting in higher levels of productivity and a more bountiful flow of social production, will usually call for and be associated with a redistribution of population between town and country and the creation of new or enlargement of old urban centers. Some of the investment needs of this ramifying course of new economic development must be anticipated by the investment plan itself if it is to be optimal. Therefore, in a dynamic and progressive economy investment planning must work out not only the input–output networks of the present stock of resources but also the networks of the augmented and transformed stocks of resources for a series of future periods. Thus present investment plans must allow for the feedback effects of the investment activity being envisaged.

Obviously the scope and meaning of planning in the socialist economy is radically different from that carried on by businesses and governments in the nonsocialist world. Long-term planning is institutionalized for all business and government establishments and these long-term plans are themselves then drawn to a single center, where they are reviewed, dovetailed, and modified to even out discontinuities that would otherwise occur and to bring local planning into necessary balance with national requirements. What is achieved by prevision in the socialist economy may also be achieved by the trial-and-error method of the market operative in the nonsocialist world. This necessarily works by fits and starts as new input–output patterns called for by new technology need to be experienced empirically as shortages or surpluses

[69]The annual rate of growth of the stock of fixed productive assets in the 1951–1970 period declined from 10.1% to 8.2%. For 1926–1970, excluding war years, the average rate of growth was about 8%. See Berri, *Planning a Socialist Economy*, 1973, pages 129 f.

before responsible capitalist or corporate managers can prudently take account of them and devise suitable responses. Since these responses will be contrived by individual firms, each in his own bailiwick, the responses will be delayed and erratic, often overshooting the mark to lead to a cycle of booms and depressions.[70]

As a specific technique of resource and product coordination it is clear that socialist growth planning is a higher form of economic planning. It vastly extends the horizons of planning and permits a more rapid development than would otherwise be possible. As a higher form, it has emergent properties of its own. The failure of J. K. Galbraith to realize this, his assimilation of economic planning carried out within the enterprises of the West and of the socialist economies of the East as "variant accommodations to the same need," alike involving supersession of the market, was a theoretical blunder of first magnitude and one that vitiates many of the conclusions reached in that otherwise able work.[71]

But though a socialist economy is quite possible with socialist growth planning, it by no means follows that this planning will be optimal or ideal. In an earlier discussion, I noted that the success of early Soviet growth planning sparked the enthusiasm of the non-Soviet world "despite the blunders of policy-making embodied in the plans, the crudities of much of the planning, and the authoritarian character of the economy."[72] The planning was crude in nearly every respect. The criteria for designing investment projects had no way to scale for investment productivity beyond the crude payout-period calculations predominant in the Western business world at the time. Since the ideological shadow of Marxian economics blotted out any recognition of capital and land costs in price setting, pricing norms ignored capital costs or the necessity to discount for roundabout methods of production.[73] An equally important defect of Soviet investment planning was an uneconomic preference for giant establishments with excessive reliance upon long-distance trans-

---

[70]It was the great achievement of Joseph Schumpeter in his *Theory of Economic Development*, 1912, and in the enlarged treatment in his later treatise, *Business Cycles*, 1939, to have shown that business cycles have their origin and take shape out of the process of innovation and industrial development. He conceived of this process in apologetic terms, as I argued in my critique of Schumpeter. See Gottlieb, "Ideological Influence in Schumpeter's Thought," 1959, pages 1–42. But his central conclusion was very correct.

[71]"The modern big corporation and the modern apparatus of socialist planning are variant accommodations to the same need." See Galbraith, *New Industrial State*, 1967, page 33. See also on the implied theme of "convergence," pages 392 ff.

[72]Gottlieb, "Pluralist or Unitary Economic Systems," 1972, page 86.

[73]"The category of production costs in socialist enterprises must not be confused with the category of capitalist production outlays. It does not express outlay of capital." Institute of Economics *Political Economy*, 1954, page 625.

portation. Clearly indicated was a tendency to overinvest by launching more construction enterprises than could be carried through with the existing or projected building industry, so that around 1959–1960 when the Soviet state operated some 200,000 enterprises they had 100,000 construction sites in operation with an average of 11 workers per project or site.[74] There is also evidence that especially in the earlier years of Soviet planning, investment judgments of an important kind could be made by top political leaders or by the supreme dictator himself without adequate staff clearing or research to eliminate eccentricities of judgment. A tragic instance of this kind is the project of the 140-mile long canal linking the Baltic Sea near Leningrad with the White Sea—a project initiated by the Soviet government in the late winter months of 1930–1931. There is every indication the project was cooked up outside the framework of long-term planning under the special circumstances that had developed because of mass imprisonment which had filled Soviet prisons and labor camps.[75] One hundred thousand prisoners were to provide corvée labor, with work to be directed by the state police. Mainly local materials were to be used, and no foreign exchange was to be expended for imported equipment so that much of the work was done by pick and shovel with the wheel barrow and the horse-drawn cart the main transportation vehicles. A peremptory time limit was imposed of 20 months with instructions to force the pace of work and surmount all obstacles.[76] The canal was completed apparently within 2 years at great human and material costs which have been described in detail by Solzhenitsyn in his "Gulag Archipelago" series. Because of haste and impromptu planning, it was built too shallow and a reconnaissance along the Baltic–White Sea Canal in 1966 disclosed that it had fallen into nearly complete disuse.[77]

[74]Novosti Press Agency Publishers, *Soviet Economic Reform*, 1965, page 33.

[75]This was substantially recited in the dedicatory volume that was compiled and published by the Soviet government shortly after the work on the canal was completed. See Maxim Gorki *et al.*, *Belomar*, 1934. The work was a collaborative account by a group of Soviet authors and the translation was an authorized Soviet translation. In its introductory account, the volume recites the activity of "wrecking" which developed in the early years of the five-year plan and it was noted that the GPU "carried out mass arrests among the wreckers." But there was already a shortage of labor to man the "new enterprises" produced by the plan. Under these circumstances could a surplus of idle labor in detention camps be tolerated? "Stalin proposed that the construction of this Canal should be entrusted by the Communist Party to the GPU" (page 20).

[76]"The basic directions for the elaboration of the project laid down in three points: to build the canal in 20 months, to apply the simplest and cheapest designs, and to use materials for construction of which there was no shortage in the country." See Gorki *et al.*, *Belomar*, 1934, page 44.

[77]The canal was the second major labor camp work project in the history of the Gulag Archipelago, so that Solzhenitsyn in *The Gulag Archipelago* has an extensive review of the project 1973–1978, vol. 2, pages 80–102.

Khrushchev told the story of how Stalin made the determination to use fabricated reinforced concrete on big construction projects.[78] Soviet leaders had to learn the hard way that to try to go too fast ultimately meant going slower—and that overbuilding was as critical a deficiency of socialist growth planning as underemployment and periodic recession were in capitalist expansion processes.

The result of Soviet experience with industrialization is that they did learn to recognize much of the crudity embodied in earlier planning. It is worthy of note that the histories of allied socialist economies have not recapitulated the whole sequence of errors that marked the initial Soviet experience. Finally, Soviet growth planning has begun to utilize some of the major principles of Western non-Marxian economics, including the critical notions of the marginal productivity of capital or investment and the need for an economy-wide rate of interest as a pricing device to charge for use of capital— a scarce and valuable resource.[79] They have begun to utilize Western mathematical methods of econometric modeling, linear programming and input–output analysis.[80]

[78]Khrushchev, *Khrushchev Remembers*, 1976, pages 106–108. Actually, the recommendation by Khrushchev was well-supported and probably made sense.

[79]"Standard Methodology for Determining the Economic Effectiveness of Capital Investments" (a translation of a Soviet document published in 1969) and a commentary by A. Bouchar, "The New Soviet Standard Methodology for Investment Allocation." See Bornstein and Fuseld, *The Soviet Economy*, 1974, pages 327–347.

[80]Adoption of mathematical methods of economic analysis was facilitated by the work of Oscar Lange, a distinguished Western economist who was also an outstanding Marxist and Polish national leader. See Lange, *Introduction to Econometrics*, 1957. On the Soviet side, there were pioneer developments of linear programming and input–output analysis that facilitated their reentry into official intellectual life after the death of Stalin. On the computerization of planning and the formal use of econometric modeling that is transforming Eastern planning both in the Soviet Union and the smaller socialist states, see Nove, *Soviet Economy*, 1961, pages 318 ff.; Liebermann, *Economic Methods*, 1973; Rumyantsev, *Categories and Laws*, 1964, pages 57–69; Koval and Miroshnichenko, *Fundamentals of Soviet Economic Planning*, 1972, pages 38 ff.

6

Functions of the State in the Economy

INTRODUCTION

We have so far resolved economic systems chiefly into shifting complexes of modes of production and the different ways by which resources are coordinated within or between modes and for use over time. Here or there we have encountered the state as custodian or operator of one of the modes—to perform public services and as an agency to carry out national economic planning as a higher form of resource coordination to achieve accelerated industrialization. However, these encounters with the state as a component part or agency of the economic system have provided only a partial picture of its role in economic life. In this chapter and the two following chapters we shall attempt a more extended view of the state's economic role.

We will deal at first with those more discrete functions of the state impacting directly on the economy. These economically related state functions are presented under three broad headings: (1) regulation of trade and production, (2) provision of essential public works, and (3) taxation both to support the state, its public works, and the public mode, and to provide for income redistribution to benefit favored classes or groups of high or low social status. There are, of course, other state functions—including provision of national defense, maintenance of internal law and order, and facilities for the pursuit of learning or the propagation of community faiths. These all have some economic effect because they consume valuable economic resources, affect class relationships and morale, and influence overall levels of economic achievement and income distribution. The work of the state in all its endeavors is organic and its influence tends to be permeative. It will be convenient, however, in a work dealing not with the total society but with one of its subsectors, the economic system, to confine our analysis of the functions of government to those that have immediate and direct impact on economic systems. Thus we shall reserve the present chapter to the presentation of the three major economically related state functions designated. In the two chapters following we will be concerned with the development of the institutions of property and money and the associated role of the state. In those two chapters we shall encounter some of the broader aspects of the state excluded from immediate review in this chapter.

It will be helpful at the outset to consider two general aspects of the economic functions of the state. The first relates to the many ways and means for carrying out state functions. The second relates to the standard for evaluation of these functions in terms of legitimacy or worth.

Ways and means will always include some use of the public mode of production—if only to issue laws or decrees, adjudicate controversies, enforce laws by police or other administrative action, and use hired labor to provide some public service. A second major way involves the working of a tax system, a set of revenue laws under which general revenue is collected to carry out the state's functions. These revenue laws—and, even more, their actual administration—will rarely be neutral in their impact upon the distribution of income and wealth or the pattern of economic behavior.[1] By means of exemptions, graduated tax rates, limiting of the objects of taxation, raising revenue by taxes provides many opportunities to regulate productive activity carried out within the modes, to encourage some modes of production and discourage others, and to limit or curtail productive activity in many fields. The *Ordnungssteuer*—"ordering tax" as it is known in German—is and was a much-used instrument for carrying out state policy ever since the late medieval or mercantilist period of European economic life. It includes high taxes on luxury articles specifically to discourage their use, the head tax to mobilize labor for plantations or estates, the protective duty to discourage foreign imports, and the tax on bank notes issued by certain kinds of financial organizations.[2] It heightens incentives in some directions and dampens them in others. It affects the makeup of security portfolios and planning for estate settlement. The larger the share of national income taken in taxation, the more potent the influence of the mode of taxation on economic life, because some ordering effect is almost inherent in taxation.

Just as important as the regulatory role of tax collection may be the regulatory role of the ways in which tax monies are used or expended. Stipends paid to students widen the scope of higher education. Tithes permitted a favored church may establish a form of religion as a social bond. State revenue transferred to the elite of the state may permit the most unrestrained luxury and the most fantastic extravagance by those selected for honorific state posts. In the modern social security systems established in most Western nations in

---

[1]For a convenient presentation of the "principle of economic neutrality" in tax matters, see Due, *Government Finance*, 1954, pages 103 ff.
[2]Gerloff, *Die Öffentliche Finanzwirtschaft*, 1942, pages 161 ff.

the twentieth century, a considerable fraction of payroll charges are paid out not to the workers immediately involved but into a social security fund that is in turn redistributed to retired or disabled workers or their surviving dependents, who draw benefits varying with need and amounts contributed.

The second aspect of state functions deserving special attention is the standard for evaluation of functions. This standard does not presuppose that state functions actually promote in some optimum fashion the welfare of the society or that the functions embody a desirable balance between public and private activities. Nor does it assume that the state is managed by its operators who hold or wield state power in the interest of society or necessarily in the interests of the class directing the predominant mode of production. The standard is adapted neither to the requirements of advanced Western states nor to those of the socialist economies that have evolved in our time. Instead, we are interested in what states have actually done for reasons of good or ill in relation to economic life, without regard to whether state policies or objectives were ill-founded or had unintended adverse effects.[3] In this regard, state structures tend to evolve modes of behavior that are not too dysfunctional, because states that are careless and casual with the use of public resources will be less able to survive. Productive activity in such states will decline, capital will not be accumulated, and the ability of the states to provide resources adequate for national defense will be undermined.

Regimes that are too unpopular or oppressive can always be overthrown by revolution or be fissured by schism from within or without. State systems that elicit the support of their people and respect inherited laws and customs will tend to survive—and thrive in the competitive struggle of state systems with each other. Throughout the whole of the history of the societies with which we are concerned in this work such competitive struggle has always appeared. This competition of state systems with regard to historically evolved functions of their economic life is the major focus in this chapter. Where it is relevant we will, of course, take note of the effectiveness of the means used to carry out the assumed functions or the manifest analytical shortcomings or flaws in the reasoning that justified these means.

The functions of the state apply to all states in historical societies. But societies will attach different values to these functions leading in some to their

[3]Thus we can make only limited use of the classical treatises on the economic functions of government that appeared in the work of Adam Smith and John Stuart Mill. See A. Smith, *Wealth of Nations*, 1776, bk. 5, pages 653–906; Mill, *Principles of Political Economy*, bk. 5, especially ch. 1, and chs. 8, 9, 11. Both treatises are exceptionally valuable because they were written from a broad background of historical knowledge and close acquaintance with current political life in Great Britain and Western Europe. However, both treatises were essays in persuasion for the brands of liberal philosophy attractive at the time. For a helpful guide through nineteenth century classical economics as it dealt with the functions of the state, see Samuels, *Classical Theory of Economic Policy*, 1966, especially chs. 3, 4.

comparative neglect. Even when assigned the same value, the functions will be carried out in different ways. Where the state has taken over all or most of the operations of industry and assimilated them into the public mode of production, then certain state functions may be carried out by enterprise management. Though overt taxation plays a role in the socialist economy, its scope is much narrower since the state may choose to obtain funding for general state purposes in other ways, as by widening profit markups inherent in state pricing norms or by increasing the rate of money issuance withdrawn by quasi-compulsory state loans. In some forms of socialist economic organization, a very large proportion of expenditure for housing, basic cereals, schooling, health care, and social security is financed out of state budgets, leaving a much narrower role for self-support by households from current income. Correspondingly, the money wage levels for households will be on a much lower scale relative to total social product. Wage payments earned by employed wage earners reimburse only a fraction of the outlays required for their provisionment. Among other things, this tends to favor the use in industry of labor-intensive techniques, causing the regulatory and redistributive functions of the socialist economy to be distinctive in many ways. They can best be understood in the context of a specialized analysis of the socialist economy not undertaken in this work. Hence much of the discussion that will follow in the remainder of this chapter about functions of the state in economic systems will pertain generally to the nonsocialist economic systems.

REGULATION OF FOREIGN TRADE

The regulatory work of the state is found on a more or less extensive scale in nearly all economic systems though the means of regulation vary considerably. Commencing first with regulation of foreign trade, we find that nearly everywhere foreign trade is subject to special regulation if only for the purpose of gathering information about the movement of trade and of collecting state revenues, because ingress or egress of goods across frontiers is convenient for purposes of tax collection. In the archaic societies from which our historical systems have emerged, a governmentally regulated "port of trade," established usually on riverine sites where inlets and extensive lagoons eased transportation by land, was the principal channel for the movement of goods between different societies or communities.[4] The great early empires of Rome and China both established special port facilities where overseas foreign trade would be carried on under strict state regulation.[5] On their more extended

---

[4]Polanyi, "Ports of Trade in Early Societies," 1963, see *Primitive, Archaic and Modern Economies,* pages 238 ff.

[5]Bury, *Later Roman Empire,* 1923, vol. 2, page 3.

land frontiers touching peoples typically migratory or only just turning to settled agricultural life, both the Roman and Chinese states could not implant state control as easily as they could at ocean ports.

The immediate purposes of trade regulation are various. Sometimes the motive has been to assure importation of necessary cereals—which Athenian ship owners were required to bring back on return cargoes.[6] Again there is the interest of national security, which according to Adam Smith outranked opulence as a national objective.[7] When the first Tokugawa Shogun fully realized the extent to which Western powers used facilities of trade as well as missionary activities to establish footholds in a country leading to foreign conquest or internal subversion, he drastically limited all intercourse with Westerners, suppressed Christianity, and channeled trade to its smallest possible confines.[8] The tactic of trade boycott has been revived in the twentieth century by American efforts to isolate and hamper trade with leading communist countries, this trade being sometimes totally prohibited or minimized by high rates of taxation and by exclusion of broad categories of industrial or even agricultural products deemed to have strategic importance. One by-product of this campaign of commercial isolation against the communist world after World War II was to force the communist countries into closer dependence upon each other and especially upon the Soviets, thus strengthening the Soviet hegemony considered harmful by the Americans.[9] Even when total boycott is abjured, trade regulation in partial spheres has been used to injure

[6]Weber, *General Economic History,* 1923, page 203.

[7]A. Smith, *Wealth of Nations,* 1776, page 431.

[8]The detailed history of the early Tokugawa regime—now introduced to American fiction readers in the memorable novel *Shogun*—makes very clear that the decision to shut off intercourse with the Western world was reached only after extended experience had indicated the dangers to national independence in maintaining open relations with the European powers. See closing chapters of Sadler, *Maker of Modern Japan,* 1937; Boxer, *Christian Century in Japan,* 1951.

[9]The critical year for the development of trade restrictions with the communist world was apparently 1948 during the Berlin crisis, the springboard both for the mobilization of the NATO Alliance and for the formation of the Bonn Republic. All this tightened up more during the Korean War struggle, when American trade with the Eastern bloc was brought to a virtual halt and American aid or assistance was only extended to countries that cooperated in our trade boycott policy, confined formally to so-called strategic goods. See on this the extended footnote on the role of German interzonal trade in Gottlieb, *German Peace Settlement,* 1960, page 264 n. 53; and see further various annual volumes of the Council on Foreign Relations, for example, *United States in World Affairs,* 1952, pages 40 ff., 299; 1957, pages 60 ff.; 1958, pages 116 ff.; 1960, pages 96 ff. Over the years our trade boycott has been increasingly relaxed for certain communist countries (such as Poland and recently Rumania and Yugoslavia) believed more independent of Soviet control or more open to Western influence. And since the recognition of China, trade and capital investment has been facilitated there. But against such communist ne'er-do-wells as Vietnam, Cuba, and North Korea, the U.S. trade boycott is still unrelenting.

the trade of an imperial opponent. Thus as far back as the thirteenth century a French king forbade the export of wool in order to weaken the textile industries in bordering countries.[10]

In the old struggle between England and France for imperial power in the continent of Europe and overseas, each country strove to weaken the other by various measures of trade restriction. By the third quarter of the eighteenth century Adam Smith could declare that "mutual restrictions have put an end to almost all fair commerce between the two nations. . . . Smugglers are now the principal importers, either of British goods into France or of French goods into Great Britain."[11]

Regulation has more often been aimed not at hurting some enemy power but at promoting some domestic interest. This interest has sometimes sought to reduce unemployment by taking measures to restrict importation of products for which the domestic capacity to produce is not fully utilized. Where the same effect of favoring domestic production can be achieved by other means, such as currency devaluation, the latter is often favored as a more "neutral" expedient and one sanctioned by international agreement. Where currency devaluation is resisted or is not available, the attractiveness of protective measures is enhanced.[12] More commonly trade restrictions are motivated by the desire to increase domestic employment by building up the protected industry. Thus it was the century-old policy of the English state to promote the development of a woolen manufacturing and cloth industry in England. This was achieved both by bringing into the country skilled foreign producers and, even more, by making raw wool cheap in England and expensive abroad—and later by express prohibition of the export of raw wool in any form. This had the long-run effect, Adam Smith argued, of reducing farmer returns from sheep herds but it also led to a powerful domestic producing and export industry of woolen fabrics that gave key trading products to British merchants. In order to police the prohibition of wool export, "the whole inland commerce of wool is laid under very burdensome and oppressive restrictions."[13]

[10]Emmanuel, A., *Unequal Exchange*, 1969.
[11]A. Smith, *Wealth of Nations*, 1776, pages 441, 462 f.
[12]Thus Keynes finally broke down and advocated that Great Britain impose protective duties in the early years of the Great Depression, because exchange devaluation from the historic gold parity of the pound was resisted and with trade unrestricted no other policy could be effective in fighting the depression and increasing employment. Keynes, *Essays in Persuasion*, 1919–1931, pages 271 ff. Similarly, in the current depression (1979–82) protectionist sentiment is reviving in the United States, though the hold of free-trade dogma is still strong and the leaders of industry, compromised by their vast foreign investments, are reluctant to support tariff action that may boomerang against them elsewhere.
[13]By the end of the fourteenth century, the domestic price of raw wool in England was less than half the price of the same wool in the Low Countries or Italy, due in large part to state export duties worked into the administration of a regulated trade monopoly, The Com-

For similar reasons, to promote building domestic industry by preventing the export of critical raw materials, England prohibited the export of fuller's earth (needed for preparation and cleansing of woolen cloth), raw hides and tanned leather, horns of cattle, woolen yarn, and cases and dial-plates for clocks and watches—and at times the exportation of various crude metals.[14] Where the domestic raw materials are not of strategic consequence, the objective of fostering the growth of domestic industry may be achieved not by an export ban on the raw material but by a bounty on import of the raw material or, more commonly, by a tax or tariff charge on the import of the manufactured product making it more expensive than its domestic counterpart.[15] This simple, widely prevailing use of import charges to "protect" a domestic industry from competitive foreign producers is the standard means of achieving the goal of promoting domestic industry. "Year after year and decade after decade, the governments of every country in the world have practiced without interruption a policy of protection."[16] The need for protection to foster domestic industries is obviously minimal in countries with a strong lead in advanced industrial technology, and such countries commonly are in the forefront of movements to reduce "protection" and corresponding "restrictions" to mutual trade. But it is rare for even these countries on their own initiative to scale down prevailing protective tariffs except in return for corresponding reductions in the tariffs of their trading partners.[17] Developing countries with a need to develop domestic industry will of course have an interest in using devices of protection to foster their "infant industries." Such countries—whose exports consist chiefly of raw materials for which demand is inelastic price-wise—have a collective interest in imposing export duties provided these can be applied by all producers or in undertaking, as have members of OPEC, measures to reduce product supply.[18]

---

pany of the Merchants of the Staple, with headquarters in Calais. See Postan, *Medieval Economy and Society*, 1972, pages 117 f., 215 f., 245 ff. Early in the seventeenth century the British enforced a total prohibition of the export of raw wool or yarn from England and developed the oppressive system described by Adam Smith for controlling the wool trade. See A. Smith, *Wealth of Nations*, 1776, pages 230 f., 613 ff.

[14]See A. Smith, *Wealth of Nations*, 1776, pages 619 ff.

[15]On bounties on imports of industrial materials see A. Smith, *Wealth of Nations*, 1776, pages 609 ff.

[16]Emmanuel, *Unequal Exchange*, 1969, page xiii.

[17]The great reduction in effective American import duties brought about in the past 30 years has been due largely to various rounds of tariff reduction achieved by multilateral agreement. See Emmanuel, *Unequal Exchange*, 1969, pages 229 ff.

[18]Emmanuel's book is an effort to enlarge upon the statement of Marx in 1848: "If the free traders cannot understand how one nation can grow rich at the expense of another, we need not wonder, since these same gentlemen also refuse to understand how within one country one class can enrich itself at the expense of another." See Emmanuel, *Unequal Exchange*, 1969, page vii.

REGULATION OF DOMESTIC PRODUCTION

We turn now from regulation of foreign to domestic trade and production. In this sphere earlier state intervention was by local officials authorized to prevent abuses in trade or commerce.[19] Bourgeois mercantile republics of the medieval period and emerging national states assumed a more complete responsibility over the whole process of the production and distribution of wealth. Magistrates would be petitioned to prohibit some industrial practice regarded as pernicious or harmful.[20] The states served mainly as an agency for enforcing guild regulations that had more finality and scope if issued under the imprint of the state and enforced by its sanctions.[21] Commodities in wide use—such as ironware, beer, wine, and fabrics—were especially subject to regulation with regard to methods of production, standard widths and lengths, density of weave, quality of dyes, and finishing and packing.

A later generation of public servants and economists was inclined to sweep away this entire structure of regulation as so much oppressive control by an overzealous state holding back the thrust of innovation and protecting corporate monopoly. Even the fair-minded and socially inclined John Stuart Mill, who had one foot in the socialist camp, did not hesitate to declare, after citing a description of state regulatory control of textile production, that the "time is gone by, when such applications as these of the principle of paternal government would be attempted in even the least enlightened country of the European commonwealth of nations." He was inclined to trust the general rule that "the business of life is better performed when those who have an immediate interest in it are left to take their own course, uncontrolled either by the mandate of the law or by the meddling of any public functionary." The enterprises carrying out production "are likely to be better judges than the government of the means of attaining the particular end at which they aim." And Mill felt that the mature consumer is "generally the best judge of the material objects produced for his use."[22]

[19]The market supervisor has broad authority to prevent abuses: he prohibits obstruction of roads, orders the tearing down of buildings in peril of collapse, and generally acts to prevent fraud and deception with food and weights and measures. Ibn Khaldun, *The Muqaddimah*, 1377, pages 178 f. The market superintendent in Old Cairo was not, however, much of a bother to the large Jewish mercantile and craft community during the some 300 years for which Geniza records are available. See Goitein, *A Mediterranean Society*, 1967–1971, vol. 2, page 369.

[20]Le Roy Ladurie, *The Peasants of Languedoc*, 1966, page 70.

[21]Nef, *Industry and Government*, 1957, pages 14 ff.

[22]Mill, *Principles of Political Economy*, 1848, bk. 5, ch. 11, no. 7. Mill's generalization that the consumer is a competent judge allows for "numerous abatements and exceptions" concerning education designed "to raise the character" of a person, judgments about "some future and distant time," business that is tended to by quasi-public corporations (whose management is hardly better than the state's), and finally a class of action calling for public concert "which

Since that liberal text was written, experience and investigation of the results of unfettered *laissez faire* led most of the industrially developed nations of the world again to litter their statute books with regulatory control over industry. Controls have served various objectives. One has been to promote simplification and standardization of sizes and technical specifications to widen the field of substitution of different brands and styles of component parts widely utilized in different products or structures. Another objective has been to protect the environment from pollution by waste products or fumes that individual producers may release into the atmosphere or into surface waters unless specifically impeded by law. Regulation has been called for to prevent products from coming into the market with dangerous health hazards to users. Regulation is also needed to provide fair disclosure of contents and exact weight as well as clearly stipulated warranties for durable goods or of fuel efficiency, as is the case for automobiles. Regulation is even needed to provide adequate and detailed information to investors about new investment securities being floated on the market and to police the relations between corporate management and stockholders by requiring corporate management to make detailed periodic financial disclosure of corporate accounts, to assure proper access by stockholders to corporate records and to prevent manipulation in public securities markets. There is literally no aspect of the process of production or exchange in the modern economy free from call on good grounds for state regulatory controls.

Regulated Wages and Working Conditions

Wages and working conditions had to await the shaping influence of the regulatory state after the wage laborer had become an important social force. He appeared in the wake of the dissolution of the feudal mode of production and of medieval guilds chiefly in the fields of capitalist agriculture and hired artisan trades. The first notable wave of regulation appeared as a specific response to the near-disastrous shrinkage of the labor force by over one-third in Europe following the Great Plague and associated famines occurring in the first half of the fourteenth century. In England and in France the first form of a "wage freeze" was employed, prohibiting payment of wages or artisan prices higher than those prevailing in the pre-Plague period.[23] In later centuries the same objective was achieved by statutes that empowered local gov-

---

concert cannot be effectual unless it receives validity and sanction from the law" (ch. 11, nos. 8, 10, 11, 12). Mill goes on to emphasize "that the intervention of government cannot always practically stop short at the limit which defines the cases intrinsically suitable for it" (ch. 11, no. 16).

[23] Marx, *Capital* I, 1867, pages 272 ff., 738 ff.

erning boards, composed chiefly of landowners and farmers, annually to set maximum wages for agricultural and artisan work. Local officials could impress into forced labor workingmen found without proper means of support or wandering "vagrants" without employment.[24] Any form of coalition of laborers to obtain higher wages or improved working conditions was categorically outlawed. This form of regulation of wages and working conditions was applied variously in Western Europe through the eighteenth century.[25] Only in 1813 in Great Britain was the law fixing maximum wages repealed to be followed 12 years later by repeal of the laws prohibiting "combination" or "coalition" of workmen.[26]

This oppressive form of labor regulation had barely come to an end when it was found necessary to interpose state power with opposite objectives: to boost, not to depress, wage levels and to improve, not to worsen, working conditions. This first took the form of measures to reduce the excessive hours of work developed in the first generation of English and Scotch cotton textile mills, which predominantly employed women and juveniles with a small contingent of children. Through the earlier centuries, the length of the working day was set in summertime from 5 A.M. to 7:30 P.M., minus $2\frac{1}{2}$ hours for food and recuperation—or for a net workday of 12 hours. In winter a reduced workday was set from dawn to dusk.[27] The workday in the nineteenth century textile mills was often in excess of these standards. The first effective textile factory law, enacted in 1833, prohibited the employment of children under 9 years of age, limited to 8 hours the workday of juveniles under 13 years of age, excluded nightwork for all employees under 18 years of age, and limited the workday of juveniles between 13 and 18 years of age to no more than 12 hours in any one day.[28] Between 1844 and 1850, amidst the clamor of sharp debate, the restricted hours of work applicable to older juveniles were extended to adult women workers and reduced to $10\frac{1}{2}$ hours daily, with a short workday on Saturday. The law was tightened to prevent evasion, thus making a reduced work week effective for the factory work force in the textile industry.[29] The English bourgeois state led by the landed

[24]The rather cruel vagrancy laws are copiously extracted and set out in Marx, *Capital* I 1867, pages 734 ff.; for a fuller account, see Webb and Webb, *English Local Government*, 1927, vol. 7.

[25]For the United Kingdom, see different accounts in A. Smith, *Wealth of Nations*, 1776, pages 136 ff.; Karl Polanyi, *The Great Transformation*, ch.9.

[26]Clapham, *Economic History Modern Britain*, 1926–1938, vol. 1, pages 198 f., 205 ff.

[27]Marx found it useful to detail this early workday legislation. See *Capital* I, 1867, pages 271 ff.

[28]Marx's account is both accurate and succinct. See *Capital* I, 1867, pages 279 ff.

[29]Though later historical accounts are available, Marx's account of this legislation—interspersed with side-comments on the extra-parliamentary struggle and debate—is accurate and illuminating. See *Capital* I, 1867, pages 280–294.

aristocracy acted to reduce factory work hours to meet minimal health and safety needs of immature or weaker workers obviously unable to protect their own interests by market action.[30] The cause was aided by the vigorous working class Chartist movement, by grievances felt by landowners "panting for revenge" at the abolition of corn tariffs, and very possibly by a change of the state of consciousness gradually taking shape in the nineteenth century causing an increased sensitivity in the cultivated classes to pain and suffering and hence an enhancement of humanitarian sentiment.[31]

Industrialists soon learned that the shorter workday and work week reduced accidents, breakdowns, and absenteeism and permitted the intensity of work to be increased. They stepped up the speed of the machines and stretched out operator responsibilities so that per unit costs of production under the new factory regime were only slightly if at all increased.[32]

---

[30]Medical reports made up a large body of the official investigations that prompted the English government to adopt factory legislation; and in the nineteenth and early twentieth centuries American courts were only induced to accept restrictive labor legislation by strong recommendations on health and sanitary grounds. In his "preface" to the first German edition of *Capital* I, 1867, Marx justly included in his praise of the English factory inspectors English "medical reporters on public health" (page 9). He cited by name no fewer that 19 doctors who had offered testimony, made reports, or collected information relevant to factory legislation (pages 245, 246, 254 n. 2, 255 n. 2, 255, 258 n. 3, 280, 265, 658, 667, 481. See also Commons and Andrews, *Principles of Labor Legislation*, 1916, pages 196 ff., 237 ff.

[31]Marx, *Capital* I, 1867, page 283. John Stuart Mill sensed this very well in an early essay: "One of the effects of civilization . . . is, that the spectacle, and even the very idea of pain, is kept more and more out of the sight of those classes who enjoy in their fullness the benefits of civilization. The state of perpetual personal conflict . . . necessarily habituated every one to the spectacle of harshness, rudeness and violence, to the struggle of one indomitable will against another and to the alternate suffering and infliction of pain. These things, consequently were not as revolting even to the best and most actively benevolent men of former days, as they are to our own. . . . In our own time the necessity of personal collision is . . . almost at an end. All those necessary portions of the business of society which oblige any person to be the immediate agent or ocular witness of the infliction of pain, are delegated by common consent to peculiar and narrow classes: to the judge, the soldier, the surgeon, the butcher and the executioner." See Mill, *Essays on Politics and Culture*, 1831–1870, pages 57 f. Commons and Andrews called attention to the same trend, which they termed "humanitarian." See *Principles of Labor Legislation*, 1916, page 26. Marx put it a little differently. Commenting on the marked change of views exhibited by Nassau Senior—whose philippic against the Factory Act of 1833 had been notorious but who approached the subject in 1863 in a quite different frame of mind, Marx noted "how modern industry when it has attained to a certain pitch is capable by the revolution it effects in the mode of production and in the social conditions of production of revolutionising people's minds." See *Capital* I, 1867, pages 483 n.3.

[32]Dramatic evidence for the above was copiously set forth by Marx in *Capital* I, 1867, pages 411–417. In his recent paper Douglas Booth is able to cite good contemporary authority for his assertion that "Daily wages in the cotton industry did rise in the decade following passage of the Factory Acts . . . and productivity suffered little." See Booth, "Marx on State Regulation," 1978, page 154.

A careful but caustic foreign contemporary observer noted the "wonderful development" of the conditions of labor with the newly regulated work week and the "physical and moral regeneration" it produced.[33] Hence the regulated work week for children, juveniles, and women was extended over the years to other industries, mining, and even smaller workshops.[34] Although state intervention refrained from touching the workday of adult male workmen, wherever they were employed in juxtaposition with women and juveniles the regulated workday was generally made applicable to them. And skilled workmen, many factory operatives and artisans through their burgeoning unions were able to win the 10-hour and later the 9-hour and even the 8-hour day and to move on to the partial time-off on Saturday.[35]

The English lead in interposing the power of the state to regulate the industrial workday was followed in the other countries in which modern industry developed—more slowly where the power of the judiciary, as in the United States, held back the movement, more rapidly where bold innovators like Bismarck held power or where external events or disasters called for national unity and induced ruling classes to undertake popular reforms.[36] In no country was the work week so drastically curbed as in the United States during the 1930s, when a rigorous 40-hour work week was established with high premiums for overtime. This was intended to curb unemployment rampant in the Great Depression by spreading the available work among more workers.[37] Only a poor case can be made for a prescribed uniform national workday applicable to all pursuits—considering the wide differences in work-

[33]Marx, *Capital* I, 1867, page 295. His judgment was more fully rendered in his near-contemporaneous Inaugural Address of the First International: "The immense physical and intellectual benefits hence accruing to the factory operatives, half-yearly chronicled in the reports of the inspectors of factories, are now acknowledged on all sides." See Marx, *Karl Marx on the First International*, 1864–1872, page 10.

[34]The early phase of factory legislation was treated by Marx in *Capital* as a process of "generalization of the Factory Acts, for transforming them from an exceptional law relating to mechanical spinning and weaving . . . into a law affecting social production as a whole"— a "conscious and methodical reaction of society against the spontaneously developed form of the process of production." See *Capital* I, 1867, pages 295 ff., 480 ff., 490. The legislative development of the next 30 years is well-portrayed in Webb and Webb, *Industrial Democracy*, 1897, vol. 1, ch. 4.

[35]Webb and Webb, *Industrial Democracy*, 1897, vol. 1, ch. 6, especially page 352 n. l.

[36]The struggle in America to achieve adequate factory legislation was for nearly a century on tenterhooks because of constitutional issues raised by a hostile judiciary.

[37]The 1938 Fair Labor Standards Act has been amended several times extending coverage and raising minimum wages and is competently reviewed in standard labor texts. See, for example Turnbull, Williams, and Cheit, *Economic and Social Security* 1957, ch. 16. The original intention to spread work among the unemployed was soon overtaken by the booming war economy of 1942–1945. But in the prosperous America which emerged from the war the reduced workweek was found acceptable.

ers' capacity, in the severity and strain of various jobs, and in worker preferences for leisure.[38]

Once the eyes of the masters of the state were focused on the industrial world, they saw other abuses beyond those of an excessive workday that could not safely or wisely be left to the interests of those immediately concerned. Mutilations caused by the whirring knives and wheels of unguarded machinery at work, explosions or cave-ins in deep mines, an excessive number of persons working in small quarters without adequate ventilation, unclean and unsanitary work conditions were all duly noted by factory inspectors and other observers. All called for corrective legislation.[39] This was meager enough at first but the appetite fed on the feeding, and with the aid of a strong labor movement in most Western countries an elaborate code of protective legislation emerged.[40]

The Germans pioneered in a system of accident compensation for medical costs of work-related injuries and further compensation for work-related disability.[41] Though trade unions shouldered a good deal of the burden of developing a code of safe working conditions, legislation was almost everywhere required.

From these beginnings what was earlier called "factory legislation" broadened into a comprehensive program. Some form of public charity was needed to give temporary support to the employable unemployed and to care for the unemployables afflicted by age, sickness, injury, or mental incompetence and to the destitute because of devastations by flood, fire, or natural catastrophe. At the outset of modern industrial development in Great Britain a dominating problem of public policy was to avoid impedance to labor mobility arising from rights to receive local parish relief. Many farm laborers in the early 1800s were getting parish relief because of low wages.[42] The early English resolution of this problem involved a nationwide network of semipenal "poor houses" and the consequent planned abolition of "out-door relief." Because that harsh regime was hardly sustainable, by the end of the century it was formally withdrawn in England and elsewhere in the Western

[38]See on this the careful analysis of that master of applied economics, Pigou, *The Economics of Welfare*, 1920, pt. 3, ch. 7.

[39]See Marx's trenchant account in *Capital* I, 1867, pages 480 ff.

[40]Webb and Webb, *Industrial Democracy*, 1897, vol. 1, ch. 7; Commons and Andrews, *Principles of Labor Legislation*, 1916, ch. 7; Turnbull, Williams, and Cheit, *Economic and Social Security*, 1957, ch. 9.

[41]The German insurance of industrial accidents countrywide was enacted in 1884; modified versions of it were adopted by other European countries and, more slowly, by the American states. Commons and Andrews, *Principles of Labor Legislation*, 1916, pages 363 ff.

[42]Webb and Webb, *English Local Government*, 1927, vol. 7; Marx, *Capital* I, 1867, pages 601 f.; Polanyi, *The Great Transformation*, 1944, 78 ff.; Hammond and Hammond, *The Bleak Age*, 1934, pages 91 ff.

world for most classes of welfare recipients.[43] In time that was followed by unemployment insurance for those able to work and retirement pensions for elderly or disabled workers. To facilitate orderly marketing of labor power, labor exchanges were established to collect information and match job vacancies and job seekers. Mediation and conciliation services helped reduce the costs of industrial conflict, become endemic with the rise of mass trade unionism.

Price Control and Rationing

The regulatory role of the state extended not only to wages and working conditions but frequently to prices, especially of essential foodstuffs marketed in urban communities to minimize the threat of famine in times of poor local harvest. Every session of the Athenian assembly was required to consider "corn and the defence of the country," as Finley remarks, "a most interesting bracketing." A committee of "corn-guardians" had the duty of seeing that corn, meal, and bread were sold at proper prices; and in times of extreme shortage public corn-buyers would undertake direct purchasing or requisitioning and arrange for distribution of grain at regulated prices.[44] In nearly all historical economic systems and even in some of their precursors, the concern of state authorities to regulate prices for essential provisions in short supply, especially in urban communities, crops up again and again until the nineteenth century. Thus an old Celtic code of laws fixed prices of provisions expressed in the then current measure of market values—a female slave.[45] Legend has it that to prevent famine and regulate food distribution in time of shortage a program of stockpiling and regulated food distribution was carried out in ancient Egypt.[46] Episodes of concern over price control for essential foodstuffs was one of the phases of the long struggle between the patrician and plebeian classes that marked the early history of the Roman Republic.[47] In the great metropolis of Byzantium the prefect of the city was required to keep a close hand on market dealing including prices.[48] Medieval

[43]The gradual admission of "out-door" relief for increasing classes of welfare recipients and the lifting of welfare standards is carefully described in Webb and Webb's *English Local Government*, vol. 9, 1929.

[44]Finley, *The Ancient Economy*, 1973, pages 169 f.; Mitchell, *The Economics of Ancient Greece*, 1940, pages 273 ff.

[45]See *Encyclopedia of Social Sciences*, 1930–1934, vol. 12, page 356.

[46]See *Gen.* 41:14–46.

[47]Livy, *History of Rome*, bk. 2, sec. 2.34–2.35.

[48]Bautier, *Economic Development of Medieval Europe*, 1966, pages 67 f. For excerpts from the well-known Book of the Prefect at Constantinople and a brief commentary, see Lopez and Raymond, *Medieval Trade*, pages 19 ff.

European towns were continually prepared to intervene in food markets, to use state resources to mobilize imported supplies, and to undertake rationing with price control if necessary to assure adequate distribution.[49] The late Tudor and early Stuart regimes in England were especially zealous in activating price and wage controls.[50]

This persistent appearance of episodes of price control and rationing, especially for foodstuffs, suggests that it met deep needs and is relatively effective to meet conditions of acute shortage. After all, an urban population has become dependent upon its food supplies and if these fall short, regulation prevents the virtual extortion that otherwise channels available supplies to the well-to-do, resulting in starvation for the poor whose continued existence is essential for the economy and state. Actual or threatened starvation frequently produced "riots."[51] The moral sense of the community supports price control and rationing under such circumstances to tide the community over and preserve public order until better times.

It is a different matter with recurring attempts at price control either to suppress inflation generated by substantial increases in quantities of circulating moneys or to enforce the circulation of a degraded coinage or paper currency set equal to higher-valued coins to which market prices had become adjusted. The best-known example of the first category is the vain effort of Spanish authorities in the sixteenth century to prevent with price controls the flood of New World gold and silver money and plate from greatly increasing the scale of market demand and boosting price levels. The effort was unavailing. Since it hampered the legal use of precious metals in market transactions it encouraged their emigration to other countries and led to the paradoxical emergence in the seventeenth century of a token (vellum) coinage becoming the standard money for market use.[52] The earliest known major instance of the second category is the effort of Diocletian in the early years of the fourth century A.D. to enforce acceptance at par of a flood of newly minted purely copper coins bearing a denomination equal to that of a higher-valued silver coin over the whole range of market commodity dealings spelled out in a

[49]Waley, *The Italian City-Republics*, 1969, page 93; Rórig, *The Medieval Town*, 1955, page 114; Pirenne, *Medieval Europe*, 1933, pages 175 ff. Even as late as 1740 in France, Parisian authorities put into action a far-reaching program to head off famine—including a regional census, a local tax on the well-to-do, search and requisitioning of surplus grain stocks, purchase from abroad, and prohibition of brewing to conserve grain. See Appleby, "Grain Prices and Subsistence Crises," 1979, page 885.

[50]Webb and Webb, *English Local Government*, 1927, vol. 7, pages 69 ff., 73 f.

[51]Charles Tilly in "Food Supply and Public Order in Modern Europe" gives details on food riots in Milan in 1628, Paris in 1775, and Ely and Littleport in 1816. See Tilly, *Formation of National States*, 1975, pages 381 ff.

[52]See Hamilton, *Price Revolution in Spain*, 1934, pages 150 f., 245 ff. For the later period, see Hamilton, *War and Prices in Spain*, ch. 10.

code of prices of which a partial text runs to over a hundred printed pages. The edict was enforced chiefly in the eastern Mediterranean with "numerous sentences of death" and many disturbances.[53] But within a few years enforcement lapsed and the edict was in effect withdrawn, the entire effort an egregious failure. So too the effort failed to enforce circulation at par of the *assignat* issued on a lavish scale by the revolutionary French government to finance the new republic at war with its enemies. That effort helped to undermine support for the Jacobin regime of Robespierre which had vigorously implemented the program of growing dependence upon paper money, grain requisitioning, food price control, and rationing.[54]

Food availability in later years in Western Europe was partly achieved indirectly by careful regulation of grain exports, which in England were prohibited when domestic prices became abnormally high, indicating domestic shortage—while conversely with low grain prices grain exports were then permitted.[55] Tending in the same direction were measures designed to limit food and grain hoarding by food processors and grain dealers who bought grain to resell. Adam Smith looked with favor on the "inland grain dealer" who when he foresees that "provisions are likely to run short" will put consumers "upon short allowance" by an anticipatory increase of hoarding and raising of prices. Conceding that "from an excess of avarice . . . the inland corn merchant may sometimes raise the price of his corn somewhat higher than the scarcity of the season requires," yet Smith believed the resulting "inconveniences" inconsiderable in comparison with those resulting from a "more liberal way of dealing."[56] Government rules that dealers sell their corn

[53]The partial text of the edict is reproduced in English in T. Frank, *Economic Survey of Ancient Rome*, vol. 1, 1933, pages 305–421. The careful studies of S. Bolin, *State and Currency*, 1958, 317 ff., make it clear that the edict was an effort to prevent devaluation of the purely copper 2D coin minted on a "massive" scale. See also Heichelheim, *An Ancient Economic History*, 1938, vol. 3, pages 294 f.; A. H. M. Jones, *Later Roman Empire*, 1966, vol. 1, pages 61, 433, 438.

[54]A first-class economist has given us a masterful interpretation of the tangled skein of currency issuance, public finance, speculation, and price and exchange control exhibited during the French Revolution. See Hawtrey, *Currency and Credit*, 1919, ch. 17. Enforced circulation began only in 1793, when a violent depreciation of the assignat occurred (page 393). After the fall of Robespierre (July 1794) circulation was no longer rigorously enforced, and within a few months it was repealed—though it took some time to restore a working monetary system and to liquidate the heritage of the assignats. For a vivid account of the Jacobin policy in action, see Forrest, "Condition of the Poor," 1973, pages 164 ff.

[55]On this sliding-scale grain trade policy, see A. Smith, *Wealth of Nations*, 1776, pages 501 ff.; Coleman, *Economy of England*, 1977, page 177. Restraints on export of grain in the continent in time of dearth especially were common. See Cipiolla, *Economic History of Europe*, 1972–1976, vol. 1, page 352.

[56]It was against these restrictions on grain dealing and speculative stocking that Adam Smith contended with special force in his famous "Digression concerning the Corn Trade and Corn Laws." See *Wealth of Nations*, 1776, pages 490–510.

at a regulated price hindered the movement of corn to market or encouraged excess consumption at the beginning of the season.[57] The Smithian counsel presupposed that a highly developed and ramified source of grain supplies on a going world market made any "cornering" of the market difficult or impossible and discouraged private hoarding by wealthy consumers or processors. Over most of recorded history it was not possible for rulers of states to take this hazard with public provisioning that they could not afford to leave to grain speculators.

Nearly everywhere from time to time the state has imposed price controls on a broad range of commodities. An English basic statute for centuries ordered local authorities to fix the local price of bread and ale by fixing the markup over the changing price of wheat and barley, the two key materials used.[58] Cloth was especially singled out for price control wherever standards and specifications by weight, composition, and texture were controlled.[59] The widely prevailing concept of a "just price" rationalized the practice of guilds and public authorities in setting prices where commodity standards had been specified.[60] This, of course, served cartel purposes of local producers, but it also had the advantage of facilitating business dealing wherever a zone of price was indicated by fixing a salient figure that could be readily accepted by buyer and seller alike as a prevailing price.

The contemporary experience with nationwide price control, put into effect for most of the wartime periods for major participants in the two World Wars of the twentieth century, raises somewhat different issues than this earlier experience. The administrative resources for handling price controls were much more adequate because of the relatively large number of professionals who could be inducted into the administrative service of the wartime state. A much larger share of the volume of commodity traffic was handled by large-scale business concerns, and throughout the business world of the capitalist and corporate modes a uniform preticketed price was developed. This was published in schedules and bulletins and maintained as a basis for doing business for relatively long periods often standardized at a full year, making universal or near-universal price control more feasible than in centuries past. The exigent need was felt by wartime governments to mobilize a high fraction of social product and manpower for war purposes and to make this product available in new shapes and forms often calling for new production facilities in new locations. It was simply not feasible to seek to achieve this objective in a short time period by the method of the market, letting

---

[57] Adam Smith, *Wealth of Nations*, 1776, pages 491 f.

[58] On this famous "Assize of Bread and Ale" traceable to the mid thirteenth century, see A. Smith, *Wealth of Nations*, 1776, pages 178 ff.; Nef, *Industry and Government*, 1957, pages 28, 48.

[59] Nef, *Industry and Government*, 1957, pages 18 ff.

[60] Tawney, *Religion and the Rise of Capitalism*, 1926, pages 112 f., 180 ff., 85, 39 ff.

prices rise for goods and services most urgently needed with compensating price falls elsewhere.

Even high taxation of the resulting profit windfalls—and this was utilized as an adjunct method—would not achieve the objective sought because of widespread stimulus to the tendency to hoard scarce goods. Wage earners would necessarily seek through their unions to obtain compensatory wage increases, which would of course feed the flames of general inflation. The use of market methods to resolve the needs of a war economy was thus excluded in all the major warring countries. Various forms of universal price control with accompanying schemes of rationing were adopted in World War I.[61] Techniques of price control—ranging from the simple "price freeze" to the tailored regulation based upon customs of the trade—were developed, sometimes geared to some critical raw material whose price was set at the primary product level or a maximum price could be imposed and advertised at the retail level. While price control weakened the incentives to divert resources to the making of scarce goods, this was largely counteracted by the abnormal activity of the state. Under these circumstances and allowing for the effectiveness of the appeals to patriotism, it was the sober judgment of an outstanding classical economist, who carefully watched the process of the war economy, that "price control in the peculiar circumstances of the war caused very little damage to the volume of the national dividend."[62] The method of price control and rationing was sufficiently successful in World War I so that it was noncontroversial in World War II. It even was mustered into service in the United States for the "brushfire" Korean war of the early 1950s, and waiving aside the need for a war, it helped to produce the prosperity and expanding national income that reelected a Republican President in 1972.[63]

---

[61]The full reasoning behind this was worked out in the outstanding little book of J. K. Galbraith, *A Theory of Price Control*, 1952. On the English side the analysis of Pigou, *Economics of Welfare*, 1920, pt. 2, chs. 12, 13, is outstanding though confined to the experience in 1914–1918. See also his anticipatory *Political Economy of War*, 1921, chs. 10, 11. The American experience in World War II was effectively summarized in Seymour Harris, *Price and Related Controls*, 1945.

[62]Pigou, *Economics of Welfare*, 1920, page 241.

[63]The program of price control—installed in August 1971 with the act of devaluing the foreign-exchange value of the dollar (partly achieved by a temporary import tax on manufactured goods) and dropping gold convertibility—enabled the economy to resume its suspended growth, which the Federal Reserve authorities accommodated by an easy credit policy rendered tolerable because of the slowing down of the inflation process and the improvement in the foreign balance of payments. The retrospective analysis in the *Economic Report of the President*, 1974, ch. 3, is extremely one-sided and inadequate. Among professional American economists J. K. Galbraith probably stands alone for his strong defense of comprehensive price controls as an instrument of national policy to curb the process of inflation. See especially Galbraith, *The New Industrial State*, 1967, ch. 22.

In Western countries in the twentieth century price control ordinarily becomes a state function only in times of abnormal stress such as prolonged periods of major war. In the socialist economies price control as a central state function is called for by a double set of reinforcing pressures as a normal method of economic management. One of these pressures grows out of state socialization of industry, which usually takes the form of comprehensive industrial trusts or combines managing all enterprises that make the same line of products or perhaps use the same manufacturing technology. Even when more than one trust operates in a given commodity field, they cannot be expected to compete with each other for markets, patronage or supplies. And certainly other enterprises in a well-organized socialist economy will not be attracted to a given field that appears profitable and be able to set themselves up in business. Nor can competition be expected from foreign producers who are not allowed free entrance into the economic system with the right to establish enterprises, make profits, and withdraw them as they please. Industrial undertakings will thus possess an uncommon degree of monopoly power in their commodity area. If they could set prices with a free hand, their monopoly power would take a frightful toll at critical points in the commodity field. If industrial profits, however, are all commandeered by higher state authority, then the motive to exercise this monopoly power would be weakened but the incentive for efficient management would be weaker.

Such commandeering brings into play the second set of pressures that in the socialist economy call for price control. As their industrialization proceeded, the leaders of the Soviet economy realized that they needed to provide incentives up and down the line in socialized enterprises to manage resources efficiently and to strive for cost reductions or for improvements in quality. These incentives, it was found, could best take the form of "profit-sharing" arrangements with which the Soviet economy is littered. Profit sharing involves bonuses for meeting state targets. One of the best available and most generalized targets is precisely the earning of extra profits or the achievement of cost-cutting goals while aiming for output and quality targets. Bonuses for meeting these targets are paid out and provide incentives not only to management personnel but to the entire regular work staff of the enterprise. If management is not constrained as to the prices that may be charged, there is no assurance that additional profits earned are not the result of use of monopoly power in pricing rather than of efficient management or high work morale.

The two pressures converge to the same outcome. If competition cannot become the organizing force to control price levels and if profit is to serve as a motivating force for innovation and improved productivity, then pricing must be taken out of the hands of enterprise management and converted into a central state function operating by uniform principles through the entire economy.

OTHER REGULATORY FUNCTIONS

We can treat more briefly other regulatory functions that have lesser impact on overall economic conditions, or pertain chiefly to local affairs, or are of comparatively recent origin. Civilized states have often sought to regulate the rate of interest on money loans either by prohibition of giving or receiving interest or by fixing of maximum rates of interest. Loans were chiefly sought by distressed small commodity producers—craftsmen, dealers, and farmers— to tide over a bad harvest or to make up for losses in implements, seed, or livestock caused by natural disaster or sometimes to pay for a wedding feast or some other special need. Among upper classes loans would occasionally be sought by prodigal gentry or aristocrats or notables seeking to obtain funds for political campaigns or for needed public performances periodically called for in the Graeco-Roman world.[64] Only much later did states or their rulers enter loan markets and feel the sting of usury-capital. Business borrowing— except in the capitalist, corporate, or other advanced modes of production— was limited and was usually accommodated by credit arrangements granted by fellow merchants or by partnership arrangements with a share in the profits.[65]

Even in sophisticated credit markets exigent borrowers are dependent upon the goodwill and grace of lenders. In earlier conditions and for almost all small borrowers, needy borrowers are *unusually* dependent upon the few possible lenders who are in a position to monitor a loan, to know about the borrower's credit-worthiness, to be knowledgeable about the security proffered, or to be able to enforce the sanctions offered by the law to compel debt payment. Under these circumstances usury emerges with interest rates so high that small producers become impoverished and tend to lose their land, tools, or animal stock needed to carry on their work, and sometimes even their simple household goods, and so be forced into the position of dependent tenancy or outright slavery. Spendthrift aristocrats or gamblers lose their estates or patrimony. Usury becomes a branch of capital, or as Marx called it, an antediluvian form of capital that has a dissolving effect on the simple com-

---

[64]These two classic borrower types made up what Marx called the "characteristic forms" of usury capital in periods antedating capitalist production. See Marx, *Capital* III, 1864–1865, page 594. Adam Smith humorously noted that the "country gentlemen" scarce ever borrowed "merely to spend." The sum borrowed is "commonly spent before they borrow it." See *Wealth of Nations*, 1776, page 334. On money-lending among Roman notables, see Finley, *Ancient Economy*, 1973, pages 53 ff.

[65]The intermixture of deferred terms of payment and foreign-exchange elements in mercantile transactions made it easy for business men to disguise interest-taking in their mutual transactions when it could not take the form of a profit share or partnership return. Thus for disguised interest in the Jewish mercantile community of Cairo in the thirteenth century, see Goitein, *A Mediterranean Society*, 1967, 1971, vol. 1, pages 252 ff.

modity mode of production, particularly peasant proprietorship and village communities.[66]

Under these circumstances public sentiment against usury is very strong—especially in societies closer to emergence out of tribal and village communities with their sentiments for mutual help and solidarity. Early religious prophecy in the Near East banned taking of interest as sinful, and Greek philosophy put this sentiment in rational form.[67] Hence many economic systems had a total *verbot* on giving or taking interest on money loans. There is no way to tell whether (1) total *verbot* of interest was helpful to borrowers in preventing wealthier neighbors or relatives from taking advantage of their need and thus ameliorating the burdens of indebtedness and possible loss of collateral pledged as security for the loan; whether (2) the *verbot* tended to dry up willingness to lend on obviously unprofitable terms; or even (3) whether the *verbot* raised the costs of borrowing by making the transaction illegal and forcing interest rates to higher levels to allow for possible legal penalties. Of the three outcomes (1) seems more likely in more solidaristic guild or rural communities or among coreligionists,[68] (2) would apply to

[66]Marx, *Capital* III, 1864–1865, pages 593 ff.; and for a similar version, see Marx, *Theories of Surplus Value*, 1862–1863 vol. 3, pages 527 ff. The evidence for the oppressive burden of usury on small producers, when usury is not effectively combatted or offset, is extremely impressive. See especially Moore, *Dictatorship and Democracy*, 1966, pages 359 f.; G. Myrdal, *Asian Drama*, 1968, vol. 2, pages 104 ff.; T. C. Smith, *Modern Japan*, 1959, pages 158 ff.; Balazs, *Chinese Civilization and Bureaucracy, 1932–1961*, pages 23 f., 43 f.

[67]For the Old Testament see Exod. 22:25; Lev. 25:36; Deut. 23:20. For the Koran, see Sûrah II. par. 275; Sûrah III, par. 130; Sûrah IV, par. 161; Sûrah XXX, par. 39. According to Weber, early Brahmin texts speak similarly. See Weber, *General Economic History*, 1923, par. 268. Aristotle's interesting rationale for the interest *verbot* is found in *Basic Works*, "Politics," bk. 1, ch. 10. Though only a slim basis for an interest *verbot* is found in the New Testament (see Luke 6:35), Christian doctrine gradually evolved one which became very strong throughout the medieval period. See especially Tawney, *Religion and the Rise of Capitalism*, 1926, pages 39 ff., 45 ff., 137 ff.

[68]Thus Goitein's research disclosed widespread credit and loan activity within the Jewish mercantile community of Cairo from the tenth to twelfth centuries but conformity with the religious injunction not to take interest from coreligionists. Goitein, *A Mediterranean Society*, 1967–1971, vol. 1, page 262. Weber reported that Chinese clan monies would be loaned to clansmen at low interest rates. See Weber, *Religion of China*, 1916, pages 90 f. In East Africa detailed budget surveys showed that in 1969 the 2.5 million rural households of Tanzania—with a total gross agricultural production (including foods grown and consumed on the farm) valued at about 3 billion shillings—obtained by loan some 271 million shillings, mostly (88%) for a one-year term. For two-thirds of the country no interest was charged at all, with moderate interest rates for some loans in the remaining third; 80% of the loans were obtained from relatives. Borrowers in urban communities touched relatives for half their loans. Such is the solidarity of a generation of villagers where traditions and obligations of kinship are still vital and compelling. See Gottlieb, "Tanzanian Agricultural and Rural Society," 1973, pages 250 f. For a similar pattern in communal village society of the borrowing from friends and

longer-term loans which in general were rare in earlier times, while (3) would tend to occur in the more sophisticated mercantile communities where moneylending had been set up as a business, as in Adam Smith's eighteenth century world.[69] This *verbot* was not too hurtful to business borrowing, which could readily be classified as profit taking by a partner or as a commenda-participation.

At more advanced levels of economic life, the resemblance between interest on money loans to house rent on leases of urban homes or land rent on farm leases or profit earned on business capital made it difficult to uphold the legitimacy of the total *verbot*; and yet the need was felt to curtail the abuses of usury. Hence states set interest rates. The early Roman legal rate of 10% or 8.33% was apparently enacted in the infant stages of the young republic and pioneered in fixing interest rates.[70] That probably fit the maxim of Adam Smith that a maximum rate should be set "somewhat above the lowest market price commonly paid for the use of money by those who can give the most undoubted security."[71] Other maximum rates have spread all over the map.[72] Even better than a simple maximum rate is a schedule of maximum rates for different classes of borrowers or loans of the type enacted by Justinian in the latest law code of the classical Roman empire. That specified a rate of 4% for loans to notables in high positions, 6% for loans to the general public, 8% for loans invested in manufacturing or mercantile projects, and 12% for nautical loans.[73]

Care must be taken to allow for handling charges and for loans not backed by adequate collateral where the risk of loss of capital is appreciable. Otherwise imposition of lending maxima simply exclude many borrowers from the loan market or force them into collusion with illegal lenders. Best of all are interest rate regulations backed up by loan funds available to borrowers

---

relatives of small amounts carrying no interest, see Belshaw, *A Village Economy*, 1967, page 179.

[69]The interest *verbot*, says Adam Smith, "instead of preventing, has been found to increase the evil of usury; the debtor being obliged to pay not only for the use of the money, but for the risk which his creditor runs by accepting a compensation for that use." See *Wealth of Nations*, 1776, page 339.

[70]This maximum interest rate goes back to the Twelve Tables. *Corpus Juris Civilis*, A.D. 528–553, vol. 1, page 62. Scholars interpret the maximum rate set at 8.33%. Heichelheim, *An Ancient Economic History*, 1938, vol. 3, page 25. This effort at rate regulation broke down in the later years of the Republic.

[71]Adam Smith, *Wealth of Nations*, 1776, page 339.

[72]See various rate maxima for various medieval communities in Marx, *Capital* III, 1864–1865, page 597.

[73]Radin, *Handbook of Roman Law*, 1927, pages 185 f.; *Encyclopedia of Social Sciences*, 1930–1934, vol. 15, page 194; *Corpus Juris Civilis*, A.D. 528–553, vol. 2, "Opinions of Paulus," page 274.

or cooperative credit facilities on nonusurious terms. These had their beginnings in late medieval times among dedicated church orders.[74] Later in coming was assistance organized or fostered by government for aid or relief to victims of famine, flood, earthquake, or other disasters. Fire and related disaster insurance is a private commercial method for meeting possible future needs that in earlier times were accommodated by usury.

The state combats usury partly by imposition of restraints and prohibitions and partly by constructive facilities of its own devising. In the same way it functions in relation to urban planning by a mix of restraints, prohibitions, and constructive facilities. The latter are as old as the city itself, which almost everywhere in earlier times had walls and gates built as the city's outer boundary, thus defining its limits and potential size. As cities grew, boundary walls were extended.[75] At the city center another organized central facility was planned for public meetings, encampments, festivals or sports, adorned with temples, shrines and public buildings, and equipped with commercial market facilities.[76]

A city can hardly function unless arrangements are made for passageways by which residents in different parts of the city can get from one area to another. These through passageways must in some cases accommodate wheeled vehicles for bulk transportation. Roman cities were generally laid out with two major principal streets running north and south and east and west at right angles to each other and crossing at city center.[77] It was a de-

---

[74]For the effort by ecclesiastics to turn the flank on the usurer by establishing loan facilities for small borrowers, a movement later led by the Franciscans and widely spread on the Continent, see Tawney, *Religion and the Rise of Capitalism*, 1926, page 53. Also see the sardonic comments of Marx, *Capital* III, 1864–1865, page 601. A recent treatise by a contemporary Jesuit economist has nothing to say about these Franciscan institutions, though he comments much about usury and the stand of the Church. See Dempsey, *Functional Economy*, 1958.

[75]Mumford, *The City in History*, 1961, pages 39, 66, 78, 359. Early Greek cities are believed not to have been walled, though of course the construction of walls around Athens after the Persian Wars was a significant event (131f). Chinese, Roman, Near Eastern, and medieval European cities were all walled. Aristotle ridiculed the pretention that avoiding walls was a mark of civic courage, but he advised that walls could also be "ornamental" as well as useful. See *Basic Works*, "Politics," bk. 7, ch. 11.

[76]Aristotle, with his distaste for merchants, recommended that the marketplace be separated from the civic center. From the agora proper "all trade should be excluded and no mechanic, husbandman or any such person allowed to enter unless he be summoned by the magistrates. There should also be a traders' agora, distinct and apart from the other, in a situation which is convenient for the reception of goods by sea and land." See Aristotle, *Basic Works*, "Politics," bk. 7, ch. 12. As Mumford points out, the civic center is also usually a marketplace. *The City in History*, 1961, pages 149 ff.

[77]Mumford, *The City in History*, 1961, pages 207 f.

batable issue whether all streets should be laid out in a rectangular grid.[78] Municipal zoning separating commercial, industrial, and residential areas of a city came much later; homes at that time were built alongside or on upper floors of stores and workshops. Spacing of municipal baths and freshwater sources were planned and provided in conjunction with channeling of fresh water flows through the city.[79] Just as important as freshwater networks is disposal of those human and animal sanitary wastes not carefully collected for reuse on farms as fertilizer. In ancient times the oldest monument to Roman engineering, we are told, is the Roman sewer, the Cloaca Maxima, still in use today though planned and built in the sixth century B.C.[80]

Negative restraints would come by way of ordinances or rules relating to placing buildings on lots or construction to meet safety or fire-prevention requirements. One of the original Roman laws inscribed on the Twelve Tables contained a building setback requirement.[81] In the thirteenth century Lübeck enforced the use of fireproof roofing and the fireproof party wall, and London twice had to try to reduce fire hazards by first encouraging and later requiring construction of city buildings with fireproof outer walls and roofs.[82] Amsterdam with its building ordinance of 1565 probably led the way in regulating building to fit into a broadly conceived plan of urban construction involving a canal and road network with a form of zoning for location of buildings with different uses.[83] Urban planning since then has made great

---

[78]Aristotle commended as "agreeable and generally more convenient, if the streets are regularly laid out after the modern fashion which Hippodamus introduced, but for security in war the antiquated mode of building, which made it difficult for strangers to get out of town and for assailants to find their way in, is preferable." He therefore recommended that a "city should adopt both plans of building: it is possible to arrange the houses irregularly, as husbandmen plant their vines in what are called 'clumps.' The whole town should not be laid out in straight lines, but only certain quarters and regions; thus security and beauty will be combined." See *Basic Works*, "Politics," bk. 7, ch. 11.

[79]Aristotle stated that the town site should contain "a natural abundance of springs and fountains"—or, in their absence, "great reservoirs may be established for the collection of rainwater." See *Basic Works*, "Politics," bk. 7, ch. 11. Roman bath works were especially elaborate. "As early as the second century B.C. the habit of going to the public baths was established in Rome; and by 33 B.C. Agrippa introduced free public baths in the form that this institution was finally to take: a vast enclosure holding a great concourse of people, one monumental hall leading to another, with hot baths, tepid baths, cold baths, rooms for massage. . . . The religion of the body was as near as the Romans ever got to religion . . . and the public bath was its temple." Mumford, *The City in History*, 1961, page 226 f; for later medieval baths, see page 293.

[80]Mumford, *The City in History*, 1961, pages 215 f.

[81]Corpus Juris Civilis, A.D. 528–553, vol. 1, page 72.

[82]Mumford, *The City in History*, 1961, page 283.

[83]Mumford, *The City in History*, 1961, page 441.

progress, especially in the twentieth century in both the socialist and non-socialist worlds.

Local urban planning is complemented by national economic planning to promote economic development, a late state function.[84] In the late medieval and early modern period it began to take form among more aggressive states undertaking interconnected measures to promote economic development. The measures varied: bounties to reward producers of needed goods and services, efforts to attract artisans or mechanics possessed of special industrial skills, special rewards for inventors or innovators, state factories financed by the royal purse, and of course tariffs to protect domestic industries from foreign competition.[85]

In the nineteenth century national economic planning had chiefly a two-fold focus. It was exercised about such projects as railway development, which everywhere called for state action and sometimes for extensive use of state resources. Railways were a catalyst of industrial growth and market development. A second focus developed around efforts by central banks (in outer form, quasi-public corporations, but increasingly in substance quasi-state agencies) for banking regulation, taking the first steps to ameliorate the worst effects of the instability that plagued the growing world of capitalist and corporate enterprise, sometimes merely intervening at moments of panic. By the start of the twentieth century public central banking emerged with greater clarity, functioning—largely in isolation but sometimes in concert with other central banks—alternately to stimulate and check credit expansion in maintaining more stable economic conditions. This regulatory action by monetary authorities was joined by fiscal action from states that learned from the Great Depression of the 1930s that with central bank support the variation of deficit state spending could help to stabilize the economy. Thus the state assumed a leadership function—stimulating the rate of economic growth at a time of stagnation or slowing it down if too exuberant. Only after World War II was it learned that states could—by varying rates of taxation, again with the cooperation of central bank authorities—inject or withdraw new streams of purchasing power and thereby decisively influence rates of private spending and production and therefore the overall course of economic development.[86] This ability to guide economic development presupposes certain policy and

[84]"For the state to have an economic policy . . . continuous and consistent is an institution of exclusively modern origin." See Weber, *General Economic History*, 1923, page 343.

[85]"The seventeenth and eighteenth centuries saw most of the governments of continental Europe—foremost among them France, Prussia and Austria—engage in extensive and costly programmes of industrial development." See Landes, *The Unbound Prometheus*, 1969, page 135.

[86]Though the decisive event here was the Kennedy–Johnson tax cut of 1963–1964, fiscal policy and tax action played a significant role in previous recession periods (especially 1953–

institutional conditions which have lately come into question even though the technical feasibility of economic guidance has been strengthened by (1) the development of a complex system of national accounts, (2) an up-to-date comprehensive network of statistical reporting of current economic conditions, and (3) the further development of techniques of projection and forecasting.[87] Even the strongest monetary-fiscal policy is helpless unless the armoury of policy includes (1) an active incomes policy and willingness at times to use general wage and price controls and (2) a resolute facing of the problem of the foreign balance of payments to be coped with by an active exchange-rate policy and even a willingness at times to employ protective tariffs. Of course in socialist economies the function of the state to chart the course of economic development is institutionalized with the development of what we have earlier called "central economic planning" (see ch. 5, pages 229 ff.).

If national economic planning is a lately arrived state function, environmental protection is more newly born. Even in the nineteenth century and earlier, spasmodic efforts were made to stem the tide of environmental degradation that industry brought in its wake.[88] Smokestacks were pushed up to thin out and dissipate noxious fumes.[89] In Germany forests were carefully

---

1954), and the election campaign of 1980 made tax stimulatory action a celebrated instrument of national economic policy, though unfortunately in isolation from central bank policy—which holds the supreme veto power over state fiscal action.

[87]These conditions are fourfold. (1) There must be *awareness* of the power and scope of fiscal–monetary action and the diverse means by which it may be realized in action. This conscious awareness was brilliantly developed by J. M. Keynes and his followers, though in recent decades the development of so-called "monetarism" highlighted by that triumphant figure, Milton Friedman, has increasingly obscured the field and crippled the practice of fiscal–monetary policy. (2) There must be going systems of corporate and income taxation with withholding at the source to make tax action a feasible weapon. (3) The central bank must play an active banking role and have broad power to operate in debt markets of varying maturities and qualities and to influence loan policies of banks. The American central bank, judged by this standard, is vastly short of the mark. With its outlook and working practice twisted by "monetarism," it is virtually incapable of playing any role other than that of killing a boom and enforcing stagnation. (4) Fiscal policy must be free to incur deficits. The rising conservative consciousness in America, which has come close to enacting a constitutional amendment to prohibit deficit financing except in time of war, will make that exceptionally difficult while parodoxically it is indulging in irresponsible deficit finance.

[88]Some precursors of modern efforts to restrain pollution of ambient air or surface waters are traceable to medieval cities, which tried to hold down smoke pollution by proper location of industrial ovens or kilns using coal and of industrial facilities that commonly dumped waste products into nearby streams or shores. See Gimpel, *The Medieval Machine*, 1976, pages 85 ff.

[89]Marx, *Capital* I, 1867, page 505. Urban agglomeration, wrote Marx, "disturbs the circulation of matter between man and the soil i.e. it prevents the return to the soil of its elements

husbanded by state action. Elsewhere, however, great timberlands were given over to lumber concerns that unhesitatingly stripped them of their forest cover, changing the ecologic balance of vegetation and converting immense areas of wilderness into hideous wasteland. Unrestricted hunting in the forest country or rough uplands and unrestricted fishing in domestic or international waters wiped out entire species of birds, fish, and mammals and placed others near extinction.

Well into the twentieth century it was counted as urban improvement for sanitary wastes washed down by heavy rains to be expeditiously transported by great sewer systems to the nearest watercourses.[90] Dangerous toxic industrial wastes would be conveniently and carelessly led into public sewer systems or into adjacent streams or creeks—or else would be buried without protection of underground reservoirs or surface waters. Wastes in smaller towns and most commercial or industrial wastes were placed in open rat-infested dumps—constantly smouldering with submerged fires and pouring leachate into surface waters. At best, municipal solid wastes were burned in municipal incinerators, but without any effort at treating for fume discharge. Nor was attention given to the poisoning of the ambient urban atmosphere by exhaust fumes released by engines or by the great electric power stations, gas works, or industrial plants.

In the United States concerted curative efforts to regulate and abate pollution and spoliation of the environment began notably in the 1950s. The first act of regulation at the federal level was in 1956, when a government agency was empowered to control discharges endangering health or welfare into bodies of water. In 1963 an initial Clean Air Act set in motion a chain of research and further legislation that established control over important sources of air pollution, stationary and mobile. A new federal agency empowered to enforce environmental controls was established and stringent standards were laid down both in statutes and in implementing regulations.[91] Environmental groups were given special access to courts to question any action of government that would have a major impact on the environment. Each such action must be taken only after issuance of a comprehensive analysis of direct and indirect environmental impact that also examines alternative

consumed by man in the form of food and clothing; it therefore violates the conditions necessary to lasting fertility of the soil."

[90]In 1912–1920, the city of Milwaukee took great pride in constructing a sewage treatment plant and a network of intercepting sewers that collected sanitary wastes, which heavy rains would wash into outflow conduits emptying into the rivers circulating in the city. Previously, *all* sanitary wastes were simply sewered to the nearest river outlet. A conduit was built to pump Lake Michigan fresh water to flush the wastes quickly through the city, down the river, and out to the harbor.

[91]See E. S. Mills, *Economics of Environmental Quality*, 1978, ch. 7.

methods of achieving the objectives sought and shows evidence of concern for protection of environmental quality.[92]

A near-universal standard is now imposed on industry and municipalities to adopt the "best available technology" for pollution abatement.[93] And this regulation has borne its fruits in improved waters and a reduced pollution of the atmosphere. In the later years of the 1970s 2–2.5% of GNP has been invested annually in pollution abatement. Total expenditure, both public and private, for the purpose for 1978 was $47.6 billion. In a recent year 118 recalcitrant industrial plants were forcibly closed.[94] The regulatory effort to check pollution of the environment has even entered in a significant way into the resolution of the energy crisis confronting the United States by preserving wilderness areas, checking oil development in shorelands, curtailing strip mining of coal and the burning of sulphurous coal, and sacrificing in some instances fuel efficiency to promote pollution abatement.[95] A new environmental consciousness is sweeping over other advanced industrial countries of the Western world and has even made an impact on the socialist countries.[96]

ESSENTIAL PUBLIC WORKS

The state function of providing essential public works was judged by Adam Smith the "third and last duty of the sovereign or commonwealth"—coming after only defence and administration of justice.[97] Before considering their rationale, it is essential to consider their far-reaching scope and diverse forms. Public works as related to economic systems may be comprehended under four broad fields: (1) transportation, (2) national protection, (3) waterworks, and (4) recreational, cultural, or aesthetic appreciation. The latter class include palaces, capital buildings, or royal sepulchers which figure largely in public display and symbolize the authority and majesty of the state.

[92]Reference is to the National Environmental Policy Act of 1970. Up through 1977, over 10,000 EISs have been filed and some 938 court actions were instituted against federal agencies. In 202 cases injunctions were issued under NEPA delayed actions. Council on Environmental Quality, *9th Annual Report*, 1978, pages 396 ff.

[93]See the informed discussion of this standard and its variant forms of expression in E. S. Mills, *Economics of Environmental Quality*, 1978, pages 186 f., 216 f., 255 ff. Automobiles have been generally subject to specific statutory standards incorporating Congressional notions of the "best available technology." Abatement of water pollution is expressly subject to that standard.

[94]U.S. Council on Environmental Quality, *9th Annual Report*, 1978, pages 418, 424, 432.

[95]Stobaugh and Yergin, *Energy Future*, 1979, pages 91 ff.; Office of Technology Assessment, *The Direct Use of Coal*, 1979, ch. 5.

[96]See E. S. Mills, *Economics of Environmental Quality*, 1978, ch. 10 for an interesting review of environmental policy in Sweden, South Korea, and Japan.

[97]See A. Smith, *Wealth of Nations*, 1776, page 681.

Facilities for public transportation probably make up the largest category of public works. These primarily embrace a network of city surface roads that enable the population gathered together in a city or town to utilize its different facilities, to have ready entry to its markets, and to participate with their neighbors in public meetings, courts, festivals, and local defense. Without such a network the town would be economically and socially dead—a random agglomeration of persons with limited ability to cooperate with each other, obstructed by their own mass and isolated in their own quarters. This road network will commonly differentiate between local pedestrian passageways or alleys following meandering routes and wider thoroughfares commonly passing through the city center and exiting at town gates. Even farming villages must have planned roadways, generally centering on a single main street, to accommodate the traffic of animals and wheeled carts, beside which houses and adjunct buildings are sited. Depending upon local need, such city roadways may be improved by providing drainage ditches, by installing hard surfacing to facilitate passage for vehicles in rainy weather, and with bridges or crossways over rivers and streams. Whether the road network will be labeled to facilitate giving directions or finding particular structures will depend upon the literacy of the population, the development of an orderly mapping technique, and the relative number of migrants or visitors to the city.

In some economic systems, of course, the road network of a metropolitan community extended into the adjacent countryside, to serve an entire local economy. But in the more developed forms of economic life, the territorial embrace of an economic system will go far beyond that of a single major urban community and its immediate hinterland. Many urban communities will then be included—with their differing environments, resources, and potential for economic development. If this development is to occur, the various urban communities must be linked together into a larger society by facilities for transportation that permit movement of people and products throughout the entire society. This enables the members of the society to feel more unified and drawn together to their common advantage and strength. Movable resources can then be tapped by taxation and made available for public purposes. The beginnings of territorial division of labor may then emerge, enabling regions to specialize along lines of true comparative advantage, thereby enhancing the prosperity and productivity of the entire society. These lines of specialization may be based upon varying environmental endowment, developed artisanship skills, or the mere economies of mass production where the proper technology has emerged.

For inland territories facilities of transportation are best provided by waterways, inland seas, navigable rivers, and man-made canals. But these cannot extend in many directions or provide access to many upland territories or mountainous regions, nor will they commonly enable populations settled in different riverine basins to have adequate inland connection with one another. Hence there is need for a network of highways providing arterial transportation for wheeled vehicles or pedestrian traffic. Since these highways will need to include costly structures bridging rivers, gorges, and streams or providing roadbeds through lowlands or marshy areas or climbing mountain passes, it is wise and prudent to build these arterial ways well, providing them with drainage ditches and a secure rock foundation and surfacing of a character that will not wash away. The Romans were famous for their long-lasting highways excavated from a roadbed some 5–6 feet deep and with layers of crushed or broken rock or rubble of different sizes—the whole being topped with flat stone slabs and often accompanied by curbs, ditches, or embankments and with retaining walls along the side of steep slopes.[98] The Chinese built highways almost as well as the Romans, even with greater ingenuity through the mountainous terrain across the great rivers, which they crossed with their remarkable beam, cantilever, and arch bridges—some with a span of up to 200 feet.[99]

An improved form of highway with hard surface will enable a horse to pull a wagon three times as heavy as on a soft road surface. But far more efficient is an iron or steel rail that minimizes friction and is four times more efficient than the best hard surface road.[100] Thus the railroad permits distant inland regions not linked by waterways to exchange bulk goods with each other and develop the full economies of specialized production. The railroad is, of course, only a specialized kind of road that to support heavier vehicles and loads must have sturdier foundations and be laid out on steadier grades. Thus railroads are more constrained by their site and grade requirements than highways so that between any two points to be connected suitable rail right-of-way will be relatively limited. Whereas other roadways and waterways are commonly traversed by many vehicles whose operations are uncoordinated with each other and with diversified points of ingress and egress, railroads are commonly required by their limitations of trackage to permit only a single vehicle operator with complete authority over track operations. Railroads thus by their nature enjoy a double transportation monopoly: first, over choice rights-of-way and terminal facilities, and secondly over rights to operate trains on the railroad. This monopoly, however, can only be achieved and optimized by dint of heavy investment in preparing a well-built, well-drained right-of-way and maximum reduction of grade stress.

Monopoly is presupposed since a proper and well-selected right-of-way cannot be obtained except by grant of public domain or by use of the coercive

[98]Needham, *Science and Civilization in China*, 1954–1978, vol. 4, bk. 3, page 1 f. and copious references to special authorities.

[99]Needham, *Science and Civilization in China*, 1954–1978, vol. 4, bk. 3, pages 147 ff.

[100]Needham, *Science and Civilization in China*, 1954–1978, vol. 4, bk. 3, page 216.

power of the state to expropriate land. Its prior owners are pushed aside with minimal compensation that does not allow for the cost of resettling in other communities, the inconvenience of splitting a property with limited access routes, or sentimental values associated with a homestead or kinship ties. The state is itself a monopoly organization that brings to life a railroad by its sovereign power. The monopoly power of railroads is further attested to by the traditional and habitual reliance for setting rates not on cost of service but on ability to pay as if a tax were levied.[101]

This natural monopoly of the railroad is not only local but national. The first railroads were only local roads connecting a few well-traveled points. But as soon as many railroads were constructed it became highly desirable for them to form regional trunk systems and ultimately a continuous network permitting through transportation from any one shipping point to another in the system. For this to be achieved, railroad operations throughout the system have to be unified.[102] Through traffic must be managed by different lines without constant repacking or handling of cargo or loaded cars at division points. Traffic schedules everywhere must be worked out in advance and published so that shipments may be appropriately routed. Payment for traffic must be administered with a single billing. Common terminal facilities and switching yards need to be provided in major metropolitan centers where many railroad lines can come to a common center to economize on use of valuable urban land, to facilitate transfer of cars and makeup of new trains between lines, and to make rerouting of passengers more convenient. Finally, there must be ready movement of rolling stock over all lines because cars loaded at one end of the system may wind up at the opposite end.[103]

---

[101]The authoritative Board of Investigation and Research in one of its reports characterized the freight-rate structure of common carriers as an outgrowth of the monopolistic theory of charging "what the traffic will bear" deformed by competition into a "crazyquilt of inequalities and discriminations." Our value of service-rate structure, related chiefly to ability to pay and not long-run marginal costs, is thus a "device of income redistribution not unlike the federal income tax." Board of Investigation and Research, *Economy and Fitness of the Carriers*, 1944, page 6; Nelson and Greiner, "Relevance of the Common Carrier," 1965, pages 352 f.

[102]In a single chapter of his interesting treatise on inland transportation, Stuart Daggett seeks to describe the pattern of "operating cooperation which contributes to the functioning of American railroads as a single transportation system." See Daggett, *Principles of Inland Transportation*, 1928, ch. 23, page 461. The operation of this inherently unified system by a congeries of individual railroad corporations—some with giant networks, others with key local routes—leads to massive wastes and diseconomies, system malfunctioning, induced regulation with its binding rules and elaborate red tape, and withall much opportunity for gouging of captive shippers and pillaging of railroad stockholders by speculative insiders.

[103]Indicative of the tendency for rolling stock dispersal over a ramifying rail network optimally managed is the fact that after two years of government operation in World War I, only 317 of the cars reported by large railroads were owned by the reporting railroad. See Daggett, *Principles of Inland Transportation*, 1928, page 471.

Since rarely do any two regions have a balanced flow of shipments or a flow with the same seasonal patterns, individual links in the railroad network would be unlikely to reverse the flow of car movements so that freight cars of origin could be promptly returned loaded to the sender. For optimal handling even the decision to add rolling stock to the system can best be taken after evaluating traffic requirements of the whole system and not merely any individual link in it. Likewise, the management of traffic flows and scheduling must be centralized to make optimal use of existing rolling stock and trackage with a minimization of empty or idle rolling stock and a maximum speed of movement of traffic through the system. Due allowance also has to be made for seasonal needs such as moving the agricultural harvest or, in years past, the winter coal supply for space-heating. It is not accidental that linear programming models were first put to practical use in the solution of transportation problems involving optimal use of transportation resources where alternative routing or transportation techniques were available for choice.[104]

Still competing with railroads and highways are inland waterways, which under favorable conditions offer unexampled economies of fuel efficiency. The tractive effort to move at slow speeds a given weight in vessels that are floating on water is much less than for vehicles moving on wheels.[105] Adam Smith regaled his readers by noting that six or eight men sailing between London and Leith, Scotland, can transport the same quantity of goods as 50 broad-wheeled wagons attended by 100 men and drawn by 400 horses.[106] The economy of water transport is, of course, highest in moderate latitudes that have no winter freeze and on open inland or coastal waters or on river channels in their lower basin with suitable water depth and few natural obstructions. To create extended networks of navigable inland waterways suitable for large craft, considerable investment is usually required for dredging silted-up areas, removing snags or other obstructions, constructing low-level storage dams to raise the level of water flow in the natural channel—combined of course with locks to permit boat passage—or building great storage reservoirs in high-basin areas to even out yearly water flow. In suitable terrain it is even desirable to construct man-made waterways or channels on excavated beds in areas where freshwater sources can be tapped. Locks or lifts accommodate a considerable change of grade in crossing ridges or traversing hilly areas. Distant riverine basins, like those of the Hudson River and the

---

[104]Lange, *Introduction to Econometrics*, 1957, pages 310–347; Kantorovich, 1959, pages 435 ff.; Veinshtein, 1966, pages 469 ff.

[105]Needham specifies a fourfold advantage in barge traffic on a river over a vehicle traveling on iron rails and a sixfold advantage on canal traffic, assuming in each case a horse is pulling a loaded wagon, barge, or vessel. See *Science and Civilization in China*, 1954–1978, vol. 4, bk. 3, 216.

[106]See A. Smith, *Wealth of Nations*, 1776, page 18.

Great Lakes, can be joined together by summit or contour canals—now found all over the world. Although heavy initial costs of construction are encountered with canals, once they are built their upkeep is moderate, wear and tear with use is negligible, and in their basic structure they have a near-perpetual service life.

Canals, navigable rivers, and inland seas or lakes are first improved with dock and lock facilities, ports, navigation aids as individual projects with a primary eye to local use. Hence these facilities vary widely in the size and depth of shipping that can be accommodated. As waterway linkages are extended and joined together, permitting through traffic and a more nationwide circulation of commercial shipping, diversity of design handicaps carriage and calls for nationwide development including standardization, surveillance, and planning. Absence of a national consolidation of waterways may, as in England, paralyze water-borne commerce.[107] In the United States the construction of the Panama Canal and the existence of a remarkable matrix of natural or man-made riverine channels and waters connecting ports on the Great Lakes, Atlantic Ocean, and Gulf Coast with the river networks of the Mississippi, Missouri, and Ohio rivers—extending north–south and east–west for a thousand miles or more in each direction—stimulated the adoption of a national plan for the development of America's inland waters.[108] That plan was made possible by an old tradition of national responsibility for improvements to navigable waters, by the favorable experience of the Erie Canal built early in the nineteenth century, by the Panama Canal built in the early years of the twentieth century, and finally by the need to improvise inland water-barge transportation during World War I.[109]

Like all national transport systems, waterways require elaborate navigational aids and terminal facilities. Harbors in protected inlets or bays where

[107]Marshall, *Industry and Trade*, 1919, pages 497 ff. The "numerous companies that were responsible for individual canals seemed perversely to ignore one another's practise." Some locks were made long and narrow, others short and broad so that "many journeys were possible only for boats that were short and narrow, and therefore wasteful of the labour of man and horse" (498). This diversity of gauge was also experienced on American railways as late as 1865—when "there was no uniformity of gauge and great inconvenience and expense was involved in the transshipment of freight at connecting points between railroads having different gauges." See Dewing, *Financial Policy of Corporations*, 1919, vol. 2, page 951ii.

[108]See the summary sketch of the plan for waterways improvement developed by Herbert Hoover when he was Secretary of Commerce in Daggett, *Principles of Inland Transportation*, 1928, pages 37 ff. The Hoover plan involved a 9-foot channel east–west from Pittsburg on the Ohio to Kansas City on the Missouri and from New Orleans to Chicago, later extended to Minneapolis by the construction of a series of 26 low-water dams.

[109]A federal barge service on the Mississippi and Warrior rivers was commenced in 1918 under the stress of war conditions. That barge service was later operated as a commercial corporation under the War Department and was only denationalized in 1953. See Daggett, *Principles of Inland Transportation*, 1928, pages 42 ff.

boats can be protected from storm waters; docks or piers where boats can be conveniently unloaded with suitable warehousing space; lighthouses to assist navigation and markers to guide pilotage through narrow channels or passes; maps and radio beacons—are all necessary for waterways to function for transportation purposes.

The waterway system cannot be developed in isolation from rail and highway networks. Each of the three has marked advantages in certain terrain, over certain areas, and for certain types of loads. Highway carriage is convenient and economical especially for short-haul trips in and out of urban places where pickup and delivery can easily be made. Railroads are more economical for bulk shipments going a longer distance over land where improved waterways are not available. Waterway traffic itself, though ideal for bulk cargo, can rarely undertake carriage all the way on water. Each of the three systems will encounter areas where rapidly rising costs of carriage per mile make use of the system unsuitable.[110] To function efficiently, the three systems should be interconnected—standardized as far as possible for easy handling by containers and with arrangements for through shipments and billing with joint terminal facilities. Alfred Marshall pointed out the great advantages for system design and operation if the three systems were integrated. Integration should allow for locational decisions to site industry, especially with electric power generation that essentially converts energy in coal to electricity.[111] In the United States the principle of unified national trans-

[110]One curious manifestation of this uneven cost level in railroads is indicated by the wide variation in cost per mile of the seven railroads participating in the formation in 1848 of the New York Central Railroad: it ranged from $22,410 to $94,985 per mile. On the Mississippi River from the mouth of the Ohio River to New Orleans, the ton-mile cost over a 50-year period (all expenditures included) was 1.7 mills per ton-mile; from the mouth of the Missouri River to the mouth of the Ohio River it was 4.9 mills. On the Missouri River from Kansas City to its mouth the cost was 107.8 mills, and from Sioux City to Kansas City it was 319 mills. See Locklin, *Economics of Transportation*, 1935, page 759; Dewing, *Financial Policy of Corporation*, 1919, vol. 2, page 947.

[111]Marshall pointed out the "diminuitive scale of Britain's geographical features brings many of her industrial centers, which are not easily to be approached by waterways, into close connection with them by motor traffic." Whenever a road comes near "to any part of a busy network of canals, contact can be made between water traffic and roadmotor traffic." Moreover, he pointed out, the need for traction on canals—especially where lifts in place of locks were employed—could now be achieved by means of electric power and this could economically be provided if central electric power stations were sited on canal networks thus bringing inexpensively freighted coal to the power stations. Such traction "has the incidental advantage of adaptability to single boats and trains of boats of various sizes." He also pointed out that standardization of electric power produced in grid networks for regional distribution with a uniform frequency was itself very desirable and much needed. Use of canal banks as routes for main wires would be serviceable. Containers for load carriage were already developed and they seemed "to contain the germ of a method by which transport by road, motor, railway and canal may be worked into organized unity, with the result of greatly lowering the costs

portation planning was accepted and given institutional support in 1940 but the mixed makeup of our transportation system and its predominant private carrier basis made that principle largely an empty generality.[112]

Waterways and especially inland waterways are only one form of water works. Other types are designed to serve quite different purposes: (1) to abate damage to human settlements caused by flood waters, (2) to provide water for irrigating farmlands, and (3) to conduct fresh water into cities from suitable sources and to conduct waste waters out of cities into some suitable outlet.

Flood abatement is needed because farmers in their search for good farmland are prone to settle in the fertile flat silt-rich plains formed by great rivers constantly liable to flood with seasonal rainfalls or spring thaws. Quite apart from prohibiting settlement of areas prone to flood, three types of public works may abate flood damage. The most common form of abatement is, of course, building dikes to protect flood plains. In the Yellow River valley— especially prone to silt and flood because of the high seasonality of rainfall, 80% of which occurs in the three summer months—various sets of dikes have been constructed, with an average width at the top of 50 feet. Because the bed of the Yellow River in its flow through the alluvial lands has risen about 3 feet per century due to silting, it has been necessary continually to raise the dikes. The bed of the river is now generally at the level of the plain and in some places as much as 12 feet above it. In high flood the river in the lower basin runs in an elevated channel above the surrounding land surface. The disaster of a break in the dike wall and a release of the flood waters over

---

of handling traffic." Lapsing from his normal caution, Marshall could not help expressing a conviction that the "full development of a canal system in association with electricity [and road and railway networks] might gradually go far towards enabling Britain to maintain her high place as a leader of industry, in spite of her great inferiority in natural resources. . . ." All this was developed in a complex argument with the following summary: "The relations of Britain's railways to heavy goods traffic may possibly be considerably modified by her exceptional facilities for the cooperation of road motors with her canals and for electric haulage on her canals." See Marshall, *Industry and Trade*, 1919, pages 500–506. Marshall's conclusion for nationalization of railroads and canals—and, by implication, electric power generation— was only faintly indicated in the text.

[112]For citations to and an evaluation of the 1940 policy enactment of the Congress establishing the goal of a comprehensive transportation policy that would allow a fair place for all modes of transportation, see Daggett, *Principles of Inland Transportation*, 1928, ch. 35; Dewey, "The Transportation Act of 1940," 1941; Locklin, *Economics of Transportation*, 1935, pages 265 ff. One of the major tasks of Soviet transportation planning is to work out an "optimal distribution of goods carriage among the different modes of transport." See Koval and Miroshnichenko, *Soviet Economic Planning*, 1972, page 169. How effectively this is carried out is another question, especially before the economic reform of 1965, when money costs of production and charges were an unimportant socioeconomic indicator.

the adjacent plain may become permanent, because as the velocity of the river movement slows down in the riverbed, the silt deposition increases so that return to the old channel after the flood may be precluded if it is plugged with silt. In the past one thousand years some eight major changes in channels occurred after disastrous floods that breached the dikes.[113]

Beside dikes to hold back flood waters, those waters can be impounded in suitable terrain by constructing storage reservoirs with diversion canals for irrigation projects. In the upper reaches of the river where silt-deposition is less of a menace, construction of dams with waters released for purposes of generating electrical power may also serve to restrain flood flows. And beyond these there is the more extended work of seeking to undo the work of deforestation that increases surface water runoff and causes gullies and silt erosion. This work is carried on chiefly by planting trees on mountain slopes or along wastelands and by terracing fields on arable slopes.[114] It has even been possible by incredible field labor in communist China to level out gullied land and turn it into contour strip fields. Public works of this character can only be motivated by a deep-seated loyalty of people to country and a widespread willingness of the rural population to improve their lands.[115]

The simplest model of a flood-control reservoir used for irrigated farming is probably that erected in the Nile River Valley. There, beginning about 4000 years ago, the cultivated area of alluvial plain was divided by massive man-made banks into retention basins averaging some 7000 acres. With the river in high flood, water was led upstream by canals into the basin from which smaller channels distributed water throughout the area. When the soil was thoroughly soaked, the surplus water could be let into another basin; the extent of inundation was subject to regulation by the calculated amount of available flood waters as indicated by upstream measuring devices. The average water depth in the basins was 3 feet when the river at its maximum was 30 feet above its bed. The basins were on the average filled with water only 45 days of the year, during which period the deposition of silt would yield a fertile moist surface for farming purposes.[116]

---

[113]For these facts about the Yellow River flood-control system we are indebted to Needham, *Science and Civilization in China*, 1954–1978, vol. 4, bk. 3, pages 217 ff. and the more recent account Huang Wei, *Conquering the Yellow River*, 1978, pages 12–48. The lower Mississippi River has in modern history changed its course six times. *New York Times*, November 21, 1980.

[114]When mountain slopes are burned, overgrazed or cut to a cover of under 10%, almost two-thirds of falling rains become water runoff, as against 2% for well-covered slopes. See Kerr, *Land, Wood and Water*, 1963, page 50.

[115]Wei, *Conquering the Yellow River*, 1978, pages 35 ff.

[116]Needham, *Science and Civilization in China*, 1954–1978, vol. 4, bk. 3, pages 365 f.; Hawkes, *The First Great Civilizations*, 1973, pages 327 ff.

In the Tigris–Euphrates valley, however, such short-term inundatory canals were not feasible. There it was necessary to build diversion canals with perennial flow, sometimes commenced in the upper reaches of the river, conveying away water from diversion dams or weirs and conducting it for long stretches—in one case 250 miles, along which water was drawn off for farming purposes by lateral diversion ditches or canals. Such canal systems over arid lands proliferated in the Islamic culture area. Similar diversion canals now irrigate immense areas in the Colorado River basin in Southwestern United States, the upper courses of the Yellow River in China, and many other rivers all over the world.

Another whole category of waterworks is designed to serve the needs of urban populations. Where the city is not constructed on a site equipped with ample fresh water as it enlarges, water must be brought in by an aqueduct system—sometimes over a considerable distance, as with two great American metropolitan centers, Los Angeles and New York City.[117] Aqueducts were distributed all over the Roman world.[118] Even cities fortunately sited on the edge of relatively clean clear water lakes, such as Chicago, must still send their water intake lines deep into the lake to obtain usable water supplies. These must be filtered and treated for pollution and then distributed over the city in high-pressure pipelines.[119]

An equally elaborate system of public works is required for orderly disposal of sanitary wastes. However, this has not been so universal a need as fresh water supply, because in the past many cities of the world collected urban sanitary wastes for use on nearby farms, or else they were simply deposited in a nearby pit, dumped into the nearest watercourse, or even left unattended on public streets. The Romans had a passion for sewers exhibited early in the Republic. Not until modern times has the Roman sewer-building record been equaled—though only in the recent Western world has man deliberately set about to treat his sanitary wastes and to discharge only a relatively harmless effluent to local watercourses. That undertaking in the United States is

[117]Los Angeles draws water from the distant Colorado River; New York City scours the Catskills. Mumford, *The City in History,* 1961, pages 477 f., 549.

[118]By A.D. 300 Roman engineers had constructed 14 aqueducts, which brought to the immense city some 400,000 gallons per day. Roman cisterns and aqueducts were built in such cities as Nimes, Lyons, Segovia, Athens, Istanbul, and Tunis. The Roman historian Frontinus wrote proudly, "With such an array of indispensable structures carrying so many waters, compare, if you will, the idle Pyramids or the useless, though famous, works of the Greeks." See Kerr, *Land, Wood and Water,* 1963, page 18.

[119]When Milwaukee experienced water shortage in the hot dry summer of 1955, the city projected a major waterworks expansion program involving a second intake line into Lake Michigan, a second filtration plant, and a new set of reservoir facilities and pipelines altogether costing $55 million. See Gottlieb, "Milwaukee Waterworks Expansion," 1964, pages 217–225. See also an earlier study on municipal waterworks, Gottlieb, "Urban Domestic Demand for Water," 1963, pages 204–210.

a goal imposed upon industry and urban collectivities with a probable cost of well over $100 billion.[120]

To achieve that goal, we have to construct not one but two sewer systems. One collects the runoff of surface waters from roofs and street drains, which generally can be carried untreated to the nearest local watercourse. The other collects sanitary wastes that need to be carried by separate sewers to some central treatment facility before discharging as harmless effluent into a local watercourse or body of water. Both sewer systems will involve a comprehensive network of local collecting sewer lines running along the streets and connected either to roof or street drains or to sanitary lines, which in turn must feed into intercepting or main sewers that discharge into treatment plants or watercourses. The older, unsegregated sewer lines made effective sewage treatment difficult because the intercepting sewers designed to carry all collected wastes to a sewerage treatment works would be oversize for use in dry weather and would be grossly undersized for handling heavy rain waters.[121]

Let us turn now to the third class of public works—the one that furthers purposes of protection from domestic and foreign enemies. Beside providing amenities for good urban housekeeping, a primary early task confronting the city was to build walls to protect itself from those who would seek to pillage or destroy it. After the Persian invasion of the fifth century, Athens led the way in building defensive walls that followed the practice of other urban communities of the Near East.[122] Even in Aristotle's time people debated whether cities should be walled. The strongest wall, he advised, "will be the

[120]A recent (1976) biennial survey of state and local governments to determine funds needed to meet the 1983 goals of the Federal Water Pollution Control Act estimated an investment of $150 billion for collection, treatment, and intercepting sewers or works. That did not include many completed sewer treatment projects locally funded or financed in part by federal grants commenced in 1957—of which 2345 projects had already been completed. Council on Environmental Quality, *8th Annual Report*, 1977, pages 27 ff.

[121]Nearly one-half of the water basins in the Great Lakes and northeastern regions of the United States are adversely affected by combined sewer outflows; for the entire country, one-third of the cost of pollution abatement is due to the cost of remedying the combined sewer system. Council on Environmental Quality, *9th Annual Report*, 1978, pages 109 f.

[122]The story of the building of these walls, which greatly angered the Spartans and entered into the making of the Peloponnesian War, was told by both Thucydides and Plutarch. See Thucydides, *Peloponnesian War*, bk. 1, par. 89–94; Plutarch, *Lives*, "Themistocles," par. 19 (page 145 of cited edition). Mumford presents the matter as if Athens innovated in building its walls. See *The City in History*, 1961, pages 131 f. But according to Thucydides' cited account, the Athenians set about "rebuilding" their "city and their walls." The Spartans held that in the event of another Mede invasion, absence of walls in the ultra-Peloponnesian cities would deprive the Mede invaders of strong points and the Peloponnese wall "would suffice for all as a base both for retreat and offense." Obviously this strategy did not appeal to the Athenians, who knew of the wall that the Spartans had hastened to build earlier to guard the Isthmus approach to Spartan territory. Herodotus, *The Histories*, bk. 9, par. 8. It is not that the walls were always wanted; the Athenians themselves tore down walls of defeated Greek enemy states. See Thucydides, *Peloponnesian War*, bk. 1, par. 108–110.

truest soldierly precaution more especially now that missiles and siege engines have been brought to such perfection."[123] Without learning from philosophy, Roman, Chinese, Near Eastern, and medieval cities were invariably walled and often moated as well. Even the monumental double walls and deep moats described so vividly by Herodotus did not save the great city of Babylon from Persian conquest. It made the conquest more difficult and perhaps delayed its advent, just as at a later time the great walls around Constantinople for so long held off the Muslim assailants.[124]

City walls are only the first form of public works designed for purposes of protection. From then on the array is endless: fortifications, commanding port entrances and at stategic mountain passes, outlying military bases, weapons-producing plants and arsenals, networks of scanning devices on ground and in space. In 1958 the value of all U.S. military structures, stated in the current prices of the day, was some $56 billion. Much larger amounts were invested in movables such as Atomic Energy Commission (AEC) equipment or in nuclear stockpiles.[125] The development of more complex defense and attack systems—like the sensory, reporting, and launching devices connected with space weaponry—would tend to increase investment in military structures. In the last decade Defense Department real property inventories have escalated by some billion dollars per year, and defense construction in progress since 1975 has amounted to over $4 billions annually.[126] The world total for military public works in 1958 was near $100 billion and is probably double that now, since the American share of worldwide military expenditures has been running during the past two decades between 25% and 50%.[127]

It is pleasant to turn our attention from protective public works serving military purposes to public works serving cultural, recreational, or aesthetic purposes. Our deepest enjoyments often come from public works built and designed to produce aesthetic effects. Included here are the shrines, museums, temples, memorials, and great public buildings that both bring large numbers of people together on meaningful occasions and exude a constant sense of monumental art. Architecture was for Hegel the most basic of the fine arts.[128]

---

[123]Aristotle, *Basic Works*, "Politics," ch. 7, par. 11.

[124]Herodotus, *The Histories*, bk. 1, par. 181–191.

[125]Goldsmith, *The National Wealth of the United States in the Postwar Period*, 1962, Table B-172B.

[126]U.S. Bureau of Census, *Statistical Abstract*, 1978, page 376.

[127]U.S. Bureau of Census, *Statistical Abstract*, 1978, page 376. The estimate in the text of course presupposes that military public works have the same relative military importance elsewhere as in the United States.

[128]Listing the individual fine arts, Hegel commences with architecture, "the beginning of all, whose foundation reposes in the very nature of its subject-matter." See Hegel, *Philosophy of Fine Art*, 1835, vol. 3, page 18. He cited approvingly a definition of architecture as "frozen music" (page 65).

The Greeks and later the Romans and medieval Italians lavished infinite care on their civic centers and main public avenues. In this parade of public beauty that blended together painting, sculpture, and architecture, Pericles in fifth century Athens led the way. He turned a public works program to relieve unemployment into a colossal beautification program—which, he claimed, "will provide inspiration for every art, find employment for every hand and transform the whole people into wage-earners so that the city will decorate and maintain itself at the same time from her own resources." This program

> would involve many different arts and industries and require long periods to complete, his object being that those who stayed at home, no less than those serving in the fleet or the army or on garrison duty should be enabled to enjoy a share of the national wealth. The materials used were stone, bronze, ivory, gold, ebony, and cypress-wood, while the arts or trades which wrought or finished them were those of carpenter, modeller, coppersmith, stone-mason, dyer, worker in gold and ivory, painter, embroiderer and engraver, and besides these the carriers and suppliers of the materials. . . . There were also ropemakers, weavers, leatherworkers, roadbuilders and miners . . . with its own corps of unskilled labourers . . . and through these various demands the city's prosperity was extended far and wide and shared among every age and condition in Athens.

So the buildings, we are told, arose "as imposing in their sheer size as they were inimitable in the grace of their outlines, since the artists strove to excel themselves in the beauty of their workmanship." The director and supervisor of the program was the incomparable Pheidias, who personally directed the making of the great golden statue of Athena, the patron goddess of Athens, and his name was duly inscribed upon the marble tablet on the Acropolis as its creator.[129] The exuberance of this public display of beauty was quite in contrast with the simple character of Greek private dwellings. As Hegel put it, "They entirely devoted the splendor and beauty of art to public objects."[130] Private appropriation and seclusion are, of course, not needed for enjoyment of beauty. Though modern societies have been unable to replicate this early Athenian model of aesthetic achievement in public works, many at least take care to unify the architecture and style of civic centers, which are laid out commonly in a setting of walkways, colonnades, and grassy knolls. And in modern urban communities throughout the nations great parks have been created where another and more natural kind of beauty is made available in woods and water and landscape.

---

[129]Plutarch, *Lives*, "Pericles," par. 5 (pages 191 ff. in the cited edition). The program met domestic opposition, but Pericles shamed his critics by offering to finance the program privately and that gesture turned the assembly. He was told to draw freely on the public funds and to spare no expense in his outlay (page 194 in the cited edition).
[130]Hegel, *Philosophy of Fine Art*, 1835, vol. 3, pages 64, 88.

THEORY OF PUBLIC WORKS

The rationale for public works as a state function was put on an elementary basis by Adam Smith, who said that "though they may be in the highest degree advantageous to a great society," the profit to be gained by constructing and maintaining them "could never repay the expense" to any private undertaker of the works.[131] That is true of many public works of which the diffuse benefits cannot be appropriated by individuals and which are collective goods in the specific sense that they must be shared by all alike or by none. Examples are defensive and protective fortifications or military facilities, aesthetically laid out public memorials, edifices, or ornaments, and measures undertaken for flood abatement or protection. Since the benefits are collective and indivisible, the planning, designing, and providing for such public works are prime functions of the state as a guardian of the social interest.

The rationale for public works as a state function is more complicated for those projects in which private appropriation of benefits is possible, such as highways, communication networks, roads, canals, bridges, ports, waterworks and sewerage systems, and hydroelectric facilities. Beneficiaries of the works may then be charged accordingly, thus permitting public works to be undertaken as private, profitable ventures—usually by a quasi-public corporation. Most such works could not be constructed without the power of eminent domain by which the necessary real estate can be commandeered from private users. That power, however, may be and has been turned over to private capital, providing suitable compensation is involved and usually stipulating that the public works offer service to all who ask it at uniform rates without apparent discrimination.[132] Only later—in the United States especially—were efforts made to impose sufficient regulations that could prevent charges that yielded excessive profits or enforce adequate levels of public service, thus bringing about the hybrid mode of production (presented earlier in Chapter 4).

It is of course possible for state-constructed and -operated public works to be designed, built, and maintained on a self-financing basis through commercial tolls and charges, thus making up a kind of state public utility. That was in fact the basis recommended for all "commercial" public works by Adam Smith. He argued that the "greater part of such public works may easily be so managed as to afford a particular revenue sufficient for defraying

[131]A. Smith, *Wealth of Nations*, 1776, page 681.
[132]Discrimination need only not be apparent or crude, for if a railway tried hard to delay or obstruct service to certain customers or districts, it was easy to contrive excuses that would pass muster in courts. That is why cities that sought railroad connections offered in many cases princely inducements, assuming that the favor of access to transportation was for the railroad to give or deny at pleasure.

their own expense, without bringing any burden upon the general revenue of the society." A highway, a bridge, a navigable canal, a harbor, and a post office may all be constructed and maintained "by a small toll" upon those who use them. Tolls charged in proportion to use or benefit seem equitable and ensure that public works will be constructed where the "commerce requires them." Their "grandeur and magnificence" must then be suited "to what the commerce can afford to pay."[133] This raises two questions: (1) What is the comparative suitability of the public mode of production or the hybrid regulated utility mode for handling public works with appropriable benefits? (2) Is the principle of self-financing desirable—as Adam Smith argued?

No universal formula suitable for all societies and all historical periods can settle the first question. Outright public mode has major advantages: a broader base for raising finance, a greater interest in the care and safety of future generations, an ability to allow for military or strategic interests frequently touched by public works, and finally greater accessibility to regions or classes with legitimate concerns about public works operations or design. As for any narrow calculation of operating efficiency, such good judges as John Stuart Mill and Arthur C. Pigou—two of the finest English minds after Adam Smith to consider applied political economy—both maintained that in their time and place construction and administration of "commercial" type public works by a suitably designed executive agency of government or by a regulated quasi-public corporation was a choice between "fiddledum and fiddledee."[134]

Adam Smith believed that a tax system that made it to the financial or

---

[133]Adam Smith, *Wealth of Nations*, 1776, pages 682 ff. The full passage is perhaps worth citing:

> When high roads, bridges, canals, etc. are in this manner made and supported by the commerce which is carried on by means of them, they can be made only where that commerce requires them, and consequently where it is proper to make them. Their expence too, their grandeur and magnificence, must be suited to what that commerce can afford to pay. They must be made consequently as it is proper to make them. A magnificent high road cannot be made through a desert country where there is little or no commerce, nor merely because it happens to lead to the country villa of the intendant of the provide or to that of some great lord to whom the intendant finds it convenient to make his court. A great bridge cannot be thrown over a river at a place where nobody passes, or merely to embellish the view from the windows of a neighboring palace: things which sometimes happen in countries where works of this kind are carried on by any other revenue than that which they themselves are capable of affording (page 683).

[134]Mill, *Principles of Political Economy*, 1848, bk. 5, ch. 11, par. 11; Pigou, *Economics of Welfare*, 1920, pages 386 f. Pigou went beyond the issue of "technical efficiency" to look at more diffuse and long-run if intangible comparative advantages of quasi-public corporations rather than a well-designed and laid-out government authority. At this level he found the pros and cons so mixed that no general answer can be provided (pages 405 f).

fiscal interest of a general government to produce an effective transport and communications and irrigation network would give a direct stimulus to efficient management of the public works concerned.[135] But the tax system that evolved in England at Smith's time satisfied that criteria; the modern tax system oversatisfies it. Much depends upon the spirit of the society, the attitude of its dominant classes, the quality of its civil service, the institutions of government permitting the assumption of public works responsibility by properly designed agencies exposed to public view but with sufficient autonomy and professional capabilities to carry out complex public works, and finally a fiscal or credit system that will produce the necessary surpluses. In the America and England of the late eighteenth and early nineteenth centuries there probably was no feasible alternative to letting out essential public works to be financed and carried out as profit-making ventures. Voices were raised, to be sure, for the state to assume the responsibility for "internal improvement."[136] But there was a general reluctance to have the state take on operational responsibilities involving large sums of money and direct business management of concerns. It was so easy to "farm out" the business of the state. Furthermore, the pressure of those certain to gain by obtaining franchises and grants was overwhelming and could not be withstood. Said the philosophic Marx: "The separation of public works from the state and their migration into the domain of works undertaken by capital itself indicates the degree to which the real community has constituted itself in the form of Capital."[137] That turned out to be not completely true for all Western nations even in the nineteenth century. In France and in Germany people were more reluctant to separate the state totally from its public works functions. By the end of the century the German system of publicly operated and designed waterways, canals, railroads, and communication networks was well-developed.[138] Since then public works have generally, apart from the United

[135]Adam Smith argued that a Chinese land tax or tax on land produce—"which rises or falls with the annual produce of the land"—provided a proper stimulus for good public works management by the executive power. See *Wealth of Nations*, 1776, pages 688 f. The English land tax of his time had been assigned a fixed quota for delivery to the central government.

[136]John Quincy Adams and certain leaders of the Whig party strongly defended a policy of "public improvements," and in many states a vigorous policy of public improvements was carried out to build canals, railroads, and turnpikes. See Hartz, *Economic Policy and Democratic Thought*, 1948.

[137]Marx, *Grundrisse*, 1857–1858, page 531.

[138]Clapham, *Economic Development*, 1921, pages 339 ff.; Engels, *Anti-Dühring*, 1877–1878, pages 311 f. At a certain stage of development, wrote Engels, even the quasi-public corporation "no longer suffices; the official representative of capitalist society, the state, is constrained to take over their management"—first made evident "in the vast institutions for communication: the postal service, telegraphs and railways." Elucidating further in a footnote, he declared that when production and communication have "actually outgrown management by share com-

States migrated outside "the domain of works undertaken by Capital" even where the quasi-public corporation has been further developed as a form of business organization.

On the second question regarding self-financing the issue is far more complex than Adam Smith stated. Full-cost pricing does have many of the advantages of which Smith spoke, and it is a principle widely acclaimed in current American-style Western economics. It is not practicable in the form of tolls for road systems where there are many points of ingress and egress—i.e., which are not isolated from their adjacent hinterland—because the cost of monitoring traffic and billing or collecting charges would be prohibitive. Even on so-called turnpike highways with very limited access, collection costs can be considerable, reaching up to 11% of the toll revenues concerned.[139] Beyond the cost of collection there is the trouble of collection. Even where access is naturally limited to two places of entrance, as on bridges, the necessity to halt a line of traffic to pay the toll limits appreciably the use of the facility.

Toll charges really amount to a distinctive kind of tax, and it is questionable whether tax books should be cluttered with a variety of such comparatively small excise charges rather than financing the total work of government through a few more general taxes, often combined with withholding at the source. Of course taxation of motor fuels and vehicle license fees enables user charges to defray many of the costs of providing and maintaining roads and highways. Going beyond this business of user charges is the larger question of the tendency of any full-cost pricing system—inclusive of both capital charges and operating costs—to limit use unduly. In most public works for which toll-reimbursement is feasible there is a wide gap between the charges for actual wear and tear and operating costs and those for recovering full costs. Otherwise put, most of the costs of providing and surfacing a bridge, of designing and laying out a highway network, or of bringing into existence the 9-foot channel operational on most U.S. internal waterways are sunk costs only slightly increased or diminished by changed usage. This is most readily seen in improved waterways and highways that are open for use by independently operated carriers. As Alfred Marshall put it: "The abolition of tolls on highways is now universally recognized as good policy; because the revenue yielded by them would be small in comparison with the excess value of the services rendered by a free road over those rendered by a tolled

---

panies," their "transfer to the state has become inevitable from an economic standpoint" and thus signifies an "economic advance" even for the "state of today." Engels did not explain why the German state was constrained to nationalize railways, while the English and American states with far more developed railway networks retained the private corporate form.

[139]Locklin, *Economics of Transportation*, 1935, page 671.

road. . . ."[140] This is the logic of the century-old American policy of favoring toll-free highways and waterways even when costly investments were required to make them serviceable. The same principle, of course, applies to all public works subject to tolling—such as museums, parks, bridges, and ferries. However, charges are suitable to cover variable costs incurred in providing incremental services involved in operating a ferry train or in producing electric power. Likewise, charges are suitable to avoid congestion and regulate access when other methods of curtailing or limiting access and usage are clearly unsuitable.

The toll-charge-minimizing approach is only one application of a much broader principle developed by Alfred Marshall: that there is *prima facie* advantage in using income taxes to provide bounties to certain vital industries, such as public utilities, that are generally subject to increasing returns (or falling supply price). Obviously, this principle is not suited for application where the economies of scale are relatively slight or transient or where need for the service is so inelastic that very little demand is turned away by full-cost tolls. Likewise, the application of the principle presupposes unused fiscal potential for raising taxes and must allow for the "direct and indirect costs of collecting a tax and administering a bounty."[141] Comment is not needed

---

[140]Marshall, *Industry and Trade*, 1919, page 506.

[141]Reference is made chiefly to the two chapters (12 and 13) in Book 5 of Marshall, *Principles of Economics*, 1890, dealing chiefly with "difficulties connected with the relations of demand and supply as regards commodities the production of which tends to increasing returns"—i.e., toward falling supply price or falling or relatively low marginal costs (page 455). That, of course, is the condition of supply of most public utilities characterized by increasing returns to scale. Kahn puts this categorically: "The critical and—if properly defined—all-embracing characteristic of natural monopoly is an inherent tendency to decreasing unit costs over the entire extent of the market." See Kahn *Economics of Regulation*, 1971, vol. 2, page 121. Marshall pointed out that a tax on a commodity that obeys the law of diminishing returns (or rising unit costs to scale) would, by raising its price and diminishing the scale of its production, lower its unit costs apart from tax—"so that the gross receipts from the tax may be greater than the resulting loss of consumers surplus." A bounty given to a commodity that obeys the law of increasing returns would have the opposite effect on price. Marshall generalized: "In the case then of commodities with regard to which the law of increasing return acts at all sharply [as it does in most public utilities] . . . the direct expense of a bounty sufficient to call forth a greatly increased supply at a much lower price would be much less than the consequent increase of consumers' surplus. And if a general agreement could be obtained among consumers, terms might be arranged which would make such action amply remunerative to the producers, at the same time that they left a large balance of advantage to the consumers." See Marshall, *Principles of Economics*, 1890, page 472. This objective could readily be accomplished by levying a tax on community incomes or on the production of goods with diminishing returns to scale. With all due caution Marshall urged not to forget "the direct and indirect costs of collecting a tax and administering a bounty; the difficulty of securing that the burdens of the tax and benefits of the bounty were equitably distributed; the openings for fraud and corruption; and the danger that in the trade which had got a bounty and in

on what a pickle a country is in when portions of its transport facilities (like highways, waterways, and airways) are not subject to full-cost tolling whereas other sets of facilities (like railroads and pipelines) are subject not only to full-cost pricing but to property taxation to boot.

INCOME AND WEALTH REDISTRIBUTION

The third major economic function of the state is to modify the pattern of income and wealth distribution generated by the modes of production. This function—which Karl Polanyi made into a pivotal concept of comparative economic systems—is carried out in all societies but to differing degrees, using different methods and with varying beneficiaries.[142] In part this function is a by-product of the pursuit by the state of other primary objectives. Thus state regulation of foreign trade through the protective tariff or other devices tends to foster industries and sometimes distinct modes of production, thereby rendering the associated enterprises and the resources or products more valuable. This source of redistribution built up the sense of regional economic grievance which entered into the making of the American Civil War.[143] The systems of agrarian protection that sustained landlord incomes in England and Junker estates in Prussia are similar examples of the potent redistributional effects of agrarian tariff protection.[144] Less effective in the long run was the protection from the decomposing effects of usury afforded clan society and the simple commodity producers of town and country in societies where the ban on usury was made effective or from time to time implemented by scaling down indebtedness.[145]

Turning now to the capitalist mode of production in its industrial homeland, England, we can see in the much-acclaimed factory legislation a redistributive process at work—especially when it later set minimum wages. This increased the relative share of national income received by the weakest class of wage laborers, forced some investment of capital to improve harsh working conditions, and raised the reward of labor on an hourly earning basis and in many cases on a weekly basis. All schemes of inheritance that require distri-

---

other trades which hoped to get one, people would divert their energies from managing their own businesses to managing those persons who control the bounties" (page 473). All this is quite relevant to the issue of full-cost pricing of regulated industries.

[142]Polanyi, *Primitive, Archaic and Modern Economies*, 1944–1966, pages 9 ff., 24 f., 209ff.

[143]An older but classical and still impressive case for this hypothesis is found in Charles Beard and Mary Beard, *Rise of American Civilization*, 1927, vol. 1, pages 678 ff; vol. 2, pages 31 f.

[144]Gerschenkron, *Bread and Democracy in Germany, 1943*.

[145]The young Athenian and Roman republics experienced major rounds of debt repudiation to ease the burden of indebtedness.

bution of estates equally among all children will tend over time to exert a potent influence on patterns of wealth distribution and even on the relationship of competing modes of production.[146]

A final example of a class of state action that has important redistributive by-product effects is taxes themselves. By permitting revenue to be raised for direct redistribution, they indirectly have potent redistributive effects through their express exemptions, the particular sources earmarked for taxation, and even the method of tax administration with its tolerated or built-in evasions.

Most redistribution is not achieved indirectly or as by-product but is brought about by use of tax monies or resources made available by the tax and revenue levies imposed by a government. The scope for this redistribution is provided by fiscal potential—i.e., by ability to raise taxes in transferable form expressed best as a fraction of gross social product. Gross fiscal potential has three broad determinants: (1) *tax acculturation*—or the prevailing consensus on the validity of, as well as the culturally shaped attitude toward, taxation and claims of the state; (2) efficiency of *tax administration* as a branch of civil service, partly depending upon practices of record-keeping of incomes and property and the degree and form of monetization prevailing in the economy; (3) balance and carefulness with which *tax laws* are drafted and conformity with the norms of fiscal science as a branch of political economy.

Tax acculturation is a peculiar process. It is weakened by social and economic localization. Tax acculturation is kept alive by repeated use and is weakened by disuse. Some state authorities with nominal state power have only minimal ability to impose and raise new tax levies without obtaining assent and cooperation from communities or classes being taxed.[147] Wars usually promote tax acculturation both by accustoming the community to new forms or higher rates of taxation and by revivifying love of country and community support.

Tax administration is greatly facilitated if taxes can be collected in money. This ultimately brings about a larger role for merchant capital and transportation facilities to work out more fluid forms of interregional division of labor and balance of payments into which taxes can be fitted as one element. Monetization greatly reduces expenses for collection of taxes and their transmission to central and regional capitols. Where heavy taxes were collected in kind—as in the Chinese and Roman empires of classical times—a substantial fraction was utilized in handling, storage, transportation, and necessary wastage. Where tax proceeds in the main stay in the local area, as with church tithes, a convenient arrangement is to assess taxes as a share of the local crop

---

[146]See this volume, ch. 8, pages 374 ff.

[147]A fascinating though at times twisted account of tax acculturation is found in Joseph Schumpeter, "The Crisis of the Tax State," 1918, pages 8–16.

or harvest which, sold in nearby market towns, readily transfers purchasing power. Monetization that takes the form of public record-keeping and accounting, provided by modern commercial and deposit banking, greatly widens the field of tax administration and steps up the amount of taxes that can be successfully drained out of current income.

Tax administration is, of course, best handled in the modern state with a salaried professional staff. In many societies, however, the makings for such a staff were not on hand, and the state was too hungry for funds to await the process of its formation. Authorities—especially in imperial states—extensively farmed out, sometimes by use of auction bidding, revenues for collection to merchants or companies of merchants whose operations were coordinated with local police or army authorities. That arrangement was widely employed for collection of taxes in the late Roman Republic and early Empire, through much of the Muslim and Turkish world, and in Western Europe up to the eighteenth century, especially in Mediterranean areas.[148] Adam Smith's indictment of tax farming pointed up the wastes of the system. The profit of the farm is always exorbitant. Few ethical and disinterested citizens have the capital or credit and knowledge of the field to seek the post, and collusion in bidding tends to develop of its own accord among the greedy. Tax farmers also tend to employ severe methods of tax collection that arouse public resistance to taxation. "In countries where the public revenues are in farm, the farmers are generally the most opulent people."[149] Yet the tax collection by bureaucracy organized in imperial states over extensive territories proved exceedingly dfficult, even in well-socialized societies; over time, taxes enriched tax collectors local and provincial as much or more than they provided revenues for public functions or central state services.[150]

Even the best and most honest tax administration will have a poor yield if taxation is poorly conceived or is imposed on objects or on bases difficult to ascertain or evaluate. Thus any agricultural tax—whether expressed as a levy on the crop and animal yields or upon acreage cultivated or rents paid— that is not based upon a carefully tended set of land records, which reveal ownership and dealings in land, and a cadastral map showing location of holdings, will tend to be inefficient and subject to leakage. All schemes of flat per-acre or per-holding or per-capita taxation, without regard to earning ability, will tend to be grossly inefficient because the amount of tax levied must be adjusted to the large class with little ability to pay.

Taxation of commodities, both imported and domestically produced, has

[148]Goitein, *A Mediterranean Society*, 1967–1971, vol. 1, pages 73, 272; vol. 2, pages 354 ff., 380 ff., 363; Braudel, *The Mediterranean*, 1949, vol. 2, pages 685, 696, 722 f.
[149]See A. Smith, *Wealth of Nations*, 1776, pages 853 ff.
[150]Noteworthily in the later stages of the Chinese empire.

been widespread from the earliest times; but the net revenue yield of such taxation varies widely, if the object taxed can be readily produced in isolated areas or on a small scale or is easily smuggled. The wide variety of rates at which customs duties are levied likewise makes the classification of a given product a matter of considerable consequence—thereby boosting the expense and arbitrariness of customs administration.[151] The modern system of tax-withholding at its very source, from the current flow of incomes, has greatly enlarged a government's taxation scope. Through a massive direct tap on payrolls and earnings individual needs are reduced for accumulating funds throughout the year to meet the annual tax assessment. But by routing incomes from their productive source directly to government, the tie between the taxpayer and his money is weakened.

Even the most skillful tax administration cannot overbalance gross errors in tax policy that do not allow for the appropriate shifting of the incidence of taxes from where they are first levied, and perhaps paid, to those by whom they are ultimately *borne*, usually in veiled forms. The ability to shift taxes depends upon the mobility of resources used in different modes of production and branches of industry—land being the least mobile of the resources of production, and merchant and usury capital by its nature being the most flighty. The shifting of the incidence of taxation is still a long-term process often concealed from the parties most directly involved and usually neglected by authorities of state seeking simple practical solutions to immediate fiscal problems. The mechanics of shifting involve relative movements of price, and these movements exert an influence that depends upon the proportionate response (or elasticities) of supply and demand for the articles affected. Hence, not until a rather sophisticated theory of price and value was developed in the eighteenth and nineteenth centuries could a fiscal science of tax shifting evolve, making possible a maximum use of fiscal potential with full awareness of the ultimate as well as immediate distribution of tax burdens. That the theory of tax shifting was not always well digested by first-rate economists is seen in the comment of Marx that the income tax levied on merchants and businessmen could be shifted onto price, thus resulting in "diminished wages or increased prices."[152]

---

[151]Adam Smith—who had practical experience with customs administration—believed that unification of the customs schedules that in his time proliferated with commodity classes, and especially reform of the overlapping excise taxation of beer, ale, distilling, and malt, would considerably improve fiscal administration in England. See *Wealth of Nations*, 1776, pages 825, 829 ff., 836 ff., 847 ff.

[152]Marx's comment was made in 1853 in one of a series of newspaper articles commenting on the tax and budget messages of Disraeli and later of Gladstone. See Marx and Engels, *Collected Works*, 1841–1860, vol. 12, page 164.

Improved fiscal administration, the greater enmeshment of the population in sophisticated income and tax-recording networks, higher levels of income, and a much higher degree of tax acculturation—all have tended to boost considerably the fraction of social product that may be extracted by a skillful government and used for income redistribution or other purposes without working undue harm to the economic process. In the socialist economies this fraction is, of course, highest. But it is nearly as high in the mixed economies of present-day Western vintage, with a considerable blend of modes of production and relatively good-sized public modes with a well-developed system of government that has organic ties to a broad electorate. Some years ago the validity of a limit of taxes for mixed economies at 25% of national income was widely debated, but there was little evidence to bear out any flat percentage rule. It has proven much easier for a government to take a *greater* share of growing income rather than a *higher* take of a constant income.[153]

Fiscal potential will primarily be utilized for carrying out the main functions of government: provision of internal order, construction of public works, administration of justice, support of the church, and above all provision for national defense or aggression. But even when the fiscal balance is tight some redistribution will always be squeezed in. At the outset this redistribution strongly favors princes (or their republican surrogates) and their spouses, children, and close kin—who must be well attended to, housed in suitable edifices, and removed from any temptation to consider the cost of things an obstacle to acquiring them. The philosophy that the first aim of the state was to magnify and glorify its chief executive and symbolic head was well entrenched in classical monarchy of the Graeco-Roman world, their Persian and Assyrian forbears, and their successsors in Europe, as well as displayed in Asia, Africa, the budding Amerindian civilizations of the New World, and the Polynesian peoples. Luxury without stint was likewise to be made available to the entire court of those who attend or assist the royal family and who altogether constitute the pinnacle of society—sometimes concentrated in the capital city, sometimes dispersed over a number of subsidiary centers. In some societies an unconscionably high proportion of social product goes to the pinnacle of society, for their palaces, their elaborate service, their subservient female retinues, their monumental sepulchers, their hordes of retainers, eunuchs, servants, and guards.

The sharp struggle constantly breaking out in such pinnacled societies over the succession to royal power is quite understandable considering the attraction of controlling and redirecting the flow of largesse to the apex. No notion of a "ruling class" should expunge from view the distinct line drawn between

---

[153]Due, *Government Finance*, 1954, pages 504 f.

the relatively small group at the pinnacle, enjoying themselves while wielding the power of government, and other members of their class outside the charmed circle, who commonly draw benefits too but of a lesser degree. These outside—insiders will usually be favored in tax legislation through frequent exemptions. They may be granted choice portions of public domain available for redistribution. And they will not be conscripted for road service or for labor on public works—though they are often on call for military service as leaders. And of course the well-salaried higher offices of army, state, and church will usually be reserved for this so-called ruling class. But for them the scope for income redistribution is on a much smaller scale than at the pinnacle.

Even in this older social world, however, a share of fiscal potential was occasionally transferred downward for the support and good living of the society's proletariat who had little status and access only to ordinary living. Perhaps the nearly five centuries of feeding the poor of Rome with bread, oil, and meat—supplied most of that time from public tax monies—was a harbinger of things to come. Public feeding was attempted for a few other cities elsewhere in the Roman Empire but not on such a prolonged scale.[154] In the United States, the new Rome of our time, public feeding with tax monies available for redistribution at the bottom of the society has reappeared. This commenced in the 1960s at two ends of the age spectrum—the very young and the very old. The young are fed in public schools, where all children get some assistance at a noonday meal and many get the entire meal subsidized. The old are transported on government vans to noonday luncheons that draw them together for a well-balanced feeding and communal association—with government picking up from one-half to two-thirds of the tab. Public housing for the elderly has virtually replaced all other forms of public housing in the United States. Medical care for the elderly is provided wholly at government expense for those without or who have drawn down their private assets and who are lodged in nursing homes; costs of physician service for those elderly who are still self-supporting are paid a third or more from general government revenues.[155]

The dominant form of social redistribution of fiscal potential in our time is undoubtedly carried out by social security, under the auspices of which 11—25% of the payroll flow of a country will be intercepted, placed in a

[154]See earlier this work, ch. 5, page 198.

[155]In the last year (1977) for which statistical data is conveniently at hand, the child nutrition program cost some $3.01 billion and supplementary medical insurance some $5.4 billion. U.S. Bureau of Census, *Statistical Abstract*, 1978, pages 328, 337. Late congressional action in the closing days of the 86th Congress reduced child nutrition programs 10%, to amount to some $5 billion for fiscal year 1981. See *Congressional Record*, December 12, 1980, S. 15354.

special fund, and from there redistributed to those retired by old age or disability or to their survivors qualifying for benefits.[156] These schemes commonly embody an element of insurance, for additional benefits beyond those entailed by contributions are paid to survivors or dependents. Redistribution everywhere tends to build up the benefits of those whose contributions were low because of their low earnings, and conversely it cuts down benefits at the upper end of the salary scale. Social security does not merely embody a redistribution of wage incomes but also of payroll taxes placed on the employer. Though these taxes may be shifted forward to price or backwards to wages, they will utilize some of the margin for fiscal potential and thus foreclose some other use of it. Western schemes for social insurance on this scale would appear to reverse or invalidate the theorem of Marx that the distribution relations that rest directly upon capitalist production—such as relations between wages, profits, interest, and rent—may at most be "modified in inessentials by taxation" but cannot be threatened in its "foundation." When 25% of payroll income, as in Western Germany, is directly redistributed to social beneficiaries according to social need and not price relations, the modification of income distribution achieved hardly involves "inessentials" though assuredly the "foundation" of the distribution may remain untouched.[157]

Redistribution has, however, gone far beyond public feeding or support for the elderly and organized schemes for social insurance. In the earlier period of capitalist production, as modern industry was beginning to develop, income redistribution was mainly achieved in favor of upper-income groups by relative tax exemption of landed estates and profits and by extensive use of indirect taxes whose "pivot" is formed, in Marx's words, on "the most necessary means of subsistence."[158]

[156]For an interesting Marxist look at comprehensive social security as it developed chiefly in the twentieth century, see Varga, *Twentieth Century Capitalism*, 1961, page 138. Social security as a fraction of national income is lower in the United States than abroad. The German system is most comprehensive, taking 25% of payroll incomes for redistribution, but the rest of Europe and Japan is not far behind. See Klein, *Management of Market-Oriented Economies*, 1973, pages 117 f.; Bureau of Statistics, Office of the Prime Minister, *Statistical Handbook of Japan*, 1972, pages 128 f.; Baum, *French Economy and the State*, 1958, pages 122 ff., 201 ff., 272 ff. For the U.S. see Derthick, *Policymaking for Social Security*, 1979. Under recent legislation the percentage of payroll income taxed for social security will rise to over 90% of payroll income covered and the combined rate of taxation by employees and employer is set to rise from 11.7% of payroll income taxed to 15.3% in the year 1990. Helpful brief review of the 1977 amendments to the American Social Security Act is found in the *Economic Report of the President*, 1978, pages 235 ff.

[157]That general formula was twice given out by Marx, in 1850 and again in 1866. See Marx and Engels, *Collected Works*, vol. 10, 1841–1860, page 331; Marx, *On the First International*, 1864–1872, pages 29 f.

[158]Marx, *Capital* I, 1867, page 756. In France the landed nobility was exempt from the heaviest direct tax, the Taile; and the English land tax that bore on real estate owners was

In Marx's day a shift had begun to direct taxation of income and property by national government. A partial tax on inheritances (landed property excluded) and flat income tax payable only by upper-income classes was already instituted during the Napoleonic Wars. The income tax was promptly abolished at that war's end, but the partial inheritance tax lingered on.[159] In the 1840s fiscal stringencies made it necessary for the British government to invoke again a flat income tax again applicable only to upper-class incomes. Its rates were doubled during the Crimean War to help finance the war. A parallel effort was made to tax landlord and not only bourgeois inheritances. British statesmen were then declaring that it was necessary to shift from indirect taxation, which burdened industry and trade, to more comprehensive schemes of direct taxation.[160] Marx noted that "if the probate and legacy duties had been paid on real property since 1796, by far the greater portion of the public debt might have been paid off."[161] And he heralded the rise of income taxation in which allowance was made for different degrees of risk or precariousness of income. His final words on the subject in contemporary newspaper articles were: "Let the machinery of a direct property tax be once properly established, and the people, with political power in their hands, have only to put that engine into motion in order to create the Budget of Labour."[162]

The progressive income tax did not appear until the end of the century, and in the United States it had to await a constitutional amendment adopted only in 1913. Progression at first was very slight in taxing income, corporation profits, or inheritances. But once a major war created real fiscal strain, a breakthrough in taxation occurred.

---

fixed or settled in 1693 at a set national amount and hence could not contribute to the rising cost of government and the expense of building empire (and fighting for it). Customs and excises became the main source of state revenues. In England these concentrated upon imported bread grains, salt, leather, soap, candles, and beer and other malt beverages. Smith pointed out that the rates of excise taxation were heavy, adding markups over cost of 300% for salt. See A. Smith, *Wealth of Nations*, 1776, pages 825 f., 840 f. Reliance upon indirect taxation was virtually made compulsory for the American republic, because the Constitution required that all direct taxes be allocated among the states on a per-capita basis, a requirement only withdrawn by constitutional amendment in 1913. On the rise of English excise taxation, see Coleman, *Economy of England*, 1977, pages 190 ff.

[159]Hicks, *British Public Finances*, 1954, pages 82 f.; Deane and Cole, *British Economic Growth*, 1962, pages 323 ff.; Marx and Engels, *Collected Works*, 1841–1860, vol. 11, pages 458 ff.; vol. 12, pages 60 ff.

[160]This stand was most clearly enunciated in the famous Disraeli budget message of 1852, which Marx commented on in his contemporary newspaper writings. See Marx and Engels, *Collected Works*, 1841–1860, vol. 11, pages 463 ff.

[161]Marx and Engels, *Collected Works*, 1841–1860, vol. 12, page 73.

[162]Marx and Engels, *Collected Works*, 1841–1860, vol. 12, page 81.

By the second World War the mixed economies of the Western world drew a large fraction of their public tax revenues from progressive income, inheritance, and corporation taxes. A high proportion of local government revenue was drawn from property taxes—which are, of course, borne more heavily by wealthier people who live in or utilize extensive services from taxable property. Assuredly, the "foundations" of wage, price, and profit relations were not removed by progressive taxation. But the "relations" themselves of income distribution were significantly changed.

7

The Institution of Money

CONCEPT OF THE INSTITUTION

The work of the state in regulating economic life, constructing and operating public works, and carrying forward a scheme of income redistribution does not exhaust its functions in shaping and operating economic systems. Beyond this multifaceted work yet closely tied in with it is the more diffuse activity of the state in carrying forward and formalizing the institutionalization that permeates all spheres of sociocultural life—including, of course, the economic. Institutionalization and its finished product, the institution, is a fundamental concept of sociological theory. Yet it was late in emerging in formal analysis and is now given a broad range of meanings.[1] At one extreme the term is applied to any widely prevailing social usage that conforms to a society's accepted norms and values. In this loose way one of the founders of "institutional economic theory" in America defined institutions as "habitual methods of carrying on the life process of the community."[2] It makes only a slight variation of this approach to consider an institution as a complex of behavior regulated by a consistent set of laws, mores, and folkways.[3] Still another version of the concept virtually identified institutions with distinctive and pervasive "law-norms." Other versions speak of institutions as "established forms or conditions or procedures characteristic of group activity," "a form of concerted behavior," "rules of behavior," "popular usages and traditions" with societal pressure to conform, "traditional values for which human beings come together," and "organized relationships purposively established by the

---

[1]The main founders of the discipline of sociology a generation ago—Max Weber, Durkheim, Pareto, and Sumner—did not develop the concept of institution though it was certainly implicit in their thought. For a criticism of the use in sociological theory of the concept of institution by second generation theorists, see Sorokin, *Society, Culture and Personality*, 1947, pages 85 ff.

[2]Veblen, *Theory of the Leisure Class*, 1899, page 193.

[3]Kingsley Davis, *Human Society*, 1949, pages 70 ff.

common will."[4] This cacophony of voices has led one major theorist of comparative economic systems to avoid the use of the term altogether.[5]

We shall not follow that latter course—certainly not without at least attempting to reconcile these different viewpoints on institutions. We must boil down the approaches into ultimate or irreducible elements and then see if they can be fitted together in a logically acceptable way. The following list of elements that might be included in the concept of institution may prove useful: "patterning of authority," role and status, "operative organization," "law norms" and social consensus, "custom and tradition." The core of the concept of institution then becomes the patterning of authority to be wielded in organizations or groups by persons with socially accepted status positions and operating in socially defined role capacities in accordance with prevailing law norms. These role and status positions must be widely accepted by the parties involved in terms of prevailing value standards and norms. To a degree these expectations must be "internalized"—i.e., integrated with the motivation of role actors and onlookers, thus becoming self-reinforcing. Obviously the process of institutionalization must extend over time so that custom and tradition can lend or appear to lend sanction of usage memorialized in legend and/or mythology. In historical societies—with which we are concerned in this work—the process of institutionalization can only take shape and mature under the guidance and with the aid of the state, because through its courts and legal powers it possesses the ability to shape its citizens' behavior by fines, sanctions, and formal decrees. At the very least the state must give the institution a seal of approval by tolerating its facilities, respecting its investment of authority, and affirming its value standards. Our concept of institution thus involves a triple focus: (1) community and class action to achieve need-satisfaction in motivated roles; (2) an inherited culture with its beliefs, usages, and customs internalized in personality; and (3) the power of the state with its ability to compel behavior and to command allegiance.[6]

---

[4]Sorokin virtually identifies "institutions" with "organized groups" and the classification and analysis of these groups by their concrete characteristics (size, age, kind of ties, degree of internal organization, structural varieties). See *Society, Culture, and Personality*, 1947, pts. 3, 4, 6.

[5]Montias, *Economic Systems*, 1976, states that "the word 'institution' (almost) never appears in the book" chiefly because he "could not give it a precise meaning that would fit into the constructive vocabulary that I tried to develop" (xi). The cacophony of definitions of institutions is drawn from a collection assembled by Sorokin, *Society, Culture, and Personality*, 1947, pages 85 f.

[6]See especially Parsons, *The Social System*, 1951, pages 39–51, where institutions are reduced to the patterning of interactive behavior by the "definition of the structure and roles of the parties to the interactive process" and to a set of "role expectations" which has become integrated with a set of "value-standards." More illuminating is the reduction of institutions, proposed by a young theorist in the field of social geography, to "prototypical role relations

All institutions, especially economic institutions, are relatively stable; they change slowly, sometimes almost imperceptibly, and tend to persist over long periods of time. Stability comes partly from the fact that institutions are worked into the tissue of daily life of the community and eventually become canonized by cultural prescription. Then too, since institutions involve an ordering of authority, those who have high status in the institutional order cling to their privileges and usually seek to retain them.

In the case of economic institutions interaction takes place between a complex of classes functioning in a set of production modes in the midst of an inherited cultural milieu and a government that has its own public mode of production, a regulative authority, a system of public finance, and its own objectives and interests. In any given economic system many particular economic institutions can be identified, and the closer the inquiry the more numerous these institutions become. But institutions must be mutually adapted to each other. As they persist over time they will tend to form a configuration in which the needs served by particular institutions are fitted together. Two of these institutional gestalts are focal in the economic sphere and embrace the most basic needs of all modes of production: property and money. "What in terms of process is seen as division of labor must appear as property to the individuals concerned in defining their relations to their products and the facilities of production." So it is with money, which emerges "whenever indirect exchange achieves a certain degree of complexity and stability."[7] Once a commodity money is extruded by the exchange process, it tends to become conventionalized and refined—and therefore becoming an object of social control, taking a wide variety of concrete forms. When closely looked at, property and money can be decomposed into many interacting institutions, but for present survey purposes they are best treated as gestalts covering broad fields of action. In the remainder of this chapter we shall consider money, and in the following chapter we will deal with property.

COMMODITY MONEY AND COINAGE

Money is basically a means of unilateral payment or of indirect exchange to permit a network of trade to develop when direct exchange or barter is not

---

which develop in the mind of each individual through his or her social relations and exposure to media images." See Kohlenberg, "Social Interaction," 1982, page 11.

[7] I cite here from my early paper in which the role of institutions in the theory of an economic systems was first worked out. See Gottlieb, "Theory of an Economic System," 1953, page 357. "The institution upon which by general agreement the institutional weight of the modern economy chiefly rests is that of property." See Ayres, *Theory of Economic Progress*, 1944, page 194.

feasible. A process of indirect exchange exists when goods are taken in exchange contemplated or intended by the receiver only for use at a later time via some future exchange or transaction. Products most serviceable for purposes of exchange or payment must be relatively durable, conveniently portable, readily divisible, and widely desired or sought after for their uses within or without the household. Though utilitarian uses to meet physiological needs or to cope with exigencies of the environment usually rank high, ornamental needs involving beauty, the exotic, or the sacrosanct have often been given precedence in settling upon the type of product used for indirect exchange. Thus various tortoise, clam, or cowrie shells were widely used among Asiatic, North American Indian, and African communities.[8] Just as often, however, utilitarian products that were relatively durable were used in unilateral payment and in indirect exchange, such as cocoa beans, cereal, cattle, bark or silk cloth, iron bars, fur, grain, salt bricks, and coconuts.[9]

When precious metals—gold, silver, and copper—were discovered for use, they were collected and admired both for their ornamental and utilitarian properties. Malleable, they were readily hammered into a variety of shapes, and when properly alloyed they acquired considerable firmness so they could be employed in cutting edges or utensils. Being exceedingly ductile, they could be given a high polish or reduced to a thin leaf or stretched out into a fine thread. These metals are still outstanding for their glitter and color. Silver does not readily oxidize and gold not at all. They resist most acids, and they are noncorrosive to the touch. As the first metals for two or more thousand years, they were used for household goods, table service, animal gear and trappings, and decoration.[10] Hence either singly or in combination—depending upon the relative supply of the metal available—the precious metals were put to service as a means of payment and as an indirect means of exchange. They met supremely well the governing standards for such exchange, as they were (1) almost indefinitely storable, (2) conveniently portable because very valuable for their bulk, (3) durable, and (4) readily divisible.

[8]Plain or exotic and ornamental shells were developed as money in 28 different areas, mostly islands, according to the recent comprehensive survey of Einzig, *Primitive Money*, 1949. For shell money in Africa, see pages 131, 154, 159; in Latin America, 181, 182; North America (as wampum), pages 170 ff., 165 f., 280 f., 406 f.); Asia, 245 f., 272. Other examples of primarily ornamental or exotic substances being used as money are the famous stone money of Yap (pages 36 ff.), the feather money of Santa Cruz (pages 52 ff.), whale teeth currency of Fiji (page 33), dogs' teeth in the Admiralty Islands (pages 64 ff.), and bead money of Tanzania (page 119).

[9]Einzig, *Primitive Money*, 1949, pages 29 f., 47 f., 82 f., 87 f., 94 f., 100 f., 113 f., 116 f., 128 f., 41 f., 160 f., 164 f., 175 ff., 180, 211 f., 260 f., 264 ff., 273, 286 ff., 304.

[10]Nomadic pastoral people such as the Massagetae, according to Herodotus, knew and used gold for headgear, belts, girdles, bridles, bits, and cheek-pieces, while bronze was used for spearheads, arrowheads and horse breastplates. See Herodotus, *The Histories* bk. 1, par. 215 f.

Precious metals did not immediately displace other means of exchange. At the start there was a plurality of means of exchange suitable for different purposes requiring payment: commodity purchase, taxes, gifts, wedding arrangements, land rents, and so on. Such schemes of plural moneys disappeared, however, wherever economic life developed on any scale with settled agriculture and the evolving modes of production analyzed in this work. The more commonly used means of indirect exchange tend to become a money of account in which relative prices or price offers will be expressed. This facilitates optimal use of resources by reducing them to a common scale of values, as Aristotle long ago perceived.[11] The precious metals could only have taken on a monetary use in areas where their supply was comparatively plentiful. Though relatively scarce among metals, gold was widely distributed on the earth's surface—especially in upland river valleys cutting through rock strata, where over long periods of time small particles of gold, deposited because of their heavy weight, abound in gravel beds. Copper and silver, usually found in compounds, were more difficult to work than virgin gold. However, outcroppings containing these two metals were much more productive than gold finds, so that these metals became available in much larger quantities than gold and therefore serviceable for a wider range of uses. Because all three metals were unusually mobile, their use spread over wide cultural areas. The hierarchy of relative values mirrored that of relative scarcity so that over most of the Mediterranean basin in Graeco-Roman times an ounce of silver exchanged for .10 to .075 ounces of gold but from 100 to 400 ounces of copper. Those ratios have been surprisingly stable over historic time.[12] Early forms of metal money were thus pieces of precious metal in convenient shapes transferred by weighing or balancing on scales, using some local standard weight such as food grains. In many languages the word signifying payment literally was an expression for "weighing out."[13]

[11]Aristotle, *Basic Works*, "Ethica Nicomachea," bk. 5, ch. 5 (pages 1010 f. of the cited edition).

[12]As Marx pointed out, discrepant ratios were possible for isolated territories in an early stage of development and for the entire Far East until opened up to currents of trade and contact with European peoples. See Marx, *Grundrisse*, 1857–1858, pages 183 ff; *Critique of Political Economy*, 1859, pages 156 f. See also Heichelheim, *Ancient Economic History*, 1938, vol. 3, pages 15 ff.; 21 f., 215 f., 290 ff.; Bolin, *State and Currency*, 1958, pages 49 f., 303 n. 6, 311; Weber, *General Economic History*, 1923, 243 ff. Of course the ratios between the individual precious metals were continually changing with new discoveries and with improvements in mining and refining technologies. However, because the preexisting stocks of precious metals used both in money and plate are very large relative to the current ouput, the effects of these discoveries and improvements were greatly diluted in force and, given time, were mutually offsetting.

[13]"The idea of payment was expressed in Arabic, as it had been before in Akkadian, Hebrew, and Aramaic by the verb 'weighing.'" See Goitein, *A Mediterranean Society*, 1967–1976,

With this early money there was not only the trouble in making exact weights, but also the handicap of determining the fineness of the metal. Though gold often occurred in pure form, silver and gold were often combined with other metals in ores. In learning how to refine and separate the metals, men also learned how to alloy, to blend, and to gild. Thus it was necessary both to weigh the amount of the metal and to ascertain its fineness or purity—a task not easily achieved if the metal pieces were not worked up at a known time, place, and manner. The work of assaying and refining gold or silver involves cupellation, but it would clearly be intolerable to resort to cupellation with every metallic exchange. Though Keynes suspected that Semitic peoples—"whose instincts are keenest for the essential qualities of money"—were able to grade metals by "touch and weight," that is risky business.[14] Some of the earliest specimens of coinage—that of Lydian electra coins, made with a weight of 4.7 grams of gold and silver compounded in natural ores and stamped with the head of a lion—were, in the judgment of Sture Bolin, deliberately degraded by artfully increasing the proportion of silver and lowering that of gold.[15]

To facilitate the circulation of money and free it of the need to be verified

---

vol. 1, page 230. Readers of the English Bible will recall the "weighing out" of money passed in payment by Abraham and some 500 years later by Jeremiah. See Gen. 23:16; Jer. 32:6–12. The scales perennially used in Roman payment of bronze money almost became a symbol of state in the early Roman Republic. "In trade between independent parties gold coins and even silver coins were invariably weighed on each occasion. . . ." See Einzig, *Primitive Money,* 1949, pages 95, 196, 203 f., 216. Weber notes that nearly everywhere grain kernels were used for weights. See Weber, *General Economic History,* 1923, page 241. An eighteenth century report tells us that the everyday Chinese shopper carried a precision scale and scissors to cut gold or silver leaf. See Braudel, *Capitalism and Material Life,* 1967, page 342. The practice of weighing out means of payment in China was amusingly expressed in an old Chinese text which said that the ancients used goods "which they weighed to serve as money and the subsequent ages used money which they weighed to serve for goods." See Vissering, *Chinese Currency Coins and Paper Money,* 1877, page 16.

[14]Keynes's exact words are: "The Semitic races, whose instincts are keenest for the essential qualities of Money, have never paid much attention to the deceptive signature of Mints, which content the financial amateurs of the North, and have cared only for the touch and weight of the metal." See Keynes, *Treatise on Money,* 1930, vol. 1, page 12. I am not sure Keynes was correct. The Phoenician peoples (both in Carthage and on the Palestinian coast), with their penchant for commerce, refrained from coining money. See Einzig, *Primitive Money,* 1949, pages 215 ff. But then innovation has historically often come from newer peoples with less settled traditions. The immediate stimulus to coinage in Greek Asia Minor was probably locally abounding supplies of gold and silver, an innovating spirit, and a taste for ostentation.

[15]Bolin, *State and Currency,* 1958, pages 24 ff. Of 61 surviving coins of that Lydian denomination early seventh century B.C., the deviation of weight from standard was found very slight compared to modern coin specimens recovered after use. The gold content varied widely from 31% to 55%.

at every turn for both its exact quantum and degree of fineness, the state intervened, perhaps at first merely to facilitate making payments from the state treasury and to standardize collection of dues and taxes. In its simplest beginnings coined money was a standardized piece of bar of metal bearing an emblem indicating magnitude and fineness. It ended up a much more elaborate affair: a series of standardized shapes making up various denominations, each bearing a distinctive emblem or image, often an indication of the place of minting, and a name which at first was a measure of weight. Coin making involved quite an exercise in the arts of metallurgy: preparing set quantities of the refined molten precious metal and alloy; devising molds that set the shape, size, and sometimes the pattern of the coin; designing metal dies that impressed the pattern on the surface of the coin; and finally cleaning, filing, and polishing. The Greeks took special care to have beautiful engravings on their coins. The Muslims who, like the Jews, detested graven human images, replaced these with compact mottoes of faith.[16]

Even in its most advanced form, coined money preserves its association with those rare qualities of precious metals that enabled them in early days to become a money form. This association is retained chiefly through widespread use of precious metals in articles of adornment, such as wedding bands or watch cases; in table service like plate, goblets, and implements for handling food; as thread in fabrics or book bindings or gilding of works of art; and in modern times by widespread industrial use as electronics conductors, as noncorrosive paint surface, or in photographic work. Then there is widespread accumulation of coins in collections valued chiefly for symbolizing different ages of man or the vanity of innumerable rulers. In Asia, especially India, ownership of precious metals as a "form of wealth is still considered as a final goal."[17] To this day, the visitor in India will be surprised at the abundance of gold and silver—or their facsimile—in the clothing and ornamentation of women.

All this gold or silver held as treasure or laid out in ornaments is readily available for service as money in case of family need. Goldsmiths and silversmiths stand ready at all times to purchase these objects so readily reduced to ingots as wholesale commercial money or to coins for circulating money. In emergencies the state has called on its citizens to surrender their gold and

---

[16]The Americans have inscribed one of these ancient mottoes on their coins and currency notes in the Latin text. In one congressional hearing a Senator's attention was drawn to the exact text on a silver currency certificate, "Annuit Coeptis", noting the same motto was inscribed over the Senate chamber. No one attending the hearing knew the meaning—which the editor put into the record, "He has smiled on our undertakings." See U.S. Senate Hearings, *Repeal of Silver Purchase Acts*, 1963, page 63.

[17]Marx, *Critique of Political Economy*, 1859, page 135.

silver treasure to serve the monetary needs of the state.[18] The available supply of precious metals in most economic systems—the socialist alone excluded—has thus always been divided between indirect exchange use as coins or bullion, and between ornamental or utilitarian use; and the amount held or used in the two latter forms has often been estimated to exceed that held in monetary form.[19] The interchange in form has its own cycles: the conversion of gold and silver to luxury goods predominating in times of peace, in Marx's judgment, while return to monetary use is favored in "turbulent periods."[20]

Coined money was thus the first improved form of the institution of money by which it moved from a simple commodity used as means of payment and of indirect exchange into a socially prescribed measure of value with a set of denominations passing current as money by sanction of the state. Coined money was the first massive exercise in standardized weights and measures, and it stepped up the process of monetization that makes for a more rational use of resources. Each piece of money advertised the sovereignty of the state and the benevolence of its ruler. Hence states became jealous of foreign moneys, usually prohibited their free circulation, and required that they be turned in for reminting—with some charge for the operation to boot.

The operative organization of the institution of money is the mint—an office of the state endowed with the monopoly privilege of preparing precious metals for circulation by certification of their weight and fineness according to set standards. The Arab word *sikkah* refers to the iron die that impresses

[18]One famous example was the Roman financial crisis six years after the disaster of Canae in 216 B.C., when each of the senators pledged to bring to the treasury all his gold, silver, and coined bronze—sparing only a ring for each family member, an amulet worn around the neck of his son, an ounce of gold each for his wife and daughters, if any, a pound of silver and 5000 asses of coined bronze for each senator. Certain Senate officers could retain some extra silver ornamentation. Livy records that senators promptly adjourned the Senate session "and everybody proceeded to bring his silver and gold and his bronze money to the treasury." See Livy, *History of Rome*, bk. 26, par. 36.

[19]Marx, *Critique of Political Economy*, 1859, page 136; Braudel, *Capitalism and Material Life*, 1967, page 350. Industrial use of gold and silver in the United States has exceeded domestic production during the entire postwar period by ratios which in 1977 were fivefold for gold and fourfold for silver. On a world scale, industrial uses of silver were approximately double that of coinage use for 1958 and 1972. See U.S. Bureau of Census, *Statistical Abstract*, 1978, page 773; U.S. Senate Hearings, *Repeal of Silver Purchase Acts*, 1963, page 131. Much of this latter-day industrial use of silver and gold is nonrecoverable as it is used in batteries, as solder, as a brazing alloy, and in photographic reproduction.

[20]Marx, *Critique of Political Economy*, 1859, page 135. This was still true in our time. During the years of Depression and war (1931–1943), private holdings of gold were reduced by 42.9 million ounces; in the following less turbulent 9 years (1944–1953), approximately 128.7 million ounces flowed into private use. Federal Reserve Board, "Private Demand for Gold," 1954.

the pattern upon the blank coin; but according to Ibn Khaldun, the word came eventually to "designate control of the process of engraving and supervision of the whole operation, of everything dealing with coinage and all the conditions that govern it." It is an office, continues the great Arab philosopher, "necessary to the royal authority for it enables people to distinguish between good and bad coins in their transactions."[21]

One Chinese emperor grew weary of the problems of managing mintage and threw open the minting of copper coins to the general public. The exercise in freedom was quickly relinquished.[22] Mint authority over coinage was a near-universal mark of effective sovereign power, partly because the coinage bore the emblem of the state and testified to its presence, and partly because the mint was a fiscal asset that could yield a revenue in time of need.[23] Degeneration of authority over minting or devolution of such authority to subordinate offices or agencies bears witness to the disintegration of state power.[24]

The office of the mint was not simple. In large empires such as the Roman and Chinese the number of operative mints was up to 40 or 50; in Anglo-Saxon England 86 mints in different locations functioned variously before the Norman Conquest.[25] Significantly, the first public building of the fledgling American republic was the mint in Philadelphia, built in 1792 pursuant to a plan laid out in the report of Alexander Hamilton "On the Establishment of a Mint." His prefatory words bear witness to the gravity of the function of the agency: "A plan for an establishment of this nature, involves a great variety of considerations—intricate, nice and important. The general state of debtor and creditor; all the relations and consequences of price; the essential interests of trade and industry; the value of all property; the whole income, both of the state and of individuals, are liable to be sensibly influenced, beneficially or otherwise, by the judicious or injudicious regulations of this in-

---

[21]Ibn Khaldun, *The Muqaddimah*, 1377, page 217.

[22]Ku Pan, *Hans Shu*, first century A.D., pages 232 ff.; for a later experiment in 958 B.C. in North China, see Elvin, *Pattern of the Chinese Past*, 1973, page 152.

[23]"Near"-universal because states founded by conquest by peoples at a lower cultural level—such as the Germanic and Arabian peoples who took over vast areas of the Persian and Roman empires—allowed mintage offices to continue with little supervision for some considerable period.

[24]This was noted especially by historians of the seventh and tenth centuries A.D. in Western Europe.

[25]See this volume, ch. 5, footnote 2. In the tenth century, an Anglo-Saxon king required that every borough have a mint using centrally prepared dies. See Clapham and Power, *Cambridge Economic History*, 1941–1978, vol. 3, page 582. Strikingly enough, there were 36 mints in Tang China coining copper coins. See Twitchett, *Financial Administration*, app. 4.

teresting object."[26] The scope of the institution of the mint is indicated by the questions which Hamilton sought to answer in his report:[27]

1. What ought to be the nature of the money unit of the United States?
2. What the proportion between gold and silver, if coins of both metals are to be established?
3. What the proportion and composition of alloy in each kind?
4. Whether the expense of coinage shall be defrayed by the Government or out of the material itself as a charge on minting?
5. What shall be the number, denomination, sizes and devices of the coins?
6. Whether foreign coins shall be permitted to be current ir not; if the former at what rate and for what period?

On none of these questions was there any unambiguous weight of tradition or wisdom of policy established by the young science of political economy. Hence as a prelude to the consideration of the questions, Hamilton had to demonstrate that the need for action was sufficiently exigent to venture with intricate policy questions for which there were no settled answers—his own report becoming a classic document in the science he helped to launch.

Regarding the expense of coinage, though it was a relatively small fraction for high-valued and large-denomination gold coins, the expense was considerable for silver coins, especially for the smaller denominations. When copper coinage became established as the main money in classical China, the efficiency of mint operation became a major issue, since even with limited techniques of mass production utilized in Chinese minting the expense of coinage would run from one-quarter to one-half the value of mint output. The attempt to load the expense of mintage along with what amounted to a royal mintage tax on mint operations resulted there in continuous struggle with counterfeiting.[28]

When handicraft molds and dies were used in minting, the variability in the finished coin output in fine metal was sufficient to cause the near-immediate secreting or clipping of full-bodied or overstandard coins. But those coins which were short-weight due to the fault of the mold, the fit of the die, or flaws in the annealing or excessive vigor of polishing were immediately sent into circulation. Even as late as the mid-eighteenth century, a range of variability in gold coins up to 40 grains upon a pound of standard was allowed

---

[26]The text of Hamilton's report on the mint to t. e House of Representatives, Jan. 28, 1792, is cited here from the version reprinted in the U. S. Senate Hearings, *Additional Mint Facilities*, 1963, page 154.

[27]See A. Hamilton, "Mint Report," 1792, page 156.

[28]This is one of the major themes of Ku Pan, *Hans Shu*, first century A.D., pages 232 ff.

for any random sample of newly minted coins tested for accuracy by the English mints.[29]

Nearly everywhere gold and silver were regarded as unique monetary metals and suited for monetary use even if only one of the two was regularly coined and established, as in Carolingian Europe, as a money of account. This derived not only from tradition and usage—in which, for example, the gold solidus of the Late Roman Empire was continually minted and kept in circulation in adjoining culture areas—but also out of a fundamental economic constraint. This constraint owed to the greater value of gold over silver, which ranged in the European world from Graeco-Roman times onward between 10–15 to 1 and in the world of the Orient 5–6 to 1. This value differential mirrors the relative scarcity of the metals in the workable mining surfaces of the time. The difference in value caused mining effort to continue for recovery of gold in ores where effort with other metals would have long been relinquished. In that sense the marginal cost in labor and equipment of mined gold, silver, and copper was proportionate to their values, permitting the inference running through classical economics from Smith to Marx: that the relative value of gold and silver derived from their respective costs of production.[30] The greater values of gold over silver and of silver over copper everywhere gave the more valuable metal a monetary advantage. The expense of the work of portage, assaying, weighing, and minting was proportionately less for the more valued metal. Hence gold had a supreme desirability as a form of money for state and church treasuries or for use in wholesale merchant traffic.

Coined money was thus the second improved form of the institution of money by which it moves from a commodity base to become a socially prescribed measure of value with a set of denominations passing current in its time and place. It has its inherent problems. The process of circulation promoted by coined money contributes in part to its own undoing. "The coin which comes into contact with all sorts of hands, bags, purses, tills, chests and boxes wears away, leaves a particle of gold here and another there, thus

[29]See A. Hamilton, "Mint Report," 1792, page 192. By contrast in the mid-1850s, the Bank of England had devised weighing scales so sensitive that they could detect $\frac{1}{100}$ of a grain of weight. A coined sovereign then lost legal tender if it was below standard by $\frac{3}{4}$ of a grain. The machine would weigh coins mechanically and fling lightweight coins onto a board "where it drops into another machine that cuts it into pieces with oriental cruelty." See Marx, *Critique of Political Economy*, 1859, page 111.

[30]Thus Ricardo flatly declares that gold is "about 15 times dearer than silver, not because there is a greater demand for it, nor because the supply of silver is 15 times greater than that of gold, but solely because 15 times the quantity of labour is necessary to procure a given quantity of it." Ricardo, *Principles Political Economy* B 347.

losing increasingly more of its intrinsic contents as a result of abrasion sustained in the course of its worldly career."[51] The English experience through the eighteenth century was that a few decades after minting gold coins would be 2% and silver coins 8% short; another informed estimate of shrinkage of coins by abrasion over a 20-year period was 5%.[52] If coinage was neglected over a long period of time, the discrepancy between new full-bodied and older worn coins would be so great that the former could not circulate at all for their nominal value. It is thus understandable that this process of degradation of the coinage would be accelerated by action of both mint-masters and money-changers. Mint-masters would adjust, or add, to the degraded standard of the coinage by reducing the size of newly minted coins labeled with the same denomination. Occasionally they would even increase the mixture of alloy in the coins, thus seeking to conceal from immediate view the alteration of coinage value. Money-changers would systematically withhold from circulation full-bodied coins or clip them before release. The alternative to continuous degradation of the coinage or of its nominal set of denominations is to engage in recoinage at great cost to the state and maintain the old parity (for which John Locke contended in a famous exchange) or else to charge the loss to holders of old coin who are bound to feel burdened by the shrinkage in value.[53] The only system of coins that can hold to its standard for a long period of time is one like the Roman gold solidus, which for centuries was continuously reminted by the treasury on every receipt, when it was weighed and honored only for its gold content.

The continuous degradation of coinage due to use and abuse by minters and clippers is only one of the major problems of coined money. The second involves variability in the value of money or its stability due to variations in the relative or absolute value of the precious metals. Changes in absolute value occurred only rarely—chiefly upon the incidence of the discovery of some immense cache of precious metals, as when the precious metal mines and collections of the New World passed into the hands of Spanish conquerors.[34] Twice in the nineteenth century immense new supplies of gold generated waves of almost wild inflation—one in 1848, following gold discoveries in California and Australia, and the other in the last decade of the century pro-

[31]Marx, *Critique of Political Economy*, 1859, page 108.
[32]Marx, *Critique of Political Economy*, 1859, page 109; A. Smith, *Wealth of Nations*, 1776, page 517.
[33]The silver recoinages in England in the 16th and 17th centuries are illuminatingly treated by Hawtrey, *Currency and Credit*, 1919, ch. 16.
[34]See the still classical account of E. J. Hamilton, *American Treasure*, 1934. More recently we have the comprehensive measures and analysis of Braudel and Spooner, "Prices in Europe," 1941–1978, vol. 4, pages 374–486.

ceeding from the invention of the cynanide process for treating gold ores and the discovery of gold in South Africa and Alaska.[35]

Changes in relative value of the precious metals to each other were more common, because they could be caused by any change in the supply of a precious metal or by a change in the parity ratio for the precious metals enforced in different countries for minting and payment purposes. As silver coinage predominated in the moneys of account and usage for low-income persons virtually since Graeco-Roman times in the Near East and in Europe, any change in the relative supply of gold or silver would cause a change in the bullion value of the two metals—to make it either harder or easier for the poor to meet their gold obligations often imposed for payment of taxes and certain kinds of unilateral payments such as dowries, gifts, or tithes.[36] Equally troublesome was the alternation in the prevailing state of the currency of countries on a bimetallic standard—i.e., where the two precious metals were coined with a fixed parity in relation to the prevailing money of account. If any country with whom there was open trade enforced a different parity between the two monetary metals, available supplies of gold and silver would become redistributed in the countries concerned, so that one would end up with a predominantly gold, the other a predominantly silver, coinage.[37]

Just as disturbing have been the problems caused in the past century by having the commercial world divided between regions where silver is the standard money, such as the Orient, and those where gold has become the standard money, as in the Western world. Changes in the bullion value of the two metals appeared as variations in the foreign exchange rate of the two regions, having all the effects of currency devaluation or appreciation without any semblance of governmental control or planning.[38] These troubles could

[35]Writing in 1859, Marx testified to the "remarkable influence" which the California discoveries of gold exerted on international trade in the 19th century. See Marx, *Critique of Political Economy*, 1859, page 152. Already in 1850 he predicted these gold discoveries would have "more impressive consequences" than the discovery of America itself, creating a "general prosperity" and an immense investment boom. See Marx and Engels, *Works*, 1841–1860, vol. 10, pages 265 f., 504 ff.

[36]In Old Cairo gold coins in the Fatimid period (969–1171 A.D.) were locally minted. Silver was widely used for small denomination payments. The exchange rate of the two metals was "in constant fluctuation," major changes being felt as a "calamity." See Goitein, *A Mediterranean Society*, 1967–1971, vol. 1, app. D, especially pages 390 ff. The same situation existed in 14th and fifteenth century Florence. See De Roover, *The Medici Bank*, 1963, pages 31 ff.

[37]This was pointed out classically by Locke in the 1690s, shown by Adam Smith, recognized as an axiom of mintage policy by Hamilton in his famous *Report*, and asserted by all later economic analysis.

[38]China was on a silver standard and insulated from the 1929–1933 world depression but was later painfully affected by the American policy of bidding up the world price of silver. See Friedman and Schwartz, *A Monetary History*, 1963, 361 f., 489 f.

have been largely avoided by international agreement on a common parity for gold and silver—or, even better, a scheme of "synmetalism" advocated by Alfred Marshall whereby the money of account would be convertible into set quantities of bullion of both metals.[39] Because neither of these solutions had much of a chance in the nineteenth century, the instabilities inherent in a bimetallic world monetary standard seemed endemic. Proclaimed the sharp-eyed contemporary observer Karl Marx: "Within the sphere of home circulation, there can be but one commodity which, by serving as a measure of value, becomes money. In the markets of the world a double measure of value holds sway, gold and silver . . . which serve as international means of purchasing chiefly and necessarily in those periods when the customary equilibrium in the interchange of products between different nations is suddenly disturbed."[40]

Before the ink had dried on the second edition of the work in which the bimetallic standard was proclaimed as a binding law, the shift from a bimetallic to a single gold standard—achieved by dropping the unlimited minting of silver coin at a fixed mint parity with gold and treating silver coinage as a "subsidiary" money like copper coin—was visibly in process. Coming into existence at first not by set design or plan but almost by accident, a single gold standard was statutorily established in England in 1816. It was established de facto in the United States by the minting in 1853 of subsidiary silver coins of inferior fineness, and formally 20 years later by a statute that omitted the authority for unlimited coinage of silver dollars. In 1871–1872, by quick drift, Germany, Holland, and the Scandinavian countries shifted to gold. In 1873 the Latin Union of bimetallic countries, headed by France, suspended silver coinage because of the falling market price of silver. Other European countries shifted to a gold standard later. A powerful silver-mining interest and the experience with paper money in the Civil War kept the

---

[39]"Although coinage of gold and silver at a fixed ratio causes movements of prices to be governed chiefly by the production of gold and silver alternately, a plan can be devised which would make the two metals work together . . . Synmetalism." See Marshall, *Money, Credit and Commerce*, 1923, pages 60 ff.

[40]Marx, *Capital* I, 1867, pages 142 ff. (section entitled "Universal Money," maintained unchanged through the 1872–1873 edition of *Capital* prepared by Marx). The section on bimetallic "Universal Money" is a shortened version of a longer text, "World Money," published earlier. See Marx, *Critique of Political Economy*, 1859, pages 149 ff. Added only in the later version was a footnote in which Marx jibed at the "absurdity" of "every law prescribing that the banks of a country shall form reserves of that precious metal alone which circulates at home." Engels, however, took note in the still later fourth German edition (1890) of the new technology of silver mining, the fall in silver prices, and the tendency of silver to "forfeit its money function more and more in the markets of the world," exposing the "utopianism of the bimetallist idea" that his alter-ego Marx in the text being reissued enshrined into a binding law of money.

bimetallic issue alive in the United States, but in the 1890s the choice for the gold standard was tied down.[41] This momentous shift from a bimetallic to a single gold monetary standard—combined with the use of token silver and copper coins—requires for its full understanding an analysis of "token money."

TOKEN MONEY

As soon as the institution of money begins to rely heavily upon the state for its certification, arrangement for denominations, and issuance, the state begins to wonder whether the certificate itself might be denominated and issued as money without precious metal accompaniment. That practice is slipped into for small-denomination coins because their wear and tear is relatively greater and they easily pass current by tale rather than by careful weighing and assaying of value. Variously in the Roman Empire, the Carolingian period, or in the later Islamic world when only silver or gold was the official money of account—a kind of copper coinage readily evolved by way of degradation of small-denomination silver coins. Since copper was the common metal for alloying of silver, mint-masters had a fiscal motive for raising the proportion of copper in the alloy, thus often causing low-denomination silver coins to take on the red copper hue.[42] This low-denomination copper token money, not generally struck in Western Europe until the late 1400s, was a new stage in the evolution of the institution of money. This coinage, not freely minted, was usually valid only for small payments. Controlled by government, the supply provides a significant fiscal resource.[43]

In the eighteenth century, England led the way in beginning to convert its silver coinage into a subsidiary money—legal tender only for small payments. Action in this direction was very hesitant because silver coinage was maintained only at a small discount from full parity.[44] As other Western countries followed the British lead, unrestricted coinage of silver bullion in

[41]The history of this momentous institutional development that led to adoption of the gold standard by the leading countries of Europe and North America is well told by Hawtrey, *Currency and Credit*, 1919, ch. 19, 20, "The Gold Standard."

[42]Henry VIII was especially notorious for his issue of silver coins heavily alloyed with copper, so that the king, it was said, had been made "with a red and copper nose." See Hawtrey, *Currency and Credit*, 1919, page 280. On silver-copper "vellon" or "Billon" coins, see Usher, *Deposit Banking in Mediterranean Europe*, 1943, pages 202 f.

[43]Clapham and Power, *Cambridge Economic History*, 1941–1978, vol. 3, pages 576 f. In 1963 the cost of production of pennies (including metal and minting costs) was 27.6% of its nominal value. See U.S. Senate Hearings, *Content of Silver Coins*, 1964, page 63.

[44]Hawtrey, *Currency and Credit*, 1919, page 348; A. Smith, *Wealth of Nations*, 1776, pages 40 ff.

most Western countries was stopped during the nineteenth century. Gradually silver coins became more heavily alloyed, so that now most silver coins are merely plated with silver and have a metal value far below their nominal value. Virtually all coinage in the world today is of this plated token variety, a survey showing that only some 10% of the metal content of all coins outstanding in 1962 consisted of gold or silver.[45]

But why stop with subsidiary coinage good only for small payments? Token money would in earlier days be coined, but after the Chinese invented the art of block printing, it could also be printed on fine paper with fancy engraving and usually given the denomination or name of a full-bodied coin. Paper money in circulation will have a much shorter physical lifetime than a well-alloyed coin, but printing is cheaper than minting and the material costs much less.[46] For these reasons none other than David Ricardo has declared that a currency is in "its most perfect state when it consists wholly of paper money" properly limited.[47] That followed the finding of Adam Smith that the substitution of paper currency for gold and silver money "replaces a very expensive instrument of commerce with one much less costly and sometimes equally convenient."[48]

But will token paper money issued by government be acceptable by the people? In many economies the act of payment often follows by a considerable period the purchase or shipment of goods, giving rise to an appreciable standing volume of short-term debt. An equally large or larger volume of debt liabilities exists at any time of future payments due on account of taxes, land rents, and church tithes or for payments on marriage contracts, dowries, or inheritances. If the state by proper enactment makes the token money valid for settling outstanding debts—including, of course, taxes—then a significant number of people will be willing to receive and utilize such token money for purposes of settling outstanding debts. Creditors paid off by such money will in turn pass it on.

Willingness to use paper currency will thus depend upon the relative in-

[45]The weight of metals embodied in the 1962 coinage of noncommunist nations was 43,689 short tons, of which 9.83% was gold or silver. Copper made up 66% of the weight, followed by declining shares for nickel, steel, zinc, iron, aluminum, and tin. See U.S. Senate Committee on Banking and Currency Hearings, *Content of Silver Coins*, 1964, pages 117 f.

[46]The respective lifetimes of a U.S. currency $1 bill and a silver dollar in 1962 were 1.5 and 30 years. The full cost of manufacturing 1000 paper dollars was $9.20 and for minting 1000 silver dollars was $12.50 (not counting material costs). A full-bodied dollar silver coin with interest compounded for 30 years at 6% per year and allowing for 10% wear and tear over the 30-year period would cost the state much more than the expenses over the period in printing currency notes of the same nominal value. See U.S. Senate Committee on Banking and Currency Hearings, *Content of Silver Coins*, 1964, pages 50, 64.

[47]Ricardo, *Political Economy*, 1817, page 355.

[48]A. Smith, *Wealth of Nations*, 1776, page 276.

tensity of use of credit in ordinary business life, the volume of outstanding payment indebtedness, the attitude of people towards the state, the relative importance of tax obligations, and whether acceptance of paper currency is associated with advantages such as easier reckoning or ability to make long-distance transfers of purchasing power. When paper currency was introduced to the Chinese during the Sung dynasty in the eleventh century A.D., it arose in a commercial setting to facilitate long-distance transfer of funds or to serve variously as a deposit-reserve basis for what in effect were commodity moneys (such as tea, silk, and iron).[49] Only under the later Mongol (Yuan) regime was use of gold, silver, or copper prohibited in exchange, with a whole set of well-engraved paper currency denominations introduced. Witnessed and described by Marco Polo, this new paper money in its heyday spread from China proper to Burma, Siam, and Annam.[50] For a few decades, we are told, the currency "enjoyed the full confidence of the people."[51] But even the harsh Mongol power, upheld with a large standing army, could not keep the system thriving when currency emissions were continuously accelerated. Within a century of its first nationwide employment, the currency became valueless; the government that sponsored it was faced with nationwide rebellions that led to the Ming dynasty in 1368 A.D. Though later efforts were made in China to print paper currency as compulsory money, the Mongol abuse of the instrument destroyed the possibility until recent times of its reintroduction.

Governmental paper currency came much later in the West, in the footsteps of the successful development of bank currency that took the form of a commercial credit instrument founded on quite different principles than fiat paper money. In its earlier versions in the American and French revolutions, failure of the paper currency was chiefly due to the inability of the revolutionary governments to mobilize by taxation the resources needed for the successful prosecution of the war on which the success of their revolutions depended. These experiences with government paper currency were reflected in the famous generalization of David Ricardo that "neither a State nor a Bank ever had the unrestricted power of issuing paper money, without abusing that power . . . ."[52]

Other experiences in the eighteenth century and even more in the nineteenth showed that a government or a governmentally sanctioned paper currency could successfully negotiate an extended period of warfare—though not

[49]For details of the Sung paper money, see Lien-Sheng Yang, *Money and Credit in China*, 1962, page 51 ff. For a fuller account which traces out the precursor of paper money in the late Tang regime, see Elvin, *Pattern of the Chinese Past* 1973, pages 155 ff.

[50]Marco Polo's account, *The Travels*, thirteenth century, pages 147 ff.

[51]Lien-Sheng Yang, *Money and Credit in China*, 1962, page 64.

[52]Ricardo, *Political Economy*, 1817, page 350.

without generating in the process a significant but potentially reversible wave of inflation. That was surely the case with the paper pound currency issued during the Napoleonic Wars by the Bank of England. Though bank credit was given out to both government and business too liberally at low interest rates, yet wartime inflation was very limited, making it possible within six years of the wars' conclusion to restore the paper pound to full gold convertibility at the old parity. A half-century later during the Civil War the United States federal government exhibited a similar utilization of paper currency; these "greenbacks" launched a wave of inflation, to be sure, but not on a scale that ruled out returning 14 years later to a convertible currency again at the old parity. Not every national experience with paper currency, however, came out so favorably—as witness the German mark inflation after World War I, the nearly continuous inflations in major countries of Latin America, and episodes of paper currency inflation in central Europe. Even if there is the will and perception, responsible action by national governments driven by resource needs and limited ability to raise funds in taxation is not always easily arranged, especially in time of war. Nor is there universal perception among state rulers as to the overriding need to limit issuance of token money to what can be absorbed either by economic growth or the needs of circulation so as to avoid an inflationary process. The socialist economies— for whom management of token money is almost a minor branch of state central planning and economic administration—have frequently shown that they do not appreciate the vital principle of limiting token money. Eventually, however, monetary stability has been generally maintained in the socialist world due to the exceptional ability to raise taxes, hold down wages, and impose rationing and price control on scarce supplies.

All this is the background for the central finding of classical economics that a paper currency is only feasible as a political reality if paper currency is issued primarily by a banking establishment through the process of making loans or giving credit and subject to keeping their currency convertible at all times into coin or bullion at the request of any currency-holder.[53] Even when the all-powerful Soviet economy sought in its early years to establish a new "sound" paper currency, it took care to have this currency issued by what was labeled a banking institution—and nominally, at least, convertible into

[53]The text from Ricardo cited in footnote 52 held that because of the danger of abuse, "the issue of paper money ought to be under some check and control; and none seems so proper for the purpose as that of subjecting the issuers of paper currency to the obligation of paying their notes either in gold coin or bullion." It is characteristic of David Ricardo that he could at times transcend his limitations. He believed that the British parliamentary state was sufficiently stable and responsible to be entrusted, via some special fiscal agency, to issue currency and thus save interest charges on that segment of its public debt and keep the currency continuously convertible into bullion (pages 355 f.).

gold coin money of the day.[54] The Western world was nurtured to the ready acceptance of paper currency during the eighteenth and nineteenth centuries only on the safeguard that the issuing institution—whatever its governmental involvements—was a bank operating on mercantile principles and that the currency itself as "legal tender" would be instantly convertible into precious metal on demand.[55]

THE COMMERCIAL BANK AND ITS DEPOSIT OR NOTE MONEY

Banking evolves from money-changing, a form of business enterprise automatically generated by widespread use of coined money. With little need for laboring assistants, the money-changer himself belongs to the mode of simple commodity producers. His means of production are a strongbox where his working inventory of gold and silver moneys are kept, his shop where he sits at his table or bench (from which the term bank is derived) with a kitty of cash handy, an abacus for quickly calculating sums, an accurate balance or scales for weighing, and various records and papers for keeping accounts or recording debts.[56] His principal assets beside his working capital of moneys are his knowledge of the precious metal content of the different coins or

[54]Zauberman, "Gold in Soviet Economic Theory," *American Economic Review*, 1951, pages 880 ff.; Levchuk, "Money Circulation," 1979, pages 73 f.

[55]The banking establishment can have important governmental intermediation, as in the Napoleonic Bank of France (where the governor and deputy of the bank were appointed by the central government) or as in the first Bank of the United States (where 20% of the voting stock was held by the U.S. government). The most complex form of intermediation was worked out in the latter-day American Federal Reserve system, in which a regional network of banker-controlled banks were subjected to vague forms of control, chiefly through requiring approval for the level of loan rates charged on certain classes of loan by a regulatory board, whose members enjoyed an unusually long term of office but were a standard governmental regulatory agency appointed by the President and confirmed by the Senate. Still more complex was the arrangement worked out in the 1935 revision of the Federal Reserve system whereby the Open Market Committee, which had been controlled exclusively by the banker-controlled Reserve banks, was reconstituted with a majority of the Presidentially appointed regulatory board joined with a lesser number of selected Reserve bank chief executives; but critical again was the institutional arrangement that the New York Reserve Bank serve as manager of the Open Market account, subject only to loose guidance formulas from the full committee. Even when the Bank of England was a wholly stockholder-controlled corporation, it functioned in close association with government; it came to serve government as a fiscal and payment agent, and government in turn was a large borrower from the Bank.

[56]The ancient Greek, Italian, and Hebrew designations for banker as money-changer related to his operations at his table (*trapeziti*—Greek; *tavola* and *banchi*—Italian; and *Shulhan*—Hebrew). See De Roover, *The Medici Bank*, 1963, pages 2, 14 f.; Goitein, *A Mediterranean Society*, 1967–1971, vol. 1, page 248.

coins of different vintage that can pass his way, his ability to gauge the degree of fineness of precious metal objects and to have these formally assayed where necessary, his knowledge of the continually varying terms of exchange in the local money market for gold and silver bullion, and his ability to serve as a safe depository for clients' surplus cash. At all times he is ready to exchange money into different denominations or forms more acceptable for certain kinds of transactions—such as payment of taxes often required in gold or locally minted silver, or even taking low-grade coins and providing high-grade coins for use abroad. He also stands ready to convert precious metals worked up as ornaments or jewelry or plate into their money equivalent. In larger financial centers the money-changers will be located close together to facilitate the making of a better market for their services and for their mutual protection and safety. The genus was well-known in the Graeco-Roman world and was abundant in Jerusalem at or near the Temple around the time of Caesar-Augustus. It became very well-established in Muslim cities, and showed up as one of the larger guilds in the Mediterranean commercial cities of the tenth through fifteenth centuries.[57]

For the money-changer to become a banker proper, he needed to deal not only in moneys but also in one or more classes of debts. Four kinds of debts, which ordinarily increase in importance when the money economy becomes rooted, became available for him.

First of all, there is debt arising because payment for purchases is deferred—being usually held on book account or in the records of the seller. At a surprisingly early stage of commercial development, possibly going back to the latter-day Roman world and certainly existing on a surprising scale in medieval times, the practice began of documenting such debt in the form of what becomes a credit instrument—an order for *deferred payment* (essentially a bill of exchange) or promise to pay (essentially a promissory note). This latter formalization of debt is significant because it facilitates payment for debt by clearing, offset, or third-party financing. In mercantile centers where sellers and buyers from different countries or financial centers come together, or in the great fairs that are centers for regional exchange, most wholesale transactions since early medieval period have been handled on a deferred-payment basis.[58] Recent close study of business life in a Muslim mercantile center of

---

[57]De Roover, *The Medici Bank*, 1963, 16, records that 80 money-changers were registered in the Florentine guild records for 1338. The printed extracts from early Genoa records of the twelfth century contain references to 13 money changers. See Usher, "Origins of Banking," 1953, pages 262 ff.; Goitein, *A Mediterranean Society*, 1967–1971, vol. 1, pages 229–262; Clapham and Power, *Cambridge Economic History*, 1941–1978, vol. 3, pages 66 ff.

[58]Clapham and Power, *Cambridge Economic History*, 1941–1978, vol. 2, pages 284 ff.; Usher, "Origins of Banking," 1953, pages 269 ff.; Lopez and Raymond, *Medieval Trade*, 1967; Mitchell, *Economics of Ancient Greece*, 1940, pages 335 ff.

the tenth through thirteenth centuries has shown that a good deal of retail trade was handled on this basis, at least in the Jewish quarters.[59]

Other categories of debt are equally important. The second and largest category is *accrued liabilities* outstanding at any time for obligations for unilateral payment; these gather over time but are discharged at one time or intermittently, like taxes, land rents, marriage dowries, inheritance settlements, and pensions or annuities. Some of these payments involve local transfers, but others may necessitate transfers between different financial centers, involving major international fund movements from points of collection to points of final disposition—as was the case with the Catholic Church.

A third class of debt arises out of personal borrowing from friends or neighbors, or sometimes from moneylenders, with the evidence of debt usually carried in the memories of the parties involved but often reduced to some form of record—occasionally in more mercantile centers to formal written instruments. Such borrowings, nearly always initiated by borrowers, were frequently encountered in the older Semitic and Persian societies of the Middle East, and were well-known in the Graeco-Roman world. They appear nearly universally in both Oriental and Western societies. The occasion for borrowing is twofold. Distress debt is negotiated to compensate for losses or injuries derived from illness, accidents, or the results of natural catastrophes or famines. Debt may also be sought to meet the needs of upper-class prodigals or impecunious notables whose social status demands a suitable show.

A fourth kind of debt is a *deposit loan* that comes from placing funds on deposit with a moneylender or rich merchant. Such a debt is usually initiated by the creditor, not the debtor, as with borrowing generally. In the Assyrian and Graeco-Roman civilizations, temples as privileged sanctuaries often took on this deposit function. Its purpose is not to succour the needs of the borrower but to accommodate the creditor by providing a place of safekeeping for his funds—and increasingly, in developing mercantile centers, by supplying facilities for payment in suitable coin, for distant financial transfer, and for overdraft privileges. Hence the deposit loan was not a bailment in which the funds turned over were to be kept separate as a special trust. Only at a later stage would deposit funds emerge with payment of interest on account, which usually had to be concealed by various devices because of the widespread interest *verbot*.

Debt from one or more of these categories has been so prevalent throughout recorded history that some of the earliest sociopolitical struggles characterizing early economic systems—their prehistory so to speak—revolve around efforts at debt settlement or adjustment. Special concern for distress borrowers is evident in the abhorrence of usury embodied in most world

---

[59]Goitein, *A Mediterranean Society*, 1967–1971, vol. 1, pages 197, 262.

major religions. This concern, however, did not mitigate the sharp feeling of nearly all traditional societies that the obligations of indebtedness should not be shirked and that severe punishment must be meted out to those who default on debt obligations, sometimes incurring forfeiture of liberty or limited servitude. The sanctity of debt was sufficiently great in the dispersed Israelite communities resident in the Islamic world so that if one of their members became bankrupted, the community often would seek to raise funds by subscription to honor defaulted obligations.[60]

In its primitive state, the simplest form of bank is achieved when the moneychanger takes on a depository function, i.e., becomes a borrower on a deposit account. This action enlarges the fund of working capital that he administers and permits him to participate more actively in short-term business dealings—usually as participant in the widely used form of commenda or trading partnership which developed in the entire medieval world. Even more importantly, the moneylender can now supply overdraft or loan facilities to his depositors or make payment transfers on their behalf to distant financial centers through arrangements he has developed. Occasionally this primordial banker will be able to clear on his own books financial transfers to different depositors dealing with him. This utilization of the bank deposit as a medium of payment rests on the experience that a promise to pay money, if generally accepted, may be as serviceable for the settlement of obligations as money itself.[61] Detailed records of such banks are available as far back as the tenth century for major Muslim centers in the Jewish–Arabic world. Such institutions probably functioned in the incipient European mercantile communities of the same period. The Jewish–Arabic banker even honored checks, or written orders for payment to named parties, copies of which have actually survived. In contemporaneous European mercantile centers, however, this procedure of transfer by written order was resisted and allowed only as a special privilege.[62] This is, of course, private banking on a fractional reserve basis since deposit moneys were not treated as warehoused bailed property

---

[60]Goitein, *A Mediterranean Society*, 1967–1971, vol. 1, pages 259 f.

[61]"The Use of Bank-Money depends on nothing except the discovery that, in many cases, the transference of the debts themselves is just as serviceable for the settlement of transactions as is the transference of the money in terms of which they are expressed." See Keynes, *Treatise on Money*, 1930, vol. 1, page 15.

[62]Goitein, *A Mediterranean Society*, 1967–1971, vol. 1, page 241. The local term for a written order for payment to a named party a stated amount was *ruq'a*, an Arabic word generically denoting a piece of paper or note. Though occasionally used in North Italian cities by 1400, transfer of funds solely by written order was not generally practiced and was in some places (e.g., Venice) expressly prohibited until late in the eighteenth century. See De Roover, *The Medici Bank*, 1963, pages 18 f.; Usher, *Early History Deposit Banking*, 1943, pages 7, 8, 22, 90.

and hence were utilized either in mercantile undertakings carried on by the banker or in overdraft facilities extended to other depositors or clients.

A still higher stage of banking is achieved when the bank also makes loans either by direct lending or indirectly by assumption of debt, by the purchase or "discount" of bills of exchange tendered by client depositors. Though earlier Italian banks had engaged in this style of banking, which is overt fractional reserve banking, the Bank of England became in 1694 the first major public institution permitted to make loans. It was prohibited from dealing in goods except to dispose of pledges or collateral acquired as security on loans. Beside these commercial loans, the Bank was obligated from time to time to accommodate the state treasury by accepting at par negotiated quantities of interest-bearing treasury bills, which in the earlier years occasionally strained the lending resources of the Bank while being potential forms of competitive paper currency.[63]

The Bank of England was among the pioneers in another essential respect. Its ability to lend would have been limited to a fraction of the coin or bullion deposited with it but for its use of a curious form of promissory note it gave out obligating itself to pay a certain sum of money to the bearer. Since the note was due at any time, it was virtually due on issuance. The advantage to a bearer of holding it or using it for payment was that it was issued in relatively large denominations easy to transfer; unlike gold coinage or bullion, it did not need to be evaluated by assay. With confidence in the issuing bank, a holder would not present the notes for conversion to coin or bullion except when needed to obtain currency for payroll purposes, petty cash needs, or transfer abroad. This, then, permitted a given amount of gold or silver coin or bullion deposited with the Bank to sustain many times its value in circulating notes.

A parallel phase of the development of the commercial bank, widely used by predecessor public and private banks, was the partial supersession of the circulating bank note itself, by which a deposit liability of the bank could be transferred by written order to a stated party for a designated amount. The circulating note—good to bearer and subject to transfer without endorsement—was an advantage over coined metal. But the deposit liability transferable by check had decided advantages over the circulating bank note. (1) It could not be stolen. (2) It could be written to the exact amount of payment needed. (3) It was transferable by mail. (4) It cut down costs of engraving

---

[63]Though the available histories of the Bank do not make too clear the use of the Bank's lending resources, constant pressure on the Bank to finance state-issued short-term interest-bearing bills (denominated usually as Exchequer or Deficiency bills), especially in times of war, is indicated. See Clapham, *The Bank of England*, 1945, vol. 1, pages 38 f., 54 ff., 66 ff.; vol. 2, 136 f., 251 f., 275 f. These state overdrafts plagued banking in Barcelona for some three centuries. See Usher, *Early History Deposit Banking*, 1943, 369 ff.

and printing of bank notes elaborately designed to minimize counterfeiting. However, it required identification by the bank of the validity of the signature inscribed on a bank transfer order. Bankers assumed the risk of loss in an inaccurate handwriting identification because experience indicated that trained cashiers familiar with the depositors' usual payment practices could detect most improper uses or forgeries of transfer orders. Creditors of the Bank of England generally preferred to hold their claims on the Bank in the form of its circulating notes. But even in the Bank's very early days, large account holders—including joint-stock corporations, government agencies, and various private bankers—utilized bank resources by holding their bank liabilities in the form of current accounts that they used by writing transfer orders. This was soon facilitated for private depositors when the Bank furnished printed transfer or check forms for its depositors.[64] It does not matter whether a bank's liabilities are transferred to settle payment obligations by handing over bank promissory notes or by ordering transfer of deposit indebtedness; for in both instances bank liabilities are being utilized as a form of money, the promise to pay superseding the object promised in payment.

As thus evolved, the commercial bank carries on three major functions: (1) It creates a flexible and economical form of money brought into existence by the action of giving credit in business transactions, which thereby are made more self-financing. As Adam Smith pointed out, use of this money reduces the quantity of gold and silver needed for monetary purposes and thus enables the capital resources of the community to be invested in more productive forms.[65] (2) The bank can arrange for settlement of indebtedness of its depositors by offset or clearing in the books of the bank or in the exchange market. And (3), the commercial bank concentrates the liquid working capital of its depositors where it can be readily loaned out to business users on a revolving basis—subject, of course, to the market test of providing adequate security for loans and the ability to use the loan resources profitably enough to pay interest charges, which help in turn to finance services extended by the bank.

As soon as these money-handling functions of the money-changer are joined with the credit and payment clearing functions of the depository or note-issuing institution, the bank has evolved far beyond the bounds of the simple commodity producer. The bank has become a capitalist enterprise that requires an extended network of agencies or branches in different financial centers, a facade of impressive buildings and offices to bear witness to its financial solidity, specialized equipment for handling, sorting, and storing moneys and

---

[64]Clapham, *Bank of England,* 1945, vol. 1, pages 141 ff.
[65]A. Smith, *Wealth of Nations,* 1776, pages 276.

bullion, and books of account for record-keeping. It has need for employing many assistants with special duties and with some aptitude for the various tasks. Over time and with specialization, bank personnel develop unique skills at quick handling of moneys, talent for detecting counterfeits and forgeries, an almost photographic memory for signatures and types of handwriting, and ability to scrutinize financial statements or bills of exchange for possible weakness in the enterprise or transaction. The great Italian banks of the thirteenth through fifteenth centuries are veritable prototypes of capitalist enterprise with their extended sphere of operations taking them all over southern and northern Europe, their keen sense of profitability, their varied clientele, their exact calculations, and their conglomerate-style dealing in wholesale trade and manufacturing.

As a capitalist form of enterprise, the bank generates its own competition so that it is no longer simply an enterprise—but an industry, competing for trade, customers, and deposits. Since the banker's gain is largely made up in his financial operations from interest collected on loans or profits earned by investment, he is driven to lending or investing on as large a scale as possible with his given reserves on hand, keeping only enough cash to serve for money-changing purposes and a contingency reserve for deposit withdrawals. But that reserve, gauged to allow for emergencies experienced in the past, in an everchanging world may prove inadequate for the emergencies of the future. The fortunes of war, with its destruction of old state systems by emergent new peoples or empires, will periodically throw a set of leading financial centers into a dither, set up a panicky demand for cash and expose the inadequate reserves carried by most bankers. Food shortage too or a series of poor harvests will tend to cause the merchants in a community to search the known food markets of their trading world for possible surpluses that can be bought up; and this action will require not bank credit but hard cash—which then must be drained, in part at least, out of the banks, revealing their scanty reserves and thus adding bank failures to the anguish of famine. But even apart from these disasters the steady pursuit of banking profit—especially when it induces bankers to keep company and give service to impecunious monarchs with favors to give—can lead to banking failure if default is encountered on state debts.[66] Once stock exchanges are established where corporate securities and wholesale commodities are regularly traded, bankers have another source of grief: namely, unwise lending to imprudent speculators.

Presumably on these accounts the records of Italian banking from the thirteenth to the sixteenth centuries are so frequently punctuated with accounts of bank failures, especially in Florence, where two waves of failure wiped out

---

[66]On the hurtful effects of defaults by English monarchs in the fourteenth and fifteenth centuries, see De Roover, *The Medici Bank*, 1963, pages 329 ff., 372 f.

great financial institutions in the fourteenth and fifteenth centuries.[67] In the first quarter of the sixteenth century six of the ten functioning Venetian banks failed.[68] In the second decade of the eighteenth century a fantastic experience in credit banking held back for nearly a century the development of banking in France.[69] Each bank failure is another nudge to the memory, forecasting in other banks a possible shortage of funds and creating a latent fear—out of which a sense of panic readily develops. And since it was in the very nature of a bank to be secretive about its affairs—to whom it was lending and on what terms, and how much cash reserves were actually on hand or readily available—confidence in the safety of banks in general could readily lapse despite the valued services they were rendering. This latent distrust of banking was at times so keen that political authorities even in advanced mercantile areas forbade money-changers to accept bank deposits or to make payments by book transfer.[70]

Even if all external shocks are avoided, the very success of the banking enterprise can accomplish its undoing, especially in its early phases. For bank credit can unleash a wave of prosperity, with its familiar outcome of rising prices and thriving business, that is undermined by two fatal drainages: (1) into the domestic circulation to provide specie or coins for meeting larger payrolls, and (2) abroad, because the prosperity generated by banking has made the country with its higher price and income level less suitable to purchase *from* and more suitable for sale *to*. These drainages capped the climax of the wave of "overtrading" that Adam Smith traced in Scotland when commercial banking first spread, terminating in a major period of recession

[67]In the 1340s the three leading Florentine banking houses—with numerous branches and employees or partners numbered nearly to three digits—collapsed, chiefly due to overextension of credit and excessive loans to sovereigns. See De Roover, *The Medici Bank*, 1963, pages 2 f.; Clapham and Power, *Cambridge Economic History*, 1941–1978, vol. 3, pages 76 f.; Miskimin, *Economy of Early Renaissance Europe*, 1975, page 151. Of the succeeding generation of Florentine banks, headed by the great Medici bank, most had failed or collapsed by the end of the 15th century. By that time only a half-dozen banks were registered in the guild, while earlier in the century, there were some 72. See De Roover, *The Medici Bank*, 1963, pages 374 f. In the 13th century a great banking firm in Siena, Bonsignori, failed in 1298—"and it is said that Siena never completely recovered from this blow" (page 2). A public Genoa bank chartered in 1408 failed in 1444 and was not revived again until 1586. See Clapham and Power, *Cambridge Economic History*, 1941–1978, vol. 3, page 97.

[68]Six out of the ten banks active in Venice in the late 1400s failed by 1530. See Lane, *Collected Papers*, 1966, ch. 5, "Venetian Bankers 1496–1533," pages 69–86. In the three centuries preceding, Galbraith recounts that a hundred or more banks came into existence and "a very considerable number also failed." See Galbraith, *Money*, 1975, page 18, n. 2.

[69]Galbraith, *Money*, 1975, pages 22 f., gives a somewhat lurid account of the John Law fiasco in France treated very accurately by E. J. Hamilton, "John Law of Lauriston," 1967, pages 273–282.

[70]Clapham and Power, *Cambridge Economic History*, 1941–1978, vol. 3, pages 97, 358.

and bank failure which had international repercussions.[71] This phase of crisis was merely one of a long series which in the eighteenth century recurred irregularly, usually as the climax of a period of business prosperity and in association with many of the characteristic phenomena of what later came to be called "business cycles."[72] Each crisis left in its wake a wave of bank failures, usually of smaller proprietorial institutions.[73] In the United States, bank failures were endemic through the third decade of the twentieth century.

To cope with this chronic problem of bank failures, the intervention of the state is required. In one form of intervention, it can restrict the activities of the bank to its most essential functions of money-changing and assaying, holding deposits, and making financial transfers by book credit. At the same time, it can give these functions their widest possible scope by making the bank a public institution that all local merchants and business enterprises must utilize. This solution—worked out in Barcelona in 1401, in Amsterdam in 1609, and in a number of other Continental financial centers later in the century—was on the whole successful. The monopoly of banking that it enforced was not too harmful because the facilities of the bank were available to all. Minimally or not at all involved in lending, the banks were fairly solid institutions. But though this form of banking is safer, it obviously does not economize very much on the use of precious metals and there is little monetary flexibility to accommodate changing monetary needs.[74]

[71]A. Smith, *Wealth of Nations*, 1776, pages 284–301; Clapham, *Bank of England*, 1945, vol. 1, pages 158 ff., 242 ff.

[72]Ashton, *Economic Fluctuations in England, 1700–1800*, 1959, discloses a vigorous trade cycle, as usual irregularly interlarded with financial crises, with most of the familiar features of cyclical behavior. So-called "long swings" in urban real estate and development, which plagued the nineteenth and early twentieth centuries, also rocked the 18th century in England. See on this works cited and data and charts reproduced in Gottlieb, *Long Swings in Urban Development*, 1976, pages 215 f., Charts 7-1, 7-2, 7-3; and this volume, ch. 3.

[73]Some 100 banks are alleged to have failed in the English "crisis" of 1793 and some 73 banks again in the more severe 1825 crisis. See Marshall, *Money, Credit and Commerce*, 1923, page 305; Kindelberger, *Manias, Panics and Crashes*, 1978, page 114. For some details of these two crises and their corresponding phases of cyclical movement, see Gayer, Rostow, and Schwartz, *Growth and Fluctuation of the British Economy*, 1953, vol. 1, pages 7 ff., 21 ff., 84 ff., 190 f., 202 ff. As Clapham rather casually notes, in the eighteenth century especially "men went into it [banking], came out of it or failed at it very frequently." See Clapham, *Bank of England*, 1945, vol. 1, page 158. He reports that of the 733 issuing banks functioning in 1813–1814, only 585 were operating in 1816–1817 after a sharp commercial crisis of 1814–1815 (vol. 2, page 60). He later notes that in "quiet times" annual attrition of bank failure was around 2% (vol. 2, page 90).

[74]On these public deposit, transfer-account and assay banks, see Jan De Vries, *Economy of Europe 1600–1750*, 1976, pages 229 ff.; Braudel, *The Mediterranean*, 1949, vol. 1, pages 530 f. For an account of the complex development of the Barcelona Bank of Deposit, which apparently money-changers were not permitted to use, see Usher, *Early History Deposit Banking*, 1943, pt. 2, pages 237–504. Of the Amsterdam bank, beside authoritative recent ac-

A second kind of state intervention seeks to strengthen the individual bank—making it bigger and better by throwing it into corporate form and allowing branches to sprout freely to facilitate fund transfer. That course was followed in England and later on the Continent where large-scale private banks, deprived of the privilege of note issue but subject only to minor regulation, became stronger and in time able to withstand the storms of the business cycle. A way out used in the United States allowed free and easy formation of banks that are also put under constant surveillance, prohibited from their spreading out in branches, and required to hold substantial cash reserves against their deposit liabilities. This rigidly circumscribed their lending ability, by limiting loans to any one borrower and frequently prohibiting mortgage loans or other loans of seemingly unsound character. Although such restrictions helped, they could not undo the work of the business cycle, correct for unwise management, or enable institutions to survive for communities whose economic base was highly unstable.

A third kind of state-sponsored solution, readily joined with the other two, is to seek to turn a commercial bank into a governmentally associated institution wrapped around with the flag and given the privilege of note issue. The first institution of this type was the Bank of England launched as a private bank in 1696 to raise funds for the Whig Revolution which put a new dynasty on the throne. It was endowed with the power of note issue and the right to make loans or buy bills as well as accept deposits and make payments. The joint-stock features enabled a considerable equity capital to be collected. The collegial form of quasi-corporate government developed by a stockholding community primarily residing near the Bank permits the privileged position of the Bank to be tolerated by the business community serviced by it.[75] The Bank of England was managed with reasonable conservatism. A

---

counts, we have the classic contemporaneous account of A. Smith, *Wealth of Nations*, 1776, 446 ff. The resources of the Bank were secretly utilized by the dominant city fathers, resulting in the closing of the Bank in 1819. See Galbraith, *Money*, 1975, pages 15 ff.

[75]The stockholders were mostly London business firms and even as late as 1833, of the 2846 stockholders only 63 lived abroad. In most of the eighteenth century, the stockholder list was under 1000. In the first quarter-century of the Bank, stockholder meetings were held at least four times yearly and played an important policy role. Directors were chosen young and generally reelected until they reached by seniority their term of service for a 2-year term as deputy and then as chief executive. Private commercial bankers were carefully excluded from directorships. Executive posts of the Bank were carefully rotated on a seniority basis. See the fascinating account by Walter Bagehot, *Lombard Street*, 1873, ch. 7, "The Government of the Bank of England." For the role of stockholder meetings, most important in the first half century of the Bank, see Clapham, *Bank of England*, 1945, vol. 1, page 41, 42, 46, 55, 58, 63, 67 ff., 75, 95, 100, 108 f. Even the strong Tudor monarchs did not try to manhandle London merchants in their money and exchange dealings. These merchants in turn appreciated

generous cash reserve margin was kept on hand. From the outset and through to the Napoleonic Wars circulating notes were confined to large denominations—thereby requiring all English payroll payments and most retail trade to be conducted with silver or gold coins, thus reducing the relative danger of internal drainage. Lending was launched in many directions, which at an early phase included some mortgages and some cash advances to notables, but in the main loans were short-term and involved purchase or discounting of trade bills issued by known parties of good credit standing.

The Bank of England, however, did not have a monopoly of the banking business in England. It had a monopoly rather of the quasi-corporate form that permitted high visibility, a banking asset, and a large amount of liquid capital to be concentrated in a single enterprise. Other banking enterprises were established both in London and in the upcountry and with them all the vitality and disadvantages of the unregulated commercial bank were manifested: wild growth, flourishing for a period, and widespread failure in time of financial crisis or trade depression.

A similar pattern of a major quasi-public corporation with government involvement was worked out, with interesting variations, in the first and second Bank of the United States and in the Bank of France. Both were given precedence in a world where private or local banking had a free rein. Again, the central institutions demonstrated relative durability so long as their charters and government involvement were maintained. Again, massive instability was experienced at the periphery of the system.

Because of the peripheral banking instability this early form of commercial banking developed in France, England, and the United States was bound to evolve further. Opened to all banking enterprises was the quasi-public form

---

the need for a state authority as was interestingly shown in a plan by Thomas Gresham for utilization of London's merchants to help raise foreign exchange to pay the queen's foreign creditors. See Burgon, *Sir Thomas Gresham*, 1839, pages 257 f. The detailed portrayal by the Webbs of the corporate City of London shows the city a proud capable burgeoning "ratepayers democracy," with a population in 1689 of nearly 150,000 persons and an extended community subject to its jurisdiction outside its borders, over 100 charters granted over seven centuries, nearly complete self-rule within its borders, direct access to the throne and special representation in the House of Commons, and a jealous regard for its rights and privileges. "From 1689," right down to 1835, report the Webbs, "the Corporation of the City of London stands forth as a sort of unofficial mouthpeice of the people of England, as against their National Government—carrying on indeed a continual criticism, sometimes insolent in its irresponsible independence of the whole policy of the National Executive in finance, in Foreign Affairs, and in domestic legislation." See Webb and Webb, *English Local Government*, 1908, vol. 3, ch. 10, "The City of London," pages 569 ff. The secret of the power of the City was its thriving business activity and its many wealthy citizens who in 1696 raised the 1.2 million pounds (25% paid up) for the stock of the corporation of the Bank of England within 12 days, less time a contemporary pamphleteer stated than "could have been imagined." See Clapham, *Bank of England*, 1945, vol. 1, page 19.

of corporate organization that is suitable for banking where capital concentration is needed and where some public disclosure of operations and financial standing is desirable. At the same time the favored central institution slowly retired from commercial banking proper. Formally invested with the monopoly of note issue, it was gradually turned into a bankers' bank or a central bank, making loans to other banks and accepting their deposits of the main monetary reserve supply of coin or bullion collected by banks. It also served as a national clearing institution in which all or most banks had deposits and as fiscal agent or banker of the central government whose loan issues at critical times might need support. Finally, it served in times of financial crisis as a lender of last resort, and, hopefully, as a stabilizing force in crises.

This evolution of a banking system in which commercial banks with primarily private motives of business gain are headed by a major governmentally established central institution, in which public purpose is supposed to be paramount, had its first sproutings in the eighteenth century. It gradually developed through the nineteenth century and was not really completed or formalized in the Western world until well along in the twentieth century. In the American case, a central banking institution, shattered in the fourth decade of the nineteenth century by President Andrew Jackson, was not recreated until the second decade of the twentieth century with the Federal Reserve banks. The priority of public purpose is not fully assured in the central institution to this day since important central banking powers are ultimately controlled by representatives of private banking institutions. The Bank of England strongly fought the entrance of joint-stock banking in the London area; i.e., it clung to its private London banking business that was uppermost in its attentions. It and the Bank of France were relatively slow to develop a network of branches—preeminent in the earlier American planning for central banking. One of the most formidable powers of a central bank, that of modifying bank reserves or selling bills or investment securities, was only rarely and imperfectly used in the nineteenth century. Moreover, changes in the discount rate by which the central bank made its loans were within a relatively modest range.

In the basic legislative mandate of the Bank of England in 1844, apart from establishing the principle that variations in note issue were to be rigidly modeled after variations in coin and bullion reserves on a one-to-one basis, the Bank of England was supposed to operate like any private institution. Its privacy would be invaded only by the requirement that it give out an abbreviated weekly financial summary of its operations. Nor did it always take the initiative in managing a financial crisis. The crisis of 1793 was handled by special issuance by the treasury of short-term government bills treated like bank notes. In the crises of 1847 and 1856 the Bank likewise made no noteworthy initiative.

Hence it is understandable that Marx, in his extended analysis of British banking and of the evolving role of the Bank of England, unlike his contemporary, Walter Bagehot, did not expressly recognize that the Bank of England was not just a preeminent commercial bank but also a central bank with special public functions in guiding the banking or credit system. At different times he came close to this recognition but it slipped away from him—partly because the Bank in his day tended to play, with all its "immense power . . . over commerce and industry" a "passive" role which at best worked to mitigate the outbreak of overt financial panic.[76] Not until well on in the next century would the central bank become endowed conceptually with the more formidable functions of cooperating with fellow central banks and of managing the national money supply of paper and token money to try to keep it aligned with the gold standard. We shall now turn to this subject because it marks the further evolution of the institution of money.

CENTRAL BANKS AND THE GOLD STANDARD

The relationships of central banks to each other and to their underlying commercial banks on the one hand, and to government on the other—as well as to their gold holdings, obligations, and currency or note issue—make up a developing phase of the institution of money that is presently experiencing an accelerating pace of change. Let us commence with treatment of the constitutional relationship by way of ownership and control of the central bank and the degree to which the crucial reserves of the banking system are effectively centralized under its authority. We will next consider the ability of a central bank to enforce its will as to monetary and credit policy by various instruments for action—some of them inherited from the nineteenth century and others devised in the twentieth century. Then we shall discuss the relationships of central banks to their gold holdings under the gold standard and to its evolution, 1945–1975, under the Bretton Woods Agreement whereby

---

[76]Walter Bagehot's great work, *Lombard Street*, 1873, followed by about a decade the basic writing of Marx on the British banking system in *Capital* III, 1864–1865. Understanding of Marx's view is hampered because his analysis stops short of attempting an "exhaustive analysis" of the credit system." He dealt with banking only in a preliminary and almost casual way—though he felt constrained by the importance of his subject and the liveliness of his interest in it to present his views at length. For the caveat, see Marx, *Capital* III, 1864–1865, page 400; *Critique of Political Economy*, 1859, page 116. Conceding the "immense power of an institution such as the Bank of England over commerce and industry," he yet found "their actual movements remain completely beyond its province and it is passive toward them." See Marx, *Capital* III, 1864–1865, page 606. He spoke almost incidentally of the "central bank" as the "pivot of the credit system," while in turn the "metal reserve is the pivot of the bank" (page 572). But the implications of the central bank role were not elucidated except merely to note that as a 'public institution under government protection [it] cannot exploit its power as ruthlessly as does private business" (page 543).

the role of gold was progressively diminished until in 1971–1975 the coup was given and demonetization of gold was carried through. Finally, we will conclude with the relationships of central banks to each other and the emergence in this century of a finer and more lasting coordination of authority in international monetary matters as embodied chiefly in the International Monetary Fund (IMF). These different phases of central banking are all related to each other but it will be convenient to treat them in the sequential order indicated.

Ownership and control over central banking has varied widely in the Western world. The democratic currents of the twentieth century, swelled by two long wars that centralized power in the hands of government, have nearly eliminated the form of central bank as a privately controlled quasi-public corporation endowed with monopoly privileges of note issue and playing the role of overseer of banks and organic link between the business–financial community and government. The Bank of England, like the Bank of France and nearly every central bank in Europe, the Americas, and the newly formed countries of Asia and Africa, was established as a government institution or quasi-independent agency, with executive heads nominated and controlled by the executive branch of government. The West German Central Bank was in its inception in 1948 a federated institution, resembling in that respect the American Federal Reserve System but free of participation by commercial banks themselves. These play a dominating role in the American scheme of central banking with the Federal Reserve Bank of New York playing still a pivotal role.[77] Nearly everywhere the central bank shares control over monetary matters with the heads of state. It is not always true that even 100% governmental control carries the day invariably against the tradition of independent judgment habitually assumed by central banking executives responsive to some degree as they must be to the sentiments of the financial community.[78]

Authority of the central bank over financial institutions carrying on com-

[77]The pivotal role of the New York Federal Reserve Bank in the U.S. Federal Reserve System partly grew out of its relatively large share in the reserves and deposits of the system, its handling from the early 1920s of investment purchases on system account in the New York financial market, its service as negotiating partner to European central banks in the 1920s and 1930s, the greater sophistication of its staff and leadership, and the tradition of financial leadership generally devolved in the national banking system (commenced in 1863) on the New York City reserve banks. See on this occasional comments in Friedman and Schwartz, *Monetary History*, 1963, 254 ff., 362 ff., 269, 380, 413 ff. The redoubtable Wright Patman, who was quite perceptive on many banking issues, once blurted out: "We have all these buildings all over the United States, and there is only one building that really operates the Federal Reserve system and that is the Federal Reserve Bank in New York." U.S. Congress, House, Hearings, *Federal Reserve System after Fifty Years*, 1964, page 1164.

[78]U.S. Congress, House, Hearings, *Federal Reserve System after Fifty Years*, 1964, pages 944 f., 989 f.

mercial banking functions is by no means completely established. By tradition in Great Britain there is no requirement that financial institutions hold their reserves with the Bank of England. A higher percentage of English reserves than elsewhere are held as vault cash or deposited abroad.[79] Only the larger American banks have chosen to accept the privileges and obligations of "membership" in the American central banking scheme. Members must make a capital contribution to the common stock of the Federal Reserve bank in their district, deposit reserves which they are required to keep with that bank; become entitled to free check-clearing and related services of that bank and to possible loan support to meet temporary financial needs.

In 1980 a break was made in the American tradition of voluntary membership in the central bank by requiring every depository institution to maintain reserves that are deposited in part at least with Federal Reserve banks and are subject to up or down variation by the central bank. The new arrangements are part of a comprehensive reform package of financial institutions to be phased in over a seven-year period, thus to become fully effective only in 1987.[80] Nearly all Western countries have adopted the American system of requiring financial institutions that carry on commercial banking to hold a stated fraction of their deposit liabilities in deposits with the central bank. This depositing action effectively centralizes banking reserves in a commercial banking system in a single central institution.

Power of the central bank to enforce its leadership in credit markets and to chart the course of banking policy rests upon three different procedures that may be used separately or in combination.

1. One method is to raise or lower rates of interest charged on loans or purchases of credit instruments. It is effective to the extent that the central bank has played an active role in credit activity by lending operations carried

[79]In his informed 1930 survey of the degree of control exercised by the Bank of England over English commercial banks, J. M. Keynes was almost apprehensive about the looseness of the control, the high fraction of its reserves held directly by the so-called "clearing" or joint-stock banks, inadequate financial reporting, recognized "window-dressing" in these reports. He believed there was no "substantial obstacle to their nibbling at their conventional [reserve] ratios as the result of concerted or sympathetic action continued by slow degrees over a period." See Keynes, *Treatise on Money*, 1930, vol. 2, pages 68 ff. The 1930 pattern has persisted in England through the mid-1950s. See Fousek, *Foreign Central Banking*, 1957, pages 46 f.

[80]Membership in the Federal Reserve was essentially voluntary since National Banks could readily obtain State Charters and membership in the Federal Reserve was voluntary for state-chartered banks. On the recommendation to require all insured commercial banks to belong to the Federal Reserve System, see Commission on Money and Credit, *Money and Credit*, 1961, pages 76 ff. Not until 1980 was action taken to eliminate over a phased time-period ending in 1987 the American "dual banking" system. See Federal Reserve Bank of New York, "Highlights," Summer 1980, pages 12 f.

on independently or by rediscount of credit instruments acquired by commercial banks and sold to the central bank. This mode of action was habitually relied upon in the first century of central banking, when a substantial part of the loan resources of the credit system passed through the portfolios of the central bank or involved central bank resources. It is not effective if commercial banks have ready access to loan markets abroad or if foreign borrowers have ready access to domestic loan markets. Under circumstances such as those usually prevailing in the United States, where the central bank engages only in peripheral and incidental credit market activity by way of loans and discounts to its member banks, the variation in so-called central bank terms of discount has chiefly a symbolic or bellwether effect, indicating the policy of monetary authorities with little direct impact on terms of credit dealings except as it may provide an excuse for financial institutions to raise their loan charges.[81] But on the Continent and elsewhere, central bank lending or rediscounting is carried on more actively; accordingly, terms of lending throughout the credit system will be directly affected by changes in the official central discount or loan rate.

The channels of influence of changes in short-term interest rates upon economic activity are many and diverse. They have frequently been debated in economic literature and to some extent have been evaluated in econometric models. The influence varies according to the circumstances of the business cycle, the strength of attitudes toward investment spending by business firms, whether the "fringe of unsatisfied borrowers" seeking credit accommodation is of large or small dimension, and the degree of insulation of domestic from international credit markets.[82]

Central banks have developed two additional potent techniques for bringing about changes in lending resources of banks and thus indirectly inducing changes in credit availability and easing or stiffening of terms of lending.

[81]Each Federal Reserve bank was authorized in the basic 1913 enabling act to "extend credit to each member bank such discounts, advancements and accommodations as may be safely and reasonably made with due regard for the claims and demands of other member banks," subject to general regulations established by the Federal Reserve Board. Over the years member banks developed a reluctance to borrow and the governing Federal Reserve Board restricted reserve bank discounting. The detailed breakdown of individual discounts and advances and number of banks accommodated for the years 1960 to 1963 indicated that though one-fourth or one-fifth of the member banks were accommodated in individual years, the total number of accommodations averaged between 5 and 10 per bank. The duration of the accommodation must have been only a few days because the dollar value of discounts and accommodations granted (for 1960—$18.8 billion) is so much greater than the value of the same item cited on monthly and weekly balance sheet reports. See U.S. Congress, House, Hearings, *Federal Reserve System after Fifty Years*, 1964, pages 310 ff.; Friedman and Schwartz, *Monetary History*, 1963, pages 268 f., 513 ff.

[82]Still classical is the presentation in Keynes, *Treatise on Money*, 1930, vol. 1, ch. 13, "The 'Modus Operandi' of Bank-Rate."

2. These changes in credit availability may be brought about by purchases or sales of high quality credit instruments handled in investment markets, chiefly debentures, bills, and notes with short maturity and issued in standardized amounts by government, public agencies, or utilities and quasi-public corporations. This method was virtually unknown in the nineteenth century and only slowly assumed importance in the American Federal Reserve scheme. When the central bank buys such instruments it makes available additional cash facilities that will end up as bank reserves that will support by established principles an expansion of credit and creation of new bank money as a multiple of the initial reserve increment. Selling such instruments withdraws bank reserves and constricts bank lending power. Use of this method does require that a well-organized investment financial market be in existence for instruments of the credit class concerned and that the central bank has a good-sized portfolio of such credit instruments.

Unless a well-organized market exists, any sizeable change in central bank portfolios will unduly affect market price and may adversely affect the investment interests of the issuers of such securities whose value is thus being artificially manipulated. If government securities are to be thus handled, treasury officers who are responsible for public debt management will feel very uncomfortable if the central bank is depressing or upsetting the market for its securities by dumping securities to draw cash facilities out of the market. Nor does it help if losses thus induced are offset by converse central bank campaigns to buy securities, because on investment management grounds it is always desirable to encourage a stable market with a minimum of special fluctuations. Many central banks, moreover, have been categorically restricted in holding or dealing in government debt to check possible abuse of credit facilities to finance deficit spending by governments. It is thus not surprising that so-called open market operations are widely carried on only in England, Canada, and the United States.[83] If the central bank were prepared to deal in debts of all maturities and with varying degrees of risk, the relationship between the complex of bond and investment market yields and the quantity of bank money would be direct, and large changes in the stock of money could be negotiated with minimum adverse impact on special kinds of investment securities. For that reason Keynes asserted in his famous 1936 *General Theory* that a "complex offer by the central bank to buy and sell at stated prices gilt-edged bonds of all maturities, in place of the single bank rate for short-term bills, is the most important practical improvement which can be made in the technique of monetary management."[84]

[83]Fousek, *Foreign Central Banking*, 1957, page 33.

[84]Keynes, *General Theory*, 1936, page 206. Predictably, Friedman and Schwartz disagree for reasons that do not meet the issue. See *Monetary History*, 1963, pages 632 ff.

3. The third method varies the reserves that banks are required to hold either in bank vaults or eligible depositories. The first major monetary theorist to call attention to the desirability of giving the central bank the power both to fix a reserve requirement and with suitable notice to modify the same was J. M. Keynes—who now, strangely, is regarded as one who underestimated the resources of central banking. He recommended that the Bank of England have the power to fix reserve requirements, which he suggested could run at 15% for demand deposits and 3% for time deposits, with a play of 5% in the case of demand and 3%, plus or minus, for time deposits.[85] His recommendation was embodied in the revision in 1935 of the American Federal Reserve system. By the mid-1950s some 30 countries had formally empowered central banks or monetary authorities to vary reserve requirements. "Though it may seem revolutionary now," Keynes wrote in 1930, some suitable provision for varying reserve requirements, "duly safeguarded, should I think be added to the powers of the ideal Central Bank of the future. It goes straight to the root of the matter, instead of relying on the indirect and roundabout influences which our empirical systems have evolved for themselves. If the member banks are lending too much and increasing cash balances without due regard to the requirements of their customers in the existing equilibrium, or if, on the other hand, they are lending too little, the variation in their reserve proportions puts on them the directest possible pressure to move in the desired direction."[86]

The power of a central bank is greater in negative than in positive undertakings. To slow down an upward business expansion is more easily done than to slow down a business contraction. A prosperity or boom movement can readily be choked off by tight credit because it is in need of greater working capital than it generates. It is more difficult by easy credit to reverse a business contraction that has gotten under way and developed its special psychological contagion. And this easy credit must not be just for working capital but also for long-term commitment to finance fixed capital in slow-paying investments for heavy industry, real estate development, or transportation or utilities. Central banks can make short-term bank credit available on very low terms, but terms of long-term lending are more difficult to bring down. Institutional and other investors, whose own sense of the likely course of long-term rates has been nurtured over generations of experience, will simply balk at the investment of funds at low yields unless they have become conditioned to expect lower yields as the normal course of business development. Long-term interest rates can thus be held up by their own state of

[85]Keynes, *Treatise on Money*, 1930, vol. 2, page 77. Milton Friedman again disagrees. Friedman, *A Program for Monetary Stability*, 1960, pages 45 ff.

[86]Keynes, *Treatise on Money*, 1930, vol. 2, page 261.

expectation.[87] However, there are major linkages between short- and long-term rates since many investors hold mixed portfolios. As yields on short maturities fall off, a necessary tendency to substitute longer for shorter instruments will be experienced, so that long-term yields will tend to fall too, though in more sticky fashion and with uncertain response by way of investment spending.

Conceding the power and authority, however limited, of the central bank, what are its objectives—presupposing that as a public institution profit-making as such, beyond a normal average rate of profit or dividend return, cannot be its primary objective? The immediate objective was assuring or maintaining stable credit markets and "accommodating" business and commerce in their credit and payment needs. The ultimate objective, however, has been to maintain ready convertibility of its deposit and note liabilities into whatever precious metals were current means of international payment—and for most of the nineteenth and twentieth centuries that meant gold. Neither bank nor central bank money was conceived or purported to be other than an economical substitute for gold subject to the ready and continual test of convertibility on demand. The masterful David Ricardo had asserted that no check on issuers of paper money was so suitable as that of subjecting them "to the obligation of paying their notes either in gold coin or bullion."[88] The Charter Act of 1844—which J. M. Keynes believed to be the "first important attempt to lay down scientific principles for the management of managed money"—required that every variation in central bank holdings of gold or bullion be duplicated by a like variation in the supply of paper money for general circulation.[89]

The 1863 bank act that established both the American scheme of national banks and the new national bank currency supported by interest-bearing government bonds provided for liabilities of the banks to be backed by a cash reserve of no less than 25% payable on demand in "lawful money"—which at that time was both specie and U.S. Treasury notes given during the Civil War limited legal tender privileges. After 1879, when convertibility of U.S. Treasury notes into gold was achieved, the national banks were thus established fully on a gold standard. This became unambiguous in the declaration of the Gold Standard Act of 1900 that "the dollar consisted of 25 and $\frac{8}{10}$

---

[87]This was of course the Keynesian case indicated in *Treatise*, and spelled out in the *General Theory*.

[88]Ricardo, *Political Economy*, 1817, page 351.

[89]Keynes, *Treatise on Money*, 1930, vol. 1, page 16. The Act did not require 100% reserve specie banking. Rather by the clever device of a fixed "fiduciary issue" of notes which could be backed by outstanding holdings of public debt, all additional or marginal variations in gold holdings were to be matched with a counterpart variation in note circulation.

grains of gold, $\frac{9}{10}$ fine . . . shall be the standard unit of value and all forms of money issued or coined by the United States shall be maintained at a parity of value with this standard, and it shall be the duty of the Secretary of the Treasury to maintain such parity."[90] After the creation in 1913 of the Federal Reserve system with its new form of ultimate money, the Federal Reserve note, and deposit liability, the special role of gold in that system was expressed in the requirement that these note and deposit liabilities were not to exceed 2.5 and 2.87 respectively times the amount of gold in coin or bullion held by the Reserve banks.[91]

In 1945 these limits were raised to a multiple of four for both note and deposit Federal Reserve liabilities. Since in 1934 all monetary gold in the country had been called in and nationalized by the U.S. Treasury, Reserve bank gold holdings were in "gold certificates" issued by the Treasury.[92] The gold would be released pursuant to the 1934 parity at $35 per ounce only to foreign governments or monetary authorities. In the Bretton Woods Agreement approved by the Congress in 1945, the U.S. Treasury accepted an obligation to maintain continuous convertibility of its currency with gold at the stated parity for purposes of settling international transactions with members of the International Monetary Fund (IMF).

Although the same option of continuous convertibility was open to other countries, few emerged from the disastrous Second World War with gold reserves large enough to undertake this task. Other IMF members instead chose to accept the obligation to make their currency generally convertible with other Fund currencies, without exchange restrictions on current transactions, and to prevent exchange rate variations greater than 1% from stated parities. Once this form of convertibility was achieved—and for Western European countries it was generally accomplished by 1958—it signified that gold convertibility was achieved for all by second remove. Gold and dollars were indeed made uniform or equivalent common denominators of value in the

[90]*United States Code*, Sec. 314, Title 31.

[91]The 1913 reserve requirement for notes was unambiguously 40% in gold, but the reserve requirement for deposit liabilities was set at 35% in gold or lawful money (which included greenbacks, treasury notes, treasury gold and silver certificates, and silver coin). See Friedman and Schwartz, *Monetary History*, 1963, page 781. In 1914, approximately one-half of the lawful money held outside the Treasury consisted of gold. It was the gold that tended to concentrate in bank reserves and ended up in Federal Reserve vaults, especially after inflow of gold during World War I. Moreover, the Treasury held a special gold reserve to guarantee the convertibility of U.S. notes, silver certificates, and treasury notes. Hence in practice, the statutory requirement for a reserve in "lawful money" beyond Reserve deposit liabilities constituted a gold reserve requirement (page 179).

[92]Friedman and Schwartz, *Monetary History*, 1963, pages 462 ff., relate fully the details of this—to their mind—sad story.

international agreement that set up the IMF, which became operational in 1947.[93] This formal equivalence only reflected the strong American position in the world economy after 1945 due to the thriving condition of its industry, its stockpile of some three-quarters of the world's known gold reserves, and its balance of payments yielding continuously a dollar and gold surplus in the prewar and early postwar years.

This common convertibility to gold, or to one or more currencies convertible to gold, meant that under the Bretton Woods Agreement—as under the traditional nineteenth century gold standard—the territories where these currencies circulated had in effect a common money, gold, and a single set of commodity prices scaled in units of gold weight, making up a unified economic space. Industrial investment and production of marketable commodities would tend to move to areas where gold costs of production were lowest or where, at equivalent gold prices, product serviceability was greater. Under the old gold standard, national moneys were permanently bonded to gold at fixed rates of exchange rarely if ever changed. Under the Bretton Woods Agreement these rates of exchange were subject under international surveillance to alteration—extensively experienced between 1946 and 1971, with over one hundred exchange-rate alterations in parity being recorded in that 26 year period. Parities were revised to improve prospects for balancing payments on current account by making imported goods and services more expensive and correspondingly cheapening access to export goods and services.

Most monetary authorities utilized gold-convertible dollars to operate their international payments because these dollars, besides being easy to transfer, were interest-bearing assets. Central bank management in a gold-standard system with fixed or infrequently adjusted parities tends to induce central banks primarily to keep in step with each other or with "the average behavior of the banking systems of the world as a whole."[94] That is certainly true for discount or interest rates because raising rates above those prevailing in other financial centers will tend to draw short-term capital. And if the movement of national income and expenditures is too much out of alignment with the predominant drift of movements abroad, the balance of payments will tend to turn. Any country leading the pack in economic growth rates tends to have an unfavorable balance—conversely true for those that lag behind, however uncomfortable slow growth may be domestically. Thus major fluctuations in the business economy since early in the nineteenth century have been

---

[93]"The par value of the currency of each member shall be expressed in terms of gold as a common denominator or in terms of the United States dollar of the weight and fineness in effect on July 1, 1944." IMF, *Articles of Agreement*, 1944, art. 4, sec. 1(a).

[94]Keynes, *Treatise on Money*, vol. 2, pages 222, 279 f.

international and readily propagated through the international trading and monetary system. Hence the fallacy of any purely national account of major economic fluctuations—or, we would note parenthetically, of any strategy of dealing with them that does not somehow insulate the economy being treated from its international environment.

Though gold became the ultimate and accepted international means of payment, standard of value, and monetary reserve for the Western economies, yet to varying degrees in different countries the linkage between gold-reserve holdings and the national stock of money grew increasingly tenuous and indirect. During the early 1920s, when the United States with its favorable balance of payments continued to draw gold from abroad, the effects of this gold were largely "sterilized"—to use the wording then current—by offsetting Federal Reserve credit policy, to give further stability to American economic life and to avoid the overstimulation to the economy that overt gold inflation would have added to the prosperity and stock market boom then in course. It was the first example in American history of "managing" the nation's monetary system not in direct response to gold signals.[95]

During the 1930s gold signals were likewise disregarded in the United States—not willfully but rather because the Depression-wracked economy could not generate enough use of credit by credit-worthy borrowers, apart from the government itself, to utilize the flood of gold that migrated into the country, responding to the devaluation of the dollar in 1934 by 66% and to capital flight seeking safe haven from Europe. Gold signals were further disregarded during World War II, when the monumental rise in Federal Reserve and bank credit was not due to gold signals but to the need to finance the war and provide the war economy with its necessary liquidity and means of exchange at very low pegged, almost nominal, interest rates. The gold abun-

---

[95]As expected, this first constructive achievement of the U.S. Federal Reserve scheme of central banking earns the reproof of Friedman and Schwartz, who manage to find—despite the evidence of the harmful effects of the stock market boom before their very eyes—that the sterilization made matters difficult for the British who had, they concede, overvalued the pound when they returned in 1924 to *their* gold parity. It is quite in line with the style of conjectural history replete in that volume to feel assured that it "probably would have been better either to have permitted the gold-standard rules to operate fully . . . or to have replaced them completely by another alternative." See Friedman and Schwartz, *Monetary History*, 1963, pages 284 ff. What historical evidence backs up the conclusion that in the real world rules operate fully or are replaced with a "complete" alternative? Compare Friedman and Schwartz's treatment of this period with that of Keynes's analysis of 1925–1929. See *Treatise on Money*, vol. 2, pages 190–195. Keynes recognizes that, though wholesale price indices were falling because international farm prices were falling, American industrial prices were—in light of current productivity—yielding a substantial profit boom, amidst a "prodigious volume of construction" and the greatest stock market boom in recent history. No wonder Keynes did not complain that the Federal Reserve in the American 1920s was too stingy.

dance characterizing the American economy of 1945–1946 did not cause the monetary managers of the American economy to relax credit or generate an inflationary wave. And they ignored the gradual and slow decline of monetary gold holdings, which after 1959 began to set the course for central bank policy largely because until 1958–1959 our foreign exchange deficits were of very moderate dimensions, effecting a desirable redistribution of gold holdings throughout the Western world. Then, as in the 1920s, "the gold position gave much leeway and seemed an almost irrelevant consideration for short-term policy."[96]

Though gold holdings were more closely regarded outside the United States, they were valued not so much as signals or determinants of domestic policy action but as the central core of an international monetary reserve to finance unexpected turns in the balance of payments. Nor was monetary gold so much used for day-to-day payments. It was generally more convenient for that purpose to utilize American dollar balances or to draw upon the International Monetary Fund for currencies needed for payment purposes. Despite their attachment to and their investment in gold—given a crowning expression in the high place of gold in the Articles of Agreement of the IMF—Western nations drifted into a set of usages permitting the demonitization of gold as a monetary metal by formal international agreement while increased scope for its use in private speculation and hoarding was being provided.

U.S. EXTERNAL DEFICIT: THE UNDOING OF THE GOLD STANDARD

The key to the undoing of the gold standard under the Bretton Woods Agreement is unquestionably the persistent and cumulative U.S. deficit in the balance of payments. From a small trickle in the early 1950s, this deficit became sizeable and visible in 1957–1958 and steadily persisted through the 1960s. The deficit resisted all the minor therapies administered by economist-doctors and nurses, and finally rose in magnitude in the 1970s into the two-digit billion class. *Balance of payments* means, of course, the net balance spent, invested, paid, or donated at home and abroad by commodity or service purchases, by gifts, transfers, and remittances, by earnings on foreign investment, and by both short- and long-term capital outflow. If Americans spend, pay out, transfer, or donate abroad dollars on a larger scale than they are paid in, a deficit will show up in their international balance of payments.

On the narrowest possible scale—considering only the deficit's appearance

[96]Friedman and Schwartz, *Monetary History*, 1963, page 627.

as official transfers either of gold reserves, other U.S. Treasury monetary assets, or short-term dollar claims held by foreign monetary authorities—the total deficit thus circumscribed between 1950–1979 amounted to no less than $168 billion, with deficits recorded in 24 of the 29 years and tending to increase over time both absolutely and relatively to national income.

Of the aggregate deficit, only some 5% was paid out in U.S. reserve assets, chiefly gold, during the first two decades of the period. In contrast, foreign official claims on the United States, reported at less than $3 billion in 1949, amounted in mid-1971 to $31 billion—and to $143 billion in December 1979. The remaining transfer is chiefly accounted for by the $61 billion held by foreign monetary authorities in the form of Eurodollar deposits resting ultimately upon American bank claims.[97] In addition, considerable net private holdings were accumulated over the period in dollar claims held by foreign business establishments and banks, including of course branches or subsidiaries of American-owned companies operating abroad.

The deficit had three broad major sources: (1) a higher level of labor costs of production in gold units, (2) massive foreign spending or transfers abroad in pursuit of imperial supremacy, (3) a widespread drift of American capital abroad chiefly by way of direct investment of multinational corporations and private speculative capital outflows. Working in the same direction but of lesser import were a number of more specialized factors which will be mentioned later.

The industrial competitiveness of American industrial products in world markets was gradually undermined during the postwar period by the relatively high hourly American wage levels measured in gold units. For the first two decades this wage level was between 4 and 5 times that prevailing in our major industrial competitors of West Germany and Japan and from 5 to 10 times the wage levels prevailing in such low-wage enclaves as South Korea, Singapore, Taiwan, or Hong Kong. Wages are of course not paid in gold but in local currencies. But when these local currencies at IMF parities became convertible into gold on call of the responsible monetary authorities, then the wage-rates became effective in gold units. The gold wage-rate which is lower, without offsetting lesser efficiency, has decisive advantages in the world market.

This gold wage differential has steadily narrowed with wage inflation abroad and dollar devaluation in 1971–1973. The differential has now disappeared in countries like West Germany, Sweden, and Switzerland. Yet it still persists on a significant scale (up to 25%) for such a major industrial competitor as

[97]Clarke, "United States External Position since World War II," 1980, pages 21–38.

Japan and it is still very substantial for all the low-wage enclaves to which our industry and industrial know-how, as we will see, has fled.[98]

If a higher gold wage-level is offset by greater labor efficiency, then relative costs of unit production will be unaffected. American high levels of labor efficiency were gradually undermined by a number of forces. One was the 40-hour work-week with high penalty overtime charges established in the mid-1930s to spread around the available work. This leads to higher unit costs of production than the more common 44- or 48-hour work-week generally prevailing abroad.[99] Reinforcing that cost disadvantage is the greater militancy of American trade unions compared with the more docile state of unionism abroad, especially in the war-devastated or developing countries. The American advantage in higher productivity growing out of our technological know-how, our industrial organization, and management methods was gradually eroded by the massive transplantation abroad of American industry and technology licensed for foreign use.

While our export prowess was being undermined by high gold labor costs of production, our government was carrying on a diversified, never-ending program of foreign spending or transfers abroad to fight communist movements coming to power in former colonial territories, to bolster up weak allies, to win over foreign governments and leaders, and to build up a network

[98]Manufacturing average hourly wages including fringe benefits as of 1960 were: United States $2.68; Netherlands, Italy, $0.57–$0.61; U.K., West Germany, France, Belgium, Switzerland $0.71–$0.78; Sweden $1.08. See First National City Bank, *Letter*, December 1960. The same comparison was made for four different periods in the *International Economic Report of the President*, 1974.

Average Hourly Wages—Manufacturing

	U.S.A.	Japan	Italy	France	U.K.	West Germany
1960	2.65	0.30	0.65	0.80	0.85	0.85
1965	3.15	0.50	1.10	1.15	1.15	1.40
1970	4.20	1.05	1.80	1.65	1.50	2.30
1973	5.05	2.25	3.15	2.95	2.25	4.20

[a]Converted to dollars at current exchange rates

In 1980 the Japanese figure was $5.71 compared to $9.89 in the U.S. See Congress Joint Economic Committee Symposium, *U.S. International Economic Policy*, 1982.

[99]A detailed study in 1968 of prospects for the American balance of payments did take note of our disadvantaged work week. It cited the manufacturing work week in 1950 and 1962: France, 44.5, 45.8; Italy, 38.3, 39.4; West Germany (inclusive of building), 48.4, 44.9; U.K., 47.5 46.4; U.S. 40.5, 40.4. See Salant *et al.*, *Balance of Payments in 1968*, 1963, page 45. Though average work-week differentials had narrowed by 1979, when computed for all nonagricultural work the U.S. average of 35.6 hours for first quarter of 1979 compares with 40.5 (Japan), 41.4 (France), 41.6 (W. Germany), 41.4 (Netherlands), 44.2 (U.K.). The work weeks for Belgium, Israel and Sweden were close to the American. See International Labour Office, *Bulletin of Labour Statistics*, 1980.

of military bases abroad. Commencing with a loan to Britain in 1946 and assistance ladled out to occupied enemy territories of Japan and Germany, this foreign spending continued in the form of Marshall Plan aid to Western Europe, assistance to Greece and Turkey, aid to our "allies" in Latin America and to the young state of Israel beginning to fight its way out of Arab encirclement. In the first decade of the deficit, one of its leading analysts, Edward M. Bernstein, noted that the principal foreign payments and transfers of the U.S. government averaged nearly $8 billion yearly for the decade.[100] In the following decades with the explosion of spending in Southeast Asia and for the Arab-Israeli wars the bill grew commensurately. In the 1960s an effort was made to cut down military expenditures abroad. Our West German ally was induced to underwrite some of the American army expenditures incurred by our divisions hosted in their country. American aid outlays were tied to American procurement and there was muttering about withdrawing the six Army divisions and Naval forces stationed in Europe.[101] In an unstable world new occasions for military spending and aid programs sprang up as fast as old programs could be narrowed down.[102]

The third broad factor generating deficits is capital outflow involving funds sent abroad for many purposes. These funds may be on short-term account only and hence kept in liquid form, or they may go abroad on long-term account to build or buy out foreign plants, to purchase foreign securities, to make investments in foreign properties or enterprises, or to build working capital in foreign properties. Measured long-term direct investment has stead-

---

[100]Harris, *The Dollar in Crisis*, 1961, pages 75 ff.; Bernstein, *International Effects of U.S Economic Policy*, 1960, pages 67 ff. See also Morley, *The Patchwork of Foreign Aid*, 1961.

[101]The program of mitigation of the government, chiefly military, balance of payment deficit is candidly outlined in a special U.S. Treasury report, *Maintaining the Strength of the Dollar*, 1968, pages 77–90. One such device of "mitigation" was to arrange for redeployment of 35,000 of the U.S. forces then (and now) stationed in Germany to be "based" in the United States but "earmarked for use in Germany and will return there at regular intervals for training"—adding to the deficit a foreign exchange component in back-and-forth transportation costs and housing upkeep in the two countries. Another was to seek "compensation" for our European military expenditures by offsetting sales of choice items of armament, which of course was a prime U.S. export item of "high technology." In June 1968, a new offset agreement was negotiated with the German government by which the Germans agreed to "buy" $625 million of treasury bonds coming due in a few years. A strange "mitigation" of our deficit abroad, noted Senator Mansfield, who put into the Congressional Record various documents relating to the offset agreement. The treasury bonds "carry interest at the market rate prevailing at the time of their purchase . . . but they must also be redeemed or renegotiated in the not too distant future." See *Congressional Record*, June 19, 1968, S7438 ff.

[102]Viet Nam foreign military expenditures were officially described as higher during 1966–1967 by $1.4 and $1.8 billion over 1964 levels. Surely that understates the explosion of foreign spending in the Asian theater than accompanied mass warfare there. See U.S. Department of the Treasury, *Maintaining the Strength of the Dollar*, 1968, page 89.

ily risen over the years, both in absolute terms and as a fraction of domestic GNP. This increase has occurred despite restraint exerted for nearly a decade in the mid-1960s and early 1970s on domestic purchase of foreign-issued bonds subjected to a 15% tax and limitation between 1966 and 1973 of direct foreign investment by established American corporations, usually expressed as a fraction of their 1962–1964 outflow with requirements for repatriation of earnings. This investment in the more recent period has not been a major direct drainage on the balance of payments because a substantial portion of its high annual earnings have been repatriated and because gradually foreign investment in American properties and securities has added positively to the American balance sheet and current account.

More menacing to the balance of payments has been short-term capital outflow motivated on various grounds: to escape American taxation, to benefit from expected currency revaluations, to participate in gold hoarding when that was illegal in the United States, to make ordinary banking loans, to help furnish foreign-owned properties with working capital, or to acquire real estate or equity interests abroad. Short-term capital outflows are usually timed to make speculative investment in foreign currency or gold markets for the sake of short-term gains.[103] Much of this capital movement has escaped detection and shows up only in a miscellaneous adjustment for "errors and omissions." It moved abroad in great swoops, running high between 1960–1964 and again in 1969–1971, and 1973–1976. Though short-term in its initial impact, most of this capital movement has been long-term in effect, because even after limited devaluation of the dollar was achieved in 1972–1973, there was very limited return flow of capital. The dollar balances apparently were invested in gold, business properties, or stock market securities—or were being held as working capital for business use.

The migration of short-term capital was the more anomalous because it was completely unimpeded, even though the Bretton Woods Agreement contemplated that member states adopt measures to restrain capital transfers that built up inconvertible monetary balances in other countries and would there-

---

[103]The later Watergate investigative hearings disclosed that American multinational corporations, through the intracacies of their many-sided corporate setups—with a host of incognito accounts, dummy "fronts," and offshore intermediaries—could easily transfer billions of dollars abroad nearly at will, the Euro-dollar market being a convenient vehicle for this purpose. An economist in the legislative reference service, Library of Congress, described the arrangements for housing outflow dollars in Switzerland and buying gold, estimating that in the speculative market of October 1960 "more than 50% of the buying orders were of U.S. origin." See U.S. House Committee Hearings, *Removal of Gold Cover*, 1968, pages 146 ff. The U.S. Treasury spokesmen testified that "we have had Secret Service checking this out ourselves to see if Americans have been violating the statute for holding gold overseas, and the indications were that Americans were not concerned" (page 59).

fore threaten to break down currency parities. Without expressly being made obligatory, utilization of such controls was variously indicated. Thus the purposes of the International Monetary Fund were to "promote exchange stability" and "orderly exchange arrangements" and to "assist in the establishment of a multilateral system of payments in respect of current transactions between members." Current transactions were defined to exclude payments "for the purpose of transferring capital." A member of the Fund was prohibited from making "use of the Fund's resources to meet a large or sustained outflow of capital." The IMF may even "request a member to exercise controls to prevent such use of the resources of the Fund" unless the member could claim ability to finance the capital movement "out of a member's own resources in gold and foreign exchange." Specific authority was given for imposing "such controls as are necessary to regulate international capital movements." The whole premise of Bretton Woods was that with the ease of transferring monetary capital between countries and with the large amount of liquid capital held by multinational business organizations having ample foreign payment and transfer connections, orderly exchange arrangements and the development of a multilateral trading system with unimpeded use of funds arising out of current transactions would be endangered by unrestricted flow of monetary capital.[104] But the IMF charter did not require control of capital transfers, and the increasingly conservative and nationalistic state of opinion in the United States precluded any interference with business practice on the scale required by regulation of capital transfers.

Some of the more specialized factors which widened the American tendency to deficit may be briefly mentioned. One was the progressive dissolution of American tariff barriers bargained away in a series of trade negotiations in which the United States led the way in cutting back on our tariff barriers just as movement toward European regional economic unity, embodied in the European Common Market, effectively raised barriers to U.S. trade.[105] That promoted the loss to American industry of much of our domestic market for manufactured products and stimulated a substantial boost in our imports. Commercial exportation by producers of agriculture, an industry most favored by comparative advantage, was handicapped over most

---

[104]IMF, *Articles of Agreement*, 1944, art. I, secs. ii–iv; art. VI, sec. 3; art. VII(a)(b); art. XIX(h)(i).

[105]"A common market demands the reduction or elimination of the barriers to trade among the nations concerned. This of course eases the difficulties of trade inside the common market; but at the same time it increases the difficulties of outsiders who wish to penetrate the market with their goods . . . ." The very creation of a European Economic Community means "an economic wedge . . . between the two main Atlantic entities." See Bowie and Geiger, *European Economic Community*, 1961, page 39. See also Humphrey, *United States and the Common Market*, 1962.

of the deficit period by maintenance of subsidized high levels of farm prices which, however suitable for domestic consumers, made it difficult to market farm surpluses abroad except on a "give-away" basis or on soft-currency reimbursement not usable in the world market. For nearly three decades the balance of tourist payments became heavily adverse because with an overvalued exchange rate for the dollar our tourist services for foreign travellers were as overpriced as European and other foreign tourist markets were underpriced for American travellers.

The impact of the American deficit on the ability of the U.S. Treasury to serve as gold banker for the Western IMF Community became a major concern by the early 1960s. Under General Charles De Gaulle's leadership, the French central bank instituted a policy of converting up to $150 million per month of her dollar claims into gold, resulting altogether in a build-up of French gold reserves of some $2–3 billion.[106] Since the Viet Nam war stepped up the pace of government deficit spending on both domestic and foreign accounts, deficits worsened in the domestic budget and the balance of foreign payments. Speculative opinion then targeted on gold, which could be freely bought and sold by speculative hoarders in the London gold market—where

[106]Gold–dollar conversion was instituted partly to carry out a more or less traditional French policy of holding at least 73% of her monetary reserves in gold but also partly to allay discontent expressed publicly at the undue buildup of dollar holdings reflecting American investment in European industry and real estate. There are indications that gold–dollar conversion began in 1963 when the French agreed to limit conversion to $30 million monthly. But conversion was stepped up to $150 million monthly in January 1965. This step-up was not anticipated by the Treasury at the time of the 1965 legislation removing the gold cover for U.S. Federal Reserve deposit liabilities. And apparently gold conversion stopped in June 1976. See U.S. House Hearings, *Removal of Gold Cover*, 1968, pages 64 ff.; U.S. Senate Hearings, *Gold Reserve Requirements*, 1968, pages 55 ff., 149 f. *IMF Reports* inform us of limited Treasury gold conversions for the years 1963–1966 in million dollars on French account of $518 (1963), $884 (1965), $601 (1966). See *IMF Report*, 1964, page 105; 1968, page 89. But then, indirectly by purchasing openly or sub rosa through the London gold market, France was indirectly withdrawing from U.S. gold holdings. Thus a detailed statement of gold imports and exports out of the London gold market showed that between 1962 and 1966, the French withdrew out of the London gold market $2.2 billion, or more than they converted from the U.S. Treasury over the same period, *IMF Report*, 1967, page 123. But this was partly on private as well as government account, for private importing and holding of gold was permitted in France. In the United States, during this period there was an unmistakable and open outbreak of hostility to the French. It came out in congressional debate trying to hold the French to their World War I debt obligations to the United States, which including accrued interest would run to $5.1 billion, though the French in accepting the World War I debt settlement added a reservation that the French promise to pay was dependent upon receipt of reparations payments from Germany of like amount. Nonetheless, in the U.S. Congress the proposal to limit U.S. Treasury gold redemption to satisfactory performance on all debt obligations held by the U.S. Treasury including World War I unsettled obligations was defeated only by a Senate 39–37 vote after interesting debate. See *Congressional Record*, March 14, 1968. The proposal would have hurt not only the French but also the British and Italians with net World War I accrued debt outstanding of $7.3 and $1.1 billion dollars, respectively.

since early 1959 its price had been pegged at the American parity price to reassure world opinion as to the solidity of the U.S. gold parity. The U.S. Treasury and six central-banking confreres stood ready to supply or take off gold in that private market when industrial, ornamental, and hoarding demand for gold was not fully matched with either recovery of old gold or newly mined output put on the market chiefly from South Africa and the Soviet Union. Western world output of newly mined gold together with sales of gold from Soviet sources ranged between $1 to $1.5 billion annually. Demand for gold for industrial, ornamental, and hoarding purposes through the 1950s and early 1960s ran generally to half of that, so that on balance monetary authorities in the Western world were able to increase their gold holdings from new production.

The London gold pool conveniently distributed among its pool members new gold acquisitions and stabilized their gold purchase operations. But under adverse market conditions the London gold pool could be a source of drainage.[107] That is clearly shown in the attached Figure 1, which graphs the sharp increase in gold hoarding—begun in 1965. This reached a climax in 1967, to withdraw altogether $2.3 billion of gold from IMF monetary gold holdings. The American loss from the operations of the London gold pool during 1967 and 1968 was booked at $1.7 billion.[108] That forced the first break in the Bretton Woods gold-standard system. At an emergency meeting in March 1968 the central banks concerned announced that they were suspending any participation in the private gold market and they would not, moreover, sell gold to any other monetary authority that did participate. This move established the so-called "two-tier" market for gold—a private market where newly mined and old gold privately owned was bought and sold at fluctuating prices—and a pegged monetary market governed by a fixed parity with the U.S. Treasury as gold banker for IMF members. The private market was prevented from dropping below $35 per ounce since newly mined South African gold was still available for purchase by the IMF through redemption of IMF rand holdings by gold exchange at the $35 parity and by a later 1969 agreement to permit IMF to buy South African gold if needed for balance of payment purposes or to provide gold to IMF members for paying gold subscriptions required by the IMF Charter.[109]

---

[107]On the London gold pool, see *IMF Report*, 1964, page 131; the detailed report of transactions for 1962–1966 cited in footnote 106; and U.S. Treasury Department, *Maintaining the Strength of the Dollar*, 1968, page 23.

[108]*IMF Report*, 1970, page 126; 1971, page 19.

[109]*IMF Report*, 1968, page 83. The IMF decision on South African gold purchases was a compromise from a test of wills between France, the United States and South Africa. An interesting commentary is provided by U.S. Congress Joint Economic Committee, *The Pedigreed Gold System*, 1969. See also U.S. Congressional Joint Economic Committee Hearings, *Proposed IMF Quota Increaese*, 1969. *IMF Report*, 1971, described how during 1970 57% of

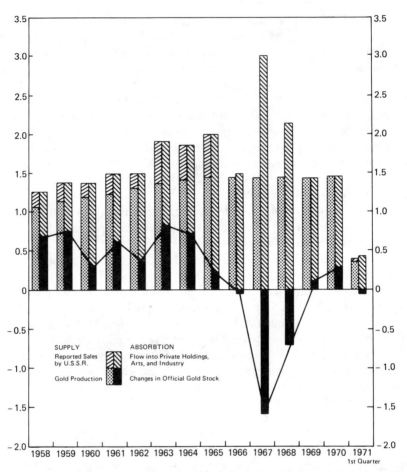

Figure 1 Estimated new supplies of gold and absorption, from 1958 through the first quarter of 1971 (billions of U.S. dollars at US$35 a fine ounce). Flow into private holdings, arts, and industry includes purchases by mainland China amounting to the equivalent of $150 million in 1965, $75 million in 1966, $20 million in 1967, $43 million in 1968, and $17 million in 1969. Changes in official gold stock exclude CMEA countries, mainland China, etc. (Source: IMF Report 1971, chap. 27.)

Speculative capital outflow then appeared to turn away from the London gold market, which was no longer pegged, onto the dollar-exchange market where rates were pegged, especially for currencies whose appreciation seemed most likely: German, Japanese, Swiss. A veritable flood of dollar funds pre-

---

South African gold went to the private market and 43% was absorbed at the parity price by IMF or national monetary authorities. All other newly mined output and all Soviet sales went to the private market.

sented itself to banks in those countries in which dollars were still being purchased at the pegged exchange rates. From those banks the dollar claims were passed on to central banks or monetary authorities—where reserves in foreign, almost all dollar-based, exchange in the year 1970 increased by $14.1 billion, or by almost 50% in one year. These flows continued in April and early May 1971, when they were accompanied by heavy movements of funds into a few other countries. In those five weeks, official foreign exchange holdings of Germany alone grew by an additional $3.2 billion. In an almost spasmodic response, the central banks of five countries suspended their support operations in the dollar exchange or instituted an official appreciation of the parity to abate the dollar flood. An acceleration of capital inflow in the second quarter of 1971 led to the floating of the Deutschemark in May 1971.[110]

Under these disturbed conditions the U.S. Treasury was requested by the English ambassador to convert into gold $3 billion of dollar exchange held by British monetary authorities. That triggered off a complete shift of strategy on the American side: to renounce gold conversions, proclaim the dollar overvalued, put on a temporary wage-price freeze, and impose a temporary 10% tariff on all imports of manufactured goods.[111]

The American strategic shift labeled the New Economic Policy did miracles in galvanizing a sluggish economy that had settled down to staginflation with 6% unemployed and moved it through a historic boom into the highest employment level relative to total labor force experienced in over a decade.[112] The action also provoked a storm cloud in world monetary and capital markets. Speculative interest turned wildly on various exchange rates and ran up the London gold price, the thermometer of distrust of all Western currencies. The various stabilizing actions taken—like the limited set of parity readjustments negotiated in December 1971, by which the dollar–gold price was raised by 8.6% to $38 per ounce, matched by upward revaluations of the Japanese and German and other European exchange parities, which altogether

---

[110]*IMF Report*, 1971, pages 19, 22.

[111]Richard Nixon, *Memoirs of Richard Nixon*, 1978, vol. 1, pages 640 ff. The inner staff of advisors under Connally's direction had early in August 1971 mapped out a bold strategy of economic advance involving price-wage freeze and a tariff surcharge when the British ambassador presented his request. With only Arthur Burns dissenting, the strategy was approved and publicly announced on August 15, 1971.

[112]The American action was reviewed in lengthy hearings conducted by the U.S. Congressional Joint Economic Committee Hearing, *New Economic Policy*, 1971; and of course in the annual economic reports of the President. It was near miraculous that price and wage control, in the hands of its professed enemies, survived their imperfect administration for nearly two years. The GNP "gap" between actual and potential GNP was eliminated in 1973. See the U.S. Congressional Joint Economic Committee, *Report*, 1973, pages 17 f. Commentary is extensive but see especially Galbraith, *Money*, 1975, pages 288 ff.; Solomon, *The Anxious Economy*, 1975.

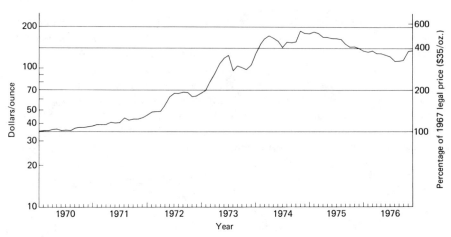

Figure 2   Wholesale price of refined gold (dollars per ounce), U.S. monthly average, 1970–1976. (Source: U.S. Department orf Labor, *Wholesale Prices*, various issues, #1022.)

resulted in a trade-weighted dollar exchange devaluation of 12 to 15%—were rejected by the market as totally inadequate.[113] Also rejected was a later 10% devaluation announced unilaterally by the American authorities in February 1973, raising the "official" dollar gold price to $42.22 per ounce, by then about one-third of the London market price.[114] "It took three successive waves of unimaginable proportions, with the countervalue of billions of dollars moving from one country to another in a single day, sometimes in a single hour, to finally move the world in March 1973 to flexible exchange rates, at least for an 'interim' period."[115]

The erratic and soaring gold price and the wild outflow of dollar foreign exchange are shown in Figures 2 and 3, and their effects were connected. For one thing, the soaring gold price—rising much faster than world commodity prices and values of corporate stock or real estate—made it very difficult to utilize the vast official reserves of gold with a book value (based on the American parity) of some $40 billion but a market value between two and three times that amount. No central banker could part with gold, except to fulfill contractual obligations, at the low old parity. And because there was no assurance that market values would hold up, few central bankers could afford either to buy gold at the market price or accept gold tendered at market

[113]On the December 1971 so-called Smithsonian Agreement, see *IMF Report*, 1972, pages 38 f. The American dollar–gold revaluation was officially made on May 8, 1972. See *IMF Report*, 1973, page 74; Solomon, *The Anxious Economy*, 1975, pages 48 f.

[114]The new parity was enacted 8 months later on October 18, 1973.

[115]De Vries, "Jamaica," 1976, pages 108 f. De Vries was a deputy director of the IMF.

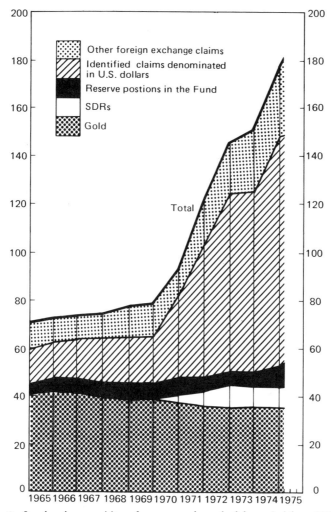

Figure 3 Level and composition of reserves at the end of the period from 1964 through March 1975 (billions of SDRs). (Source: IMF Report, 1975, Chart 10.)

values to satisfy current obligations.[116] Hence as the gap widened between the official parity and market price, transfers of gold at the official level, except pursuant to specific obligations such as "quota" subscriptions to the IMF to pay "charges" on IMF drawings, ceased and were replaced by oc-

---

[116]"As the gold price on the free market rose further after 1971, reaching multiples of the official price, the gold holdings of the monetary authorities in effect became unusable." See De Vries, "Jamaica," 1976, page 117. De Vries attributes this unusability to the *verbot* em-

casional pawnings of gold used as collateral for central bank loans one to another.[117] The country-by-country holdings of gold reserves reported to IMF through most of 1972, 1973, and 1974 showed generally identical quanta.[118]

A deflationary impact came from the immobilization of gold reserves because of lack of any assured level of value that could withstand market pressures. This impact, however, was more than offset by the avalanche of dollar claims that worked its way into monetary reserves at an accelerating rate after 1969. If these reserves are now tabulated and if the gold reserves as of the end of 1972 are cut in half and are phased out by the end of 1973, we see that total usable reserves by the end of 1974 nearly kept pace with both price inflation and real economic growth, which for industrial countries between 1970–1975 had risen about two-thirds. By 1975 total active official reserves considerably outpaced nominal world GNP (Table 1).

Neither IMF assets nor dollar exchange was as valuable as gold promised to be. But their use in current transactions could cause no loss and their

TABLE 1
Official Reserves IMF Members 1970–1975 (year-end, in billion SDRs)[119]

Year	Gold	Fund reserve assets	Foreign (chiefly U.S.) exchange	Total
1970	37.2	10.8	44.5	92.5
1971	36.1	12.3	73.9	122.2
1972	17.9	15.0	94.9	127.7
1973	—	15.0	100.7	115.6
1974	—	17.8	124.7	142.5
1975	—	21.4	158.9	180.4

bodied in the Articles of Agreement on buying or selling at other than its official parity. But the parity agreement was lapsed after August 15, 1971. With more insight, the Reuss-chaired Subcommittee of the Joint Economic Committee of the U.S. Congress, in a November 1972 report, correctly noted that ". . . the high private price of gold had made official monetary institutions reluctant to use the metal in settling balance of payments deficits." See U.S. Congressional Joint Economic Committee, *Gold, SDR's and Central Swaps,* 1972, page 3. For the same judgment see De Vries, "Jamaica," 1976, page 118; Habermeier, *Operations and Transactions in SDR's,* 1973, pages 14, 21; *IMF Report,* 1974, page 40.

[117]U.S. Congressional Joint Economic Committee Hearings, *The IMF Gold Agreement,* 1975, page 36. Official gold transactions of the IMF with members dwindled in million IMF credit units from 96.5 in 1973 to 7.0 in 1974 and .3 in 1975. See *IMF Reports,* 1973, page 56; 1974, page 62; 1975, page 58.

[118]See any statistical tabulation of monthly gold holdings of monetary authorities, 1972–1975, allowing for effects of U.S. revaluations. For a misleading account, see Cochrane, "Gold: The Barbarous Relic," 1980, pages 385–400.

[119]*IMF Reports,* 1975, page 34; 1977, page 38.

current value was market-tested for settlement of international obligations. Reserve fund assets that consist largely of various forms of special credit claims on IMF or on member countries—conveying the right to buy with one's own currency the currency of other nations—were usable chiefly to meet international payment needs or deficits being experienced. Dollar exchange had no restrictions on use, was readily transferable, was acceptable not only to IMF confreres but also to communist countries, and earned relatively high interest. Obviously the creator of dollar exchange—the multinational corporate business and banking community and their principal agencies and instrumentalities in the Federal Reserve Bank of New York and the U.S. Treasury, and behind them the entire American economy—benefited from the continuous use of their national obligations for international payment purposes. They enjoyed the privilege of incurring deficits virtually at will, and thus of borrowing from creditors whose sufferance did not need to be solicited.

Great hope was expressed that the scope for Fund-related assets—such as various schemes for expanding use of special drawing rights—could be enlarged, so that international business could become self-financing, as the medieval world mercantile business had done through using the bill of exchange. Finally, there was special resistance to building up the use of gold as an international money by boosting its accepted value, because this would reward gold hoarders who bought in the private market, or those nations who either drained the U.S. Treasury (like the French, who were not holding their "proper" share of dollar exchange) or, like the Soviet Union and South Africa, were the principal producers of newly mined gold to whom any boost in official gold values would be a free and undesirable gratuity. All this activity was reflected in the newer abstruse monetary theories that in their fashion idealized the American interest in continuous use of our national money for international payment purposes and our willingness to permit the German and Japanese central banks to continue accumulating our dollar exchange to avoid excessive drop in their exchange rates.[120]

[120]This recasting of economic theory to rationalize the new arrangements and the discard of the gold standard was spearheaded by Milton Friedman. Friedman led the way by an early essay advocating flexible exchange rates wholly unpegged by government. Behind his flexible exchange rates was, however, a practical nugget of advantage urged in terms of American national interest: ". . . let the balance of payments do whatever it wants and then it is the responsibility of other countries, of France, Britain, Germany what they want to do. If they want to let the price of the dollar decline, they can. If they don't want to, they will have to hold the dollars." See U.S. House Hearings, *Removal of Gold Cover*, 1968, page 164. Milton Friedman, of course, knew that the German and Japanese central banks held far too many dollar claims to let their external value depreciate excessively, especially since in the process American export goods would become more competitive. See also Friedman, *Dollars and Deficits*, 1968; *Essays in Positive Economics*, 1946–1953, pages 157–203; and many other writings and speeches.

Demonetization of Gold

This array of interests and ideas finally resulted in a negotiated agreement in August 1975 on a comprehensive package that (1) legalized the interim arrangements which had evolved around managed floating rates; (2) made them subject to minimal IMF surveillance; (3) expanded the role of IMF credit assets to meet temporary payment needs; and (4) finally ended the anomalous status of gold. An orderly demonetization of gold was to be achieved as follows:

1. Abolition of an official price for gold.
2. Elimination of the obligation to use gold in transactions with the Fund and elimination of the Fund's authority to accept gold in transactions unless the Fund so decides by an 85% majority.
3. Sale of one-sixth of the Fund's gold (25 million ounces) for the benefit of developing countries without a reduction of other resources for their benefit, and restitution of one-sixth of the Fund's gold to members. The proportion of any profits or surplus value of the gold sold for the benefit of developing countries would be transferred directly to each developing country in proportion to its quota. The rest of the gold would be subject to provisions in an amendment of the Articles that would create enabling powers exercised by an 85% majority of the total voting power.
4. That there be no action to peg the price of gold; that the total stock of gold then in the hands of the Fund and the monetary authorities of the Group of 10 would not be increased; and that each party to these arrangements would report semi-annually the total amount of gold bought or sold.
5. That acceptable solutions be found on the subject of the exchange-rate system under the amended Articles, so that these agreed solutions could be combined with those on quotas and gold.[121]

The agreement formulated a broad consensus. The provision on gold was to be combined in a single package with other agreements elsewhere being negotiated—expanding the scope for IMF credit and working out a net code

[121]Paragraphs 1, 2, 3, and 5 of the text are cited verbatim; paragraph 4 is summarized and refers to undertakings agreed by the negotiating parties to hold for two years only, though it has been indefinitely extended. The agreement was reached by an Interim Committee of the IMF Board of Governors and the text is readily found in IMF documents. See U.S. Congressional Joint Economic Committee, Hearings, *The IMF Gold Agreement*, 1975, pages 67–69; see also the illuminating exchange of letters between Henry Reuss and the principal American negotiator, William Simon (pages 74–85).

of rules to guide surveillance of managed floating rates. Broadly speaking, the agreement would actually legalize the international monetary system—based chiefly upon use of credit assets and dollar exchange—that had already evolved. Central-bank utilization of gold holdings was approved for sale to the gold market for profit-taking and to depress gold prices. Central-bank purchases of gold from the private market were precluded at least for a forward two-year period. So that developing countries would favor adoption of the new arrangements and of gold demonetization, they were given the prospect of significant sharing in the profits of gold disposition under terms controlled by the leading IMF powers. Further use of Fund gold would, however, be blocked without the nearly unanimous agreement of member countries. Any action by monetary authorities to codify a new gold price for use in monetary transactions was specifically outlawed. The contemplated sale of gold to the private market by the Fund and approved for central banks harbored the promise of interjecting some "uncertainty into the gold market" and thus could only tend to "encourage funds to shift back to other assets" and "help to restore confidence to currencies."[122] Agreement was obtained on the general principle that "the role of gold in the international monetary system would be gradually reduced."[123]

The new monetary agreement was approved by a conference of heads of state in November 1975. The articles embodying the revised IMF agreement that virtually abolished the gold standard were formally presented to the IMF board of governors in mid-1976. They were approved without controversy by the U.S. Congress.[124] As the IMF agreement was being considered by IMF members, the program of gold sales for the distribution of one-third of the Fund gold stock—1555 tons over a four-year period—was commenced. The sales for the benefit of developing countries were held in near-monthly auctions with a monthly profit for the Development Trust Fund averaging

[122]I cite from one of those extraordinarily illuminating presentations developed by the Trilateral Commission, *Renovated World Monetary System*, 1973, page 36. The Task Force Report favored "gradual abandonment of gold as an official monetary medium" and hence it opposed establishing "an official higher price of gold." It also ventured the suggestion that the capital gains of central bank sales of gold "would represent an attractive source, during the transition period, of development assistance," 37. The commission favored a reconstitution of the then functioning monetary reserves of IMF members by conversion of outstanding dollar exchange balances into IMF reserve assets.

[123]Report of Interim Committee, U.S. Congressional Joint Economic Committee Hearings, *IMF Gold Agreement*, 1975, page 68.

[124]Though there was a flash of controversy when the gold agreement hit Washington in September 1975, by the time the official text of the IMF Charter Amendments were prepared, they slid through the Congress with little controversy though with some partisan debate. See U.S. Congressional Joint Economic Committee Hearings, *IMF Gold Agreement*, 1975; IMF Amendments, 1976; *Congressional Record*, 1976; H6386 ff., H7734 ff.; H7762 ff.

nearly $150 million, promising a total Fund of nearly $4 billion.[125] There was no question about the outcome. In April 1978 the Fund announced that 83.97% of the voting power of the Fund had approved the IMF amendment, which then formally entered into force.[126]

Thus went the succession of the events leading to the collapse of an institution as old, venerable, and traditional as the gold standard—"part of the apparatus of conservatism" and as such "one of the matters which we cannot expect to see handled without prejudice."[127] But however solidly emplaced these events may appear, we might pause to consider (1) whether this collapse was deep-rooted or owed chiefly to an adventitious flux of events, and (2) whether it will prove temporary or permanent.

Events played a role in the gold-standard collapse, especially the outbreak of the new Arab–Israeli conflict in 1973, which hastened militant price action by OPEC, itself adding a powerful upward impulse to the wave of inflation then in course and furthering disturbance in gold and currency exchange markets. The OPEC price boost itself was in part considerably instigated by dollar devaluation and the institution of floating rates that derogated from the real purchasing power of OPEC oil receipts normally payable in dollars. But all the essential elements of the collapse of the gold standard—the outflow of dollar exchange, building up of monetary reserves, and the inflated speculative course of the London gold price—were already well under way before the OPEC price boost in late fall 1973 pushed the process onward. The dollar deficit in the balance of payments and capital outflow had gradually evolved in the three decades before the collapse. It became ever more embedded as America increasingly glorified itself as an Imperial Power and took on planetary responsibilities as Cold War fighter. It is not accidental, of course, that the two powers who most easily gorged themselves on our dollar exchange had been occupied militarily by the United States after World War II and still were held in U. S. Defense embraces, albeit now by their own consent. And the dollar deficit itself was only the obverse side of the process by which American business interests had spread over all IMF territories and acquired

[125]The Trust Fund to distribute the profits of gold sale to developing countries was established in May 1976. *IMF Report*, 1976, pages 111–117. Resources were made available by the Trust Fund for "additional balance of payments assistance on concessional terms to 61 eligible developing members that qualify for assistance." Concessional lending began in 1976 with twelve loans. The loans bearing interest at $\frac{1}{2}$% are to be repaid in 10 semi-annual installments beginning not later than the end of the first six months of the 6th year. The Trust Fund was thus designed to operate permanently on a revolving basis tending to attach qualifying developing countries to the IMF system. The record of the gold auctions was set forth in *IMF Report*, 1979, page 79.

[126]*IMF Report*, 1978, page 55.

[127]Keynes, *Treatise on Money*, 1930, vol. 2, page 291.

properties, business interests, corporations, and gold. In this sense then, the gold standard collapsed due to deep-rooted causes.

As for the second question: Is the collapse likely to be permanent or temporary? In a disturbed and troublesome world the price of gold still fluctuates wildly and can be expected to behave so in the future. Investors in the Western world, who have been allowed by many Western governments to buy and import or export gold freely, increasingly turn to the gold market. They do this out of distrust of paper currencies, because of the fascination that a pure gambling market holds for certain temperaments, and finally in a search for safe-haven assets that will hold their value in a postdisaster world. The groundwork for this scenario was laid in the postwar period by the gradual resumption of minting of gold bars or gold coins by many governments—notably South Africa, Great Britain, Hungary, Netherlands, and Switzerland, as well as various countries in the Persian Gulf where gold coins were in use as a current exchange medium. Areas touched by war—such as Laos—almost immediately witnessed a renewed interest in gold trading. The number of markets where at various times gold was officially traded is itself quite remarkable: Zurich, London, Beirut, Hong Kong, Paris, Milan, and Brussels. Gold holding and trading both in bars and coins was opened up in most West European countries during the 1960s.[128]

In late 1974 the United States removed all restrictions on American residents' ownership of gold. In consequence, recorded American activity in buying gold coins and bars and trading gold futures spurted, so that the $3 billion of gold imports to satisfy gold hoarding was about four times the volume of gold sold in U.S. Treasury gold auctions of the same year.[129] Thus there has been a remarkable change from a half-century ago, when gold no longer passed from hand to hand "and the touch of the metal has been taken away from men's greedy palms." "The little household gods who dwelt in purses and stockings and tin boxes" have again come to life and it is doubtful that they can be exorcised.[130]

Moreover, all the real interests that propelled the Western world to destroy its gold standard give promise of long life. The United States will not willingly renounce the privilege which it gradually assumed of creating international money to finance its payment deficits. Differential holding of dollar exchange relative to gold will also raise a barrier to any legalization of a higher gold price, which could then be pitted against the private market. The central

---

[128]I cite here from a number of IMF reports: 1954, page 16; 1958, pages 148, 151, 153; 1961, pages 127, 131, 132; 1962, page 163; 1967, page 120; Federal Reserve, "Private Demand for Gold," 1954, pages 2 ff.

[129]*New York Times*, March 3, 1979.

[130]Keynes, *Treatise on Money*, 1939, vol. 2, page 127.

banks, each in its own way, can balance domestic budgets by selling off some of their gold stock and reaping capital gains. And any restoration of the gold standard at a much higher market value would create the monetary basis for another wave of inflation, one form of money being added to another that already suffices for the need. Possibly a post-World War III world might see the restoration of some form of a gold standard—probably with renewed use of gold coin for a greatly reduced world population and volume of trade. But short of major disaster or a conversion in the USA to a new political philosophy, the restoration of a gold standard does not seem likely, even though the centralized gold reserves needed for the purpose have as yet been retained.[130a]

RELATIONS OF CENTRAL BANKS TO EACH OTHER

The same process that leads to the formation of centers of central banking and monetary authority within national economic systems tends to weave cooperative relationships among these centers of authority. It became apparent early that losses of monetary and gold reserves within a nation are often the counterpart of gains to reserves of other nations. The resulting in-and-out movement of coin and bullion in national reserves was conspicuous already by the time of Adam Smith.[131] Like commercial bankers, central bankers learned that banking setbacks anywhere at home or abroad were disturbing to all. Hence it is not surprising that cooperative behavior among central banks was exhibited particularly in periods of commercial crisis. In 1837 the Bank of England gave support to New York City banks struggling with financial crisis. Two years later when panic struck in London, the Bank of France gave a substantial loan to the Bank of England.[132] The financial crisis of the 1890s also witnessed some important episodes of financial cooperation.[133] In the United States, during most of the nineteenth century, official

---

[130a]The compendius 1982 report of a Commission on Gold indicated that, apart from a noisy group of doctrinaire "gold-bugs" who clamored for restoration of some pure form of "gold standard," America's top economic leadership in Congress, in Wall Street, in the banking world, and in the economics profession shows few signs of adopting a "new political philosophy" of which the text speaks. See *Report to the Congress of the Commission on the Role of Gold in the Domestic and International Monetary Systems.* 2 vols. Washington D.C.: GPO 1982.

[131]A. Smith, *Wealth of Nations,* 1776, page 413.

[132]Mathews, *Trade Cycle History,* 1954, pages 69, 90 f.; Clapham, *Bank of England,* 1945, vol. 2, pages 168 ff.; Bagehot, *Lombard Street,* 1873, page 170.

[133]Clapham, *Bank of England,* 1945, vol. 2, pages 329 ff. In more general terms, see Hawtrey, *Currency and Credit,* 1919, pages 187 ff.

relations between international banking systems would be negotiated or handled by major private financial leaders. Thus after World War I many of the financial settlements by which the new European states or the defeated Central Powers began to resume normal business operations with convertible national currencies were handled on the American side partly by the New York Federal Reserve Bank and partly by top Wall Street financial leaders who were able to negotiate the loans critically needed for the settlements.[134] Apart from these settlements, the central bankers of the leading Western countries began mutual consultations, which at times led to significant policy actions by giving temporary loan credit or changing money market conditions in ways intended to be helpful abroad, if not at home.[135]

In the 1930s these relationships between national monetary authorities took on two distinct forms. In the early 1920s, as an outcome of the financial settlements with the defeated Central Powers—revolving as they did around collecting by fiscal means reparation funds and devising appropriate facilities for international transfer of these funds—the Bank of International Settlements (BIS) was established under the control of the central banks (CBs) of the leading Western powers concerned with payment or receipt of reparations and related international war debt settlements. The BIS was to be strictly a CBs' bank with capital provided by CBs, with the right to accept CB deposits, to make loans to CBs, and to buy and sell gold, securities, and foreign exchange. The BIS organizational form and charter were designed to permit its growth into an international institution with broader membership and wider concerns. But the U.S. never officially joined it; and though functioning to this day, it remains a banking organ more or less restricted to Common Market central banks.[136]

A second form of international monetary relationship grew out of the currency devaluations experienced in the Great Depression from 1931–1936. These resulted generally in substantial devaluation "profits" usually placed in

---

[134]Thus the now-forgotten conferences of "experts" held under the auspices of the League of Nations or of the wartime Allies to work out reparation agreements for the remnant of the defeated Central Powers included prominent American bankers who usually participated in the financial agreements resulting. Thus the Dawes Plan, which included a critical $100 million gold U.S. bank loan to the Reichsbank to commence the plan's operations on domestic German taxes and foreign transfers, and the later 1929–1930 Young Plan, which codified the final reparations agreement and established a partner of J. P. Morgan, S. Parker Gilbert, as the Allied supervisor of transfer arrangements. See some references in Gottlieb, *German Peace Settlement*, 1960, 145 f., 244 n. 19, 20; Mikesell, *Economic Policy and International Relations*, 1952, pages 51 f.

[135]Friedman and Schwartz, *Monetary History*, 1963, pages 269, 361, give only brief, almost cursory attention to this development, though it resulted in sizable international loans and credits.

[136]Keynes, *Treatise on Money*, 1930, vol. 2, pages 402 ff.

the hands of a treasury "Stabilization Fund" charged with continuing responsibility for managing the exchange rate. An exchange rate is, of course, a price shared between currencies of two or more countries. When one country changes its exchange rate, that automatically changes in the opposite way the exchange rate of partner countries—which naturally have the same privilege of independently setting the price for their own currency either in relation to gold or to other widely traded currencies. Hence the managers of the Stabilization Funds learned to have certain relations with each other, to agree substantially to abide by certain exchange parities, and to guarantee the gold value of that parity for balances of currency acquired by a partner Stabilization Fund over a short period. Some of these relationships were codified in an agreement reached between the monetary authorities of the three leading Western powers (Tripartite Agreement).[137] Out of this experience a project to work out a broader form for international monetary cooperation was born during World War II.

The war setting for the extended negotiations on a framework for international monetary cooperation was important in several respects. First, it gave unquestioned authority to the preeminent role of the U.S. dollar, which until the outbreak of war had been convertible into gold at the 1934 parity. Secondly, because the key negotiating states were in the embrace of a tightly organized war economy loaded with direct controls over production, foreign trade, and banking, it was possible to base contemplated international monetary cooperation upon a charter that would accommodate wide diversity in socioeconomic arrangements—extending even to state-controlled economies of a communist type.[138] Thirdly, wartime negotiation by the Allies in the Anti-Axis War heightened the sense of common concern for the future peace and made it a bit easier jointly to take a common step forward and lay the foundation stones of what might well evolve into a supranational central bank with major responsibilities for building and maintaining an orderly international financial system. An accidental but important asset of these negotiations

---

[137]On the American side, these developments are reviewed rather carefully in Mikesell, *Economic Policy and International Relations*, 1952, ch. 5. From a broader perspective, see League of Nations, Economic Financial and Transit Department, *International Currency Experience*, 1944, ch. 6.

[138]Though the Soviet Union did not play an active role in the Bretton Woods negotiations, they subscribed to the agreement and they booked themselves at the time for a quota contribution of $1.2 billion, the third largest quota then scheduled with 13.6% of the voting power of the Fund. They withdrew from IMF as a casualty of the Cold War. Yugoslavia has remained a member continuously and Rumania became a member in the 1970s. It has proved quite feasible for economic systems with a high degree of state control and nationalization to function in IMF. This at the time was closely questioned by R. F. Mikesell, "International Monetary Agreement," 1947, pages 56–83.

was that they brought together two seminally creative minds in applied political economy who were entrusted with major negotiating responsibilities by two leading governments, the U.S.A. and Great Britain.[139] One of the two had sketched the broad philosophical basis for supranational central banking some 15 years before.[140]

The shared premises for the negotiations became very clear both from the arrangements embodied in the final agreement and contemporary discussions. The negotiations assumed that member countries would normally centralize custody of international payment reserves made up chiefly of gold and balances of convertible currencies usable for settling adverse international payments. These reserves correspond to balances of working cash ordinarily kept by an operating business firm to provide for unanticipated changes in either the flow of receipts or unexpected expenditures or changes in credit arrangements. To facilitate international trade and commerce based upon multilateral and not bilateral balance of payments, it was believed that payment balances resulting from international current transactions should be convertible into all participating currencies—thus providing members with the widest range of choice for using their resources in international markets. However, only *current* transactions arising out of the current flow of purchases and sales of goods and services, or income transfers related to them, would be subjected to this high standard of convertibility. Except for a country with very large reserves and with a favorable balance of payments trend, such as the United States, it was presupposed that most countries could not generally allow capital to flow freely out of their country. Also, countries were expected to maintain stable mutually agreed exchange rates for their respective currencies, to facilitate business planning on prospective price levels at home and abroad

---

[139]Reference is, of course, to J. M. Keynes and H. D. White, who authored the respective British and American plans and who chaired their national delegations to the Bretton Woods conference held in 1944. See the extended discussion of the Keynes–White plans in Williams, *Postwar Monetary Plans*, 1943–1946, pts. 1, 2. Keynes's own tribute to the caliber of his negotiating partners at Bretton Woods is worth citing. "I wish I could draw back the veil of anonymity and give their due to the individuals of the most notable group with which I have ever been associated, covering half the nations of the world, who from prolonged and difficult consultations, each with their own interests to protect, have emerged, as we all of us know and feel in our hearts, a band of brothers." See Keynes, "Address to the House of Lords," May 23, 1944, page 378.

[140]It is a "waste of time," wrote J. M. Keynes in 1930, "to draw up an elaborate paper constitution for such a Bank [a supranational Bank to which the central banks of the world would stand in much the same relation as their own member banks stand to them] long in advance of its entering the field of practical politics. But an outline constitution may be the best way of indicating the kind of thing that is desirable." And so Keynes went on with his amazing sketch of 12 themes, some of which are quite prescient of what actually came about. See Keynes, *Treatise on Money*, 1930, vol. 2, pages 399 ff.

and to make it possible to hold some balances of foreign currency without fear of instant depreciation. But to cope with persistent and cumulative payment deficits, countries would be permitted to establish a higher purchase price (called *currency devaluation*) in terms of their national currency for other currencies or for gold, thus giving their producers a competitive edge in world markets and hopefully tending to make the balance of payments favorable. Apart from these cumulative deficits, it was presupposed that the balance of payments would nearly always be fluctuating—now turning positive, now negative in almost a random fashion, with payment deficits or surpluses being financed by transfer of international reserves or by suitable credit arrangements.

These premises more or less corresponded to relations prevailing shortly after the war among nations chiefly in the Americas but included also major British Commonwealth countries not seriously damaged by World War II.[141] Countries of Europe, Asia, and North Africa directly visited by the long and damaging war could not at all fit into the arrangements contemplated—which for them could only embody a goal of economic policy to be striven for while the damage of war was repaired, armies demobilized, and civilian economic interests given greater precedence.

These premises were worked over at an extended conference convened in 1944 by the Allied powers at Bretton Woods, New Hampshire, where the Articles of Agreement of the International Monetary Fund (IMF) were worked out. The Articles provided a broad and elastic framework capable of enduring the long transition period dominated by "relief and reconstruction." The Articles were adapted gradually by experience and went through two major rounds of amendment. One in 1968 established a new form of international reserve asset. The other in 1978 ratified the abolition of the gold standard and accommodated itself to managed floating exchange rates. As negotiated, implemented, and subsequently amended, these Articles provide the basis for a major international institution which may be described briefly under five broad headings.

1. *Resources.* Member countries were obligated to make capital subscriptions amounting to $7.2 billion, according to "quotas" that had been previously negotiated and were accepted by the parties concerned as appropriate

---

[141]The critics of the IMF Agreement, such as J. H. Williams, did not clearly grasp that the IMF Charter was more or less directly suitable in the immediate postwar period to some Latin American countries and to Canada, Australia, New Zealand, and other British Commonwealth areas not severely damaged by war. Thus a group of Central American republics, followed in 1952 by Canada, accepted the obligations of Article VIII of the Charter, pledging to avoid all restrictions on the making of payments and transfer for current international transactions or use of discriminatory currency arrangements or multiple exchange-rate practices unless approved by the Fund. See *IMF Report*, 1979, page 116.

in relation to ability to pay, prevailing reserves, and importance in international trade. These quotas were payable one-quarter in gold and three-quarters in national currency or claims thereto to be maintained at their gold value to offset any currency devaluation. These capital subscriptions are of critical importance because they govern the scale of borrowing to which members might be entitled (at the most double the quota). They also govern the contribution made to Fund decisions and management, which are accomplished by weighted voting by members in proportion to their capital subscription. New members would pay a mutually agreeable "quota"; and periodically the Fund would organize an increase in capital subscriptions, which are now going through their seventh round, building up the capital resources of the Fund to well over 10 times the level reached in current purchasing power when the Fund commenced operations.[142]

These subscribed funds, made up essentially of a collection of currency claims and gold supplemented by reserves built up out of accumulated earnings, are the main source of credit facilities offered by the Fund. They have been supplemented in the last two decades by special borrowing facilities from the more well-to-do Fund members to provide balance of payments loans on concessional terms to needier members to help meet balance of payments needs for which short-term credit assistance was manifestly unsuitable. Since 1974, when exploding oil prices created special balance of payments need, the Fund has borrowed or made arrangements to borrow the equivalent of some $25 billion in high-grade convertible currencies or half of the capital subscriptions. The last major round of borrowed facilities became operational only in 1979 and makes possible loans at fully commercial interest rates. Oil-producing nations have only contributed 42% of the borrowed capital though petroleum pricing boosts created the need to borrow.[143]

---

[142]It is difficult to compare 1947 and 1979 Fund resources because the gold unit of measure, applicable until 1970, has now disappeared. In 1970, Fund resources in gold units were $21.3 billion in subscriptions and altogether $23.2 billion including borrowed assets and accumulated earnings, or about three times the original capital. The measuring unit shifted to SDR's after gold convertibility was abolished. In this looser measuring unit, capital subscriptions in 1979 were 39.0 billion SDR including gold measured at book value ($42.22 per ounce) and total resources including borrowed funds were 45.1 billion SDR. In the seventh round of quota increases the IMF is in process of implementing a September 1978 decision to expand "quotas" generally by 50% with special increases for 11 members (chiefly oil-producers) that would altogether boost subscriptions to over 60 billion SDR. See *IMF Report*, 1979, pages 120 f.

[143]The first major borrowing facility started in 1962 was the so-called G.A.B. (General Arrangements to Borrow) financed chiefly by Common Market countries and Switzerland, making available funds controlled by particular lending states up to a maximum of 6.5 billion SDR with outstanding balances drawn usually less than a billion SDR. Two major facilities were generated by OPEC price boosts. The Oil Facility with 6.9 billion SDR was created in September 1974 with 72% petro-state financing. Within two years, it was loaned out and

2. *Organization.* The Articles of agreement contemplated Fund organization in three tiers. At the bottom there is an annual almost ceremonial general assembly of members represented usually by their treasury minister or their top central banker representing the government concerned in its combined monetary-banking arrangements. Only the assembly can act to amend the charter (which requires separate ratification by governments), admit new members, approve a revision of quotas, create reserve assets, require a member to withdraw, dispose of Fund gold assets, and make other critical decisions.

At the middle level is a smaller board of directors, made up of representatives of six states—holding either the largest quotas or, as in the case of Saudi Arabia, possessed of unusual financial power—and 15 regional groups of members, each of which elects its director. The directors are full-time residential officers who, in the words of the charter, are "responsible for the conduct of the general operations of the Fund"—such as grants of Fund credits or dealing in Fund holdings, acceptance of parities or parity alterations, resolution of conflict between members on exchange-rate questions, and release of members from Fund obligations.[144]

All voting by directors and by the assembly is proportioned to "quotas" of the country or the group represented. On most operating Fund decisions a simple majority of voting power decides but on critical issues such as quorum, increase of quotas, distribution of Fund credit assets, disposition of Fund gold holdings, and the like a qualified majority of voting power is now required up to 85%, giving various groups of countries such as the British Commonwealth, the Common Market, or the United States by itself the veto power.

The managing director of the IMF is appointed by the board of directors from outside their body and holds office at their will. Functioning under the general supervision of the board of directors, the managing director is responsible for the organization, appointment, and supervision of a large staff of experts in the fields of economics, finance, and accounting who carry out the research and routine work of the Fund and who contribute substantially to its policy decisions. With clerical personnel, this staff drawn from 97 countries as of 1982 numbers 1525 persons.[145] The charter expressly rules that the managing director and the Fund staff shall function as international civil

---

was (in 1979) 30% repaid. The second major loan facility was opened up only in 1979, the so-called "Supplemental Facility" with 7.8 billion SDR available. The petro-state share was only 42% with interest charges on loans starting in 1979 at 9.25%. See *IMF Report,* 1978, pages 67 f, 75; 1979, pages 71 ff.

[144]IMF, *Articles of Agreement,* 1944, art. XII, sec. 3(a).

[145]*IMF Report,* 1982, page 97.

servants and shall "owe their duty entirely to the Fund and to no other authority." Each Fund member is enjoined by the charter to "respect the international character of this duty" and to "refrain from all attempts to influence any of the staff in the discharge of his functions."[146] So far the international character of the Fund staff appears to have been respected outwardly at least.

3. *Lending Policy*. Fund resources are available for use by members who may draw upon the currencies held by the Fund to meet temporary balance of payment needs. As loan policy has been developed by Fund management, credit accommodation will be automatically granted any member up to the level of its so-called "gold tranche" or the share of its "quota" payable originally in gold. This borrowing right is now considered part of the monetary reserves of Fund members to be used only as needed because its use is subject to interest charges. Thereafter, additional loans of usable or convertible currency may be sought up to the limits of the "quota" (so-called *credit tranche*) with a convincing demonstration that there is genuine need of additional reserves and that national economic policies are in process of implementation aiming at redressing the balance of payments in not later than three to five years. Loans will be made with due recognition of the need for credit accommodation by other members if Fund management is satisfied that the deficit is not likely to be cumulative or persistent—and hence more suited for redress by other means than Fund credit accommodation. Loans are repaid by returning to the Fund an equivalent value of convertible or reusable balances that had been withdrawn by the loan. In its first 31 years of operation, Fund members obtained in loan arrangements nearly $60 billion and have repaid over half that.[147]

The Fund has developed over the years a large staff of banker-economist experts who consult with member countries regarding the alternative lines of action that may be taken to restore international payment balance equilibrium. In the main these alternative lines will involve currency devaluation, programs to suppress capital outflow, or programs to slow down domestic economic expansion of business, government spending, or credit—which increases the volume of spending on foreign goods and services and ties up resources that might be used to service customers abroad. Though IMF balance of payments therapies often are not liked, they are clearly the only ways by which a limited fund of reusable credit resources can be maintained. Over the years Fund therapy has proven sufficiently helpful that membership in the Fund has been continued and capital subscriptions have been increased.

4. *Exchange Rate Policy*. The charter requires its members to designate to

---

[146]IMF, *Articles of Agreement*, 1944, art. XII, sec. 4 (e).
[147]*IMF Report*, 1979, page 111.

the Fund upon accepting membership a parity for its currency or arrangements by which that parity would be governed. The charter broadly requires that Fund members have a single operative exchange and not multiple rates for transactions in different fields such as tourist spending, food imports, or services. While a Fund member may gain some advantage by charging more for its currency when used for certain purposes or selling its currency more advantageously for certain uses, this advantage is broadly balanced or largely offset if the same device is used by other Fund members—to the common detriment of all.

The charter mandates exchange devaluation to cope with cumulative and sustained tendencies to balance of payments deficit that cannot be dealt with by other means. Until 1971 over a hundred individual parity changes were approved or authorized by the Fund. Under the pressure of wild capital outflow triggered by the disappearance of the gold standard in August 1971, the attempt to maintain mutually fixed exchange rates broke down. The Fund approved a philosophy of floating rates for groups of currencies managed by day-to-day intervention. In a basic amendment to the Fund charter approved by member countries in 1977–1978, exchange rates were open for member determination subject to consultation with the Fund. However, the option of devaluation still remains as an approved policy instrument to assist members in reaching a better balance of payments.

5. *Reserve Creation.* As the Fund was originally established, international reserves consisted essentially of gold holdings of members and such convertible foreign exchange as they were willing to hold. The Fund charter did authorize action by the Fund to raise all currency parities upward in terms of gold, thus increasing the volume of reserves that gold holdings would convert to. Such action, however, was opposed by the United States because it would yield differential benefits to Fund members who had, like the French, converted their dollar holdings into gold and because it would appear to strengthen the role of gold vis-à-vis dollars. The Fund then sought to make more efficient use of existing reserves by deliberate creation of new supplemental credit facilities.

In 1968 an amendment to the Fund charter authorized creation by qualified voting majorities of a new credit entity with sufficient usability in international payments to qualify as a reserve asset. This new entity was called Special Drawing Rights (SDR), allocated as a fraction of capital subscribed by all Fund members. These rights were means of acquiring reserves on the occasion of balance of payment need by informing the Fund of need and the desire to convert a given quantum of SDR. The Fund would then be obligated to designate a Fund member whose holdings of SDR are not excessive and whose reserves are sufficient to enable the member to accept the tendered quantum of SDR and give in exchange usable convertible currencies of equivalent value. The recipients must pay interest to the converting partner, which of course adds to the willingness of members to augment their SDR holdings. Like the use of Fund credit facilities, the use of SDR is supposed to be temporary. Over a five-year period a member must maintain an average holding of 30% of its original SDR allocation, now lowered to 15%; members who early in the period need to use all of their SDR holdings will have to anticipate later readjustment of reserve holdings to enable them to "reconstitute" a minimum SDR position.

Beside being thus convertible at will into usable convertible currencies, SDR may be used directly by members to pay interest charges incurred in the use of SDR or in the use of Fund credit facilities or to pay the crucial 25% share of Fund capital subscriptions originally payable in gold but since 1978 payable in SDR. Holdings of SDR may also be used to acquire member currency held by another member.

An SDR unit was originally defined as the same weight of gold that constituted the 1934 parity of the American dollar. That simple measure of value had to be relinquished when gold was demonetized for international payment purposes in 1975. The Fund then redefined SDR as a composite of fractions of leading currencies, weighted for their respective importance in international trade and obtaining a determinate value at any given set of exchange rates. This measure of value is complex, but it will not be affected appreciably by exchange rate changes—though its real value is subject to erosion by any broad tendency to inflation in prices prevailing in the world economy.

The fundamental principles which govern the creation of SDR is worth citing from the amended Fund charter:[148]

> In all of its decisions with respect to the allocation and cancellation of SDR the Fund shall seek to meet the long-term global need, as and when it arises, to supplement existing reserve assets in such manner as will promote the attainment of its purposes and will avoid economic stagnation and deflation as well as excess demand and inflation in the world.

In accord with that high global standard the creation of SDR was begun in 1970 by crediting Fund members in proportion to their "quotas" over a three-year period with a total of nearly 9.3 billion SDR, amounting at the time to an addition of some 12% in Fund usable reserves. Some 116 Fund members participated with quotas equivalent to 98.5% of total Fund subscribed capital.[149] Over the three-year period the heaviest net users of SDR were the United States and The United Kingdom, who used between 30 to 40% of their original allocations. Less developed areas in Africa, Latin America, the Middle East, and Asia used some 62% of their allocations. The principal recipients of SDR were industrial Europe, Canada, and Japan—who all

---

[148]IMF, *Articles of Agreement*, art. IV(a).

[149]Habermeier, *Operations and Transactions*, 1973, pages 4 f. Holdouts who chose to "opt out" included Arab Gulf states (like Saudi Arabia, United Arab Emirates, Kuwait) and Libya.

ended up with larger SDR holdings. Fourteen of the countries had a need to
"reconstitute" at the end of 1972. Use of SDR varied over the period for
different countries. There were all together 109 transactions with designation,
mostly for small amounts, and a handful of transactions of agreement by
which SDR were transferred chiefly to large European dollar holders for excess dollar claims. There was an even larger use of SDR to repay Fund loans
or to pay Fund interest charges; and the Fund in turn used its SDR receipts
to buy individual currencies needed for its operations. Aggregate use of SDR
for all uses total over 3.1 billion. SDR's on occasion were even felt more
desirable to hold than gold and there was a general willingness both to receive
and use them.[150] Interest rates on use of SDR were boosted to improve incentives to hold or to accept SDR's and to somewhat deter their free use—
which was, however, in case of need given greater leeway by reducing the
average balances of SDR allocations that must be retained unused.[151]

World central banking is a helpful but not a miraculous instrument. It
cannot function successfully in a world economy in which large groups of
Fund members have continuous and massive balance of payment surpluses
and deficits. The tendency toward bifurcated imbalance arising out of the
early period of "dollar scarcity" was overcome by special U.S. programs for
distributing dollars in relief, military spending, and capital outflow. It remains
to be seen whether the much stronger tendency to imbalance arising out of
the massive, one-sided continuous surpluses by OPEC oil exporting countries
since 1974—and which in 1979 reached a record level of $68 billion—can
be likewise overcome. Those surpluses have as their counterpart in a closed
trading system balance of payment deficits. Those deficits were especially
difficult to handle and service because all but a small fraction of them ended
up as short-term debt of developing countries—those which were moderately
well-off but especially those that were very poor. The process by which these
deficits in the Western trading system shifted from points of original incidence
among oil-importing nations to developing countries is complex and need not
be elucidated here. The total external debt of the non-oil exporting developing
countries runs end-1979 at over $250 billion. Debt service requirements for
these countries run to between 10 and 15% of current exports. As interest
rates rise and as fresh borrowing occurs to finance accruing deficits, the burden of debt service continues to mount. Most of these countries have very
limited external monetary reserves which can be drawn upon.[152]

The first stage of default is now being experienced in the form of borrow-

---

[150]Habermeier, *Operations and Transactions*, 1973, Tables 3, 4, 6, 8, pages 26 ff., 30 ff.
"There existed for much of the three-year period a general willingness to receive SDR's through
designation" (page 37).

[151]*IMF Report*, 1979, pages 68 ff.

[152]IMF, *World Economic Outlook*, 1980, pages 5 ff. IMF staff estimates that in 1980 and
1981 OPEC surpluses on current account will rise $115 and $87 billion respectively. The

ing by non-oil-developing countries to meet debt service requirements on older loans.[153] The burden of debt service has been temporarily eased by continuous inflation of world price and nominal income flows—which for this group of countries has been running in both 1979 and 1980 at 30% per year and for the leading industrial countries between 10 to 15%. The bulk of the borrowing to finance this "distress" debt has come from the multinational banks, whose deposit balances have primarily in recent years come from petro-dollars, and whose loans are generally in short maturities at fully commercial interest rates, yielding all together a high and rising debt service. Though this debt is essentially a petro-debt and the dollars loaned out are petro-dollars, the immediate creditors are the multinational banks and financial institutions that will bear the immediate onus of any default or breakdown in this structure of debt.

IMF loans and credits have financed only a small fraction of this indebtedness.[154] Thus defaults on developing country indebtedness that involve linked defaults on major international banking systems and thus deeply affect credit systems in major IMF countries may leave IMF as a credit institution substantially undamaged. Whether IMF can survive the readjustments to be called for in a world where debt structure has collapsed—like the set of international debts growing out of World War I, which collapsed early in the 1930's—remains to be seen.[155]

---

aggregate deficit of non-oil developing countries for 1980 and 1981 is projected at $68 and $78 billion.

[153]*IMF Report*, 1979, pages 75 ff.

[154]See IMF, *World Economic Outlook*, 1980, for an appraisal of the debt service problems of the non-oil developing countries and especially a group of 38 "low income" countries with 1977 per capita GDP's of under $300. They have had limited rates of real economic growth over the past decade, and their debt service payments—relating only to outstanding public and publicly guaranteed medium- and long-term external debt—have risen from 10% to 15% of current exports. Total external debt of the non-oil developing country group as a whole ran at end-1979 to over $150 billion (pages 29–38).

[155]I have touched up but have not sought to expand and bring up-to-date (October 1982) the last three paragraphs of text and footnotes drafted on the basis of research completed $2\frac{1}{2}$ years ago. The tendency toward "bifurcated imbalance" of which the text speaks, has grown worse since that time. The debt of developing countries has grown by about $100 billion; at end-1981 it amounted to $436.9 billion. That debt has become more difficult to manage because of the world economic slowdown and depression that has had devastating results for many Third World countries, even some like Mexico with oil exports. "Monetarist" therapy has taken a terrible toll in at least two advanced countries, the United States and Great Britain. The first overt defaults at the weakest links in the world economy have now broken out. A submerged process of crisis is working its way. Very obviously further analysis of the prospects and role of IMF in this world financial crisis, which promises to be drawn-out and which has already generated a large periodical literature, would require a separate monograph. May I refer however to the constructive analyses found in two recent IMF publications: Killick, *Adjustment and Financing*, 1982; IMF, *World Economic Outlook*, 1982.

8

Institution of Property

INTRODUCTION

The institution of property in a well-developed form is implied by the defining characteristics of an economic system already presented in previous chapters. Thus if money is to become widely used as a medium of exchange in markets and for measuring values, it necessarily follows that possession of money must be honored and accepted as a personal possession that can be used in exchange so that markets become possible.

Similarly, the operation of an established mode of production in agriculture—whether that of a slave plantation, a village community, a capitalist farm, a peasant proprietorship, or a landlord–tenant arrangement—will call for a definite scheme of land tenure and established rights of ownership or possession in farm stock. The parties involved must recognize the relationships in which they are involved relative to their implements, cropland, and pastures.

The functioning of markets analyzed in Chapter 5 implies that would-be buyers and sellers recognize their respective rights of possession and the shared code that establishes these rights. Even the making of highly particular contracts by voluntary agreement of the parties presupposes the use of accepted procedures for interpretation of their agreement and for adjudication of controversy about it. This was strikingly expressed in the utterance of the great French sociologist Durkheim, that "everything in the contract is not contractual."[1]

The determination of what contracts are valid, who are proper contracting parties, the means by which other party's assent may be obtained, the language for signifying agreement and witnesses for the same, and various consequences of the contract and procedures available for enforcement—all are

[1]Durkheim, *On the Division of Labor*, 1893, page 211.

presuppositions of the contract. They make up a considerable part of the institution of property.[2]

As soon as accumulated wealth—such as cleared and improved farm land, stocks of raw materials, fleets of boats and trading vessels, precious metals and valuable works of art—becomes important, then a plan of disposition upon death will need to be established if economic life is not to be continually disrupted by armed conflicts or feuds about succession to possessions of the deceased. Nor can this succession safely be left to parties most immediately involved, because certain larger interests of the community or of the society itself are at stake. Those who inherit many properties must be able to resume roles in the social order. That order in turn will have an interest in arranging a succession that satisfies prevailing cultural norms about what is right and proper and also contributes to effective performance in that order. So regulation of inheritance of possessions is vital in any code of property.

Marxian economics has, of course, emphasized the role of property in economic systems. But it has tended to identify the two or treat the juridical fact of property as a mere reflex of economic relations. In his prefatory remarks to the theory of "exchange," Marx noted that exchange in the market is only possible if exchangers recognize "in each other the rights of private proprietors." He then said: "This juridical relation, which expresses itself in a contract, whether such a contract be part of a developed legal system or not, is a relation between two wills and is but the reflex of the real economic relation between the two." He concluded: "It is the economic relation that determines the subject-matter comprised in each such juridical act."[3] Of course

---

[2]See Durkheim's own treatment, in the form of a critique of Herbert Spencer in pt. 2 of his chapter "Organic and Contractual Solidarity," Durkheim, *On the Division of Labor*, 1893, pages 206–219; Parsons, *Structure of Social Action*, 1936, pages 311 f.

[3]Marx, *Capital* I, 1867, page 84. This reflex relationship was enunciated in Marx's writings of the mid-1840s. See especially *The Holy Family*, 1845, pages 127 ff.; Marx, *Poverty of Philosophy*, 1847, page 197; Marx and Engels, *German Ideology*, 1845–1846, pages 77f., 373 ff., 395 ff. These are variously discussed in Marxist compendia, especially in the writings of Plekhanov, *Selected Philosophical Works*, 1883–1913, vol. 1, pages 540 f., 663 ff., 679 f. See Hazard, *Soviet Legal Philosophy*, 1951, pages 145 ff. In his fullest statement (in *German Ideology*) Marx conceded that since "the State mediates in the formation of all common institutions . . . the institutions receive a political form." But then to Marx, the State "is the form in which the individuals of a ruling class assert their common interests" (78f). In his critique of Proudhon, Marx dismissed "bourgeois property" as "nothing other than . . . all the social relations of bourgeois production" and asserts that to "give a definition of property as of an independent relation, a separate category, an abstract and eternal idea, can only be an illusion of metaphysics or of jurisprudence." See Marx, *Poverty of Philosophy*, 1847, page 197. As against German idealism—which represented social development as following from the ideas which marked its course—this viewpoint has validity. But to view the state and its work as a simple instrument of the dominant class by which their common interests are asserted is to overlook that usually there is only a very loose relationship between the dominant class and

the juridical form evolves from the life interest, usages, and needs of those whose labor, devotion, and enterprise make a mode of production possible. The first driving force in the evolution of law—as far as it gives shape to the institution of property—will be rules and usages that are generated in the mode of production itself by its primary actors be it a tribal society, a village community, a feudal manor, or a capitalist–merchant community.

Even in a homogeneous social and ethnic milieu and within a single mode of production, rules and usages do not sustain themselves of their own accord. They are constantly being upset or challenged by novel situations, diverse interests, or changing circumstances. Hence, even in very simple societies there will be established facilities and procedures for hearing complaints and controversies and attempts to settle them by various forms of adjudication applying shared rules and norms. Surveys of peoples as widely separated and unrelated as the Eskimos, Amerindian tribes, Trobrianders, Ashanti, and Ifugao show very clearly a well-defined legal code at work and established facilities for adjudication and conflict resolution.[4] Through the sixth decade of this century, courts in Tanzania and other countries in Africa were making decisions based upon "customary law," administered in East Africa under the control of tribal chiefs and councils. So law and usage go hand in hand; they evolve with each other and support each other or take the lead in change by turns.[5] This was expressed in institutional economic theory by John R. Commons, who believed the irreducible unit of economic analysis was an exchange transaction in which, besides interested market performers negotiating and dealing, a fifth party also was present—a "judge, priest, chieftain, paterfamilias, arbitrator, who would be able to settle disputes."[6]

In more complex societies with uneven social development and with divergent production modes and communities participating, a broader form of law and more complex method of adjudication must emerge corresponding to the new social conditions, the greater density of population, and the new social interests involved. Of course the law that settles controversies cannot be merely a juridical thing. The system of law giving final form to the institution of property must be capable of laying down decisions which can be

---

the state and no practicable way for the class as a whole to impose its will on the state. Beside the dominant class there are also the armed forces of a society and those forces are often not made up of the dominant class. The armed forces are the backbone of the state and will often come to dominate it completely as for extended periods in the Roman Principate, in the later Roman Empire, and later periods of Seljuk, Mamluk, and other Turkic periods of dominance in the Near East.

[4]Hebel, *Law of the Primitive Man*, 1964, page 29.

[5]For an authoritative review of the customary law of property in East Africa, see James, *Land Tenure in Tanzania*, 1971, pages 61–87, 261–302.

[6]Commons, *Legal Foundations of Capitalism*, 1924, pages 68 ff.

enforced by the highest organs of the state. The state with its effective monopoly of violence in a given society and the assent of its subjects must act through judicial organs which *adjudicate*—and thus tend to shape the law—and then seek to enforce the decisions, thus constituting "a means of coercion and a means of persuasion."[7]

From time to time the state may formally alter by published proclamation or decree the law bearing on particular property rights. The state with this great power may itself be an organ of a dominant economic class, as was clearly the case in the emergent mercantile communities of Italy in the early medieval period. Or the state—as in the period of the early Roman Republic—may be a compromise state in which both plebeian and patrician classes had balanced rights and duties and participated in state power.[8] Or the state can become the mere organ of the armed forces, sometimes their plaything used to maximize their own exploitation and buttress their position—as in much of the later Roman or Islamic empires. But however the state is organized—even when only one dominant class rules through the state—the institution of property that is *mediated* by the state will be quite different from a property institution shaped directly by naked class interests. Marx himself characterized "the power of the State" as "the concentrated and organized force of society, itself an economic power."[9]

Thus mediated, it is possible for the institution of property to be shaped by *the longer view* and *the broader needs* of the class or society in which the adjudication occurs. These needs are: (1) to reinforce the power of the state and the ruling class, (2) provide adequate motivation at all levels of society, (3) seek to assure steady reproduction and growth of the society, and (4) to respect widely shared values and norms. Above all, state mediation facilitates orderly change. Hence it is our belief that the legal relation is no mere legal "reflex" of the economic relation, as Marx asserted, but is shaped by and through the power of the state—and class or group or clique rule exercised by the state—via the force of law and through juridical processes in continuous interplay with pressures arising in the society and within modes of production. The power of the state is not unlimited and the extent to which it

[7]Hazard, *Soviet Legal Philosophy*, 1951, page 62.

[8]For a clear enunciation of the early state of the Roman Republic as a "compromise state," see Hazard, *Soviet Legal Philosophy*, 1951, pages 60 ff. For a deeper analysis, see conventional histories of Roman society and the full portrayal of a qualified historian of Roman public law, Jolowicz and Nichols, *Roman Law*, 1932, pages 10–54. The decisive features which bring about the mixed-class state were recited by the Roman historians Polybius and Livy. The plebeian assembly, convened by its own officers whom it elected as tribunes, elected a consul, had veto powers over actions of the Senate, could enact ordinances (plebicites) with the force of law, and had sole authority to declare war and to validate judicial sentences of death.

[9]Marx, *Capital* I, 1867, page 751.

will influence the development of the institution of property via either law-making or juridical processes will depend upon the character of the state, class relationships in the society, the stage of the development of law as a juridical force, and the degree of rationality embodied in the law. In early Rome, the composition and enactment of a code of civil law was a memorable historic act, couched in a highly rational form and freed from priestly ritual. The code of law itself became a venerated symbol of national unity and of the civil power of the society. It was studied by children as a school exercise well until the time of Cicero and it was memorized by law students for centuries afterward. The power of the law as an organ of the state in Rome and as a shaper of social institutions ranks exceptionally high.[10] Understandably enough, one of the attractions of Roman domination to the conquered Mediterranean peoples was precisely this veneration by the Romans as a people for generalized law, especially after Roman citizenship was extended first among all Latins and later throughout the empire. Nor is respect for written law unique only to the Romans. Ancient Israel was solidified as a state by the veneration given the code of civil law—variously distributed in the sacred books—setting up the national and religious leader, Moses, as the lawgiver. The attachment of ordinary Athenian citizens for the law courts—where large numbers of citizens were empaneled early in the day for jury duties—was memorialized and lampooned by the great dramatist, Aristophanes, in *The Wasps.* The famous Akkadian law code of Hammurabi deriving from the Bronze Age (1792 B.C.) was a logical accompaniment to the emergence of a supraurban state power embracing many urban areas and city states and drawing upon a succession of earlier legal codes.[11]

[10]I refer of course to the famous Twelve Tables enacted in the late 400s B.C. and which we can reconstruct from innumerable citations come down to us, though no copy or fragment of the original Tables has been recovered. See the English text available in *Corpus Juris Civilis,* A.D. 528–553, vol. 1, pages 57–80. School boys recited the Table text. See Radin, *Handbook of Roman Law,* 1927, page 23. Every student of Roman law was compelled to memorize them "before he could proceed to prepare himself for his profession." See *Corpus Juris Civilis,* A.D. 528–553, vol. 1, page 213 n. The respect shown Roman citizens throughout the Empire is brought home to us in the New Testament account in Acts 22–28, the high point, of course, being the instant respect for the right of a Roman citizen to appeal to Caesar against a tribunal decision and the evident fairness of the successive hearings, including those before King Agrippa and his wife Bernice (Acts, 25–26). My first direct contact with Roman law came in 1949. After returning from three years of service with military government in Germany, I chanced to read one of Cicero's great legal orations—his indictment of Verres for abuse of power of military government in Sicily, robbed of its treasures and art works. The American republic, I felt, was not as diligent in enforcing the rule of law in its conquered territories as the Roman Republic.

[11]Our understanding of the Hammurabi code is necessarily imperfect because of the remoteness of the language and the restricted number of case documents on tablets that have survived and have been discovered. See Hawkes, *The First Great Civilizations,* 1973, pages 170 f.; Driver and Miles, *The Babylonian Laws,* 1923.

If the forms of property or their legal vestments have an independent development in law, it becomes possible for a legally precocious people to develop a legal culture regarding property that could exert an influence on other societies with different modes of production and cultures. Precisely that possibility seems realized in the Roman case because of the rationality of Roman law, the diversity of modes of production to which it applied, and the tendency among Roman legal theorists to express in completely secular terms and very clearly legal relationships such as those involved in bankruptcy, corporation (which only existed in very special form in Roman life), contract, lease, inheritance, fraud, and good faith. Hence though the actual institution of property was shaped in each society and generation out of the social and class struggles and the modes of production evolving in that society, those struggles were carried on by classes, parties, state rulers, and civil servants whose consciousness and ideas were influenced by Roman legal culture. This frequently influenced the nomenclature, the forms, and the devices embodied in the evolving institution of property. This culture was given special prominence in Europe because from the earliest days the Roman language remained the language of worship, sacraments, and literary expression—even amongst Germanic, Celtic, and Slavic peoples—and over a large part of Europe the Roman language survived in modified form as the spoken tongue down to our day.

ASSETS, TANGIBLE AND INTANGIBLE

What, then, is property as an institution? It is best regarded as an ordering of recognized protectible interests in economic assets. A comment on each term in this definition—in reverse order—is needed.

The economic assets to which protectible interests relate vary in different societies. The broad defining characteristics of these assets appear in the properties of appropriability, value, or worth for human purposes, and in scarcity.[12] Appropriability and worth are absolute requirements. An object or a claim cannot be an object of property rights if it is not scarce and does not appear to have worth or value for some human purpose. And if valuable things like fresh air, rainfall, horizons, tides, national protection, or sunlight are not appropriable, or cannot be rendered appropriable, they cannot become under ordinary conditions objects of property. Many valuable and ap-

---

[12]On this trinity, see Walras, *Elements of Pure Economics*, 1877, pages 65 ff. Scarcity was defined as a condition when "things are available to us only in a limited quantity insufficient to permit everyone concerned to completely . . . satisfy his desires." Worth was rather casually described as predicated whenever a thing "can be put to any use at all."

propriable things in an early stage of economic development are not
sufficiently scarce to become objects of property.[13] Similarly, most societies
have experienced the process by which previously valueless things become an
object of property after knowledge is gained of how to use them directly or
intermediately.[14]

Of this universe of valuable, scarce, and appropriable things, the first major
segment of objects of property will be movable goods for which market facilities exist. Conversely put, all movable things ordinarily handled in markets
and thus treated as alienable will for that time and place be regarded as property. Nearly everywhere in the list will be precious metals, domesticated livestock, bread grains, jewels, cloth, metals and metallic goods, building materials,
herbs, spices, salt, hides and leather. Where humans are bought and sold,
they too will constitute a species of property.

We turn now to a broad class of special economic assets that fall into four
major headings: (1) land—both urban and rural, (2) moving or stationary
waters, (3) mineral sites or subsoil riches, and (4) radiation. It was not a simple
or direct process by which land on which man lives—which provides most
of his food and which is the center of his family and community life—becomes converted into numbered parcels of real estate rendered alienable and
bought and sold like movable goods. Even in societies where this process has
long been completed, as in the United States and Great Britain, the law of
property, by the presence of archaic survivals in procedures for handling and
recording real estate, betrays the once-pregnant distinction drawn between
personal and real property. The land that is everywhere useful, scarce, and
appropriable will often in earlier economic systems not be readily alienable.
Sometimes the ban on alienability will apply to sales outside the kinship or
tribal community, as with ancient Israel where the legal code prohibited real
estate transfers outside the tribe.[15] East African rural communities until this
century did not permit holders of appropriated and bounded parcels to sell
or alienate these parcels. If no longer put to use, the land was reallocated by
village elders to other suitable village claimants, this being a cardinal feature
of communal land property that also persisted in the Russian village com-

---

[13]That may include workable farmland, drinking water, pasture for domesticated stock,
fruit in season, and so on. For a perceptive analysis of how property rights in land evolve
with growing scarcity and with greater demand for the produce of land, see Ault and Rutman,
"Individual Rights to Property," 1979, pages 171 ff.

[14]A definite form of property rights in hunting territories in eastern Canada evolved in the
seventeenth and eighteenth century. As the fur market developed, Indian interest in safeguarding their hunting terrain was intensified. See Demsetz, "Theory of Property Rights,"
1967, pages 350 ff.

[15]See Bible, Num. 36:5–9. This embodied an amendment to a previous ordinance (27:5–
11) that permitted inheriting daughters to marry outside their tribe.

munity into the twentieth century.[16] In many societies contingent lineage claims to land holdings make alienation very difficult. The Graeco-Roman world was distinguished by the quickness with which such lineage ties were cut away and alienability was given to holders of real estate, thus enabling such holders to rearrange their personal possessions and change their locations and to borrow on the strength of their land holdings. The same tendencies were manifested in the early phases of the classical Chinese empire but they were less fully realized. For extended periods through to the eighth century A.D., alienability of land parcels was restricted and control of many land holdings devolved upon the state bureaucracy.[17] The classical law of feudal property barred the sale of real estate that had been assigned for beneficial use only to particular holders in exchange for rendering defined services. The process by which holders of feudal property gradually appropriated to themselves and their family successors other incidents of property and finally claimed full ownership rights including alienability is the central thread in the sphere of property relations in the long history of the dissolution of the feudal institution of property.[18]

The property status of moving or stationary waters is similar to that of land in that waters are valuable for human purposes and often scarce at choice locations, but they are more difficult to appropriate. Flowing water as a "moving, wandering thing" was once believed by qualified legal observers (Blackstone), to "of necessity continue common by the law of nature."[19] This doctrine was in unique form written into the basic ordinance that governed the constitutional development of the Old Northwest territory of the United States. That ordinance specified that "the navigable waters leading into the Mississippi and Saint Lawrence and the carrying places between the same, shall be common highways, and forever free, as well to the inhabitants of the said territory as to the citizens of the United States, and those of other states which may be admitted into the confederacy, without any tax, impost or duty therefore."[20]

---

[16]James, *Land Tenure in Tanzania*, 1971, pages 61 ff. This customary law was reenacted by the Nyerere regime to slow up commercial rural development in Tanzania; sale was commonly allowed, however, for the unexhausted value of improvements on the land, including cultivated tree crops (pages 63 f., 88 ff., 288 ff.).

[17]See Elvin, *Pattern of the Chinese Past*, 1973, pages 60 ff.; Balazs, *Chinese Civilization*, 1923–1961, ch. 9.

[18]The issue of feudal succession and the patrimony of "fiefs" is brilliantly treated by Bloch, *Feudal Society*, 1939–1940, vol. 1, ch. 14.

[19]Blackstone, *Commentaries on the Laws of England*, 1776–1779, cited here from Anderson and Hill, "Evolution of Property Rights," 1975, page 176.

[20]See Hurst, *Law and Economic Growth*, 1964, ch. 3, especially for the Northwest Ordinance of 1787. The essential text of this and related statutory provisions of the congressional acts that governed the territory of Wisconsin and admitted her into the Union were written into

Even though the water itself was commingled and flowing, some of it could be diverted and channeled for agricultural, industrial or domestic uses. Flowing water when diverted over mineralic or acidic or salty channels could be degraded. Waters when dammed have greater exposure to evaporation or soil absorption and hence become lost to downstream use.[21] Moreover, we have learned that drawing water from deep underground reservoirs may affect the flow of water in springs and streams and the water level in ponds and lakes throughout the drainage basin. Hence the rights to use water, to divert running streams or rivers, and to draw from underground reservoirs all make up a specific form of property increasingly valuable and complex.

Water in large lakes or oceans has distinctive status as an object of property for somewhat different reasons. The oceans are not yet subject to national appropriation and hence access to them except in time of war is not appropriable by long-standing international agreement. But inland oceans such as the Black or Baltic Seas—reachable only through narrow straits that may be fortified, controlled, and appropriated—may become a species of collective (national) property. For centuries the Black Sea was a closed Byzantine lake from which both the state and the merchant guilds drew large profits from water courses draining into that lake and from adjacent shore settlements. After Byzantine control was shattered in the Fourth Crusade in 1205, Venetian and later Genoese mercantile power exercised dominion. To a lesser degree the Baltic Sea was subject to profitable control by those who were established on the straits. Other narrow shipping channels have played a similar role of governing access.

While metallic goods bought and sold in markets are of necessity alienable objects of property, the sites from which the mineral ores are extracted have a more ambiguous status. When only surface ores could be worked to shallow depths, mineral sites were valuable "finds"; therefore in earlier historical systems state rulers tended to seek to appropriate the fruits of such finds by

---

the Wisconsin Constitution. Water carriage of lumber was critical for the first 30 years of the state. Log transport on the state's inland waters brought 69 cases to the Wisconsin Supreme Court, clustering in the years 1875–1895 when the lumber industry came to major growth. The waters were open to navigation without toll but traffic was frequently hampered by booms, dams, and other water-control devices so that the courts ruled that "mutual accommodation" was required (pages 149, 161, 699 f.).

[21] Such degradation has noteworthily been the case with the Colorado River. The increased salinity of the downstream flow entering Mexico led to strong Mexican complaints and to agreement with the United States to construct a desalinization facility. For a general background to the river and its problems, see Burness and Quirk, "Water Laws," 1980, pages 111–134. On the negotiations with Mexico, reports of the U.S. international negotiator with Mexico and various state agencies and officials involved, see U.S. Senate Hearings, *Salinity Control Measures*, 1974.

converting these sites into public property and placing the whole category of subsoil mineral wealth outside the reach of private appropriation. The wealth of Lydian kings—to which Herodotus testifies and which is known from other sources—was derived directly from the mines worked under regal control. The Laurium silver mines of Athens, worked by slave labor under contractors, were managed directly by the Athenian state and the revenues returned to the state treasury. Those revenues helped to build the naval fleet which defeated the Persians at Salamis.[22] The Roman state did not seek to work or handle copper mines, but the more valuable gold and silver mines in Spain, developed and worked before Roman control was established over the territory, were appropriated by the state and worked as public property.

The doctrine that mineral wealth belongs to the state does not tend to encourage subjects to make undue efforts to locate and work mineral deposits. Hence in later economic systems state claims have been reduced to the formula of a special tax, a regal half or fifth, becoming attenuated as mines grew deeper or had to be worked under more difficult conditions.[23] English landlords, merchants, and industrialists through the centuries have been able to confine the claims of the crown for a special share in mineral wealth to gold or silver—of which very little was found in Great Britain. That left mineral enterprise and mineral sites free to develop and become capitalized—after discovery, of course—as private property, like other real estate.[24]

It was fateful that the United States as an erstwhile child of British society inherited her legal traditions regarding mineral property, for those traditions conditioned the later development of our petroleum industry. The subsoil riches of the petroleum and natural gas deposits widely scattered through the American domain were considered private property, the windfall of the owner

---

[22]Herodotus, *Histories*, bk. 7, pars. 143 ff.; Plutarch, *Lives*, "Themistocles," par. 4 (page 135 in edition cited). The Laurium revenues on the proposal of Themistocles were withheld from the accustomed distribution to citizens and spent on the construction of 200 ships actually used in the naval battle at Salamis. The ups and downs in the administration and development of the Laurium mines (which are still being worked but not for silver) for over a century and a half, are pieced out by H. Mitchell, *Economics of Ancient Greece*, 1940, pages 104 ff.

[23]Quite amusing is the way Adam Smith notes how the Spanish crown cut down its regal claim from one-half to one-third—and ultimately, as far as gold was concerned, to one-twentieth when the yield of their New World mines fell in the later sixteenth and early seventeenth centuries. With the gold strikes in Brazil the Portuguese king was able to claim a half. See A. Smith, *Wealth of Nations*, 1776, pages 169 ff., 214 f. French royalty asserted the power of the crown over mining and was able to enforce it on iron and coal properties. See Nef, *Industry and Government*, 1957, pages 68 ff.

[24]Weber, *General Economic History*, 1923, page 183. For the important English coal mining property, the story is told in detail by Nef, *British Coal Industry*, 1932, vol. 1, pages 265–343.

of the surface land. Never did greater wealth come about with so little effort or enterprise, the landowner being usually a passive party who merely was the lucky recipient of the fortunes that happened to fall his way.[25] Nationalization does not always avoid this calamity. In the case of the Persian Gulf states, which are practically the personal property of the elite rulers of those states and their extended families, nationalization merely throws the cloak of the nation about the collective wealth of the ruling plutocracy. In the United States, even when oil or gas finds were discovered on nationally owned property—so that royalties and benefits of development might be deemed the intrinsic property of the nation, or at least an offset to its swollen national debt—it is striking that efforts were made to cheat the nation out of its possessions, as illustrated by the Teapot Dome scandal of the 1920s. Later, the nation was swindled by systematic alienation of its oil- or gas-bearing lands with little or no tested knowledge of their geologic properties or determination of the amount of oil or gas likely to be recovered. The method of disposition, that of an auction market, ensured that only the largest of the oil companies would be able to make the necessary cash bids—on the foolish presupposition that companies in that highly syndicated and cartelized industry operate responsibly and would assign to government by auction bidding its full share of the expected proceeds.[26]

Even more distinctive than water or mineral rights as an economic asset subject to property rights are radio waves generated by man. These are at the very borderline of tangibility—as detectable, electromagnetic, modulatable pulses of radiation that travel at the speed of light at a limited set of frequencies. The strength of signal attenuates with distance, subject to some directive control. These signals cannot in any literal sense be consumed, confined, or appropriated. The capacity to generate and emit these signals that can be cheaply converted to sound and picture is, in any receiving area beyond the shortwave band, quite limited, yet the potential use of them as carriers of information, propaganda, news, entertainment, and advertising is very great. Police, military, telephonic, and industrial uses of these signals are growing. The ordinary household throughout the Western world, increas-

---

[25]In a paper some time ago on the distribution of wealth in America among households, I noted that the "millionaire class of princely estates" worth more than 50 million [1957] dollars, of which some 150 [at the price levels of 1957] had been listed by *Fortune* magazine in 1957: "The smell of the oil-field hovers over their listing." See Gottlieb, "Household Wealth," 1959, page 6.

[26]The alienation is by method of leasing. By statute, except in naval oil reserves, staff of the Interior Dept. are not permitted to engage in test drilling to evaluate the lands put on the "market" for leasing by auction. On this complex subject, see Blair, *The Control of Oil*, 1976, pages 138 ff.; Engler, *Brotherhood of Oil*, 1978, pages 150 ff.; Freeman, *Energy: The New Era*, 1974, pages 174 f.; U.S. Senate Hearings, *Federal Leasing and Disposal Policies*, 1972.

ingly in the Eastern world, and to a limited degree in the Third World depends upon these signals for news, views, and entertainment. To some extent these signals can be rendered appropriable by limitation of the kinds of receiving devices that can translate their signals into sound, pictures, or both. In any country in which radio repair shops are widespread and where amateurs are accustomed to assemble their own receiving sets, if only as a hobby, any attempt to limit severely or specially to tax receiving devices to create capitalizable property rights in radio signals is bound to generate widespread "bootlegging" of receiving devices. Hence a form of property in radio waves has been created in the United States by licensing broadcasting stations permitted to use given radio frequencies at a given strength of signal. Receiving sets owned by the public are free of user tax and are generally available. The licensed station derives a capitalizable return, and hence a property right, from the radio signal emitted by associating (some would say prostituting) music, drama, entertainment, news, and ideas or opinions to advertising so that the listener's attention gained for one purpose will be inadvertently shifted to another. Needless to say, because the advertiser funds the station that emits the signals, the advertisers' interests and phobias control the programming and dominate the viewing and listening media in America outside of a small circle of public (educational) stations.[27]

So far we have dealt with property as relations of persons to more or less tangible things or facilities—stationary, movable, flowing or radiant. But property can also relate to wholly intangible things. One entire category of such intangible things is called by Noyes "quasi-material objects, protected processes." They may be defined as "certain exclusive processes, capable of being appropriated and protected because, while immaterial, they are, in spite of that fact, capable of transfer; because they are special and not general, and therefore distinguishable and identifiable; and because they are processes which can persist independently of persons."[28] Some are based on a temporary kind of monopoly—as, for example, patents and copyrights that are monopoly privileges granted by law and which have value, are readily exchangeable, and make up in the Western world an important class of property. Akin to these

[27]The Chicago School has given very luminous treatment of this form of property created by government regulation and licensing, to them an abhorent and inefficient instrument. They do not seem to find fault with the forced marriage of programming to the tender mercies of the advertiser or the propaganda artist inherent in the present broadcast media pattern in the United States. Rather, they ask only that the slight public control, which now through the Federal Communication Commission seeks to protect public interests, be abolished and that broadcasting licenses be sold at auction to the highest bidder. See Coase, "The Federal Communication Commission," 1959, pages 1–40; Minasian, "Property Rights in Radiation," 1975, pages 221–274.

[28]Noyes, *Institution of Property*, 1936, pages 440 f.

is business goodwill built up as a going concern with a patronage and supplier following. It is intangible and possibly unsaleable but with a value nonetheless, and if it is damaged a suit for recovery will ordinarily be allowed.[29]

Beside the protected processes, then, there is a vast universe of assets made up of *claims* to what Noyes accurately characterizes as "indeterminate objects." The rights of a creditor do not relate to the specific thing given to create the indebtedness; these rights are converted into a claim for an equivalent value—a "floating charge," as Noyes put it, against a total mass of property.[30] Of a similar character are the rights of a stockholder in the great public corporations which, as we have seen in Chapter 3, have become the dominant form of business enterprise in the Western world. Those rights boil down to a prorated share in such benefits as the control group in the corporation choose with discretion to make available to stockholders.[31] Bank deposits, our predominant form of money, represent only a creditor claim to the assets of the bank. The claim to a Social Security benefit is an important item of property—now reduced in the United States, because Social Security reserves are nearly exhausted, to a share governed by statutory formulas to the current inflow of such payroll taxes as Congress and the President choose to impose upon the active labor force and make available for redistribution to those who have retired because of old age or disability, or to their dependent survivors. Claims to income or to a stream of income available in the future now make up a dominant category of property for most retired persons, for most persons living on invested capital, and for virtually all so-called benevolent institutions and organizations.

In addition to the main core of property objects, there will be a floating margin or nimbus of objects of property rights realizable under special conditions or stress which hence make up a potential class of economic assets. Children in China were not ordinarily sold nor were there markets for children, but in times of famine or disaster over wide areas significant numbers of children would be sold as domestic or industrial chattels. Feudal estates held in vassalage were not ordinarily alienable, but sometimes there were ways to transfer at least portions of them for consideration. So it doubtless was under Roman law in the Republic and Principate for land in provinces where Roman citizens held occupancy and benefit but formally were not able

---

[29]Noyes, *Institution of Property*, 1936, pages 447 ff.

[30]Noyes, *Institution of Property*, 1936, pages 326 ff., 370 ff., 397 ff.

[31]I say with "discretion" since it has been established that courts will not interfere with business judgments on the policy of paying out dividends as shaped by boards of directors unless "there is clear evidence of fraud" or of a grossly unconventional business philosophy. See Dewing, *Financial Policy of Corporations*, 1919, page 747 and the entire chapter "Distribution of Profits—Principles," pages 743–796; Berle and Means, *Modern Corporation*, 1932, page 190.

to sell land.[32] So likewise with that ambiguous practice of "bride-price," which in many early societies is the quantum of valuable goods transferred to the family of the bride as a condition of relinquishing control of the young female (commonly required to be a virgin).[33] Other kinds of potential or quasi-property are made up of licenses to operate a business, public service franchises in the United States (with questionable saleability, especially when Public Service Commission controls are operative), and public offices and appointments—which in many political systems have been "farmed out" or sold.[34]

A more contentious and problematic type of quasi-property consists of

[32]Though that was the rule in the Republic and through the early Principate, it apparently became relaxed in the Empire though the land remained subject to land tax. See Jolowicz and Nichols, *Roman Law*, 1932, page 267.

[33]Payment of "bride price" was considered by Briffault "the most widespread mode of acquiring a wife . . . not only among uncultured and barbaric peoples . . . but . . . in most advanced cultures." He finds the practice among the ancient Semites, Vedic Indians, Bantu Africans, Merovingian Europe, and elsewhere. See Briffault, *The Mothers*, 1927, vol. 2, pages 212–229. Even in Africa, where Briffault believed "marriage by purchase" had "degenerated into a mercenary bargain" (pages 224 ff.), wives might readily leave the compound of the husband and return to their families, though often this involved return of "bride-price." And among many African peoples the cattle given in bride-price accompany the young bride when she moves to her husband's dwelling; or an equivalent fund of cattle are put under the custody of the bride as her patrimony. But even where the bride is "purchased" she is hardly vendible and her relations with her mate and her own family do not have the character of appropriability. Consideration of the case of the Roman wife shows that the formal position of the wife in man-made law may vary considerably from her real position. In theory the Roman wife passed after marriage under the total power of her husband, subject to corporal punishment or sale. Few Roman wives were sold. Far from being in a position of subjection, Briffault pointed out, the "position of women in Rome was from the first to last more independent and dignified than among any other patriarchal people." There was no oriental seclusion, she was educated with boys in mixed schools, and she entertained with her husband at parties (349f). The elder Cato complained that "all mankind rule their wives, we rule all mankind and our wives rule us." See Plutarch, *Lives*, "Cato the Elder," par. 8 (page 416 in the edition cited). That these Roman "rulers" despite their low legal status could kick up a public fuss is shown by the commotion Roman matrons created over Lex Appia, a female sumptuary ordinance. See Livy, *History of Rome*, 29 B.C.–A.D. 17, bk. 34, pars. 1–8 (195 B.C.). Aristotle shrewdly said a man ruled his wife "as a stateman" but his children "as a King." See Aristotle, *Basic Works*, "Politics," bk. 1, ch. 12 (page 1259b).

[34]As late as the mid-19th century John Stuart Mill could castigate his country for retaining fuedalistic property in such public trusts as "a commission in the army and an avowson, or right of nomination to an ecclesiastical benefice." See Mill, *Principles of Political Economy*, 1848, bk. 2, ch. 11, par. 7. According to Aristotle "the offices of king and general" in Carthage were filled by sale. See Aristotle, *Basic Works*, "Politics," bk. 2, ch. 11. Responsible historians estimated that in eighteenth century France there were some 51,000 venal offices with a capital value (in 1778) of 600 million livres. See Taylor, "Noncapitalist Wealth," 1967, pages 473 ff.

claims for compensation for loss or injury caused by public action deemed beneficial or productive of good for many, if not all, members of the society but which is damaging or hurtful to a few persons. In the case in which damage is caused by taking of property or goods for public use, compensation in the legal code of most Western countries is nearly always granted, though it reimburses only for the fair-market value of the goods taken, not for moral or sentimental losses or for inconvenience. The issue of compensation arises, however, when the injury involves imposition of higher costs of production due to imposition of environmental requirements or health standards, or else prohibiting land uses that have been deemed aesthetically blighting. Awarding compensation, minimally and grudgingly given in some cases, thus brings into existence a new property right, undisturbed enjoyment of a preexisting benefit or privacy or occupation.[35]

Not all readily alienable things commonly handled in markets, however, will be property. The leading excluded category is human services—menial, professional, or industrial—in most societies at some times and places regularly subject to hiring for performance. If enslaved, the performer may be a species of property. The service itself is an economic asset, but it is hardly a species of property, though the promise to pay or contract for a service and the obligation to pay after a performance is certainly a form of intangible property. Of course the free performer could be said to have property rights over his own service-yielding capability. But that is to impute to him a form of relationship alien to him and to suppose that he reckons with himself as an alien object, as if the person and his serviceability are different things. The performer values his time and effort and will only give his service for consideration. That no one can coerce him and compel the performance against his will means that he is not converted into an object of property for others and certainly not for himself. If property is a social relation between persons regarding things, their access, and use, then to impute this social relation to a person and his own activity is to commit the venal sin of fetishism castigated by Marx. It is to strip a "social relation" from the human interaction to which it relates and to subsume it under the relation between a person and his own activity.[36]

[35]See on this subject the provocative paper by F. I. Michelman, "Property, Utility and 'Fairness,'" 1968, pages 100–144.

[36]"A social relation of production appears as something existing apart from individual human beings, and the distinctive relations into which they enter in the course of production in society appear as the specific properties of a thing—it is this perverted appearance, this prosaically real and by no means imaginary mystification that is characteristic of all social forms of labour positing exchange-value." See Marx, *Critique of Political Economy*, 1859, page 49. Marx protested the way of thinking that treated an independent farmer as his own employer who hires himself as a laborer and pays himself rent as landlord. "Assuming the cap-

Schematically, we can list these broad classes of economic assets, all useful and appropriable and related to property interests:

1. Alienable goods handled in markets
2. Human beings if coercively controlled and readily alienable
3. Land, water rights or access, and subsoil minerals
4. Radio signals
5. Inalienable public properties and means of production, village community lands, and feudalized property tied up in vassalage
6. Quasi-material processes typically monopolistic
7. Claims to income or funds
8. A residual class of contingent claims

CONTROL AND BENEFICIAL USE

These assets are in a scheme of property related to a polarity of *interests* held by various classes of persons or organizations. The interests in economic assets run a broad spectrum involving at one end the distribution of *control* of the use of objects, sites, buildings, and facilities or immaterial processes and the right to exclude others from trespass. Control includes the power of management to coordinate the use of economic assets to reach meaningful results. This control is essentially exerted by the masters of the great quasi-public corporations that dominate Western industrial economies today. *Control* is exerted over the vast amounts of goods and assets held and managed in trust for the beneficial use of other parties. And control over large amounts of capital is entrusted to the typical bank, to enable banking enterprises to carry on. The stockholder typically has little or no control over the modern quasi-public corporation beyond a prorated share and use of such funds as the control group direct for payment to stockholders. Organizations may be set up in the United States and elsewhere in the West under self-perpetuating boards that have unlimited authority to manage and control assets dedicated, so far as beneficial use is concerned, for so-called benevolent, educational, or charitable purposes.

At the other end of the spectrum of interests is *beneficial use*. Organizations

---

italist mode of production and the relations corresponding to it to be the general basis of society, this subsumption is correct." See Marx, *Capital* III, 1864–1865, page 875. Thus from Marx's point of view, Walras committed a cardinal sin for he subsumed labor in a capitalist society as an owner of personal-capital yielding labor-services, thus positing three classes of capital: landed capital, personal capital, and capital proper. See Walras, *Elements of Pure Economics*, 1877, pages 213 ff.

holding property as trustee have ample powers of asset-management but have no valid claim to beneficial use of the property. That use is reserved for the stipulated beneficiaries of the trust. The holder of an easement giving access to a roadway has essentially a beneficial use of the facility but without power of control or sale except for the purpose of extinguishing the easement.[37] A typical leasehold interest has very restricted control and usually has no power of alienation but gives full possibility of beneficial use subject of course to some offsetting payment. A small class of leasehold interests, where vacant sites are leased for purposes of improvement and long-term use, was widely utilized in England up to the twentieth century. It surrendered all control of a site projected for a certain class of improvement for a long term set commonly at 100 years—subject, however, to making regular rental payments and also subject to the surrender of the properly maintained site to lessor at the termination of the lease.[38]

Beneficial use can be combined with control with an exclusion of rights of both alienability and disposition after death. That is the case of the lifetime estate managed by the beneficiary—subject, however, to the ultimate surveillance of a court or of some community agency to protect the interests of other beneficiary parties. Entailed property gave the holder both control and beneficial use but without the power of alienation. In primogeniture, limitation of alienability and disposition and partition was necessarily joined with fixing of lines of succession, usually running to firstborn male heirs or, lacking that, brothers or ascending male collaterals of remoter degree. The device has been used essentially to keep intact and undivided landed estates belonging to an aristocracy after the feudal mode of production and the assignable fief was dissolving. In various forms this scheme of landed property prevailed in Western Europe in the late medieval period. It somewhat weakened in the nineteenth century; in France, however, where the Great Revolution of the eighteenth century broke most of the estates, a new law of succession was established. The entailed estate with promogeniture persisted in Spain, Germany, England, and Scotland until the democratic changes associated with the twentieth century.[39]

As a form of property the entailed estate is a highly artificial creation because it denies the needs and interests of all children other than the main heir. It assumes that the pattern of land use can be frozen for long periods and hampers raising capital by borrowing to finance improvements. It guar-

[37]Noyes, *Institutions of Property*, 1936, pages 194 ff.
[38]Marx, *Capital* III, 1864–1865, pages 621, 775.
[39]For an excellent review of entailed property or its equivalent term, fideicommissum (a related device in Roman estate law), see *Encyclopedia of Social Sciences*, 1930–1934, vol. 5, pages 553 ff. and the reference provided therein.

antees that landed property will often be in the hands of persons with little interest or talent for its proper management. In Mill's words, its natural effect is "to make landlords a needy class."[40] Hence entailed property can only be a persistent form where it is developed by a class-conscious landed aristocracy with a privileged state position determined to keep the institution intact and ward off assailants from within and without who would seek to gain rights of disposition and alienability. The regime of monarchy and of a titled aristocracy with state privileges such as prevailed in England, Spain, Scotland, Germany, and central Europe during the nineteenth century provided a state and judicial culture where the property form of the entailed estate could survive though in attenuated form.[41] In the United States, France, and in most of the New World there was no role for a landed aristocracy and the state and judicial culture was hostile to its principles.[42]

A special form of a kind of modified entail is found in those Western nations, most prominently in the United States and Great Britain, that permit wealthy persons to set up endowments of wealth with indefinite duration with complete separation between control and beneficial use. These endowments must be dedicated to benevolent, educational, or religious uses under the control of a self-perpetuating body of trustees initially appointed by a donor to carry out a mission. The impulse to dedicate wealth to service of others in some socially appropriate form has been felt in nearly all societies. It accounts for the performance at private expense of public rites and games and the building of lavish monuments in the Graeco-Roman world of antiquity, for the continual impulse to set aside surpluses and windfall earnings to worshipful and prayerful purposes, and for the fact that through the ages the

[40]Mill, *Principles of Political Economy*, 1848, vol. 5, ch. 9, page 2.

[41]Thus the courts in England struggling against the device of entail tried to limit its scope to no more than lives in being at the time the entail was imposed plus 21 years in addition. That so-called ban on perpetuities passed into American common law of trusts. However, "by means of elaborate methods known to lawyers as contingent remainders, shifting and springing uses, executory devises and powers of appointment, it became possible so to settle property that it must for an indefinite period continue to be enjoyed by a series of limited owners, no one of whom had complete powers of alienation." See *Encyclopedia of Social Sciences*, 1930–1934, vol. 5, page 555. For the same, see Coleman, *Economy of England*, 1977, page 129; J. S. Mill, *Principles of Political Economy*, 1848, bk. 5, ch. 9, par. 3.

[42]American revolutionaries who triumphed in 1776–1783 were hostile to the principle of entailed property and primogeniture and one by one succeeded in outlawing the principle in their state law codes. Rhode Island was the latest state to so act. In the same spirit the Northwest Ordinance of 1785 provided for division of estates to children in equal parts, save only the rights of widows. See *Encyclopedia of Social Sciences*, 1930–1934, vol. 14, page 439; Beard and Beard, *Rise of American Civilization*, 1927, page 512. A clause of the Wisconsin Constitution adopted in 1848 prohibited all feudal tenures of land and declared that lands in the state must be held in allodial tenure, which bars entail (art. I, sec 14).

great churches of the world have tended to become wealthy from gifts offered them by wealthy believers seeking perhaps to propitiate for their sinful lives. These motives have in a world of high wealth taxation been reinforced in the mixed economies of our time, in which endowments are often invested in precisely the nest of securities that continue to yield control of corporate empires which might otherwise be undermined by heavy inheritance taxation.[43]

Even if control is not deferred or shared with others, it is rarely complete and without restriction. The state or an agency harbored or authorized by the state may impose a wide range of restrictions on the control and use of the objects and facilities subject to property claims. Thus even where parcels of agricultural land are privately possessed and worked by individual parties with substantial rights of hereditary transmission and beneficial use in other respects, the farming of the land can still be coordinated by the village or manorial community with regard to crops to be seeded, siting of house and garden plots, time of plowing and harvesting, and obligation to fence with hedges the fields used for common pasture.[44] The erection of buildings was already in the early Roman code of the Twelve Tables subject to specified setbacks from a lot line.[45] Since that early time restrictions on building have multiplied, so that in most settled places buildings must be erected only of certain materials, not exceeding a certain height, in a certain style, and for set purposes and uses. The right to burn rubbish or waste—once taken for

---

[43]There is abundant enumeration. We know, for example, that in the U.S. as of 1977–1978 there are some 19,000 small general-purpose foundations with assets under $1 million and that, exclusive of captive trusts allied to particular churches, colleges, or other benevolent organizations, there are 3138 trusts with assets over $1 million and commanding altogether $32.8 billion in assets. See U.S. Bureau of Census, *Statistical Abstract*, 1979, page 362. Compendious facts have been collected in annual reports of foundations and foundation-societies and they have been related to the entire world of philanthropy by F. G. Dickinson, *Philanthropy in the American Economy*, 1970. Policy discussion by economists may be found in Dickinson, *Philanthropy and Public Policy*, 1962. The British in the nineteenth century established an administrative agency with powers of control and supervision; this authority in the U.S. is exercised chiefly by the U.S. Department of Treasury. Endowed wealth in colleges was given a critical review by Adam Smith, *Wealth of Nations*, 1776, pages 717 f. Although many foundations have played a creative and imaginative role, many have remained in close association with the family interests of the donor and served presumably as a means for inheritance tax exemption. Experience with endowed benevolent trusts extends now for a thousand years or more but little overall monographic study is available on uses of benevolent endowed wealth, influence of aging, role of secular versus religious control, and in modern times tendencies with regard to control of corporate wealth by donor influences through trustee boards.

[44]Homans, *English Villagers*, 1941, ch. 5.

[45]*Corpus Juris Civilis*, A.D. 528–553, vol. 1, page 72.

granted as an inalienable privilege of the owner of a parcel of land—has been restricted and in many places prohibited.

The operation of vehicles on a road, the speed with which those vehicles may be driven, and the equipment with which such vehicles are operated are all now subject to widespread regulation. The medieval craftsman was bound by his guild and frequently by statutory authority to produce or do his work only with certain tools, on certain materials, in prescribed widths and measures, satisfying certain standards of thickness and texture. Labor legislation has grown in scope and volume in the Western world ever since British factory legislation of the mid-nineteenth century (to which reference was made in Chapter 6) put under growing restriction the operation of industrial plants regarding the hours worked, sanitary conditions, educational facilities for juvenile workmen, and safety conditions.

INHERITANCE, PARTIBLE OR CONCENTRATED

We have already indicated that, beside beneficial use and control, an important cluster of interests relating to economic assets, will be disposition on death. Patterns of disposition and procedures governing the same are protean. Nearly every society with a distinctive legal culture and an extended course of historical development will exhibit distinctive codes of custom and law regarding inheritance that enter into the institution of property. The hand of the state here is a telling one both for fiscal reasons—to seek a share in the assets of the departed—and to provide clearcut formulas of distribution that satisfy prevailing social norms, command assent, and keep the peace. Even in the juristic culture of eighteenth century England, with its veneration for the rights of property and for property owners, it was recognized that those rights terminated on death and that the validity of wills and testaments was wholly a "creature of civil right and law."[46] Similarly, in that erstwhile child of England, the republic of the United States, even in the height of its Gilded Age when the respect for property ownership was most compelling, the Supreme Court found that inheritance "was a creature of law and not a natural right" and hence was "subject of reasonable regulation and taxation."[47] The power of the state is, of course, limited by the large number of persons whose expectations of succession have already been formed and who would be outraged at any prejudicial change that touched them. Hence, even in economic systems with rapid patterns of change, the institution of property in its handling of succession and inheritance has an unusual inertial tendency.

[46]Ely, *Property and Contract,* 1914, vol. 1, page 416.
[47]Ely, *Property and Contract,* 1914, vol. 1, page 416.

Inheritance is primarily governed by law and custom—and, to a much lesser extent in most economic systems, by bequest. Therefore, we shall first examine patterns of intestate inheritance (without will) principally with regard chiefly to tendencies to disperse or concentrate ownership rights by providing for single or multiple heirs. We will note arrangements for sharing by female heirs and widows that also influence degree of dispersion and are tied in with the form of family and marriage institutionalized in the society. We shall then turn to give some attention to scope of bequest—unusually wide in some societies but very narrow in most.

The inheritance arrangement that appears to accomplish the fullest dispersion of ownership and works to cut down persistent patterns of concentration is unquestionably the Arab arrangement codified by Muhammed and tending to shape the property patterns of Islamic societies. He prescribed not only equal portions to all male children and, as we shall see, shares for daughters and some provision for widows but also a generous giving "unto parents and near relatives in kindness."[48] If there are no surviving children, parents, brothers, or sisters, then the heritage is dispersed among near and remote relatives in rough proportion to degree. One consequence of this was a distinct tendency for family accumulations to be dispersed and equalized among the lineage, thus impeding the accumulation of capital in rich merchant families.[49]

Similar to the Arab arrangement but with a lesser tendency to dispersion is that of most agricultural peoples among whom the heritage is equally divided among surviving heirs, usually males; failing these, among immediate surviving male kinsmen of first degree (father or brothers); and failing these, a more general distribution to all kinsmen of higher degrees usually proportioned to the degree or nearness of the relation. These schemes thus all contemplate *partible* inheritance and promote dispersal of property interests. Agricultural communities with partible inheritance tend in the later phases of their development to multiply the small parcels of land that will go into particular holdings. Where land holdings are not periodically equalized by reallocation, a large number of very small holdings will tend to accumulate. Partible inheritance cultures have apparently predominated among most settled agricultural peoples. Included are the Latin peoples of Italy in the early phase of their development before testamentary freedom, Russian and apparently Slavic peoples, Turkish peoples, the population of classical China,

---

[48]Koran, Surah 3, pars. 180, 240; Surah 4, pars. 7–12.

[49]Competent authorities are quite clear on this. See Ashtor, *Social and Economic History of the Near East*, 1976, page 113; Hodgson, *Venture of Islam*, vol. 1, 1974, page 343; vol. 2, pages 124, 389. So numerous were the heirs that apparently a "science of inheritance laws" developed involving in special cases algebra, and exponents especially for the recalculation of shares. See Ibn Khaldun, *Muqaddimab*, 1377, pages 346 f., 377 f.

early Greek societies, East African agricultural peoples, the Welsh, the Irish, some English districts, most early French provinces and all of France after the Revolution and under the Napoleonic Civil Code, and the advanced Amerindian villagers before the Spanish Conquest.[50]

The rule of impartible inheritance, apart from the special patterns of inheritance devised for a landed aristocracy and royalty, was followed or evolved among a smaller range of peoples. Patterns of impartible inheritance appear among Vedic Indians, many German-speaking peoples in or around what is now Germany, Scandinavian peoples, and the dominant agricultural communities of Norman England practicing open-field husbandry in what is sometimes labeled "Champion country."[51] Although inheritance here usually goes to the eldest son, a variant minority pattern of the youngest son is also known, and there are records of communities petitioning the manorial authority to change the rule of impartible descent from the eldest to the youngest or even to allow the holder of the land to arrange for his own successor among his sons regardless of their order.[52] The clear intent of impartible inheritance was to preserve farm holdings intact at a size sufficient to support a household and pay the rents and deliver the services that were called for. The switch from oldest to youngest son is thus explicable since the youngest might be the only son remaining in the household at the time of succession.

[50]James, *Land Tenure in Tanzania*, 1971, page 64; Shanin, *Peasants and Peasant Societies*, 1971, pages 34, 39, 172; Homans, *English Villagers*, 1941, pages 109–120; Malefakis, *Agrarian Reform and Peasant Revolution of Spain*, 1970, page 68 n. 5; Myers, *Chinese Peasant Economy*, 1970, pages 125 ff.; Belshaw, *A Village Economy*, 1967, pages 18 ff.; Lewis, *Life in a Mexican Village*, 1951, page 178; Goldthwaite, *Private Wealth in Renaissance Florence*, 1968, page 256; Aristotle, *Basic Works*, "Politics," bk. 2, ch. 6, 1265b4 (the Jowett translation speaks of property distribution among "citizens" which the Sinclair [Penguin] translation refers to as "children"). Russian princes and boyars, except the Grand Duchy of Moscow, "adhered to the rule of division among all sons in keeping with Russian private law." See Bendix, *Work and Authority*, 1956, page 120. That equal division of an estate among children was imposed by the French law of the Revolution and codified under Napoleon is well-known and will be further discussed. It is not as well-known that traditional pre-Revolutionary practice and law at least in many provinces of France involved equal shares among male sons of holdings on death. See Duby, *Rural Economy and Country Life*, 1962, pages 182, 198; *Early Growth of the European Economy*, 1973, pages 36, 79, 184 f.; Kemp, *Economic Forces in French History*, 1971, pages 88, 103, 236; Le Roy Ladurie, *Peasants of Languedoc*, 1966, pages 92, 95 ff., 111 f. The early Roman law of intestate succession prescribed partible inheritance with equal sharing of all immediate family heirs including the widow, unmarried daughters, and male children living in the household, all inheriting as tenants in common with rights of partition if requested. See *Corpus Juris Civilis*, A.D. 528–553, vol. 1, pages 67, 150 ff.

[51]Homans, *English Villagers*, 1941, ch. 9, "Impartible Inheritance of Land," especially page 127. The Laws of Manu in ancient India specify that the legacy of the parents is dividable only with the permission of the eldest son, though other sources say that division can be arranged by family members during the lifetime of the parents but then the eldest son "gets more" and the youngest son less. See Krader, *Asiatic Modes of Production*, 1975, pages 363 f.

[52]Homans, *English Villagers*, 1941, pages 113 f.

Clearly also, impartible inheritance tends to generate a stream of young male migrants set adrift or apprenticed to a nearby town.

A mixed pattern of inheritance sharing characteristics of the partible and impartible is found among the Japanese and ancient Israelites. The Japanese pattern was very close to the impartible since the main family holding with its choice fields, dwellings, graves, and plaques was left intact together with the important post of "headship" that devolved upon a single heir except when a bona fide will or testament otherwise prescribed. In the latter case only a small fraction of the holding would be devolved upon a "branch" family with a fraction in terms of acreage of one-quarter down to a one-tenth and even less, while livestock and bigger pieces of equipment were as a rule retained in the main establishment.[53] The ancient Israelite pattern was more of a compromise between the two types because it involved a double portion for the eldest son with an abridged portion for the youngest son.[54]

In only a few of the historical economic systems with which we are concerned in this work did rules of inheritance applicable to intestate succession completely control inheritance. These rules left some room for bequests by will. Athenians under Solon introduced testamentary freedom but only with no children.[55] The earliest full regime of testamentary freedom is found in ancient Rome, where rights of testamentary disposition quickly evolved in the young Republic. Wills with their surprises were regularly expected of large property holders. An elaborate code of law necessarily developed regulating the formalities by way of witnesses and signatures required for validity, role of the estate executor (in Latin designated the heir), grounds for rendering provisions of a will invalid, special provisions regarding wills of soldiers, and the like.[56] The English followed the Roman practice, and the Americans followed the English practice. In the three countries the act of opening and reading the will or testament of a wealthy person just deceased aroused considerable public interest precisely because of broad testamentary freedom.[57] Elsewhere only a limited range of testamentary freedom has been

---

[53] See T. C. Smith, *Agrarian Origins of Modern Japan,* 1959, pages 37 ff.

[54] The earliest tradition of Israel seemed to call for equal division among sons. Hence Sarah made Abraham send away the son of Hagar so that he "shall not be heir with my son Isaac." See Gen. 21:10. But the later Deuteronomy expressly called for absolute impartiality among sons and a double portion, where there was more than one son, for the eldest, giving him two-thirds with two sons, one-half with three sons, etc. Deut. 21:17. And that rule was carried out in later Judaism. See Goitein, *Mediterranean Society,* 1967–1971, vol. 2, page 399.

[55] Plutarch, *Lives,* "Solon," par. 21 (page 110 of cited edition).

[56] See Radin, *Handbook of Roman Law,* 1927, chs. 22–25.

[57] Because of the element of suspense and the revelation of character both of the will-deviser and interested potential inheritors, the making and reading of wills often became a favorite climactic of novels. See many of Balzac's novels and the striking climax scene in George Eliot's *Middlemarch.*

permitted. In Spain, for example, a third of the estate may be given as a bequest.[58] The French under the Code Napoleon mathematized it more carefully. Bequest is allowed equal to the share of half of the estate if there is only one child inheriting, of one-third of the estate if there are two children inheriting, and so on.[59]

Treatment of unmarried daughters and widows is an important but somewhat obscure feature of the institution. The Roman rule for intestate disposition testified to their respect for women for the unmarried daughters and widow received a full portion along with the sons.[60] The Vedic Indian formula respected the rights of unmarried daughters.[61] Islam allowed daughters to share in estates but at a half-rate compared to men, and widows could not be turned away without provisions for a year.[62] The inheritance code that grew out of the French Revolution prescribed equal shares for all children, whether male or female, married or unmarried. Probably most of the arrangement for widows in most marriage systems was worked out in the wedding ceremony and the premarriage settlement, in which what in old English texts were called rights of "dower" or "free bench" were tied with the marriage along with the contribution of goods or lands the would-be wife brought to the marriage.[63] In English law the terms of a marriage settlement were governing if in conflict with the terms of a will. In that sense the law of marriage settlement was a significant part of the law of inheritance. In the same way the apparent neglect in the inheritance code of many peoples as to the interests of daughters in the inheritance of fathers is explained because it was the duty of inheriting brothers to provide unmarried sisters with a

[58]Malefakis, *Agrarian Reform and Peasant Revolution*, 1970, page 68, n. 5.

[59]*Encyclopedia of Social Sciences*, 1930–1934, vol. 14, page 440.

[60]*Corpus Juris Civilis*, A.D. 528–553, vol. 1, pages 66, 150 ff.

[61]Krader, *Asiatic Modes of Production*, 1975, pages 363 f.

[62]Muhammed was very clear. Husbands were adjured to give wives the "free gift of their marriage portions", were to give "provision for the year without turning them out" otherwise they shared at a half-rate with male heirs. See the Koran, Surah 2, par. 240; Surah 4, pars. 7–11.

[63]These arrangements for thirteenth century English villagers were carefully worked out by Homans, *English Villagers*, 1941, chs. 12, 13, "Trothplight and Wedding," and "Free Bench, Curtsy and Wardship." For latter-day Jewish communities living under the rabbinic (Talmud) code, an important part of marriage was the written document embodying the wife's marriage settlement; it spelled out what she was entitled to receive in event either of divorce or death of her husband. *Mishna*, A.D. 200, 3rd div. "Nashim" (Women), especially "Ketuboth" (Marriage Deeds) pages 245–264. The rules of Mishna were variously elaborated in the Babylonian Talmud and carried out in Jewish communities until modern times. A Jewish bride from an Orthodox home until recently was given a Ketuboth prior to marriage (though this instrument no longer governs inheritance by the wife, at least in most Western states). Goitein surveys these arrangements at length in *Mediterranean Society*, 1967–1971, vol. 2 and at length in vol. 3, 1978.

suitable dowry, arranging a sufficiency of goods or lands for their marriage settlement. The institution of property is in that respect closely linked with the institution of marriage and the family, which themselves are central to the social order.

RECOGNITION

To be of use, property interests need to be *recognized* by persons who will be touched by the interest or concerned by it. The mere assertion of a property interest does not of itself activate the interest. *Your* belief that your property interest is valid must be complemented or mirrored by the same belief held by relevant *others*. This reciprocal recognition is essential for neighbors who live near the site or sites where a property interest may be housed or domiciled or to business firms that supply provisions or materials which are incorporated into the assets associated with the property interest. If the interest is an incorporeal claim arising out of an obligation or contract, then of course the most important relevant others will be the obligee or debtor. Beyond these persons there will be a small universe of local officials, including policemen or constables keeping some kind of public order and local magistrates who have authority to deal with controversies. Mercantile interests are often embodied in a special community of merchants and traders organized in some local guild, chamber, or fraternity—and *their* belief as to the validity of the interest will be critical. For even if that association is not the ruling power in the society, it will at any rate have direct access to high authorities, so it often is allowed to settle claims arising in its midst.

To obtain recognition under challenge, it is particularly useful that proper written records be maintained, that transactions be so arranged that they are properly witnessed, and that important contracts be inscribed and kept in public records. To eliminate any confusion about sale transactions in a broad class of saleable objects, early Roman law prescribed that these transactions be witnessed by five Roman citizens and that the purchase money be then and there weighed on scales.[64] Partnership or investment contracts in the growing world of medieval commerce and trade were usually written in front of witnesses by professional notaries and copies were kept in public records. To facilitate identification of ownership claims, English law early in its course required that contracts to buy and sell real estate must be in writing, in proper form, witnessed and at a later stage abstracted in a public record. Although such records do not themselves produce recognition, they facilitate making claims and hence give assurance that claims will be respected. Among most Germanic peoples the medieval manor had its institution of hall-mote, in

[64]*Corpus Juris Civilis*, A.D. 528–553, vol. 1, page 98.

which at least twice a year all adult men of the manorial community—including villeins, lord, and freemen—assembled in the great hall and juries were impaneled to hear suits of trespasses, grievances about land use, and violation of customary order. Records were kept in what the historians now call "court rolls"—long strips of parchment, less than a foot wide, many of them surviving to this day. The outcome of many manorial suits was determined by search of the records for what was "customary" practice. For the same reason medieval peasant rebellions often targeted on seizing and burning court rolls because "in them was evidence of their bondage."[65]

PROTECTION OF INTERESTS

An interest to an economic asset will not be realizable if it is not reciprocally recognized. But recognition alone will not avail unless facilities for compulsory inquiry and adjudication are available so that, if necessary, the interest can be protected by established authority. The authority may be a meeting of clan elders or a local priest, chief, or ruler. Or it may involve the right to initiate an action or suit at law against a fellow citizen, and to summon adversary parties and witnesses before a hearing by the magistrate. Heading up the Twelve Tables of Roman law was the statute that "when anyone summons another before the tribunal of a judge, the latter must, without hesitation, immediately appear." If he failed to respond to the summons, specific procedures were laid down including arrest or conveyance on an animal or covered litter. Both parties were to state their case and on that same day the magistrate would either make a decision or collect sureties or pledges and determine that a more proper trial should take place before a specially appointed judge.[66] Response to the summons was not subject to argument and much of the ritual of complaint and response by defendant was intended to assert the power of law over controversies.

If a Roman citizen had a property interest with reasonably good evidence and witnesses to back it up, he could in most of the Republic and during the best years of the Empire feel quite certain that by invoking legal remedies his interest was protectible. In the merchant communities of the medieval period, especially in the wholly independent mercantile Italian republics or wherever a ruling monarch, as in England, had endowed a city with power to hold court over its citizens, controversies between merchants about property rights could be brought before magistrates with every presumption that

[65]Homans, *English Villagers*, 1941, "The Hallmote," pages 309–317.

[66]*Corpus Juris Civilis*, A.D. 528–553, vol. 1, pages 57 f.; Jolocwicz and Nichols, *Roman Law*, 1932, page 176.

rights of hearing and remedies were available to protect any valid interest. But of course where parties to a controversy had standing in different jurisdictions or states, remedial powers of local magistrates might not be adequate. The canon law of the Church would be applicable in territories controlled by the Church or if a cleric was a party.[67] As the bounds of the national state widened, as merchant law became applied internationally, and especially as imperial sway was developed providing for special avenues of conflict resolution, conflict of jurisdiction was less of an impedance to providing protection for property interests. However, the mere process of appellate procedure in federal states with a dual judicial system, like the United States, has put property rights of economically weak parties in jeopardy. And since higher courts do not always clearly resolve matters brought before them, a property interest could be significantly weakened by interminable delays. Weaker parties could not afford to keep issues in suspense for long periods of time. This enabled economically strong parties—such as the emergent monopolistic corporations in the later decades of the nineteenth century—to work their will and virtually defy legislation by their power to utilize an overrefined judicial system permeated with their influence.[68]

A unified court system with ready access and higher tribunals for appeal only constitutes the formal basis of the expectation that property interests could be protected in case of legal controversy. Equally important is the principle of *rational public jurisprudence*—i.e., that judicial decisions should be accompanied by a written and public statement of justification with respect for precedent so that the implications of a decision could be taken into account by students of law and later by jurists or higher tribunals. This process in turn entails development of a legal profession with centers for teaching law and housing juristic literature, in which practitioner, lawmaker, and judge are all at home. On its formal side this centralization emerged first among later

[67]A haberdasher from southern France seeking to purchase some goods from a merchant in Nice agreed in the event of a lawsuit over the contract to submit to the jurisdiction of the Chamber of Accounts of Aix (a royal court); the Royal court of the Chatelet of Paris; a municipal court in his own town; a merchant court in Marseille; the court of the Pope and the Apostolic Chamber; and the court of the ducal city of Nice. See Tigar and Levy, *Law and the Rise of Capitalism*, 1977, pages 9 f.

[68]This is clearly shown in the extended efforts to check monopoly by various parties: capitalists squeezed out of the petroleum business by unfair competitive tactics, state governments seeking to outlaw monopoly or contracts in restraint of trade (such as the trust agreement among 41 refining and pipeline companies and marketing organizations, which joined together in the initial Standard Oil Trust) or the fledgling Interstate Commerce Commission seeking vainly to enforce nondiscriminatory railroad tariffs and access to rail transportation by giant monopolists and their struggling competitors. These efforts failed partly because the governing statutes were loose, and partly because monopoly power could indulge long delays in court proceedings believing time was on their side.

Romans, among whom an extensive legal literature and juridical public opinion became widely developed.[69]

Modes of production like the capitalist or corporate require the far-reaching cooperation by long-term contract of innumerable suppliers of loanable or investable capital or of land resources. Relations of indebtedness invariably permeate the economy in a network of credit and debt. Therefore, to carry on business operations according to prudent expectations it may be of critical importance to count on a rational system regarding legal access, procedures, and substantive law that is not subject to frequent upsets or random change.

Ordering of Interests

The final component of the institution of property involves the *ordering* of interests to minimize conflict, so that norms cherished by the community or society are preserved and that loyalty to the legal order is not undermined. Because the interests in economic assets by individuals and groups inevitably

---

[69]In this procedural sense Max Weber declared that "the rational law of the modern occidental state, on the basis of which the trained official renders his decisions, arose on its formal side, though not as to its content, out of Roman Law." See Weber, *General Economic History*, 1923, page 339. This applied especially to the literature of jurisprudence, which was revived in medieval Europe by the 10th century, and to the emergence in Italy of the profession of "notaries"—who, Weber noted, together with the universities "have on their conscience the revival of Roman Law" (page 340). On this revival, see the interesting treatment by Tigar and Levy, *Law and the Rise of Capitalism*, 1977, pages 10 ff.; and the fuller treatment in Weber, *Economy and Society*, 1921, vol. 2, "Sociology of Law," pages 852 ff. So far as substantive interests go, bourgeois groups "were much better served by the institutions of the medieval law merchant and the urban real estate law" (page 853). "It was only the general formal qualities of Roman law which, with the inevitable growth of the practice of law as a profession, brought it to supremacy. . . . A very important factor in this respect was the formalistic training of the lawyers, on whom the princes were as dependent as their officials, and which was largely responsible for the fact that in the West the administration of justice acquired the juristically formal character which is peculiar to it in contrast to most other systems of patrimonial administration of justice. . . . The reception of Roman law created a new stratum of legal *honoratiores*, the legal scholars who, on the basis of an education in legal literature, had graduated from a university with a doctor's diploma" (page 853). The high honor accorded the legal profession is indicated by the treatment as legally valid of written legal opinions of the more outstanding or reputable jurists and attorneys when these opinions (Responsa Prudentum) were published, a treatment begun by Augustus and continued by his successors. See *Corpus Juris Civilis*, A.D. 528–553, vol. 2, pages 221 f. For a detailed recitation of legal science during the early Empire, see Jolowicz and Nichol, *Roman Law*, 1932, ch. 22, pages 374–394, ch. 27, pages 451–460. In the later Empire, the *responsa prudentum* ceased to be "a living source of law" (page 451) and with the shift of the imperial center to Constantinople, interest in law receded and theology became more important (pages 451 f.).

come into conflict, the resulting controversies appear before the community's magistrates, lawmakers, or judges for adjudication. If naked class interests of a particular class dominate the entire state, permitting this class to ride rough-shod over other groups, the ordering will tend to reinforce class domination, privilege, and control over economic assets and the underlying population. But such naked and complete class rule is not the invariable case. The dominant class will usually need the support of other classes, whether emergent or declining, and if this class wishes to inspire not only obedience but assent and some measure of loyalty, it must then show some respect for the needs and concerns of others whose function in the state might be to grow food, to provide soldiers, to pay taxes, or to supply needed services and provisions.

Ordering is achieved in two ways: (1) by applying old rules to new cases of controversy and thus, piecemeal, making new law; or (2) by promulgation of a new rule or law, usually alone but sometimes in the context of a general codification.

It is not possible to apply a standing rule, even if very tightly drawn, to specific cases without making judgments that amplify the rule or turn it in one direction or another, if only by widening or narrowing the meaning of the terms in which the rule is expressed. The scope of judicial interpretation is widened by all rules that predicate a quality or condition described by a general perjorative term—such as injury, hurt, discrimination, nuisance, defamation, and abuse. The concrete content of such words has to be filled by the magistrate or court in each specific case in a manner believed appropriate and perhaps consistent with previous recorded decisions that catch his attention and are believed to be relevant. Early Roman law was a model of tight, even curt drafting. Yet many of its provisions made such predications. A law specified a minor fine for a not "serious injury" caused another person. Another law provided the death penalty for "public abuse" of another person emitted "in a loud voice" or expressed in a poem "for the purpose of insulting him or rendering him infamous."[70]

Accordingly, virtually the entire American law of tort deals with injuries or hurts inflicted by one or more person on others or rules which hinge on establishing intent or purpose where latitude for construction or interpretation is self-evident. The vagaries of judicial interpretation made possible are indicated by the history of even such an instrument held in high reverence as the United States Constitution. Amendments to the Constitution, for example, limit the power of the Congress to do a number of things described in vague words ("free exercise of religion," "peaceably to assemble," "unreasonable searches and seizures," "due process of law" or "just compensation," "excessive bail," "cruel and unusual punishments"). An even wider

---

[70]*Corpus Juris Civilis*, A.D. 528–553, vol. 1, page 70 (Table 7, laws 6, 7).

scope for meandering is exhibited in the interpretation of legal norms by rabbinic scholars who had the deepest respect for the integrity of those norms and the need to hold rigorously to their true meaning (the Talmud). That is why rules originating in one epoch can by gradual interpretation under changing conditions be transmuted into norms of another character and scope.

Interpretations of the written law become strained and divergent when changed conditions and perhaps an altered consciousness have emerged, or a new class demands recognition, or a new ruler or leader wishes to memorialize his rule perhaps at the instigation of a creative advisor. Then the making of law by judicial interpretation will be accompanied and shifted in its course by new laws or edicts that may establish a new legal basis. Conscious and express lawmaking habitually indulged over a long period of time was a major achievement of the Roman state from its earliest days as a small Latin provincial power to its rise to Mediterranean empire. Although other societies knew changes in the law and the issuance of new laws, the building up of a more or less coherent body of legislation carried in the books of record and embodied in a working jurisprudence of the day was a unique achievement of the Roman polity for the ancient world.[71] In the medieval period this use of formal proclaimed law greatly declined because of the decline of literacy and a weak central state structure. For an extended period in England the central function of the king within Parliament was not allegedly to make laws but to apply old law as a court. A growing body of express law did cumulate and the habit of lawmaking to deal with new conditions gradually revived and helped in England as elsewhere to shape the changing institution of property.

The role of law regarding property is to permit this institution to function over a wide territory with reasonable uniformity of application according to norms or rules that from time to time are changed to suit new conditions and are gradually flexed by interpretation. In nearly all societies law performs this role with a conservative bias. As Harold Laski has correctly charged, the judicial mind "is largely engaged in the study of precedent"—which is to say,

---

[71]The Chinese polity in its classical imperial pre-Mongol period, had its codes of law (in the third century the published code ran to 60 volumes containing 126,300 characters). Western observers believe enforcement of this law had "an arbitrary character." In the eyes of the authorities "every accused person was assumed to be guilty." See Balazs, *Chinese Civilization and Bureaucracy*, 1932–1961, pages 17, 254. Weber flatly states that "rational and calculable administration and law enforcement did not exist" and that there was no official collection of precedents. Weber, *Religion of China*, 1916, pages 100 ff. A massive collection of case histories was compiled in the 1830s involving over 5000 cases which have been made the object of a careful study by American investigators. Bode and Morris, *Law in Imperial China*, 1967. They reached the "general conclusion that Ch'ing legal procedure was systematic [and] reasoned." See also Needham, *Science and Civilization in China*, 1954–1978, vol. 2, pages 204–215, 521–532 on the "legalist" philosophy and the history of law in Chinese civilization.

it looks to the past. "What it can do is most often set by the statutes of a preceding generation. Its chief exponents are, as a rule, men already well past middle age who come to positions of authority just when new wants they have not known are coming to be expressed."[72] The bar—the organized profession of practicing attorneys—can only make its living by serving the masters of the state or the rich and well-to-do, who have money to pay for legal services, and not the poor. If a property-owning class is actually leading a movement for political change with revolutionary ideas uppermost, the lawyers and jurists may then play a more radical role—as they did in the eighteenth century by making brave pronouncements on natural law, really revolutionary law.[73] But in settled times under-classes of unlettered men or women with little organization and few resources have very little influence and participation in legal process and jurisprudence, so that their interests tend to be neglected in the ordering process of the law. Under-classes will exercise influence only if by their assertive spirit, resolution, and bearing they instill respect for their rights and privileges. Often they must enforce that respect by withdrawal of cooperation, slowdown on the job, sabotage tactics, running away, or infliction of damage by incendiary actions—or, in the last resort, by insurrection. As class differentiation hardened in later Roman society, the tradition of equal treatment of Roman citizens under the law increasingly weakened. The legal status of free citizens in a low economic position—such as tenant farmers or craft workers—deteriorated, and a sharp contrast was drawn between the legal standing of the upper and lower classes. "Since the influence of rank was so potent in the litigants in the courts,

---

[72]Laski, *Grammar of Politics*, 1925, page 572.

[73]In his sociology of law Weber aptly characterized "the formal qualities of revolutionary law" as "natural law." Natural law which was the bourgeois creed in the seventeenth and eighteenth centuries "has been the specific form of legitimacy of a revolutionarily created order . . . the method by which classes in revolt against the existing order have legitimatized their aspirations." See Weber, *Economy and Society*, 1921, page 867. He correctly points out "the rise of socialism at first meant the growing dominance of substantive natural law doctrines in the minds of the masses and . . . the intelligentsia" (page 873). The prominent role played by lawyers and juridical thinking in the American and French revolutions of the 18th century has been noted by many observers. Edmund Burke noted that the "intractable spirit" of the rebellious North American colonies was in part due to the widespread study of law with a legal profession "numerous and powerful." See Burke, *Speeches and Letters*, 1774–1781, pages 94 f. When Burke discovered that the bulk of the elected members of the French States-General in 1789 were composed of lawyers and not the "leading advocates" or "renowned professors" but the "inferior unlearned . . . merely instrumental members of the profession . . . obscure provincial advocates, stewards of petty local jurisdictions, country attorneys," he wrote, he "saw distinctly and very nearly as it happened, all that was to follow." See Burke, *Reflections on the French Revolution*, 1790–1791, pages 40 f. August Comte also gave somewhat later a pinched interpretation of the role of lawyers in the French Revolutionary period. See Comte, *Positive Philosophy of August Comte*, 1830–1842, vol. 2, pages 180 f.

humble litigants naturally sought the patronage of a great man, transferring to him the nominal ownership of their property, if their title was disputed, so that the defence could be conducted in his name."A sharp line became drawn between the upper and lower classes in all criminal proceedings, the *honestiores* and *humiliores*, with harsh penalties readily laid down for *humiliores* who were also liable to torture if the judge believed testimony offered was inaccurate or unreliable.[74]

SIGNIFICANCE OF PROPERTY FOR ECONOMIC SYSTEMS

The institution of property is central to economic systems if only because each mode of production can only be carried on with a suitable form of property. The village community in its stricter form calls for common property in farmland and associated pastures and woodlands used by the village. Though land is divided into parcels for individual cultivation and harvesting, with tools, plows, harvest, and livestock usually treated as private property, the land itself will not be regarded as appropriable and as subject to individual control. Generally, land will be allocated by village elders or chiefs or clan leaders according to need. Individual parcels often tend to adhere to particular families but changes in parcel holdings sometimes may be induced by "gifts."[75] Quite clearly this common land tenure enhances the solidarity of the community and slows down tendencies to dissolution by internal differentiation— some people getting richer and some poorer.

But there are decided drawbacks to this communal property system. Since a person cannot count on using the same land for a long period of time and on being rewarded for special efforts to improve the land, the motive for improvement is consequently reduced. Thus commonage freezes farm husbandry in a fixed pattern by impeding individual innovation in methods of cropping, and it reduces incentives to building up soil fertility by applying fertilizers, by ditching or draining, by changing crop rotations, by planting tree crops, by interplanting or by other means that take effect over much time. Where scope for innovation is limited and the need for solidarity is great, the village community will hold its own for many years. But it tends to become untenable in a society in which attitudes of individual enterprise are widespread, the solidarity of the family and village group are being un-

[74]Jones, *Later Roman Empire*, 1966, vol. 1, pages 503–519 f.

[75]On the role of gift transfers associated with land allocations, see some treatment in Gottlieb, "Extent and Character of Differentiation in Tanzanian Agricultural and Rural Society" (page 253, n. 20).

dermined, and family ties are weakened.[76] The institution of property not only links the mode of production to the state and to the economic system; it links all three to culture—which is the totality of knowledge, rites, practices, beliefs, and ideals ambient in the society.

The relationship between the capitalist mode of production and the institution of property is also mutually interwoven and reinforcing. This mode calls for far more than mere private property in the means of production, in purchased supplies and raw materials or component parts, and in finished product—with freedom to market the product at will and in accordance with terms that may be agreed between buyer and seller. There must also be protection of lease agreements because frequently the producing capitalist will not own all the means of production but will lease or borrow some, especially land or mineral or timber rights, from landlords, bankers, or merchants. Transactions involving loan capital must be protected as a special form of property with recognition of the need to pay interest, however disguised, on money loans.

The ready use of loan capital at remunerative rates enables it to be shifted between financial or trading centers or firms as business needs indicate, and it facilitates the use of capital where it can be most productively employed. Critical in this connection was the release of a money debt from the general form of a personal obligation to named parties, thereby permitting ready transfer or sale by endorsement.[77] Producing capitalists will often merge their capital in single enterprises managed with their joint skills and talents, so that a special form of property in partnership must be developed. Because this can encourage the emergence of younger or newer capitalists with much potential ability but little capital, it is a way to provide for a continuity of individual enterprises beyond the life cycle of the dominant capitalist personality involved.

Finally, the capitalist mode of production requires that a special sanctity be given in law to the wage relationship (including the authority of the employer to direct and control the labor of the hired worker) and to the emergent flow of profits which, because they may be long delayed or may only emerge near the end of the enterprise, need special protection as a form of property rights. Thus the form of property and contract required for the capitalist mode of production to develop is both complex and diversified, involving a host of relationships with suppliers, landlords, bankers, laborers, customers, management, and fellow capitalists. The mode of production may,

[76]Tendencies to disintegration of Russian communal land tenure were carefully noted in investigations in pre-1914 Russian agrarian problems.

[77]Development of the "bearer" bond and ready alienability of debt was traced by Sombart to Jewish influences. See Sombart, *The Jews and Modern Capitalism*, 1911, pages 91 f.

of course, spring up with a very restricted form of property derived from or adapted to other modes of production. But the capitalist mode can develop in depth and can unfold with greater productive power and develop its full genius only if the institution of property is adapted in large part to its needs.

The form of the institution of property adapted to a given mode of production will not necessarily be unfit for service, with or without minor modifications, in other modes. Thus the forms of property adapted to the needs of the direct commodity mode are nearly all of them quite suitable for use in the capitalist mode because both modes share the categories of market, price, and exchange; also, both call for private property in means of production and product. The direct commodity mode even experiences elementary forms of loan and lease agreements in use of land and loan capital and in incipient form it experiences the form of hired labor, though this is usually assimilated to household help or apprenticeship. But the capitalist mode of production needs to cut down drastically impediments to use of loan capital at remunerative interest rates. The form of property in craft partnership—whether in the Moslem, Roman, or early medieval urban communities—needed further development to suit the needs of capitalist partnership property. And because interfinancial developments through a network of business credit envelops any capitalist mode of production, a formal law of bankruptcy was needed to cut the burden of debt and to prevent the total destruction of the economic assets embodied in the skill and energy of a bankrupt capitalist.

Between the forms of property of the capitalist and corporate modes there is a similar organic relationship. The first form of the public corporation arising within the capitalist mode involved a means by which an association of capitalists, with unlimited liability for its debts, could develop a formal structure of government with limited powers, and operating in a well-defined field by a charter bearing state approval.[78] Individual investing capitalists still had their main focus of property in the business itself and not in their securities.

Gradually, as the corporation grew in size and stockholders multiplied and diversified their portfolios, a cleft developed between control groups and the investor. Powers of control were augmented by a gradual evolution that gave control groups more freedom to innovate, to dilute investor equities, to divert earnings into preferred channels, to invest in other corporations, and to de-

---

[78]Limited liability for stockholders was a privilege of some 18th century English charters but was rarely found in American corporate charters. Courts generally applied the traditional rule that if the assets of the corporate purse were insufficient, funds of associated stockholders were liable for assessment. See Handlin and Handlin, "American Business Corporation," 1953, pages 111–118.

velop an intricate network of corporate subsidiaries functioning without any review or even possibility of control by stockholders. Government intervention established new rules of corporation accounting, disclosure, and elections. And nearly everywhere in the Western world where the quasi-public corporation has been established, a partial socialization of the fruits of the enterprise has been achieved by corporate income taxation. The final outcome is that the quasi-public corporation is a more or less permanent autonomous quasi-public body under control of a self-perpetuating body of oligarchs held under close surveillance by family dynastic foundations and trusts, by major investment banking oligarchies, by financial institutions that have acquired substantial voting power of corporate stocks, by sundry individual buccaneering capitalists.

Perhaps the reciprocal influence of modes of production and patterns of inheritance woven into the institution of property are the clearest way property affects economic systems. The well-being and relative position of peasant proprietors, the backbone of the direct commodity mode, is critically associated with inheritance patterns. Partible inheritance has a potent double-acting effect. It tends to multiply tiny farm properties thus pauperizing a substantial fraction of peasant proprietors but also giving a strong stimulus to direct accumulation in order to round out the landholding to a more suitable size. Means of accumulation may be found by sending children to labor for wages in near-by estates or available towns.[79] Partible inheritance is continually working at the other end to subdivide richer peasant or gentry properties because precisely in these strata will tendencies to larger family size flourish, especially in countries like China where until the socialist revolution plural marriage was available for those able to afford the luxury.[80] The threat

[79]This frequently occurred in the sample of families studied over three generations in representative villages of two districts of China over the period 1890–1940. See Myers, *The Chinese Peasant Economy*, 1970, pages 159–160. "When a son is born to a poor family, he is not looked upon as someone who will further divide the family's land but as someone who will add to it" simply by going out to work without supporting a wife until the extra cash permits the purchase of a little bit of land.

[80]The land inheritance system "made it impossible for large farms to remain extant for more than 1 or 2 generations." The progeny of a "successful and big landowner become small holders" fairly quickly. See Myers, *Chinese Peasant Economy*, 1970, pages 162 f. That tendency was actually traced out for a large number of well-to-do landowners. Another local survey reported: "the big landholder will raise more children, consequently the size of their holding will be reduced within a few generations." See Fei Hsiao-Tung, *Peasant Life in China*, 1947–1948, page 196. The influence of plural marriage is sometimes underscored in English commentaries because second and third wives are often called concubines. "Little wives" would be a more suitable term. A monograph on comparative economic systems in preparation by the present author contains a case study on Tang China which traces out the roots of plural marriage, the actual character of these additional wives and the status of their offspring or of "adopted" children.

of multiple heirships induced among some Western peoples at least cautious attitudes toward child rearing and marital fertility.[81] Partible inheritance has been regarded by many competent observers of Chinese agricultural life as the ultimate reason why peasant proprietorship was able to survive over the centuries as the dominant agricultural mode of production, though it was continually destroying itself by subjection to usurers and had little ability to cope with severe crop failures or adverse weather conditions.[82]

With regard to capitalist enterprise in mercantile and industrial fields, any strict form of partible inheritance—as that institutionalized in France by the Great Revolution with the intention of undermining the surviving landed aristocracy by forcing partition of their land holdings—would seem to be damaging unless family reproduction is very much curtailed. Thus, all children in the post-Revolution French family had an imprescriptible right, valid except for some extreme disability, to an equal share in the estate after allowing for a modest set of bequests. Whichever survivor took over the business might inherit it stripped of liquid assets and burdened with indebtedness to fellow heirs; or, worse, he might be punished with a set of co-partners without talent or zest and a probable tendency toward sibling rivalries. The heirs' position could thereby be almost as bad as in the current practice of highly progressive inheritance taxation that virtually compels the liquidation of successful capitalist enterprise by sale to corporate combines in order to gain the liquidity to satisfy heirships and bequests as well as a heavy-handed estate tax. So careful and penetrating an observer as Alfred Marshall was convinced that the French pattern of equal partition in inheritance division "made for industrial quietism" because it "lessened the inclination . . . to get together expensive plant, since it was almost sure to be broken up at . . . death."[83] An equally damning indictment of the blighting effects of the opposite kind of inheritance pattern, that of primogeniture, on capitalist enterprise was that it burdened this enterprise in its later phases with "weak and stupid leadership" of "third-generation men."[84]

We thus conclude that inheritance arrangements—together with inheritance taxation—may have profound effects on the character of the economic

---

[81]That had noteworthily long been believed to be the principal explanation for the considerable drop in overall fertility and completed family size beginning early in the 19th century in France. See Spengler, *France Faces Depopulation*, 1938. An American researcher found similar tendencies operative in the American rural community in northern states between 1760 and 1870. See Schapiro, "A Land Availability Model of Fertility Changes," 1982, pages 577–610.

[82]Weber, *Religion of China*, 1916, page 83, n. 85; Kolb, *East Africa*, 1963, pages 113, 145; Moore, *Social Origins of Dictatorship*, 1966, page 170.

[83]Marshall, *Industry and Trade*, 1919, pages 113 f.

[84]Keynes, *Essays in Persuasion*, 1919–1931, page 327.

system, its growth dynamics, and the relative strength of the different production modes. We are still a long way from the position of certain strands of nineteenth century radical thought that the "abolition" of inheritance or its taxation at 100% rates could revolutionize the character of the economic system. Marx was quite correct in denying that. But neither can we accept his simplicistic generalization that "like all other civil legislation, the laws of inheritance, are not the cause but the effect, the juridical consequence of the existing economical organization of society."[85] It is striking that this flat generalization was made in view of the radically differing structures of "economical organization" in the field of agriculture in France, Switzerland, and England—partly due to different institutions of inheritance as fixed in the law of property in the three countries.

---

[85]This statement was the climax of Marx's report and speech recorded in the Minutes of the London Council of the First International in 1869 on the proposal of the Bakunin organization in Geneva to "abolish inheritance." Marx, *First International,* 1864–1872, pages 107–112.

9

The Economic System as a Whole

In the preceding chapters the essential principles and components of an economic system have been defined and elucidated. However, the interconnections between these principles and components have not been systematically spelled out, especially in an international context. It would thus be helpful to present a summary review of the theory of an economic system—showing how the whole fits together and applies to different kinds of societies with distinct sets of economic arrangements variously linked together in overarching multinational gestalts or orders. We will first seek to present (a) a summary view of an economic system for a more or less isolated society. We will then review three related questions: (b) how economic systems evolve or change over time; (c) how they are related to each other by international or interregional trade, capital and labor movements, and dependency relationships in larger multinational orders; and (d) how systems more or less unique may be grouped into broad classes or family types.

SUMMARY VIEW OF AN ECONOMIC SYSTEM

As defined in this work, an economic system for a more or less distinct society with given functional priorities is made up of a complex of modes of production functioning in various fields of production with resource allocation within and among modes coordinated by a combination of market methods, rationing, and planning. Associated with these modes is an institutional overlay made up of a given form of public economy, a scheme of state regulation of economic behavior, a set of revenue sources, a pattern of income redistribution, and two major economic institutions—property and money.[1] This

---

[1] I closed my 1952 paper, "Theory of an Economic System," with the following definition: "An ideal type-form resolvable into a family of hybrid stages and types of systems united more or less loosely in civilizational complexes and identified individually in terms of a more or less integrated pattern of functional priorities, ways and means and institutional Gestalt." See Gottlieb, "Theory of an Economic System," 1953, page 363.

institutional overlay is no mere adjunct or outgrowth upon the modes of production. Its integrating and coordinating function conditions and affects the operation of production modes, modifies the distribution of beneficial services and income, and shapes the course of economic development.

As is common in sociocultural systems, not all components of an economic system are equally important. The lines of causal interconnection are not one-way but interrelated and reciprocal. Thus the capitalist mode of production, once clearly in place in a given society, cannot function well except with an institution of property and with a set of functional priorities and modes of resource-allocation favorable to it. Likewise it is clear that establishing a frame of laws regarding property that gives security to capitalist earnings and min-imizes state interference with capitalist operations will tend to promote the growth of the capitalist mode. Yet the capitalist mode in the late medieval period grew and expanded in societies governed by noncapitalist elites prone to close and minute regulation of industry and trade. Nor will favorable in-stitutions or cultural climates necessarily induce the capitalist mode of pro-duction. In many phases of Roman history both the cultural milieu and institutions would seem to have favored the rise of capitalist production. The institution of property was clearly predisposing, and the propertied qualifi-cation to suffrage and to officeholding invested owners of capital with dom-inance in the political arena. The cultural values of the society were highly rational, and though slave labor obtained from military victories provided a competitive labor force, the tendency to emancipate was so widespread that a considerable scope would have been allowed for the hired worker for whom the "client" or "freedman" status would have been quite consistent with wage-earner relationships. Roman engineering in public works construction was quite skilled. Yet the capitalist mode of production advanced very slowly even in epochs when trade was nearly unrestricted and considerable territorial division of labor resulted over large territories reached by navigable water-ways—most significantly the Mediterranean, the Black and Aegean seas, and the Indian Ocean.

The defining features of an economic system have variable impacts on the structure of the system. Thus the public economy and its tax sources and scheme of redistribution may play a very important role in an economic system and clearly affect the mode of life of the society but may hardly have major impact on other features. The Roman economic system in the early Empire illustrates the point. Imposition of tribute on the conquered provinces and an extensive tax scheme generally provided the basis of support for a substantial redistribution of income that funded a mercenary army, a wasteful and luxury-mad pinnacle establishment with its palaces, temples, and extrav-agant displays, and the public feeding of a sizable urban lumpen-proletariat.

These characteristics were distinctive in the Roman economic system of the time—but did they have much impact on related features of the economic system?

Are all the features of an economic system necessarily bound together? Some scope for necessity is clearly to be found. Thus if in any system agriculture—which with food-producing technologies before 1800 was necessarily determinative of much of the social and political structure of the society— was organized along feudal, slaveholding, or landlord–tenant modes, necessarily the societies could not have functional priorities that favored economic progress and innovation by means of industrial development. Dominant classes generated by these agricultural modes and the governments or state systems they would sustain carried with them normative and value schemes that disparaged industrial effort or investment in resources for industry or commerce. In these societies the employments classed as worthy or honorable would involve ceremonial learning, exploit, or aggression; whereas commercial or industrial behavior would imply subservience or inherently unworthy or debasing submission. Of course industrial effort would be welcomed to obtain gold or silver, to build and operate navigable ships, or design and produce weapons and utensils. But practitioners of these crafts would not have high standing and gentlemen would not invest their resources in supporting activity with a view to industrial efficiency.[2]

The capitalist mode of production can come into existence in scattered fields, such as wholesale trade and navigation, banking, and mining. But it cannot become generalized and a dominant mode of production in the economy without predisposing institutions of property and money. The latter fosters a stable coinage in precious metals, ready access to the mint, the development of commercial banks, and the use of bank credit and clearing— helping to create a world market with ready facilities for payment. The institution of money brings into existence a mobile fund of liquid capital that can be shifted to support capitalist production according to need and can efficiently handle and negotiate payments between financial centers. Likewise the capitalist mode of production, which generates a hothouse pace of technological change, cannot coexist in a society with a scheme of functional priorities that does not lay considerable emphasis on efficiency and market forces as guides to the allocation of economic resources. These examples merely illustrate the diverse tie-ins found between the elements of an economic system.

---

[2]Veblen emphasized "that the concept of dignity, worth or honor as applied either to persons or conduct, is of first-rate consequence in the development of classes and class distinction." See Veblen, *Theory of the Leisure Class*, 1899, page 15.

But if there are constraints in the patterning of the elements of an economic system, so also is there a wide range of freedom. Thus the modes of production sets that can stably coexist for considerable periods within the same kind of economic system are exceptionally diverse. The capitalist mode of production on a restricted scale and in a very few fields is found in the earliest societies above the primitive and archaic: in many phases of Roman economic history, throughout the medieval world, and in Islam and classical China in such fields as farming estates, wholesale trade and shipping, tax collections, mining, and certain kinds of mills and craft enterprises calling for a larger labor force than a family or apprentices could readily provide. Closely associated with this mode is also the direct commodity producer in such economic activities as retail trade, petty finance, farming enterprises, fishing and various urban crafts involving work with metal, leather, and wood, products of stone, clay and glass, wineries, and beverage production. It is common in agriculture to find varied sets of agricultural modes coexisting with different combinations of plantation, village serfdom with varying degrees of subordinated labor, landlord–tenant farming, and capitalist estates with managed hired labor.

The two countries of Western Europe in the nineteenth century with similar bourgeois societies and the most closely related economic systems—France and England—had utterly different modes of production in agriculture. In France the petty proprietor predominated as a product in part of the French Revolution and of several generations of partition of landholdings among all children. In Great Britain, by contrast, the capitalist farmer rented land and hired labor to operate a farm on the basis of capitalist production. Going across the ocean to the then third largest bourgeois society in the Western world—the United States—two modes of production coexisted, though as fierce rivals in the development of available vacant land: the slave plantation, using black enslaved labor, and the independent farmer using primarily family labor. Even within the South there was diversity in the modes of agricultural production: small-scale peasant proprietorships, using primarily family labor but with some slave assistance, working usually together in the field, barn, or shop, competed with the plantation in bidding for farmland and use of productive resources.

We thus conclude that there are elements of determinateness which constrain the variation that may be found in the defining elements of an economic system but that there is also a surprising degree of freedom. Hence we are likely to find few economic systems contemporary over space presenting the same set of defining features or the same concrete kind of economic system. This in turn means that each distinctive society will in all likelihood be associated with a unique economic system.

HOW ECONOMIC SYSTEMS EVOLVE OR CHANGE OVER TIME

Since all elements of an economic system—modes of production, functional priorities, public economy and schemes of regulation and income redistribution, institutions of money and property, and modes of resource coordination—are products of historical evolution and are continually evolving, any given economic system will change as it advances through historic time. But rates of change over time vary widely. For some societies substantial change is marked only over millennia. For other societies one century may be a significant milestone. Where the pace of historic change as in the twentieth century has accelerated, one quarter-century to another may exhibit significant change.

Some of the modes of production under certain conditions metamorphose into related modes. Thus a setup in agriculture of petty proprietors with feasible sets of small landholdings often differentiates into larger and smaller proprietors—based partly on who can avoid a drought or pestilence that destroys herds, partly, where there is partible inheritance, on the number of surviving male children who may inherit rights to the land, partly on native ability and industry or capacity for hard work that bears fruit and generates a small surplus over the years. These surpluses in turn can be put to use in profitable mortgage-lending to neighbors who need to be staked for a season or to celebrate properly a wedding or pay back taxes, with failure to pay leading to forfeiture of the land pledged or other suitable assets.

The same tendency toward differentiation takes place among wholesale traders or merchants; some tend to be handicapped by mishap or accident while competitors grow in affluence with lucky merchandising strikes. Under conditions in which the volume of trade is increasing, the scope of trade is widening, or a taste for distant articles and goods is developing, differentiation usually works its way. Since it is easier for merchants to accumulate by way of profitable investment as well as usurious loan, the pace of differentiation in commerce is accordingly increased. Of course accumulations both in landed property or among town merchants can become a target for persecution or expropriation from a hostile regime. Large estates may be split up among many heirs or get cut down by bequests to favorite endowments and charities. Upper-class wealth is also readily squandered by "prodigals" or wasted in "misconduct," as Adam Smith noted two centuries ago.[3]

Metamorphosis may evolve a new mode or perhaps what can be regarded as a higher form of an older mode. It was in that way that Marx viewed the progression of the capitalist mode of production from its simplest form, that

---

[3]A. Smith, *Wealth of Nations*, 1776, pages 321 ff.

of the handicraft shop, enlarged to permit the simultaneous employment of many workmen under the mastership of one capital but using the traditional craft methods to produce the traditional craft product. That was, Marx believed, "both historically and logically the starting point of capitalist production."[4] Even in this simple form without alteration in the actual work process, significant economies were achieved in the common use of buildings, storehouses, and equipment that could be given more intensive use, reducing costs of operation per unit of production. Moreover, combined labor permitted many tasks to be carried through by coordinated efforts such as raising a heavy weight, turning a winch, or removing an obstacle. The mere social contact, Marx believed, begets an emulation and stimulation of the animal spirits that heighten the efficiency of labor. Cooperation, noted Marx, "ever constitutes the fundamental form of the capitalist mode of production." It was the "prevalent characteristic form . . . throughout the manufacturing period roughly speaking from the middle of the 16th to the last third of the 18th century" and it remains the characteristic form in those branches of production where "division of labor and machinery play but a subordinate part" even where "capital operates on a large scale."[5]

In the European context the manufacturing form was swiftly evolving. Increasingly each worker was confined to a related subset of the operations formerly carried on and for which he could be provided with specialized implements "giving to each special implement its full play only in the hands of a specific detail laborer." The use of machines, especially for "the first simple processes that have to be conducted on a very large scale and with the application of great force sprang up here and there"—as in paper manufacture the tearing up of rags, in metallurgy the pounding of ores, or in mining the pumping out of water. Thus in the early stage of the industrial revolution a higher form of the capitalist mode of production with greater productive power than simple cooperation was developed whereby the craft workman was stripped of his general skills and turned into a detailed operator carrying out only a given phase of the craft work and with a widened form of the division of labor within the enterprise.[6]

The third and, for Marx, final form of the capitalist mode of production developed with a prime mover that could exceed man's limited power of producing uniform continued motion, that was "entirely under man's control, that was mobile and a means of locomotion, that was urban and not, like the waterwheel, rural, that permitted production to be concentrated in towns instead of, like the waterwheels, being scattered up and down the

[4]Marx, *Capital* I, 1867, page 322.
[5]Marx, *Capital* I, 1867, pages 335 f.
[6]Marx, *Capital* I, 1867, pages 363 ff.

country, and that was of universal technical application."[7] With such a prime mover, which became available in the late eighteenth century with the perfection of Watt's second and so-called double-acting steam engine, it was possible to operate the machines, mills, and pumps that were becoming available or were being devised to supersede the workman who handles a single tool by a mechanism "operating with a number of similar tools and set in motion by a single motive power." Machines in turn could be connected together into a chain of machines of various kinds, with one supplementing the other. "As soon as a machine executes, without man's help, all the movements requisite to elaborate the raw material, needing only attendance from him, we have an automatic system of machinery and one that is susceptible of constant improvements in its details," turning into "a mechanical monster whose body fills whole factories and whose demon power at first veiled under the slow and measured motions of his giant limbs, at length breaks out into the fast and furious whirl of his countless working organs." This is the form of the capitalist mode of production embodied in "machinery and modern industry," for Marx the ultimate form of the mode.[8]

Another sequence by metamorphosis of forms of a given mode of production was traced by Marx out of the feudal mode in which labor service in kind on the manorial estate at various seasons of the year was gradually converted into rent-in-kind by phasing out the demesne estate converted into small farms with crop-sharing. Without any necessary lessening of the surplus product extracted from the producer, his burden in rendering that product was lessened by giving him greater freedom to plan his husbandry to avoid the frequent calls for labor service on the lord's estate or buildings at times when his own holdings called for work.[9] A further stage in the sequential development commutes rent-in-kind to money rent, from which it may then be converted—as in Russia and Japan—into state tax levies. The Russian levy was instituted at the time of serf liberation in the 1860s when peasant tax obligations for homestead grants were settled. Japanese feudal rent imposed by daimyo lords was converted into a state-assessed and -collected land tax in the Meiji Restoration. This tax provided some 80% of government revenues in the late nineteenth century.[10]

However, feudal rent in labor service after changing into rent-in-kind may not go the tax route. Money rent does not bind the husbandry of the pro-

[7] Marx, *Capital* I, 1867, page 377.

[8] Marx, *Capital* I, 1867, pages 376 ff.

[9] Marx, *Capital* III, 1864–1865, pages 790–796. See Lenin's interesting review of this sequential development in *Capitalism in Russia*, 1899, pages 174 ff.

[10] Liu and Fei, "Land Tax Burden in China," 1977, page 379. Moore, *Dictatorship and Democracy*, 1866, pages 270 f., 275 ff.

ducer to predetermined staples, and it allows the producer to make his payment with any portion of his product or of his assets which he finds convenient. It spares the rent receiver the onerous duty of counting out his collections-in-kind and of arranging for transportation and storage. Thus it is convenient for both parties. Commutation also enhances the incentive of the producer, who can benefit from improvements carried through in his husbandry or on his land because the rent need not grow, at least immediately, with the product or productivity of the holding. Thus commutation commonly increases the sense of personal independence and freedom of the producer. But it does impose upon the producer a fixed payment based upon both average prices for staple products and average yields, thus subjecting both producer and rent receiver to uncertainty because the tax may be onerous the year crops have been deficient, and receipts may be scanty with crop shortage. Where as in Japan and Russia, the commutation was of feudal payments converted into land taxes, and where places of collection may differ significantly from places of expenditure, regional arteries of transportation and a suitable division of labor must be evolved for commutation to be made effective. Marx believed that commutation to money rent presupposes "a considerable development of commerce, of urban industry, of commodity circulation in general."[11] Careful study, however, has disclosed that the process of commutation of service and product rents into money rent was not directly associated with commercial development, though obviously market processes and trade was a precondition for it.[12]

The key to commutation is the mutuality of advantage to tenant and landlord. The landlord could then afford to shift to hired labor or to lease demesne land to capitalist farmers who could organize more efficient production. The producers were willing to make sacrifices by way of onerous money payments to obtain freedom in their work and marketing. Marx rightly pointed out that this commutation to money rent is "nevertheless the final form and simultaneously the form of dissolution" of feudal rent imposed coercively.[13] For though unfree status may linger and though some of its special disabilities in peripheral matters may remain, in nearly everyplace where commutation occurs market forces grow stronger and rent payments are adjusted to condition of the land and its fertility and expected returns that it will yield. The final outcome need not be capitalist estate farming, which in its complete

[11]Marx, *Capital* III, 1864–1865, page 797.

[12]Dobb, who has gone over the issue carefully, states that "the connection" between the commuting of the seigniorial demesne for a money-rent or working it with hired labour and the growth of the market and money dealings is not "simple and direct." It was not areas close to London that in the 14th century witnessed commutation but more distant areas farthest from great markets. See Dobb, *Development of Capitalism*, 1947, pages 38 ff.

[13]*Capital* III, 1864–1865, page 798.

form with labor hired and land leased by capitalist farmers emerged only in Great Britain. Peasant proprietorship can also emerge or various kinds of landlord–tenant farming with either share-cropping or money rent as a mode of rent payment.

The pattern of the modes can thus change by metamorphosis of some modes into advanced forms or into other related modes. But the pattern of modes may also change by way of changes in the relative strength of the modes competing with each other for limited resources and markets. In the modern Western world there is ceaseless competition under way in many fields of service, industry, commerce, and professions and in some branches of agriculture between three distinctive primary modes of carrying on production: (1) small craft enterprises using family labor or partners; (2) capitalist production organized by owners of capital who assemble the other productive factors; and (3) corporate enterprise operating vast networks of bureaucratically managed establishments. This century in America has witnessed the virtual supersedure of the small retail merchant handling groceries in a small store operated by himself and family helpers by chains of large capitalist or corporate supermarkets operated impersonally with hired labor. The main focus of competition in the grocery trades is between the capitalist firms operating a limited set of supermarkets and great supermarket corporate chains. So too the small capitalist banker is being crowded out by the corporate chain, the small capitalist stock broker is crowded out by national brokerage syndicates, the capitalist hotel and the small locally operated motel is pushed to the wall by national corporate hotel and motel chains, and the independent capitalist newspaper is swallowed up by media corporate chains or networks.

Then again new products or the use of new materials may tend to shift the balance between modes. Thus the proliferation in the 20th century of durable household engineering products using either electricity or the internal-combustion engine have created a world of small-scale service callings in the form of repair shops and service dealers who by their expertise may keep alive the radios, TVs, appliances, stereos, typewriters, and automobiles abounding in local residences. This labor in repair and maintenance may actually come to outweigh the original labor of initial production generally carried on in a large corporate enterprise. By its nature this service work must be scattered in the housing communities of the nation and will often favor the direct commodity producer owning his own shop and equipment.

Other examples readily illustrate the theme of technological changes and improvements shifting the balance between modes of production. The inventions in the late eighteenth century of power spinning, carding, and weaving combined with the steam engine as a mobile source of power to give the large capitalist factory an enormous advantage in textile production over craft spinners, carders, and weavers. The invention later in the 19th century of the sewing machine played an equally revolutionary role in displacing the enormous mass of cottage industry and craft labor employed in the wearing apparel industry making straw hats and other millinery, shirts, corsets, dresses, gloves, suits, neckties, collars, coats, undergarments, etc. As Marx pointed out, the "revolution in the industrial methods which is the necessary result of the revolution in the instruments of production, is effected by a medley of transition forms." These forms vary, Marx found, "according to the extent to which the sewing machine has become prevalent in one branch of industry or another, to the time during which it has been in operation, to the previous condition of the workpeople, to the preponderance of manufacture, of hand-icrafts or of domestic industry." In dressmaking—e.g., where the labor was for the most part already organized, chiefly by simple cooperation—the sewing machine formed merely a new factor in that manufacturing industry. But in tailoring, shirtmaking, or shoemaking, all the forms are intermingled. Here the "factory system proper. There middlemen receive the raw material from the capitalist en chef and group around their sewing machines in chambers and garrets from 10 to 50 workwomen. Finally, as is always the case with machinery when not organized into a system, and when it can be used in dwarfish proportions, handicraftsmen and domestic workers, along with their families, or with a little extra labour from without, make use of their own sewing machines." The most prevalent system, Marx found, was the concentration by the capitalist in his factory of large numbers of these machines with distribution of the produce to domestic workers for further manipulation. This was favored by the rapid development of the sewing machine and its specialization for different uses and its adaptation to operation by steam power.[14]

For any mechanical product with many working parts, a similarly revolutionary technical change was the development of techniques and devices on metal-working machines that could fabricate parts sufficiently identical to be assembled without special fitting. The musket, devised for manufacture and assembly by Eli Whitney, was an early example of such an assembled product. In Marx's judgment the two essential conditions for this development were a "prime mover capable of exerting any amount of force and yet under perfect control," such as the steam engine, and secondly the "slide rest," a tool that was necessary to produce the shapes required in the detailed working of machines. This tool was soon made automatic and applied to tools other than the lathe, for which it was originally intended. "This mechanical ap-

---

[14]We draw from the memorable account in Marx, *Capital* I, 1867, ch. 15, sec. 8, "Revolution effected in Manufacture, Handicrafts and Domestic Industry by Modern Industry" subsec. e, pages 470–480.

pliance replaces, not some particular tool, but the hand itself, which produces a given form by holding and guiding the cutting tool along the iron or other material operated upon." The consequence of these two developments that applied steam power to guided metal-working machines made it possible, in Marx's epoch-making words, to "make machines by machines" and thus give to the capitalist mode of production in its "modern industry phase" "a fitting technical foundation" enabling this mode to "stand on its own feet."[15] Obviously this stance permitted that mode to spread to new branches of production or to give existing branches larger scope for operations.

Not all inventions, however, strengthen larger enterprise. For example, the development of the electric motor, which comes in a wide spectrum of sizes, combined with the centralized generation of electric power distributed over a wide area to make it possible for very small enterprises to have the same facility of powered prime movers as the large plant.

Change occurs not only within the mode of production and in the relations among modes, but also in all the other components of an economic system: functional priorities, modes of resource coordination, intensity and scope of state regulation, patterns of income redistribution achieved by the public economy, and the institutions of money and property. These relate to qualitative forces oriented to the cultural world and less amenable than modes of production to quantitative measurement. Generally speaking and for most societies, these more cultural components of an economic system change more slowly than the complex of the modes of production. In historic periods that have witnessed major changes in the forms or patterns of predominant modes, little change may be observed in the concurrent cultural components. Thus in the middle period of the Roman Republic, in the half-centuries before and after the Punic Wars that completed the Roman conquest of northern Africa and of major portions of Spain and Macedonia-Greece, there was considerable change in the modes with the major rises in the slave plantation, commercial trade, and merchant activity. There had to be some shift in the holding of property and income redistribution because large landed estates were derived mainly from use of public lands obtained through conquest, which also yielded by-products of looting and spoliation for soldiers but above all for officers, commanders, and governors. Yet the institutions of property, the scope for state regulation, the form of coined money made up of copper and silver coins, the functional priorities, and modes of resource coordination— all these seemed little affected.

As another example, during the nineteenth century the United States experienced a truly massive change in the order and makeup of the modes of production. The century was commenced with very little capitalist enterprise,

[15]Marx, *Capital* I, 1867, pages 384 f.

a few corporations chiefly in finance, a solid belt of plantation slavery in the South, and primary reliance on the direct commodity producer in agriculture, retail trade, much commodity production, and some transportation. The century ended with the slave plantation transformed into a hybrid landlord–tenant–peon mode, with massive capitalist production increasingly dominated by large monopoly corporate enterprise in railway transportation, banking, and heavy industry—and with petty bourgeois modes chiefly found in farming, retail trade, and local urban or rural services. Yet the century terminated with nearly the same set of functional priorities and the same heavy reliance on market forces with no central planning. Rationing and the public service were confined mostly to defense and elementary schooling. Our institution of property and money was nearly the same—except that there was one privately operated central bank in 1800 and in 1900 a set of New York City metropolitan banks covertly playing the central bank role. In 1900 the public economy and pattern for income redistribution relied as in 1800 upon indirect taxes and tariff import duties to provide federal public revenues.

But in later years the nonmodal components of the American economic system altered rapidly. In the 35 years between 1933 and 1968 in the United States revolutionary changes occurred in nearly all the nonmodal components. The level and intensity of state regulation of economic activity—now covering investment and security markets, wages and hours of work, agricultural production, banking and credit—greatly increased. The institution of money was dramatically changed when precious metals were substantially evacuated from coinage and paper currency in dollars became an internationally accepted money without any state-determined linkage to gold at home. The functional priorities were considerably modified to allow enhanced importance for conservation of the environment and better support for the underprivileged and poor. A beginning was made in peacetime central planning to set the framework and goals for the market economy. Finally, the massive rise of progressive income and inheritance taxation to nearly one-half of corporate net income, reaching the level of socialization, has provided the fiscal base for a scheme of income redistribution that has had far-reaching social effects. For payroll incomes a similar scheme of income redistribution has marked the Social Security system, which now draws in nearly 13.5% of payroll incomes redistributed nearly as much on the basis of need as of contribution.

For the Soviet Union it required only a decade—in the 1920s—to experience two sets of far-reaching changes in the institution of property and of money, in the pattern combination of central planning, markets, and rationing, and of functional priorities, with growth via industrialization becoming the dominant goal. The first set occurred with the shifts—guided by Lenin's New Economic Policy with its major emphasis on a unique combination of central planning and market forces—to a currency based on gold money and an institution of property that established access to open markets for Russia's urban craft enterprises, merchants, and peasant proprietors. At the end of the decade a revolutionary policy turnabout—inspired by Lenin's successor, Joseph Stalin, and the governing Russian Communist Party—created a manipulated paper currency with an inflationary bias, a nearly complete exclusion of open markets, widespread rationing guided by a universal form of central planning, and the virtual expropriation of the peasant farm properties grouped into state-managed and -controlled collective farms. These farms embodied a hybrid form of a producer cooperative joined with a state plantation.

For these two countries in this century—the United States and the Soviet Union—the pace of change in the nonmodal elements has been rapid. Much of this rapid pace follows from major wars. Again and again throughout history wars have played a hothouse role by forcing social and institutional change. During these recent periods of war the power of central economic planning in market societies was first demonstrated, pervasive rationing schemes were put to use—displacing for many products the role of markets in resource allocation—and the constraint of coined money and gold-standard-related bank credit was superseded by state-controlled credit money founded on public debt disguised by bank loans and deposit-creation. The war periods with their mass conscription for military service also introduced the use of progressive income taxation—a conscription of income as well as of labor.

But quite apart from war, and from technological changes that support new modes of production or enhance the older modes, and from the slowly acting but powerful influences generated by increased density of settlement and population, there is the distinctive and at times overwhelming impact of changes in public opinion. At its deeper levels this may be perceived better as a change of consciousness—a special mode of awareness and sensitivity taking over in a society. Such a change occurred among the peoples of the Roman Empire, for whom in a relatively short period the Christian mythos acquired central importance to millions of persons. An equally significant change resulted from the teaching and leadership of the prophet Muhammad, about whom the new Islamic faith and community crystallized in the seventh century among Arab peoples near Mecca and Medina. An equally remarkable change of consciousness has been experienced in the United States in the last two decades when concern for the environment—to cleanse it of its pollution, to protect it from further deterioration—became an accepted faith of millions, cut through opposition in the governing parties and changed the balance of priorities that govern economic policy. This change in consciousness was partly a delayed reaction to the cumulated build-up of environmental deterioration, especially in American cities where millions of internal-combustion engines poisoned the atmosphere as their charges of burnable gas and oxygen exploded under high pressure. Hardly a lakefront on which a city bordered or a river or creek passing through it was not polluted from the concentrated filth of the city's sanitary and industrial wastes. In prior decades environmental concern had very low priority and rarely was allowed to impede industrial development or the full use of modern technology; now with its priority greatly enhanced, pollution-abating equipment of the best kind was to be installed, and legislation was enacted with enforcing agencies to constitute practically a new layer of government over industry and transportation. All forms of commercial and intrusive land use by humans were proscribed in large portions of the national territory set aside as wilderness areas. The intensity of the reaction and its sustained power have introduced a new factor into the economic arrangements of the American economy by markedly changing its functional priorities and by giving new scope to the regulatory power of government.

HOW ECONOMIC SYSTEMS ARE RELATED TO EACH OTHER

In the whole of this chapter and in most of this book we have assumed that economic systems relate to a body of economic behavior organized in societies coterminous with a given national state assumed to be fairly well-defined. We have at different points recognized that societies are not isolated from each other but are part of a larger intersocietal community often having well-knit relations and frequently even a common sense of identity derived from a shared ethnic origin, language base, literary heritage, or shared religious faith. All this makes for ready cultural mobility. Culture enters into economic systems by shaping functional priorities and patterns of resource allocation.

We have recognized that national states take shape not in isolation but within a system of states, thereby generating the need for substantial allocation of resources for national defense or aggression—one often leads to the other. This allocation influences patterns of income redistribution by preempting tax potential from other possible uses, often making the military the dominant factor in the state itself. The system of states inevitably involves a *ranking* of states in terms of power and strength, frequently creating networks of dependency or subordination so that the very boundary lines between states thins out.

We have also considered wholesale trade as an important branch of production that is often carried on internationally by the marketing of products among different societies. This international trade was first conducted generally by capitalist merchants using hired labor and buying and selling in markets for money, manifesting the categories of price, market, value, profit, and wages—and to that extent being the first examplar of the capitalist mode of production. Likewise we have seen that an important function of the institution of money in a given society is to facilitate the process of international exchange. During the capitalist period proper, the gold standard became virtually an international institution.

In all these ways, then, we have recognized that each economic system is not isolated but has relations more or less extensive and intimate with other systems. When trade is continuous and production capabilities have long been oriented to it, these interstate economic relations tend to make for an international division of labor and for a mutual dependency among the trading states. So far as strictly national needs are concerned, different branches of industry, services, and agriculture become over- or under-developed.

Interdependency may, of course, go further than that. In earlier societies trade was the main linkage between economic systems, but in modern times other linkages have developed. The very labor force active in an economy derives not from a local indigenous population but from far-reaching currents of migration that redistribute people away from areas of low productivity with poor opportunities for enterprise and jobs. These currents of migration were one of the main connections between countries experiencing worldwide capitalist business and building cycles during the nineteenth and twentieth centuries. Paralleling the migration of labor in the modern world has been the migration of capital, which moves abroad with exceptional ease and has facilitated the international spread of newer forms of production and technology. Because much industry within a society will use materials drawn from abroad, because the states that are the very capstones of the entire economic system are themselves tied up in dependency relationships with other states, and finally because the institutions of money and property will be oriented to foreign as much as to domestic needs, in what sense can we speak of an economic system as if it were coterminous with a given society and state? May not the economic system stretch beyond a local society and state?

Reasoning along this line, many recent theorists have virtually given up the notion at least in modern times of a national economic system. Wallerstein actually contends that there are "no socialist systems in the world-economy . . . because there is only *one* world-system, it is a world-economy and it is by definition capitalist in form."[16] Even complete nationalization of all productive enterprises within the bounds of the nation-state "is not and theoretically cannot be a sufficient defining condition of a socialist system" as long as this nation "remains part of a capitalist world economy" and continues to "produce for this world market on the basis of the same principles

[16]Wallerstein, *Capitalist World Economy*, 1979, page 35.

as any other producer"—i.e., mindful primarily of its own advantages. Earlier he defines a "world system" as one "in which there is extensive division of labor" geographically; and a "capitalist world system," which, he argues, rewards "accumulated capital, including human capital, at a higher rate than 'raw' labor power."[17]

As talented a theorist as Samir Amin concurs with Wallerstein that "with capitalism having already assumed a planetary dimension and having organized production relations on this scale, socialism can only come into existence on a world scale." The world economy is polarized between an advanced "center" with high levels of technology and income and a dispersed subordinated "periphery" characterized by the "dominance of agrarian capital and ancillary (comprador) commercial capital."[18] Amin makes very clear that the peripheral economic systems, while associated with common traits such as extraversion (distortion toward export activities), hypertrophy of the tertiary sector, and underdevelopment generally, may differ significantly from each other depending on "the nature of the pre-capitalist formations that were there previously" and the "forms taken by the external attack when subjugation occurred." He allows for major differences between peripheral formations in Latin America, in the Near East and Asia and Africa. Though Amin recognizes and treats many advanced autocentric centers (of which North America, Japan, and Western Europe are directly enumerated), he argues that the advanced centers have a single capitalist mode of production.[19]

The fundamental question concerns implications of a stable division of labor by which many economies become tied to each other by mutual dependence in an international trading network with corresponding flows of international payments and some set of international moneys generally held or accepted throughout the system. Does the mere fact of such a trading network—crystallized into a division of labor with specialization in different types of products or services or degrees of technology and fabrication—bring into existence a higher or multinational overarching economic "system" of some type? Such trading relations, whereby dependent branches of economy developed in different countries tied together by mutual exchange and trade, first occurred in the ancient world in the areas linked by coastal trade in the navigable waters of the Mediterranean basin in the Graeco-Roman world, developed to a higher degree in the medieval world, to a still higher degree in the mercantilist period of the 17th and 18th centuries, and of course to the highest degree in the 19th and 20th centuries.

---

[17]See Wallerstein, *Capitalist World Economy*, 1979, pages 73 f.; *Modern World-System Capitalist Agriculture*, 1974, pages 15, 347 ff.

[18]Amin, *Unequal Development*, 1973, pages 202, 383.

[19]Amin, *Unequal Development*, 1973, pages 77, 202 f., 294 f., 298 ff., 317 f.

Obviously, something new comes into existence with such trade. It creates a mutual dependence that is often uneven because there is not always reciprocal intensity of demand for products supplied for export trade and demanded as imports. Countries with developed commerce and financial centers, which tend to organize and finance the trade, are in a position to use trade for their special advantage. A gross disparity exists between staples produced in many places but marketed on a multinational scale in international auction markets, and manufactured or craft goods or services produced only on order or to suit customer demand under the control of the producer. Trade itself will widen the sphere of economic fluctuation running its course in the trading network, and naturally it engenders cultural mobility and stimulus as merchants, sailors, diplomats, and travelers make mutual contacts. Finally, trade readily opens new functions for the state power to regulate trade and international payments and also creates further opportunities for it to collect revenues by taxation of goods either leaving or entering national frontiers traditionally policed by the state.

These effects on economic systems of mutual trade will, of course, be reinforced in special ways if beyond trade there is opportunity for migration of capital or persons within the trading network. The unified conjuncture of the 19th century business cycle over most of the participating advanced countries induced major worldwide cyclical movements that reflected not only common price movements generated out of trading capabilities but also powerful movements of capital lured by higher rates of return or of labor attracted by expanding jobs. This obviously made it difficult for any individual country to seek a more stable economy when its money, capital, and commodity markets were linked to the dominant world market. The endeavor to prevent internal prices from falling when the world price level is falling would merely cut off export trade shared with other producing centers; and any attempt to maintain income and employment at a time of world downward movement would create a deficit in the balance of payments and induce an outward flow of the nation's gold supply. For at a higher level of income and employment, imports would be attracted; with ample domestic markets, the urge to export would be diminished.

Moreover, financial centers in trading countries tend to be linked by a network of debts and credits. Because the same securities will be sold in many international security markets, financial crisis in any one center often produces corresponding crises in related centers. Rarely do these financial centers have equal capabilities. Dominant centers have the smoothest functioning, aggressive organizations, well-developed markets for goods and securities, accumulated or readily attracted financial reserves of large magnitude, and the widest range of access to other markets. Satellite centers are more or less dependent and passive. Dependency and dominance patterns are both increased when the currency of the dominant financial center becomes the international reserve of other trading centers or, even worse, when that currency becomes the international means of payment readily held and used as money by individuals, enterprises, and governments. In all these respects economic life becomes profoundly transformed when economic systems are linked by trading relationships and financial dependency into a world system dominated by the strongest economic powers.

An international system may be reinforced by institutionalization of various reciprocal obligations and ties linking states together. The most elementary form of institutionalization is that achieved by so-called commercial treaties, which provide for fishing rights in adjacent waters, rights of navigation, reciprocal consular stations with established authority, arrangements for travelers or visitors to obtain mutual access, and relative level of customs payment required by applicable customs duties. Overt institutionalization in the Western world came mainly after World War I with the establishment of the League of Nations, and later the Bank of International Settlements, established in 1930 as the first form of international central banking among the advanced industrial powers. American hegemony over the Western system was firmly established after World War II with its armed forces triumphant in Asia and in Europe and its military arsenal fortified by the atomic bomb—the near-ultimate terror weapon that forced Japan's surrender in 1945. U.S. economic supremacy was clearly indicated in 1946 by holding of some 70% of the Western world's gold reserves and vast export surpluses of foodstuffs, industrial goods, and fuels. The high point of power imbalance in the Western world was probably reached with the concurrent institutionalizations of the International Monetary Fund (in its earlier years virtually an extralegal organ of the U.S. Treasury using diplomatic means) and the NATO agreement, which in 1948–1949 fixed the American military presence in Europe with command over West European military forces. Since then disbalance has been diminished by the growing economic strength of America's two prime industrial competitors, the European Common Market and Japan (who together now hold gold reserves exceeding the U.S. reserves) and by the overt institutionalization of the European economic community, which is in the process of establishing a form of genuine federal union. This revision of politico-economic power in the Western world has led to a tripartite arrangement with Japan, Western Europe, and the United States playing similar roles, though the burden of strategic defense is still borne primarily by the U.S.

It is clear, then, that international trade and finance, as well as the overt institutionalization of agreements, controls, and authorities that are the beginning of state power in the Western world, have greatly influenced the economic systems of member countries. These systems have changed in this constrained environment, but the limits of institutional change will be increasingly set by the multinational complex that has become established by treaties, money ties, credits, and the layout of export industries and trading access. It would be nearly impossible for a major Western country to go the socialist route—not in the sense of limited nationalization of the kind that Britain carried out in 1945–1949, but by cutting off open access to and from its markets to world markets and subordination of national production and investment to central economic growth planning. Such a country could hardly still remain a member in good standing of the Western alliance and of Western economic institutions. If it closed its markets to enable national economic planning and separated its price levels from world market price levels—i.e., if it wrenched its national economy away from the dominant world economy—there would be resistance and disruption all along the line. Tariff levels against its goods would necessarily be boosted because access to its markets would now be impeded. Its international credit would become suspect. The multinational corporations operating in that country would become so many agencies for disruption of any national planning that might run counter to their private interests. Capitalists would tend to send their capital out of the country by any available means, including use of ordinary payment networks or sale of securities and other assets abroad, which would generate the financial crisis always signified by cumulative foreign deficits. In this sense, then, the institutionalized economic system is broader than a national state, so that a state may play a subordinate role, similar to that of a state government in the American scene—incapable of making major economic decisions or giving national leadership to its people. The national economic system, as we have defined it in this work, still exists, developing and changing in all the dimensions that have been outlined. But its path of evolution will be constrained by the multinational system of which it is a part and which has its own line of evolution. With virtually revolutionary effort a society in the Western world may, of course, wrench itself away from these constraints— as the French have done to a limited extent.

A corresponding Eastern imperium dominated by the Soviet Union has set similarly broad parameters that define the paths of evolution open to the socialist societies of the world. These parameters were breached by two socialist regimes—Yugoslavia and China—that had come to power primarily through domestic efforts. The Yugoslavs were the first to assert independence during the late 1940s. The Sino–Soviet split in the early 1960s was marked by even more rancor and became public over a decade later. Aid was withdrawn, trade agreements were suspended, and a condition of virtual nonintercourse shading into economic warfare was instituted between the socialist bloc led by the Soviet Union and the two defecting states. These in turn were able to establish economic ties with the vast nonaligned world and with individual countries within the Western bloc and eventually even with the Western imperial center, the United States. Hence a distinctive pattern of evolution marked the development of socialist economies in both mainland China and Yugoslavia.

But even within the bloc of socialist states tightly tied to Soviet apron strings, divergent patterns of development are perceptible. In Poland, where the peasant proprietor had been well established and resistance to Russian control was a historical tradition, it became impossible to push ahead with collectivization. The peasant proprietor remained there the dominant mode of production in agriculture. In Hungary a far-reaching reform of the planned economy was carried through, greatly weakening the role of rationing and increasing the importance of market processes and incentives. All through the Eastern satellite socialist states where collectivization was made effective, the relative size and role of the "private plot," the residual peasant holding, was much larger than in the Soviet economy, and the scope for private enterprise markets was much broader.[20]

PREINDUSTRIAL SYSTEMS

From the analysis of this and previous chapters, it is apparent that a determinate, but for practical purposes, virtually indefinite, number of unique economic systems are organized above the primitive and archaic levels in historic economic life. In earlier periods the scale of a relatively self-subsistent society with its own state and set of economic arrangements was much smaller than in modern times. Though a few great empires and state formations stretched across continents and embraced millions of persons, there were also numerous smaller areas with more homogeneous populations, fairly well-defined societies, and polities that had some sort of economic system as defined in this work. And for all these societies, both large and small, historic changes in modes of production, technologies, states of consciousness, political organization, and culture were constantly altering one or more of the components that make up an economic system. Each distinct society will thus have a more or less unique economic system at any one time. At varying rates that system will change over time. The reality of this innumerable variety of economic systems found in history has been diminished by the tendency to group concrete systems into broad classes or family types. Some form of grouping is indispensable to cope with the fact that though systems are all unique they are simultaneously similar in some respects. Where these respects are suffi-

---

[20]See the authoritative presentation in Shmelv, "Private Household Plot," 1975, pages 79 ff.

ciently important and critical, it becomes helpful to group systems sharing a given number of features into a broad class. But the class itself is not the historic reality; only real are the concrete systems—all different in significant respects.

It would be best to work out schemes of classifying economic systems after a sufficient number of them have been precisely identified or catalogued in terms of carefully defined criteria. One could then contrive different sets or models of system characteristics, yielding different groups of systems. The most specified sets of criteria would, of course, yield the largest number of family types; and, conversely, use of only a few defining criteria would permit a few broad classes to emerge with many essential features of systems omitted from view. Such a scheme of classification was provided in its simplest possible form by the first major theorist of comparative economic systems. Karl Marx selected only one system criteria for system classification—the predominant mode of production. While useful for certain purposes, it omits too much of reality to have explanatory force or to permit analysis of how concrete systems function or change over time. It would be nearly impossible to predict system behavior under stipulated conditions with such a simple classification. But once we decide to add features other than the predominant mode of production, we are embarrassed by the riches before us; we lack clues to make it easier to form models with a wide range of explanatory power but yielding only a limited number of family-type systems. If there were a catalogue of systems showing values for all defined features properly quantified or ranked, one could search out cluster groups of defining features that would empirically have a maximum of explanatory power but a workable set of system classes.

But we have no such catalogue nor do we have a simple list of systems recognized as such. And we do not have on hand any effort to quantify or rank by suitable measures those more intangible culture-related qualities of economic systems that enter into their makeup and affect their operation in critical ways. Under these circumstances, we are forced to rely upon broad classifications worked out by generations of economic historians who have filtered for us out of the historical record the images of broad historical classes of economic systems and societies loosely grouped in culture areas or "civilizations."

Perhaps the most fundamental of these historical classifications is that of the relatively small-scale societies involving an ethnically homogeneous population dependent chiefly on agriculture, livestock-tending, or fisheries but with a limited set of urban centers where commercial and manufacturing activities are concentrated and where governmental, cultural, and related services are provided. The governing class was sometimes concentrated in the leading urban center as in the classical Graeco-Roman and medieval city-state;

at other times it was dispersed over the countryside, to gather together periodically in assemblies or councils. This form of socioeconomic system predominated in the ancient world and continually tended to reappear as empires or larger state systems would break up. The characteristic modes of production in the countryside were village communities of direct commodity producers, landlord–tenant, or some form of serfdom or slavery. The predominant mode of production in metal work and manufacturing was the simple commodity producer drawn together for mutual protection into regulatory guilds used by government both to maintain order and collect taxes. The capitalist enterprise appeared chiefly as an outgrowth of direct commodity production to carry out wholesale trade or operate incipient forms of deposit banking.

City-states were sometimes leagued together under the leadership of the strongest state for mutual defense. But generally the cohesive power of city-state federations or leagues was weak. This form of socioeconomic system preceded the formation of the great empires, persisted on the fringes of the empires, and constantly reappeared when empires broke up both in the ancient world and repeatedly through the medieval period. Where irrigated agriculture was not developed the level of productive forces was relatively low. Agricultural surpluses that could sustain urban populations normally permitted no more than 10% of the total population to live in cities. But irrigated agriculture produced much larger surpluses so that urban life accordingly developed more complex patterns and more refined levels of performance. Money evolved primarily in the form of coined precious metals with rudimentary forms of banking. Commodity traffic moved chiefly along coastal waters or on navigable waterways. Except for river-control systems public works were chiefly urban in form and location: civic-centers for worship, recreation, and public meeting, city walls, water-distribution methods, harbor and port facilities, roadways in and out of cities.

Repeatedly city-states and small principalities were swept up by a strong warrior people—sometimes using novel military technologies—into large empires or a class of imperial redistributive systems that Immanuel Wallerstein has properly set up as a major class of socioeconomic systems.[21] The class is a broad genus with many species falling under it, and it involves expansion

---

[21]The term was elucidated mainly in essays where the category was defined as "World-Empire with a Redistributionist Economy." Specifically included is Byzantium, China, Egypt, Rome, feudal Europe, and feudal Japan. There a kind of "world-economy" developed, involving "vast areas" with a "sophisticated division of labor" headed up into a "single political structure" that collected by a variety of channels an agricultural surplus sufficient to maintain "artisans," a large military, and an "administrative stratum." See Wallerstein, *Capitalist World Economy*, 1979, pages 5, 22, 37, 71, 136, 142, 156 ff. The idea, of course, is a commonplace in historical literature.

considerably beyond a narrow tribal community with shared kinship and language. Empire in a persistent form entails erection of a formalized state system with a layered authority over imperial domains and high levels of taxation chiefly from agriculture. Modes of production encompassed within the genus include nearly all modes except the modern corporate and cooperative: slavery, feudal, village community, direct commodity producer, capitalist, landlord–tenant, and public. High tax potential makes possible schemes of income redistribution that vary widely in different systems. Many of these imperial redistributive systems, especially in the vast Euro-Asian plains and in the early medieval European period developed instability so that system characteristics were not matured within a stable and well-anchored state system. We simply do not know very much about very early systems in this genus, under Persian, Assyrian, or Greek-Macedonian auspices. The leading systems that extended over a considerable historic period, about which we have both archaelogical and extensive literary records, are the various dynastic epochs of classical China, the Mogul Empire in India, the early and late Roman Empire, a succession of Muslim–Turkic imperial states, the Byzantine empire that dominated the Aegean and Black Sea littoral and adjacent lands for nearly a thousand years, and possibly the brief Carolingian empire that disintegrated shortly after it was established.

Another broad class of economic system with distinctive characteristics illuminated by historical writing and economic research is the European medieval system that ran its course in the some thousand years which elapsed between the breakup in the fourth and fifth centuries A.D. of the Western half of the late Roman Empire and the gradual emergence variously in the thirteenth to the fifteenth centuries A.D. of newer, more homogeneous Christian societies at a higher level of technology and culture. This emergence was speedier for the more precocious southern areas of Europe, where the Roman inheritance was more rooted, to be revived through contacts with Arabic and Byzantine societies. This dawning after the Dark Ages was delayed for northern European peoples, who were only newly Christianized. The first half of that thousand-year period was dominated by the absorption into Europe of the successive waves of chiefly Germanic but also Slavic migrations, which could quietly infiltrate or else devastate large areas of settled countryside and urban centers. This cultural engulfment resulted in the weakening and gradual fade-out of Western Roman imperial administration and the tangled emergence of highly unstable new state systems and political configurations. The Slavic, Bulgar, and Turkic migrations chiefly impacted on the Eastern Roman empire, which absorbed them and maintained its integrity for most of the medieval period. The second half of the medieval epoch was dominated by the gradual emergence of new language communities derived from mixtures of migrating peoples and older settled populations, the full Christianization of the core European population and its peripheral societies, increase in levels of agricultural productivity stemming from a set of interacting technical improvements in agriculture which significantly boosted gross farm yields, and the consequential development of new autonomous centers of urban life, trade, and craft—especially in metallurgy, textiles, and navigation.

Running through the whole medieval epoch was the integrating role of a multinational, well-organized priestly order; functioning as the Catholic Church, it controlled worship, social services, learning, and much government administration. The medieval epoch also witnessed the gradual crystallization of a military warrior class of armored horsemen (knights) closely associated with and giving service to the great landlords on their manorial estates. An enserfed peasantry provided the surplus of food and raw materials that supported church, military, nobility, and prince.

Even the Marxists, with their propensity for simple schemas of broad historical succession, have come to recognize that the medieval epoch for Western Europe does not embody a single "feudal" economic system but a "variegated typology of social formations."[22] That typology rests upon the broad distinction drawn by most medieval scholars between an "early" and a "later" feudalism (with the line drawn approximately towards the middle of the eleventh century)—"very different from one another in their essential character."[23] The feudal mode of agriculture in its classical form is far more predominant in the first period. In the later period the level of productive forces is much higher due to a remarkable advance in skills and technology. Simple commodity producers and merchants in the earlier period circulated only small amounts of commodities, rarely traversing long distances. Moreover, these producers and merchants functioned as a suppressed order of feudal society. The feudal institution of property had unrivaled scope and prevalence in the earlier period. The essential principle of this form of property is that holding of land or office and its beneficial use up and down the social ladder was subject to services rendered to higher authority. Thus society was given a pyramidal form, making insecure the transmission of property rights to immediate family successors. The nature of the services rendered was usually more expansible and onerous for holders of lower status, such as enserfed peasant villagers. Inheritance succession was possibly taxed more heavily among high-status holders. In the earlier period the public economy was relatively undeveloped and very little income redistribution shifted income from those dominating its immediate production. State structures were

[22]Perry Anderson, *Passages from Antiquity to Feudalism*, 1974, page 154. Anderson proceeds to contradict his own finding by claiming that a generalized "feudal synthesis" with its own developed "feudal mode of production" itself "produced" the "typology" of concrete, highly divergent systems (pages 155 f.).

[23]Marc Bloch, *Feudal Society*, 1939–1940, vol. 1, pages 59 ff.

fluid and porous in the early period and essential governmental power—over customs, administration of justice, taxation, minting, frontier administration—either lapsed or devolved to local authority. The bounds in the early period between polity, social order, and economic system were correspondingly fluctuating and undefined.

The later medieval period encompasses not a single system but a whole typology of systems. One was a highly developed complex of Italian urban trading communities centered in the well-barricaded valley of the Po River, draining the southern Alps and Apennines and controlling potentially the entire Adriatic region. These urban communities were led by a town bourgeoisie centered in a town artisanry and a town merchantry which operated a powerful merchant marine. Those communities broke out of feudal power in the 11th and 12th centuries. The modes of production involved were primarily simple commodity producers organized in strong guild associations, landlord–tenant and capitalist farming using hired labor which replaced the enserfed manorial village, and a richly developed regulatory town public economy that organized defense, regulated trade and markets, and built up the public facilities permitting efficient transportation and communication. In its political form this artisan-peasant-landlord mercantile society could never outgrow its urban chrysallis and build a larger state system that could suppress internal divisiveness and defend itself against the older state systems. Strength was often wasted in prolonged internal civil war. At best these burgeoning urban republics could occasionally league together sufficiently to resist external Germanic or Muslim aggression. As the medieval epoch drew to a close, the economic basis of the Italian city-states and their mercantile power was undermined by the loss of trading territory swallowed up by Turkish conquests in Asia Minor and the Balkans and eventually Byzantium itself, by the development of a more powerful merchant marine by states to the west (Portugal, Holland, France, Spain, and England), and by the displacement of industry to northern Europe.

A second quite distinct category of late medieval economy is the powerful centralized English state that developed, along with its classical form of manorial agriculture cast in the feudal mode, a self-governing, chartered town democracy made up of artisan guilds led chiefly by mercantile capitalists. The chartered towns comprised one of the three estates, with a distinct and nearly coequal voice in the governing of the realm under a strong monarchy. The development of a viable central state and as well of the commercial towns was accompanied by a tendency to commercialize the feudal mode, to turn it, with commutation of feudal dues and services into money rents, in the direction of landlord–tenant and capitalist forms of agriculture based on rent and wage relationships. The public economy was invigorated by a considerable growth of taxing power extended over both the manorial and the urban economy—partly due to the fiscal exploitation of wool exports, which both enriched the crown and the rising merchant class given a trading monopoly. The quite remarkable freedom from the internal river and road tolls that impeded commercial development everywhere on the Continent promoted a unique sense of national unity. Yet all this coexisted with an outward form of manorial agriculture, a persisting role of feudal exploitation in the countryside, and a military still relying on mounted armored knights.

The rest of Europe at this period falls into quite different categories. The central state was poorly developed in France and Spain and had practically disappeared in most of Germany, so that the English category does not fit. Yet town development both in the economy and polity was too strong— though falling radically short of the sovereign power achieved in Italy—to employ simply the "feudal" label, especially because in wide areas of Germany and Scandinavia an impressive independent peasant proprietorship was still maintained as a minority mode of production in agriculture. The situation varies even more in the adjoining societies—Poland, Hungary, Bohemia—which became part of the European community long after the early age of "feudalism." Here we can accept the typological suggestions worked out for the most part quite brilliantly by Perry Anderson in his chapters "The Far North," "East of the Elbe," "The Crisis in the East," and "South of the Danube."[24] If that multiplies economic systems unduly, it nonetheless testifies to the complexity of the historic process.

MERCANTILIST SYSTEMS

Our next suggested broad class of economic system is the mercantilist economy whose characteristic features broadly reflect a West European economic development of the 16th and 17th and first half of the 18th centuries. This development achieved its classic form in Holland, England, and France, but extended partly to Spain, Portugal, Prussia, and Sweden. The mercantilist economy embodies a period of transition between a late medieval and a more purely capitalist class of economic system drawing strength from the overseas expansion of Europe and the first beginnings of the industrial revolution, all organized and powered by coercive state measures. The overseas expansion owes to the enhanced military and navigational skills by which Europeans achieved mastery of the oceans and brought under European subjection vast indigenous populations in Asia, Africa, and the Americas. The more advanced Amerindian societies chiefly in Mexico and Peru became subjugated, with their ruling classes wiped out or assimilated and their people peonized. The

[24]Anderson, *Passages from Antiquity to Feudalism*, 1974.

more primitive populations were generally extirpated or driven to a wild frontier. West Africa was drained of its able-bodied population—hunted out by local African rulers and sold to European slavers established in African coastal areas. Slaves were shipped to the New World to carry on gold and silver mining or to cultivate the vast plantations growing sugar, coffee, tobacco, and other tropical products which became major staples of merchandise in European commodity markets during the mercantilist epoch. The subcontinent of India and the stretch of tropical islands that in historical times sustained the spice trade were given over to systematic plundering. While the societies of Japan and China could more adequately deal with Europeans and preserve their integrity, European trading footholds on the periphery of their territory were established, permitting a profitable trade to develop enriching European consumption with Asian silks, tea, and fine porcelain.

Overseas expansion was critical in several respects for the development of the capitalist mode of production. This expansion called for an enormous enlargement of the European merchant marine, a capitalist means of production, to carry the migrating peoples of Europe and Africa and the products of three continents around the world. Construction of merchant shipping involved capitalist enterprise free from guild restrictions and feasible only with wage labor. Then the slave trade at both the acquisition and dispersing ends called for mercantile enterprise because slaves were bought by suitable offers of attractive merchandise that appealed to African slave-catchers. After migration slaves were not dumped but carefully auctioned off in American slave markets to assure profitable sale.

Once slaves were put in place in the New World or an equivalent labor supply organized by peonization of more advanced Indian peoples, then the products of slave and peon labor—chiefly cotton, sugar, hides, precious metals, cocoa, coffee—needed to be transported back to Europe and after necessary processing and packaging marketed in various ports for inland distribution. This created new industries which, like shipbuilding and the merchant marine, were organized as capitalist enterprises.

Apart from its stimulus from overseas trade and the new world market that it created, the capitalist mode of production was directly stimulated by technical renovation both in agriculture and in industry. Farm productivity was boosted, especially in Holland and England, by the abolition of serfdom. Manorial estates were increasingly leased to commercial farmers and improved farming methods were introduced with the drainage of wetlands, enclosure of open fields, and the conversion of arable land to pasture. Crop diversity was promoted by cultivation in Europe of two Indian staples acquired from New World farmers, the potato and maize plants—both high-yielding in terms of both acreage and calories, suited for temperate European climates, and capable of withstanding weather conditions that would injure staple wheat or rye plantings. The nutritional base of the European urban economy was further widened by the development of deep sea fishing which yielded a rich harvest especially in the North Atlantic and by sugar and other edibles drawn to Europe by trade chiefly from the New World.

Technical renovation in industry was even more noteworthy. New sources of readily mined quality iron in Sweden and Russia were discovered. Iron output boomed in the mercantilist epoch, rising over fourfold between 1500 and 1750. Enough heat was generated in smelting to make for a continuous blast and to liquefy the metal, making cast-iron products for the first time in Europe. Improved methods for milling and fabricating iron were developed in wire-drawing, rolling, and slitting mills using water power for the first time. New and powerful sources of energy were made available, especially in England, through a vast development of coal mining that revolutionized economic life by providing fuels for space heating and for boilers used in such industries as salt-making, breweries, glassworks, brick and lime-making, ironworks, dyers, smithies, and sugar refining. As coal mines were sunk to lower depths, calling for the investment of considerable capital to provide drainage and facilities for coal transport, large-scale mining enterprise developed, drawing together both titled landlords and mining capitalists. Between 1551 and 1690 estimated output of coal rose over tenfold reaching a level of some 3 million tons for England and Scotland, counting only coal shipped any distance, usually by water.[25] Beside coal mining and industries dependent upon coal as boiler fuel, fine mechanical skills of the kind illustrated by the making of watches and clocks were developed in a wide variety of fields. The textile industry where the "putting out" system flourished in the woolen trades spawned a whole set of developments that brought about the capitalist workshop centered around dye-houses, fulling mills, and silk-throwing mills operated by water power. Scientific thought was carried to new levels in the work of Bacon, Galileo, and Descartes. This age saw the first beginnings of true chemistry. The most important scientific instruments—the telescope, the microscope, barometer, thermometer—took form, and the first scientific so-

---

[25]The rise of coal mining in Great Britain and the associated developments in transportation, marketing, industrial technology, and business enterprise were painstakingly researched and comprehensively traced out by Nef, *British Coal Industry*, 1932, vol. 1. Estimated tonnage by districts between 1551 and 1790 is summarized (vol. 1, pages 20 f.) Further, Nef spells out the various ways in which coal production, transportation, and distribution and the use of coal as boiler fuel furthered the development of the capitalist mode of production and the complex forms of business partnership that foreshadowed the modern corporation and cartel (pages 347 ff.). For sketches of "an early industrial revolution," see how the use of coal as boiler fuel transformed salt-making, glassmaking, breweries, brickmaking. This early account was deepened and extended in his later publications. See especially "The Industrial Revolution Reconsidered," 1943, pages 8 ff.; *Industry and Government*, 1957.

cieties were established. The printing press multiplied and cheapened writings, which became readily available to common people for the first time and inspired a more general education.

This extended and hothouse capitalist development did not, of course, spring up only by its native energies. Throughout its course is seen the guiding role of strong monarchies with ruling elites openly fostering the industry and trade of a rising bourgeoisie. Aristocratic landlords were being weaned away from feudal habiliments and were turning into bourgeois property holders managing estates for rental income. The methods of fostering industry and trade were various. They involved the development of naval power to seize colonial outposts of competitor mercantile nations, to open up trading stations in the Pacific and along the African coast, and to conquer territories suitable for colonial development. They included the establishment of privileged corporations to carry on long-distance trade, to organize overseas plantations, and to enable the landed aristocracy, crown, and bourgeiosie to share in the profits of the ventures and participate in colonial control. These corporations were at the same time profit-making business organizations to assemble capital and entrepreneurship and state agencies to control territories, rule subjects, and fight wars. The state encouraged new industry with bounties and aids, suppressed competition from abroad by ruinous tariffs, restricted the importation of luxuries and products that could be made at home, and fostered exports with bounties and grants, thus tending to bring money into the kingdom and prevent it from leaving once there. Idle workers were to be driven into relief workshops to earn a bare subsistence. These coercive state actions were characterized by Marx as elements of "primitive accumulation" which "distribute themselves now more or less in chronological order over Spain, Portugal, Holland, France, England"—and by the end of the seventeenth century in England arrived at a "systematical combination."[26] There, too, the economic theory of a mercantilist economy and its essential regulatory principles was most fully developed in tracts, theoretical treatises, and essays, marking out a major phase of the development of economic theory.[27]

[26]This subject was treated by Marx in his famous part 8 of *Capital* I, 1867, "The So-called Primitive Accumulation" (pages 713–774), especially the passage cited on page 751. The combination embraces "the colonies, the national debt, the modern mode of taxation and the protectionist system." These methods employ the power of the state and "depend in part on brute force . . . to hasten hothouse fashion the process of transformation of the feudal mode of production into the capitalist mode and to shorten the transition." For an alternative formulation, see Marx, *Capital* III, 1864–1865, page 785.

[27]The fact that these regulatory principles might lack theoretical coherence or rest upon faulty logic under the circumstances of later times or that they were often applied irregularly does not mean, as has been widely argued, that "mercantilism" did not exist. The distinguished

MODERN SYSTEMS[28]

The next major form of economic system growing out of mercantilist economy may be called, following Karl Marx, the "capitalist" system. This may
be said to exist if the capitalist mode of production has become predominant.
Following our account of the capitalist mode of production and the succession
of forms in which it is embodied, ending up in powered machinery controlled
by capital, it would appear improper to label any economic system as "capitalist" unless that mode of production clearly predominated in the employment of labor or flow of commodity output in the fields of manufacturing,
mining, and wholesale trade and had at least substantial footholds for the use
of powered machinery in manufacturing and transportation. The domestic
economy would then be opened up to the pricing standards and market opportunities for internationally traded goods of the world market and its pricing norms. This presupposes that the hold of the chartered guilds or town
corporations over local markets would have been substantially broken and
that restrictions on free movement of the domestic labor force were abolished. These criteria involve treating as a "capitalist economy" Great Britain
and the United States between the fifth and sixth decades of the 19th century,
with a somewhat later set of decades for Germany, France, and the Low
Countries—and still later decades for Poland, European Russia, and Sweden.
To those accustomed to think about "capitalist economy" less restrictively
than is laid out here, let me add that our concern is for that form of capitalism

---

economic historian D. C. Coleman, argued that it was "born as the brainchild of an economist [Adam Smith], the concept in its life has been abused by historians, mishandled by
economists, transmuted into Mercantilismus and variously paraded for praise or blame by
anyone seeking historical illustrations of the latest nostrum in political economy." See Coleman, *Economy of England*, 1977, page 173. Nor can mercantilism be palmed off, following
Wallerstein, as merely a "defensive mechanism of capitalists located in states which are one
level below the high point of strength in the system." See Wallerstein, *Capitalist World Economy*, 1979, page 19. Mercantilist practices were widely applied by states that were both leaders
and followers. We concur with the observation of C. H. Wilson, an exceptionally thoughtful
student of the period, that it is "dangerous to deny that certain principles informed both
thought and policy in this period." See Wilson, *Economic History*, 1969, page 75. For theorists
and historians who join with us in claiming that something akin to a mercantilist system
actually existed as a phase of European economic development, as an institutional scheme,
and as a policy drift, see Dobb, *Development of Capitalism*, 1947, page 209; Amin, *Unequal
Development*, 1973, pages 31, 64; Procacci, "A Survey of the Debate," 1976, page 129. Sombart in his conceptual category of "Frühkapitalismus" portrays the substance of the mercantilist
system.

[28]The text following as well as the preceding section are tightly drawn summaries of the
principal findings of the companion volume to this work noted in the Preface and nearly ready
for publication. That volume lays out the evidence glossed over in this summary.

analyzed by Marx under "machinery and modern industry"—which is relatively mature and using both mechanized industry and transportation. It would be quite consistent with the theory of an economic system developed in this work to structure a definition of capitalism with broader ambit, reaching back farther in time and including a wider range of societies within the class. Clearly, the broader the class, the more diversified the patterns of behavior encompassed within it.

The classes of economic systems remaining for identification are the mixed economy, the socialist economy and the Third World economy. The distinction between the mixed economy and capitalist economy is deep, many-sided, and pervasive. The predominant mode of production in industry, mining, wholesale commerce, and finance has become the public corporation—now increasingly internationalized with a major role in many of the urban services and in retail trade, long the home of the direct commodity producer. The capitalist mode has lost to the corporate mode but has taken over much of the field of the direct commodity producer and in many countries has won an important role in agriculture to supplement the family farm or peasant proprietor. The more oppressive modes of open or peonized landlord–tenant farming more or less faded out of the mixed economy, especially in the United Kingdom, the United States, and Japan. The direct commodity producer is still strong in the professions, in retail trade, in urban services, in many of the creative arts, and of course in farming and fishery.

The mixed economy has evolved a more advanced form of money than the typical capitalist economy still dependent upon precious metals. The central bank has more clearly emerged as a guiding agency to stabilize the course of economic growth and prevent crises. In the more advanced mixed economies the central bank is now joined to state planning and fiscal agencies with an overall function of guiding economic life along a steady course. The precious metals have been evacuated from working moneys and now linger as a form of gilding on coins or since 1975 as an ultimate treasure reserve with a value too high and uncertain to utilize for payment purposes. The supply of effective national moneys is determined by action of the banking system on the basis of reserves provided by the central bank or treasury. As explained earlier (Chapter 7), these agencies collaborate with each other through an international Western central Bank (IMF) to stabilize and regulate the exchange rates prevailing in money markets between these national moneys and the American dollar, which plays a kingpin role in the Western world economy. The IMF in turn is governed by its member countries in accordance with the capital contributed to it, with the dominant voice and vote cast by the United States, which has an effective veto on IMF actions.

The regulatory scope devolved on government in the mixed economy is wide indeed. Inherited from the capitalist economic system was the beginning form of regulation of industry to prevent overwork and unsanitary, un-healthy, or dangerous working conditions. These early beginnings of factory regulation were extended into a comprehensive code that typically sets min-imum wages, maximum working hours, and standards of protection against dangerous equipment or unsafe working conditions. Regulation now extends to reshaping industry to prevent pollution by waste products or gases of the ambient air or ground waters and to retain where possible untouched wil-derness. The growing and the marketing of agricultural products are now closely regulated to assure food and fiber producers a steady market at fair prices for their products. The conduct of banking enterprise, behavior in investment markets, the development of new products that might prove dan-gerous or unsafe for human use—these are merely a small sample of the wide field of regulatory action now on the agenda of state action in advanced Western countries.

The public mode of production has extended into vast new areas, such as the construction and operation of schooling facilities to educate the entire youth of the nation. Laboratories and institutes are built up for the devel-opment of science. Vast public networks of distributive services providing power, communication, and transportation on land, water, and air have been constructed and operated nationwide. Farm inventories of major crop staples are largely held in government storage to stabilize farm price levels. Multi-purpose resource developments of river networks have been constructed to minimize flood damage, generate power, or regulate water flows. In the United States the expansive force of the public economy has been largely channeled, as previously noted (Chapter 4), into hybrid forms of the corporate–public mode. One of these now encompasses the huge composite armament, space-technology, and nuclear industry engaged in its deadly race with the Soviet Union to achieve sufficient technical proficiency in devas-tation to break the will of its adversary. The other hybrid mode encompasses the more standard public utilities, providing services of transportation and communication or delivering on ready-made distributive networks energy flows for instant utilization. An appreciable segment of the housing supply in most mixed economies is now provided by public enterprise or public financing. Much health care is now delivered in public facilities or is managed by public agencies obligated to set standards of care and safety and to provide for funding. In many mixed economies a significant fraction of banking, most power generation, and much large-scale corporate enterprise have been so-cialized and are managed and operated on a commercial basis as public sector enterprise.

In the capitalist economies income redistribution—carried out mainly by taxation, fiscal programs, and handling of public domain—was on the whole inegalitarian. Capitalist taxation rested on excises and sales taxes on consumption or industrial staples and stimulants, with sparse use of luxury levies or taxes bearing in a major way on upper-income property or earnings. In England a heavy public debt held largely by the upper-income class mortgaged a substantial fraction of tax revenues, effecting a significant redistribution of national income in fewer hands. The poor and needy, plagued by intermittent bouts of unemployment and afflicted with the usual rounds of disabling illnesses augmented by disease and injuries generated by the crude working machinery of a new industrial technology, were afforded only skimpy and often degrading forms of charitable assistance, the leading model of its kind being the English poorhouse established in Great Britain by the Poor Law Reform of 1834.

In the mixed economy a new basis for income redistribution was laid by the massive development of wealth and income taxation at progressive rates, which became outrightly confiscatory for the highest levels of income and wealth. Much of the proceeds were dedicated, especially in the United States, to paying for past wars or for the heavy burdens of the Cold War. But substantial fractions of these tax revenues were available for use in financing public administration, social programs, welfare support for the aged and disabled, and programs of public housing, community development, or resource development generally. A special program of income redistribution, aided significantly by general tax revenues, was carved out of payroll taxation bearing on employees and employers and providing for a comprehensive program of social security. This finances old-age or disability retirement pensions, pensions to survivors and dependents, stop-gap payments during unemployment, and health insurance to cover the costs of medical care. In all these ways income was redistributed in the mixed economy chiefly by state action using fiscal and tax means worked out in many-sided welfare programs.

Redistribution by state action was paralleled by another form of redistribution achieved directly by wage and salary earners organized into strong trade unions. In the capitalist economy the infant union movement barely won a foothold even in fields where craft solidarity of workmen was unusually strong. Unions functioned in a cloud of disrepute and public opprobrium and were subject to constant judicial and police harassment. In the mixed economy these movements had gradually spread their evangel of working-class action through the entire labor force. They now began to function with the aid of government, and even their crippling strike actions won a wide degree of immunity in the law. Over many fields of industry, especially when sheltered from foreign competition, unionization was so complete that negotiated wage increases would tend to be shifted into industrial price levels, leading to a new phenomenon, the wage–price spiral. In fields where unionization had little visible power, employers were careful to develop programs of employee relations that provided many of the benefits of unionism but avoided its constant prodding and willful ways. Even with extensive unemployment, wage rates tend to increase, exhibiting in operation a kind of labor market utterly different from that known and experienced in the capitalist economy.

Finally the mixed economy with its powerful central bank, extensive government budget, vast field of authority over enterprises, broad-yielding tax systems collecting now generally at the source, and transfer and welfare programs, gradually learned that it had to intervene in economic life to stabilize its course and to seek to head off the unruly movements of expansion and contraction—the specific law of motion of business enterprise operating in open markets for a profit motive. The capitalist era experienced only the first timid beginnings of this intervention—primarily exerted by the central bank or the complex of institutions playing a central banking role. That intervention mainly sought to stem the tide of financial panic. In the late capitalist period the possibilities for therapy began to be recognized through public works or unemployment insurance or the organization of public stockholding of major raw material inventories to help to stabilize their precipitous price movements. But as late as the 1920s, the business of government had not yet come to encompass as one of its current, continuous, and major responsibilities that of guiding economic life to run a steadier course on an upward gradient. That full responsibility was not generally assumed in the mixed economy until after World War II. Then the stabilizing and interventionist policies of government were writ large, and the need to avoid economic tailspins like the Great Depression became the dominant objective of the day. This stabilization and regulatory drive to guide economic life is now challenged in Great Britain and the United States by a conservative and obscurantist tide of opinion that has temporarily taken over control of government. It is very doubtful, however, that this conservative tide can be long maintained.

We shall deal in shorter compass with the two remaining major classes of later historical economic systems—the socialist and Third World—because their distinctness and uniqueness is already widely recognized. Only the most doctrinaire could question that the Soviet Union and the dozen or so states that have been shaped by it or have followed its lead—making up the present-day socialist world—have unique economic systems differing categorically from those evolved and maintained in the nonsocialist world. The socialist world trades with the nonsocialist world only sparsely—and irregularly with the United States, that paramount home of the mixed economy. In nearly all socialist countries this trade is filtered through governmental agencies specially chartered for trading purposes. The patterns of mutual dependency emerged in trade with the nonsocialist world are woven very loosely. The driving force of the socialist economies is political control by a well-organized communist party and various forms of central growth planning, combined with wholly socialized industry, wholesale trade, banking, and all public utilities. Capitalist enterprises organized chiefly as licensed foreign concessions have only a limited field of operation in a few socialist states. The direct commodity producer still lingers on with his limited private markets in some urban craft services, in the professions, food bazaars, and the family-owned and -operated farm. The farm in most of the socialist world has been reduced to a private plot with the main cultivated fields—especially those planted in grains—worked by hybrid forms of producer-cooperative and state-plantation using modern farm machinery. The principal modes of resource coordination are planning and rationing. But market methods are variously used for distribution of consumer goods and services, in labor markets, and even to some degree in housing markets.

The Third World economies consist in large part of the former colonialized empires built up during the overseas expansion of mercantilist and capitalist systems between the 16th and early 20th centuries. The peoples involved were the dark-skinned or colored or sometimes Mestizo peoples of Southeast Asia, Africa, the Middle East, and Latin America. These peoples had in some cases long been subjugated in various imperial redistributive systems before passing under mercantilist or capitalist control. Independence and some form of autonomous self-rule were achieved generally in waves. The first occurred early in the 19th century, when mainland Latin America nationalist elites threw off Spanish and Portuguese imperial control and organized independent state systems, which with Anglo-American protection maintained their independence. The second wave resulted from the breakup of the Turkish imperial state after World War I, when the more advanced of the Arab peoples were sooner or later able to achieve some kind of formal independence, usually with their oil resources well-mortgaged to Western corporate power. The third wave followed from the turmoil of World War II, which shook up the empires at a time when nationalist sentiment was high and the ability of Western countries to hold peoples in subjection became questionable, especially since the Soviet Union was able to give liberation movements economic and military assistance. In long-fought struggles, the once-colonial peoples demonstrated their determination to end this subjugation. Hence through the decades following 1946 nearly all of the colonial peoples who wished to or fought for it achieved their independence.

The level of production forces in the Third World is low on the whole, due to limited formal schooling, a weak development of industry and underlying resources, and generally unstable state systems lacking reliable means for peaceful succession of rulers. Predominant modes of production in agriculture range from inefficient forms of subsistence farming or parasitic forms of landlord–tenant farming with near-servile forms of tenancy to the more efficient but antagonistic forms of capitalist plantations. Industry is carried on in three modes: (1) domestic capitalist enterprise, (2) nationalized or state industry financed by outside loans, and the most ambitious scale (3) large enterprises established by multinational Eastern or Western corporations using modern technology and operated usually in partnership with local capitalists or with the local host government. An outstanding example of the last type is yielded by the petro-states where, by bold action and international organization (OPEC), host governments have gradually taken over control of the production, marketing, and pricing of the rich petroleum and natural gas resources in their countries. By a striking economic coup these host governments have within a few years raised manyfold the net incomes generated by the facilities of the multinational corporations that for moderate fees have raked in from world markets the vast incomes now generated by oil exports, turned over for the larger part to the oligarchies controlling the petro-states. These incomes have brought into existence a new plutocracy in the Persian Gulf whose investments are now creating a new industrialized and luxury consumption world in their own societies and a vast network of investments abroad bringing under petro-control commercial, industrial, and corporate resources in the mixed economies and above all in the United States. These petro-states—at least in the Persian Gulf—are in the process of moving out of the class of Third World economies into a special category of system with a dual character: a unique dependence upon international monopoly power and partnership with multinational corporations, and a flow of rentier income nearly entirely divorced from any sustained productive effort carried on within the domestic modes of production.

EACH SYSTEM UNIQUE

Inclusion within a class of economic system should by no means be allowed to expunge recognition of the unique character of all systems and the imperfect homogeneity of systems found within the class. Though by restrictive definition we have sought to draw closely the confines around such systems as the mercantilist and capitalist, yet in significant response these systems vary widely. The Netherlands rested on an underlying rural population predominantly made up of peasant proprietorships; by contrast, their counterpart in England were capitalist farms carved out of great landed estates operated with wage labor. While the absolute monarchy was the dominant party in the larger states of the European continent where mercantilist patterns are found— witness Louis XIV of France and Phillip II of Spain—the corresponding form of state system in that foremost land of mercantilist experience, England, was basically a parliamentary government struggling for supremacy with a succession of royal masters. The industrial revolution that marked the mercantilist economy in England and Holland was quite absent in mercantilist Spain, where the unbridled import of precious metals ironically produced not industrial renovation but industrial decline.

Diversity within the capitalist and mixed economies was equally noteworthy. In the capitalist heyday protectionism withered in Great Britain but flourished in Germany and the United States. The independent family farmer was at home in the United States and France but was disappearing from Great Britain, the classical home of the landed estate and capitalist farm. A second agricultural mode in Great Britain was a classical form of landlord–tenant farming developed in Ireland. The slave plantation flourished in the American South.

The mixed economies run an equally prominent diversity. The corporate mode is nowhere in the Western world so well established as in the United States, where it has infiltrated via its hybrid forms into the most essential public services. The urban cooperative—which plays a prominent role in leading European democracies, especially in Scandinavia and in Great Britain—has mere toeholds in the United States. Only in the United States is the great public regulatory program of economic stabilization—which requires intimate and sustained collaboration of monetary and fiscal policies—undermined at its source by the wholly separated administration of money and budgets and by the still strong remnants of private control of central banking, an awkward inheritance from the early stages of the mixed economy. Moreover, the American mixed economy clearly gives priority to achievement of military power, whereas social welfare is the predominant goal of the mixed economy in those Western states that do not assume the obligation of policing the world and giving total devotion to the struggle against communism.

Diversity is also the hallmark of the socialist class of system. In the six decades of Soviet experience three nearly distinct forms of socialist economy followed in succession in Russia once the new regime was securely established there in 1921 in its post-World War I borders. Two of the socialist economies functioning outside of the U.S.S.R. itself now permit the family farmer to dominate the countryside. Socialist systems have run a gamut between totally regimented economies with few market processes to well-developed market economies, with cooperative worker-controlled enterprises, as in Yugoslavia. Since emerging in the late 1940s, socialist China has experienced revolutionary shifts in its patterns of economic organization.

In the Eastern as in the Western world economic systems are diverse and multiform. Processes of historic change and development, once set in motion, cannot be arrested. Hence the principal conclusion of this work: that economic systems are many-faceted and evolving forms—constantly changing.

References

The year or years after the full title records the year of original publication of the first edition or, in some cases, the period of composition.

Abrahamsen, M. A. *Cooperative Business Enterprise* New York: McGraw-Hill, 1976.
Abrahamsen, M. A., and Scroggs, C. L., eds. *Agricultural Cooperation: Selected Readings*. Minneapolis: University of Minnesota Press, 1957.
Abramovitz, M. *Inventories and Business Cycles: With Special Reference to Manufacturing Inventories*. New York: National Bureau of Economic Research, 1950.
Allen, G. C. *Japan's Economic Policy*. New York: Oxford University Press, 1980.
Amin, S. *Unequal Development: An Essay on the Social Formations of Peripheral Capitalism*, 1973; trans., New York: Monthly Review Press, 1976.
Anderson, Perry. *Lineages of the Absolutist State*. London: New Left Books, 1974.
Anderson, Perry. *Passages from Antiquity to Feudalism*. London: New Left Books, 1974.
Anderson, T. L., and Hill, P. J. "The Evolution of Property Rights: A Study of the American West," *Journal of Law & Economics*, April 1975.
Appleby A. B. "Grain Prices and Subsistence Crises in England and France, 1590–1740," *Journal of Economic History*, December 1979.
Aranow, E. R., and Einhorn, H. A. *Proxy Contests for Corporate Control*. New York: Columbia University Press, 1957.
Aristotle. *The Basic Works of Aristotle*, ed. R. McKeon. New York: Random House, 1941.
Ashton, T. S. *Economic Fluctuations in England, 1700–1800*. New York: Oxford University Press, 1959.
Ashtor, E. A. *Social and Economic History of the Near East: The Middle Ages*. London: Collins, 1976.
Ault, D. E., and Rutman, G. L. "The Development of Individual Rights to Property in Tribal Africa," *Journal of Law & Economics*, April 1979.
Ayres, C. E. *The Theory of Economic Progress*. Raleigh, N.C.: University of North Carolina Press, 1944.
Bagehot, Walter. *Lombard Street*. London: John Murray, 1873.
Baker, Jacob. *Cooperative Enterprise*. New York: Vanguard, 1937.
Balazs, E. *Chinese Civilization and Bureaucracy: Variations on a Theme*, 1932–1961; trans. New Haven: Yale University Press, 1964.
Baron, P., and Sweezy, P. *Monopoly Capital: An Essay on the American Economic and Social Order*, 1966; New York: Monthly Review Press, 1968.
Baruch, B. *My Own Story: The Private Years*, 1957; New York: Cardinal, 1958.
Baum, W. C. *The French Economy and the State*. Princeton, N.J.: Princeton University Press, 1958.
Bautier, R. H. *The Economic Development of Medieval Europe*, 1966; trans. New York: Harcourt, 1971.

Beard, Charles, and Beard, Mary. *Rise of American Civilization*, vols. 1 and 2, 1927; New York: Macmillan, 1930.

Becker, G., and Landes, W. M. *Essays in the Economics of Crime and Punishments*. New York: National Bureau of Economic Research, 1974.

Beckett, J. C. *The Making of Modern Ireland, 1603–1923*. New York: Knopf, 1966.

Belshaw, M. *A Village Economy: Land and People of Huercorio*. New York: Columbia University Press, 1967.

Bendix, R. *Work and Authority in Industry: Ideologies of Management in the Course of Industrialization*, 1956; New York: Wiley, 1974.

Benton, J. F., ed., *Town Origins: The Evidence from Medieval England*. Lexington, Mass.: Heath, 1968.

Bernstein, E. *International Effects of U.S. Economic Policy*, U.S. Joint Economic Committee Study Paper 16. Washington, D.C.: Government Printing Office, November 1961.

Berle, A. A., and Means, G. C. *The Modern Corporation and Private Property*. New York: Macmillan, 1932.

Berri, L. Ya., ed. *Planning a Socialist Economy*, 1973; 2 vols., trans., Moscow: Progress Publishers, 1977.

Bettelheim, C. *India Independent*. New York: Monthly Review Press, 1968.

Beveridge, Lord (W. H.). *Voluntary Action: A Report on Methods of Social Advance*. London: Allen & Unwin, 1948.

Blair, J. M. *The Control of Oil*, 1976; New York: Vintage, 1978.

Bloch, Marc. *Feudal Society*, 1939–1940; trans., 2 vols., Chicago: University of Chicago Press, 1964.

Block, William J. *The Separation of the Farm Bureau and the Extension Service*. Urbana: University of Illinois Press, 1960.

Blum, J. *End of the Old Order in Rural Europe*. Princeton: Princeton University Press, 1978.

Bodde, D. and Morris, C. *Law in Imperial China. Exemplified by 190 Ch'ing Dynasty Cases. With Historical, Social and Judicial Commentaries*, 1967. Philadelphia: University of Pennsylvania Press, 1973.

Bolin, S. *State and Currency in the Roman Empire to 300 A.D.* Stockholm: Almquist & Wiksell, 1958.

Booth, Douglas. "Karl Marx on State Regulation of the Labor Process: The English Factory Acts," *Review of Social Economy*, October 1978.

Bornstein, M., ed. *Comparative Economic Systems*, 3rd ed. Homewood, Ill.: Irwin, 1974.

Bornstein, M., and Fuseld, D. R., eds. *The Soviet Economy: A Book of Readings*, 4th ed. Homewood, Ill.: Irwin, 1974.

Boulding, K. E. *The Organizational Revolution: A Study of the Ethics of Economic Organization*. New York: Harper, 1953.

Boulding, K. E. *Principles of Economic Policy*. Englewood Cliffs, N.J.: Prentice Hall, 1958.

Boxer, C. R., *Fidalgos in the Far East, 1550–1770*. Nijhoff: The Hague, 1948.

Boxer, C. R. *The Christian Century in Japan*. Berkeley: University of California Press, 1951.

Bowie, R. R., and Geiger, T. *The European Economic Community and the United States* (study paper prepared for U. S. Congress Joint Economic Committee). Washington, D.C.: Government Printing Office, November 1961.

Braudel, F. *The Mediterranean and the Mediterranean World in the Age of Philip II*, 1949; trans. from 2nd rev. ed., vols. 1 and 2. New York, Harper, 1973.

Braudel, F., *Capitalism and Material Life, 1400–1800*, 1967; trans. New York: Harper & Row, 1974.

Braudel, F., and Spooner, F. C. "Prices in Europe from 1450 to 1750," in *Cambridge Economic*

History of Europe, vol. 4, eds. E. E. Rich and C. H. Wilson. Cambridge: Cambridge University Press, 1967, pp. 374–480.

Briffault, R. *The Mothers*, vols. 1–3. London: Allen & Unwin, 1927.

Bronfenbrenner, Martin. "Two Concepts of Economic Freedom," *Ethics*. April 1955.

Brzezinski, Z. K. *The Soviet Bloc: Unity and Conflict*, 1960; rev. ed., New York: Cambridge University Press, 1967.

Bukharin, N. *Historical Materialism: A System of Sociology*, 1922; trans. from the 3rd Russian ed., New York: International Publishers, 1925.

Bureau of Statistics, Office of the Prime Minister. *Statistical Handbook of Japan*. Tokyo: Bureau of Statistics, 1972.

Burgon, J. W. *The Life and Times of Sir Thomas Gresham*, 1839; vols. 1 and 2, New York: B. Franklin, 1969.

Burke, E. *Speeches and Letters on American Affairs, 1774–1781*; Everyman's Library ed., London: Dent, 1908.

Burke, E. *Reflections on the Revolution in France and Other Essays, 1790–1791*. Everyman's Library ed., London: Dent, n.d.

Burke, Edmund. *Burke's Works*, vols. 1–5, (a series devoted to papers, addresses, and reports 1783–1794, associated with the indictment of Warren Hastings and with Indian affairs). London: Bohn's Library, 1910–1917.

Burkhead, J. *Government Budgeting*. New York: Wiley, 1966.

Burness, H. S., and Quirk, J. P. "Water Laws, Water Transfers, and Economic Efficiency: The Colorado River," *Journal of Law & Economics*, April 1980.

Bury, J. B. *History of the Later Roman Empire: From the Death of Theodosius I to the Death of Justinian*, 1923; vols. 1 and 2, New York: Dover, 1958.

Cairncross, A. K. *Home and Foreign Investment, 1870–1914*. Cambridge: Cambridge University Press, 1953.

Cairnes, J. E. *The Slave Power: It's Character, Career and Probable Designs*, 1862: republished in *Did Slavery Pay?* G. V. Aitkens, ed., Boston: Houghton-Miflin, 1971.

Carr, E. H., and Davies R. W. *Foundations of a Planned Economy, 1926–1929*. New York: Penguin, 1974.

Carus-Wilson, E. "The Woolen Industry," in *Cambridge Economic History of Europe*, vol. 2, M. Postan and E. E. Rich, eds. Cambridge: Cambridge University Press, 1952.

Carus-Wilson, E. *The Merchant Adventurers of Bristol in the Later Middle Ages*. 1962; 2nd ed., London: Merlin Press, 1967.

Carus-Wilson, E. *Medieval Merchant Venturers: Collected Studies*, 1954; 2nd ed., London: Methuen, 1967.

Chamberlin, E. H. *Theory of Monopolistic Competition: A Re-Orientation of the Theory of Value*, 1933; 5th ed., Cambridge: Harvard University Press, 1946.

Chamberlin, E. H. *Toward a More General Theory of Value*. Oxford: Oxford University Press, 1957.

Chase, S. and Schlink, F. J. *Your Money's Worth: A Study in the Waste of the Consumer's Dollar*. New York: Macmillan, 1928.

Chayanov, A. V. *The Theory of Peasant Economy*, 1925; trans., Homewood, Ill.: Irwin, 1965.

Ching-Tzu, Wu. *The Scholars*. (A 17th-century Chinese Novel.); trans., Peking: Chinese Books, 1973.

Chung-Li Chang. *The Chinese Gentry: Studies on Their Role in Nineteenth Century Chinese Society*. Seattle: University of Washington Press, 1955.

Chung-Li Chang. *The Income of the Chinese Gentry*. Seattle: University of Washington Press, 1962.

Cicero. *Selected Political Speeches*; trans., New York: Penguin Classics, 1973.

Cicero. *Letters to His Friends*, vol. 1; trans., New York: Penguin Classics, 1978.

Cipolla, C. M., ed. *The Fontana Economic History of Europe*, vols. 1–4. Glasgow: Collins/ Fontana, 1972–1976.

Cipolla, C. M. *Guns, Sails and Empires: Technological Innovation and the Early Phases of European Expansion, 1400–1700*. Minerva Press, 1965.

Cipolla, C. M. *Before the Industrial Revolution: European Society and Economy, 1000–1700*, 1976; 2nd ed., New York: Norton, 1980.

Clapham, J. H. *The Economic Development of France and Germany, 1815–1914*, 1921; 3rd ed., Cambridge: Cambridge University Press, 1928.

Clapham, J. H. *Economic History of Modern Britain*, vols. 1–3. Cambridge: Cambridge University Press, 1926–1938.

Clapham, J. H. *The Bank of England*. vols. 1 and 2. Cambridge: Cambridge University Press, 1945.

Clapham, J. H., and Power, E. eds. *Cambridge Economic History of Europe*, vols. 1–7. Cambridge: Cambridge University Press, 1941–1978. (After vol. 1, later volumes were published under different editorships. The first volume is subtitled "From the Decline of the Roman Empire.")

Clark, S. *Social Origins of the Irish Land War*. Princeton, N.J.: Princeton University Press, 1979.

Clarke, S. V. O. "Perspective on the United States External Position since World War II," Federal Reserve Bank of New York, *Quarterly Review*, Summer 1980:21–38.

Coase, R. H. "The Federal Communication Commission," *Journal of Law & Economics*, April 1959:1–40.

Coase, R. H. "Payola in Radio and Television Broadcasting," *Journal of Law & Economics*, October 1979:269–328.

Cochrane, P. "Gold: The Barbarous Relic," *Science and Society*, November 1980:385–400.

Cohn, S. H. "Deficiencies in Soviet Investment Policies and the Technological Imperative," in U.S. Congress Joint Economic Committee, *Soviet Economy in a New Perspective: A Compendium of Papers*. Washington, D.C.: Government Printing Office, 1976.

Cole, G. D. H. *A Century of Cooperation*. London: Allen & Unwin, 1944.

Cole, G. D. H. *The British Cooperative Movement in a Socialist Society*. London: Allen & Unwin, 1951.

Coleman, D. C. *The Economy of England, 1450–1750*, New York: Oxford University Press, 1977.

Commission on Money and Credit. *Money and Credit: Their Influence on Jobs, Prices and Growth*. Englewood Cliffs, N.J.: Prentice-Hall, 1961.

Commons, John R. *Legal Foundations of Capitalism*. Madison: University of Wisconsin Press, 1924.

Commons, John R. *Institutional Economics: Its Place in Political Economy*, vols. 1 and 2. Madison: University of Wisconsin Press, 1934.

Commons, John R. *Economics of Collective Action*. New York: Macmillan, 1950.

Commons, John R., and Andrews, J. B. *Principles of Labor Legislation*. New York: Harper, 1916.

Cook, R. C. *Control of the Petroleum Industry by Major Oil Companies*, Temporary National Economic Committee, Monograph No. 39. Washington, D.C.: Government Printing Office, 1941.

Copeland, M. T., and Towl, A. R. *The Board of Directors and Business Management*. Cambridge, Mass.: Harvard Graduate School of Business, 1947.

Corpus Juris Civilis, vols. 1–17; trans., Cincinatti: Ams Press reprint, 1932. ("The Civil Law" was originally published in Constantinople, A.D. 528–533; it was drawn up by a celebrated jurist's commission headed by Tribonius. Cited in this work are "Twelve Tables," "Institutes of Gaius," "Rules of Ulpian," "Opinions of Paulus," "Enactments of Justinian," appearing in vols. 1–3.)

Comte, August. *The Positive Philosophy of August Comte*, 1830–1842; freely translated by H. Marlineau, 3 vols., London: Bell & Sons, 1896.

Council on Foreign Relations. *The United States in World Affairs*. New York: Harper. (Appearing annually since 1931 except for 1941–1944. Prepared by the council staff with changing editorships.)

Crittenden, A. "After Wave of Mergers, Analysts Debate Plusses." *New York Times*, 31, May 1982.

Curtin, P. D. "Epidemiology and the Slave Trade," *Political Science Quarterly*, June 1968.

Curtin, P. D. *The Atlantic Slave Trade: A Census*. Madison: University of Wisconsin Press, 1969.

Daggett, Stuart. *Principles of Inland Transportation*, 1928; 4th ed., New York: Harper, 1955.

Davis, D. W. *The Problem of Slavery in Western Culture*, 1966: New York, Penguin, 1970.

Davis, Kingsley. *Human Society*. New York: Macmillan, 1949.

Dean, Joel. *Capital Budgeting*. New York: Columbia University Press, 1951.

Deane, P. and Cole, W. A. *British Economic Growth, 1688–1959: Trends and Structure*. Cambridge, England: Cambridge University Press, 1962.

Dempsey, B. W., S. J. *The Functional Economy: The Bases of Economic Organization*. New York: Prentice-Hall, 1958.

Demsetz, H. "Toward a Theory of Property Rights," *American Economic Review*, May 1967.

De Roover, R. *The Rise and Decline of the Medici Bank, 1397–1494*, 1963; New York: Norton, 1966.

Derthick, M. *Policymaking for Social Security*. Washington, D.C.: Brookings, 1979.

De Vries, Jan. *The Economy of Europe in an Age of Crisis, 1600–1750*. New York: Cambridge University Press, 1976.

De Vries, T. "Jamaica, or the Nonreform of the International Monetary System," *Foreign Affairs*, April 1976. (Reproduced in U.S. Senate Committee on Foreign Relations Hearings, *International Monetary Fund Amendments*. Washington, D.C.: Government Printing Office, June–August 1976.)

Edwards, Corwin. "Conglomerate Business as a Source of Power," in *Business Concentration and Price Policy*. A Conference of the Universities National Bureau Committee for Economic Research. Washington, D.C.: National Bureau of Economic Research, 1955.

Dewey, D. L. *et al.* "Standards for the Performance of Our Economic System," (symposium), *American Economic Review Proceedings* May 1960:1–26.

Dewey, Ralph. "The Transportation Act of 1941," *American Economic Review*, March 1941.

Dewing, A. S. *The Financial Policy of Corporations*, 1919; 5th ed., vols. 1 and 2, New York: Ronald, 1953.

Dickinson, F. G., ed. *Philanthropy and Public Policy*. New York: National Bureau of Economic Research, 1962.

Dickinson, F. G. *The Changing Position of Philanthropy in the American Economy*. New York: National Bureau of Economic Research, 1970.

Digby, M. *The World Cooperative Movement*. London: Hutchinson University Library, 1947.

Dobb, M. *Studies in the Development of Capitalism*, 1947; rev. ed., New York: International Publishers, 1963.

Dormer, P., ed. *Cooperative and Group Farming in the Economic Development of Agriculture*. Madison: University of Wisconsin Press, 1977.

Downs, R. S., "Afterword," in *The Jungle*, (1905) author Upton Sinclair. New York: Signet, 1960.

Driver, G. R., and Miles, J. C. *The Babylonian Laws*, vol. 1, 1904; Oxford: Oxford University Press, 1952.

Duby, G. *Rural Economy and Country Life in the Medieval West*, 1962; trans. New York: Columbia University Press, 1968.

Duby, G. *The Early Growth of the European Economy: Warriors and Peasants from the Seventh to the Twelfth Century*, 1973; trans., Ithaca: Cornell University Press, 1974.

Due, John F. *Government Finance: An Economic Analysis*, 1954; rev. ed., Homewood, Ill.: Irwin, 1959.

Durkheim, E. *On the Division of Labor*, 1893; trans., New York: Macmillan, 1933.

Earle, P., ed., *Essays in European Economic History*. New York: Oxford University Press, 1974.

Einzig, Paul. *Primitive Money: In Its Ethnological, Historical and Economic Aspects*, 1949; rev. ed., London: Pergamon Press, 1966.

Elvin, M. *The Pattern of the Chinese Past: A Social and Economic Interpretation*. Stanford, California: Stanford University Press, 1973.

Ely, R. T. *Property and Contract in Their Relation to the Distribution of Wealth*, vols. 1 and 2. New York: Macmillan, 1914.

Encyclopedia of the Social Sciences, vols. 1–15, ed. E. R. A. Seligman *et al.* New York: Macmillan, 1930–1934.

Emmanuel, A. *Unequal Exchange: A Study of the Imperialism of Trade*, 1969; trans., New York: Monthly Review Press, 1972.

Engels, F. *Herr Dühring's Revolution in Science: Anti-Dühring*, 1877–1878. New York: International Publishers, n.d.

Engler, R. *The Politics of Oil*. Chicago: University of Chicago Press, 1961.

Engler, R. *The Brotherhood of Oil: Energy Policy and the Public Intererst*. New York: New American Library, 1978.

Feder, E. *The Rape of the Peasantry*. New York: Anchor, 1971.

Federal Reserve Bank of New York. "Highlights of the Depository Institutions Deregulation and Monetary Control Act of 1980," *Quarterly Review*, Summer 1980.

Federal Reserve Board of Governors. "The Private Demand for Gold, 1931–1953," *Federal Reserve Bulletin*, September 1954.

Fei, Hsiao-Tung. *China's Gentry: Essays in Rural–Urban Relations*, rev. ed. M. P. Redfeld, ed. Chicago: University of Chicago Press, 1953.

Fei Hsiao-Tung. *Peasant Life in China: A Field Study of Country Life in the Yangtze Valley*, 1939; trans., New York: Dutton, 1953.

Fesler, James W., *et al. Industrial Mobilization for War: History of the War Production Board and Predecessor Agencies, 1940–1945*, vols. 1–3. Washington, D.C.: Bureau of Demobilization, CWA, Government Printing Office, 1947.

Finer, H. *Theory and Practice of Modern Government*, 1934; rev. ed., New York: Holt, 1949.

Finley, M. I. *The Ancient Economy*. Berkeley: University of California Press, 1973.

First National City Bank. *Letter*. New York: First National City Bank, December 1960.

Fisher, E., and Rapkin, C. *The Mutual Mortgage Insurance Fund: A Study of the Adequacy of Its Reserves and Resources*. New York: Columbia University Press, 1956.

Fite, G. C. *Farm to Factory: A History of the Consumers Cooperative Association*. Columbia: University of Missouri Press, 1965.

Florence, P. Sargent. "Cooperatives," *International Enclyclopedia of Social Sciences*, vol. 3. New York: Macmillan, 1968.

Fogel, R. W., and Engerman, S. L. *Time on the Cross: The Economics of American Negro Slavery*, vols. 1 and 2. Boston: Little Brown, 1974.

Ford, H. J. "Budget-making and the Work of the Government," *The Annals of the American Academy of Political and Social Science*, November 1915.

Forrest, A. "The Condition of the Poor in Revolutionary Bordeaux," *Past & Present*, May 1973.

Fousek, Peter. *Foreign Central Banking: The Instruments of Monetary Policy*. New York: Federal Reserve Bank of New York, 1957.

Frank, A. G. *Capitalism and Under-Development in Latin America: Historical Studies of Chile and Brazil*. New York: Monthly Review Press, 1969.

Frank, A. G. *Latin America: Underdevelopment or Revolution*. New York: Monthly Review Press, 1970.

Frank, A. G. "The Development of Underdevelopment;" republished in *Dependence and Underdevelopment: Latin America's Political Economy*, J. D. Cockcroft et al., eds. New York: Anchor, 1972.

Frank, A. G. "Economic Dependence: Class Structure and Underdevelopment Policy"; republished in *Dependence and Underdevelopment: Latin America's Political Economy*, eds., J. D. Cockcroft et al. New York: Anchor, 1972.

Frank A. G. *Mexican Agriculture, 1521–1630*. New York: Columbia University Press, 1979.

Frank, T. *An Economic Survey of Ancient Rome*, vol. 1. Baltimore: Johns Hopkins Press, 1933.

Freeman, S. D. *Energy: The New Era*. New York: Vintage, 1974.

Freyre, Gilberto. *New World in the Tropics*; trans., New York, Vintage, 1963.

Friedman, Milton. *Essays in Positive Economics*, 1946–1953. Chicago: University of Chicago Press, 1953.

Friedman, M. *A Program for Monetary Stability*. New York: Fordham University Press, 1960.

Friedman, Milton. *Capitalism and Freedom*. Chicago: University of Chicago Press, 1962.

Friedman, Milton. *Dollars and Deficits*. Englewood Cliffs, N.J.: Prentice-Hall, 1968.

Friedman, Milton, and Schwartz, A. J. *A Monetary History of the United States*. New York: National Bureau of Economic Research, 1963.

Friedman, Milton, and Schwartz, A. J. "Money and the Business Cycles," *Review of Economics and Statistics*, February 1963.

Furtado, C. *The Economic Growth of Brazil*, 1961; Berkeley: University of California Press, 1964.

Galbraith, J. K. *A Theory of Price Control*. Cambridge, Mass.: Harvard University Press, 1952.

Galbraith, J. K. *The New Industrial State*, 1967; 2nd ed., Boston: Houghton Mifflin, 1971.

Galbraith, J. K. *Economics and the Public Purpose*, 1973; New York: Signet, 1975.

Galbraith, J. K. *Money, Where It Came, Where It Went*. Boston: Houghton Mifflin, 1975.

Galbraith, J. K. *A Life in Our Times: Memoirs*, 1981; New York: Ballantine, 1982.

Galewski, B. "Social Organization and Rural Social Change," 1968, in *Peasants and Peasant Societies*, T. Shanin, ed. New York: Penguin, 1971.

Gandhi, Mahatma. *Village Swaraj*. 1921–1947; rev. ed., Ahmedabad, India: Navajivan Trust, 1963.

Gay, P. *The Dilemma of Democratic Socialism*. New York: Collier, 1962.

Gayer, A. D., Rostow, W., and Schwartz, A. J. *The Growth and Fluctuation of the British Economy 1790–1850*, vols. 1 and 2. Oxford: Oxford University Press, 1953.

Gee, Wilson. *The Social Economics of Agriculture*. 1932; rev. ed., New York: Macmillan, 1942.

Geiger, T. *The European Economic Community and the United States*. Study paper prepared for U.S. Congress, Joint Economic Committee. Washington, D.C.: Government Printing Office, November 1961.

Genovese, E. D. *Roll Jordan Roll: The World the Slaves Made*. New York: Vintage, 1976.

Gerloff, W. *Die Öffentliche Finanzwirtschaft*, 1942; 2nd ed., Allgemeiner Teil, Frankfurt: V. Klosterman, 1948.

Gerschenkron, A. *Bread and Democracy in Germany*. Berkeley: University of California Press, 1943.

Gerschenkron, A. "Agrarian Policies and Industrialization: Russia, 1861–1917," in *Cambridge Economic History of Europe*, vol. 6, pt. 2, H. J. Habakkuk and M. Postan, eds. Cambridge: Cambridge University Press, 1965.

Gibb, H. A., and Bowen, H. *Islamic Society and the West, in The Eighteenth Century*, vol. 1. Oxford, England: Oxford University Press, 1950.

Gide, Charles. *Consumer's Cooperative Societies*, 1917; trans., New York: Knopf, 1922.

Gimpel, J. *The Medieval Machine: The Industrial Revolution of the Middle Ages*, 1976; trans., New York: Penguin, 1977.

Goitein, S. D. *Jews and Arabs: Their Contacts through the Ages*, 1955; 3rd ed., New York: Schocken Books, 1974.

Goitein, S. D. *A Mediterranean Society: The Jewish Communities of the Arab World, As Portrayed in the Documents of the Cairo Geniza*, vols. 1–3. Berkeley: University of California Press, 1967–1978.

Goldsmith, R. W. *The National Wealth of the United States in the Postwar Period*. New York: National Bureau of Economic Research, 1962.

Goldsmith, R. W. *The Flow of Capital Funds in the Postwar Economy*. New York: National Bureau of Economic Research, 1965.

Goldsmith, R. W. *Institutional Investors and Corporate Stock: A Background Study*. New York: National Bureau of Economic Research, 1973.

Goldthwaite, R. *Private Wealth in Renaissance Florence: A Study of Four Families*. Princeton, N.J.: Princeton University Press, 1968.

Gogol, N. *Dead Souls*, 1842; trans., New York: Penguin, 1961.

Goodwyn, L. *Democratic Promise: The Populist Movement in America*. New York: Oxford University Press, 1976.

Gorki, Maxim, *et al. Belomar: An Account of the Construction of the New Canal Between the White Sea and the Baltic Sea*, 1934; New York: Harrison Smith, 1935.

Gottlieb, M. "Marx's Mehrwert Concept and Theory of Pure Capitalism," *Review of Economic Studies*. vol. 18, no. 3, pp. 164–178, 1951. (A printing error credited the authorship to H. rather than M. Gottlieb.)

Gottlieb, M. "Theory of an Economic System," *American Economic Review Proceedings*, May 1953.

Gottlieb M. "Theory of an Economic System"; rev. and extended version, in *Frontiers of Social Science: In Honor of Radhakamal Mukerjee*, London: Macmillan, 1955.

Gottlieb, M. "Toward a Sociological Economics," *Indian Journal of Economics*, April 1957.

Gottlieb, M. "Value and Price in Industrial Markets," *Economic Journal*, March 1959: 22–38.

Gottlieb, M. "The Ideological Influence in Schumpeter's Thought," in *Zeitschrift für Nationalökonomie*, January 1959:1–42.

Gottlieb, M. "Our Household Wealth in America and Its Distribution," *Kansas Business Review*, August 1959.

Gottlieb, M. *The German Peace Settlement and the Berlin Crisis*. New York: Paine-Whitman, 1960.

Gottlieb, M. "Clarence E. Ayres and a Larger Economic Theory," *Southwest Social Science Quarterly*, June 1960.

Gottlieb, M. "The Milwaukee Waterworks Expansion: A Case Study in Urban Investment Planning," *Public Administration Review*, December 1964:217–225.

Gottlieb, M. "Urban Domestic Demand for Water: A Case Study on Kansas," *Land Economics*, May 1963:204–210.

Gottlieb, M. "Perspectives for Analysis of Economic Behavior," in B. Singh ed., *Social and Economic Change*. Bombay: Allied Publishers, 1967.

Gottlieb, M. "Mortgage Credit Insurance: A Tale." Unpublished manuscript of author, January 1969.

Gottlieb, M. "Mukerjee: Economics Become Social Science," *Journal of Economic Issues*, December 1971.

Gottlieb, M. "Pluralist or Unitary Economic Systems: A Contribution to the Dialogue between Western Social Science and Marxism," *African Review*, April 1972.

Gottlieb, M. "The Extent and Character of Differentiation in Tanzanian Agricultural and Rural Society 1967–69," *African Review*, June 1973:241–261.

Gottlieb, M. *Health Care Financing in Mainland Tanzania.* Syracuse, N.Y.: Syracuse University Press, 1975.

Gottlieb, M. *Long Swings in Urban Development.* New York: National Bureau of Economic Research, 1976.

Gray, R., and Birmingham, D. *Pre-Colonial African Trade.* Oxford, England: Oxford University Press, 1970.

Grimes, B., and Clark, E. *Goals of Economic Policy.* Boston: Little, Brown, 1955.

Gutman, Herbert. *Time on the Cross, Slavery and the Numbers Game: A Critique of Time on the Cross.* Urbana: University of Illinois Press, 1975.

Habermas, Jürgen. *Knowledge and Human Interests*, 1968; trans. Boston: Beacon Press, 1971.

Habermeir, W. *Operations and Transactions in SDR's: The First Basic Period*, IMF Pamphlet Series No. 17. Washington, D.C.: International Monetary Fund, 1973.

Haines, M. R. "Fertility and Marriage in a Nineteenth-Century Industrial City: Philadelphia, 1850–1880," *Journal of Economic History*, March 1980:151–158.

Hamilton, Alexander. Report to the House of Representatives, January 28, 1792, "The Mint." (Republished in U.S. Senate Committee on Banking and Currency, Hearings, *Additional Mint Facilities.* Washington, D.C.: Government Printing Office, 1963.)

Hamilton, Alexander, Madison, James, and Jay, John. *The Federalist or the New Constitution*, 1787–1788; New York: Dutton, Everyman's ed., 1911.

Hamilton, E. J. *American Treasure and the Price Revolution in Spain.* Cambridge: Harvard University Press, 1934.

Hamilton, E. J. *War and Prices in Spain, 1651–1800.* Cambridge: Harvard University Press, 1947.

Hamilton, E. J. "John Law of Lauriston: Banker, Gamester, Merchant, Thief?" *American Economic Review Proceedings*, May 1967:273–282.

Hammond, J. L., and Hammond, B. *The Bleak Age*, 1934; rev. ed., Gretna, La.: Pelican, 1947.

Handlin, O. and Handlin, M. F. "Origins of the American Business Corporation," in *Enterprise and Secular Change: Readings in Economic History*, F. C. Lane, ed. Homewood, Ill.: Irwin, 1953.

Harris, Seymour. *Price and Related Controls in the United States.* New York: McGraw-Hill, 1945.

Harris, S. E., ed. *The Dollar in Crisis.* New York: Harcourt, 1961.

Hartz, Louis. *Economic Policy and Democratic Thought: Pennsylvania, 1776–1860.* Cambridge, Mass.: Harvard University Press, 1948.

Hawkes, J. *The First Great Civilizations.* New York: Knopf, 1973.

Hawtrey, R. G. *Currency and Credit*, 1919; 3rd ed. London: Longman Green, 1929.

Hawtrey, R. G. *The Economic Problem.* London: Longman, Green, 1926.

Hayek, F. *The Constitution of Liberty.* Chicago: University of Chicago Press, 1960.

Hazard, J. N., ed. *Soviet Legal Philosophy* (translation of Soviet works on law, 1908–1945). Cambridge, Mass.: Harvard University Press, 1951.

Hebel, E. A. *The Law of the Primitive Man: A Study in Comparative Legal Dynamics*. Cambridge, Mass.: Harvard University Press, 1964.

Hegel, G. W. F. *The Science of Logic*. Pt. 1 of *Encyclopedia of the Philosophical Sciences in Outline*, 1817; trans. by William Wallace from 2nd German ed., Oxford, England: Oxford University Press, 1892.

Hegel, G. W. F. *The Philosophy of Fine Art*, 1835; vols. 1–4, trans., London: Bell & Sons, 1920.

Heichelheim, F. M. *An Ancient Economic History: From the Paleolithic Age to the Migrations of the Germanic, Slavic, and Arabic Nations*, 1938; vol. 1–3, trans., Leiden: A. W. Sijthoff, 1957–1970.

Herodotus. *The Histories*, written early 5th-century B.C.; trans., Harmondsworth, England: Penguin, 1954.

Heyerdahl, T. *American Indians in the Pacific*. London: Allen and Unwin, 1952.

Hicks, Ursula K. *British Public Finances: Their Structure and Development, 1880–1952*. Oxford, England: Oxford University Press, 1954.

Hidy, R. W., and Hidy, M. E. *History of Standard Oil Co. (New Jersey)*, vols. 1 and 2. New York: Harper, 1955.

Hodgson, M. G. S. *The Venture of Islam: Conscience and History in a World Civilization*, vols. 1–3. Chicago: University of Chicago Press, 1974.

Holmberg, R. "Vicos: A Peasant Hacienda Community in Peru," in *Economic Development and Social Change*, G. Dalton, ed. New York: American Museum, 1971.

Holyoake, G. J. *Self-Help for the People: The History of the Rochdale Pioneers*, 1857; reprinted in *Introduction to the Cooperative Movement*, A. J. Kress, ed. New York: Harper, 1941.

Honjo, Eihiro. *The Social and Economic History of Japan*, 1935; trans. New York: Russell & Russell, 1965.

Homans, G. C. *English Villagers of the Thirteenth Century*, 1941; New York: Norton, 1975.

Hopkins, A. G. *An Economic History of West Africa*. New York: Columbia University Press, 1973.

Horowitz, D. "The Alliance for Progress," in *Imperialism and Underdevelopment: A Reader*, R. I. Rhodes, ed. New York: Monthly Review Press, 1970.

Hsia Nai. *New Archaeological Finds in China*; trans., Peking: Foreign Language Press, 1972.

Huang Wei. *Conquering the Yellow River*; trans., Peking: Foreign Language Press, 1978.

Humphrey, D. D. *The United States and the Common Market*, 1962; rev. ed., New York: Praeger, 1964.

Huntington, S. P. *Political Order in Changing Societies*. New Haven: Yale University Press, 1968.

Hurst J. W. *Law and Economic Growth: The Legal History of the Lumber Industry in Wisconsin 1836–1915*. Cambridge, Mass.: Harvard University Press, 1964.

Hutchinson, G. S., ed. *The Business of Acquisitions and Mergers*. New York: Presidents Publishing House, 1968.

Hutchinson, T. W., ed. *Africa and the Law*. Madison: University of Wisconsin Press, 1968.

Ibn Khaldun, *The Muqaddimah: An Introduction to History*, 1377; trans. by F. Rosenthal, edited and abridged by N. J. Sawood, Princeton: Princeton University Press, 1968.

Institute of Economics of the Academy of Sciences, USSR. *Political Economy: A Textbook*, 1954; trans. from 2nd ed., London: Lawrence & Wishart, 1957.

International Labour Office, Geneva. *Bulletin of Labour Statistics*, 1st quarter, 1980.

IMF (International Monetary Fund). *IMF Articles of Agreement*. United Nations Monetary and Financial Conference, July 1–22, 1944. Washington, D.C.: IMF, 1944.

IMF. *Annual Report*, since 1947. Washington, D.C.: IMF.

IMF. *IMF News Survey*, appearing weekly since 1948.

IMF. *World Economic Outlook: A Survey by the Staff of the International Monetary Fund*, appearing annually since May 1980.

Ivanov, Y. M. *Agrarian Reforms and Hired Labour in Africa*. trans., Moscow: Progress Publishers, 1979.

James, R. W. *Land Tenure and Policy in Tanzania*. Nairobi, Kenya: East Africa Literature Bureau, 1971.

Jolowicz, H. F., and Nichols, B., eds., *Historical Introduction to the Study of Roman Law*, 1932; 3rd ed., Cambridge: Cambridge University Press, 1972.

Jones, A. H. M. *The Later Roman Empire, 284–602: A Social, Economic and Administrative Survey*, vols. 1 and 2. Norman: University of Oklahoma Press, 1966.

Jones, B. *Cooperative Production*. Oxford, England: Oxford University Press, 1894.

Jurau, J. M., and Louden, J. K. *The Corporate Director*. New York: American Management Association, 1966.

Kahn, Alfred E. *The Economics of Regulation: Principles and Institutions*, vol. 2. New York: Wiley & Son, 1971.

Kantorovich, L. V. "Mathematical Formulation of the Problem of Optimal Planning," in *Socialist Economics: Selected Readings*, 1959, A. Nove and D. M. Nuti, eds., New York: Penguin, 1972.

Kelly, K. D. "The Independent Mode of Production," *The Review of Radical Political Economics* Spring 1979:38–49.

Kemp, T. *Economic Forces in French History*. London: Dobson, 1971.

Kerr, Robert S. *Land, Wood and Water*. New York: MacFadden, 1963.

Keynes, J. M. *Essays in Persuasion, 1919–1931*; London: Rupert Hart-Davis, 1931.

Keynes, J. M. *Treatise on Money*, vols. 1 and 2. London: Macmillan, 1930.

Keynes, J. M. *The General Theory of Employment, Interest and Money*. New York: Harcourt, 1936.

Keynes, J. M. "Address to the House of Lords," May 23, 1944; in *The New Economics* S. Harris, ed. New York: Knopf, 1948.

Khrushchev, N. S. *Program of the Communist Party of the Soviet Union*; trans., New York: Crosscurrent Press, 1961.

Khrushchev, N. S. *Report of the C.C. C.P.S.U. to the 22nd Congress CPSU*; trans., New York: Crosscurrent Press, October 1961.

Khrushchev, N. S. *Khrushchev Remembers: The Last Testament*; S. Talbott, trans. and ed. New York: Bantam, 1976.

Kile, O. M. *The Farm Bureau Movement*. New York: Macmillan, 1921.

Kile, O. M. *The Farm Bureau through Three Decades*. Baltimore: Wavery Press, 1948.

Killick, T., ed. *Adjustment and Financing in the Developing World: The Role of the International Monetary Fund*. Washington, D.C.: International Monetary Fund, 1982.

Kindelberger, C. P. *Manias, Panics and Crashes: A History of Financial Crises*. New York: Harper, 1978.

Klein, P. A. *The Management of Market-Oriented Economies*. Belmont, Calif.: Wadsworth, 1973.

Knight, Frank W. *Risk, Uncertainty and Profit*, 1921; reprint., Chicago: University of Chicago Press, 1971.

Knight, Frank W. *Freedom and Reform*. New York: Harper, 1947.

Knight, Frank W. *The Economic Organization*, 1933; New York: A. M. Kelley, 1959.

Knight, F. W. *Slave Society in Cuba during the Nineteenth Century*. Madison: University of Wisconsin Press, 1970.

Kohlenberg, Elizabeth. "Social Interaction: Social Institutions and Time Geography." (Paper delivered at the annual meeting of the Association of American Geographers, San Antonio, Texas, April 1982.)

Kolb, A. *East Asia: Geography of a Cultural Region*, 1963; trans., London: Methuen, 1971.

Koontz, H. *The Board of Directors and Effective Management*. New York: McGraw-Hill, 1967.

Koontz, H., and O'Donnell, C. *Principles of Management*. New York: McGraw-Hill, 1955.

Koval, N., and Miroshnichenko, B. *Fundamentals of Soviet Economic Planning*; trans., Moscow: Novosti Press, 1972.

Krader, L. *The Asiatic Modes of Production: Source, Development and Critique in the Writings of Karl Marx*. Assen: Van Gorcum, 1975.

Kress, A. J., ed. *Introduction to the Cooperative Movement*. New York: Harper, 1941.

Kroeber, A. L. *Anthropology*, 1923; rev. ed., New York: Harcourt, 1948.

Kropotkin, P. *Mutual Aid*, 1890; Gretna, La: Pelican, 1939.

Kropotkin, P. *Memoirs of a Revolutionist*. Boston: Houghton Mifflin, 1899.

Kulischer, J. *Allgemeine Wirtschaftsgeschichte: Des Mittelalters und der Neuzeit*, 1925; trans., vols. 1 and 2, Munich: R. Olderbourg, 1928–1929.

Ku Pan. *Han Shu. Food and Money in Ancient China: The Earliest Economic History of China to 25 A.D.*; N. L. Swann, trans., who sometimes is attributed authorship, Princeton: Princeton University Press, 1950.

Kuznets, Simon. *National Income and Its Composition, 1919–1938*, vols. 1 and 2. New York: National Bureau of Economic Research, 1941.

Landes, David. *The Unbound Prometheus: Technological Change and Industrial Development in Western Europe from 1750 to the Present*. Cambridge: Cambridge University Press, 1969.

Lane, F. C. *Andrea Barbarigo, Merchant of Venice, 1418–1439*. Baltimore: Johns Hopkins University Press, 1944.

Lane, F. C. ed. *Enterprise and Secular Change: Readings in Economic History*. Homewood, Ill.: Irwin, 1953.

Lane, F. C. *Venice and History: The Collected Papers of F. C. Lane*. Baltimore: Johns Hopkins University Press, 1966.

Lane, F. C. *Venice: A Maritime Republic*. Baltimore: Johns Hopkins University Press, 1973.

Lange, O. *Introduction to Econometrics*, 1957; trans. Warsaw: Pergamon, 1959.

Lange, O. *Political Economy: General Problems*, 1959; trans. from 2nd Polish ed., London: Pergamon Press, 1963.

Laski, H. *Grammar of Politics*, 1925; 4th ed., London: Allen & Unwin, 1938.

League of Nations, Economic Financial and Transit Department. *International Currency Experience*. Authored by R. Nurske, Geneva: League of Nations, 1944.

Lenin, V. I. *Development of Capitalism in Russia*, 1899; trans. from 2nd Russian 1907 ed., Moscow: Foreign Language Publishing House, 1956.

Lenin, V. I. "The Agrarian Question and the 'Critics of Marx,'" 1902; republished and translated in *Collected Works*, vol. 4, New York: International Publishers, 1929.

Lenin, V. I. *Selected Works*, vols. 1–12; trans. New York: International Publishers. (This edition is undated but was issued in the late 1920s and early 1930s.)

Lenin, V. I. *Imperialism, the Highest Stage of Capitalism: A Popular Outline*. 1917; trans., Peking: China Books, 1965.

Lenin, V. I. *State and Revolution*, 1917; trans., New York: International Publishers, 1932.

Lenin, V. I. *Selected Works*, vols 1–3, trans., Moscow: Progress Publishers, 1971.

Le Roy Ladurie, E. *The Peasants of Languedoc*, 1966; trans., Urbana: University of Illinois Press, 1974.

Levchuk, Z. "Money Circulation and the Role of Money under Socialism," *Problems of Eco-*

nomics, August 1979. (A quarterly periodical of translations of articles by Soviet economists.)

Lewin, M. *Russian Peasants and Soviet Power*. London: Allen and Unwin, 1968.

Lewis, O. *Life in a Mexican Village: Tepoztlan Revisited*, 1951; Urbana: University of Illinois Press, 1963.

Liberman, E. *Economic Methods and the Effectiveness of Production*, 1970; trans. Garden City, N.Y.: Doubleday, 1973.

Lichtheim, G. C. *Marxism: An Historical and Critical Study*, 1961: trans., 2nd ed., New York: Praeger, 1965.

Lien-Sheng Yang. *Money and Credit in China: A Short History*. Cambridge, Mass.: Harvard University Press, 1962.

Lintner, J. "Expectations, Mergers and Equilibrium in Purely Competitive Securities Markets," *American Economic Review Papers and Proceedings*, May 1971.

Linton, Ralph. *The Study of Man*. New York: Appleton, 1936.

Linton, Ralph. "An Anthropological View of Economics," in A. Ward, ed., *Goals of Economic Life*. New York: Harper, 1953.

Liu, T., and Fei, J. C. H. "An Analysis of the Land Tax Burden in China, 1650–1865," *Journal of Economic History*, June 1977.

Livy (Livius Titus). *History of Rome From Its Foundation*. His work was published between 29 B.C. and A.D. 17 in 142 books. Of these only 35 are extant. Citations to these books are from English translations, paged in the Oxford Classical Text and published at Harmondsworth, England: Penguin, under the following titles:
Early History of Rome, bks. 1–5, 1960 (rev. 1971);
Rome and Italy, bks. 6–10, 1982;
The War with Hannibal, bks. 21–30, 1965;
Rome and the Mediterranean, bks. 31–45; 1976.

Locklin, P. *Economics of Transportation*, 1935; 4th ed., Homewood, Ill.: Irwin, 1954.

Lopez, R. S. and Raymond, I. W., eds. *Medieval Trade in the Mediterranean World: Illustrative Documents Translated with Introductions and Notes*. New York: Norton, 1967.

Lundberg, Ferdinand. *The Rich and Super-Rich*, 1968; New York: Bantam, 1969.

Luxemberg, R. *Einleitung in die Nationalökonomie*. Berlin: Laubsche Verlag, 1925.

Mace, Myles L. *Directors: Myth and Reality*. Cambridge, Mass.: Harvard School of Business, 1971.

Machiavelli, N. *The Prince and the Discourses*, 1513–1521; New York: Modern Library, 1950.

Mack, R. P. *The Flow of Business Funds and Consumer Purchasing Power*. New York: Columbia University Press, 1941.

Mack, R. P. *Information, Expectations and Inventory Fluctuation*. New York: National Bureau of Economic Research, 1967.

Maine, Henry. *Village Communities in the East and West*. New York: Henry Holt, 1876.

Makhov, A. S., and Frish, A. S., eds. *Society and Economic Relations*, 1966; trans., Moscow: Progress Publishers, 1969.

Malefakis, E. E. *Agrarian Reform and Peasant Revolution of Spain*. New Haven: Yale University Press, 1970.

Malinowski, B. *A Scientific Theory of Culture and Other Essays*. Chapel Hill, N.C.: University of North Carolina Press, 1944.

Malthus, T. R. *An Essay on the Principle of Population*, 1799; republished with select chapters from the 6th ed. greatly revised in *On Population*, New York: Modern Library, 1960.

Mandel, E. *Late Capitalism*, 1972; trans. London: New Left Books, 1978.

Mao Tse-Tung (Mao Zedong). *A Critique of Soviet Economics*, 1958–1959; trans., New York: Monthly Review Press, 1977.

Mao Tse-Tung (Mao Zedong). *Selected Works*, vols. 1–5; trans., Peking: Foreign Language Press, 1961–1977.

Markham, J. W. "Survey of the Evidence and Findings on Mergers (with Comment by Walter Adam)," *Business Concentration and Price Policy*, a conference of the University National Bureau Committee for Economic Research. New York: National Bureau of Economic Research, 1955.

Marshall, Alfred. *Principles of Economics*, 1890; 8th ed., London: Macmillan, 1920.

Marshall, Alfred. *Industry and Trade*. London: Macmillan, 1919.

Marshall, Alfred. *Money, Credit and Commerce*. London: Macmillan, 1923.

Marx, Karl, and Engels, Frederick. *The Holy Family*, 1845; trans., Moscow: Foreign Language Publishers, 1956.

Marx, Karl. *The Poverty of Philosophy: Answer to the Philosophy of Poverty by M. Proudhon*, 1847, in K. Marx and F. Engels, *Collected Works*, vol. 6 (pp. 110–212). New York: International Publishers, 1982.

Marx, Karl. "Irish Tenant Rights," 1853; in K. Marx and F. Engels, *Ireland and the Irish Question: A Collection of Writings*, 1845–1891; New York: International Publishers, 1972.

Marx, Karl. *Grundrisse: Foundations to the Critique of Political Economy*, written 1857–1858; published in Moscow 1939–1941, cited in this volume from M. Nicolaus, trans., New York: Vintage, 1974.

Marx, Karl. *Contribution to the Critique of Political Economy*, 1859; trans., New York: International Publishers, 1971.

Marx, Karl. *Karl Marx on the First International*, 1864–1872; trans., New York: McGraw-Hill, 1973.

Marx, Karl. *Theories of Surplus Value*, 1862–1863; published by K. Kautsky, 1905–1910; cited in this volume from the improved version, vols. 1–3, Moscow: Progress Publishers, 1963–1971.

Marx, Karl. *Capital. A Critique of Political Economy*, vols. 1–3, each bearing a distinctive subtitle for vols. 1–3 respectively: "The Process of Capitalist Production," "The Circulation Process of Capital," and "The Process of Capitalist Production as a Whole." The basic writing of the three volumes was in the main carried out by Marx between 1863–1866. Only the first volume was published by Marx in 1867 and revised by Marx in a French translation published in 1873. The remaining two volumes were posthumously edited and compiled by F. Engels, Marx's trusted co-worker and friend in 1885 (vol. 2) and in 1894 (vol. 3). The English translations of *Capital*, cited in this work, were derived from the latest German editions prepared by F. Engels and the English translation has been corrected in Russian publications, Moscow: Progress Publishers and their English version has been accepted by the English text: New York: International Publishers, 1967.

Marx, Karl, and Engels, Frederick. *Collected Works*, 1841–1860; vols. 1–18, trans. New York: International Publishers, 1974–1982.

Marx, Karl, and Engels, Frederick. *German Ideology*, written 1845–1846, published in 1932–1933; trans., Moscow: Progress Publishers, 1964.

Marx, Karl, and Engels, Frederick. *On Britain*, 1845–1895; trans. Moscow: Foreign Language Press, 1953.

Marx, Karl, and Engels, Frederick. *Selected Works*, 1845–1895; vols. 1–3; trans. New York: International Publishers, 1968.

Marx, Karl, and Engels, Frederick. *Ireland and the Irish Question: A Collection of Writings*, 1845–1891; trans. New York: International Publishers, 1972.

Marx, Karl, and Engels, Frederick. *The Communist Manifesto*, 1848; reproduced and translated in *Collected Works*, vol. 6. New York: International Publishers, 1982.

Marx, Karl, and Engels, Frederick. *The Russian Menace to Europe*, 1848–1894; trans. Glencoe, Ill.: Free Press, 1952.

Mathews. R.C.O. *Study in Trade Cycle History: Economic Fluctuations in Great Britain*. Cambridge: Cambridge University Press, 1954.

McConnell, Grant. *The Decline of Agrarian Democracy*. Berkeley: University of California Press, 1953.

Meek, R. L. "Mr. Gottlieb on Marx: A Comment," *Review of Economic Studies* 20:1952–1953:78–83.

Melman, Seymour. *Pentagon Capitalism: The Political Economy of War*. New York: McGraw-Hill, 1970.

Menshikov, S. *Millionaires and Managers*. trans., Moscow: Progress Publishers, 1960.

Merton, R. K. *Social Theory and Social Structure*. Glencoe, Ill.: Free Press, 1949.

Metzler, Lloyd. "The Nature and Stability of Inventory Cycle," *Review of Economics and Statistics*, August 1941:113–129.

Metzler, Lloyd. "Factors Governing the Length of Inventory Cycles," *Review of Economics and Statistics*, February 1947:1–15.

Michleman, F. I. "Property, Utility and 'Fairness': Comments on the Ethical Foundations of 'Just Compensation Law,'" *Harvard Law Review*, (1968), republished in B. A. Ackerman, ed., *Economic Foundations of Property Law*. Boston: Little Brown, 1975.

Mikesell, R. F. "The Role of the International Monetary Agreement in a World of Planned Economies," 1947; republished in H. S. Ellis and L. A. Metzler, eds., *Readings in the Theory of International Trade*. New York: McGraw-Hill (Blakiston), 1950.

Mikesell, R. F. *United States Economic Policy and International Relations*. New York: McGraw-Hill, 1952.

Mill, John Stuart. *Essays on Politics and Culture*, 1831–1870; Garden City, N.Y.: Doubleday, 1963.

Mill, John Stuart. *Principles of Political Economy: With Some of Their Applications to Social Philosophy*, 1848; cited in this volume from 1871 ed., London: W. J. Ashley, 1909.

Mill, John Stuart. *Utilitarianism, Liberty and Representative Government*, 1859–1861; London: Dent, Everyman's Library ed., 1910.

Mills, E. S. *The Economics of Environmental Quality*. New York: Norton, 1978.

Mills, C. W. *The Power Elite*. New York: Oxford Press, 1956.

Minasian, J. F. "Property Rights in Radiation: An Alternative Approach to Radio Frequency Allocation," *Journal of Law & Economics*, April 1975:221–274.

Mishna, The, H. Danby, ed. and trans., Oxford: Oxford University Press, 1933. *The Mishna* was a collective work by a succession of Rabbinic sages, setting forth the evolving rules and principles of Pharisaic Judaism in the post-Biblical period. The Mishna took its present shape under the guidance of a single redactor, commonly believed to be Judah the Patriarch (also called "Prince"). The work appeared somewhere around A.D. 200. *The Mishna* is more commonly presented by individual paragraphs in the many-volumed *Babylonian Talmud*, interspersed with extended and didactic commentary.

Miskimin, H. A. *The Economy of Early Renaissance Europe 1300–1460*. Cambridge: Cambridge University Press.

Mitchell, H. *The Economics of Ancient Greece*. Cambridge: Cambridge University Press, 1940.

Mitchell, Wesley C. "The Backward Art of Spending Money," 1912; republished in *The Backward Art of Spending Money and Other Essays*, Fairfield, N.J.: A. Kelley, 1950.

Montias, J. M. *The Structure of the Economic Systems*. New Haven: Yale University Press, 1976.

Moore, B. Jr. *Social Origins of Dictatorship and Democracy*, 1966; New York: Penguin, 1967.

Morley, L. F. *The Patchwork of Foreign Aid*. Washington, D.C.: American Enterprise Institute, April 1961.

Mukerjee, P. K. *Economic Surveys in Under-Developed Countries: A Study in Methodology.* Bombay: Hind Kitabs, 1959.

Mukerjee, Radhakamal. *Institutional Theory of Economics.* London: Macmillan, 1941.

Mukerjee, Radhakamal. *Planning the Countryside.* 1946; 2nd ed. Bombay: Hind Kitabs, 1950.

Mumford, Lewis. *The City in History: Its Origins, Its Transformations and Its History.* New York: Harcourt, 1961.

Mumford, Lewis. *Technics and Civilization,* 1934; New York: Harcourt, 1963.

Mund, V. *Open Markets.* New York: Harper, 1948.

Mundy, J. H., and Riesenberg, P., eds. *The Medieval Town.* Princeton, N.J.: Van Nostrand, 1958.

Myers, R. H. *The Chinese Peasant Economy: Agricultural Development in Hopei and Shantung, 1890–1919.* Cambridge, Mass.: Harvard University Press, 1970.

Myrdal, Gunnar. *Asian Drama,* vols. 1–3. New York: Random House, 1968.

Myrdal, Jan. *Report from a Chinese Village,* 1963; New York: New American Library, 1965.

Needham, Joseph. *Science and Civilization in China,* vols. 1–5. Cambridge: Cambridge University Press, 1954–1978.

Nef, J. U. *The Rise of the British Coal Industry,* vols. 1 and 2. London: Cass, 1932.

Nef, J. U. "The Industrial Revolution Reconsidered," *Journal of Economic History* 3, May 1943.

Nef, J. U. *Industry and Government in France and England 1540–1650,* 1940; Ithaca, N.Y.: Cornell University Press, 1957.

Nelson, R. A., and Grenier, W. R. "The Relevance of the Common Carrier under Modern Economic Conditions," *Transportation Economics.* A Conference of the University of National Bureau Committee of Economic Research; Conference Series No. 17. New York: National Bureau of Economic Research, 1965.

New York Stock Exchange. *1955 Year Book.* New York: New York Stock Exchange Public Relations Department, January 1, 1955.

Nichols, Alfred. "Stock versus Mutual Savings and Loan Associations: Some Evidence of Differences in Behavior," *American Economic Review, Papers and Proceedings,* May 1967:337–346.

Nieburg, H. L. *In the Name of Science.* Chicago: Quadrangle Books, 1966.

Nixon, Richard. *The Memoirs of Richard Nixon,* vols. 1 and 2. New York: Warner Books, 1978.

Norman, E. H. *Origins of the Modern Japanese State: Selected Writings.* New York: Pantheon, 1975.

Nove, A. *The Soviet Economy,* 1961; 3rd rev. ed., Winchester, Mass.: Allen & Unwin, 1968.

Novosti Press Agency Publishers, ed. *Soviet Economic Reform: Main Features and Aims* (a collection of 1965 articles and texts); trans., Moscow: Novosti Press Agency Publishers, 1966.

Noyes, C. R. *Economic Man: In Relation to His Natural Environment,* vols. 1 and 2. New York: Cornell University Press, 1948.

Noyes, C. R. *The Institution of Property.* New York: Longmans, Green & Co., 1936.

Olson, Mancur. *Collective Action. The Logic of Collective Action and the Theory of Groups.* 1965; Cambridge, Mass.: Harvard University Press, 1971.

Parsons, Talcott. *The Structure of Social Action,* 1936; 2nd ed., New York: Free Press, 1949.

Parsons, Talcott. "Introduction" to *The Theory of Social and Economic Organization,* by Max Weber. Oxford England: Oxford University Press, 1947.

Parsons, Talcott, *The Social System.* New York: Free Press, 1951.

Parsons, Talcott. *Societies: Evolutionary and Comparative Perspectives.* Englewood Cliffs, N.J.: Prentice-Hall, 1966.

Parsons, Talcott. *Sociological Theory and Modern Society*. New York: Free Press, 1967.

Parsons, Talcott, and Smelser, N. J. *Economy and Society*. New York: Free Press, 1957.

Phillips, C. F., Jr. *The Economics of Regulation*, 1965; rev. ed., Homewood, Ill.: Irwin, 1969.

Pigou, A. C. *The Economics of Welfare*, 1920; 4th ed., London: Macmillan, 1932.

Pigou, A. C. *Political Economy of War*, 1921; rev. ed., New York: Macmillan, 1941.

Pigou, A. C., ed. *Memorials of Alfred Marshall*, 1925; New York: A. Kelly & Millman, 1956.

Pirenne, H. *Economic and Social History of Medieval Europe*, 1933; trans., London: Routledge, 1936.

Plato. *Laws*; trans., New York: Penguin, 1970.

Plato. *The Republic*; B. Jowett, trans., New York: Modern Library, 1941.

Plekhanov, G. V. *Selected Philosophical Works*, 1883–1913; trans., vols. 1–5, Moscow: Progress Publishers, 1976.

Plutarch. *The Lives of the Noble Grecians and Romans*, J. Dryden and A. H. Clough, trans., New York: Modern Library Reprint, 1864.

Polanyi, K. *The Great Transformation*. New York: Rinehart, 1944.

Polanyi, K. *Primitive, Archaic and Modern Economies*, 1944–1966; G. Dalton, ed., Boston: Beacon Press, 1971.

Polo, Marco. *The Travels*, late thirteenth century; trans., New York: Penguin, 1958.

Polybius. *The Histories* (The Rise of the Roman Nation), 155–125 B.C.; Selections, F. W. Walbank, ed. and trans. Harmondsworth, England: Penguin, 1979.

Postan, M. M. *The Medieval Economy and Society*, 1972; Gretna, La.: Pelican, 1975.

Powell, G. H. *Cooperation in Agriculture*. New York: Macmillan, 1913.

President's Commission on National Goals. *Goals for Americans*. New York: Columbia University Press, 1960.

Procacci, G. "A Survey of the Debate," in R. Hilton, ed., *The Transition from Feudalism to Capitalism*. London: New Left Books, 1976.

Proxmire, William, Senator. *Uncle Sam: The Last of the Big Time Spenders*. New York: Simon & Schuster, 1972.

Radin, M. *Handbook of Roman Law*. St Paul: St. Paul Publishers, 1917.

Ransom, R. L., and Sutch, R. *One Kind of Freedom: The Economic Consequences of Emancipation*. New York: Cambridge University Press, 1977.

Rawls, John. *A Theory of Justice*. Cambridge, Mass.: Harvard University Press, 1971.

Redford, E. S. *Field Administration of Wartime Rationing*. "Historical Reports on War Administration." Washington, D.C.: OPA, Government Printing Office, 1947.

Ricardo, David. *The Principles of Political Economy and Taxation*, 1817; London: Dent, Everyman's ed. 1911.

Robbins, Lionel. *An Essay on the Nature and Significance of Economic Science*, 1932; 2nd ed., London: Macmillan, 1935.

Robinson, D. *Slavery in the Structure of American Politics*, 1971; New York: Norton, 1979.

Rochester, A. *Why Farmers are Poor: The Agricultural Crisis in the United States*. New York: International Publishers, 1940.

Rodinson, M. *Islam and Capitalism*, 1967; trans., Austin: University of Texas Press, 1973.

Rogers, J. E. T. *Six Centuries of Work and Wages*. New York: Putnams, 1883.

Rörig, F. *The Medieval Town*, 1955; trans., Berkeley: University of California Press, 1967.

Russell, J. C. "Population in Europe, 500–1500," in C. M. Cippola, ed., *The Fontana Economic History of Europe*, vol. 1. Glasgow: Fontana, 1972.

Rumyantsev, A. *Categories and Laws of the Political Economy of Communism*, 1964; trans., Moscow: Progress Publishers, 1969.

Sadler, A. L. *The Maker of Modern Japan: The Life of Tokugawa Ieyasu*. London: Allen & Unwin, 1937.

Salant, W. S., *et al*. *The United States Balance of Payments in 1968*. Washington, D.C.: Brookings, 1963.

Sampson, Anthony. *The Sovereign State of ITT*, 1973; New York: Fawcett Crest, 1974.

Samuels, W. *The Classical Theory of Economic Policy*. Cleveland: World, 1966.

Schiller, O. M. *Cooperative Integration in Agricultural Production; Concepts and Practical Applications: an International Synopsis*. 1966; Bombay: Asia Publishing House, 1969.

Schroeder, G. "Recent Developments in Soviet Planning and Incentives," in U.S. Congress Joint Economic Committee, *Soviet Economic Prospects for the Seventies: A Compendium of Papers*. Washington, D.C.: Government Printing Office, 1973.

Schumpeter, Joseph. *Theory of Economic Development*, 1912; trans., Cambridge, Mass.: Harvard University Press, 1934.

Schumpeter, Joseph. "The Crisis of the Tax State (Steuerstaat)," 1918; republished and translated in *International Economic Papers* No. 4, New York: Macmillan, 1954.

Schumpeter, Joseph. *Business Cycles*, vols. 1 and 2. New York: McGraw-Hill, 1939.

Schurman, Franz. *Ideology and Organizations in Communist China*, 1966; 2nd ed., Berkeley: University of California Press, 1970.

Scitovsky, T. *The Joyless Economy*. Oxford, England: Oxford University Press, 1976.

Scroggs, C. L. "Historical Highlights," in M. A. Abrahamsen and C. L. Scroggs, eds. *Agricultural Cooperation: Selected Readings*. Minneapolis: University of Minnesota Press, 1957.

Seidman, A. *Planning for Development in Sub-Saharan Africa*. New York: Praeger, 1974.

Senior, N. *An Outline of the Science of Political Economy*, 1836; London: London School Reprint 1836 ed., 1938.

Shanin, T., ed. *Peasants and Peasant Societies*. New York: Penguin, 1971.

Shiba Yoshinobu. *Commerce and Society in Sung China*. 1968; trans., Ann Arbor: University of Michigan Press, 1970.

Shmelv, G. "The Private Household Plot in CMEA Countries," *Problems of Economics*, May 1979. (A quarterly periodical of translated articles appearing in Soviet economic journals.)

Sloan, Alfred P. *My Years with General Motors*. New York: Doubleday, 1963.

Smith, Adam. *An Enquiry into the Nature and Causes of the Wealth of Nations*, 1776; E. Cannan, ed., as of 5th ed., 1789. New York: Modern Library, 1937.

Smith, T. C. *The Agrarian Origins of Modern Japan*. Stanford: Stanford University Press, 1959.

Solomon, E. *The Anxious Economy*. San Francisco: Freeman, 1975.

Solzhenitsyn, A. I. *Gulag Archipelago 1918-1956: An Experiment in Literary Investigation*, 1960s; trans., vols. 1-3, New York: Harper & Row, 1973-1978.

Sombart, Werner. *Der Moderne Kapitalismus*, vols. 1 and 2. Leipzig: Duncker & Humblot, 1902.

Sombart, Werner. *The Jews and Modern Capitalism*, 1911; J. Epstein, trans., New York: Macmillan, 1951.

Sombart, Werner. *Die Ordnung des Wirtschaft*. Berlin: Springer, 1925.

Sombart, Werner. *Die Drei Nationalökonomien. Geschichte und System der Lehre von der Wirtschaft*. München: Duncker & Humblot, 1930.

Sorokin, P. *Social Mobility*. New York: Harper, 1927.

Sorokin, P. *Social and Cultural Dynamics: Basic Problems, Principles and Methods*, vol. 4. New York: American Book, 1941.

Sorokin, P. *Society, Culture and Personality*. New York: Harper, 1947.

Sorokin, P., and Zimmerman, C. *Principles of Rural-Urban Sociology*. New York: Holt, 1929.

Spence, J. D. *Emperor of China: Self Portrait of K'ang-Hsi*. New York: Random House, 1957.

Spencer, Herbert. *The Principles of Sociology*, vols. 1-3. New York: Appleton, 1896.

Spirkin, A., and Yakhot, O. *The Basic Principles of Dialectical and Historical Materialism*; trans., Moscow: Progress Publishers, 1971.

Stalin, J. *Economic Problems of Socialism in the USSR*; trans., New York: International Publishers, 1952.

Steiner, Peter O. *Mergers, Motives, Effects, Policies*. Ann Arbor: University of Michigan Press, 1975.

Stobaugh, Robert, and Yergin, Daniel, eds. *Energy Future: Report of the Energy Future at the Harvard Business School*. New York: Random House, 1979.

Schram, S. *Chairman Mao Talks to the People*. New York: Pantheon, 1974.

Summerson, J. *Georgian London*, rev. ed. Baltimore: Penguin, 1962.

Szuma Chien. *Records of the Historian: Selections*, written 20 B.C.; trans., Peking: Foreign Language Press, 1979.

Tacitus. *Annals of Imperial Rome*, written first-century A.D.; trans. Harmondsworth, England: Penguin, 1972.

Tannenbaum, F. *Ten Keys to Latin America*, 1960; New York: Random House, 1966.

Tawney, R. H. *Equality*. London: Allen & Unwin, 1929.

Tawney, R. H. *Religion and the Rise of Capitalism: A Historical Study*, 1926; New York: New American Library, 1947.

Taylor, G. "Noncapitalist Wealth and the Origins of the French Revolution," *American Historical Review*, January 1967.

Taylor, H. C. *Agricultural Economics*. New York: Macmillan, 1919.

Thierry, A. *The Norman Conquest of England*, 1825; trans., Everyman's ed., vols. 1 and 2, London: Dent, 1907.

Thomas, W. I., and Znaniecki, F. *The Polish Peasant in Europe and American*, trans., 1919; reprinted, vols. 1 and 2, New York: Knopf, 1927.

Thucydides. *The History of the Peloponnesian War*, written fifth century B.C.; R. Crawley, trans., Everyman ed., New York: Dutton, 1910.

Tigar, M. E., and Levy, M. R. *Law and the Rise of Capitalism*. New York: Monthly Review Press, 1977.

Tilly, Charles, ed. *The Formation of National States in Western Europe*. Princeton, N.J.: Princeton University Press, 1975.

Trilateral Commission. *Towards a Renovated World Monetary System: A Report of the Trilateral Monetary Task Force*. New York: Trilateral Commission, October 1973.

Tugan-Baranovsky, M. I. *The Russian Factory in the 19th Century*, 1898; trans., Homewood, Ill.: Irwin, 1970.

T'ung-Tsu Ch'u. *Local Government in China under the Ching*. Cambridge: Harvard University Press, 1962.

Turnbull, J. G., Williams, C. R., Jr., and Cheit, E. F. *Economic and Social Security*, 1957; 3rd ed., New York: Ronald Press, 1967.

Twitchett, D. C. *Financial Administration under the Tang Dynasty*. Cambridge: Cambridge University Press, 1970.

Ullmer, Melville J. *Capital in Transportation, Communications, and Public Utilities: Its Formation and Financing*. New York: National Bureau of Economic Research, 1960.

Usher, A. P. *The Early History of Deposit Banking in Mediterranean Europe*. Cambridge, Mass.: Harvard University Press, 1943.

Usher, A. P. "The Origins of Banking: The Primitive Banks of Deposit," in F. C. Lane, ed., *Enterprise and Secular Change: Readings in Economic History*. Homewood, Ill.: Irwin, 1953.

Varga, Y. *Twentieth Century Capitalism*; trans., Moscow: Foreign Language Press, 1961.

Varga, Y. *Politico-Economic Problems of Capitalism*, 1963; trans., Moscow: Progress Publishers, 1968.

Vazquez, M. C. "Vicos: The Interplay between Power and Wealth," in G. Dalton, ed., *Economic Development and Social Change*. New York: National History Press, 1971.

Veblen, T. *Theory of the Leisure Class*, 1899; New York: Modern Library, 1934.

Veblen, T. "The Country Town," in *Absentee Ownership and Business Enterprise in Recent Times* 1923; reprinted in M. Lerner, ed., *The Portable Veblen*, New York: Viking Press, 1948.

Veinshtein, A. L., 1966; in A. Nove and D. M. Nuti, eds. *Socialist Economics: Selected Readings*. New York: Penguin, 1972.

Vice, A. *The Strategy of Takeovers: A Casebook of International Practice*. New York: McGraw-Hill, 1971.

Vissering, W. *On Chinese Currency Coins and Paper Money*, 1877; Taipai reprint of Leiden original, 1968.

Waley, D. *The Italian City-Republics*. New York: McGraw-Hill, 1969.

Walker, K. R. *Planning in Chinese Agriculture: Socialization and the Private Sector, 1956–1962*. London: Cass, 1965.

Wallerstein, Immanuel. *The Modern World-System: Capitalist Agriculture and the Origin of the European World Economy in the Sixteenth Century*. New York: Academic Press, 1974.

Wallerstein, Immanuel. *The Capitalist World Economy*. Cambridge: Cambridge University Press, 1979.

Walras, L. *Elements of Pure Economics*, 1877; W. Jaffe, trans., of 1926, definitive French ed., Homewood, Ill.: Irwin, 1954.

Walras, Leon. *Études d'economie sociale: Theorie de la répartition de la richesse sociale*, 1896; definitive ed. Lausanne, Switzerland: Rouge, 1936.

Ward, A. D. *Goals of Economic Life*. New York: Harper, 1953.

Warner, W. Lloyd. *The Corporation in the Emergent American Society*. New York: Harper, 1962.

Webb, Beatrice (AKA Beatrice Potter). *The Cooperative Movement*. London: Swann Sonnenschein, 1891.

Webb, Sidney and Webb, Beatrice. *Industrial Democracy*, vols. 1 and 2. London: Longman, Green, 1897.

Webb, Sidney and Webb, Beatrice. *English Local Government from the Revolution to the Municipal Corporation Act, 1689–1835*, vols. 1–11, London: Longman, Green, 1903–1929. (A set of studies dealing with "Parish and County," "Manor and Burrough," "Statutory Authorities for Special Purposes," "The King's Highway," and "Poor Law History," and other topics.)

Webb, Sidney, and Webb, Beatrice. *Soviet Communism: A New Civilization?* 1935; 3rd. ed., London: Longman, Green, 1944.

Webb, Sidney, and Webb, Beatrice. *The Consumer's Cooperative Movement*. London: Longman, Green, 1921.

Weber, Max. "Zur Geschichte der Handelsgesellschäfte im Mittelalter," 1889; republished in *Gesammelte Aufsätze zur Social-und Wirtschaftgeschichte*, 1896–1909; Tübingen; Mohr, 1924.

Weber, Max. *The Protestant Ethic and the Spirit of Capitalism*, 1904–1905; New York: Scribners, 1958.

Weber, Max. *The Methodology of the Social Sciences*, 1904–1917; trans., Encino, Calif.: Glencoe Free Press, 1949.

Weber, Max. *From Max Weber: Essays in Sociology*, 1906–1921; H. H. Gerth and C. W. Mills, trans. and eds., New York: Oxford University Press, 1946.

Weber, Max. *General Economic History*, 1923; trans., Encino, Calif.: Glencoe Free Press, 1927.

Weber, Max. *Religion of China: Confucianism and Taoism*, 1916; trans., New York: Macmillan, 1964.

Weber, Max. *Economy and Society: An Outline of Interpretive Sociology*, 1921; vols. 1 and 2, trans. from 4th German ed., 1956, Berkeley: University of California Press, 1978.

PUBLICATIONS OF THE UNITED STATES GOVERNMENT, WASHINGTON D.C.:
GOVERNMENT PRINTING OFFICE

A. Office of the President

Message of the President of the United States. Standby Rationing Plan. 96 Congress, 1st Session, H.Doc. 96-63, March 1, 1979.
Economic Report of the President, including a report of the Council of Economic Advisors, annually since 1947.
International Economic Report of the President. February 1974.

B. The Congress of the United States

Congressional Record. Proceedings and Debates of the Congress. (Separately published for each day the Congress is in session.)
Joint Economic Committee Reports
  Report. *Gold, SDR's and Central Bank Swaps*, 1972
  Report. *The Pedigreed Gold System: Why Spoil It?* 1969.
  Report on the *Economic Report of the President for 1973*. H. Doc. 93–90, March 1973.
Joint Economic Committee Hearings.
  Hearings. *New Economic Policy*, 1971
  Hearings. *The Proposed IMF Quota Increase and its Implications for the Two-Tier Gold Market*, 1969.
  Hearings. *Fast Breeder Reactor Program*, 1976.
  Hearings. *The IMF Gold Agreement*, October 1975.
  Hearings. *International Monetary Fund Amendments*, 1976.
House of Representatives
  Hearings. Committee Government Operations, *Investigation and Study of the Federal Home Loan Bank Board*, January 1962.
  Hearings. Committee on Banking and Currency, *Gold Reserve Requirements*, 1964.
  Report, 6th Committee on Government Operations. *Investigation and Study of the Federal Home Loan Bank Board*, June 24, 1963.
  Hearings. Committee on Banking and Currency, *The Federal Reserve System after Fifty Years*, 1964.
  Hearings. Committee on Banking and Currency, *Removal of Gold Cover*, 1968.
Senate Hearings
  Senate Banking and Currency Committee
    a. Hearings. *Repeal of Silver Purchase Acts*. 1963
    b. Hearings. *Content of Silver Coins*. 1964
  Senate Committee on Interior and Insular Affairs
    a. Hearings. *Federal Coal Leasing and Disposal Policies*, 1972.
    b. Hearings. *Market Performance and Competition in the Petroleum Industry*, pt. 1 and 2. 1973
    c. Hearings. *Salinity Control Measures on the Colorado River*. 1974
  Other Senate Documents, Reports or Hearings
    a. Report. Select Committee on Presidential Campaign Activities. *The Senate Watergate Report*, 1974. (Also available, vols. 1 and 2, New York: Dell, 1974.)
    b. Report. Subcommittee on Securities. Committee on Banking, Housing and Urban Affairs, *Security Industry Study*. S. Doc. 93-13, April 6, 1973.
    c. Report. Committee on Rules and Administration. *Financial or Business Interests of Officers or Employees of the Senate*, July 8, 1964.

C. Other Publications

Report. U.S. Tariff Commission, *Implications of Multinational Firms for World Trade and Investment and for U.S. Trade and Labor*. Report to Senate Finance Committee, 1975.

U.S. Bureau of the Census. *Statistical Abstract of the United States*, issued annually.

U.S. Council on Environmental Quality. *Annual Reports*, since 1970.

U.S. Department of Agriculture. *Yearbook*, issued annually.

Federal Home Loan Bank Board. *Statement on Inquiry into Mortgage Insurance Companies*. June 26, 1964 (mimeographed).

Federal Trade Commission. *Report on Motor Vehicle Industry*, 76th C, 1st S, H. Doc. 468, 1940.

Hearings. Temporary National Economic Committee. Investigation of Concentration of Economic Power, Part 22, *Investment Banking*, 1940.

Office of Technology Assessment. *The Direct Use of Coal*, 1979.

Report. National Resources Committee. *The Structure of the American Economy*, 1939.

National Commission on Food Marketing. *Food from Farmer to Consumer*, 1966.

Atomic Energy Commission. *Annual Report* to the Congress for 1973; vols 1 and 2, 1974.

Board of Investigation and Research. *Preliminary Report on the Relative Economy and Fitness of the Carriers*, H Doc. 595, May 16, 1944.

U.S. Treasury Department. *Maintaining the Strength of the United States Dollar In A Strong Free World Economy*, January 1968.

Index

STUDIES IN SOCIAL DISCONTINUITY
(Continued from page ii)

STUDIES IN SOCIAL DISCONTINUITY